Gaps and Governance Standards of Public Infrastructure in Chile

INFRASTRUCTURE GOVERNANCE REVIEW

OECD
BETTER POLICIES FOR BETTER LIVES

This work is published under the responsibility of the Secretary-General of the OECD. The opinions expressed and arguments employed herein do not necessarily reflect the official views of OECD member countries.

This document, as well as any data and any map included herein, are without prejudice to the status of or sovereignty over any territory, to the delimitation of international frontiers and boundaries and to the name of any territory, city or area.

Please cite this publication as:
OECD (2017), *Gaps and Governance Standards of Public Infrastructure in Chile: Infrastructure Governance Review*, OECD Publishing, Paris.
http://dx.doi.org/10.1787/9789264278875-en

ISBN 978-92-64-27886-8 (print)
ISBN 978-92-64-27887-5 (PDF)

The statistical data for Israel are supplied by and under the responsibility of the relevant Israeli authorities. The use of such data by the OECD is without prejudice to the status of the Golan Heights, East Jerusalem and Israeli settlements in the West Bank under the terms of international law.

Photo credits: Cover © Moises Arias

Corrigenda to OECD publications may be found on line at: *www.oecd.org/about/publishing/corrigenda.htm*.

Foreword

The review assesses Chile's infrastructure policy system, identifies the main governance bottlenecks for the development of infrastructure projects, provides a comparison with what other countries have done to alleviate similar bottlenecks, and proposes tailored policy recommendations. While Chile has been successful in upgrading its infrastructure stock over the past decade, new demands are emerging in a more complex policy environment. Meeting the logistics needs of Chile's key export industries, managing the pressure of urbanisation on key infrastructures, limiting regional disparities in access to essential services, preparing for natural disasters, managing the risks of too much, too little and too polluted water and securing sustainable access to water services both in urban and rural settlements; these and other pressures make infrastructure policy planning and delivery particularly challenging in Chile.

The report underlines that the success of Chile's infrastructure policy can be ascribed in significant part to the strength of the country's institutions and public administration. Nevertheless, the report also emphasises that public investment processes will need to adapt to a more decentralised, more consultative and more integrated policy environment if it is to meet the very high ambitions set out in Chile's development plan, Plan Chile 30/30. To reap the maximum economic, social and environmental benefits infrastructure investments in the Plan 30/30, the report highlights that Chile would need to couple investments in hard physical infrastructure with other natural and green infrastructure and transition clearly towards better water demand management and water use efficiency.

In Chile, as in most countries, the real obstacle to effective delivery of key infrastructure is not the availability of finance, but rather problems of governance. To help Chile improve its management of infrastructure policy from strategic planning all the way to project level delivery, the report has relied on several OECD frameworks and standards. First *Getting Infrastructure Right: a Framework for Better Governance* – that addresses the key success factors for an effective infrastructure policy system ranging from planning and strategy to delivery mode choice, PPP management, citizen consultation, regulatory frameworks and project evaluation. Second, the *OECD Council Recommendation on Effective Public Investment Across levels of Government* that provides guidance to governments to assess the strengths and weaknesses of their public investment capacity across levels of government and set priorities for improvement. And third, the *OECD Principles on Water Governance*, which provide standards for effective, efficient and inclusive design and implementation of water policies across levels of government and in cooperation with stakeholders.

Acknowledgements

The *OECD Infrastructure Governance Review of Chile* is a joint report produced by the OECD Budgeting and Public Expenditure Division, and the OECD Regional Development Policy Division within the OECD Public Governance Directorate led by Rolf Alter, in cooperation with the International Transport Forum. The project was co-ordinated by Andrew Davies and Juliane Jansen, and the report was drafted by a team composed of Juan Garin, Ian Hawkesworth, and Juliane Jansen (the governance framework for infrastructure and horizontal co-ordination), Isidora Zapata and Dorothée Allain-Dupré (co-ordinating infrastructure policy across levels of government), Lorenzo Casullo, Stephen Perkins and Jari Kauppila (transport infrastructure), and Antonio Cañamas Catala and Aziza Akhmouch (governance of water infrastructure). The report draws on substantial contributions from Rachele Poggi, and Nathan Zhivov of the International Transport Forum. Guillaume Guère, Trade and Agricultural Directorates, OECD, provided valuable comments on the water chapter. We thank Bonifacio Agapin, Andrea Uhrhammer, Kate Lancaster, and Bernardo Vazquez for their help preparing the document for publication.

The report benefitted from input provided by delegates to a wide range of OECD Networks and Committees: the Public Governance Committee, the Working Party of Senior Budget Officials (SBO), Network of Senior PPP and Infrastructure Officials, and the Regional Development Policy Committee (RDPC), with particular thanks to Salim Bensmail, Director, Infrastructure Finance Unit, Ministry of Finance, France and Alain Desruisseaux, Director General of Policy at Infrastructure Canada for their contributions as peer reviewers. The transport infrastructure section benefitted from expert review by Stephen Alchin, Executive Director at Infrastructure Australia.

The OECD Secretariat is especially grateful to the Planning Department (*Dirección de Planeamiento, DIREPLAN*) of the Ministry of Public Works (*Ministerio de Obras Publicas*) for their commitment and active support throughout this review, in particular to Jocelyn Fernandez Zenteno, Fernando Aldea Godoy, Ignacio Araya Areyuna, and Roberto Riveros. Invaluable insight was also provided by a wide range of central, sub-national and other public institutions as well as civil society organisations in Chile. Special thanks are also conveyed to the General Directorate of Water, and the Directorate of Hydraulic Works (Ministry of Public Works), the Superintendence of Sanitation Services, the Ministry of Finance, the Ministry of Agriculture, the Chilean Chamber of Construction, the Council of Mining, and Aguas Andinas.

Table of contents

Tables

Figures

Executive summary

Chile's infrastructure planning and governance framework has supported the roll-out of a range of high quality and efficient infrastructure systems in areas such as intercity highways, deep-sea ports, airports and urban water services, many of which that have made key contributions to the country's rapid development over the past two decades. Chile will still need to deliver large amounts of infrastructure in the years ahead as it strives to achieve high-income status. However, changing circumstances, many of which are a consequence of the country's development, are driving a shift in the country's needs, which will require, in turn, adjustments as to what kind of infrastructure is planned and how it is governed.

This report looks at the governance framework conditions and horizontal co-ordination of infrastructure in Chile. It also examines how Chile co-ordinates its infrastructure policy across various levels of government in a context of growing decentralisation, as well as at infrastructure and government issues in the transport and water sectors.

Governance framework conditions and horizontal co-ordination

The success of Chile's infrastructure policies can be ascribed in significant part to the strength of the country's institutions and public administration. Chile's public investment system benefits from a well-institutionalised social evaluation process that has helped ensure that infrastructure investments are of good quality and generate value-for-money. The Ministry of Finance has played an important role as gatekeeper by ensuring that the projects undertaken are affordable and do not compromise financial stability. Chile has also been successful in mobilising private financing for infrastructure development. Nevertheless, Chile's public investment processes must be updated to better reflect an integrated approach to long-term development and to take into account issues such as climate change and regional imbalances. Chile's infrastructure planning system needs to articulate a clear long-term vision and a set of development goals. The Chilean Infrastructure Plan (Plan Chile 30/30) is an initiative under the leadership of the Ministry of Public Works, and it has the potential to generate such a vision and guiding framework, particularly given the inclusive and bottom-up nature of the process. Moving forward, Chile should consider:

- strengthening long-term infrastructure planning and policy making to achieve development goals
- making room for transversal issues in the project evaluation and prioritisation system
- introducing an integrated and co-ordinated view of infrastructure planning, both within and across sectors
- strengthening the analytical capacity of its planners, in order to ensure evidence-based decisions and value for money.

Co-ordinating infrastructure policy

Chile is currently at the early stages of a change in how its regions participate in the definition and governance of infrastructure investment policy. This is a major shift, as Chile has the most centralised public investment framework in the OECD: 88% of such investment is decided centrally, far above the OECD average of 41%. A place-based infrastructure policy will help Chile to address territorial disparities and enhance regional productivity by maximising the potential of urban and rural areas. A territorial approach to infrastructure investments calls for the use of certain tools needed to enable effective co-ordination between all levels of government, especially in the context of decentralisation. This co-operation can be improved by strengthening existing instruments such as contracts and inter-ministerial committees and by better connecting infrastructure planning with budgeting in order to make sure that strategic planning is effectively translated into investment prioritisation. This requires building capacity at a subnational level through a learning-by-doing process in which regions increase their capacity to plan and manage investments as they gradually gain greater autonomy. Territorial infrastructure planning also means that Chile needs to further encourage co-operation across jurisdictions to make it possible to invest at the relevant scale. This need is especially acute in metropolitan areas. Specific challenges that Chile will need to address are:

- development of a place-based strategy for the regions
- promotion of decentralisation
- use of specific tools to improve vertical co-ordination
- co-operation across sub-national jurisdictions
- strengthening of subnational capacities.

Transport infrastructure issues

Productive investment in transport infrastructure is vital for prosperity. Chile is a middle-income economy heavily geared towards exports. Investment in a high-quality transport infrastructure base has contributed significantly to the country's development. A fully co-ordinated approach to infrastructure spending, with investment driven by transport policy goals that are integrated with land-use and sectoral development objectives, must accompany Chile's transition from a middle to a high-income economy and should address the potentially negative impacts on social and territorial equality and the environment associated with this transition. Given the current and projected gaps between Chile and its OECD peers, the following policy priorities should be set to achieve the goals of Plan Chile 30/30:

- supporting trade competitiveness by completing missing last-mile motorway links, establishing inland logistics centres in conjunction with investment in port capacity in Central Chile, and aligning modal shift policies with investment priorities in relation to rail freight connectivity establishing infrastructure policies that provide more equitable access to jobs and services through targeted ***investment at the metropolitan and regional level*** ensuring ***that moving goods and people is not at odds with air quality and safety standards***.

Water infrastructure and governance issues

Over the past few decades, water demand has increased in Chile, linked to dynamic economic growth and the high degree of economic specialisation in water-intensive sectors, including mining, agriculture and forestry, and fish farming. Population growth (which in Chile is above the OECD average) and futture demands for hydroelectricity generation will exacerbate these trends in the future and raise issues of how to match supply with demand geographically, how to maintain water sustainability in the future and how to minimise competition among users. While infrastructure planning and development, as foreseen in the Plan Chile 30/30 may contribute to securing sustainable access to water in the future, infrastructure responses alone will not be sufficient to meet future needs and mitigate water-related risks. Investments in physical infrastructure will need to be accompanied stronger governance frameworks, supported by robust institutions, and improved information systems to effectively guide decision making at all levels. In order to ensure this, Chile should:

- place ***water governance high in its agenda for long-term sustainable development.*** To achieve this Chile should design and implement a consensus-based national water resources policy that involves sound consultation across water-related ministries and public agencies, between levels of government, and with the private sector and society at large. The strategy should consider establishing incentives to foster effective basin governance in order to effectively manage water at the right scale, and strengthen water information systems and use them to guide planning and decision making.
- choose ***the right water infrastructure projects, both in quantity and type, and manage demand as well as supply.*** The Plan Chile 30/30 should acknowledge both hard assets as well as soft measures that will help cope with water risks. Although some hard infrastructure might be needed, it is important to raise the effectiveness and efficiency of investments by promoting low-cost options and green infrastructure (rainwater harvesting, recovering flooding plains, etc.) as well as water demand management strategies. The latter can combine different instruments, such as reuse of rainwater and grey water or enhancing public education on water conservation through awareness campaigns.

Chapter 1

Introduction to public infrastructure in Chile

Chile has been successful in building its key transport and water infrastructure over the past 25 years, which serves as structural backbone that are essential for economic development and welfare. However, circumstances are changing with implications for the needed infrastructure investment. This Chapter provides an introduction to the development of public infrastructure in Chile and gives an overview of the challenges that lie ahead.

Background

Chile has been successful in building up its key transport and water infrastructure.

Over the past 25 years, Chile has successfully rolled out many of the key investments in the country's basic infrastructure backbone that are essential for the country's economic development and welfare. Rapid investment in infrastructure has sustained impressive economic growth rates and improvements in the Chilean population's standard of living. GDP per capita has increased from USD 4 787 in 1990 to USD 22 197 in 2015. Chile has also achieved universal access to basic services that are essential to wellbeing, such as drinking water and sewerage systems (Ferro and Mercadier, 2016). While growth has led to significant overall reductions in poverty (OECD, 2015), it has relied heavily on capital accumulation (IMF, 2015) and has been geographically uneven (OECD, 2011).

Major economic infrastructures such as the highway network and port system have been built over the past two decades. Chile boasts a high quality and well-maintained highway system that links major cities and provides good north-south connectivity over the length of the country. Within the decade from 2004 to 2014, total container capacity at Chilean ports more than doubled, and the productivity of maritime transport at the port level is among the highest in Latin America. Major urban infrastructure projects such as the Santiago metro system and the city's ring roads have sustained the capital's economic and demographic growth. Between 1985 and 2013, Chile managed to expand its wastewater treatment capacity from 0 to 100%. Finlally, Chile has managed to develop this infrastructure efficiently and to a high standard, which is a testament to the quality of the country's institutions (IMF, 2016).

This success can be ascribed, in significant part, to the strength of Chile's institutions and the capacity of its public administration. The Ministry of Public Works' (Ministerio de Obras Públicas – MOP) experience and capabilities in preparing and executing projects have been instrumental in delivering the country's high-quality infrastructure. Chile's public investment system benefits from a well-institutionalised social evaluation process that has contributed to ensuring that infrastructure investments are of good quality and generate value for money. In addition, the Ministry of Finance has played an important gatekeeper role by reviewing and approving projects to ensure that they are affordable and do not compromise financial stability. Nevertheless, Chile's processes must be refined and updated so that evaluations of projects and programs better reflect an integrated approach to long term development.

Chile has also been successful in mobilising private financing for the development of its infrastructure. It has adopted and refined the concessions model for delivering infrastructure, a major factor explaining the speed with which it has been able to build its extensive highway network. In the two decades since the launch of the concessions programme in 1992, Chile has procured 82 projects worth a total of USD 19 billion, and built or rehabilitated 2 500 kilometres of highways using this mechanism (MOP, 2016). It has also introduced innovations into the concessions model such as contracts based on the "least present value of future revenues" which helps to reduce demand risk (Box 1.1).

Box 1.1 Reducing demand risk in highway concessions

Highway concessions financed by tolls paid by users face significant demand risk. This is due, in part, to the uncertainty around the price-elasticity of demand for roads, as well as the inherent difficulty of predicting future traffic over a long time period. Such schemes are inevitably subject to the vagaries of economic cycles and other unpredictable changes in the economic circumstances affecting demand for the asset.

Traditional auctions typically involve fixed-term contracts based on the lowest toll, which leaves the concessionaire facing elevated demand risk. In order to reduce the high level of demand risk which results in an increase in the risk premium required by investors and a greater likelihood of renegotiations, the MOP in 1994 introduced a new mechanism for adjudicating concession contracts, one called least present value of revenue (LPVR) auctions. The first concession was awarded on this basis in 1998 for Route 68, the highway between Santiago and Valparaiso (MOP, 2016).

Under this system for awarding concession contracts, the contract's duration is variable, only ending once the present value of revenues has been reached. In the case of lower than expected toll revenues, the contract gets extended so that the concessionaire obtains the agreed-upon present value of revenues. The method also allows for the possibility of adjusting toll levels, for example, if demand is lower than expected, without affecting the underlying economic value of the contract. Such a system thus goes a long way towards eliminating demand risk. It also provides a transparent basis for compensating the concessionaire if the government decides to terminate the contract early (Engel, 2001).

Since its adoption, numerous highway concessions have been procured using the LPVR method. Moreover, in spite of the potential variability in the value of payments, banks and other lenders have accepted this mechanism because it reduces the likelihood of failure of the project company.

Source: MOP (2016), *Concesiones de Obras Públicas en Chile – 20 años*, Ministerio de Obras Publicas, Santiago; Engel (2001).

A changing context

The circumstances that shape infrastructure investment needs are changing.

Many of the key investments in the basic infrastructure backbone that are essential for economic development and welfare have been completed. In the road sector, the main vertical north-south highway (Route 5) and most transversal arteries linking the key cities have been built. Access to potable water and sanitation services is practically universal (99% access to improved water sources and sanitation facilities in 2015), as is access to electricity from the national grid. The increase in coverage of basic roads, rural drinking water systems and rehabilitation of fishing coves has been significant.

While these investments have had clear economic benefits, future investments choices may be more difficult and marginal returns may be lower. As will be highlighted in the chapters on transport and water, infrastructure gaps still do exist, although the nature of these gaps is shifting to issues such as regional inequality, equal access, welfare and quality of life. For instance, there are great disparities in the quality of infrastructure from region to region. The same can be said with regard to national-level and local-level infrastructure. While national infrastructure of strategic importance such as the main highways is built and operated to meet exacting international standards, urban roads are often of lower quality and poorly maintained, despite Chile's increased efforts in remote and isolated areas. Finally, there are significant gaps with regard to negative externalities such as congestion, air pollution and road safety, which have emerged as a consequence of economic development.

In response to public demands, the current government has prioritised social sectors such as education and health. This is in many ways consistent with Chile's transition from a middle income to a high-income country. However, this means that, in the future, traditional infrastructure investment may increasingly need to compete for resources with the social sectors. While it may not result in an overall reduction in infrastructure investment, Chile may experience a shift in the types of infrastructure being built, with perhaps more hospitals and schools and fewer major transport projects.

Chile's economy has experienced a slowdown in recent years as a result of lower global growth in general and a drop in demand for copper in particular. With the end of the commodity super-cycle, Chile may face lower medium- and long-term growth prospects (IMF, 2015). This reduces resources available for public investment. On the other hand, the right infrastructure investment, performed well, can contribute to productivity growth. In addition, Chile may benefit from a rebalancing of its economy from the export of natural resources to manufacturing and services. Infrastructure will have an important role to play in supporting economic diversification. Choices regarding what kinds of infrastructure to build will therefore need to be informed by a vision of the evolving structure of the Chilean economy.

Transversal issues such as climate change, pollution, natural disasters and health are becoming more important. Chile's intended national determined contribution (INDC) submitted for the Paris Climate Agreement in 2015 envisages a reduction in carbon emissions intensity of 30% below 2007 levels by 2030. Infrastructure projects will need to support this shift towards a lower-carbon economy. Moreover, with its long coastline, glaciers and dry climate in the north, Chile is highly vulnerable to the impacts of climate change. Notions such as resilience, preparedness and sustainable development therefore need to be integrated into infrastructure planning. However, when infrastructure decisions are based primarily on financial criteria they do not easily accommodate values that are not so easily captured in monetary terms.

These evolving circumstances have implications for infrastructure planning

Past choices regarding infrastructure development were relatively simple: the infrastructure needs were great, the gaps were obvious, and there was little doubt as to the key driver of the economy – principally the export of minerals. Future infrastructure choices may not be so straightforward.

Future infrastructure needs will be more localised and will require a greater ability to identify and respond to needs at a local level. Thus, while access to most basic infrastructure services in Chile is universal, significant discrepancies in quality exist between different regions and localities. For example, there are problems in access to water services in some of the urban peripheries of metropolitan areas (particularly in Santiago), and rural water services are still not universal (particularly for the case of sanitation services). Also, standard roads in the north are lacking and the motorway network does not cover the northern macro-zone stretching from Atacama to Arica.

Moreover, future projects may be less transformational in nature and large expenditures on maintenance are likely to be needed, as many of the major pieces of infrastructure have already been built (like the inter-city highway network and the Santiago airport). In order to address this greater level of complexity, future infrastructure planning will need to focus more on social infrastructure and on smaller and more localised projects, and it will have to become more inclusive in its social and spatial dimensions and take into account cross-cutting issues such as climate change, sustainability and resilience.

Future benefits from infrastructure investment may increasingly accrue from the existence of complementarities and synergies among a cluster of assets rather than stand-alone projects. Such complementarities are easier to find and manage at the regional or local level. With many of the large infrastructure investments complete, future investments will increasingly involve extensions to or linkages with existing infrastructure. A key example here is the need to enhance inter-modality, thereby facilitating the movement of goods and people across transport modes and developing "last mile" infrastructure. Intermodal strategies require better co-ordination at the planning stage, a wider lens to assess the benefits at the assessment stage and more complex interactions at the implementation stage. The marginal returns of single projects may therefore be lower and more difficult to evaluate. Project evaluation methodologies will need to evolve to take into account the impact of linkages and synergies between projects.

Furthermore, with many of the basic needs for access to key infrastructure services having being satisfied, addressing future needs may require more of a mix between supply and demand measures. For instance, digital technologies are making demand management an increasingly credible alternative for resolving capacity issues in the transport sector. When productivity improvements enhance capacity, investment in digitalisation can be an alternative, or at least a complementary measure, to infrastructure building.

Finally, decisions regarding what to build and how to build it will increasingly need to take into account certain negative externalities, whether in terms of air quality, carbon emissions, or health and safety. It will no longer be sufficient to privilege growth to the detriment of social or environmental values. Planning instruments will need to be adapted to better reflect externalities generated by infrastructure investments. Key competences will be required to address these new circumstances. The evolving nature of infrastructure needs in response to changing circumstances will have implications for the types of competences that will be required of the Chilean infrastructure planning system going forward. These will include issues such as capacity for long-term thinking, the decentralisation of infrastructure decisions, an evaluation and prioritisation process more geared towards transversal issues (e.g. climate change) and use of the whole toolbox of private sector participation.

References

Engel, E., R.D. Fischer and A. Galetovic (2001), "Least-Present-Value-Of-Revenue Auctions and Highway Franchising", Journal of Political Economy. Vol. 109, National Bureau of Economic Research, Cambridge, MA, pp. 993-1020.

Engel, E. (2016), "Infraestructura en Chile: historia de un lobby exitoso", Voces, La Tercera, May 8, 2016, Ñuñoa.

Ferro, G. and A. Mercadier (2016), "Technical Efficiency in Chile's Water and Sanitation Providers", *Utilities Policy*, Vol. 43, Elsevier, Amsterdam, pp. 97-106.

IMF (2015), Chile: Staff Report for 2015 Article IV Consultation, July 2015, Washington D.C.

IMF (2016), Regional economic outlook. Western Hemisphere, World Economic and Financial Surveys, April 2016, Washington, D.C.

MOP (2016), "Elementos de la experiencia Chilena", presentation by Jocelyn Fernandez at the OECD Annual Meeting of Senior Infrastructure and Public-Private Partnership Officials, 1 March 2016, Paris.

OECD (2011), *Water Governance in OECD Countries: A Multi-level Approach*, OECD Publishing, Paris, http://dx.doi.org/10.1787/9789264119284-en.

OECD (2015), *OECD Economic Surveys: Chile 2015*, OECD Publishing, Paris, http://dx.doi.org/10.1787/eco_surveys-chl-2015-en

Chapter 2

The governance framework for infrastructure and horizontal co-ordination in Chile

This Chapter identifies the main adjustments that should be made to Chile's central infrastructure governance and horizontal planning, with recommendations based on the OECD's infrastructure governance framework and related guidance. The first section provides an assessment of Chile's infrastructure governance framework and how well it meets a set of ten governance pre-conditions that have been identified by the OECD as important for ensuring value-for-money and affordability with regard to infrastructure investment. Section two focuses on the essential ingredients of an infrastructure planning system and identifies gaps in Chile's planning capabilities and framework. The final section of this chapter provides a number of recommendations for strengthening infrastructure planning and the governance framework. The analysis draws on best practice examples from the four country case studies (France, the Netherlands, Denmark and Australia) that are presented in the Annex to the chapter.

Governance pre-conditions: An assessment of Chile's governance framework

Infrastructure decision-making and delivery should be guided by principles of value for money, transparency and accountability. The OECD has identified nine pre-conditions for an infrastructure governance framework that can generate the right decisions regarding what to build and how to build it, as well as ensure the efficient and accountable implementation of those decisions.

Medium- and long-term planning

Getting infrastructure decisions right is crucial to ensuring that investments enhance people's welfare and contribute to productivity growth and competitiveness. A necessary condition for a successful infrastructure programme is appropriate strategic planning. The key role of infrastructure planning is ensuring that decisions related to infrastructure investments take into account needs, trade-offs, political priorities and long-term development goals, and do so in a transparent and consultative way.

Many of Chile's large projects have relied on market-based mechanisms as a way of assessing future demand and ensuring that the right projects get built. This approach works well for projects where private interests can accurately estimate future demand. However, for sectors and projects where market mechanisms may not be feasible or appropriate (e.g. as a result of non-excludability or externalities), a greater degree of planning becomes necessary.

In the context of evolving circumstances, Chile's ability to meet its future infrastructure needs is constrained by its limited capacity for medium- to long-term planning. While political cycles create incentives for focusing policymaking on short- to medium-term measures, in Chile the challenge is particularly acute because of the four-year electoral cycle combined with the single presidential term.

Unlike many OECD countries, Chile does not have an overall long-term strategic infrastructure plan (Figure 2.1). Chile's government lacks institutions and a culture that promotes more long-term thinking and evidence-based policy-making, two key competences required for developing the sort of infrastructure that will prepare the country for the future.

Figure 2.1. Planning and Prioritisation

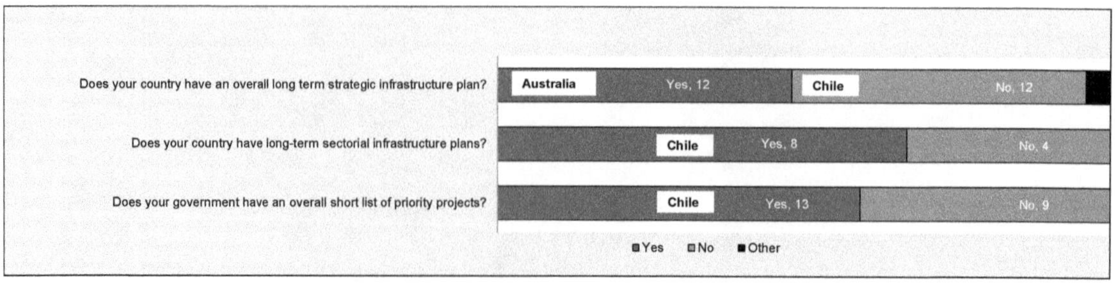

Note: 25 respondents, "others" refers to medium-term (6-7 year) plans (Ireland).

Source: OECD (2016a), OECD Survey of Infrastructure Governance.

The choice of what to build should be framed within a vision for the future of the country that is articulated through an explicit statement of long-term development goals. Some centralised guidance relating to the objectives and priorities that infrastructure policies and investment prioritisation should pursue is essential to ensuring the overall coherence of investments across sectors. Thus, infrastructure strategies should not only take into account the specific needs of a sector, but also ensure that investment plans contribute to achieving broader long-term development goals.

A key strength of Australia's infrastructure planning system, to cite an example, is its integrated strategy (Annex 4). The infrastructure plan encompasses how infrastructure is financed, delivered and used, and it is guided by a set of Australia's main long-term ambitions. This holistic approach considers all infrastructure sectors within a single plan, which encourages greater alignment across sectors and investments and creates more spaces for generating synergies.

In Chile, a number of sectoral ministries undertake infrastructure planning and investment prioritisation for their respective sectors. For example, in 2013 the Ministry of Transport and Telecommunications (MTT) produced a National Plan for Port Development that identified priority investments in the port sector over a time horizon extending 20 years. In 2014, the MTT also produced a "Master Transport Plan for Santiago in 2025", which presented a long-term integrated plan for urban transport covering all transport modes, including both public transport (regional trains, subways, tramways and buses) and motorways, urban roads and bicycle lanes. Similarly, in 2010, the MOP (see Box 2.1) published a *"Plan Director de Infraestructura"*, which looked ahead to 2020, and, applying a methodology called "Tranus", developed a combined transport and land use model which served as the basis for identifying projects in different regions of the country (Consejo de Políticas de Infraestructura, 2014). The MOP, through its Plan Chile 30/30, is initiating a new planning process for infrastructure development for roads, water and public buildings.

While these initiatives are laudable, they don't have the benefit of drawing on centralised guidance in the form of a strategic vision for the country and a connection to long-term development goals. Such a vision would provide a framework for making strategic choices, balancing trade-offs and choosing priorities from among different needs. A greater level of institutionalised centralised guidance and long-term thinking will generate more coherence across sectoral plans, ensure that sectoral investments contribute to a common set of long-term goals and reduce the potential for overlap and duplication.

Moreover, a long term framework needs to take major future risks and uncertainties into account. This will contribute to future-proofing investment plans and improving the resilience of the nation's infrastructure. The concepts of vulnerability and resilience for both the infrastructure project itself and the services that it will provide need to be addressed from the early planning stages. Weighing the risks arising from natural disasters and climate change when it comes to connectivity, the provision of drinking water, public services and other areas, will minimise potential for future disruption of productive and social activities (see Section 2 below for a more detailed discussion of the components of a long-term planning system).

The long-term framework provides a wide range of options and instruments to connect infrastructure planning to socio-cultural issues. A more integrated view of infrastructure across various sectors can contribute to the country's development. Given

Chile's indigenous and multicultural background, especially in large rural areas of the territory, an overall plan for infrastructure and water infrastructure has to integrate the needs of aboriginal people and minorities (see Section 1.3, Focusing on users' needs).

Box 2.1. The Ministry of Public Works (MOP)

The Ministry of Public Works is the central actor in governance of infrastructure projects across throughout the governance life-cycle, including evaluation and prioritization, project preparation, tendering, contracting, construction, operation and maintenance. It carries out its work through a sub-secretariat and two Directorates-General: one for Water and the other for Public Works. The latter is divided into six departments: Port Works, Water Works, National Roads, Airports, Architecture and Concessions. In addition, there are three non-executive departments: Planning, Accounting and Finance, and Legal. On the regional level, the MOP includes Regional Ministerial Secretariats in each of the fifteen regions of the country (See figure below).

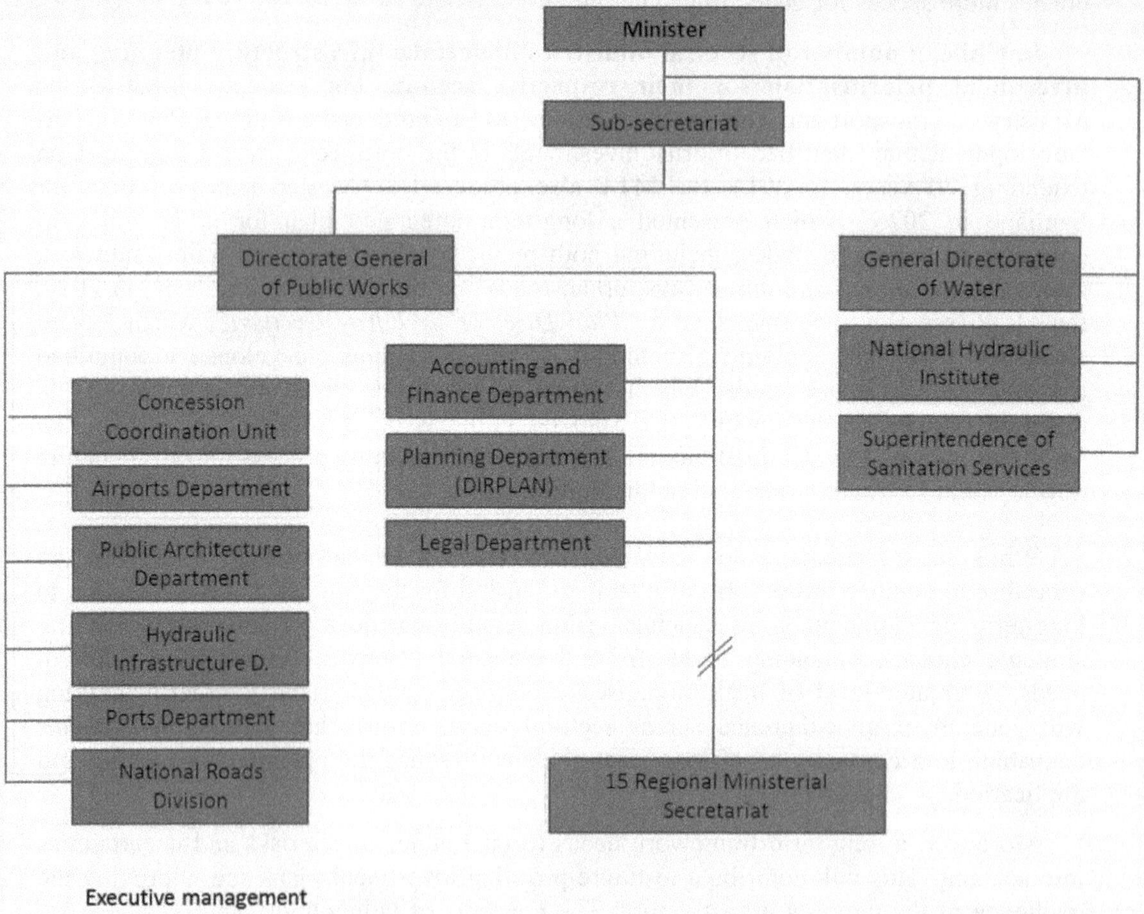

Source: MOP (2016), www.mop.cl/acercadelmop/Paginas/Organigramayestructura.aspx

Within the MOP, responsibility for evaluation of infrastructure and planning needs lies with the Planning Department (DIRPLAN) (See table below). However, the MOP's focus on the provision of infrastructure as its primarily policy goal may generate a preference for new investment as a first response to meeting needs in the roads and water sector. This focus on infrastructure provision may cause alternate ways to address users' needs (e.g. demand management) to be overlooked.

Box 2.1.The Ministry of Public Works (MOP) (*cont.*)

Functions and roles within the MOP in the infrastructure governance cycle

Function	Institutional arrangement within MOP	
Evaluation of infrastructure needs	Planning Department (DIRPLAN)	Policy making within the MOP is conducted primarily within the DIRPLAN and is focused on developing approaches and guidelines to strengthen the provision of infrastructure through new investments or conservation.
Planning and prioritisation	DIRPLAN	DIREPLAN performs medium- to long-term infrastructure planning within the MOP.
Infrastructure project preparation	Concession Coordination Unit (CCOP) Airport Department Public Architecture Department of Hydraulic Infrastructure Port Works Department Road Division	Project preparation is performed by the respective divisions within the MOP responsible for different types of infrastructure. Within the road division the Sub-division for development (Sub-dirección de desarrollo) is responsible for preparing and commissioning the various studies required for project development, such as social cost-benefit analyses and feasibility studies.
Construction, operation, delivery and maintenance	Concession Coordination Unit (CCOP) Airport Department Public Architecture Department of Hydraulic Infrastructure Port Works Department Road Division	Procurement of works within the MOP is performed by the respective divisions responsible for different types of infrastructure. Within the Road Division, the sub-division of Works (Sub-dirección de Obras) leads the procurement process in collaboration with the Sub-divison of Budget and Finance (Subdirección de Presupuesto y Finanzas).
Monitoring	Fiscal Inspector	A Fiscal Inspector from within the MOP is appointed to supervise the works and contractor performance. An engineering consulting firm advises and supports the Fiscal Inspector for the duration of the works contract. A similar structure is used for concessions. In the case of concessions, a Fiscal Inspector is also appointed to monitor contractor performance during the operational phase.

Source: Authors, based on information provided by MOP.

Finally, any long-term planning should be buttressed by a forward-looking budgeting process. Currently, Chile's only produces annual commitments which inhibit the ability of spending departments to think and plan longer-term (see Section 1.5, Mechanisms to ensure sustainability and affordability of infrastructure investment).

Co-ordination within and across sectors

There should be robust co-ordination mechanisms for infrastructure policy within and across levels of government as well as between jurisdictions. The mechanisms should encourage a balance between a whole-of-government perspective, and sectoral and regional views (see Chapter 3 for the analysis of vertical co-ordination of infrastructure policy across levels of government).

Cross-sectoral co-ordination

Horizontal co-ordination between sectoral ministries should ensure that investment across sectors contributes to the pursuit of common development goals, limits the possibilities for overlap between projects, promotes synergies between investments, and ensures that investments are mutually reinforcing. Co-ordination of all institutional stakeholders is an essential pre-requisite for efficient and effective infrastructure planning and should be ensured early in the process.

As discussed further in the Chapter 3, **Chile's central government is characterised by a high degree of compartmentalisation**. Sectoral ministries work within somewhat insulated silos with limited mechanisms for ensuring alignment and integration across policy areas and investments.

Furthermore, the organisational structure of the MOP itself is also highly siloed. Each division is focused on its own type of infrastructure (e.g. roads, ports, airports, etc.). There are no coordinating mechanisms within the MOP for developing an integrated and systemic vision of the transport sector as a whole. This is a potential weakness given the important linkages that exist between different transport modes. The challenge is amplified by the fact that the MOP only has a partial vision of the transport sector, given that its responsibilities do not cover certain transport modes (e.g. rail) or scales (e.g. urban transport).

At the national level, **a new co-ordinating mechanism** called the Interministerial Committee for Cities, Housing and Territory (COMICIVYT) has been created to co-ordinate land use and infrastructure planning across ministries (see Box 2.2). However, the regional plans (Estrategia Regional de Desarrollo – ERD) developed by this mechanism are not binding and only have a weak link with the budgeting process. As a consequence, the policies and investments of sectoral ministries are not required to conform to the priorities established in the ERD.

Box 2.2. A cross-sectoral co-ordinating mechanism at the regional level

The Interministerial Committee for Cities, Housing and Territory (COMICIVYT) was established under Decree No. 34 on 5 June 2015. COMICIVYT is responsible for formulating policies related to land use planning and for developing integrated investment plans in each of the 15 regions. Five ministries participate in the infrastructure planning dimension: Ministry of Housing and Urbanisation, MOP, MTT, Ministry of State Properties, and the Sub-secretary for Regional Development of the Ministry of Interior and Public Security. COMICIVYT thus provides a cross-sectoral platform for prioritising infrastructure investments within regions based on a long-term vision for the region's development. Regional Integrated Infrastructure Plans developed through COMICIVYT have a 5-year timeframe and provide input to the annual budget discussions held between spending ministries and the Ministry of Finance's Budget Department (DIPRES). These plans therefore have the potential to greatly improve the overall coherence of infrastructure planning within regions, thus maximising the efficiency and impact of both public and private investment.

Source: COMICIVYT (2016), Planes Regionales de Infraestructura Urbana y Territorial.

Intra-sectoral co-ordination

The co-ordination challenge is particularly acute in sectors where responsibilities are distributed across different ministries. This is the case for road transport, where the responsibility for planning, building and maintaining the intercity network lies with the Ministry of Public Works (MOP), responsibility for planning for multi-modal logistics, including road freight, and urban transport are competencies of the Ministry of Transport and Telecommunications (MTT), and responsibility for planning and executing investments in urban roads lies with the Ministry of Housing and Urban Planning (Ministerio de Vivienda y Urbanismo – MINVU).

In other words, planning responsibilities for transport are shared across different ministries. For example, the Logistics Division of the MTT performs freight and logistics planning covering major ports, railways, haulage, and maritime transport. It has produced a number of plans including a National Development Plan for Ports and a Rail Haulage Plan. The MOP, on the other hand, is responsible for planning infrastructure investments in intercity roads, ports and airports.

SECTRA takes the lead in planning for the development of urban transport systems. This unit within the MTT carries out integrated urban transport planning for cities. In developing urban transport plans for major cities and smaller municipalities, it works with regional and municipal governments and various ministries such as the MOP, MINVU and the Ministry of Social Development (Ministerio de Desarrollo Social – MDS).

When it comes to intercity transport and freight, no single planning body exists to co-ordinate the various stakeholders. The distribution of transport-related planning competences across multiple institutions increases the need for co-ordination.

However, greater co-ordination is a sub-optimal response to the lack of clarity in terms of roles and overlap in responsibilities. Instead, the initial response should involve mapping the distribution of responsibilities both in terms of sectors and functions (policymaking, planning and execution), and if necessary readjusting responsibilities in order to reduce the need for co-ordination. Ultimately, there should be an integrated transport plan that brings together all modes of transport, making it possible to weigh the merits of a range of transport alternatives and address the connections between different modes (e.g. ports and roads).

Land use planning as a co-ordination mechanism

Land use plans can be important instruments for facilitating a co-ordinated approach to infrastructure development involving various sectors (e.g. housing, transport, and water and sanitation services). These plans can help avoid conflict over competing uses of land and reduce both the potential for delays in projects caused by difficulties in obtaining land and the cost of acquiring land for infrastructure projects in the future. In Chile, land use planning is primarily the responsibility of regional and municipal governments. Municipal governments are responsible for preparing Municipal Regulating Plans (Plan Regulador Comunal – PRC), while regional governments draft Regional Plans for Land Use (Planes Regionales de Ordenamiento Territorial – PROT). A third type of planning instrument, Inter-Municipal and Metropolitan Regulating Plans (Plan Regulador Intercomunal/Metropolitano – PRI/PRM), are prepared by the MINVU's representatives in each of the country's 15 regions. These plans govern the spatial development of those urban and rural areas that are parts of a larger urban unit such as a metropolitan area (OECD, 2013a). These various regulatory plans are meant to provide a spatial dimension to regional and municipal development strategies.

The current land use planning approach suffers from a number of weaknesses, including the long time it takes to develop or amend a land-use plan and a lack of synchronisation between the processes for developing regulating plans and regional/local development strategies. This has resulted in a potential lack of coherence between spatial plans, long-term development strategies and regional infrastructure plans (OECD, 2013a).

Furthermore, **a significant proportion of infrastructure projects may bypass the land use planning system altogether**. Given that they are driven by sectoral ministries, and may not have their origins in regional or local development strategies, some large projects are the most likely to be excluded from spatial planning processes. As many of the larger infrastructure projects (e.g. highways, rail lines, and dry ports) are land intensive, it is important to identify and set aside space well in advance.

For example, land use planning will be required for identifying one or more sites for the development of intermodal freight terminals in or near Santiago to service the movement of containers to/from a potential mega-port at Valparaiso or San Antonio. Planning and reserving corridors for future rail connections to such sites and "first mile" or "last mile" roads will also be important.

This gap could create future challenges for placing infrastructure, potentially leading to increased opposition to projects, delays and higher construction costs. The problem will only worsen as metropolitan areas expand due to population pressures, leaving less available land for other functions. Land use planning will be essential for managing population growth in a manner that supports the development and operation of effective public transport systems.

It will be important to strengthen the spatial planning function in Chile in order to effectively meet future infrastructure needs. A number of OECD countries have recognised the importance of integrating land use and infrastructure planning. For example, the Netherlands has a planning system that links infrastructure planning to a long-term vision for the spatial development of the country (see Annex 2). Infrastructure Australia, an advisory body responsible for guiding infrastructure decision making in Australia, is developing a policy for protecting corridors for future investments in nationally significant infrastructure (Infrastructure Australia, 2016). The city of Auckland in New Zealand has recently developed a new transport plan that recognises the importance of land use planning and reflects the orientations of Auckland's main planning instrument, the Auckland Unitary Plan (New Zealand Ministry of Transport, 2016).

Handling transversal issues

A further co-ordination challenge relates to transversal issues such as climate change that do not have an institutional home, but cut across numerous sectors. Effectively addressing transversal issues requires a shared understanding of the challenges involved and an integrated response across the whole of government. Infrastructure planning needs to come with a built-in capacity to handle such transversal issues in a co-ordinated and integrated manner (see also Section 1.10, Resilience of public infrastructure).

Focusing on users' needs

> *The process for managing infrastructure should be user-centric, i.e. focused on users' needs. It should be founded upon broad-based consultations, structured engagement and access to information.*

Stakeholder engagement throughout a project's life cycle can contribute an enhanced understanding of user needs, which helps to strengthen the legitimacy of infrastructure investments, addresses public concerns and heads off potential opposition at an early stage, and generally improves the quality of projects by exposing them to greater scrutiny. Infrastructure services are much more efficient and effective when they are planned in consultation with other infrastructure providers and users from the early stages. Early interaction before the implementation of infrastructure projects prompts the interest and participation of citizens, thus reducing risk of later failure (see Chapter 3, Section 7.3 for further details on encouraging stakeholders and citizen participation on subnational levels).

Consultation and citizen engagement in infrastructure projects is of particular importance in Chile given the highly centralised nature of decision making in the country. In the absence of further political decentralisation it is all the more important to establish channels through which to take in citizen and user concerns, and then to reflect these concerns in the design of infrastructure projects. Moreover, Chile's economic development and maturing democratic culture will increasingly generate demands from the public and civil society to have a stronger voice in decisions that affect them.

Consultations and user engagement should therefore be incorporated into the various stages of an infrastructure project's life cycle, from the long-term planning stage to operation. An understanding of user needs should inform the development of infrastructure plans. Along these lines, the process of regional consultations proposed as part of the drafting of the Plan Chile 30/30 is a good example of this sort of structured engagement in the planning process. Like many countries in the OECD, Chile has some mandatory consultation processes for the evaluation of infrastructure needs, decision and prioritisation of infrastructure and infrastructure project preparation (Table 2.1).

Table 2.1. Mandatory consultation processes[1] for infrastructure projects in Chile and OECD countries.

	Stages of development consultation processes take place:			
Mandatory consulting processes	Evaluation of infrastructure needs	Decision and prioritisation of infrastructure	Infrastructure project preparation	Construction
Chile	Chile	Chile	Chile	Chile
Australia	Estonia	Austria	Australia	Australia
Austria	Germany	Estonia	Czech Republic	Germany
Czech Republic	Hungary	Germany	Estonia	Korea
Denmark	Italy	Hungary	France	New Zealand
Estonia	Korea	Italy	Germany	Sweden
France	Norway	Korea	Hungary	United Kingdom
Germany	Slovenia	Norway	Italy	
Hungary	Sweden	Slovenia	Korea	
Ireland	Switzerland	Sweden	New Zealand Norway	
Italy	United Kingdom	Switzerland	Spain	
New Zealand		United Kingdom	Sweden	
Norway			Switzerland	
Korea			United Kingdom	
Slovenia				
Spain				
Sweden				
United Kingdom				
Switzerland				

Note: (1) Processes that regulate engagement between the public, other stakeholders and the authorities during the development of a particular infrastructure project.

Source: OECD (2016a), OECD Survey of Infrastructure Governance.

Chile's indigenous and multicultural background, especially in large rural areas of the country's territory, lends particular importance to consultation with indigenous communities. With its recent ratification in 2008 of the International Labour Organization's (ILO) Indigenous and Tribal Peoples Convention No. 169 of 1989, Chile began to introduce the international standard on indigenous rights into Chilean legislation (Box 2.3). Good practice examples for the involvement of indigenous communities in infrastructure projects can be found in New Zealand (Box 2.4).

Box 2.3. Consultation processes for indigenous communities in Chile

In recent years, Chile has made progress toward meeting international standards on the fundamental human rights of indigenous communities. In 1993, the "indigenous" law enshrined the relationship between the state and the indigenous communities in legislation. The law aims to "establish standards on protection, promotion and development of indigenous peoples" and created the National Corporation for Indigenous Development (CONADI), housed in the Ministry of Social Development.

In 2008, Chile ratified International the Labour Organization's (ILO) Indigenous and Tribal Peoples Convention Nr. 169 of 1989, which grants the right to free, prior and informed consultation of indigenous people about initiatives that may directly affect them, especially in matters related to natural resources or investment projects in indigenous territories. However, its implementation had to wait until 2013, when Decree 66 of the Ministry of Social Development was issued to regulate indigenous consultation. The regulations described were based on almost 300 meetings with and within the indigenous communities, organised by the Chilean Government.

Infrastructure investments in territories governed by the "Indigenous Law" are subject to budget annotations (*glosas*) implemented in 2009 by the Road Administration of the MOP. These measures earmarked investments in construction, adaptation, improvement and conservation projects of community roads located in territories governed by the Law. However, agreements on the execution of projects need to be signed with the Regional Governments and Municipalities, which need to submit a list of potential projects to the Road Administration, indicating the regional, communal or private sector resources available. The Road Division then establishes the final slate of projects to be implemented.

In a move towards compliance with the Indigenous and Tribal Peoples Convention, the Ministry of Public Works in 2016 issued a guide for all public officials involved in consultation processes with indigenous communities for the designs and future works to be constructed through the Roads Division, Hydraulic Works, Port Works, Airports, Architecture and Concessions. The Unit responsible within the MOP, the Executive Secretariat for the Environment and Territory (SEMAT), ensures the compliance of public works and management of water resources with the regulations on Indigenous Affairs, providing advice in these matters to the ministerial authorities and the services involved.

Additionally, the Chilean government is currently in the process of establishing the institutional framework it requires in order to better address the concerns and needs of the indigenous peoples of Chile. These institutions will include a new Ministry of Indigenous Affairs, as well as a series of ministerial regional Secretariats, an Interministerial Committee of Indigenous Peoples and nine Indigenous Peoples Councils, which will be tasked with defending the local interests, needs and rights of each of each community.

Source: MOP(2017), based on www.mop.cl/asuntosindigenas/Documents/TerritorialCultural.pdf, www.conadi.gob.cl/index.php/noticias-conadi/1360-a-6-anos-de%20-the-ratification-of-the-convention-169-of-the-oit-conadi-highlights-current-process-of-consultation-indigena, www.mop.cl/Prensa/Paginas/DetalleNoticiaSecundaiaMp.aspx?item=2259, www.gob.cl/2016/01/11/ministerio-de-pueblos-indigenas/, www.Conadi.gob.cl/documentos/LeyIndigena2010t.pdf.

Box 2.4. Consultation processes and the Māori in New Zealand

The engagement with the Māori community in infrastructure development in New Zealand is managed under the *Resource Management Act (RMA) 1991* and the *Heritage New Zealand Pouhere Taonga Act (HNZPTA) 2014.*

Resource Management Act 1991

The Resource Management Act 1991 recognises and provides for matters of national importance, which are set out in Section 6 of the act. Public participation is one of the key principles underlying the RMA. Specifically, Section 6 (e) states that: "persons exercising functions and powers under [the act], in relation to managing the use, development, and protection of natural and physical resources, shall recognise and provide for the following matters of national importance: the relationship of Māori and their culture and traditions with their ancestral lands, water, sites, *waahi tapu*, and other *taonga*, and the protection of historic heritage from inappropriate subdivision, use, and development". Furthermore, Section 8 of the Act requires that all "persons exercising functions and powers under the Resource Management Act take into account the principles of the Treaty of Waitangi", which for example includes the duty of the Crown to actively protect Māori interests and make informed decisions which in most cases would require consultation.

Decisions under the RMA are usually the responsibility of local authorities, as they are generally responsible for making decisions about the effects of land use and activities on the surface of rivers and lakes. In cases of national policy statements, environmental standards and conservation plans, matters may also be referred to the Ministry for the Environment or the Ministry of Conservation. The Ministries have a responsibility to monitor the implementation of the RMA.

The close co-operation with the Māori community ensures that the communities can express and advocate for their needs and interests. The projects themselves also benefit largely from the holistic perception of "guardianship" by the Māori communities, which is not limited to archaeological and sacred sites, but also raises awareness of long-term water and other environmental issues.

Source: Conversation with Dr. Simon Bickler, archaeological consultant, New Zealand, www.heritage.org.nz/protecting-heritage/archaeology/standard-archaeological-authority-process, www.mfe.govt.nz/rma/, www.environmentguide.org.nz/rma/maori-and-the-rma/

Full legislation:
Resource Management Act 1991: www.legislation.govt.nz/act/public/1991/0069/latest/DLM230265.html; Heritage New Zealand Pouhere Taonga Act 2014: www.legislation.govt.nz/act/public/2014/0026/latest/DLM4005414.html.

Project preparation phase

During the **project preparation phase**, consultation with stakeholders that have an interest in or are affected by a specific project should be performed at a **sufficiently early stage** so that their feedback can be used to inform the project's design and address potential public concerns. Stakeholders that feel they have been excluded from a project's decision-making phase regularly become its most vigorous opponents.

In Chile, citizen participation in the project preparation phase takes place primarily in the context of environmental impact assessments (EIA). Once an EIA has been published online, interested citizens and stakeholders are invited to submit written comments on the document, contributions to which the relevant authority is obligated to respond. Stakeholder engagement in Chile is thus primarily focused on meeting legal requirements as opposed to being applied as a strategic tool aimed at engaging users in project design or engendering acceptance for a particular project. A one-size-fits-all methodology is applied regardless of the size, nature or sensitivity of a particular project, and the scope of engagement is limited to environmental factors.

Infrastructure quality and service delivery could be enhanced through the adoption of more proactive, interactive and participatory forms of engagement. This would involve measures to expressly identify and reach out to interested and affected groups in a process tailored to each project's characteristics. A deeper level of public participation in decision making can be achieved by expanding the participatory toolbox to include techniques such as public hearings, webinars and workshops. In addition, the scope of public engagement could be extended beyond strictly environmental factors to cover socio-economic impacts and user needs. Infrastructure planning based on user needs can be a powerful instrument for better integration, taking into account the needs of minorities living in remote areas. Involving future users in "co-producing" infrastructure services can help generate better social outcomes and reduce the likelihood of creating unwanted services (Wiewora, Keast and Brown, 2016). Finally, the development of guidelines for conducting stakeholder engagement can serve to improve its adoption and enhance its effectiveness during the project preparation phase.

France has developed a highly structured and participatory form of citizen engagement called *débats publics* (public debates), which could serve as model for other countries wishing to foster greater public participation in infrastructure decision making (see Annex 2A). These public debates are organised and facilitated by an independent commission (Commission national du débat public - National Commission for Public Debate), that ensures that public consultations are genuinely participatory and are run impartially and to a high standard.

Construction phase

During the construction phase, **mechanisms should be available to the public for submitting complaints or feedback related to the works**, and resources and expertise should be made available to respond to public enquiries. In this regard, the Comptroller General of the Republic (Controlaría General de la República), Chile's supreme audit institution, has launched an innovative online geographic information system (GIS) tool that will allow the public to access data on infrastructure projects nationwide and to submit complaints (see Box 2.5).

Box 2.5. GEO CGR: Chile's online platform for promoting transparency and public engagement in monitoring infrastructure projects

GEO CGR is a geographic information system (GIS) that provides data on public investment in Chile. The platform also enables members of the public to register complaints or request inspections relating to specific public works featured on the platform. The Comptroller General can then dispatch an inspector to a particular site in response to a complaint.

The web portal enables users to visualise and access information on infrastructure projects via an interactive map of Chile. It allows users to view the distribution of public investment across the national territory. It also allows them to zoom in and view the location of projects at a local level in their own cities or neighbourhoods. Users can then obtain information on the status of projects shown on the map. Data on the platform is provided by the various contracting authorities.

The level of completion and timeliness of the data thus depends on their own judiciousness in updating information on their investments and contracts. Beneficiaries of the platform might include regional or municipal governments that seek to compare levels of public investment with other regions, civil society organisations that monitor the use of public funds or members of the public that are affected by or concerned about public works in their area.

GEO CGR is an innovative mechanism for improving the transparency of public investment. It provides a means for engaging the public in monitoring the implementation of public investment, and a channel for citizens to report irregularities or express concerns over specific projects.

Source: Controlaría General de la República.

Operation phase

Finally, **during the operational phase of a project, systems for collecting, monitoring and analysing user feedback should be in place**, and the information and insights collected should be used to improve quality and efficiency of service.

Chile could extend and deepen the use of stakeholder engagement to solicit the views of citizens, stakeholders and users on the projects' impacts and benefits with a view to improving the quality and acceptance of projects. The adoption of guidelines for conducting stakeholder engagement during the project preparation phase could be a useful tool to support this process.

Choice of delivery mode

> *At times, projects may be chosen for reasons other than maximising cost effectiveness. Motivations might include a wish to capitalise on an existing subsidy or a desire to finance the asset in a non-transparent manner off the government's balance sheet by using, for example, a PPP. The choice of how to deliver an infrastructure service, i.e. delivery modality, should balance political, sectoral, economic, and strategic concerns.*

Since the choice of delivery mode can have important consequences for service quality, efficiency and public finances, the decision-making process over how to deliver key infrastructure merits close scrutiny. Delivery modes are often conditioned by the legacy of past choices and the institutional structure of the state. In spite of a high degree of path dependency in terms of infrastructure delivery modes, governments are capable of acting to determine how to deliver future infrastructure. Good decision making with regard to infrastructure delivery modes should seek to eliminate bias, consider multiple alternatives and give priority to value-for-money criteria, all while taking into account the circumstances in the country, including the availability of fiscal space.

Infrastructure delivery in Chile is spread across a variety of delivery modes, including traditional procurement, concessions, state-owned enterprises (SOEs) and hybrid modes (e.g. SOEs and concessions for terminals in the case of public ports). These modes are selected depending on a range of criteria (Table 2.2) The decision-making process relating to PPPs and concessions merits particular attention given their long lifetimes, and the fact that they lock their cost structure in place over a period of many years.

Some countries apply a value-for-money test, using for example a public sector comparator to determine whether a project is suitable for the concession or PPP model. The PPP unit of Victoria, Australia for example (Partnership Victoria) uses a public sector comparator that takes into account the risks that are transferable to a probable private partner, and those risks that will be borne by the government. By comparing the net present costs the comparator servers as a hypothetical risk-adjusted cost of the public delivery of the project of the output specification. The methodology of the public sector comparator is made publicly available. Other countries (such as the United Kingdom), are moving away from the public sector comparator, towards approaches that incorporate qualitative and quantitative factors, such as value-for-money and affordability benchmarks, project visibility, desirability and achievability. While Chile doesn't apply such a test, the extensive experience it has gained over a period of 20 years in operating concessions, mainly for roads, provides it with strong benchmarks for determining whether a particular project might best be approached as a concession.

Table 2.2. Decision criteria for infrastructure procurement delivery methods in Chile

Traditional public works	PPP/concession	SOE
Availability of public sector financial resources	Is the private sector able to handle these kinds of projects?	Extent of government control
Is the public sector able to handle these kinds of projects?	Strength of business case	Political sensitivity to private sector participation
Political sensitivity to private sector participation	The degree to which costs can be recovered from users	The need to share risks with private actors, i.e. ports
The level of uncertainty related to future technological or societal conditions	The need to build a market for alternative ways of procuring public infrastructure (e.g. PPPs)	
The wish to tap private finance sources to augment the public budget	The wish to use private finance sources to augment the public budget	
	The need to share risks with private actors, i.e. ports	

Notes: Criteria rated by Chile received as of great or of some importance. The criteria in bold were among the five most important criteria found across OECD countries.

Source: OECD (2016a), OECD Survey of Infrastructure Governance.

The concessions unit within the MOP (Coordinación de Concesiones de Obras Públicas – CCOP) **does not apply a formal set of criteria for framing choices**. It does, however, consider cost recovery via user fees to be a key element in the decision of whether to proceed using the concessions model[1]. Nevertheless, going forward Chile could benefit from adopting a more formal set of criteria to guide choices relating to delivery modes, particularly if it seeks to extend the concessions model to other types of infrastructure where it has less experience (such as hospitals) and where cost recovery may not be feasible.

Decisions to pursue concessions in non-traditional, social sectors should be subjected to value-for-money analyses. Ministry of Finance Concessions in social sectors will need to be financed in large part by government payments, unlike motorways which are financed through tolls. In this context, thorough value-for-money analyses must be conducted and scrutinised by the Ministry of Finance (see Box 2.6 for examples of PPPs for social infrastructure in the United Kingdom).

The placement of the CCOP within the MOP may pose an obstacle to extending the concessions model to sectors beyond roads and airports. Its expertise is naturally tilted towards traditional MOP infrastructure. Extending the concessions model to other sectors such as health or education will require close collaboration with sectoral ministries in order to conduct analyses and design contracts that are adapted to the specific characteristics and needs of each sector. Such close collaboration may be inhibited by the existing institutional structure. As a unit within the Dirección General de Obras Publicas (DGOP), administrative decisions require the approval of the DGOP, a stumbling block which could limit the CCOP's ability to engage effectively with other ministries. Irrespective of the institutional arrangement, the decision to adopt the concessions model in a given sector is a political choice that depends not only on an objective economic analysis but also relies upon buy-in from other parts of the government as well as from the general public. It therefore requires strong support from within the sectoral ministries, the Ministry of Finance and the Executive.

Box 2.6. PPPs for Social Infrastructure- practices in the United Kingdom

Investment in social infrastructure in the United Kingdom is financed in a variety of ways, from pure public procurement to regulated private investment, including Private Finance Initiatives (PFI), a particular vehicle for financing public infrastructure where the private partner finances, designs, builds, and operates the infrastructure asset.

From 1992 to 2012, PFIs were successfully used to deliver many large social infrastructure projects, such as schools, hospitals and public facilities. A review by the National Audit Office (NAO, 2010) for example, indicates that in the health sector most PFI hospitals are well managed and are achieving the value for money initially intended.

However, in response to criticism by the public and Parliament, PFI was updated in the form of Private Finance 2 (PF2) through open consultation with public and private sector representatives and is generally perceived as a positive renewal of Private Finance Initiatives.

The concerns that were voiced included:

1. The PFI procurement process has often been slow and expensive for both the public and the private sector. This has led to increasing costs and reduced value for money for the taxpayer.
2. PFI contracts have been insufficiently flexible during the operational period, so making alterations to reflect the public sector's service requirements has been difficult.
3. There has been insufficient transparency as to the future taxpayer liabilities created by PFI projects and on the returns made by investors.
4. Inappropriate risks have been transferred to the private sector, resulting in a higher risk premium being charged to the public sector.
5. Off-balance-sheet classification of many PFI projects has meant that there have been budgetary incentives for departments to use private finance.

Although the current political focus has moved from social to economic infrastructure, the emphasis on the PFI/PF2 programme remains on social infrastructure. The portfolio of current PFI projects across government (as of 31 March 2015) includes 722 PFI projects, of which 171 were carried out by the Department of Education and 125 by the Department of Health[1]. A current example for the use of PF2 is the Priority Schools Building Programme.

Priority School Building Programme (PSBP) and the Aggregator model

The Priority School Building Programme (PSBP) represents an attempt by the Education Funding Agency (EFA) to help attract private sector investment to provide for the schools most in need of urgent repair.

Funding individual schools had proved to be difficult due to the limited size of deals. Therefore, the aggregator model was introduced, grouping schools into batches to attract both bank debt and capital markets to fund required rebuilding or repair. The batches of schools served by the programme are spread across England, with each group taking into consideration geography, commercial viability and the degree of need. Schools in the worst condition were prioritised for the first batch in case of overlap of batches.

An advantage of the aggregator model is the ability to aggregate total financing requirements across all the batches, thus reducing financing costs through competition and streamlining procurement by using standardised financing documents for each batch of schools. A limitation of this model that remains is cross-default, i.e. that one project is negatively affected by other projects in the same batch. This however, can be addressed by well managed information sharing.

Currently, five batches of 46 schools with a total funding requirement of approximately GBP 700 million will be served through private finance. However, these 46 schools represent only about 20% of the 260 schools under the programme. Private finance batches are open to bids from any construction organisation. The Private Finance batches follow the "Design, Build, Finance and Operate" delivery model with an operational period that generally lasts 25 years.

Note: https://www.gov.uk/government/publications/psbp-overview/priority-school-building-programme-overview.

Source: OECD (2015a), Review of Public Governance of Public-Private Partnerships in the United Kingdom, OECD Publishing, Paris.

The criteria used to determine the appropriate delivery mode should include factors such as economic efficiency, risk transfer, cost recovery and competition, among others (see Box 2.7 for a list of such criteria developed by the OECD). The criteria should explicitly avoid introducing preferences resulting from accounting rules for financing assets off-budget or off-balance-sheet.

The decision-making process regarding the choice of delivery mode should be insulated from institutional bias. Currently, in Chile, decisions regarding whether to propose the concessions model for a particular infrastructure service are taken by the same unit that is responsible for the delivering the project, the CCOP. The decision to proceed with a concession, PPP or a traditional procurement process should, ideally, be taken by a body that is independent from the delivery units. In Chile the MoF has to approve all PPP contracts, but does not evaluate alternative options.

For example, in France, a unit within the Treasury provides support and advice to all levels of government regarding the choice of financing modality. This unit, called the Infrastructure Financing Support Unit (Mission d'appui au financement des infrastructures) also gives advise on how to structure projects from a legal and financial perspective (see Annex 1 for a discussion of the role of the French Infrastructure Financing Support Unit).

Box 2.7. Checklist for investigating the ideal delivery mode

Project size and profile

- Is there a large initial capital outlay and long payback period?
- Does project size justify the legal, technical, and financial costs of the delivery mode?
- Can quality enhancements in the design and construction phase generate savings during the operating phase of the project?
- Do these savings justify the additional transaction costs involved in bundling construction, operation, and maintenance in a single contract?

Revenue and usage

- Can user fees be charged, are they affordable for the majority of users, and are they politically acceptable?
- Are user fees sufficient to cover the majority of capital and operating costs?
- Can usage be monitored?

Quality

- Can the quantity and quality of project outputs or outcomes be specified and measured efficiently?
- Will design innovation be required to achieve improvements in efficiency and value for money?

Uncertainty and risk

- What is the level of uncertainty related to future technological conditions?
- What risks is each sector (public vs. private) most capable of influencing and managing?
- Is demand relatively predictable over the lifetime of the project?
- Who is best placed to influence demand for the infrastructure-based service?

Box 2.7. Checklist for investigating the ideal delivery mode (*cont.*)

- Is the private sector willing to and capable of bearing some or all of the demand risk?
- Are there particular integrity risks in terms of corruption and undue influence that merit attention?

Competition

- Will there be a sufficient number of qualified bidders in the case of a PPP/concession project to ensure a competitive bidding process?

Notes: This box should not be interpreted as either for or against increased public provision or private sector participation in infrastructure delivery. It is offered as a guide for reflection and attempts to compress the experience of countries and practitioners into a checklist of key issues. There will therefore be cases, countries, and sectors where experiences are not sufficiently reflected in the above.

It is also important that the decision regarding the delivery method should be separated from project evaluation and prioritisation decisions. Thus, the decision to proceed with a project should be based solely on the merits of the project (as assessed using a cost-benefit or cost-effectiveness analysis) and not the delivery mode in itself. If a project meets the standards set by the social return target or other economic criteria, it should, at that point, be subject to an analysis of the merits of alternative delivery modes. Processes that bypass this sequence are more likely to generate poor choices both in terms of projects and delivery modes.

Projects developed on the basis of unsolicited bids not only reverse this sequence, but also effectively reduce competition by favouring the project's sponsor. Contracting authorities in Chile have at times accepted unsolicited bids. This shifts the cost of project preparation onto the project's sponsor. The sponsor accepts these costs in return for a favourable outcome of the tendering process and possibly a higher price. The key to addressing this issue is reducing the dependence of contracting authorities - in this case the CCOP - on private partners by ensuring they have sufficient resources and capacity for preparing projects internally.

The necessary devolution of responsibilities and powers to subnational levels will need to be accompanied by capacity development, including in the governance of PPPs. Currently the CCOP does not have the mandate to strengthen the capacities of subnational governments to design and run PPP or infrastructure projects (Table 2.3). Therefore, it is worth exploring ways by for different governing bodies on different subnational territorial levels to manage concessions, as capacities for preparing and managing concessions are currently not present at subnational levels. However, to ensure the planning capability for the decision on the appropriate delivery modality, Chile needs to work towards gaining sufficient capacities on the subnational as well as the national levels (For more information, please refer to Chapter 3).

When choosing concessions, contracts need to clearly define the degree of risk taken on the different parties. Although Chile has increased its efforts on risk management in concessions, there is no unified procedure for identifying and allocating risks between public and private parties that takes the cost of such allocation into account. To ensure that the private partner operates efficiently and delivers value for money, a sufficient amount of risk needs to be transferred to the private party. However, it has to be ensured that risk is transferred to the party that can manage it best, i.e. the party that can manage the risk at the lowest cost. This includes *ex ante* risk management (who is best able to prevent a risk from occurring) and *ex post* risk management (best able to deal with the results of realised risk), as well as the cost of both (*ex ante* and *ex post*) options. Unlike risks that can be managed (endogenous risks), risks that are exogenous to the private sector should not be transferred to the private party. While for example political change and taxation are unmanageable (exogenous) risks for the private party, they are endogenous to government. The Global Infrastructure Hub's PPP Risk Allocation Matrix (Box 2.8) can help to identify risk allocations.

Table 2.3. Do national PPP units/or Infrastructure Units in the Central Government strengthen the capacities of subnational governments to design and run PPP or infrastructure projects in general?

Yes	No
	Chile
Australia	Austria
France	Denmark
Germany	Estonia
Italy	Finland
Korea	Hungary
Spain	Japan
United Kingdom	Luxembourg
Czech Republic	New Zealand
Ireland	Norway
Turkey	Slovenia
	Sweden
	Switzerland

Source: OECD (2016a), OECD Survey of Infrastructure Governance.

Box 2.8. Allocating risks in Public-Private Partnership contracts

A deep understanding of the risk allocation arrangements is necessary to ensure the development of robust, bankable and sustainable PPP projects in the interest of both the public and the private sector parties.

As part of the *Global Infrastructure Hub*'s (*GIH*) promotion of leading practices in infrastructure investments, the GIH, in co-operation with the law firm *Norton Rose Fulbright,* developed a set of annotated risk allocation matrices for *PPP* transactions to assist PPP practitioners and governments in their understanding of typical PPP risk allocation.

The matrices are based on leading practices in four sectors, namely the transport, energy and water and sanitation sectors, covering 12 projects in total. They show information about the different projects, including:

- risk allocation, i.e. who typically bears the risk
- mitigation measures, i.e. what can be done to minimise the risk
- government support arrangements, i.e. what other government measures may be needed to be taken
- depending on the project's location, a comparison with the emerging or developed market

The guide includes risks that can be legislated, allocated and mitigated between the public and private sectors and which are addressed primarily through the concession or project agreement. Excluded are risks such as government procurement risk, private sector financial and performance risk, third party intervention or delay and specific risks arising in unsolicited projects.

The *Allocating Risks in Public-Private Partnership Contracts* guidelines can be accessed as an online tool as well as a downloadable PDF, available on the GIH website (www.globalinfrastructurehub.org/allocating-risks-in-ppps). The tool is available in English and Spanish.

Source: www.globalinfrastructurehub.org/allocating-risks-in-ppps.

In Chile, service quality and safety standards provided by concessions are generally higher than those offered by the same infrastructure operated by the State, creating a preference for PPPs on the part of certain users and ministries. This issue should be managed by explicitly choosing those services requiring a higher standard of quality to be managed by concessions. Additionally, equality between regions and citizens should be ensured by avoiding an extensive use of concessions in one place and publicly-delivered services in another.

Mechanisms to ensure the sustainability and affordability of infrastructure investment

Regulations, practices, and policies should encourage the sustainable and affordable development, management and renewal of infrastructure.

Chile benefits from a **historically centralised budget process focused on ensuring fiscal sustainability** (OECD, 2016b). A structural fiscal rule ensures that the budget remains in cyclically adjusted balance over an economic cycle.

The calculation of the structural balance target takes into account the size of contingent liabilities. To this end, DIPRES, the Budget Directorate of the Ministry of Finance, produces an annual report on contingent liabilities that includes minimum income guarantees on concessions. The fiscal framework thus provides a strong basis for ensuring the sustainability of public investment in infrastructure, and takes into account fiscal risks arising from the concessions programme. Contingent liabilities must be authorised by the Ministry of Finance. Since 2006, these have been compiled in a registry of contingent liabilities

Nevertheless, in Chile not all projects are subject to assessment of their affordability for the public budget. While in Chile only certain projects such as road concessions are assessed, in most OECD countries an assessment of affordability for the public budget is in place for all larger infrastructure projects (Table 2.4). The institutions responsible for these assessments are often Ministries of Finance or the corresponding line ministries.

Table 2.4. Are infrastructure projects subject to an assessment of their affordability for the public budget?

All projects	All projects above a threshold	Certain projects	None
Belgium	Austria	Chile	Australia
Czech Republic	Denmark	France	
Estonia	Norway	Mexico	
Finland	Korea		
Germany	Slovenia		
Ireland	Sweden		
Italy	Turkey		
Luxembourg			
New Zealand			
Spain			
Switzerland			
United Kingdom			

Note: Total respondents: 23.
Source: OECD (2016a), OECD Survey of Infrastructure Governance.

Furthermore, the absence of multi-year budgeting creates challenges for infrastructure planners. Most infrastructure investments take place over multiple years. The lack of medium-term commitments generates uncertainty for both the procuring authority and the contractor. Moreover, without medium-term visibility as to the availability of budget resources, infrastructure planners find it difficult to develop a pipeline of projects.

The strong leadership of DIPRES, the Directorate of the Budget at the Ministry of Finance, helps align budgets with the president's medium-term strategic priorities. Progress has been made in designing operational programmes using a logical framework when submitting requests for new and additional funding. However, the budget document would benefit if its programme structure was more closely aligned with these operational programmes. Medium-term expenditure frameworks are only used as an internal management tool by DIPRES, not exploited as a tool for planning. Most OECD countries have introduced MTEFs into the annual budget preparation process. For a detailed analysis of Chile's budget system, please see OECD (2016b), Budgeting in Chile (see Chapter 3 for an analysis with regard to subnational levels).

Alternative financing methodologies such as an infrastructure fund, additional to the budget, are being discussed in Chile. In principle, the arrangements around PPPs and other infrastructure investments should take the principles of Value for Money (see Section 1.7, Value for Money), affordability and transparency as their point of departure. It is unclear whether non-traditional financing methods add value in themselves, e.g. the cost of borrowing money will always be lower for a sovereign borrower. The value added of the use of such an infrastructure fund should hence be carefully evaluated. Other examples for Infrastructure Funds can be found in Denmark (Box 2.9).

Box 2.9. The Danish Infrastructure Fund

As a part of the agreement on the new green transport policy in 2009, and as a response to large transport investment needs and the desire to provide economic stimulus in response to the global financial crisis in Denmark, a major Infrastructure Fund was established. The Fund was endowed with DKK 97.3 billion (around EUR 13.5 billion) to be invested on the basis of the priorities and specific projects identified by the Infrastructure Commission and endorsed by the political parties behind the agreement. The fund provides the means for specific projects and other infrastructural efforts that have been decided upon through 2020 as a part of the political agreements.

The Infrastructure Fund is financed partly by tax revenues and partly by other sources such as returns on the sale of public assets, road revenues (including tolls from the Oresund and the Great Belt fixed link) and tax financed means. Political priorities can be determined within the means available. The Fund is dynamic and replenished with additional means as new sustainable sources of funding are identified, as well as with savings on projects decided within the Fund. "Land value capture", i.e. increased land value due to investments in transport, is used as a part of the financing.

The Parliament originally allocated one-third of the fund to infrastructure projects in the road transport sector, while the remaining two-thirds were intended for rail projects. However, in the context of political reprioritisation at the end of 2012, the Danish government decided to use all the funds for rail infrastructure projects, including additional funding from the annual budget. In 2013, a discussion began about the establishment of a further fund, the so-called "Togfonden" (train fund) for the financing of transport infrastructure, with a draft a volume of 28.5 billion Danish kroner (approx. EUR 3.7 billion). The fund's aim was to improve the rail links between Copenhagen and other major cities and to push ahead the electrification of the Danish rail infrastructure. However, a lack of financing due to falling oil prices caused negotiations to stall, and by end of 2016 they had not been completed.

Source: Danish Infrastructure Investment, Ministry of Transport, Ministry of Transport (2013), "Best Practices Study on Transport Infrastructure Planning and Financing in the EU" (Best-Practices-Studie zur Verkehrsinfrastrukturplanung und -finanzierung in der EU), Final Report.

Cost overruns pose a risk to the affordability and value for money of infrastructure projects. Traditional infrastructure procurement processes are especially likely to face cost and time overruns (Burger and Hawkesworth, 2013). To reduce this "optimism bias" (Box 2.10), namely the tendency for *ex ante* assessments to underestimate the cost and time it will take to complete a project, Denmark (Annex 3) introduced a new approach to budgeting that has dramatically limited cost overruns. In the past, transport projects often turned out to be 40-50% more expensive than originally budgeted for. Denmark introduced a new budgeting regime, where the estimate for a project's cost is supplemented with a 50% reserve. This total sum has to be budgeted up front and appropriated by Parliament in the annual budget act. If a project goes under-budget, the remaining funds can be assigned to other projects. To avoid the risk of overpriced tenders and price-fixing under this approach, a high level of competition has to be ensured.

Box 2.10. Optimism bias for large infrastructure projects

The term **optimism bias** describes the tendency of planners to make overly positive predictions of outcomes. Especially for large infrastructure projects, the high degree of uncertainty due to the long planning horizon and the complexity of the projects represent a challenge to budgeting and timing. Conditions and ambitions may significantly change during a project's development and implementation, although uncertainty may diminish through the project cycle. However, this uncertainty cannot come as a surprise, since cost and time overruns in infrastructure projects are more the rule than the exception. A study by Bent Flyvbjerg et al. (2003) examined more than 200 transport mega projects in 20 countries around the world and showed that development costs were on average 28% higher than forecasted.

To anticipate these future cost overruns, governments may augment the estimated budgets already at the time of the decision to build a project. These budget "uplifts" (Flyvbjerg, 2004) depend on the estimated probability of cost overruns as well as on the acceptable degree of risk. The introduction of optimism bias includes three steps:

1. Identifying a relevant reference class of past projects of similar in scope and risks to the planned projects
2. Establishing a probability distribution for the selected reference class, based on sufficient and credible data (at least 10 projects)
3. Deciding on the acceptable risk, i.e. placing the specific project at an appropriate point in the reference class distribution.

The third step depends on the investors' capability to assume risk. Organisations with a large portfolio of projects and the ability to reallocate budgets between projects may use the average cost overrun as the budget uplift, accepting the 50% chance that the budget increase may be higher than the average cost overrun. On the other hand, individual large projects with no access to additional funds beyond the approved budget cannot afford to take on as much of a risk of cost overruns. In these cases the uplift needs to be higher than the average cost overrun to ensure that the probability of the final cost above the budget (including up-lift) will below the acceptable risk threshold.

If total budget reservation (including the uplifts) is perceived as being available to the project, optimism bias up-lifts may act as incentivises against cost control. Therefore it is essential to supplement the introduction of optimism bias measures with thorough risk assessments and prudent cost controls during project implementation.

Source: Flyvbjerg, B. et al. (2004), "Procedures for Dealing with Optimism Bias in Transport Planning"; Flyvbjerg, B., Bruzelius, N. and Rothengatter, W. (2003), "Mega Projects and Risk: An Anatomy of Ambition".

Competition

Competition is another important tool for ensuring the sustainability and affordability of infrastructure investments. In the case of infrastructure-based services that often have natural monopoly features, sound procurement processes are essential to guaranteeing that investments are subject to competitive forces and thus place a priority on value for money. This is particularly important in the case of PPPs and concessions that lock in costs for users or taxpayers over long periods, often reaching 30 years or more. Among the keys is taking steps to ensure and promote the proper functioning of the suppliers' market, both domestically and on the more regional markets. This means working to reduce the barriers to entry to allow for and promote greater market access for new medium and small specialists where possible while improving the processes of evaluation and monitoring of contractors and strengthening processes and market intelligence capabilities. In these respects the knowledge of regulations and alternative models to mitigate market failures should be valued.

The use of market soundings in the UK is considered a key element of developing a good PPP pipeline. The UK government engages in an ongoing conversation with domestic and international market participants in order to ensure that there is interest, that the projects are realistic from the private sector's point of view. This also gives give market participants greater confidence that a pipeline of projects is approaching. Without assurances about the quality and quantity of relevant projects, private actors will disband bidding teams and thus competition will be weakened. Various provincial Australian governments travel to other countries in Europe and Asia and present their PPP programme, procedures, and pipeline in order to entice foreign companies to bid. Even if foreign companies do not bid, the mere possibility of entry - if it is realistic- should enhance competitive bidding (Box 2.11).

Box 2.11. International competition in infrastructure projects in Australia

The emergence of new international competition in the Australian local construction industry is seen as an opportunity to build infrastructure cheaper and faster. In 2014, the arrival of six Spanish construction firms in Australia to compete for greenfields infrastructure projects broke the duopoly that had dominated the Australian market and highlighted the benefits of freer global trade.

In an interview, former Minister of Trade, Andrew Robb, said the competition had been drawn to Australia by the prospect of infrastructure investment being reinvigorated by asset sales to fund new developments.

"It is a huge opportunity to do it and have some of the best construction companies in the world bringing state-of-the-art expertise and innovation to all of this rollout of infrastructure," Mr. Robb told The Australian. "What was seen as a duopoly in Australia with major projects has now become highly competitive in the space of five years," Mr. Robb said. He highlighted the east-west road development in Melbourne, where there were Spanish companies in each of three short-listed consortia bidding for the project.

Treasurer Joe Hockey has offered the states AUD 5 billion in top-up payments if they sell assets such as ports and electricity transmission and distribution networks and use the proceeds to build new roads, rail and hospitals. Mr. Robb said the apparent certainty of funding for the projects from asset sales, combined with low financing costs and a shortfall of work elsewhere in the world had drawn international players to Australia.

Source: White, A. (2014), "More competition in building 'good for infrastructure'", The Australian, in OECD (2015), *Effective Delivery of Large Infrastructure Projects: The Case of the New International Airport of Mexico City.*

To promote the fair and equitable treatment of potential suppliers, the OECD (2015b) Recommendation of the Council on Public Procurement advocates an adequate and timely degree of transparency in each phase of the public procurement cycle. While taking into account the legitimate needs for protection of trade secrets and proprietary information and other privacy concerns, as well as the need to avoid releasing information that could be used by interested suppliers to distort competition in the procurement process, the process should ensure an adequate degree of transparency for contractors and suppliers, including the appropriate transparency in subcontracting relationships.

This may be achieved by allowing free access, through an online portal, for all stakeholders, including potential domestic and foreign suppliers, civil society and the general public, to public procurement information, especially data related to the public procurement system (e.g. institutional frameworks, laws and regulations), the specific procurements (e.g. procurement forecasts, calls for tender, award announcements), and the performance of the public procurement system (e.g. benchmarks, monitoring results). Published data should be meaningful for stakeholder uses. Furthermore, visibility of the flow of public funds, from the beginning of the budgeting process through all stages of the public procurement cycle, should be ensured to allow stakeholders to understand government priorities and spending, and policy makers to organise procurement strategically (OECD, 2015b).

Ensuring competition during contract modifications, renegotiations or extensions is more problematic than during the initial contract award. For this reason, infrastructure managers should place strict limits on the recourse to such practices. While certain renegotiations might be the consequence of unforeseeable events, others can be the result of opportunistic behaviour on the part of the operator or the contracting authority.

In Chile, modifications and extensions to concession contracts occur fairly frequently. According to research by Bitran et al. (2013), between 1993 and 2004, there were on average 3.3 renegotiations per concession, representing a total additional compensation to concessionaires of 25% of the initial cost of the projects. A majority, or 84%, of the contract modifications were government led, and 69% were for complementary works. When project additions are commissioned via this mechanism, they bypass the normal project approval processes and controls exercised by institutions such as the Ministry of Social Development. Furthermore, because they take place in the absence of competition, they are likely to come at a considerably higher cost than would be the case under competitive tendering. Although this phenomenon is prevalent for concessions, similar problems also occur for the traditional state-financed infrastructure. It should be emphasised, however, that changes to ordinary public works contracts also happen frequently across all countries often arising from optimism bias, changes in specifications from the public side or discoveries of new issues related to construction.

To reduce the occurrence of such practices, a number of reforms were made to the concessions law in 2010, including stricter limits on renegotiations, both in terms of amounts and conditions, and required bidding for works. According to the MOP(2017), these changes in coherence with the Ministry's "Plan to improve concession contracts" have resulted in a reduced number of contract modification, limited to cases were changes were absolutely necessary to secure the wellbeing of the community, and building all works[2] through public bidding procedures, all with the approval of the Ministry of Social Development (MOP, 2017). It remains to be seen how effective these reforms have been in terms of reducing the frequency of contract modifications in the long run. In addition to reforms to the legal framework governing concessions, there is a need to address some of the underlying causes – including insufficient resources to prepare new projects and insufficient analytical capacity – that drive contracting authorities (the CCOP in particular) to resort to contract modifications and extensions.

Focus on performance over lifetime of an asset

> *Systems should be put in place to ensure a focus on the performance of the asset throughout its lifespan.*

A challenge for virtually all OECD countries is applying a whole-of-life perspective to infrastructure investments (Figure 2.2). The emphasis of infrastructure planning and financing is heavily skewed towards the initial investment phase because it offers more immediate rewards for politicians, project champions and developers. When they neglect future phases of the project lifecycle including operation, maintenance and disposal, countries run the risks of over-investing in new infrastructure, under-investing in maintenance, operating infrastructure inefficiently, and underestimating the disposal costs. Countries whose Supreme Audit Institutions conduct analyses of assets over their whole life-cycle include Austria, Belgium, Czech Republic, Estonia, Denmark, Germany, Ireland, Italy, Korea, Slovenia, Sweden, Switzerland, Turkey, and the United Kingdom.

Figure 2.2. Type of audits performed by the Supreme Audit Institution regarding infrastructure assets in OECD countries

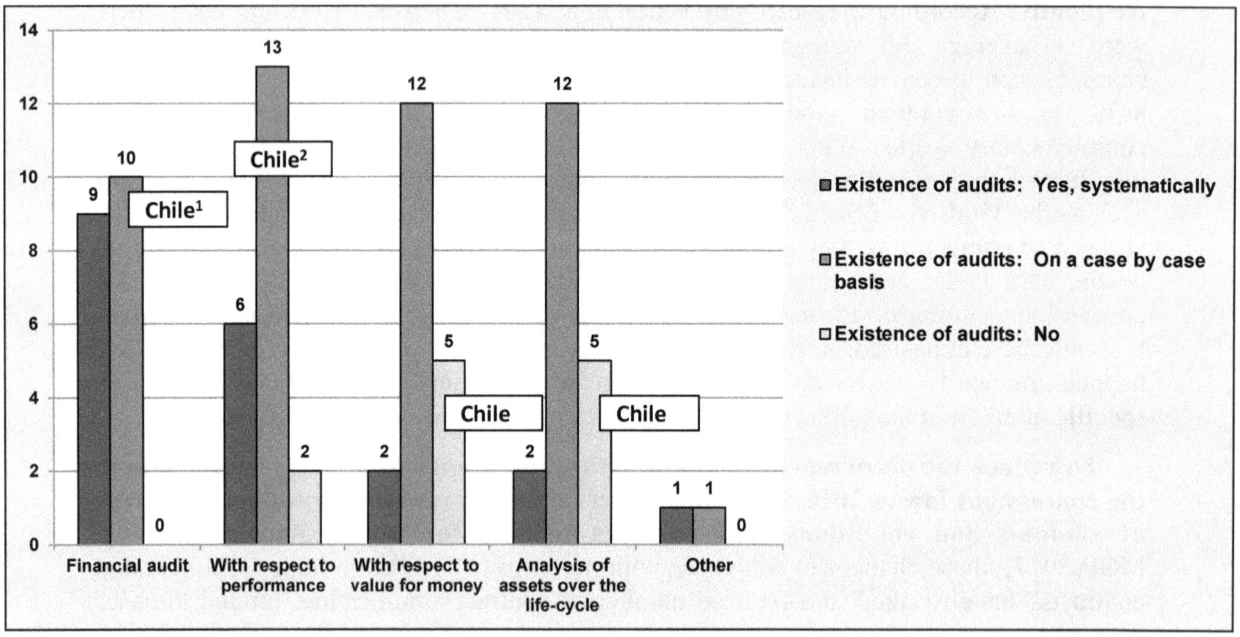

Note: Total respondents: 23; 1. As per yearly audit plans; 2. Litigation or Inquiries.

Source: OECD (2016a), OECD Survey of Infrastructure Governance

By bundling financing, construction, operation and maintenance, well-structured PPPs and concessions inject a whole-of-life approach to managing infrastructure, and provide strong incentives for ensuring that infrastructure is adequately maintained and efficiently operated. In making extensive use of the concessions model for roads, Chile has ensured that a significant proportion of its highways are maintained to high international standards. However, in contrast with a majority of OECD countries, Chile does not have a formal policy ensuring that the relevant line ministry or agency conducts a performance assessment of each project (Table 2.5). As the road network ages and becomes more subject to deterioration, it will become increasingly important to ensure that sufficient funds are allocated to maintenance. As concessions come to an end and are re-concessioned, the contracting authority should ensure that new concession contracts accommodate a greater need for maintenance by setting appropriate service-level standards and an adequate level of toll revenues.

Table 2.5. Are there formal policies ensuring that the relevant line ministry or agency conducts performance assessment of each infrastructure project?

Yes	No
	Chile
Czech Republic	Australia
Finland	Austria
Germany	Belgium
Ireland	Denmark
Italy	Estonia
Japan	France
Mexico	Luxembourg
New Zealand	Norway
Korea	Slovenia
Spain	Sweden
Turkey	Switzerland
United Kingdom	

Source: OECD (2016a), OECD Survey of Infrastructure Governance.

Moreover, the CCOP will need to ensure that it has the sufficient capacity to effectively monitor service levels with regard to maintenance and contract management. Concerns have been raised in Chile over the management of concession contracts during the operational phase. This is partly a question of insufficient resources since, over time, more and more projects enter their operational phases, thereby requiring increasing resources for overseeing the performance of the operators. Clearly defined accountability, roles and responsibilities are among the key areas identified by the good practice contract management framework in the UK (Box 2.12). Moreover, in Chile, the monitoring function for concessions has developed under a construction logic, with much of the emphasis placed on the technical inspection of works, as opposed to an operating logic focused on monitoring service levels (MOP, 2016).

This also relates to the role of the contract manager (*Inspector Fiscal*) tasked with monitoring the implementation of contracts. The World Bank has noted that, under the current arrangement, a great deal of responsibility is concentrated in this single individual, with insufficient resources, procedures and standards in place to support and guide the work of the *Inspector Fiscal* (World Bank, 2015a). Such a personalised model may result in a lack of consistency between projects. Furthermore, the *Inspector Fiscal* model is one borrowed from traditional public works, and as such it is mainly oriented towards the oversight of construction activities. However, during the operational phase, concessions are especially in need of monitoring of service levels using standardised processes and criteria.

Box 2.12. Good practice in the legal framework for contract management contract management principles in the United Kingdom

Good practice in the contract management framework was developed by the UK National Audit Office to focus on the activities that need to be undertaken during the operational phase of the contract. It is particularly relevant for contracts where services are delivered over a long period of time (five years or more) to ensure that service levels and value for money are maintained over the duration of the contract.

The framework covers 11 areas of contract management, including the planning, delivery, and development phases. Based on this framework, the Crown Commercial Service developed 11 contract management principles:

1. Ensure that contracts are known and understood by all those who will be involved in their management.
2. Be clear about accountability, roles and responsibilities.
3. Establish and use strong governance arrangements to manage risk and enable strategic oversight.
4. Adopt a differentiated approach based on risk
5. Manage contracts for business/public service outcomes.
6. Accept that change will happen and plan for it.
7. Measure and report on performance and use data efficiently to incentivise good performance
8. Drive continuous improvement, value for money and capture innovation.
9. Accept that successful delivery of major projects is best achieved through a single fully integrated team.
10. Ensure that links are made with organisation and/or government wide SRM programmes
11. Adopt and encourage mature commercial behaviours.

Source: NAO (2016), www.nao.org.uk/wp-content/uploads/2016/12/Good_practice_contract_management_framework.pdf, CCS(2014), www.gov.uk/government/uploads/system/uploads/attachment_data/file/395083/Contract_Management_Principles.pdf.

Public procurement methods lack a similar incentive structure for taking a lifecycle approach to infrastructure management. It is therefore important for project planners to estimate and budget for future operation and maintenance expenditures at the time of project preparation. Decisions regarding choices of technology should also be based on a whole-of-life approach. For example, decisions on road surfaces should take into account the impact of different paving solutions on long-run maintenance needs and road users' safety. When considering whether to opt for paved or unpaved roads, project evaluators need to consider the trade-off between investment and maintenance costs in the CBA analysis. As Chilean planners consider the appropriate standards to be applied to different categories of roads, they should consider the implications of various options on maintenance budgets. Furthermore, an analysis of ongoing costs relating to operating and maintaining the asset should also feature in the review undertaken by the Ministry of Finance.

For roads under public management, Chile currently uses a range of mechanisms for maintaining the road network. They include direct management by the MOP, global maintenance contracts covering a pre-determined set of interventions within a particular road network, and service-level contracts whereby contractors are awarded the responsibility for maintaining public road networks to certain quality and safety standards. In 2011, global contracts accounted for approximately 57% of road network maintenance (Vivallos, 2013). Service contracts have the benefit of incentivising contractors to monitor the quality of the roads and perform more preventive maintenance. They therefore have the potential to ensure roads are maintained to a high standard, as well as reduce overall maintenance costs on a whole of life basis. They are currently used only for paved roads and cover routine maintenance. Where possible, the MOP should consider expanding the use of service-level contracts as a way of improving the overall quality of the road network.

Delivery units such as the CCOP should dedicate sufficient capacity to the operational phases of projects. This should be done regardless of the procurement method used – traditional or concession. Furthermore they should ensure that the performance of assets and service levels is actively monitored.

Value for money

There should be rigorous processes for addressing absolute and relative value for money, e.g. cost-benefit analysis, affordability for the public purse and users, and transparency of key information on both the project and the overall asset portfolio.

Chile's National Investment System (SNI) has a number of well-institutionalised processes that promote value for money and transparency in the use of public investment. One of the pillars of Chile's public investment system is the social cost-benefit analysis (CBA) process that lies at the heart of project evaluation (Figure 2.3). This process has a number of strengths, including a simple and clear target rate of return, well-documented methodologies for undertaking CBA and a clear institutional separation of roles between project development, evaluation and approval. With regard to this latter point, sectoral ministries like the MOP and MINVU prepare and deliver projects, while the MDS is responsible for reviewing and approving social cost-benefit evaluations. Nevertheless, there is no formal requirement for ensuring absolute value for money from infrastructure projects (Table 2.6). As a consequence, only 40% of projects are subjected to cost-benefit analyses. Of those, 70% are assessed using the minimum-cost criteria (Ferro and Mercadier, 2016).

Figure 2.3. Approaches to determining value for money in Chile and OECD countries

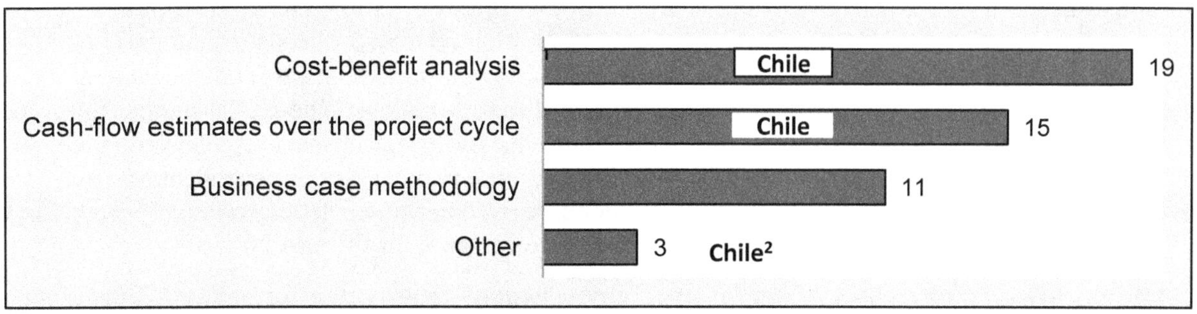

Note: 1. including Total Cost of Ownership during the life-cycle, 2. Cost-efficiency.

Source: OECD (2016a), OECD Survey of Infrastructure Governance

Table 2.6. Formal process or legal requirements for to ensure absolute value for money from infrastructure projects in Chile and OECD countries

Yes	No
	Chile
Australiaa	Austria
Germanya	Estonia
France[a 1]	Luxembourg
Italya	Slovenia
United Kingdoma	Spain
Hungary[b]	Sweden
Ireland[b]	
Japan[b]	
New Zealand[b]	
Norway[b]	
Korea[b]	
Turkey[b]	
Mexico[c]	
Czech Republic[d]	
Denmark[d]	
Finland[d]	
Switzerland[d]	

Notes: a. Yes in all cases; b. In all cases above a certain value threshold; c. On an ad hoc basis; d. Only PPP Projects; (1) Either by Infrastructure Australia or the budget department;(2). excluding projects financed by local authorities.

Source: OECD (2016a), OECD Survey of Infrastructure Governance.

A further safeguard relates to the Ministry of Finance's central role in approving key project milestones that involve commitments such as tender documentation and contract award. Like in most OECD countries (Table 2.7), the project cannot proceed if requirements set by the MoF are not fulfilled. This exerts a further check on the system, thereby helping to ensure not only that projects generate a positive social return, but also that they are well-structured in financial terms, are affordable for the public purse and do not burden the state with excessive risks.

Chile's National Investment System also exhibits a high degree of transparency. The various methodologies and processes for undertaking social evaluations are published on the MDS's website, as are the social prices used in those evaluations. An online Integrated Project Database provides information relating to the status and costs of all public investments, thereby enabling civil society, the private sector and the general public to monitor investments across sectors in different regions. The CCOP within the MOP also publishes extensive information on concessions during each of phase of the project's lifecycle. This system, which combines rigorous processes, independent review and a high degree of transparency, has undoubtedly contributed to the relatively high quality and efficiency of Chile's infrastructure investments over the past 20 years.

However, as mentioned earlier, **in the concessions field, value for money can be undermined by contract modifications and extensions, and will hence require special control.** Not only do such practices bypass the social evaluation system, but they result in infrastructure being procured at a higher cost than necessary since they avoid the disciplines imposed by competition.

Table 2.7. Does the Central Budget Authority have a formal, gate-keeping role in approving infrastructure projects?

Yes	No
Chile	
Austria	Australia
Belgium	Estonia
Czech Republic	New Zealand
Denmark	Norway
Finland	Switzerland
France	
Germany	
Ireland	
Italy	
Japan	
Luxembourg	
Mexico	
Korea	
Slovenia	
Spain	
Turkey	
United Kingdom	
Sweden	

Source: OECD (2016a), OECD Survey of Infrastructure Governance.

Robust anti-corruption mechanisms

Corruption entry points should be mapped at each stage of the public infrastructure project, and integrity and anti-corruption mechanisms should be enhanced.

Chile has some strong independent institutions and measures that work to guard against corruption in infrastructure projects (Table 2.8). The Comptroller General of the Republic of Chile plays a key role in this respect by performing *ex ante* evaluations of infrastructure projects to ensure that they comply with the contract as well as applicable laws and regulations. The remit of the Comptroller General also extends to auditing projects procured by state-owned enterprises such as the Santiago Metro company. While the office of the Comptroller General is not permitted to undertake performance audits, it has been expanding the scope of its audit reports to encompass principles like efficiency, economic use and efficacy. It has also been extending its responsibility from a narrow focus on projects to consider broader themes and processes, with a view to detecting patterns that might be indicative of systemic problems.

External experts and members of civil society have expressed concerns over the potential for public bodies responsible for infrastructure spending to be unduly influenced by private actors (Engel, 2016). In some cases, this could involve the supply of privileged information to a private party, thereby providing that party with an unfair advantage. It may also entail an excessive dependence on a private party's expertise and analytical capacity. Such practices may not always be the result of foul play, but may simply be the consequence of a lack of technical capacity and human resources within a procuring authority.

Table 2.8. Chile's anti-corruption measures in the infrastructure governance process

Measures	OECD Survey of Infrastructure Governance (No. of countries)						
	Public works		State owned enterprises (SOE)		PPP/Concession		Regulated Private Assets
Private contractors sign codes of conduct	7	Chile	4	Chile	4	Chile	2
Staff members of private contractors sign integrity pacts	5		2		4		3
Private contractors are subject to spot checks by government/outside auditors	9	Chile	6	Chile	7	Chile	3
Staff members of private contractors are subject to spot checks by government/outside auditors	4		3		4		2
There is an online warning system in place to share discovered corruption schemes and/or warning signs among relevant agencies on a real time basis	6		5		4		3
An anti-corruption monitoring board is in place with independent expert representation to analyse transaction and/or improve procedures	2		1		1		1
Others: Audits by the Contraloría General de la Republica		Chile		Chile		Chile	-

Source: OECD (2016a), OECD Survey of Infrastructure Governance.

The regular use of unsolicited bids, particularly in the domain of concessions, may be a symptom of insufficient capacity and financial resources within the CCOP to design and prepare projects. Excessive reliance on unsolicited bids raises the risk that infrastructure development will follow a piecemeal logic driven primarily by private interests as opposed to one that is based on a coherent and integrated strategy grounded in the pursuit of public interests (MOP, 2016).

Strong technical capacity within the contracting authorities will enable them to maintain a healthy arm's length relationship with private interests. It is thus important for procuring authorities such as the MOP and the CCOP to identify areas where they may lack capacity and expertise with a view to then strengthening those areas.

Collection, dissemination, and analysis of data

Infrastructure governance should be based on data. Governments should put in place systems that ensure the systematic collection of relevant data and institutional responsibility for analysis, dissemination and learning from this data.

Chile, as a pioneer in concessions in Latin America, stands in the enviable position of having a strong track record of projects that have completed their full lifecycle. In spite of Chile's relatively long experience of using concessions, particularly in the roads sector, more should be done to leverage this experience through the systematic collection and analysis of data on projects (Table 2.9). A key obstacle lies in the analytical capacities of the CCOP, whose ability to make better use of data is constrained by limited resources. The ability to take stock and learn from past experience is particularly important now that a number of concession contracts are terminating and will need to be retendered. A more systematic use of data will ensure that Chile makes use of its experience to further improve and refine its concessions systems.

Table 2.9. Mandatory systems for the systematic collection and dissemination of relevant financial and non-financial infrastructure project data

	OECD Survey of Infrastructure Governance (Yes, No. of countries)	Chile
Ex ante:		
Collection of data	16	No
Disclosure of data	12	No
Use of data	10	No
Analysis of data	10	No
Ex post:		
Collection of performance data	7	No

Source: OECD (2016a), OECD Survey of Infrastructure Governance.

The recent establishment of the Research and Financial Analysis Division within the CCOP is a step in the right direction. This division is tasked with putting in place procedures and standards for performing financial analyses during all the stages of a project, monitoring the industry, and undertaking transversal studies, all with a view to improving processes (MOP, 2016). It will be important for unit to be endowed with the capacity and resources it will need to perform its duties effectively, allowing it to serve as a mechanism for learning, feedback and dissemination of best practice, using state-of-the-art technology and tools. Furthermore, a prerequisite for generating research output is to have access to data throughout the lifecycle of projects. To this end, it will be necessary to ensure that the research unit is empowered by information systems that collect and provide access to such data (World Bank, 2015a).

It is equally important that data on projects executed through traditional means are systematically collected and analysed. A key challenge with regard to being able to compare different project delivery modes (traditional procurement vs. PPPs) lies in the generally weaker standard of scrutiny and transparency applied to traditional procurement modes.

The ITF and OECD have recommended the establishment of a Logistics Observatory to collect, analyse and disseminate data on transport and logistics, and to develop key performance indicators (ITF/OECD, 2016). A similar capability is required for infrastructure, covering the full lifecycle of planning, preparation, execution and operation. The establishment of an independent analysis unit tasked with collecting, analysing and disseminating data across all delivery modes would enhance Chile's ability to learn from its experience, and ensure that Chile remains at the cutting edge of infrastructure delivery.

Resilience of public infrastructure

Infrastructure systems should be resilient, adaptable to new circumstances and future-proof. Critical risks materialise, and technological change can fundamentally disrupt sectors and economies

Multiple disasters in recent years have demonstrated significant impacts of disasters and their consequences for citizens. Disruptions to critical infrastructure systems spread the social hardships of disasters in several ways. They can cut off access to basic lifelines (health services, food, fuel, payment systems), leave citizens for an extended period without the reliable electricity, communications, and mobility that infrastructure provides, and produce large economic impacts by preventing the mobility of labour and inventory. According to the World Risk Index (ADI, 2016), Chile is the 11th most exposed country in the world to natural hazards. However, due to its low susceptibility and well-developed coping and adaptive capacities, it only ranks 22 on the World Risks index.

In Chile, responsibility for climate change policy and environmental policy more generally lies with the Ministry of the Environment. However, aside from the obligation to perform environmental impact assessments as part of project preparation activities, the application of environmental standards, and the use of social prices in cost-benefit evaluations, there are limited incentives and instruments for incorporating environmental considerations infrastructure planning strategy and decision making. Strategic Environmental Evaluations (Evaluación Ambiental Estratégica – EAE) are used to assess the risks and effects of local and regional territorial development plans. However, their focus on risk management limits their potential to act as drivers of change, for example by promoting longer-term sustainable development objectives (OECD, 2013a). Regionalised and integrated sustainability concepts in planning throughout the project's life cycle are needed to enable compliance with international commitments to reduce emissions and to comply with the Sustainable Development Goals. Furthermore, cities are responsible for a significant share of infrastructure investments, which if invested wisely can contribute to national efforts to combine growth with environmental performance (Box 2.13).

Box 2.13. How can national governments support green growth in cities?

Cities do not act in isolation from upper echelons of government. National governments can enhance cities' capacity to act on green growth in the following ways:

1. Bridging the gap between national and local approaches to green growth. National plans often do not account for the spatial elements of green growth, nor for cities' existing contributions to green growth. Urban green growth initiatives can run the risk of being stand-alone, flagship green projects that are dependent on short-term political cycles; long-term sustainable economic growth calls for a systematic, citywide, multi-sectoral approach.
2. Providing the technical assistance, funding and knowledge needed for large-scale infrastructure projects – such as smart grids, high-speed trains, and green R&D – and to help cities measure the economic and environmental impact of green growth initiatives.
3. Setting strong national and international environmental targets and baseline standards to remove policy obstacles, prevent harmful competition among regions and promote a "race to the top" (OECD, 2010a). At the same time, cities need flexibility in how they meet these targets in order to innovate urban-level policy responses that can then be scaled up.
4. Establishing national price signals and standards – e.g. through carbon taxes or other pricing mechanisms. Such signals can enhance the incentives for firms to adopt and develop green innovations and help to indicate the commitment of governments to move towards greener growth. They can also enhance efficiency in allocating resources by establishing markets for green innovation and will lower the costs of addressing environmental challenges.

Box 2.13. How can national governments support green growth in cities? *(cont.)*

5. Creating a common set of urban environmental and economic indicators to compare best practices and measure the impact of green growth projects on environmental, economic and social priorities. National governments can help develop a common methodology and support capacity building at the subnational level.
6. Re-designing taxes and grants to subnational governments to correct incentives for unsustainable behaviour and reward cities that create environmental benefits beyond their borders.

Source: OECD (2013b), *Green Growth in Cities*, OECD Publishing, Paris.

Countries like France and the Netherlands have created greater alignment and coherence their between infrastructure plans and environmental objectives by merging the environmental and infrastructure portfolios within a single ministry (see Annexes 2A and 2B). If this isn't feasible, an alternative would be establishing a unit within the centre of government focused on ensuring a whole-of-government approach to addressing environmental challenges such as climate change.

What kind of planning framework does Chile need going forward?

A key weakness identified in Chile's governance framework is the lack of medium- to long-term infrastructure planning, particularly in central government. Investment in high quality and efficient infrastructure is an essential ingredient for ensuring a country's long-term productivity, competitiveness, and the well-being of its population. Infrastructure, more so than other government policy choices and investments, requires a particularly long-term perspective because it involves large sunk costs in highly specific assets that have long lifetimes. Investments in infrastructure can thus frame a country's development options for decades to come. Thus, while good investments can be catalytic for a country's development, bad choices can be disastrous because they represent a waste of resources, and can commit a country to a development pathway that doesn't improve welfare and generates strong negative externalities (e.g. air pollution).

The need for infrastructure planning

Unfortunately, the long-term nature of infrastructure investment sits awkwardly with the nature of modern politics. This is particularly the case in democratic systems where political cycles are short and political priorities are often driven by the urgent short-term needs of the population and the volatility of the media. Chile faces a particular challenge in this regard because of short four-year Presidential terms that cannot be renewed. This naturally creates a bias in favour of programmes and policies that generate results that can be felt in the short-term.

The highly visible nature of large infrastructure projects creates a further disconnect between politics and infrastructure investment. On the one hand, politicians have a strong incentive to privilege infrastructure investments that are highly visible, and thus leave a "legacy". On the other hand, infrastructure's contribution to economic development and wellbeing depends on far more than just the physical asset and, in particular, the construction of the asset. What ultimately generates an economic or social return is the service that is provided through infrastructure - which requires that physical assets be operated and maintained - alongside soft assets such as human capital, processes, and organisational structures. Unfortunately, when the incentives are skewed toward leaving a "legacy", these other dimensions can be neglected, resulting in inefficient investments that fail to respond adequately to the needs of the population.

In spite of the awkward relationship between politics and infrastructure, infrastructure cannot be completely de-politicised. Since infrastructure needs almost always exceed available resources, trade-offs inevitably exist between different priorities. Navigating these trade-offs often requires making difficult choices that weigh the interests of different social groups and values (e.g. current versus future generations; urban versus rural; growth versus environment). These choices cannot be reduced to a simple technocratic exercise. Consequently, politics has a critical role to play in infrastructure decisions. The question is how to ensure that politics plays a constructive role given the misalignment between political cycles and infrastructure lifecycles.

Part of the role of infrastructure planning is to align investment decisions with the country's needs and long-term development goals. It should also serve to frame and guide political choices so that infrastructure investments respond to important needs while ensuring value for money over the lifetime of an asset.

An infrastructure planning system should have the following characteristics and functions:

- guided by a long-term vision and goals for the country's economic and social development
- takes into account future trends and uncertainties relating to macroeconomic, political, technological, environmental, demographic and social issues
- addresses current as well as future needs of the population
- integrated within sectors to ensure that the full range of options for responding to needs are considered in the decision-making process
- co-ordinated across sectors to ensure that investments are aligned and generate synergies
- integrated with land use planning
- aligned with the priorities of the political leadership
- provides space for the political leadership to assess trade-offs and make choices in a transparent manner
- takes a whole-of-life view of infrastructure and focuses on the services that infrastructure enables.

Elements of an infrastructure planning framework

The key role of an infrastructure planning system is to create an enabling pathway between present conditions and a desired future state. Implicit in this particular definition is the need to have a vision for the desired future state. This definition also requires an understanding of present conditions in the form of the current needs of the population and gaps in access to key services. Decisions on what infrastructure to build can then be framed as part of a broader strategy for bridging the present and the future.

The **key dimensions of an infrastructure planning framework on the national level** therefore include: an understanding of the desired future state (the vision), a sense of the future context, an understanding of present conditions and needs, and a strategy for linking current needs and the future vision (Figure 2.4). Chile's infrastructure planning system on the central governance level can thus be assessed in relation to these various components.

Figure 2.4. Infrastructure planning framework

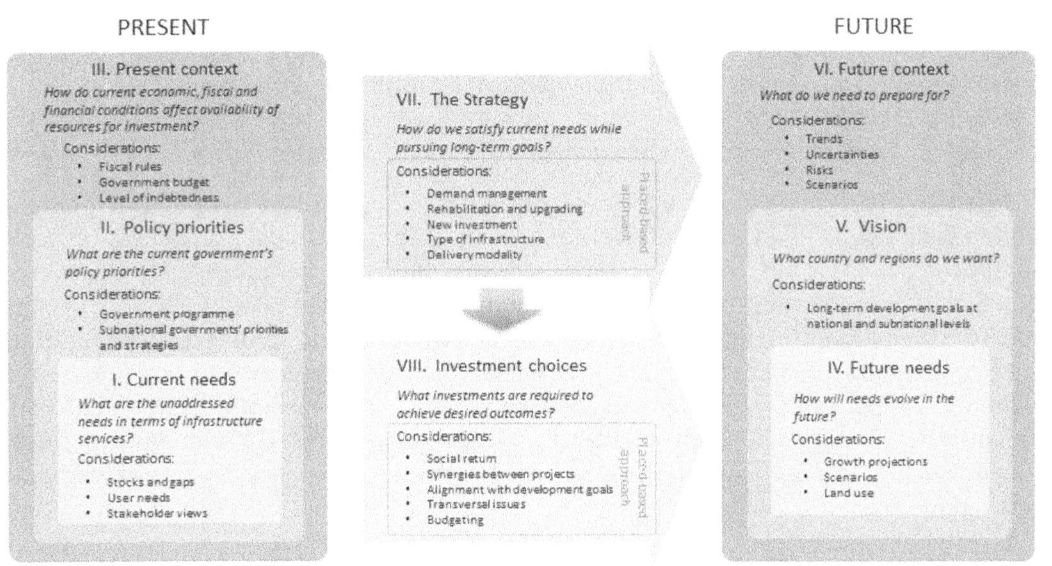

Source: Authors.

I. Needs: What are the unaddressed needs in terms of infrastructure services?

Infrastructure creates value when it contributes to addressing social needs or facilitates economic activity. Choices regarding infrastructure development must therefore be focused on user needs. Information on the stocks and quality of existing infrastructure is an important input into needs assessment. Maintaining an inventory of the country's infrastructure stocks can provide a rational basis for identifying infrastructure needs and gaps.

However, it isn't sufficient to focus solely on current needs. **Needs must be projected into the future**. In so doing, planners must to take into account the country's long-term development goals along with the impact of future trends and uncertainties (see below).

Needs are often best captured at the local level, for welfare-enhancing infrastructure, or at the sectoral level for productivity-enhancing infrastructure. It should therefore be the role of sectoral and regional planners to develop strategies for addressing those needs.

Assessment

As a result of Chile's highly centralised government, infrastructure user needs are generally determined by the central ministries that have the bulk of the spending power. However, such a centralised approach creates a gap between planners and users.

In order to better respond to the needs of the population, it would be important to improve the capacities of local and regional governments to identify needs, and design ways to meet them. Greater democratic accountability at the regional level would no doubt improve the state's attentiveness to local needs, but further devolution of capacities and resources will be required in order to strengthen responsiveness.

In the short- to medium-term, many subnational governments will not have sufficient capacity to plan and develop projects in response to local needs. In parallel with any political and fiscal decentralisation process, it is necessary to strengthen the planning capacities of subnational governments. A more proactive use of stakeholder engagement, particularly in the project preparation phase, can also improve responsiveness to user needs (see Section 3 above, Focusing on users' needs).

II. Policy Priorities: What are the current government's policy priorities?

Infrastructure investment decisions represent a significant proportion of total public expenditure. They should therefore be subject to the oversight of elected officials and reflect the priorities of the national and subnational governments. However, the influence of politicians on the allocation of investment resource should not come at the expense of value-for-money considerations. Decision-making processes should thus create opportunities for political input, yet be carefully circumscribed to limit excessive discretion, ensure transparency, and guard against the risk of corruption and clientelism. The absence of decision points requiring political input does not eliminate political influence, but rather is likely to push it into the shadows and lead to less transparent decision making.

Assessment

Chile's National Investment System has a rigorous process and a well-established methodology for evaluating projects to ensure they generate value for money. However, the current system offers limited scope for incorporating political priorities into the decision process. A more formal role for policy makers in the overall infrastructure planning and project selection process could contribute to a greater degree of transparency around infrastructure prioritisation and more alignment with overall policy priorities.

Project prioritisation methodologies such as multi-criteria analysis (MCA) can provide space for integrating political choices and policy priorities into infrastructure decision making in a transparent manner (see below for a more detailed discussion of MCA). Furthermore, MCA methodologies are able to accommodate additional priorities such as equity across regions, thus reflecting the reality that the context within which infrastructure projects are situated is often highly complex and that they are usually required to satisfy a number of policy goals (Marcelo et al., 2016).

III. Present context: How do current economic conditions affect availability of resources for investment?

The budgetary envelope for infrastructure investment is determined by the country's overall economic conditions and its fiscal status. It is these framework conditions that determine what is possible in the realm of infrastructure investment.

Assessment

Chile's strict annual budgetary process and the oversight of the Ministry of Finance ensure that project approvals are consistent with the country's economic framework conditions. On the other hand, the absence of multi-year budgeting creates challenges for infrastructure planners. Except for the very smallest of projects, infrastructure investments take place over multiple years and require staggered disbursements. While budget appropriations for ongoing projects are prioritised, the lack of medium-term commitments generates uncertainty for both the procuring authority and the contractor. Moreover, without medium-term visibility on the availability of budget resources, infrastructure planners find it difficult to develop a pipeline of projects.

IV. Future needs: How will needs evolve in the future?

Infrastructure is not meant to solely address current needs but must also anticipate how needs are likely to evolve in the future. Failure to do so could result in infrastructure that quickly becomes obsolete or fails to keep up with population or economic growth. The rapid pace of technological change is creating further challenges for infrastructure planners whose choices, good or bad, will be felt for decades to come.

While the input from users and other stakeholders is critical for determining current needs, **planners need to look elsewhere to gain insight into how needs will evolve into the future.** Infrastructure decisions should therefore take into account projections of future population growth and trends such as urbanisation. Future growth projections should also be integrated with a long-term vision for land use, particularly in metropolitan areas. Since long-term projections are, by nature, fallible, planners should consider applying foresight techniques such as scenario planning to develop alternative development pathways for future needs that could serve as a basis for generating more flexible and robust plans. Planners and policy makers will then need chart a path between satisfying today's urgent needs and developing long-term solutions that will be adapted to society's evolving needs.

Assessment

A variety of infrastructure planning tools in Chile take into account the impact of factors such as population and economic growth on infrastructure needs. For example, the "Master Transport Plan for Santiago in 2025" projects factors such as population growth, land use in terms of the distribution of residential and economic activity, and motorisation rates. These are then fed into a transport model for Santiago for the purposes of assessing the implications of different modal shares and deriving investment alternatives.

Given the timeframe required to plan and execute major infrastructure investments, **estimates of future needs could benefit from a longer-term perspective** (for example, a 30-year time frame might fully capture the scale of the changes resulting from demographic change). Developing such projections requires the collaboration of statistical institutes to ensure the availability of data and the use of appropriate methodologies. The use of scenarios could also inject greater robustness into assessments of future needs through accommodating factors that are inherently unpredictable such as the timing and impact of technological change.

V. The Vision: What country do we want?

Infrastructure decisions that will have important implications for a country's economic development during the decades ahead need to be framed by a vision for the future of the country. For example, infrastructure choices made in preparation for a more service-oriented economy are likely to be quite different from those made for an economy that remains dependent on the export of raw materials.

It is the role of the centre of government to provide such a beacon in the form of long-term development goals. These goals should be broad enough to reflect some form of societal consensus that cuts across the political spectrum and will thus be resilient to changes in government. Governments will differ in terms of how they attempt to work towards those goals, but, if the vision is sufficiently robust, they will be aiming in a similar direction.

The process for setting these goals will depend on a country's political system, culture and institutions. However, irrespective of the mechanism, it should be inclusive and serve to aggregate the views and expectations of different parts of society and regions. It should also be clearly communicated so that it may serve as an anchor for policy making across different sectors and levels of government. Infrastructure planners can thus base their choices and investment priorities on a set of long-term objectives that have broad political support.

Assessment

Currently, in Chile, there is no clear long-term vision expressed and communicated via a set of development goals. In some countries, such high-level guidance is provided by the executive or by a leading department. For example, in the Netherlands, the Ministry of Infrastructure and Environment compiles a national spatial plan (National Policy Strategy for Infrastructure and Spatial Planning – SVIR). The SVIR links spatial development and infrastructure within a broad vision for the future of the country in 2040. Moreover, the plan seeks to incorporate and balance 13 national interests defined by the central government. Since the SVIR is binding by law on all central government bodies, sectoral strategies must be consistent with it. It thus provides an overarching framework for the rest of government to develop more detailed sectoral or regional plans (see Annex 2 for a description of the Dutch infrastructure planning approach).

The Plan Chile 30/30 headed by the MOP has the potential to generate such a vision and guiding framework, particularly given the inclusive and bottom-up process employed in its creation. The challenge will be to ensure that the output of the process survives future changes in administration. Ideally, such an initiative should also be designed to serve as the guide for long-term thinking across the whole of government and not simply the MOP in order to generate alignment across sectors. For that, it requires buy-in and participation from multiple ministries and regional governments, and, most importantly, strong backing from the political leadership. Furthermore, there should be mechanisms in place to ensure that infrastructure investment decisions at a sectoral level are aligned with long-term goals.

In 2007, France undertook a similar process called Grenelle de l'environnement which consisted of a multi-stakeholder debate on the environment. This process resulted in the formation of a strong consensus around environment goals. The output of this process was institutionalised through legislation and served to frame infrastructure development over the past decade (see Annex 1 for a description of this process and how it was linked to France's infrastructure planning system).

VI. The future context: What do we need to prepare for?

In addition to being guided a by a long-term vision for the country, infrastructure investment decisions need to be future-proofed. Infrastructure planners must take into account long-term trends and uncertainties in areas such as the global economy, climate change and natural disasters, technology and demographics, among others, that will affect the types of infrastructure that will be necessary in the future. For example, investments in road infrastructure being made today will likely have to accommodate the adoption of driverless car technologies within the next couple of decades. Similarly, with Chile being a highly open and export-oriented economy, the future development paths of countries such as China and India will have a major impact on the structure of Chile's economy.

While many of these factors are impossible to predict, they should nevertheless be reflected in long-term investment decisions. Major uncertainties that have the potential to destabilise a particular sector of the economy should be the focus of research efforts. One such uncertainty is the impact of climate change on different sectors and regions of the country. Infrastructure plans in sectors such as energy, water and transport need to build in sufficient resilience to cope with the effects of climate change.

Strong scientific capabilities are a key part of ensuring that long-term thinking regarding future trends and uncertainties is integrated into decision making. However, it isn't sufficient to simply produce research. Research also needs to be integrated into policymaking and used to inform long-term public investment decisions. Platforms are required for translating research outputs into policy-relevant insights that are then fed into the policymaking and planning processes. Furthermore, since many of these critical uncertainties have systemic impacts across multiple sectors and regions, mechanisms for ensuring that research permeates across government, both horizontally and vertically, are required.

Assessment

In most democracies, electoral politics shortens the horizon of policy makers and creates incentives for politicians to prioritise short-term issues. In Chile, the challenge is particularly acute because of the four-year electoral cycle combined with the single presidential terms. It is therefore important to have institutional arrangements that can counterbalance these pressures by injecting a longer-term perspective into policy making. Some countries such as the UK have institutions at the centre of government that are dedicated to providing research and guidance on long-term trends, or generating foresight analysis in support of policy making (see Box 2.14).

Building on Chile's long-term thinking ability will support the country in its efforts to meet its international climate commitments. Including sustainability concepts in planning supports Chile's in its path towards reaching its intended national determined contribution (INDC) submitted for the Paris Climate Agreement in 2015 to reduce carbon emission intensity by 30% below 2007 levels by 2030.

Box 2.14. Institutional arrangements in the UK for encouraging long-term thinking

The UK government includes a number of institutions that serve to inject scientific research, long-term thinking and important transversal issues into policymaking across the whole of government.

Government Office for Science

The Government Office for Science is a unit with approximately 80 staff members within the Department for Business, Innovation and Skills. Its mission is to "ensure that government policies and decisions are informed by the best scientific evidence and strategic long-term thinking". Its principal responsibilities include providing scientific advice to the Prime Minister and members of the Cabinet, ensuring and improving the quality and use of scientific evidence and advice in government, and creating and supporting connections between officials and the scientific community.

The Government Office for Science produces foresight reports on major long-term public policy issues. Foresight studies use the latest scientific evidence and futures analysis to address complex issues and provide strategic options for policy. Ongoing and recent foresight studies include work on the future of cities, the ageing population, and skills and lifelong learning.

See: www.gov.uk/government/organisations/government-office-for-science.

Horizon Scanning Programme Team

The Horizon Scanning Programme Team is a unit within the UK Cabinet Office that co-ordinates strategic horizon scanning work across government departments by drawing on insights from experts from within and outside of government. The role of horizon scanning is to analyse future trends, identify future threats and opportunities, and improve the resilience of policies to different future environments.The Horizon Scanning Programme Team engages with external experts by organising roundtable discussions on specific topics, taking part in communities of interest that bring together different experts to explore a particular issue, and fostering a network of private sector horizon scanning experts.

See: www.gov.uk/government/groups/horizon-scanning-programme-team

UK Committee on Climate Change

The Committee on Climate Change (CCC) is an independent body whose purpose is to "advise the UK Government and Devolved Administrations on emissions targets and report to Parliament on progress made in reducing greenhouse gas emissions and preparing for climate change". In fulfilling this role the CCC conducts independent analysis into climate change science, economics and policy, and engages with a wide range of organisations and individuals to share evidence and analysis.

The CCC's advice on carbon budgets and targets is reflected in legislation and the Government's carbon reduction strategy. The CCC also provides analysis and recommendations for different sectors such as power, buildings, transport and agriculture.

The CCC comprises a Chairman and eight independent members who are all academics. It has a secretariat with around 30 staff members who provide analytical and corporate support to the Committee. The CCC is jointly sponsored by the Department of Energy and Climate Change (DECC), the Northern Ireland Executive, the Scottish Government and the Welsh Government.

See: www.theccc.org.uk/.

However, Chile's institutional set-up currently **lacks mechanisms such for incentivising longer-term thinking** and integrating research into policy making.

The Presidential programme includes **a commitment to establishing a Ministry for Science and Technology.**[3] This would be a positive measure for promoting the role of science in society in general and in policymaking in particular. An alternative might be to create a scientific advisory body attached to the Presidency, one that could support all government departments with research and analysis.

In addition to creating institutional homes for longer-term thinking within government, **better co-ordination between policy-making bodies and academic research institutions could serve to focus the country's research capabilities on long-term development priorities and challenges.** Incentives in the form of funding should be provided for research that addresses critical development challenges and uncertainties. While it won't eliminate uncertainty about the future, further research can certainly help to reduce it. Finally, the involvement of independent science-based research bodies in the development of methodologies helps to increase the legitimacy of decisions relating to infrastructure planning and project selection. A notable exception is represented by the Centre for sustainable urban development (Centro de Desarrollo Urbano Sustentable, CEDEUS[4]), which provides Ministries with information on urban public transport.

In Denmark, for example, close collaboration between the Ministry of Transport and the Danish Technical University (DTU) has been key to the development of a national traffic model. The participation of the DTU and its ownership of the model ensures that the Danish transport planning and project prioritisation system benefits from strong credibility and legitimacy among stakeholders and the public at large (see Annex 3 for a description of Denmark's transport planning system).

VII. The strategy: How do we satisfy needs while pursuing long-term goals?

A strategy serves to bridge the gap between current needs and policy priorities on the one hand, and a vision for the future on the other, all while taking into consideration the various uncertainties and risks that could impede progress towards long-term development goals. Without long-term development goals, strategies are likely to lack purposefulness and a long-term perspective. Moreover, in the absence of a unifying vision, different regional and sectoral strategies are less likely to be mutually reinforcing and may even work at cross-purposes.

Social needs and the provision of public goods can be addressed through a variety of mechanisms. The choice of how to satisfy specific needs should therefore take into account the full range of available options. A first choice relates to whether a particular need should be addressed by managing demand or through increasing supply. In some cases, a demand-management approach may be preferable, particularly when certain resources are scarce (e.g. water) or when additional supply may generate excessive negative externalities (e.g. air pollution). The use of smart regulation and pricing can therefore be an alternative or a complement to a supply-oriented approach. The decision to invest in infrastructure therefore needs to be framed within a broader strategy of how to address needs.

In many cases, when needs are great, a demand-focused approach will be insufficient (and indeed may be inappropriate) for ensuring that needs are satisfied. Under such circumstances, increasing supply will be critical for enhancing welfare. However, methods of increasing supply shouldn't be limited to the addition of new infrastructure, but should also encompass rehabilitation and upgrading of existing infrastructure.

Choices of what type of infrastructure to build should examine alternate infrastructure technologies for achieving a particular outcome. In the case of transport for example, alternatives could include moving goods by rail, road, ships or using a combination of modes. Chile faces a major decision with regard to the location of its new Large Scale Port. Perhaps of equal importance will be its choices regarding the type of infrastructure that will be built in order to link the new port to the country's logistics chain.

Policy makers also face choices relating to *how to increase supply*, including deciding on whether to privilege public delivery or private provision. These choices need to be conditioned by the economics of a particular infrastructure sector, and take into account a country's circumstances, including its political environment and culture, its public sector institutions and capabilities, its legal environment and its history (Hawkesworth and Garin, 2016). Chile has successfully combined a variety of modes including traditional procurement, concessions, state-owned enterprises and privatisation for delivering its infrastructure. While some sectors, such as energy production, have been completely privatised, in others, such as ports and roads, multiple delivery modalities coexist.

Decisions relating to demand versus supply measures, infrastructure technologies and delivery modalities require a deep understanding of the economics of a sector along with a systemic perspective. An integrated sectoral plan that considers investment as a component of a broader strategy for achieving specific outcomes is more likely to yield robust investment choices than one which treats different mechanisms and technologies separately. Finally, while sectoral plans need to be targeted at addressing current and future needs, they must also be guided by long-term development goals. For example, France and the Netherlands have both developed integrated transport plans which have benefited from the fact that the responsibility for all transport modes rests with a single ministry (Annexes 1 and 2). In the case of the Netherlands, the integrated transport strategy is framed by a national spatial strategy which is guided by a long-term vision for the country in 2040 and three medium-term goals (2028) designed to keep the Netherlands competitive, accessible, liveable and safe.

Assessment

In Chile, sectoral ministries typically determine needs at the sectoral level, develop strategies for responding to those needs, including the role of infrastructure investment, and identify specific investments in their sector. This is consistent with the role performed by sectoral ministries in most other OECD countries with regard to infrastructure planning.

Nevertheless, **in certain sectors significant overlaps exist between ministries, and the delimitation of roles isn't entirely clear**. As mentioned in the first section, both the MOP and the MTT have planning roles with regard to the transport sector, and there isn't always sufficient consultation between the two ministries. Thus, while the MTT undertakes freight planning on a multi-modal basis, it doesn't have responsibility for the interurban road network. This can generate connectivity problems, particularly in areas where different modes intersect, such as between the ports and roads sectors. It may also result in sub-optimal infrastructure choices.

The MTT has been tasked with developing an interurban transport investment strategy by 2017 (Consejo de Políticas de Infraestructura, 2014). This is a **promising initiative which could potentially generate a more integrated and systemic transport strategy**. However, in order to deliver such an outcome, the process of preparing the strategy will require close co-ordination between the various entities responsible for delivering transport infrastructure, including MTT, MOP, MINVU, and EFE, as well as the Ministry of the Environment. It should also address the entire policy toolkit, covering demand, supply and governance measures, and not be limited to the investment element. Finally, the preparation of the strategy should involve broad-based consultation with relevant stakeholders such as representatives of transport users, regional governments, environmental associations, academics and industry associations.

VII. Investment choices: What investments are required to achieve desired outcomes?

Infrastructure investment is an essential component of a strategy for making the leap to the future. If strategies are focused on outcomes and user needs and guided by long-term development goals, they are more likely to yield investment options that contribute to improvements in wellbeing and productivity growth.

Since in Chile, as in every other country, resources are limited, it is **critical that only good investments receive funding**. In a context of budgetary constraints, not all investment proposals can be funded and projects therefore need to be prioritised. The methodology and criteria used for selecting and prioritising projects are therefore key to ensuring that projects generate value for money and support key development objectives.

The project selection process must also provide space for making political choices that are able to weigh trade-offs and compare priorities not only within sectors, but across sectors. On the other hand, too much politics in the project selection process can undermine project quality and efficiency. It is therefore important to frame the scope for political agency in infrastructure project selection through transparent and structured processes.

Assessment

As mentioned earlier, one of the strengths of the Chilean model is its **social cost-benefit evaluation system which imposes a considerable degree of rigour on the project selection process.** The social evaluation methodology ensures that only projects that generate a minimum social return receive funding.

What the social evaluation system doesn't provide, however, is a **transparent and rational basis for prioritising projects.** Decisions as to which projects to prioritise and pursue from within a list of projects that all reach the minimum social return bar therefore becomes a result of political bargaining and budgetary negotiations between sectoral ministries and the Ministry of Finance. This approach obscures the underlying preferences of decision makers and privileges projects that have the support of the officials or politicians that are most adept at influencing the process.

Furthermore, the social evaluation methodology can only accommodate individual projects and fails to capture wider systemic benefits and costs of particular projects. This is particularly important in the case of transport since decisions inevitably have knock-on effects on the wider transport system. If these systemic effects are not accounted for, project benefits or costs may be underestimated. For example, the choice to privilege passenger transport in a rail system will have an opportunity cost with regard to freight transport which may not be reflected in a standard cost-benefit analysis. Denmark uses a national traffic model to predict the impact of new infrastructure on traffic and its effect on the rest of the network. This modelling approach enables transport planners to consider the system-wide impacts of a particular project when evaluating the benefits of an investment (see Annex 3).

In addition, the social CBA methodology discriminates against developing infrastructure in remote regions where, for example, low traffic volumes in the case of roads result in lower economic benefits. However, such infrastructure may be important for promoting economic development or reducing inequality, which are valid political goals. As a consequence, infrastructure investments targeting regional roads in Chile with low traffic volumes ("*Soluciones básicas*") are not subject to the minimum social return thresholds required by the Ministry of Social Development (see Section 1.3, Choice of the delivery modality). However, it is still important that such projects be subject to some form of prioritisation. Australia, which faces similar challenges in terms of providing accessibility to remote regions, is considering a risk-based approach for prioritising investments in upgrades for roads in remote and regional areas that do not generate high positive returns based on a CBA (see Section 1.3, Focusing on users' needs).

A further weakness of the Chilean system is that isn't sufficiently forward-looking. As a consequence, projects may not necessarily contribute to long-term goals, or they may be highly vulnerable to future contextual changes. Such a system may also discriminate against projects that might be important for preparing the country for the future, but for which it may be hard to demonstrate a high social return in the present. Thus, investments that are necessary for strengthening preparedness and resilience against climate change and natural disasters might not be prioritised under the existing approach.

Some countries apply a multi-criteria analysis (MCA) framework as a way to broaden their inputs to include factors that elude monetisation. An MCA framework can serve as a complement to CBA analysis and be used to accommodate more long-term goals and strategic issues, as well as to improve alignment with broader policy priorities. It can also help to make policy makers′ preferences transparent and ensure they are reflected in the project prioritisation process (Box 2.15). Finally, an MCA methodology can be used to rank projects on a more transparent basis, thereby reducing the scope for subjectivity and discretion in the decision-making process.

Box 2.15. Combining Cost-Benefit Analysis (CBA) and Multi-criteria Analysis (MCA)

Most infrastructure project appraisal processes typically apply some form cost-benefit analysis (CBA). CBA privileges monetary values or factors that can be easily converted into monetary values. Its strength lies in its logical simplicity and the fact that it generates a single number that can be used to compare and rank projects, even across sectors. CBA is thus an effective tool for filtering out bad projects and ensuring that a portfolio of infrastructure projects generates value for money.

The principal weakness of CBA is that it doesn't accommodate values that are not easily expressed in monetary terms. However, choices regarding what infrastructure to build can seldom be reduced to purely monetary values. Factors such as a project's contribution to strategic policy goals, impacts that can only be assessed in qualitative terms (e.g. biodiversity) or values that are difficult to quantify (e.g. resilience) will therefore be neglected in a standard CBA. This does not mean that such factors are completely excluded from the decision-making process. If preferences are excluded from formal analysis they are often incorporated upstream or downstream of a CBA in a non-transparent manner.

Multi-criteria analysis (MCA) offers a complementary approach that accommodates both monetary and non-monetary variables (quantitative as well as qualitative). It involves assigning impact scores to various factors, weighting the importance of those factors, and aggregating the weighted impacts of each factor to generate a single value and produce a ranking among projects.

Box 2.15. Combining Cost-Benefit Analysis (CBA) and Multi-criteria Analysis (MCA) (*cont.*)

Applying MCA to the Irish road sector

A combination of both techniques has the potential to retain the rigour and value for money focus of CBA while broadening the decision criteria to incorporate other strategic policy goals. The National Road Authority of Ireland developed a combined CBA-MCA framework for appraising the National Secondary Road Network in Ireland. The methodology was used to identify roads that were suitable candidates for upgrading to a higher design standard. The approach consisted in incorporating cost-benefit analysis data in an MCA alongside other non-monetised elements. This approach enabled the project prioritisation process to take into account policy objectives such as improvement to the environment, safety, economy, accessibility and integration (Gühnemann, Laird and Pearman, 2012).

Applying MCA to the Irish road sector

A combination of both techniques has the potential to retain the rigour and value for money focus of CBA while broadening the decision criteria to incorporate other strategic policy goals. The National Road Authority of Ireland developed a combined CBA-MCA framework for appraising the National Secondary Road Network in Ireland. The methodology was used to identify roads that were suitable candidates for upgrading to a higher design standard. The approach consisted in incorporating cost-benefit analysis data in an MCA alongside other non-monetised elements. This approach enabled the project prioritisation process to take into account policy objectives such as improvement to the environment, safety, economy, accessibility and integration (Gühnemann, Laird and Pearman, 2012).

MCA in New South Wales

Australia's State of New South Wales (NSW) also combines CBA with other criteria to prioritise projects. Its Major Projects Assurance Framework considers, on the one hand, projects' fit with a "Strategic Objectives" dimension which includes alignment with NSW's investment themes, value for money, the project's ability to afford citizens "a better life" (by reducing cost of living and improving liveability), and economic efficiency. The "Project Assurance" dimension incorporates cost-benefit analysis as well as professional assessments of the suitability of project management, and risk assessment. Projects are plotted on a two-dimensional plane and are classified depending on their position on the diagram (World Bank, 2015b).

Source: Gühnemann, A., Laird, J., Pearman, A., (2012), "Combining cost-benefit and multi-criteria analysis to prioritise a national road infrastructure programme"; World Bank (2015b), "Prioritization of Infrastructure Projects: A Decision Support Framework".

Policy recommendations

Chile's infrastructure planning and governance framework has supported the roll-out of a range of high quality and efficient infrastructure systems in areas such as highways, ports and airports that have been key enablers of the country's rapid development over the past two decades. Chile will still need to deliver large amounts of infrastructure in the years ahead as it strives to achieve high-income status. However, changing circumstances, many of which are a consequence of the country's development, are driving a shift in the country's needs which will require, in turn, adjustments to how infrastructure is planned and governed.

Key competences required for addressing these new circumstances

The evolving nature of infrastructure needs in response to changing circumstances will have implications for the types of competences that will be required of the Chilean infrastructure planning system going forward.

1. Capacities for long-term and systemic thinking.

Future infrastructure investments will need to be a framed by a long-term vision for the country's development. Since today's infrastructure choices will have a legacy that extends well into the 21st century, decisions cannot be made under the assumption that Chile's economic structure and trading relations will remain unchanged. Infrastructure planning will therefore need to be guided by a vision for the development of the country that takes into account the future contribution of different sectors of the economy such as tourism, along with major trends such as urbanisation and climate change. Moreover, infrastructure decisions will need to be aligned with strategic policy priorities and longer-term development goals, as well as with other policy areas such as education.

2. Better co-ordination of infrastructure planning both within and between sectors.

Chile will need to develop more co-ordinated and integrated infrastructure planning within sectors such as transport and water, including greater integration between sectoral strategies and infrastructure planning within sectors. It will also require adopting a more systemic and cross-sectoral perspective in infrastructure planning and prioritisation.

3. Decision-making capacity for infrastructure investments required at the local level.

As local needs become more important drivers of infrastructure development, it will become important to be able to identify, prioritise and respond to needs at the subnational level. Capacity for planning and managing investment within regional and municipal governments will therefore need to be reinforced. This should be supplemented by more proactive and participatory forms of stakeholder engagement to improve awareness of user needs and develop responsive solutions.

4. The project evaluation and prioritisation system will need to accommodate transversal issues.

As transversal issues such as climate change and sustainable development gain in strategic significance, they will need to be better integrated into processes for evaluating, prioritising and selecting projects. Moreover, project evaluations will also need to incorporate the impact of synergies resulting from complementary investments as well as multi-purpose infrastructure. Nevertheless, changes to project evaluation methodologies and selection criteria must not come at the expense of value for money and efficiency considerations.

5. Responses to infrastructure needs should take into account the entire policy toolbox including public investment, private participation, rehabilitation and upgrading, technology, regulation and taxation.

As marginal returns on new investments diminish, it will be increasingly important to ensure that the project selection process delivers value for money through prioritising the highest yielding projects. In some cases, increasing the supply of infrastructure will not be the optimal response to a particular need. Planners must therefore have the capability to evaluate a wide range of policy options. Thus, new infrastructure investment must be weighed against alternatives such as demand management using technology and pricing tools, or rehabilitating and upgrading existing infrastructure. Infrastructure planning must therefore be closely integrated with other aspects of sector-level policy such as regulation.

6. There should be better co-ordination between infrastructure planning and land use planning.

Land use planning is a key tool for ensuring liveability in major cities faced with the twin pressures of population growth and urbanisation. Land use planning is also critical for ensuring co-ordination between housing development and infrastructure investment in order to accommodate sustainable urban growth. Finally, as Chile moves towards a decision point on major infrastructure projects such as the Large Scale Port, better land use planning will be key to securing investment in a timely and efficient manner in complementary infrastructure such as freight corridors and dry ports.

Key recommendations

In order to deliver on those priorities, a number of reforms to Chile's infrastructure and planning system will be necessary. These reforms can be grouped into three dimensions: institutional issues, methodological issues and capacity/resourcing issues. A detailed list of governance gaps and remedies grouped by the governance pre-conditions can be found in Table 2.10.

Institutional

1. Create an institutional home for long-term thinking and evidence-based policy at the centre of government.

A fundamental mismatch exists between the long-term nature of infrastructure investing and short-term political cycles, particularly in democracies. Chile's electoral system generates particularly powerful forces that direct policy makers' attention to the short- to medium term horizon. This can be problematic for infrastructure decision making since it can skew decision criteria towards immediate needs at the expense of longer-term goals. Ideally, infrastructure planning should navigate a path between short-term needs and a longer-term vision for the country.

Policy making that is evidence-based and strongly informed by scientific research provides a natural hedge against short-term pressures. Longer-term thinking can also be given an explicit focus by providing it with an institutional home. An institutional counterweight at the centre of government, one that is mandated to develop long-term science-based policy research, can help to shift the centre of gravity away from an excessive focus on the short term. Such a body could aggregate the following functions:

- generate research and conduct foresight analysis on strategic themes and transversal issues
- collaborate with universities and research centres to research long-term strategic challenges
- shape the research focus of universities and research centres through the allocation of research funding
- co-ordinate with government departments to develop science-based policy
- support government departments in applying foresight techniques.

2. Establish a central level Infrastructure Advisory Body to guide infrastructure decision making and prioritisation.

Future infrastructure choices will need to be increasingly attuned to local needs, but also guided by more of a long-term perspective. Moreover, they will need to take into account transversal issues such as climate change, consider synergies between projects and across sectors, prioritise across sectors and make political trade-offs in a transparent and accountable way. Decisions regarding what infrastructure to invest in will need to weigh a wider range of factors and will thus become increasingly complex. As marginal returns diminish, making the right choices will become ever more important for ensuring that infrastructure continues to contribute to productivity growth and wellbeing.

In order to make the right choices going forward, Chile will need to strengthen its ability to assess long-term infrastructure needs and reinforce its planning and decision-making capacity. There is currently no institution within the central government that performs the type of long-term thinking that can inform the assessment of future infrastructure needs across multiple sectors. Further, decision-making capacity is vested within sector ministries, with no mechanisms for thinking about infrastructure in a cross-sectoral and systemic way. Key decisions regarding how much and what to build are essentially taken by the delivery units, which creates an inherent conflict of interest.

A central institution dedicated to assessing long-term infrastructure needs and to providing oversight and support for infrastructure planning could serve to strengthen the quality and robustness of infrastructure decision making. It would serve as an independent advisory body to support infrastructure planning and assist in the overall prioritisation of Chile's infrastructure spending. It would support the actions of sectoral ministries and, at times, challenge them by providing an independent perspective on infrastructure needs. Without recommending a specific home for such an institution within Chile's public administration, it should be at arms-length from delivery units and cover all infrastructure sectors. Members of the advisory body should be carefully selected so as not to privilege a particular political party or industry lobby, and thus ensure that it provides impartial advice to policymakers. As an example, in response to co-ordination challenges across government departments, Australia has created an independent statutory authority that is responsible for evaluating infrastructure needs, developing a strategy to address those needs and prioritising infrastructure investments (see Annex 2D for a description of the role of Infrastructure Australia in infrastructure planning).

Some of the functions that should be assigned to such an institution include:

- evaluate long-term infrastructure needs through undertaking research and applying foresight techniques
- work with the centre of government to develop long-term development goals that should inform infrastructure planning
- provide advisory, training and support to subnational governments to strengthen their capacity to identify and prioritise their infrastructure needs, and plan and execute investments
- develop methodologies for prioritising projects within and across sectors
- develop a national infrastructure plan and an integrated list of priority projects that reflect policy priorities and long-term development goals

- provide guidance and advice on the choice of delivery mode, such as the advisability of using concessions or PPPs in different sectors, as well as on the choice of cost recovery models
- advise on a balanced portfolio of delivery modes that ensures a continuous flow of investment arising from territorial investment plans to maintain the consistency of initiatives regardless of funding source
- systematically collect and analyse data on infrastructure investments through their lifecycle
- develop and disseminate best practices on project preparation, evaluation, selection, structuring, financing, procurement, etc.

3. Create a more integrated and co-ordinated view of transport planning.

A modern and efficient transport system must enable fluid transfers between transport modes, across regions, and between the national and local levels. Planning investments in transport infrastructure therefore requires a systemic view of freight logistics and mobility that integrates all transport modes and geographical scales. Moreover, infrastructure choices need to weigh the merits of different modes since they are often substitutes (e.g. rail vs. road).

Transport planning is currently distributed among a variety of ministries depending on the transport mode and geographic scale (e.g. urban roads vs. intercity motorways) with limited mechanisms for co-ordination. A greater level of integration and co-ordination of transport planning will be necessary to ensure that Chile's transport system supports future productivity growth and competitiveness.

A key step in this direction would be to clarify and rationalise the distribution of roles and responsibilities between the various ministries involved in transport, particularly with regard to planning functions, with a view to reducing co-ordination problems and creating a more integrated view of transport planning. Responsibility should be assigned for developing a comprehensive transport sector strategy that integrates all transport modes, including ports, roads, rail and airports. The transport sector strategy would serve as a framework for more detailed sector level plans (e.g. roads, ports, railways, and airports).

Finally, greater integration with land use planning is required to accommodate major projects of national significance. In the absence of a national spatial plan, sector strategies should incorporate a land use dimension with a view to identifying and preserving land for key infrastructure such as freight corridors, logistics platforms, and motorways.

Methodological

4. Develop a more formal process and criteria for selecting between infrastructure delivery modalities.

Chile currently does not apply value-for-money analysis or other formal criteria to select infrastructure delivery modes. The CCOP has relied on its many years of experience with concessions in the highway sector and on investor demand to allow it to identify projects that qualify as concessions. The principal criteria for determining whether an infrastructure asset gets delivered using the concession model or through traditional procurement has therefore been cost-recovery. However, cost-recovery may play less of a role in the future, particularly as the number of projects in the roads sector that can provide full cost-recovery diminish. In addition, cost-recovery criteria may not be as applicable to other sectors like health care where PPPs are being developed.

If Chile wishes to continue relying on private finance in its infrastructure development, it would benefit from adopting a more systematic approach towards selecting the appropriate delivery modality. Such an approach would formalise the criteria used to inform the choice of delivery modality, and set out a more formal process that would frame the choice of delivery mode. The criteria could include value for money analysis (VfM), keeping in mind that VfM presents its own challenges.

Since concessions and PPPs are implemented across a number of sectors (roads, ports, airports, health, etc. and by different delivery units (CCOP, and some state-owned enterprises), the guidance should be broad and comprehensive enough to apply across all sectors that are likely to implement the concessions or PPP model. The guidance could be developed by the above-mentioned Infrastructure Advisory Body (Recommendation 2) which would also provide advice on the advisability of proceeding with a particular delivery mode, along with recommendations on the appropriate financial and legal structures for projects.

5. Develop a national infrastructure plan and a shortlist of priority projects.

A national infrastructure plan that identifies strategic priorities and produces a shortlist of priority projects would help to align infrastructure investments across sectors and ensure that investments contribute to long-term development goals. Such an infrastructure plan should be developed by the above-mentioned Infrastructure Advisory Body (see Recommendation 2) and guided by formal processes to ensure that it does not privilege any one particular sector and applies a systemic view of infrastructure.

The planning process should consider the corresponding temporal scales. This includes the long-term vision to 2030, a medium-term perspective through a five-year moving instrument and finally shortlisted projects for the next year's budget.

Priority projects should be selected based on a transparent methodology and criteria. To get on a shortlist, projects would have to be shown to contribute to achieving long-term goals and not to be in conflict with other investments. Other factors that could be considered are potential synergies and complementarities with other projects. The task of developing such a shortlist should be allocated to an actor, such as the Infrastructure Advisory Body, that does not have a role in infrastructure delivery, in order to avoid possible conflicts of interest.

While the plan and priority shortlist need not be binding, they should form the starting point for budget negotiations. Discrepancies between the plan and actual investments should be identified by the Comptroller General and reviewed by Parliament.

6. Adjust the project appraisal methodology to accommodate strategic policy priorities, long-term development goals, transversal issues, and systemic effects in project prioritisation.

The social evaluation methodology used to assess and filter infrastructure projects provides a rigorous basis for ensuring that investments deliver value for money. However, cost-benefit analysis (CBA), even when it incorporates social prices, does not take into account factors that are difficult to monetise.

A multi-criteria analysis (MCA) framework could complement the existing social evaluation methodology by expanding the decision criteria to include long-term development goals and strategic policy priorities. There are different possibilities for applying MCA alongside CBA. MCA could be applied to those projects that meet the minimum social return target in order to develop a shortlist of priority projects. Alternatively, the two methodologies could be integrated (see Box 2.15 above). Regardless of the specific approach taken, a transparent mechanism that enables strategic priorities to influence project prioritisation could create a space for injecting political priorities into infrastructure decision making without compromising on value for money.

In the realm of transport, when performed on a multi-modal basis traffic modelling (see the Danish case study, Annex 3) can provide insights into the impact of specific projects on the wider transport network. While developing such a model requires extensive expertise and resources, it could make social cost-benefit analyses more comprehensive and accurate by considering systemic effects.

7. Reform budget management.

Chile currently relies on an annual budgetary process on per project basis. This strict annual process, along with the oversight of the Ministry of Finance, work to ensure that project approvals are consistent with the country's economic framework conditions. However, except for the very smallest of projects, infrastructure investments take place over multiple years. For larger infrastructure projects, the lack of medium-term commitments creates uncertainty for both the procuring authority and the contractor.

Reforming Chile's budgetary process based on the country's visions for its long-term development would help infrastructure planners to develop a project pipeline looking roughly 15 to 20 years into the future and secure funding for strategic initiatives within the framework of territorial and water infrastructure plans from MOP and other public and private entities.

Sharing DIPRES's comprehensive but internal medium-term expenditure framework with the MOP and other line ministries could help to offset the annual focus of budgets, which tends to impede effective expenditure management decisions on resource allocation covering a number of years. The forward estimates of spending beyond the budget year make clear the medium-term implications of budget decisions. Detailed recommendations for Chile's budget system are discussed in OECD (2016b), Budgeting in Chile.

Capacity/resourcing

8. Strengthen the analytical capacity of the Co-ordinator of Concessions (CCOP) in project preparation, monitoring and analysis.

The ability of the contracting authorities to work closely with private partners while retaining complete autonomy over decision making is essential to ensuring that infrastructure investments represent value for money for taxpayers and users. This is particularly relevant for concessions and PPPs because of relatively large investments and the duration of the contracts.

Insufficient capacity and resources could result in excessive dependence of the contracting authority on the private partners for performing the project preparation work. Resource constraints may also incentivise the use of contract modifications and extensions as a means of delivering infrastructure. Weak monitoring of contractor performance could result in a deterioration of infrastructure assets and a decline in service levels. Such practices could reduce competition in the concessions field, affect value for money and increase long-term costs for users and taxpayers.

The Co-ordinator of Concessions (CCOP) should reduce its reliance on private sector firms for performing project preparation work and undertake more of it in-house. It should also strengthen its capacity to provide effective oversight of concession contracts. This will require strengthening its analytical capacity along with a commensurate increase in its resources. While this will have short-term budgetary implications for the MOP and the Ministry of Finance, depending on where resources are taken from, it will have positive implications for the affordability of infrastructure investment in the long-term.

9. Increase capacity to collect, analyse and disseminate data.

The systematic collection, analysis and dissemination of data on infrastructure investment and performance is key to improving decision making. Greater data analysis capacity within the Co-ordinator of Concessions (CCOP) could improve the management of concessions, support better performance, and improve decision making and contract design.

Data should also be applied to improving the management of infrastructure procured through traditional means. A central data analysis function within the infrastructure advisory unit (see Recommendation 2 above) could serve to support infrastructure decision making and management across all planning departments and contracting authorities.

The MOP should support these processes towards more transparency and efficient management by using the state of the art technology and tools, digitalisation and the integration of digital technologies in the replacement or redesign of paper-based procedures and standardising procedures. This will not only ensure transparency and increased competition, but will also simplify processes for contract management, driving cost savings and integrating available information. These tools and standards should also be applied across subnational levels of government, where appropriate and feasible, to achieve further efficiency.

10. Strengthen stakeholder engagement, particularly in the project preparation phase, in order to identify user needs and integrate their feedback into the project design.

Stakeholder engagement can work to improve responsiveness to local needs, increase the legitimacy and quality of infrastructure decisions and pre-empt potential opposition. To generate these benefits, stakeholder engagement in Chile should evolve from a minimal one-size-fits-all approach to one that actively reaches out to and solicits the input of affected/interested stakeholders and users, with a process that is tailored to the circumstances and needs of each project. This would require, on the one hand, expanding the participatory toolbox to include a wider range of techniques that could be applied depending on the project's circumstances, and on the other hand, extending stakeholder input beyond a narrow focus on environmental issues. These changes would need to be supported through the development of guidelines and training opportunities, and potentially enforced with regulation and the institutional strengthening and administrative rules.

11. Strengthen the capacity of subnational governments to perform infrastructure planning.

The prospect of greater devolution of decision-making powers regarding infrastructure to subnational governments is a positive step in the direction of greater responsiveness to local needs. However, in order for such a transfer of responsibilities to be beneficial it would need to be accompanied by a significant strengthening of the capabilities of subnational governments to plan and manage infrastructure investments. More specifically, regional and local governments would need to gradually develop the capacity to accurately identify users' needs, evaluate infrastructure options, perform project appraisals, procure projects and monitor implementation. Such a transfer of competences would need to be supported from the centre through the provision of extensive training, advice, and coaching. A central level Infrastructure Advisory Body (see Recommendation 2) could be tasked with providing support to subnational governments.

Table 2.10. Governance gaps and remedies

Pre-conditions	Governance gaps	Remedies
Medium- and long-term planning	• Lack of institutionalised central guidance for infrastructure planning in the form of a long-term vision and development goals for the country. • Lack of medium- and long-term planning. • Lack of institutions and a culture that promote more long-term thinking and evidence-based policy-making.	• Assign responsibility for developing centralised guidance regarding long-term objectives that should inform infrastructure planning across all sectors. • Develop capacities for long-term thinking within centre of government.
Horizontal co-ordination	• High degree of compartmentalisation in central government. • No mechanism for co-ordinating infrastructure planning across sectors exists at central level. • Responsibilities for planning in transport are distributed across multiple ministries with weak co-ordination. • Insufficient integration between infrastructure and land use planning. • Lack of incentives or instruments for incorporating environmental considerations in a strategic sense to infrastructure planning and decision-making.	• Map the distribution of responsibilities both in terms of sectors and functions (policymaking, planning and execution), and if necessary readjust responsibilities in order to reduce the need for co-ordination. • Develop an integrated transport plan covering all modes. • Improve integration between land use planning and infrastructure planning at subnational, and develop spatial planning concepts and tools for nationally significant infrastructure. • Establish a unit within the centre of government focused on ensuring a whole-of-government approach to addressing the climate change
Focusing on user needs	• Highly centralised infrastructure planning creates obstacles to identifying needs at a local level. • Stakeholder engagement is limited in terms of scope • (environmental impacts), techniques (internet access and online tools), and level of participation (written contributions).	• Extend the scope of stakeholder engagement beyond environmental impact assessment. • Deepen public participation in decision-making through the adoption of more interactive and participatory techniques such as public hearings, webinars, workshops, etc. • Develop guidelines for conducting stakeholder engagement during the project preparation phase.

Table 2.10. Governance gaps and remedies (*cont.*)

Pre-conditions	Governance gaps	Remedies
Choice of delivery mode	• Lack of value for money analysis or formal criteria for determining appropriate delivery modality. • Decision to proceed with concession model is taken by the delivery unit. • Significant resort to unsolicited bids in concessions projects.	• Develop formal criteria for determining optimal delivery mode. • Establish a clear institutional separation between the choice of delivery mode and responsibility for project delivery. • Strengthen the capacity of the CCOP and ensure it has the resources to prepare projects.
Sustainability and affordability of infrastructure investment	• Frequent modifications to concession contracts, often instigated by the public sector partner. • Regular extensions to concession contracts, and delayed retendering. • Annual and per project budget process.	• Strengthen the analytical capacity of the CCOP and ensure it has sufficient resources to prepare projects. • Tighten the rules governing contract modifications and ensure they are enforced by the Ministry of Finance. • Introduce medium-term commitments to generate certainty for planners, procuring authority and contractors.
Focus on performance over lifetime of asset	• Limited capacity to monitor performance of concessionaires. • Missing life-cycle perspective for managing infrastructure assets procured using traditional means.	• Improve capacity of CCOP to monitor performance of assets and service levels. • Ensure that future maintenance costs are included in project CBA analysis. • Expand use of service-level contracts for maintaining the road network.
Value for money	• Frequent modifications to concession contracts, often instigated by the public sector partner. • Regular extensions to concession contracts, and delayed retendering.	• Strengthen the analytical capacity of the CCOP and ensure it has sufficient resources to prepare projects.
Robust anti-corruption mechanisms	• Excessive dependence by MOP on external expertise for project preparation, potentially resulting in susceptibility to influence from private actors.	• Strengthen the technical capacity of the CCOP and ensure it has sufficient resources to prepare projects.
Collection, dissemination, and analysis of data	• Insufficient use of data in infrastructure management both for monitoring ongoing projects and as a learning mechanism.	• Establish an independent analysis unit tasked with collecting, analysing and disseminating data across all delivery modes. • Put in place information systems for collecting and providing access to data across the different phases of projects.

Notes

1. Conversation with officials in the CCOP.
2. Any work that has a value higher than 5% of the official budget or greater than a certain amount (Concessions Law, Articles 19 and 20).
3. www.gob.cl/2016/01/18/ministerio-de-ciencia-y-tecnologia-los-aspectos-clave-del-proyecto-de-ley/.
4. www.cedeus.cl/.

References

ADI and UNU-EHS (2016), *World Risk Report 2016*, Alliance Development Works and United Nations University Institute for Environment and Human Security, Berlin and Bonn.

Alignment Project - *Recommended Strategic Approach*, Auckland, New Zealand.

Bitran, E., Nieto-Parra, S. and Robledo, J. S. (2013), "Opening the black box of contract renegotiations: An analysis of road concessions in Chile, Colombia and Peru", *OECD Development Centre Working Papers*, No. 317, OECD Publishing, Paris.

Burger, P. and Hawkesworth, I. (2013), "Capital budgeting and procurement practices", *OECD Journal on Budgeting*, Vol. 13/1, OECD Publishing, Paris, http://dx.doi.org/10.1787/budget-13-5k3w580lh1q7.

CCOP(2015), Minuta: Fundamentos y efectos de modificaciones a los contratos de concesión por mejoramiento de proyectos, 18 Noviembre 2015, Concession Coordination Unit, Ministry of Public Works, Chile.

CCS (2014), Contract management principles, Crown Commercial Service (CCS), https://www.gov.uk/government/uploads/system/uploads/attachment_data/file/395083/Contract_Management_Principles.pdf

COMICIVYT (2016), Planes Regionales de Infraestructura Urbana y Territorial, Comisión interministerial de "Ciudad, Vivienda y Territorio" COMICIVYT, Government of Chile, 2016

Commission Mobilité 21 (2013), "*Pour un schema national de mobilité durable*", Rapport au minister chargé des transports, de la mer et de la pêche.

CONADI (n.d.), "Six years after the ratification of ILO Convention 169 Conadi highlights the current process of Indigenous Consultation (A 6 años de la ratificación del Convenio 169 de la OIT Conadi destaca actual proceso de Consulta Indígena), Ministerio de Desarollo Social, Gobierno de Chile, Noticias, www.conadi.gob.cl/index.php/noticias-conadi/1360-a-6-anos-de%20-the-ratification-of-the-convention-169-of-the-oit-conadi-highlights-current-process-of-consultation-indigena, accessed 13.03.2017

Consejo de Políticas de Infraestructura (2014), *Análisis Crítico de los Planes de Infraestructura*, December 2014, Santiago.

Danish Infrastructure Investment, Ministry of Transport (2013), *Best Practices Study on Transport Infrastructure Planning and Financing in the EU (Best-Practices-Studie zur Verkehrsinfrastrukturplanung und -finanzierung in der EU), Final Report*, Roland Berger, Berlin.

Engel, E. (2016), "Infraestructura en Chile: historia de un lobby exitoso", *Voces, La Tercera*, May 8, 2016, Ñuñoa.

Engel, E., R.D. Fischer and A. Galetovic (2001), "Least-Present-Value-Of-Revenue Auctions and Highway Franchising", *Journal of Political Economy*. Vol. 109, National Bureau of Economic Research, Cambridge, MA, pp. 993-1020.

Environment Foundation (2014), The Environmental Guide: Māori and the RMA, www.environmentguide.org.nz/rma/maori-and-the-rma (accessed 13 March 2017).

Ferro, G. and Mercadier, A. (2016), "Technical Efficiency in Chile's Water and Sanitation Providers", *Utilities Policy*, Vol. 43, Elsevier, Amsterdam, pp. 97-106.

Flyvbjerg, B. et al.(2004), *Procedures for Dealing with Optimism Bias in Transport Planning*, Guidance Document, The British Department for Transport, London.

Flyvbjerg, B., Bruzelius, N. and Rothengatter, W. (2003), *Mega Projects and Risk: An Anatomy of Ambition,* Cambridge University Press, London.

France Stratégie (2014), *Quelle France dans dix ans*?, Rapport au Président de la République, France Stratégie, Paris, France.

Gerhard Hammerschmid and Kai Wegrich (2016), *Infrastructure Governance and Government Decision-Making*, The Governance Report 2016, Hertie School of Governance, Oxford.

Gühnemann, A., Laird, J. and Pearman, A. (2012), "Combining cost-benefit and multi-criteria analysis to prioritise a national road infrastructure programme", *Transport Policy*, Vol. 23, Elsevier, Amsterdam, pp. 15-24.

Hawkesworth, I., and Garin, J., (2016), "Good Governance and Choosing the Right Infrastructure Delivery Model", *The Governance Report 2016*, Hertie School of Governance, Oxford, U.K.

Heritage New Zealand (2016), www.heritage.org.nz/protecting-heritage/archaeology/standard-archaeological-authority-process, accessed 12.02.2017

Heritage New Zealand Pouhere Taonga Act 2014, Ministry for Culture and Heritage, New Zealand, www.legislation.govt.nz/act/public/2014/0026/latest/DLM4005414.html, accessed 13.02.2017

IMF (2015), *Making Public Investment More Efficient*, Staff Report, IMF, Washington, D.C.

Infrastructure Australia (2015), Australia Infrastructure Audit Report, Australian Government, Sydney.

Infrastructure Australia (2016a), *Priorities and reforms for our nation's future*, Australia Infrastructure Plan, Infrastructure Australia, Sydney.

Infrastructure Australia (2016b), T*he Infrastructure Priority List - Project and Initiative Summaries*, Australia Infrastructure Plan, Infrastructure Australia, Sydney.

Infrastructure Australia (2016c), Five Stages of the Assessment Framework, Available at http://infrastructureaustralia.gov.au/projects/Stages-of-the-Assessment-Framework.aspx

Infrastructure UK (2014), Markets for PPPs Growing Use, Implications and Lessons Learnt, Presentation by James Ballinghall at the IADB's "Fiscal Space and Investment Projects: The Role of Public Private Partnerships", Seminar, 3 June 2014

ITF/OECD (2016), *Logistics observatory for Chile*, International Transport Forum, Paris, www.itf-oecd.org/logistics-observatory-chile (accessed 10 September 2016).

Le Moniteur, (2016) Création de la mission d'appui au financement des infrastructures: le décret publié, www.lemoniteur.fr/article/creation-de-la-mission-d-appui-au-financement-des-infrastructures-le-decret-publie-32181831.

Marcelo, D., Mandri-Perrot, C., House, S., and Schwartz, J. (2016), An Alternative Approach to Project Selection: The Infrastructure Prioritization Framework, *World Bank Public-Private Partnerships Group Working Paper*.

Marshall, T. (2009), *Infrastructure and Spatial Planning: Netherlands Working Paper.* http://planning.brookes.ac.uk/research/spg/projects/infrastructure/resources/NLWPmay182009final.pdf

Marshall, T. (2013), *Planning Major Infrastructure: A Critical Analysis*, Routledge, New York.

MIE (2011), *Summary National Policy Strategy for Infrastructure and Spatial Planning*, Dutch Ministry of Infrastructure and Environment, The Hague.

Ministère de l'environnement, l'énergie et de la mer, (2013), *Mobilité 21, pour un schéma national de mobilité durable,* www.developpement-durable.gouv.fr/Commission-SNIT-vers-un-nouveau.html.

Ministerio de Transportes y Telecomunicaciones (2014), *Plan Maestro de Transporte Santiago 2025*, Santiago.

MOP (2012), Guia de Antecedentes Territoriales y Culturales de los Pueblos Indigenas de Chile, Santiago De Chile, www.mop.cl/asuntosindigenas/Documents/TerritorialCultural.pdf,

MOP (2016), *Concesiones de Obras Públicas en Chile – 20 años*, Ministerio de Obras Publicas, Santiago.

MOP (2016a), "Elementos de la experiencia Chilena", presentation by Jocelyn Fernandez at the OECD Annual Meeting of Senior Infrastructure and Public-Private Partnership Officials, 1 March 2016, Paris.

MOP (2016b), Organisational Structure, Ministry of Public Works, Chile, www.mop.cl/acercadelmop/Paginas/Organigramayestructura.aspx, accessed 07.01.2017

MOP (2016c), "Minister Undurraga led presentation of the "Guide of Indigenous Peoples: Consultation and Territory (Ministro Undurraga encabezó presentación de la "Guía de Pueblos Indígenas: Consulta y Territorio)", Ministerio de Obras Publica, Noticias, www.mop.cl/Prensa/Paginas/DetalleNoticiaSecundaiaMp.aspx?item=2259, www.gob.cl/2016/01/11/ministerio-de-pueblos-indigenas/, www.Conadi.gob.cl/documentos/LeyIndigena2010t.pdf, accessed 13.03.2017

MOP (2017), Second round of consultations, Ministry of Public Works (MOP), Chile, January-May 2017

NAO (2010), *The performance and management of hospital PFI contracts*, National Audit Office (NAO), Stationarey Office Limited, London.

NAO (2016), *Good practice contract management framework*, National Audit Office (NAO), United Kingdom, www.nao.org.uk/wp-content/uploads/2016/12/Good_practice_contract_management_framework.pdf, accessed 13.03.2017

New Zealand Ministry of Transport (2016), *Auckland Transport,* New Zealand Ministry of Transport, Auckland.

OECD (2013b), *Green Growth in Cities,* OECD Publishing, Paris, http://dx.doi.org/10.1787/9789264195325-en.

OECD (2014), *OECD Territorial Reviews: Netherlands 2014*, OECD Publishing, Paris.

OECD (2015a), *Review of Public Governance of Public-Private Partnerships in the United Kingdom,* Working Party of Senior Budget Officials, OECD, Paris.

OECD (2015b), *OECD Recommendation of the Council on Public Procurement*, Directorate for Public Governance and Territorial Development, OECD, Paris.

OECD (2016a), *OECD Survey of Infrastructure Governance,* OECD, Paris, (internal database)

OECD (2016b), Budgeting in Chile, 37th Annual Meeting of OECD Senior Budget Officials, Stockholm, 9-10 June 2016.

OECD (2013a), *OECD Urban Policy Reviews, Chile 2013*, OECD Publishing, Paris.

Productivity Commission (2014), "Public Infrastructure", Inquiry Report No. 71, Canberra.

RMA(1991), Resource Management Act 1991 (RMA), Ministry of the Environment, New Zealand, www.legislation.govt.nz/act/public/1991/0069/latest/DLM230265.html.

Vivallos Medina, L. (2013), *Prácticas Evaluación Comparativa de Agencias de Desarrollo de Carreteras: el Caso de Chile*, World Bank, Washington D.C.

White, A. (2014), "More competition in building 'good for infrastructure'", The Australian, in OECD (2015), *Effective Delivery of Large Infrastructure Projects: The Case of the New International Airport of Mexico City*, OECD Publishing, Paris

Wiewora, A., Keast, R., and Brown, K. (2016), "Opportunities and Challenges in Engaging Citizens in the Co-Production of Infrastructure-based Public Services in Australia", *Public Management Review*, Vol.18, no. 4, Taylor & Francis Groups, London.

World Bank (2015a), *Fortalecimiento institucional para el sistema de concesiones de obras públicas en Chile: Diagnóstico, análisis y recomendaciones*, Programa de estudios conjuntos: Gobierno de Chile – Banco Mundial, World Bank Group.

World Bank (2015b), *Prioritization of Infrastructure Projects: A Decision Support Framework*, Draft Working Paper, The World Bank, G20 Development Working Group, Singapore, May 2015.

Annex 2A

France: using public debate to build a consensus around infrastructure goals

France has developed an integrated transport strategy

France is of particular interest to infrastructure planners because few developed countries have invested so significantly in infrastructure since the 1960s. Over the past 40 years, France has invested massively in transport and energy systems. In the transport arena, France has linked the country with a web of motorways and high-speed rail lines. It has also built an impressive array of nuclear power stations, transmission lines and pipelines that supply the energy that powers the nation's industry and cities. These accomplishments consumed vast amounts of capital and land, and are a testament to the French state's capacity to get things done (Marshall 2013).

In the past decade, infrastructure development in France was shaped by two major trends. France was a relative latecomer to the environmental cause, particularly with regard to transforming its energy system. However, since 2007, France has embraced environmental concerns and, in particular, the fight against climate change, and has made the environment central to its economic development strategy, with large implications for infrastructure choices. Since the global financial crisis, it is has also faced significant budget constraints that have reduced its scope for action in the infrastructure sphere. Both these trends – environmental concerns and budgetary constraints – have influenced the way France has approached infrastructure planning in recent years.

An integrated infrastructure portfolio

The Ministry of Environment, Energy and the Sea (*Ministère de l'Environnement, de l'Énergie et de la Mer*) **is the key ministry with respect to infrastructure investments.** The ministry has responsibility for energy, transport and the environment, and it acts as the procuring authority for infrastructure projects. It is furthermore responsible for both delivering and operating infrastructure assets.

This super-ministry with a vast portfolio owes its existence to a merger of two ministries. In 2007, the Ministry of Equipment (*Ministère des Équipements*) and Ministry of Ecology (*Ministère de l'Éécologie*) merged. The energy portfolio was also transferred from the Ministry of Industry (*Ministère de l'Industrie*). In 2012, maritime fisheries and aquaculture were transferred from the Ministry of Agriculture (*Ministère de l'Agriculture*). By bringing together the environmental and infrastructure portfolios under one umbrella, France has undoubtedly forced climate change and environmental considerations into sectoral policymaking and infrastructure development.

Environmental considerations are central to infrastructure strategy

A key process which contributed to infrastructure strategy in France was the *Grenelle de l'environnement*; a broad, public, multi-stakeholder debate in 2007 on how to meet climate goals. The debate involved the participation of five "colleges", made up of representatives from the state, local and regional authorities, environmental NGOs, employers, and workers. This process generated a number of proposals, some of which were adopted in a set of two laws, *Grenelle* I and II. The passing of these laws served to institutionalise the outputs of the *Grenelle* debates.

Energy and transport were two areas that featured heavily in the *Grenelle* debates. In the case of transport, the *Grenelle* mandated a reduction of carbon emissions of 20% by 2020. It made a series of recommendations on how to achieve that target, which focused primarily on reducing car use and shifting to other modes such as rail. The *Grenelle* process has thus had a major role in shaping infrastructure policy in France since 2007, and has contributed to bringing environmental considerations to the forefront of infrastructure decision making.

The French transport strategy

The *Grenelle* recommendations in the transport arena were reflected in *the Schéma national des infrastructures de transport* (SNIT), an integrated strategy document covering all modes of transport (road, rail, aviation and maritime transport). The SNIT set objectives for different modes, with an emphasis on non-road modes, and contained a list of the main infrastructure projects required to meet those objectives. It also proposed measures relating to the modernisation and maintenance of the existing transport network. The proposed investments in the SNIT were estimated to cost EUR 245 billion over a period of 25 years.

Prioritising infrastructure projects

In 2012, the Hollande government concluded that it could not accommodate the public investment levels proposed in the SNIT as a result of the pressures on French public finances due to the global financial crisis. The government established a multi-party commission (Mobilité 21), to review the SNIT with a view to filtering and prioritising large infrastructure projects (Ministère de l'environnement, l'énergie et de la mer, 2013). While the commission was nominally under the auspices of the Ministry of Environment, it was composed of six parliamentarians, drawn from the governing parties as well as the opposition, as well as four independent experts. The role of the commission's work was not to prepare a new SNIT, but to determine how best to implement the SNIT, taking into account the constraints imposed by the state of public finances.

A key focus of the commission's effort was therefore to order projects contained in the SNIT in terms of priorities. To this end, the commission, with input from France Stratégie (see below) and the *Commissariat General à l'Investissement*[*], employed a multi-criteria analysis (MCA) methodology to prioritise the projects.The MCA evaluation considered four broad themes, including the projects' contribution to key transport policy goals, their environmental performance, their societal performance and their socio-

[*] The Commissariat général à l'investissement is a public body established in 2010 responsible for reviewing the overall coherence of public investment and overseeing the activities of organisations charged with implementing public investment programmes.

economic performance (measured according to the net present value of a project's benefits and costs). This process resulted in projects being classified into one of three groups: (1) those that should be initiated before 2030 and for which studies should be actively pursued; (2) those that should be initiated between 2030 and 2050; and (3) those with a time horizon extending beyond 2050 (Commission Mobilité 21, 2013).

Strengths of the French approach

The recent French approach to infrastructure planning, embodied by the *Grenelle* process, is an innovative example of using public debate involving multiple stakeholders. The process led to a new orientation for the country's development and a set of goals that benefit from broad consensus and legitimacy. Moreover, the outputs of the process have been institutionalised through legislation, thereby ensuring their influence extends beyond a single administration. Further, the incorporation of environmental matters into the same super-ministry responsible for energy and transport has strengthened the link between environmental and sectoral policy making.

The outputs of the *Grenelle* process have provided a broad framework for the development of sectoral strategies such as the SNIT, an integrated transport strategy covering all transport modes. The development of an integrated transport strategy has also benefited from the merging of different transport portfolios into a single ministry.

To the credit of the current administration, it created much needed continuity and stability for stakeholders. It has built on the work of the previous government in the transport arena, including regional governments, investors and contractors. Finally, the French have adopted an innovative approach to prioritising projects in the transport sector by appointing an independent commission composed of parliamentarians and independent experts, thereby reducing the potential for conflicts of interest.

Long-term thinking at the centre of government

France Stratégie provides strategic guidance to the government. The Commissariat général à la stratégie et à la prospective (CGSP), commonly known as France Stratégie, is an expert advisory body attached to the Prime Minister's office. It was established in 2013 as a replacement for the Centre d'analyse stratégique (and the Commissariat general du plan before that). The *Commissariat general du plan* was originally responsible for developing the country's economic plans, a practice that ended in 1992.

France Stratégie generates medium- and long-term thinking on social, economic, environmental and technological issues affecting French society, as a way of framing policy decisions. It also performs evaluations of existing policies and develops policy recommendations. Finally, it acts as a platform for public consultation by organising debates involving stakeholders from civil society, the private sector, and academia. At the behest of President François Hollande in 2013, France Stratégie prepared a study with an overarching vision for France in 2025, which analysed the key challenges facing the country, laid out a vision for France in the coming years and identified a number of strategic goals and priorities.

A structured and participatory process for citizen engagement

France has a highly institutionalised and transparent form of public consultation, which serves to encourage citizen participation in decision making about infrastructure projects. At the heart of this system is the National Commission for Public Debate (Commission national du débat public – CNDP), an independent public body whose mission is to inform the public and organise public debates and consultations. The CNDP is composed of 25 members drawn from various spheres of public life, including elected officials, representatives of public bodies such as the *Conseil d'État* (State Council) and the *Cour des comptes* (National Audit Office), and representatives from civil society organisations including trade unions, employer organisations and consumer associations.

Project developers are required to submit a project to the CNDP for a public debate if it meets certain criteria, particularly with regard to the size of the project (e.g. an investment above EUR 300 million). A request for a public debate can also be submitted by 10 members of parliament, a regional or municipal council, or an accredited environmental association. The CNDP decides whether or not a project warrants a public debate based on national interest considerations, and on the impact of the project (environmental, socio-economic and land use). If the CNDP determines that a public debate isn't required, it can nevertheless recommend that it be subject to a public consultation.

Once the CNDP has decided that a project warrants a public debate, it appoints a special project commission (*Commission particulière de débat public* - CPDP) tasked with organising and facilitating the public debate. The CPDP decides on the appropriate structure and participatory instruments to be used in the public debate. In preparation for the debate, the project developer must submit a report that is made publicly available, describing the project and its overall context, the project's rationale, its objectives, its estimated cost, and its environmental and social impacts.

The public debate itself takes place over a period of four to six months. The role of the public debate is fourfold: (1) to discuss the need for the project; (2) to review different alternatives for the project, (3) to examine the consequences of the project on land use; and (4) to discuss the environmental impacts of the project. The CNDP acts as an organiser, facilitator and rapporteur of the public debate, and doesn't take any position on the project's merits.

Once the debate is complete, the CPDP prepares an account of the debate covering the main arguments presented by the participants, as well as a summary report. Following the debate, the sponsor must choose between three options: (1) abandoning the project; (2) proceeding with the project along significantly different lines; and (3) proceeding with the project based on the recommendations that emerged from the public debate. Within a period of three months after the debate, the project developer is required to make public his decision on how to proceed, and, in doing so, address the issues raised during the debate. Irrespective of the outcome of the public debate, the CNDP continues to monitor the evolution of the project and acts to ensure that the public remains informed when any decisions relating to the project are made. As a result of the public debate system, approximately 10 projects have been abandoned, and numerous projects have undergone modifications, some of them substantial.

Some criticisms have been expressed, particularly in relation the fact that there is no obligation on the part of the project sponsor to make adjustments based on the contributions made by the participants during the debates. Thus, for major strategic projects such as new nuclear power stations where the state has decided on both the need for the project and its location, there is probably relatively little that a public debate can do to shift the outcome in a significant way. Some groups have also complained that this system slows down decision making. However, project developers in France appear to accept this as a part of the reality of doing business, and they build it into their project planning (Marshall 2013).

Overall, **the system of public debate in France is an impressive example of participatory democracy**. It has become a key feature of the French infrastructure planning process that, performed properly, can contribute to improving decision-making on major infrastructure projects, as well as improving the legitimacy and acceptability of projects among the public.

A dedicated unit advises on project financing modalities

Fin Infra is responsible for providing all levels of government with support and advice on how to structure projects from an economic, legal and financial perspective. In 2016, the Infrastructure Financing Support Unit (Mission d'appui au financement des infrastructures – Fin Infra) was created within the French Treasury (DG Trésor). This unit replaces a prior incarnation called the Public-private Partnership Support Unit (Mission d'appui aux partenariats publics-privé - MAPPP) and has a broader mandate than its precursor (Le Moniteur, 2016).

The roles of Fin Infra are three-fold. First, it provides advice and support to public entities on financing infrastructure investments of "general interest". To this end, it will develop and apply expertise on financing techniques, financial modelling, and market intelligence for infrastructure finance. Secondly, it must contribute to optimising value for money of projects. Third, it assists in identifying and managing legal, financial and budgetary risks relating to investments.

A key aspect of its role is to provide advice during the early project preparation phase on the choice of delivery modality. Projects that could be executed through public-private partnerships must be submitted for review to the Unit, which then rules on the advisability of using private financing. Fin Infra thus provides procurement authorities with a much needed independent and expert judgement on the critical decision of how best to deliver infrastructure projects.

Annex 2B

The Netherlands: Framing infrastructure planning with a long-term spatial strategy

Geographic and demographic characteristics demand long-term planning

In few countries does infrastructure play such a critical role for the very physical survival of the nation as in the Netherlands. Due to its topography, the country is in a constant battle with the North Sea. Thus, flood protection and water management infrastructure have long been priorities of Dutch government planning. Climate change is adding a further layer of challenges to a country with historic vulnerability to environmental forces. In addition, the Netherlands is a highly urbanised country with an elevated population density where land is scarce, which further increases its vulnerability.

This particular set of geographic and demographic circumstances and challenges has strongly influenced the nature of infrastructure planning in the Netherlands. Dutch infrastructure planning is characterised by its long-term perspective, its cross-sectoral integrated approach, and its close ties with spatial planning.

Integration of infrastructure with spatial planning

Dutch transport, energy and water infrastructures are the central responsibility of the Ministry of Infrastructure and the Environment (MIE). The ministry was formed in 2010 following the merger of the former Ministry of Transport, Public Works, and Water Management, and the Ministry of Housing, Spatial Planning and Environment (Marshall, 2013). The Ministry is also responsible for developing and implementing policy in the areas of water management, aviation and maritime affairs, spatial planning and the environment. The merger thus brought together previously separate functions of infrastructure development and spatial planning. Before the merger, inter-ministerial co-ordination was enabled by two high-level official committees which met on a three-weekly basis, and whose output informed the cabinet committee. By bringing infrastructure and spatial planning into the same department, co-ordination between these two activities should be strengthened.

Long-term thinking

The Netherlands has a long tradition of producing national spatial plans. The latest incarnation published in 2012 is the National Policy Strategy for Infrastructure and Spatial Planning (SVIR), compiled by the MIE. The SVIR links spatial developments and infrastructure within a broad vision for the future of the country in 2040. The 2012 SVIR sets out three medium-term goals (2028) designed to keep the Netherlands competitive, accessible, liveable and safe: (1) enhance the Netherlands' competitiveness by strengthening its spatial and economic infrastructure; (2) improve and secure space for accessibility; and (3) guarantee a safe environment in which it is pleasant to live, and in which unique natural and cultural heritage values are preserved (MIE, 2011).

SVIR thus creates a platform for co-ordinating planning across sectors. The SVIR covers infrastructure development for passenger and freight transport across all modes, energy (electricity transport, renewables, and oil and gas), and the water system. It thus seeks to ensure that sufficient space is available to meet the country's current and future infrastructure needs and balance the different uses of land, subsoil and the sea while safeguarding the quality of the environment. By its nature, this spatial thinking provides a holistic perspective.

The strategy outlined in the SVIR was deemed important for national competitiveness. It involves focusing central government resources and development on key sectors and urban regions, particularly around the country's main ports (Amsterdam-Schiphol airport and the Port of Rotterdam), the "brain-port" (a technology complex around Eindhoven), and "green-ports" (agricultural and horticultural clusters), and on regional development that benefits the country as a whole (MIE, 2011).

In a departure from previous strategic plans, the responsibilities for promoting regional development and land use planning are devolved under the current plan to provinces and municipalities. This follows a decentralisation in 2008 of the responsibilities for regional economic policy and spatial planning to provincial and municipal governments (OECD 2014).

The SVIR also seeks to incorporate and balance 13 national interests defined by the central government (MIE, 2011). The SVIR thus provides an overarching framework for more detailed sectoral plans such as the Multi-annual Programme for Infrastructure, Spatial Planning and Transport (MIRT). Since the SVIR is binding by law on all central government bodies, sectoral strategies must be consistent with it. The SVIR thus provides high-level guidance with regard to medium- to long-term goals, as wells as the government priorities that should inform sectoral strategies and infrastructure investment.

Evidence-based strategic planning

Strategic planning and sectoral policymaking in the Netherlands is supported by strong research institutions and close ties with academic institutions. The preparation of spatial strategies involves extensive research, public consultation, and cooperation between ministries, agencies, universities and consultancies, as well as discussions in Parliament, and negotiation at the cabinet level (Marshall, 2009). The Netherlands Institute for Transport Policy Analysis (KiM) and the Netherlands Environmental Assessment Agency (PBL) provide knowledge inputs for the preparation of mobility policy and transport plans at the MIE. A further organisation that supports evidence-based policymaking is the Netherlands Bureau for Economic Policy Analysis, a government research institution that provides input to economic decision-making for politicians and policymakers. In carrying out its work, it collaborates with academic researchers within the Netherlands and from abroad.

Investment prioritisation

The MIRT aims to improve the coherence between investments in spatial planning, the economy, mobility and liveability at the national level. The MIRT investment programme, developed by the MIE, formally extends beyond the life of a single parliament, which provides some valuable long-term continuity to infrastructure investment plans.

To assist in analysing bottlenecks and challenges, a National Market Capacity Analysis (NMCA) is underway. One of the tools used to assist in identifying current transports needs is the "accessibility indicator". The accessibility indicator will enable comparative assessments of the level of accessibility across different regions for all transport modes (MIE, 2011). Prioritisation is a matter of political consideration.

The MIRT puts forward a list of projects and programmes deemed necessary on a national level. The MIE applies a multi-criteria analysis methodology to select projects to receive funding from the national government. To evaluate project alternatives, a social cost-benefit analysis is used. The criteria include a combination of both quantitative and qualitative indicators, and reflect political priorities as well as the long-term development goals expressed in the SVIR (OECD, 2014):

- bottleneck: identified by applying National Market Capacity Analysis (NMCA)
- mentioned in government coalition agreement
- essential for safety and completion of the network
- economic costs/benefits
- SVIR target contributing to a better (international) competitiveness
- SVIR target contributing to better accessibility
- SVIR target contributing to a better liveability and safety.

Key strengths of Dutch system

Dutch infrastructure planning takes place within a **coherent framework** that balances political priorities and long-term development goals.

- **Long-term perspective:** The SVIR provides high-level guidance based on a long-term vision for the future of the country. This framework specifies the goals that should inform sectoral strategies and infrastructure plans.
- **Cross-sectoral framing:** Key infrastructure portfolios are contained within a single ministry, thereby enabling co-ordination between sectors. In addition, since the SVIR is a spatial strategy that balances various infrastructure needs, it injects a degree of cross-sectoral integration at the outset of the infrastructure planning process.
- **Coherence between strategies and investment plans**: The goals expressed in the SVIR are reflected in the criteria used to select infrastructure projects, thereby ensuring coherence between high-level strategies and investments.
- In 2016, the Dutch government set a goal, based on a civil servant study group, to examine a secure, **more flexible and adaptive infrastructure planning** with focus on short- and long-term investments. The setup of the MIRT and the infrastructure funds might change due to this.

Annex 2C

Denmark

The 2009 "agreement on green transport policy" is the main current foundation for transport investment in Denmark

In 2009, in the wake of the global financial crisis, a broad parliamentary agreement was struck regarding substantial transport infrastructure investment in Denmark. The 2009 agreement and the associated Infrastructure Fund represent an innovation in Denmark in terms of transport policy. It provides a prioritised list of projects, a dedicated funding source and defines the group of political parties that have a say as to how the agreement is to be implemented, including which projects to prioritize and how to spend any excess funding. However, no replacement for the 2009 agreement is envisioned as of now.

A key input that provided the glue for this consensus was an Infrastructure Commission Report published in January 2008 that identified key transport investment needs on the basis of the projected traffic flows in 2030. The broad agreement around this objective coincided with the desire to provide economic stimulus in response to the global financial crisis. The convergence of these pressures led to the creation of an Infrastructure Fund endowed with DKK 100 billion (around EUR 13.5 billion) to be invested on the basis of the priorities and specific projects identified by the Infrastructure Commission among others and agreed upon by the political parties behind the agreement. The Infrastructure Fund is an innovation in Danish transport policy as redundant means from prioritised projects flows back to the Fund thereby earmarking the allocated funds for further investments in infrastructure.

Figure 2C.1. Investments shares of the Infrastructure Fund

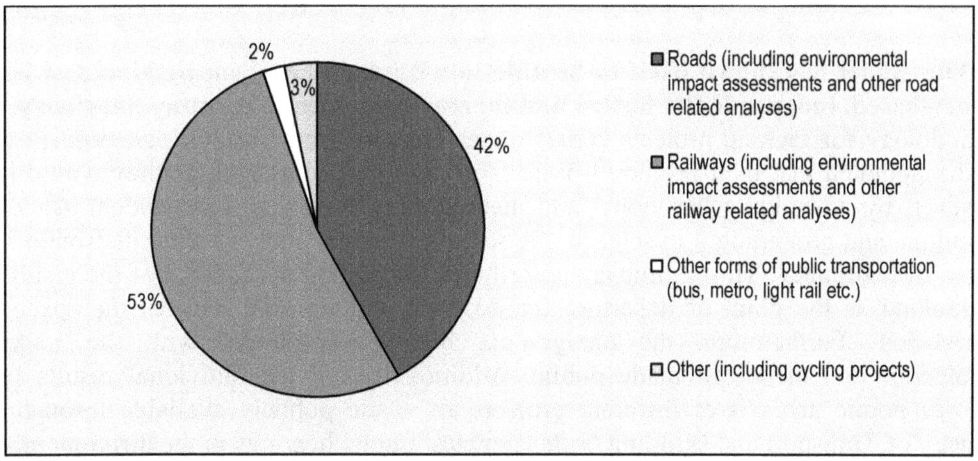

Notes: The largest projects include (2016 prices_:The Signalling Programme (total renewal of all signalling on the Danish rail network) – DKK 19.3 bn; The New Line Copenhagen-Ringsted (dual track railway) – DKK 11.7 bn; The Motorway between Funder and Låsby – DKK 6.6 bn; The Storstrøm Bridge – DKK 4.2 bn; The Holstebro Motorway – DKK 3.8 bn.

Source: Conversation with Transport-, Bygnings- og Boligministeriet, March 2017.

Investment policy is firmly based on socio-economic cost/benefit analysis

Denmark's system for prioritising infrastructure investments is based primarily on a socio-economic cost-benefit analysis methodology. Projects are ranked according to their socio-economic return. In principle those projects with the highest scores are prioritised in terms of funding, but ultimately the political level determines which projects are going to be implemented.

The system of socio-economic cost-benefit analysis relies on three elements, in particular:

- A **national traffic model,** giving a picture of the impact of new infrastructure on traffic projections and its effect on the rest of the infrastructure network. This modelling approach enables transport planners to consider the system-wide impacts of a particular project when evaluating the benefits of an investment. Smaller projects are at the moment still analysed in local traffic models.
- A **catalogue of prices** for different direct and indirect effects of infrastructure. In addition, to the direct time-value of transport, there are prices for indirect effects such as environmental effects (e.g. emissions), and health (e.g. air pollution and road accidents).
- A **science-based methodology** was developed in collaboration with the Technical University of Denmark (DTU) who continue to "host" the national traffic model and the catalogue of prices and are involved in further refining the methodology. For example, the DTU is currently undertaking research on agglomeration effects, which are currently not taken into consideration by the social-economic analysis.

In the political decision making process, local politicians and stakeholders often ensure that local considerations are brought forward. The agency in charge arranges public meetings in order to present and hear opinions on for example the specific land use, through the different phases of the final analysis.

An evidence-based point of departure for project prioritization and transport policy

The model has shown itself to be able to withstand criticism by virtue of being science-based, independently hosted and increasingly open to scrutiny. Inevitably, the methodology for ranking projects comes under pressure from various stakeholders who are disappointed that their preferred projects are not ranked as high as they would like. However, by embedding the model and methodology within an independent academic institution, and grounding it in science, the social-economic analysis benefits from a high degree of legitimacy. This legitimacy contributes to creating acceptance of the results of the ranking as the point of departure for decision making, and reduces the space for contestation. Furthermore, the analysis is highly transparent, with the ranking, calculations and model all made public. Additionally, all the individual results from socio-economic analysis of different projects are made publicly available through the Ministry of Transport and Building or its agencies. Public hearings in the different phases of the investigated projects ensure a structured process for stakeholder consultation.

Most infrastructure is funded via the national budget and user tolls are only used for two large fixed links

Private financing of infrastructure plays a minor role in financing infrastructure development in Denmark, as the government can borrow at the best sovereign rate. The fixed links over Oresund (to Sweden) and Great Belt (Storebælt) are placed in state owned enterprises, financed on the market (with a government guarantee) and are wholly user-funded. This model will also be used in two upcoming fixed links, one of which is the Femern Bælt link to Germany.

Maintenance falls under the responsibility of the sector agencies. It is financed through the agencies own budgets and typically prioritised by the agencies through the principals of socio-economics analyse. Larger reinvestments that go beyond the agencies own budgets can be negotiated and allocated separately on the annual budget upon a political agreement.

A new approach to budgeting has dramatically limited cost overruns

In the past, transport projects could turn out to be 40-50% more expensive than originally budgeted for. In 2007, Denmark introduced a new budgeting regime, where the estimate for a project's cost is supplemented with a 50% reserve at the earliest stages of planning and 30 % once the environmental impact assessment has been performed. This total sum has to be budgeted up front and appropriated by Parliament in the annual budget act. If a project comes in under-budget, the remaining funds can be assigned to other projects. To avoid the risk of overpriced tenders and price-fixing under this approach, a high level of competition has to be ensured.

Annex 2D

Australia: A structured top-down approach to infrastructure planning

Dispersed responsibility for infrastructure

In Australia's federal state structure, responsibility for most infrastructure provision lies primarily with state governments. However, even when the central government does not deliver infrastructure, it often has a role in providing funding (Productivity Commission, 2014). As a consequence, the central government performs an important steering and oversight role with regard to infrastructure investment, even when it isn't involved in its delivery.

Within the central government, responsibilities with regard to infrastructure development are distributed across a number of departments. The Department of Infrastructure and Regional Development is the lead ministry with regard to infrastructure, with a particular focus on the transport sector. The Department is responsible for the design and implementation of the Australian Government's infrastructure, transport and regional development policies and programmes. The Department of the Environment and Energy is responsible for the energy and water portfolios, and the Department for Industry, Innovation and Science also contributes to the development of energy policy, including in relation to the development of energy resources.

Improving co-ordination through institutional innovation

In 2008, in response to concerns about poor infrastructure planning, the Australian Government introduced an institutional innovation in the form of Infrastructure Australia (IA), an independent statutory body (Hammerschmid and Weigrich, 2016). IA was designed to address the issue that infrastructure decision-making, particularly decisions on new projects, was not as rigorous as it needed to be. Strategic planning and project development were seen to be weak, and the economic assessment of proposals was limited. IA is now legally separate from the Department for Infrastructure and Regional Development, and is governed by an independent 12-member board with members drawn from business and academia, who appoints the CEO.

The role of IA is to **provide independent research and advice to all levels of government** as well as to investors and owners of infrastructure on the projects and reforms needed to support Australia's economic and social development. Its responsibilities include: auditing the country's infrastructure needs and performance; developing a rolling 15-year infrastructure plan that identifies Australia's national and state-level infrastructure priorities; and reviewing the business case for larger projects (where the proponent is seeking more than $100M in Australian Government funding). Smaller projects requiring less than $100M of Australian Government funding typically do not come to IA for assessment. IA's sectoral responsibility extends beyond that of its parent department and, in addition to transport, includes energy, telecommunications and water.

Assessing future needs

The Australian Infrastructure Audit ("Audit") **takes a strategic top-down approach to identifying Australia's long-term infrastructure needs**. It analyses the drivers of infrastructure demand such as population and economic growth. The first Audit (published in 2015) identified infrastructure needs and gaps based on projections for demand growth looking out towards 2031. The Audit thus provides an evidence base for decisions relating to infrastructure reforms and investments (Infrastructure Australia, 2015).

Infrastructure Australia is required by law to conduct an audit and produce a new infrastructure plan at least every five years. While the exact scope of the next audit (currently scheduled to be released in 2020), and the next plan (currently scheduled to be released in 2021), are yet to be determined, it is likely that the opportunity will be taken to review progress against the conclusions from the 2015 Audit and recommendations in the 2016 Plan.

In addition, Infrastructure Australia's operations can be audited by the Australian National Audit Office (ANAO). In 2009/10, the ANAO conducted a review of the processes used by Infrastructure Australia to develop the first Infrastructure Priority List.

Developing a long-term strategy

The Infrastructure Audit serves as a key input to Australia's Infrastructure Plan ("Plan"), which puts forward a package of governance and policy reforms to how infrastructure is funded, financed, delivered, managed and used. The strategy proposed in the Plan is guided by four long-term aspirations: (1) productive cities, productive regions; (2) efficient infrastructure markets; (3) sustainable and equitable infrastructure; and (4) better decisions and better delivery. The Plan focuses on how to achieve those aspirations through applying a range of levers including institutional and regulatory reforms, as well as investments (Infrastructure Australia, 2016a).

By focusing on a set of long-term ambitions, the strategy developed in the Plan considers a wide range of options and instruments. This is distinct from the common more project-centred approach and goes beyond simply investing in new projects. Further, this approach enables a more integrated view of how infrastructure across various sectors can contribute to the country's development. Finally, it also provides a platform for articulating how infrastructure can provide solutions to cross-sectoral issues such as sustainability and support for Indigenous communities.

Prioritising investments

The Infrastructure Priority List ("List") complements the Infrastructure Plan by providing a list of initiatives and projects that can address specific infrastructure needs and challenges. The List is developed in collaboration with state and territory governments and industry. The List includes initiatives at various levels of development, from problems in need of a solution to projects that have undergone a full business case assessment by IA. Initiatives and projects included on the List are assessed by the Infrastructure Australia board through a structured, five-stage Assessment Framework. This framework encourages early analysis of problems and options, to maximise the prospects for arriving at economically robust project proposals. (Infrastructure Australia, 2016b):

Stage 1 - Problem Identification and Prioritisation

Nominators* engage with Infrastructure Australia, to identify and prioritise evidence-based problems and opportunities of national significance. In some instances, where a problem is identified but there is no nominator for an appropriate initiative, Infrastructure Australia may act as nominator.

Stage 2—Initiative Identification

Nominators develop initiatives that could suitably address the problems and opportunities identified in Stage 1. Infrastructure Australia assesses initiatives for strategic fit in the context of the problems and opportunities prioritised in Stage 1. If an initiative is positively assessed by the Infrastructure Australia Board after Stage 2, the initiative is added to the Infrastructure Priority List.

Stage 3—Options Assessment

Nominators looking to develop a business case analyse the options available to address the problems and opportunities identified in Stage 1. Infrastructure Australia provides feedback on the options being taken into a full business case, and arrange access to relevant case studies.

Stage 4—Business Case Assessment

Project proponents develop a full business case that objectively considers the potential solutions identified in previous stages. Infrastructure Australia then assesses the business case in line with its Assessment Framework. If a business case is positively assessed by the Infrastructure Australia Board, the project is added to the Infrastructure Priority List.

Stage 5—Benefits Realisation

In collaboration with proponents, Infrastructure Australia seeks to understand the outcomes from the project, as well as project delivery, against the benefits and costs described in the business case.

To improve the rigour of and transparency in decision-making, Infrastructure Australia publishes the Infrastructure Priority List and project assessments.

Key strengths of the Australian system

- **Insulated from political pressures.** Australia has introduced an innovative institutional framework for guiding infrastructure development. As an independent body, Infrastructure Australia is, in principle, insulated from the political process, and can therefore assess infrastructure needs and develop recommendations on the basis of objective scientific and economic criteria.
- **A structured approach.** Infrastructure Australia applies a sequenced and structured approach to infrastructure planning by framing investment choices within a long-term assessment of needs (the Audit) and a considered evaluation of the various options for addressing those needs, a process that is guided by a set of long-term goals (the Plan).
- **An integrated strategy.** By considering all infrastructure sectors within a single plan that is guided by a set of long-term ambitions, the Infrastructure Plan provides for an integrated perspective on infrastructure. Such a holistic and

integrated approach encourages greater alignment across sectors and investments, and improves the scope for generating synergies.

Areas for improvement

The Infrastructure Plan also considered the governance in infrastructure in Australia and identified some weaknesses, **particularly in long-term planning at the subnational level**. It also highlighted insufficient co-ordination between infrastructure and land use planning, specifically with regard to the identification and preservation of key corridors.

There is no direct linkage between investment budgets and the infrastructure plan. The strategy proposed in the Infrastructure Plan and the infrastructure projects contained in the Priority List are recommendations without binding legal force. Implementation of reforms and delivery of investments falls to other central government departments, or state or territory governments. It is thus the responsibility of state governments, or the central government to make the ultimate decisions regarding whether or not to proceed with a particular investment or policy reform. These are under no obligation to deliver on the recommendations proposed by Infrastructure Australia. Governments consider Infrastructure Australia's advice and recommendations on projects, but also consider other factors, including advice from their own 'line agencies'.

* *Nominators*: any individual or organisation who suggests a potential infrastructure solution as an initiative.

Chapter 3

Co-ordinating infrastructure policy across levels of government

This Chapter assesses the current multi-level governance framework for infrastructure investments and identifies actionable recommendations based on the OECD Recommendation on Effective Investment across Levels of Government (OECD, 2015b). Like many other OECD countries, Chile needs to strengthen some co-ordination instruments across the national and subnational governments to invest more efficiently in its territory. A better connection between the infrastructure planning and budgeting processes, to date almost totally disconnected, could also improve the effectiveness of infrastructure investments as the country moves towards programme –based budgeting. A more integrated, programme-based approach, contrary to a project-based financing, allows for turning strategic planning into effective investment prioritisation. Finally, greater horizontal co-operation across jurisdictions is needed to invest at the relevant scale.

Co-ordinating infrastructure policy across levels of government

Chile is currently in the early stages of a paradigm shift in its governance of infrastructure investments, granting regions a new role. This is a major turning point, as Chile has the most centralised public investment framework in the OECD, with 88% of that investment decided upon at the central level – compared to 41% on average in the OECD (OECD, 2016b). This change requires strengthening the appropriate tools to enable effective co-ordination between levels of government, especially in the context of decentralisation reforms aimed at transferring more competences and resources to subnational governments.

Chile's special and diverse geographic characteristics make it particularly important for the country to look at infrastructure investments through territorial lenses. Place-based policies would enable Chile to address territorial disparities and develop infrastructure projects that can improve connectivity and access to services and communication by maximising the potential of urban and rural areas. Governance arrangements are critical for the implementation of effective place-based policies (OECD, 2016a).

Infrastructure investments that improve connectivity between rural and urban areas, foster intermediary cities, reduce territorial disparities and boost productivity in lagging regions could allow Chile to overcome the middle income trap. Recent analysis from the OECD has shown that in all OECD economies the first-year effect of public investment in stimulus amounting to 0.5% of GDP is significant and translates, for example, into 0.6% GDP growth in the United States, and 0.5% in the Euro area (OECD, 2016c). With the current macro-economic context (notably low copper prices), the catching-up process of Chile depends largely on its capacity to invest smartly to boost competitiveness across its territory.

The impact of infrastructure investment depends on how it is managed. While the financing dimension of infrastructure investments is important, the broader public governance dimension is equally important. OECD evidence has shown that substantial benefits can be realised by better managing public investment throughout its "life cycle" and across levels of government, and that the quality of public governance correlates with public investment and growth outcomes, at both national and subnational levels (OECD, 2013c).

Marked geographic heterogeneity and strong territorial disparities

Territorial characteristics and economic activity vary widely across the country

Chile has particular territorial characteristics that have led to a concentration of economic activities and settlement patterns in a few areas. Chile is over 4 300 km long and has an average width close to 180 km, which explains the great heterogeneity throughout its territory. It has a wide range of soil types and of climatic and environmental conditions, ranging from deserts in the north to lakes, fjords and glaciers in the south. The country's geographical and topological characteristics have resulted in the concentration of economic activities and settlement patterns in a few areas, and these factors represent a significant challenge for infrastructure in terms of connectivity, access to services and access to communication. Chile's unique geography creates challenges when it comes to developing and managing connections, firms and regions throughout the country and to delivering goods and services, especially to remote areas. According to the geographic concentration index, demographic concentration in Chile (61) is almost twice the OECD average (32) and is only surpassed by Iceland (62). Almost half of the Chilean population live in Santiago, and almost 60% in Santiago and Bio-Bio. Similarly, economic activity is highly concentrated in Chile, with the country displaying highest level of geographic concentration of GDP (52) in the OECD (OECD, 2013a). With important urban hubs and vast rural areas, governance structures that enhance the linkages between those areas are among the keys to maximising the territorial potentials for development.

The Chilean economy depends on a few sectors that are largely concentrated in certain regions. Economic activity in Chile varies strongly throughout the country. Mining, one of the engines of the Chilean economy, is concentrated in the north of the country. Further south, the Metropolitan Region represents nearly 45% (Banco Central de Chile, 2015) of national GDP and specialises in financial and entrepreneurial activities and services like transport and telecommunications. The centre-south engages in agricultural activities, while the south is specialised in fishery, contributing much less than the central region to national growth. This heterogeneity calls for differentiated infrastructure investment strategies tailored to the place that investments aim to serve in order to boost productivity while also promoting inclusiveness.

Chile needs to diversify its economic activities to boost growth and productivity. Chile's economic activity has the potential to be much more diversified than it is at present. During the last years, Chile's vulnerability has become very clear due to its strong reliance on the export of primary commodities (Ahmad and Zanola, 2015), which may constrain its growth potential in the long term. With the slow-down of the economy, the debate around its dependence on primary resources has become a top priority. Diversifying Chile's productive base is crucial to adding value to existing sectors and to mobilising regional resources instead of depending on top-down development strategies. To avoid the middle income trap, Chile needs to develop a medium-term perspective with new economic hubs throughout the country that will allow for a greater balance of economic activities and achieve a considerable potential for additional domestic production (Ahmad and Viscarra, 2016). For this to happen, it is necessary to develop higher skills and innovative activities that can increase productivity in different territories (OECD, 2009b).

Unequal performance and territorial disparities

Urban areas are the economic engines of the Chilean economy. Santiago, Valparaíso and Concepción account for the largest share of national growth. Santiago was responsible for 48.14% of the national GDP in 2013, while Valparaiso and Concepción, Chile's other two most important Functional Urban Areas (FUAs), accounted for 5.01% and 3.25% of GDP, respectively. The rest of the urban system displays a more modest economic performance (OECD, 2013a). The concentration of activities in urban areas, especially in port cities and Santiago, has led to regional inequalities and had strong consequences in terms of congestion and pollution. Urban hubs also attract migrants from the less developed regions, causing a concentration in peripheral townships with poor facilities (Ahmad and Zanola, 2015). Santiago attracts a considerable share of business activity and labour demand, mainly owing to the benefits of agglomeration. People want to live where firms – and therefore job opportunities – are concentrated (OECD, 2009b).

Concentration of economic activities has brought with it important territorial performance disparities. Heterogeneity in regional performance is a widespread fact among OECD countries (OECD, 2009b), both among similar type of regions (e.g. urban, intermediate and rural) and across regions within the same country; this heterogeneity is nonetheless much greater in Chile. Although inequality in GDP per capita across regions in Chile has been diminishing over the last decade, the Gini Index across TL3 regions (corresponding to Chile's *provincias*) remains the highest among OECD countries (Figures 3.1 and 3.2). In Chile, while some regions are at least three times richer than the national average, others have per capita GDP values of less than half the national average. Inequality is not only driven by leading regions (Santiago, Antofagasta and Tarapacá) but also fuelled by low performance in a number of other regions. GDP per capita in La Araucanía, Aysén, Bío-Bío, Coquimbo, Los Lagos, Maule and Valparaíso is less than 75% of the national average (OECD, 2016a). This suggests that economic performance has not benefited regions in the same way; some regions of the country could be better mobilised in the overall development process.

Figure 3.1. Gini Index of inequality of GDP per capita across TL3 regions, 200 and 2013

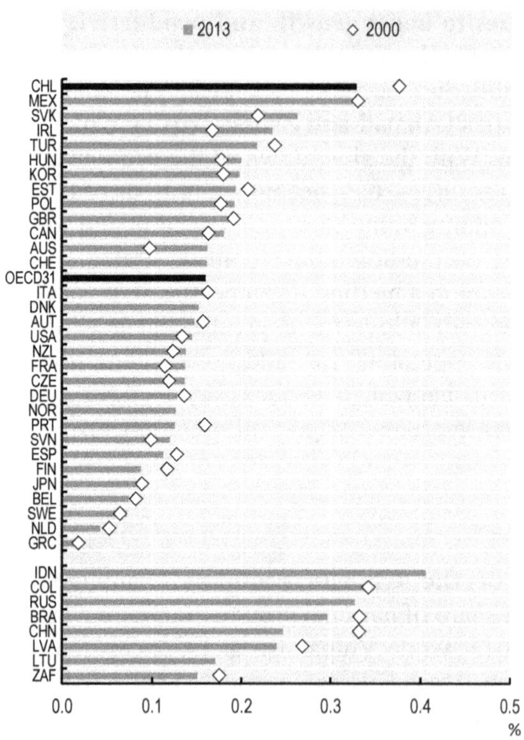

Source: OECD (2016e), *OECD Regions at a Glance 2016*, http://dx.doi.org/10.1787/reg_glance-2016-en.

Figure 3.2. Regional variations in GDP p.c. (as a % of national average), 2013 (TL2)

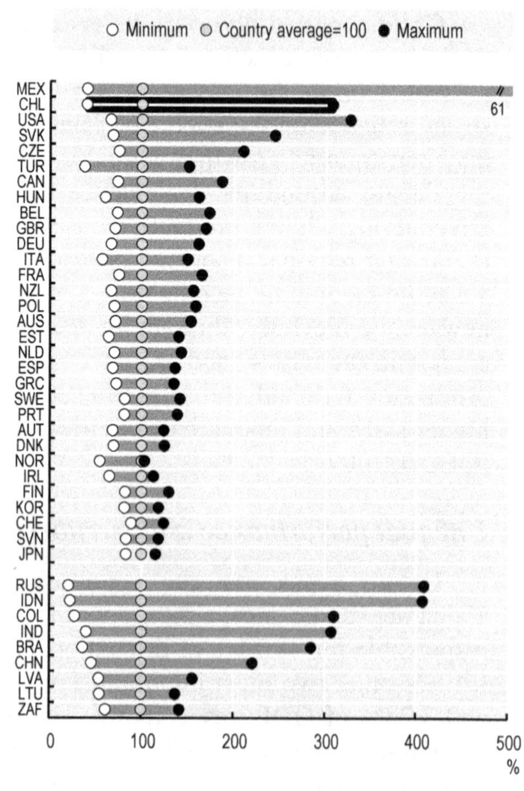

Source: OECD (2016e), *OECD Regions at a Glance 2016*, http://dx.doi.org/10.1787/reg_glance-2016-en.

In terms of a broader regional well-being measure, regions are also highly unequal in Chile (Figure 3.3). The OECD Regional Well-being Index reveals that Chile has the largest regional disparities among OECD countries when it comes to the environment; the Magallanes y Antártica region ranks in the top 5% of OECD regions, while Tarapacá is in the bottom 20%. Antofagasta is the best among Chilean regions in education and access to services, but the worst in health and housing (OECD, 2014c). Well-being disparities suggest that the development strategy of the country has not been delivered efficiently throughout the territory.

Interregional disparities in infrastructure are significant, with specific challenges related to access to basic services and communications, especially in remote and peripheral regions. Road infrastructure coverage and quality is uneven across Chile. It is not just that Chile lags behind some other OECD countries in road surface quality and safety standards, but that there are also disparities between Chilean macrozones and within these zones, as evidenced by large differences in road paving and road accident rates. Even starker differences are evident across areas of large cities like Santiago where poorer neighbourhoods are not only located further away than richer ones from jobs and services, but also suffer from lower quality infrastructure such as the lack of pedestrian streetscapes (see Chapter 4). In terms of communication, the percentage of households with internet broadband access is not only an important challenge for extreme regions, but also an issue for more developed territories. While close to 50% of households in the metropolitan region and the mining regions of Arica, Parinacota and Antofagasta have Internet access (a figure close to that of some OECD countries like Hungary, Italy and Spain), the figure is only 16% for households in Maule and Araucanía (two of the agriculture-intensive regions). Geographical characteristics mean that especially rural and remote areas are the most affected by connectivity and as such remain disconnected and sometimes isolated from urban areas.

Figure 3.3. Relative performance of Chilean regions by well-being dimension

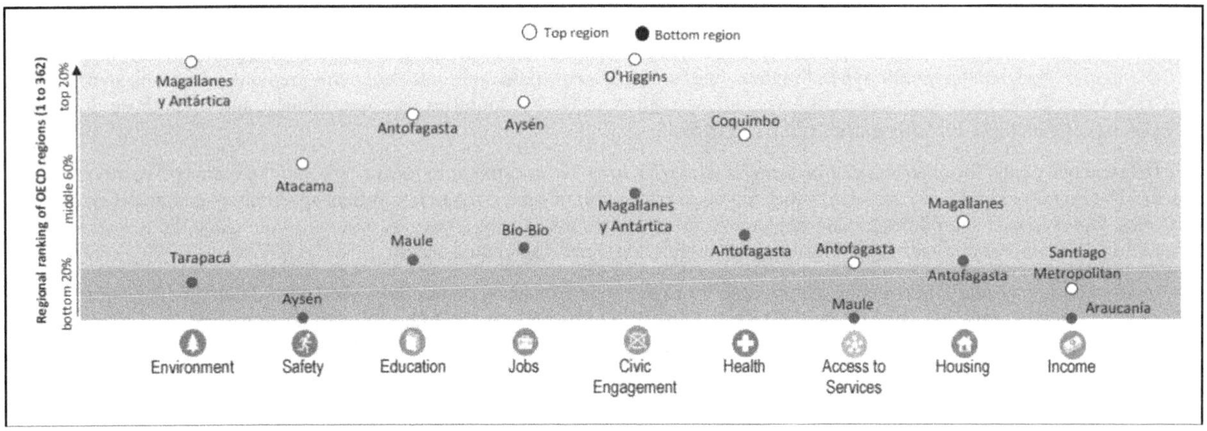

Source: OECD (n.d.), Regional Well-being database, www.oecd.org/gov/regional-policy/CHI.pdf.

Towards a place-based investment strategy

Infrastructure investments are crucial to the enhancement of economic performance in all Chilean regions. Infrastructure choice, independent of its size, should be linked to a development strategy based on assessments of the potential opportunities for and impediments to growth in each locality, as recommended by the OECD's *Recommendation on Effective Public Investment* (Boxes 3.1 and 3.2). Investment in infrastructure can facilitate development and help to diminish regional disadvantages; however, it needs to be implemented along with parallel measures such as innovation educational improvements to ensure that a region, especially a lagging one, can take full advantage of the opportunities that improved infrastructure creates. Chile's heterogeneity calls for differentiated investment strategies tailored to local needs and regional competitive advantages.

Strong inequalities require a discussion on the kind of country, cities, regions and localities Chile wants to develop (see Chapter *2*). This has two direct implications: (1) the need to generate links between different sectors; and (2) the need to develop a place-based approach to planning infrastructure investments and regional development, as has been documented in previous OECD Reviews (OECD, 2009a; OECD, 2013a; OECD, 2014b). Place-based policies will allow Chile to consider differing territorial needs and adopt investment mixes that respond differently to challenges in metropolitan areas and lagging remote regions, and that promote urban-rural linkages, and boost intermediary cities.

Box 3.1. Infrastructure and territorial productivity

Infrastructure investment is the backbone of productivity, supporting the delivery of effective public services in a myriad of policy areas that affect people's lives. High-quality infrastructure is key to both raising productivity levels and improving social inclusion. Infrastructure can help in reducing territorial disparities by bridging the existent gap that distances urban and rural territories.

Various econometric studies from the OECD, IMF and World Bank show that investment spending has a significant multiplier effect. Recent analysis from the OECD show that the first year effect of a 0.5% of GDP public investment stimulus by all OECD economies is significant and translates for example in 0.6% of GDP increase in the United States, and 0.5% in the Euro area (OECD, 2016c).

The impact of infrastructure investment depends on how it is managed. While the financing dimension of infrastructure investments is important, the broader public governance dimension is equally important. OECD evidence has shown that substantial benefits can be realised by better managing public investment throughout its "life cycle" and across levels of government; and that the quality of public governance correlates with public investment and growth outcomes, at both national and subnational levels (OECD, 2015b). One calculation estimates that globally USD 1 trillion per year could be saved from better governance of expected public infrastructure investment needs (McKinsey, 2013).

Infrastructure investments have an important spatial dimension. Infrastructure needs differ across regions depending on their density, economic structure and distance from the productivity frontier. There is strong heterogeneity in regional performance among OECD countries both among similar type of regions (e.g. urban, intermediate and rural) and across regions within the same country (OECD, 2014a). Differences in productivity levels across regions in OECD countries vary enormously, and often those differences are much larger than those across countries (OECD, 2016a).

Heterogeneity calls for differentiated investment strategies to tailor investment to local needs and the competitive advantages of regions. The investment mix will inevitably vary among urban, rural, or mixed regions to reflect specificities and assets of different territories. Governments should design and implement infrastructure investment strategies tailored to the place the investments aim to serve in order to boost productivity while also promoting inclusiveness and equal access.

Investment in physical infrastructure is important for regional performance, particularly when co-ordinated with other strands of policy. Infrastructure alone has little impact on regional growth unless regions are endowed with adequate levels of human capital and innovation (OECD, 2015b). When undertaken in isolation, it can yield poor results, and it seems to be subject to diminishing returns.

Place-based approaches are demanding from a governance point of view, since co-ordination across sectors or jurisdictions to achieve complementarities or invest at the relevant scale do not occur spontaneously. They need to be managed, through effective governance mechanisms, both vertically and horizontally. Whether through shared policy competencies or joint funding arrangements, public investment typically involves different levels of government at some stage of the investment process, making its governance particularly complex.

Effective public investment requires substantial co-ordination across levels of government to bridge any gaps in information, policy or financing that may occur. Effective co-ordination among levels of government helps to identify investment opportunities and bottlenecks, to manage joint policy competencies, to minimise the potential for investments to work at cross-purposes, to ensure adequate resources and sufficient capacity to undertake investment, to resolve conflict and to create trust (OECD, 2015b). Governance instruments to support co-ordination include for example financial incentives to support co-operation, co-financing mechanisms, joint investment strategies, conditionalities, platforms of dialogue, or specific instruments such as contractual arrangements.

Sources: McKinsey (2013), *Infrastructure productivity: How to save $1 trillion a year*, www.mckinsey.com/industries/infrastructure/our-insights/infrastructure-productivity; OECD (2016a), *OECD Regional Outlook 2016: Productive Regions for Inclusive Societies*, http://dx.doi.org/10.1787/9789264260245-en; OECD (2016c), *Stronger Growth Remains Elusive: Urgent Policy Response is needed, Interim Economic Outlook* http://pac-files.oecd.org/acrobatebook/1215071e.pdf; OECD (2015b), *Recommendation on Effective Public Investment Across Levels of Government*, *www.oecd.org/gov/regional-policy/recommendation-effective-public-investment-across-levels-of-government.htm*; OECD (2014a), *OECD Regional Outlook 2014: Regions and Cities: Where Policies and People Meet*, http://dx.doi.org/ 10.1787/9789264201415-en.

Chile has made important progress in the definition of a place-based strategy for infrastructure investments. The Ministry of Public Works has followed previous OECD recommendations to undertake a process *from* and *for* the territories in the design of its Plan Chile 30/30 The Plan is innovative in various dimensions, as it calls for an in-depth consultative process with local actors to validate infrastructure projects, and at the same time, expresses a commitment to developing a long-term vision for the development of the so-called macrozones. This last factor is particularly relevant, as a macrozone planning of infrastructure investments recognises territorial heterogeneity across the country and at the same time permeates planning with a territorial dimension that goes beyond regional administrative boundaries. The recently approved Law on Contributions to Public Space also reflects Chile's move towards viewing infrastructure projects through territorial lenses by improving the administration and management of urban spaces. While this law neither changes governance mechanisms for urban spaces nor accentuates administrative or financial decentralisation, it recognises that infrastructure investments have impacts that go beyond the pure physical work, in that they change the dynamics of a territory. The law requires that when new urban projects are executed, they contribute to the construction of parks, public spaces and the transport infrastructure needed to serve urban growth.

To be successful in the design and implementation of a place-based infrastructure strategy, **Chile needs to pay special attention to how investments are managed**. While the financing dimension of infrastructure investments is important, the broader public governance dimension is equally important. Moving towards a place-based approach in the country requires strengthening some existing multi-level governance arrangements to increase communication and collaboration both between the national government, regions and municipalities and among different sectors and jurisdictions, all in order to achieve complementarities or ensure that investments are made on the relevant scale (Box 3.2). The Multi-level Governance Indicators recently developed by the OECD based on the Recommendation on Effective Public Investment across Levels of Government show that Chile is below the OECD average for a series of dimensions, including the existence of coherent planning (see also Chapter 2), and of regular dialogues on regional development policy and investment priorities between the national and subnational levels of government. Even when a country has better than average vertical co-ordination instruments, performance monitoring and co-financing arrangements, the mere existence of such tools does not guarantee their effectiveness (Figure 3.4). As will be seen later, Chile needs to further develop these tools in order to adapt them to the new challenges of the country.

Box 3.2. Effective public investment across levels of government

The OECD Recommendation on Effective Public Investment across Levels of Government adopted in 2014 targets the systematic obstacles that countries, regions and cities face when managing public investment, notably challenges in vertical and horizontal co-ordination, across sectors, and bottlenecks in sub-national capacities. It highlights three systematic challenges for managing public investment across levels of government limit efficiency and effectiveness:

1. **Co-ordination challenges:** Cross-sector, cross jurisdictional and intergovernmental co-ordination is necessary, but difficult in practice. Moreover, the constellation of actors involved in public investment is large and their interests may not be aligned.
2. **Sub-national capacity challenges:** Where the capacities to design and implement investment strategies are weak, policies may fail to achieve their objectives. Evidence suggests that public investment and growth outcomes are correlated to the quality of government, notably at the subnational level.
3. **Challenges in framework conditions:** Good practices in budgeting, procurement and regulatory quality are integral to successful investment, but not always consistent across levels of government. The purpose of these Principles is to help governments assess the strengths and weaknesses of their public investment capacity across levels of government and set priorities for improvement.

Source: OECD (2015b), *Recommendation on Effective Public Investment Across Levels of Government – Implementation Toolkit*, www.oecd.org/effective-public-investment-toolkit.

Figure 3.4. Multi-level Governance Indicators in Chile and the OECD

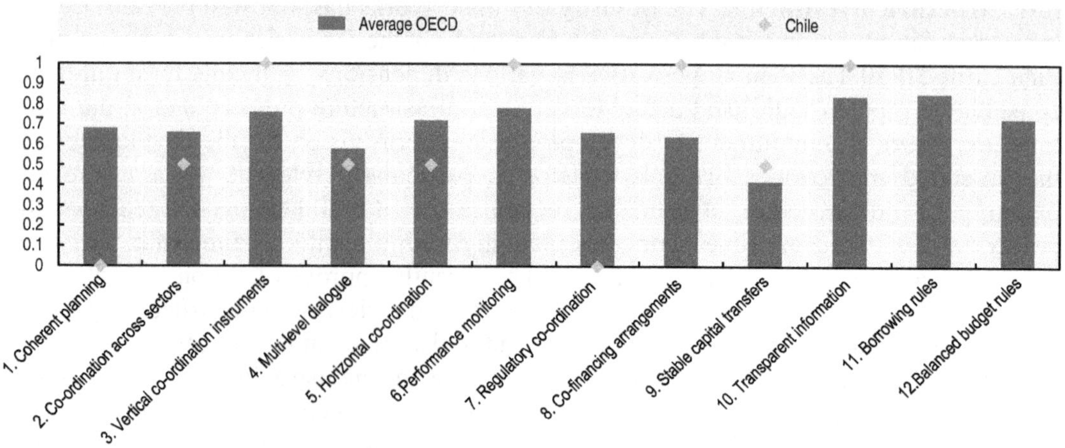

Source: OECD (unpublished), Regional Outlook Survey 2016.

Chile: a highly centralised country

Chile is the most fiscally centralised country in the OECD

Chile is a highly fiscally centralised country compared to other OECD countries. Subnational governments face constraints on their ability to raise their own revenues, they have limited room for expenditure, and there are significantly fewer investments decided upon by regions and municipalities than the OECD average. The limited fiscal autonomy of subnational governments contrasts strongly with the country's heterogeneous productive structure. The diverse territorial characteristics call for a more autonomous management of revenues, expenditures and investments in different regions and municipalities, as their needs vary markedly across the country. Centrally driven investments can only partially respond to local needs.

Figure 3.5. SNGs expenditure as a % of GDP and public expenditure in 2014

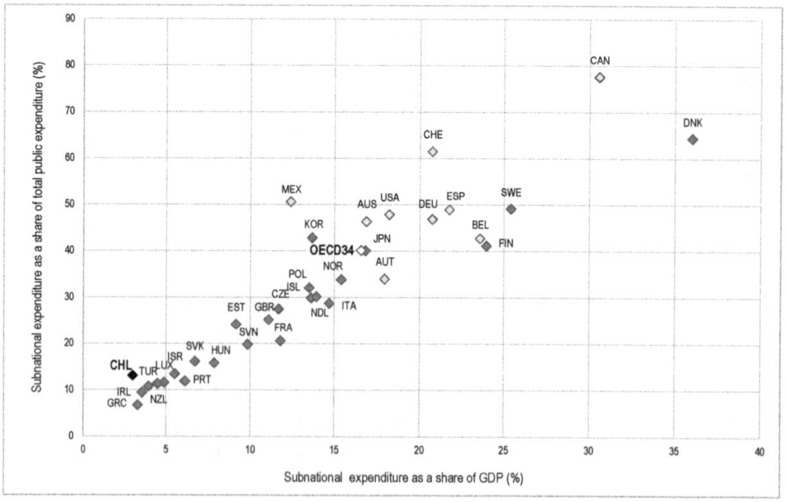

Notes: The statistical data for Israel are supplied by and under the responsibility of the relevant Israeli authorities. The use of such data by the OECD is without prejudice to the status of the Golan Heights, East Jerusalem and Israeli settlements in the West Bank under the terms of international law.

Source: OECD (2016b) *Subnational governments in OECD countries: key data*, www.oecd.org/gov/regional-policy/Subnational-governments-in-OECD-Countries-Key-Data-2016.pdf.

Chilean subnational governments have a limited ability to raise revenues and limited spending responsibilities, which are substantially lower than in other OECD unitary countries. In 2013, subnational own revenues in Chile represented 3.2% of GDP, compared to 16% on average in OECD countries. While taxes constitute a higher than average proportion of municipal revenues in Chile (see Figure 3.5), municipalities exert limited authority over these revenues. Municipalities had full discretion over the rates for only 17% of tax revenues in 2011. Property tax, which constituted approximately 43% of municipal tax revenues in 2011, is strongly controlled by the central government, which sets the base, rate, frequency of adjustments, and exemptions (OECD, 2013a). Development of sub-national revenue collection is important not only to finance investment but also to bolster financing for long-term operations and maintenance and to permit full participation in co-financing arrangements (OECD, 2015a). Subnational governments have also limited expenditure responsibilities, which[1] represent 3% of GDP in Chile, compared to 13.3% on average in unitary OECD countries. Spending autonomy is limited by constraints on their revenue sources, and most expenses are earmarked for education and health.

Subnational governments (SNGs) play a secondary role in public investments, unlike in most OECD countries. When looking at subnational investments, Chile ranks as the most centralised country: subnational governments are responsible for only 12% of total public investments, while in the OECD they are responsible for almost 60% (Figure 3.6). When looking at these figures from a world-wide perspective, this is also true. SNGs represented almost 40% of public investment worldwide in 2013 (OECD/UCLG, 2016), and Chile is amongst the unitary countries with the lowest levels of subnational investment, at the same level as Costa Rica and Jordan (Figure 3.7).

Figure 3.6. Subnational governments' share of public investment

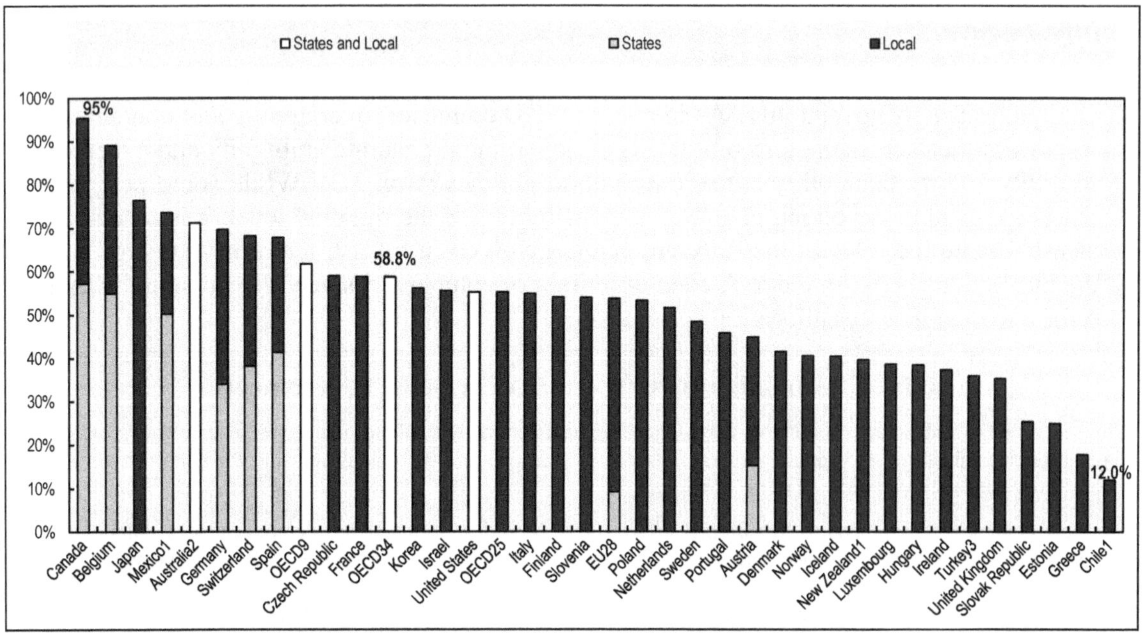

Notes: 1. 2013 figures. 2. 2012 figures. 3. 2011 figures. The statistical data for Israel are supplied by and under the responsibility of the relevant Israeli authorities. The use of such data by the OECD is without prejudice to the status of the Golan Heights, East Jerusalem and Israeli settlements in the West Bank under the terms of international law.

Source: Authors' elaboration based on OECD (2016b) *Subnational governments in OECD countries: key data*, www.oecd.org/gov/regional-policy/Subnational-governments-in-OECD-Countries-Key-Data-2016.pdf and OECD (2016f), "Subnational government structure and finance", OECD Regional Statistics (database), http://dx.doi.org/10.1787/05fb4b56-en.

Figure 3.7. SNG investment as a % of GDP and public investment

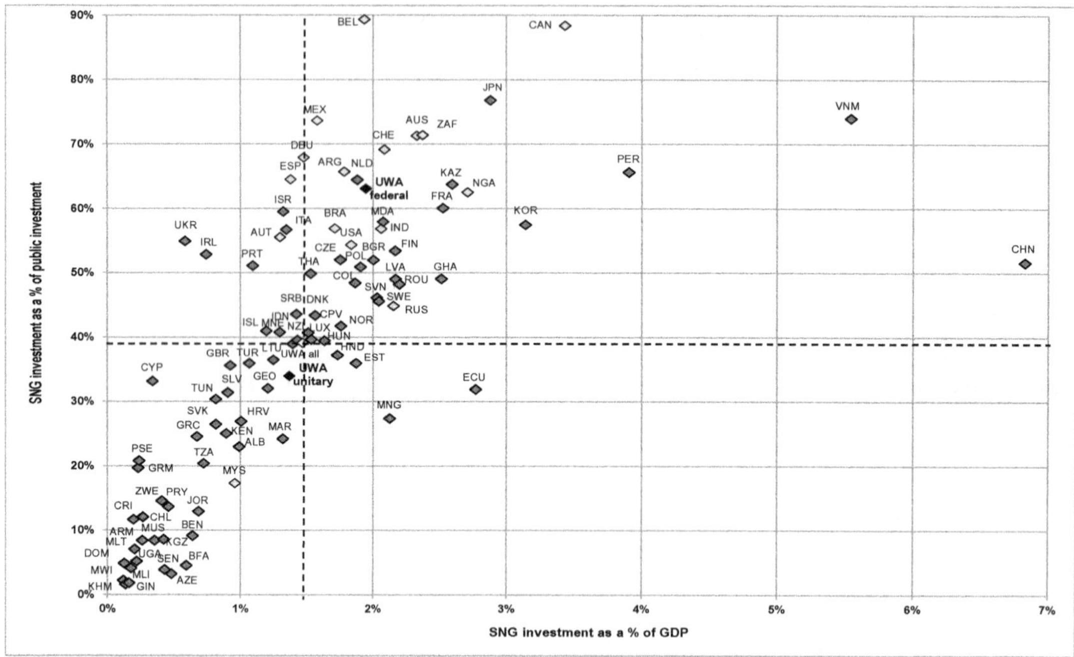

Notes: The statistical data for Israel are supplied by and under the responsibility of the relevant Israeli authorities. The use of such data by the OECD is without prejudice to the status of the Golan Heights, East Jerusalem and Israeli settlements in the West Bank under the terms of international law.

Source: OECD/UCLG (2016), *Subnational Governments around the world: Structure and finance.*

SNGs have limited and overlapping responsibilities over infrastructure investments

The administrative structure of Chilean regions brings along significant challenges for its governance. As in many OECD countries, overlapping and concurrent responsibilities across the different levels of government generate ambiguity and a lack of visibility and accountability concerning public policies (Box 3.3). While some progress has been made in devolving planning responsibilities to the regional level, it is crucial to clearly define the roles of the different actors involved in infrastructure investments and the interactions between them. A clear definition of competences needs to go along with a reform to the resources allocation system.

Box 3.3. Administrative structure of regional governments

Chile is a centralised unitary state with two tiers of government at the subnational level. The first tier consists of 15 regions and the second tier of 345 municipalities. Between the regions and municipalities, and for administrative purposes, there are 54 provinces with very limited responsibilities.

Regional governments (*Gobiernos Regionales, GOREs*) are both decentralised and de-concentrated units of the central state. Regions are led by the *Intendente*, a representative of the President at the regional level who oversees development initiatives and the co-ordination of sectoral policies in the region. The Regional Council (*Consejo Regional, CORE*), whose members have been democratically elected for four-year terms since 2014, works with and supervises the *Intendente*. The GORE is responsible for the regional public administration and since 2009 it has also been responsible for regional planning.

The CORE is the main decentralised actor in the region and has a central role in the planning of infrastructure projects. These bodies approve the regional budget and a variety of planning instruments with implications for infrastructure: regional development strategies, municipal regulating plans, regional urban development plans, Programme Contracts (*Convenios de Programación/CP*) and the distribution of the major source of regional investment - the National Regional Development Fund (FNDR) (see below).

Box 3.3. Administrative structure of regional governments (*cont.*)

Implementation of sectoral policies is the responsibility of the national ministries' representatives in the region (Secretarías Regionales Ministeriales, SEREMIs) and their services, which work directly with the *Intendente*. The Ministries with subnational competencies and some infrastructure implications are the Ministry of Housing and Urban Planning, Transportation and Telecommunications, Public Works, Education, Environment, Finance, Health, and Social Development. They are responsible for implementing national policies within their jurisdiction, responding to line ministries and co-ordinating initiatives with the *Intendente*. Depending on the political will, co-ordination between SEREMIs in the regions can be close, or it can be non-existent, as no permanent institutional framework for collaboration has been established.

The SEREMI of the Ministry of Housing and Urban Planning (MINVU) are responsible for developing regional, inter-municipal and metropolitan plans, as well as overseeing the development of municipal land-use plans (OECD, 2013a: 144). The Housing and Urban Development Agency (SERVIU) MINVU is the service in each region that is responsible for the construction and maintenance of urban roads and has played a major role in the Transantiago transport project (OECD, 2013a).

Regional actors and main competences

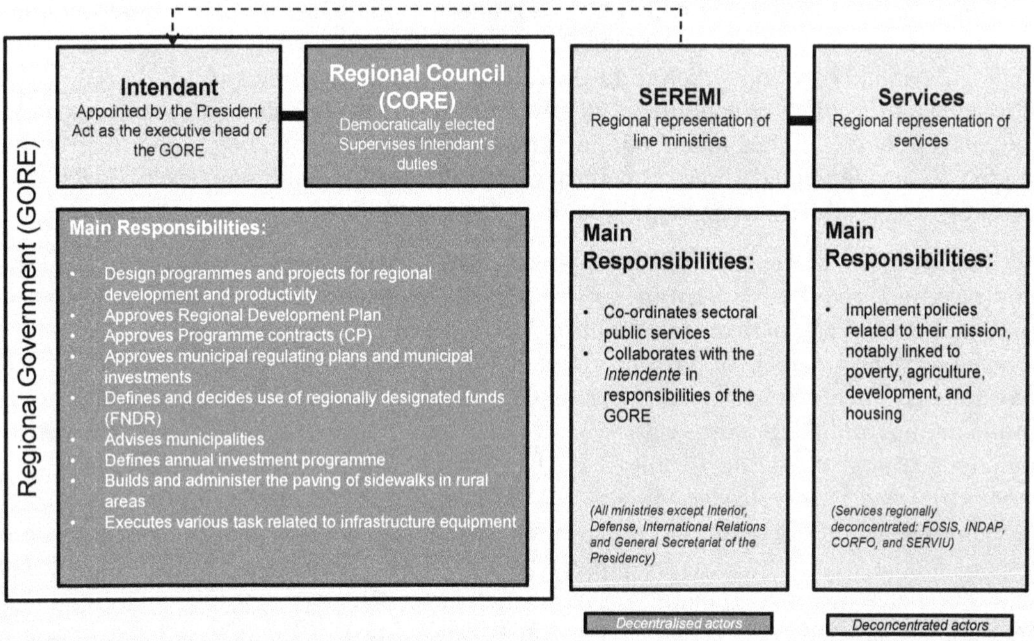

Source: OECD (2013a), *OECD Urban Policy Reviews, Chile 2013*, http://dx.doi.org/10.1787/9789264191808-en; Government of Chile (2005), Ley Nro 19.175, Orgánica Constitucional sobre Gobierno y Administración Regional.

The picture of the relationships and accountability among the different regional actors is fuzzy. The coexisting mandate of the *Intendente,* who is both a representative of the state and the head of the CORE, generates a problem of divided loyalties (to the central and to the region) that can undermine the process of designing place-based infrastructure agendas (OECD, 2009a). As the head of a regional government, the *Intendente* has to work on developing a region's territory from the local level, and as the president's representative he is responsible for implementing national policies and guidelines. In most regions, as a consequence of the centralised culture of the country, the de-concentrated role takes precedence, with these figures implementing central mandates in regions. A high turnover of *Intendentes* in a vast majority of regions also hampers the communication and co-ordination the *Intendente* may have with regional public servants. The proposed reform that would allow for the direct election of the *Intendant* would partially solve this dilemma. As an elected official, the *Intendente* would respond directly to the interests of the region, along with the elected Council, acting as a counterweight to the future Regional Governor (still representing the president in the Region). For these officials to appropriately carry out this role, the central government will need to give them additional competences and resources; otherwise, regional autonomy would be constrained.

The relationship between the GORE and the SEREMIs is also unclear. SEREMIs work directly with the *Intendant* and implement sectoral initiatives in line with the *Intendant*'s priorities, but they answer directly to the line ministry. While in theory the priorities of all parties should align as the SEREMIs are responsible to their ministries and the ministries to the President, and the *Intendant* is carrying out the President's programme at the regional level, in practice SEREMIs will tend to align priorities with their ministry with a limited comprehensive approach for regional policies. Such alignment is to be expected, not only because the SEREMIs are branches of line ministries and not direct departments of GORE responsible for executing regional priorities, but also because SEREMI civil servants and their line ministers tend to outlast the average mandate of an *Intendant*. This means that following ministerial priorities lends greater stability and structure to their actions and programmes (OECD, 2013a). At the same time, policy execution is mostly carried out by subnational public agencies (*servicios públicos*) linked to and administratively dependent upon national ministries but headed by an appointed director with a certain degree of autonomy as to the use of resources and implementation of policies in the jurisdiction.

The division of responsibilities between the national and SNGs is particularly complex and requires a strong co-ordination framework to develop a coherent approach to infrastructure investments. The structure sometimes leads to overlapping competences and a lack of visibility and accountability with regard to infrastructure investments. Local roads are a clear example of this, as the central government, regions, municipalities and the private sector all have responsibilities over planning, construction, maintenance and operation (Table 3.1). In general, the *Ley Orgánica Constitucional sobre Gobierno y Administración General* defines GOREs as responsible for the design and approval of programmes and policies for regional development: this implies indirect responsibilities over infrastructure projects framed by these development strategies. The Law stipulates in very general terms that the GORE decides the distribution of investments targeted to regions, notably the *Fondo Nacional de Desarrollo Regional* (FNDR), and participates in programmes or projects for the provision and maintenance of infrastructure and equipment in the region. At the same time, the Law specifically determines that the GORE is also responsible for the construction, maintenance and administration of sidewalks and roads in urban areas. The GORE also should promote and ensure the correct functioning of transport services and the development of rural or isolated areas of the region. These last few competences can also have an indirect impact on infrastructure investments. At the same time, as the law does not clearly specify the scope for GOREs to get involved in infrastructure investments, the articulation of investment might be their key – and often underutilised – competence. This unclear institutional framework and ambiguity with regard to the responsibilities of the different actors intervening in defining investments make collaboration in the planning process particularly relevant. Mapping the distribution of responsibilities across levels of government in terms of policy making, planning and execution would help to better develop co-ordination tools. If necessary, taking advantage of decentralisation reforms (see below), a readjustment of responsibilities could be envisaged in order to reduce the need for co-ordination.

Table 3.1. Responsibilities over infrastructure investments

Processes						
Category		**Central Government**	**Regions**	**Municipalities**	**State-owned public companies or agencies**	**Private Sector**
Aviation/ airports	Main network	P, C, M&O			O, Ow (Dirección General de Aeronautica)	F, C, M&O (Concession of terminal areas and land).
	Small Aero-dromes (publicly owned)	P, C, M&O	P, F (FNDR)		O, Ow (Dirección General de Aeronautica)	
Maritime ports	Major Public Ports	PF: In state-owned ports, the investment is made by terminal concessionaires. The port makes investments only in common areas. The existence of private ports for public use is acknowledged, but does not enter into this scheme			P, F, C, M&O, Ow	C, F, O&M (Concession of terminal areas and land).
	Minor Public Ports		P, F (FNDR)	O (Occasionally)		
Railways		P, M&O (railways)			P, F, C, M&O, Ow (EFE, CODELCO)	C, M, Ow (Private carriers and other freight companies pay for use, renovation and rehabilitation of railways)
National highways	Road Network	P, C, M&O, Ow				
	Concessions Roads	P,Ow,F				F, C, M&O
Local roads		P, C, M&O (for public registered roads)	P, C, M&O	P, C, M&O (for most local roads- registered as public or not-connected to public network)		P, C, M&O, Ow (built on private land)
Public Transport	Transit System	P, F, C, M&O, R (Santiago)		P, F, C, M&O, R (Rest of cities)		O - Ow
	Metro System	P			P, F, C, M&O, Ow	
Tele-communications		R, (Subsidies, in some cases)				P-C-O&M-F-Ow
Electricity Supply		R, (Subsidies, in some cases)				P-C-O&M-F-Ow
Irrigation facilities	Model 1. traditional	P,C,M&O (for major maintenance),Ow				O&M
	Model 2-Concessions	P, PF, R				Finance-Construction - Major Maintenance -Ow
Drinkable water supply	Urban Systems (Public Network & Private Network)	F, C (most of the public network), R (new housing and connection to existing networks; subsidies in some cases), Ow			R: (Superintendence of Sanitary Services)	P,F, C, Ow (private network),M&O (for major maintenance)
	Rural Systems	P, Finance, C, M&O (only major maintenance)	P, F (FNDR)			M&O, Ow
Sewage/ sanitation	Urban Systems (Public Network & Private Network coexist)	P, Finance, C, M&O (only major maintenance)				

Notes: P: Planning F: Financing PF: Partial Funding C: Construction M&O: Maintenance and Operations R: Regulation Ow – Ownership.

Source: Ministry of Public Works (2016), "information provided by the Ministry of Public Works", First round of comments by Government of Chile, December.

The authority and autonomy of regional governments is highly limited in Chile. Regional governments have limited autonomy over their expenditure and investments, as they act as mere vehicles for the transfer of central resources to municipal governments. As shown in Figure 3.8, when compared to the OECD in terms of regional power as measured by the Regional Authority Index (Box 3.4), Chile ranks very low, far below the Latin-American average (Hooghe et al., 2016).

Figure 3.8. Regional Authority Index 2010

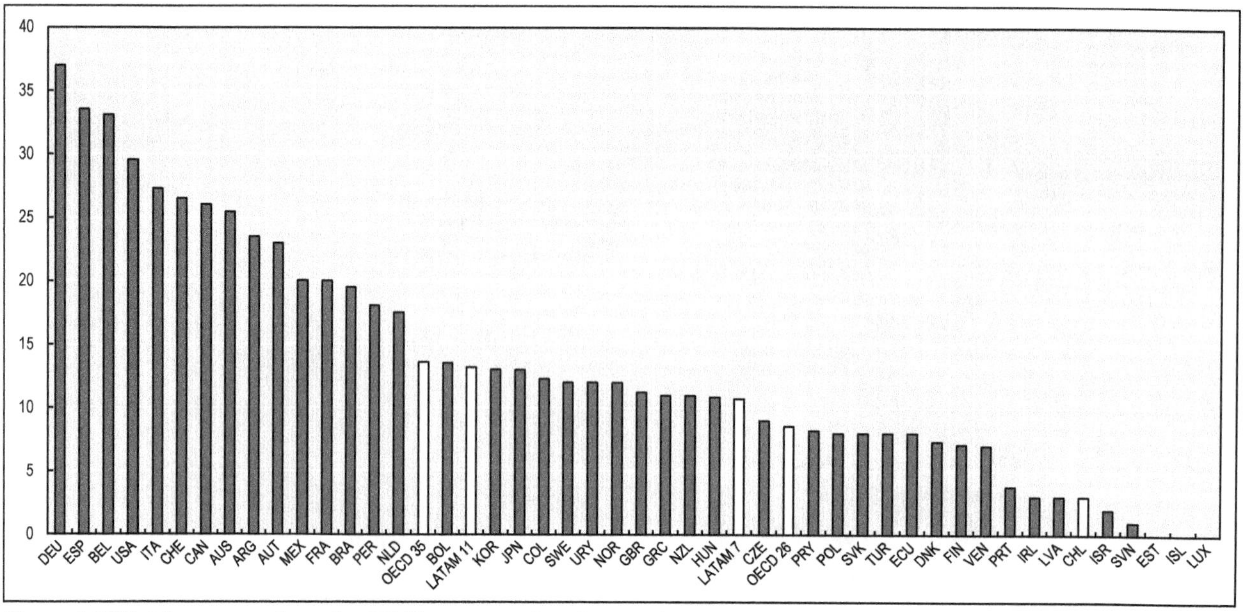

Notes: OECD 34 corresponds to the OECD average; 6 Latin American countries corresponds to the average of unitary Latin American countries. This index synthetises the five dimensions of self-rule (institutional depth, policy scope, fiscal autonomy, borrowing autonomy and representation) and shared rule (law making, executive control, fiscal control, borrowing control and constitutional reform).The statistical data for Israel are supplied by and under the responsibility of the relevant Israeli authorities. The use of such data by the OECD is without prejudice to the status of the Golan Heights, East Jerusalem and Israeli settlements in the West Bank under the terms of international law.

Source: Hooghe et al. (2016), *Measuring regional authority*, Volume I: a postfunctionalist theory of governance, www.arjanschakel.nl/regauth_dat.html.

Box 3.4. The Regional Authority Index

The *Regional Authority Index* is a measure of the authority of regional or intermediate governments in 81 countries. The Index has annual records for the period 1950–2010. The sample considers the 35 OECD countries as well as the EU member states, all Latin-American countries, some European, and Pacific and South-East Asian countries. The dataset encompasses subnational government levels with an average population of 150 000 or more.

Regional Authority is measured along ten dimensions: institutional depth, policy scope, fiscal autonomy, borrowing autonomy, representation, law making, executive control, fiscal control, borrowing control, and constitutional reform. These intend to capture two dimensions of regional authority: “self-rule”, which is the authority that a regional government exerts within its territory, and “shared rule”, the authority that the regional government has in the country as a whole.

The Index does not attempt to identify optimum levels of regional power. Instead, it is a valuable tool to codify information on the extent to which different tiers of government across the world exert their authority in order to have a picture of which groups at which scale have the authority to make different kinds of decisions. Further, this Index can be used to investigate the character, causes and consequences of governance structure within the state.

Source: Hooghe et al. (2016), *Measuring regional authority*, Volume I: a postfunctionalist theory of governance, www.arjanschakel.nl/regauth_dat.html.

Municipalities have relatively greater autonomy than regions, but the homogeneous allocation of competences might be contributing to large disparities in investments and service provision. At the local level, the Constitutional Organic Law defines municipal competences by distinguishing their exclusive and shared responsibilities (see Box 3.5). All municipalities, regardless of their size or capacity, are responsible for delivering the same public services, notably health and education. There is some evidence that this homogeneous competence allocation, despite a high degree of heterogeneity in municipal capacity, makes such uniform service delivery very difficult for some municipalities. In some cases, delivering health and education services consumes the entire municipal capacity in terms of human resources and budget, restricting the possibility of investing in hard infrastructure, notably in roads or urban planning. The misalignment between the resources available and the competences granted in a homogenous fashion across the territory creates horizontal inequalities in the types, level and quality of services provided, further entrenching spatial segregation (OECD, 2013a).

Box 3.5. Municipal structure and competencies

Chile has 345 municipalities governed by a mayor and a municipal council, both directly elected for a four-year term. Unlike regions, municipalities are constitutionally autonomous and have two categories of competences, exclusive and shared, with implications for infrastructure development. According to the Constitutional Organic Law of Municipalities (Law 18695) municipal governments have exclusive responsibilities to create their own development (PLADECO) and land use plans, and to implement the norms linked to transport, construction and urban planning dictated by line ministries. Shared competencies with implications on infrastructure include carrying out functions related with urban planning and urban and rural roads; construction of social housing and sanitary infrastructure; public transportation and transit. However, in practice municipalities have limited autonomy, as local authorities depend on higher levels of government both for funding and for approval of development plans (OECD, 2013a).

Municipal Structure and competencies

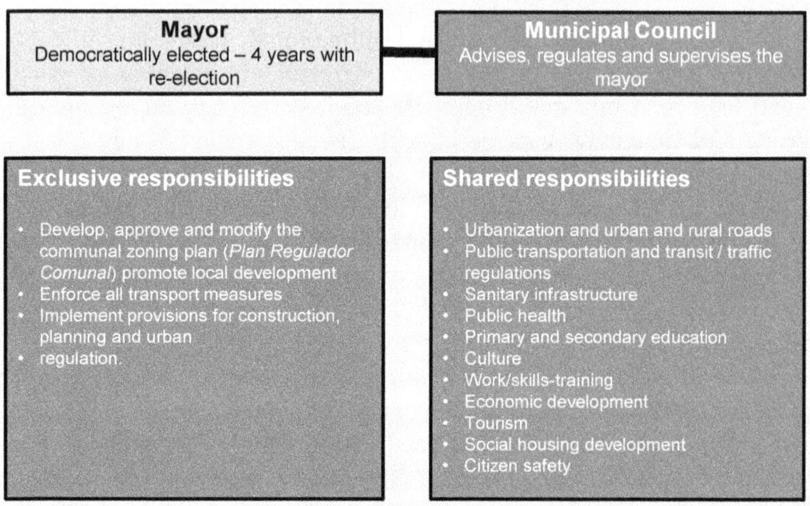

Source: Government of Chile (2006), DFL1, Ley Nro 18.695 Orgánica Constitucional de Municiaplidades.

Involvement of private actors at subnational level is limited

The private sector plays an important role in infrastructure development at the national level but its involvement in subnational investments is limited. The concessions system has contributed to a significant improvement in Chile's infrastructure and in access to basic public services, particularly for rural and remote areas (see Chapter 2). Responsibility for airports, ports and highways, has sometimes shifted to the private sector via concession arrangements[2]. While by definition these types of large-scale infrastructure investments have a territorial dimension, concession promotion, preparation, award, and supervision are largely the responsibility of the central government, namely of the Ministry of Public Works' Concessions Co-ordination Unit, with no representation in regions. Despite notable successes at the national level, the concession system can also be a factor behind inter- and intra-urban segregation when evaluated at a municipal level. Local authorities have the technical ability to enter into concession agreements with the private sector, for example, providing public parking garages. The actual capacity of municipalities to enter into such agreements, however, varies, and tends to be more common among wealthier municipalities (OECD, 2013a).

The 2014 LAC Infrascope of the Economist Intelligence Unit show that **Chile is the leader in Latin America in PPP-readiness and capacity but clearly lags behind in terms of subnational activity**. The Infrascope also shows that Chile is in the top category in regulatory and institutional framework. However, it shows clear lags in terms of subnational activity in PPPs (see also Chapter 2, Section 1.2). Although the regulatory framework allows for subnational PPP contracts, most PPP activity is still centralised at the national level (EIU, 2014). Some examples of local concessions contracts exist, particularly for waste removal or security of public spaces, but also for infrastructure projects like parking lots. However, concession infrastructure projects are still limited and concentrated in richer municipalities, and they depend largely on the local capacity to undertake PPP contracts. This is a critical challenge in the Chilean context, where these contracts play an important role. While national policies clearly favour public-private associations, subnational governments lag behind. To improve SNGs' involvement in PPPs, regional representations of the Concessions Co-ordination Unit could be created.

Weak relationships between private and subnational actors in Chile contrast with decentralised systems elsewhere in the OECD. Greater involvement of private actors at the subnational level in Chile could help the country take full advantage of the private sector expertise and financing, especially with the important funding constraints at the subnational level (Box 3.6). Even in decentralised countries, PPP structure in the OECD relies strongly on the central government level; in Canada for example, the Federal Government is committed to ensuring that investments in public infrastructure contribute to Canada's long-term economic growth and deliver maximum value for Canadians. With the help of the P3 Canada Fund, PPP Canada has positioned itself as an enabler of public–private partnerships (P3) projects, incenting provinces, territories, municipalities and First Nations to consider the P3 model and generate better value for taxpayers. P3s are a long-term, performance-based approach to procuring public infrastructure that can enhance governments' ability to hold the private sector accountable for public assets over their expected lifespan. P3s work because they engage the expertise and innovation of the private sector and the discipline and incentives of capital markets to deliver public infrastructure projects. Colombia is another interesting example. The PPP model there is significantly more decentralised than in other countries in the region. In Colombia, every level of government has responsibilities over the planning, implementation and supervision of PPPs, receiving support from the central level, which has set up a database to register PPP projects.

Box 3.6. Mobilising private actors at the subnational level

Principle 6 of the *OECD Recommendation on Effective Public Investment across Levels of Government* is to "Mobilise private actors and innovative financing arrangements to diversify sources of funding and strengthen capacities".

Involvement of private actors can help to bridge the infrastructure financing gap. Private engagement can also strengthen capacities of governments at different levels by adding expertise, enhancing ex-ante assessment of projects, strengthening analysis of the market and credit risks, and achieving economies of scale and cost-effectiveness. Sub-national governments (especially smaller ones with limited access to finance) could consider creating specific agencies for joint borrowing (municipal bond banks), mutualising capital funding, or mutualising guarantee funds to facilitate access to finance, and thereby enhance their capabilities for financing and managing public investment projects.

Careful consideration of private engagement includes informed consideration of public-private partnerships (PPPs) at sub-national levels of government. Decisions regarding PPPs should be co-ordinated with the budget process and based on their potential value for money. PPPs should be affordable *and* generate value-for-money (VFM) in excess of traditional procurement (See Chapter 2, Section 1.7).

The complexity of PPPs can require technical capacity that may be lacking at sub-national levels. This can be bolstered through support from higher levels of government, through bench learning, targeted training, creation of dedicated PPP units (which can exist at different levels of government), and promulgation of good practices.

Source: OECD (2015a), *Recommendation on Effective Public Investment Across Levels of Government*, www.oecd.org/gov/regional-policy/recommendation-effective-public-investment-across-levels-of-government.htm.

During the definition and tendering phases of infrastructure investments with the private sector, the local level should be included. While private entities are present at the local level thanks to their involvement in investment with the national authorities, their collaboration with territorial actors remains limited. Integrating private actors into the definition and execution of the agenda at the local level as well is crucial to managing inter-dependencies and shared responsibilities. This could allow local level to unlock new sources of finance, and it may also offer other benefits in terms of project design and management. Still, when involving private actors, the risk of capture by specific interest groups that needs to be managed, particularly where firms prioritise the creation of future markets for themselves rather than the best strategies for the particular region (OECD, 2013c).

Decentralisation reforms for territorial investments

Chile has a deeply rooted centralist culture that has slowed down decentralisation initiatives. The centralist culture in Chile is widely known and has been widely documented (Raczynsky and Serrano, 2001; Waissbluth and Arredondo, 2011; Marcel, 2008). This centralist tradition, along with an organisational culture that privileges legal procedures over results, favour standardised solutions to diverse and complex problems (Raczynsky and Serrano, 2001). The centralisation of decisions hinders productive development, democracy and citizen participation in decisions that directly affect them. More territorially balanced development requires stronger subnational governments, which can be achieved by transferring responsibilities and resources they need to properly exercise new competences.

Decentralisation reforms aimed at strengthening regional and municipal autonomy have been on agenda for several years. In 2009, an important step was taken towards strengthening the institutional power of the GOREs. To be precise, there was a transfer of responsibility for regional planning to regional governments (Law 20.390, amending the 1992 Constitutional Law on Regional Governments). Resulting from this reform, a new division for regional planning was created within the GORE. However, the capacity to carry out this responsibility is unequal throughout the territory. Notably, this reform allows GOREs to enter into annual or longer-term Contract Plans (*Convenios de Programación*, CP) with each other, with one or more ministries, or with municipalities. Some years later, in 2013, Regional Councils were directly elected by citizens for the first time, deepening their local representativeness[3]. Since then, decentralisation has progressed at a slow pace.

The slow progress of decentralisation reforms in Chile is partly due to some doubts on the part of the central government as to the capacity of regional governments to take over more responsibilities and successfully manage more resources. It is argued that subnational governments do not have the necessary skills and capacities to take on more responsibilities. At the same time, advancing down the road of fiscal decentralisation by giving more autonomy to regions and municipalities to administer their resources could jeopardise the country's fiscal accounts (Rodríguez and Granados, 2013). However, international experiences show that fiscal unsustainability resulting from decentralisation reforms is mainly due to weak institutional arrangements, low accountability and weak subnational capacities. As long as the country avoids these pitfalls, Chile has space to make responsible advancements toward greater fiscal decentralisation.

Decentralisation reforms are currently on the agenda of OECD countries like Netherlands, France or Norway. Like several other OECD countries, the current Chilean administration has prioritised a decentralisation agenda with the aim of providing subnational governments – especially regions – with the tools, capacities and legitimacy they need to improve their autonomy and performance. The current decentralisation agenda suggests a move towards greater emphasis on a territorial dimension, strengthening planning and implementation competences of regions. The package of decentralisation reforms promoted by the government is based on four main bills; three of them are focused on strengthening the regional tier (see Box 3.7). The transfer of competencies needs to go along with transfer of resources; otherwise, it would create bottlenecks for investments.

Box 3.7. Current decentralisation reforms in Chile

Projects on decentralisation under discussion during the 2015-2016 period are based on 5 pillars:

1. **Constitutional reform for the direct election of the "*Intendente*"**, now the Regional Governor, who will be the head of the Region and the Regional Council. At the same time the current Provincial Governor will be called the Presidential Delegate, representing the President in the region. This project is in the final stages of discussion in congress.
2. **Devolution of competences from the Central Government to Regional Governments.** This project modifies the administrative structure of the GOREs by creating new divisions: Productive Development and Industry, Social and Human Development, and Infrastructure and Transports, each of which will take charge of some of these new competences. This measure also creates a new Regional Manager. It opens the possibility for the GORE to manage urban areas, especially for urban mobility and residual management. This project is in the final stages of discussion in congress.
3. **Strengthening municipal management and professionalisation of municipal staff.** The project gives more flexibility to mayors to manage contracts according to municipal needs. The project was recently approved by Congress and its implementation is ongoing.

Box 3.7. Current decentralisation reforms in Chile (*cont.*)

4. **Reform of the financing system of Regional Governments**. This bill has not been written yet, but the government's objective is to present the project to the Congress once the Constitutional reform for the election of the "*intendente*" has been approved

5. **Pilot Experiences**. Regarding the transfer of competencies, the project defines a preliminary pilot model to transfer the competence of productive development in 2015 to certain regions in order to gradually strengthen regions and learn from experiences. The Sub-secretary for Regional Development (*Subsecretaría de Desarrollo Regional*, SUBDERE), together with the Ministry of Economy, the Production Development Corporation (Corporación de Fomento de la Producción, CORFO) and the Service for Technical Co-operation (Servicio de Cooperación Técnica, SERCOTEC), are in charge of co-ordinating the initiative. By this year, pilot programmes to transfer competences over infrastructure and transport should be in place.

Source: SUBDERE (2016a), "Descentralización", www.descentralizacion.subdere.gov.cl.

Figure 3.9. Breakdown of responsibilities across levels of government: A general scheme

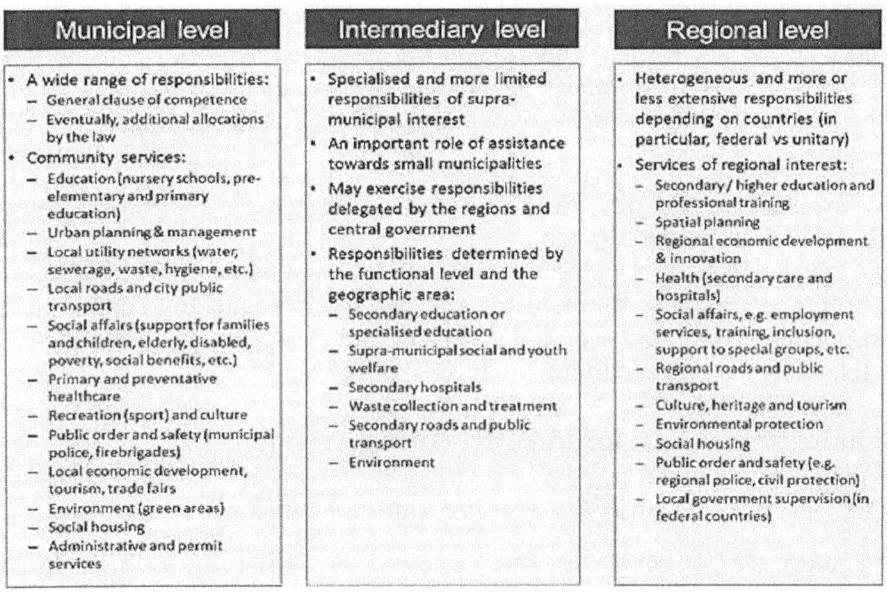

Source: OECD (2016e), *OECD Regions at a Glance 2016*, OECD Publishing, Paris, http://dx.doi.org/10.1787/reg_glance-2016-en.

Decentralisation reforms are an opportunity to better define competences across levels of government. Current discussions on decentralisation reforms to reinforce the regional level need to be accompanied by a clear and detailed assessment of the assignment of responsibilities among sectors and across the different levels of government. The Organic Law on Regions (*Ley Orgánica Constitucional de Gobierno y Administración Regional*) indicates the specific competences of regional governments linked to territorial organisation, promotion of productive activities, and social and cultural development (Figure 3.9). However, the Law is unclear in specifying concrete responsibilities; it mixes functions with specific powers and links powers to specific tasks or objectives instead of pining down the areas where governments have concrete powers (*Comisión Asesora Presidencial en Descentralización y Desarrollo Regional,* 2014). It is thus crucial to clearly set out the exclusive and shared competencies, as well as those that will be delegated. At the same time as these issues are defined for regions, a re-definition and clarification of competencies also need to be done at the central and local levels. Indeed, in OECD countries, laws normally define whether a subnational responsibility is exclusively reserved to local government, a delegated task from the central government or another subnational government (SNG), or a shared responsibility with another institutional government level (OECD, 2016e). In the OECD, national or regional regulations go into different degrees of detail on local governments' responsibilities, as they often refer to the general clause of competence or the "subsidiarity principle", especially for the municipal level, which gives local authorities the explicit freedom to act in the best interests of the local level.

The democratic election of the *Intendente* is a key step toward greater representativeness. The direct election of the *Intendente,* who will now be directly answerable to his or her constituency, helps to deepen democracy and accountability. Accountability processes could thus incentivise the *Intendente* to pursue regional strategies with closer links to the projects included in the budget; regional agendas could be then enforced. However, the direct election of the *Indentende* will not create the right incentives if it is not complemented with the delegation of competences (item 2 of the current decentralisation agenda) and granted the resources needed to execute these new responsibilities and avoid unfunded mandates. If this latter condition is not met, the democratic election of the *Intendente* could become a de facto straitjacket for the future *Intendente*.

Pilot experiences for the devolution of competences should be pursued to diminish transition costs, especially in less developed regions. The Ministry of Economy, for example, is currently devolving competences related to productive development and industry. Similar pilot experiences could be conducted for the delegation of responsibilities over infrastructure and transport, as contemplated by the projects following the model currently in place (see below).

Improving planning framework for infrastructure investments

Weak cross-sectoral co-ordination at the national and subnational levels

As in many OECD countries, cross-sectoral co-ordination both at the national and subnational levels is a major challenge for Chile. Co-operation between sectors is crucial to uncovering complementarities and reducing conflicts among different sectoral strategies. However, in Chile, like as in several other OECD countries, infrastructure investments at different levels of government follow a strong sectoral approach (see Chapter 2). At the regional level, SEREMIs are in a position that does not facilitate cross-sectoral co-ordination. Each SEREMI answers directly to its ministry, while also serving individual *Intendentes* by working together to implement sectoral initiatives in the region in line with the local official's priorities. While in theory the priorities of all parties should align, in practice SEREMIs tend to align their priorities with their ministries, thus harming co-ordinated programmes within the region (OECD, 2013a). To increase efficiency of infrastructure investments a combination of investments in both "hard" and "soft" infrastructure are needed to maximise potential for long-term growth. Such complementarities often need to be constructed through appropriate governance arrangements (OECD, 2015b).

The siloed approach to infrastructure investments is also hampered by a project-based budgeting process. National, regional and local strategies and infrastructure plans are not binding, and their links with financing and budgetary instruments are limited. Even for regional investments, budget is allocated on a sectoral basis, which discourages collaboration among the different sectors. Instead, sectors are encouraged to compete for funding (see below).

Inter-ministerial committees have made some important progress in addressing the siloed structure of the decision-making process in the country. An example of an interesting multi-level governance arrangement is the regional project of the Interministerial Committee for City, Housing and Territory (COMICIVYT), which has deployed regional committees to the 15 regions to involve SNGs in the planning of investment policies. The regional efforts of the COMICIVYT are aimed at co-ordinating land use and infrastructure planning across ministries at the regional level, raising the profile of local priorities at the central level, and producing the Regional Investment Plans of for 2015-2022 (*Plan Regional de Inversiones 2015-2022*). The experiences of these committees were heterogeneous; in some cases a real co-ordination took place, but in others the Regional Investment Plan was the no more than an aggregation of various sectorial policies, with these differences depending largely on the political will of the actors involved and the *Intendente*. However, regional COMICIVYTs are still a strong tool to enhance co-ordination at the subnational level, as they can help to identify investment opportunities and bottlenecks, thus minimising the potential for investments to work at cross-purposes. Avoiding the Chilean tendency to create new bodies for new problems, it would be important to take advantage of this existing institution to further develop its scope. Chile could envisage extending the planning competences of the COMICIVYT to monitoring the implementation of regional plans, institutionalising its existence. Regional COMICIVYT could become regular committees with monitoring competences and accountability to citizens.

To improve collaboration between ministries and public agencies at the subnational level, the government should strengthen the role of the Sub-secretariat for Regional and Administrative Development (SUBDERE). In Chile, SUBDERE is the national unit in charge of promoting regional development. It is under the Ministry of the Interior and has a great degree of autonomy to deal directly with different ministries on issues under its responsibility. One of the areas of activity of SUBDRE is the administration of public investment programmes, especially regional allocation and oversight of resources linked to the FNDR and the Municipal Common Fund (FCM). SUBDERE also supports institutional strengthening at the sub-national level and helps to incorporate a regional vision into the activities of other central government institutions. However, it is currently very difficult for SUBDERE, in practice, to act as the national co-ordination unit. Firstly, public investment destined for the regions is regulated by the National Investment System and is delivered on a sectoral basis. Additionally, the initiatives proposed by national ministries and public agencies normally follow a top-down approach, sometimes without enough consultation and co-ordination with SUBDERE (OECD, 2009a). Within this framework, SUBDERE could act as "arbiter" to facilitate and foster integrated place-based approaches for infrastructure investments, co-ordinating both sectoral initiatives and national and subnational investments.

Multiplicity of planning tools

Regional level

Regional infrastructure investments are shaped by a multiplicity of instruments with limited linkages among them. Development planning in regions is articulated through a combination of instruments, which together are supposed to guide the selection of a regional investment portfolio. Regional governments are responsible for designing Regional Development Strategies (*Estrategias Regionales de Desarrollo*, ERD) and establishing the main socio-economic guidelines for regional development for a period of six to ten years. Yet in terms of investments, there is no requirement for public entities that present initiatives to follow the guidelines set out in these strategies, a state of affairs that acts as a disincentive for regional planning (OECD, 2009a). The Regional Land Use Plan (*Plan Regional de Ordenamiento Territorial*, PROT) provides a spatial dimension to the objectives outlined in the ERD and addresses issues related to sustainable urban development and the management of watersheds and coastal areas, whose implementation requires cross-sectoral co-operation and municipal input (OECD, 2013a).

Line ministries also have their own investment plans, but their true linkages with the ERD are limited. Within the MOP, three different types of plans shape infrastructure investment planning (Box 3.8). In addition to these three main planning instruments, the MOP is developing a long-term plan for infrastructure Plan Chile 30/30 that will introduce some elements of territorial planning involving regions into the process of setting of priorities. While this Plan represents an important step forward in the involvement of regional and local actors, it is unclear how this strategy relates to other national plans from the same or different sectors and how it is articulated with regional and local plans. In parallel, other line ministries like MINVU also have plans or strategies for subnational infrastructure investments (Figure 3.10). SUBDERE also has also developed some planning instruments and implemented a number of programmes for subnational infrastructure, such as the Programme for Rural Infrastructure for Territorial Development (*Programa de Infraestructura Rural para el Desarrollo Territorial*, PIRDT) and the Investment for City Development Program (*Programa de Inversión Desarrollo de las Ciudades*).

Box 3.8. Planning instruments within the MOP

The Infrastructure Master Plan guides investment in the long term (20 years); this master plan is complemented by 9-year Regional Plans for Infrastructure and Water Resources (*Planes Regionales de Infraestructura y Recursos Hídricos al 2021*, PRIGRH) for each of the 15 regions of Chile. Each PRIGRH contains a portfolio of investments that are intended to contribute to ministerial goals and each region's Regional Development Strategy (MOP, 2014). In order to align national and subnational planning, the PRIGRH were developed between 2010 and 2012, following the drafting of the national Infrastructure Master Plan between 2008 and 2010. The MOP also develops short-term plans to achieve specific objectives within the Special Plans, specify infrastructure or water resource management of for a specific area (Villagran et al., 2013) and address particular and focused issues (Figure 3.10).

Municipal level

At the municipal level, planning authority is limited by a reliance on higher levels of government for funding and approval of development plans. Each municipality develops a Municipal Regulating Plan (*Plan Regulador Comunal*, PRC) and aMunicipal Development Plan (*Plan de Desarrollo Comunal*, PLADECO), which are supposed to guide the development of the town. These plans have the greatest potential for sub-national engagement, but they are not binding and not required for annual project-by-project fund allocation. Plans developed by municipalities can be overruled by central government authorities (OECD, 2013a), as their implementation requires that municipalities apply for and receive annual project approval and funding from higher levels of government, such as the GORE and the Regional Council. Thus, in practice municipalities have limited planning autonomy; local authorities depend on higher levels of government both for funding and for approval of development plans (OECD, 2013a).

Limited articulation between national, regional, and municipal planning leads to poor prioritisation of infrastructure investments at the municipal level. The current planning and funding systems also lead to discrepancies in priorities and uncertainty that local priorities will be heard and respected. In Antofagasta for example, the PLADECO has 39 strategies and 75 lines of action, built around municipal concerns voiced by residents and other stakeholders and information gathered in surveys/questionnaires and interviews. For a municipality of Antofagasta's size and current capacity, this is highly ambitious, and potentially unrealistic. In addition, having too many lines of action combined with low capacity for execution at the municipal level risks leading to weaker policy outcomes due to energy, attention and resources being spread too thin (OECD, 2013b). Given the current planning and financing mechanisms, without an agreed-upon investment strategy, there are guidelines to establish and align priorities among the different actors involved in subnational development. A further obstacle to prioritisation is that many municipalities lack the adequate capacities to design their development plans and lack data on infrastructure needs.

Figure 3.10. Examples of infrastructure-related planning instruments at different levels of government

Central government	Region plans and plans for regions	Municipalities and Metro areas
Agenda Chile 3030 Master Infrastructure Plan Emergency Programme for Reconstruction and Infrastructure Special Plan for Development of Outlying Areas Special Plans • Connectivity Plan Austral • Plan Chiloé • Plan Red Interlagos • Plan Rapa Nui • Plan Arauco Infrastructure plan for connectivity of indigenous rural communities National Port Development Plan EFE Master Plan and Three-year plan (2014-2016)	Regional Plans for Infrastructure and Water Resources (PRIGRH) Regional Development Strategies (ERD) Regional land-use plan (PROT)/ Regional Plan for Urban Development (PRDU) Plans for outlying areas: • Arica and Parinacota Region • Green Patagonia (Region of the Lakes) • Aysén Region • Region of Magallanes and Chilean Antarctic	Municipal development plan (PLADECO) Municipal zoning plan (PRC) Sectional plan Inter-municipal Zoning Plan (PRI) Metropolitan Zoning Plan (PRM) Master Plans of Urban Transport Master Plan for Traffic Management Strategic Urban Plans (PRU and PRES)

Source: Villagran V. (2013), Regional Plans of Infrastructure and Water, Resource Management to 2021 (PRIGRH); Current Challenges to reach the Development of Integrated Regional Planning of Infrastructure, www.uncrd.or.jp/content/documents/1058IRDP%202013%20-%20P11_Chile.pdf; OECD (2014b), OECD Rural Policy Reviews: Chile 2014, http://dx.doi.org/10.1787/9789264222892-en; OECD (2013a), OECD Urban Policy Reviews, Chile 2013, http://dx.doi.org/10.1787/9789264191808-en; OECD (2013b), OECD Territorial Reviews: Antofagasta, Chile 2013, http://dx.doi.org/10.1787/9789264203914-en; CPI (2014), Análisis Crítico de los Planes de Infraestructura; Undurraga, A. (2015), Agenda Chile 3030: Hacia un país con desarrollo equilibrado.

Articulating national, regional and municipal planning tools

Turning strategic planning into effective investment prioritisation is a major challenge for Chile. Like in many other OECD countries, regional and local planning instruments in Chile are of limited use. The ERD and PLADECO, for example, should provide a basis for community deliberation, discussion, and planning, but their non-binding, unfunded nature appears to limit their usefulness, particularly given the annual, project-by-project approval process. Prioritisation of infrastructure investments is hindered by the use of multiple planning instruments, which may generate more confusion than clarity regarding the short-, medium- and long-term needs and priorities of subnational governments.

The capability to overcome weak co-ordination of planning instruments is limited by political cycles that create incentives for national and local actors to prioritise a short-term agenda. In Chile, the challenge is particularly acute because of the four-year electoral cycle combined with the single presidential term. At the local level the problem is even more acute: municipal elections take place in between the election of the Regional Council (at the same time as the president) and the 4-year designation of an *Intendente*. Regional councillors work with different mayors in their period, and the election of mayors is potentially politically overshadowed by the elections of Councils. There is a potential risk of local actors becoming political actors in campaign during their entire term.

Some efforts at co-ordination and prioritisation between the regional and municipal levels in the planning process do take place. To partially co-ordinate ERDs and PLADECOs in the budgetary process, each region must prepare a Preliminary Draft on Regional Investment (*Anteproyecto Regional de Inversiones, ARI*) as part of the regional budget process. The ARI lists regional investment projects which need to be considered when formulating the region's budget and those of ministries. Once the annual national budget law is approved, the ARI becomes the Public Programme for Regional Investment (*Programa Público de Inversiones Regional*es, PROPIR), both available via the online platform *ChileIndica*. In this process, the budgetary co-ordination carried out by SUBDERE through its Co-ordination of Public Expenditure Unit (*Unidad de Coordinación del Gasto Público*) is aimed at reducing divergences or contradictions between sectoral investments.

A sectoral and top-down approach for co-ordination is more the rule than the exception. While the ARI and PROPIR reduce the tendency for investments to work at cross-purposes, they follow a centralist and top-down approach (Box 3.9). Ultimately, it is the national budget office (DIPRES) that has the final say on which regional investments are included in the budget law, and this decision is primarily based on a project-by-project logic. The non-binding nature of planning documents and the central definition of funding may disincentive the design of technically proficient documents seeking to integrate stakeholder's priorities. These phenomena also stand in the way of the appearance of rural and urban cross-cutting approaches to planning and do not encourage the consideration of such territorial specificities as natural risks, the presence of an indigenous population and climate change. A key step forward would be to provide improved technical assistance for subnational governments in the design of integrated investment programmes/projects, including financial plans, financed by different and articulated funding sources (see below).

Box 3.9. The ARI and PROPIR

Decree N. 3876 of 2000 stipulates that is the responsibility of the Ministry of Interior and Public Security, through SUBDERE, to co-ordinate regional public investment. This duty is the responsibility of the Co-ordination of Public Expenditure Unit (*Coordinación Gasto Público,* CORGAPU), with the support of *Intendente*s, with the latter figures responsible for co-ordination with Public Services and Ministries within their regions.

The *Intendente*, together with the Regional Council, SEREMIs, and the Regional Directors of the different public services in the region, develop the *Anteproyecto Regional de Inversiones* (ARI), including a financial estimation of the projects to be undertaken, in order to accomplish their institutional objectives. The ARI needs to be sent to the Unit of Co-ordination of Public Expenditure in SUBDERE via the online ChileIndica platform. Any discrepancies between the priorities of the *Intendente* and the regional authorities of the sectoral ministries must be resolved in the evaluation phase of the ARI or in the budgetary discussions carried out in DIPRES.

The preparation of the ARI is strongly guided at the central government level. National ministries and services give their regional representatives specific guidelines as to which policies, programmes and institutional goals should be considered for the regional ARI. In parallel, to design the ARI, *Intendente*s have to consider the non-binding Regional Development Strategy (ERD), the presidential commitments, the Special Development Plans for Extreme Zones, and the PLADECOs. However, the official memorandum which provides instructions for the preparation of the ARI and PROPIR specifically mentions that the *Intendente* may consult the mayor when appropriate.

Once the ARI is approved at the central government level and by the DIPRES, national ministries and services inform regional representatives of the details of investments and programmes to be considered in the PROPIR. This information is also available on the ChileIndica online platform. This platform has to be updated regularly by Regional Governments, as it is the instrument used by the central government to monitor execution of investments. However, the information of this platform is not publicly available, which represents a significant restriction on the possibilities for monitoring by citizens and ensuring accountability.

Source: SUBDERE (2016d), *Sistema de Información Territorial para las Regiones de Chile,* www.chileindica.cl.

The Ministry of Public Works is moving forward in integrating subnational priorities into the National Infrastructure Plan 30/30. The inclusion of the different levels of government in the dialogue to design the final Plan 30/30 which will identify the main infrastructure regions by macro-zones represents a very innovative process for OECD countries. The inclusion of subnational governments is relevant to improve alignment and co-ordination. However, it is still unclear the extent to which municipalities are being involved and how other ministries are integrated into these regional planning processes. Planning on a territorial perspective needs to ensure the participation of all levels of governments but also of different sectoral ministries.

Chile should strengthen the role of the ERD as an instrument to guide and articulate regional and local infrastructure investments. The ERD can provide a strategic regional development framework articulated with a national strategy that identifies long-term regional development goals including all relevant sectors. A unique strategy for infrastructure and spatial planning co-ordinated among sectors at the national and subnational levels can help Chile to streamline its infrastructure planning. This is necessary to give to the Gore's new planning division the opportunity to play a greater role in guiding regional development in a comprehensive way (OECD, 2009a). A unique strategy for infrastructure and spatial planning co-ordinated among sectors at the national and subnational levels, as the Area Agendas in the Netherlands (Box 3.10) can help Chile to streamline its infrastructure planning.

Box 3.10. Area Agendas in the Netherlands

Since June 2012, the National Policy Strategy for Infrastructure and Spatial Planning (SVIR) has been in force. This plan represents a strategic agenda for spatial planning policies. One of the aims is laying down the baseline programme of investments. The SVIR sets out a list of national priorities to be followed by the central administration (various ministerial departments and government agencies). A related instrument, the Multi-Year Plan for Infrastructure, Spatial Planning and Transport (MIRT), is an investment programme set up by the national government with the goal of improving the coherence between investments in spatial planning, economic development, mobility and livability at the national level. Overall, infrastructure and accessibility are adequate in the majority of regions.

National and local officials meet annually to discuss a "regional agenda", a vision shared by national and regional authorities. In this sense, the MIRT is a national programme which contributes to the regional agenda, providing a long-term investment framework for the Netherlands and its regions. The MIRT programme formally extends beyond the term of a single parliament and therefore provides a coherent framework for ensuring consistency and concentration in investments

The different layers of government have their own vision documents: the SVIR (national government), Provincial Structural Vision (provinces) and zoning plans (municipalities), all serve as input into the Area Agendas. Area agendas are the most important instruments to discuss and align questions and projects in the physical domain (housing, industry, infrastructure, public transport, nature, water) between national, regional and local governments. Each MIRT region has its own collective area agenda. The Area Agendas outline the vision, ambition, questions and projects of each specific MIRT region, shared by national, regional and local governments. The alignment of vision, goals and projects leads to better solutions, more efficiency and, in the end, greater effectiveness. Dialogues and platforms take place multiple times a year. Decision making on the content of the area agendas takes place in an annual meeting at political level (BO MIRT), and the outcome is discussed in Parliament.

Source: OECD (2014d), *OECD Territorial Reviews: Netherlands 2014*, http://dx.doi.org/10.1787/9789264209527-en.

Linking budgeting and planning

SNGs depend largely on central transfers for investments

The strong centralisation in Chile limits the autonomy of SNGs to invest in infrastructure. Most regional investments are decided upon at the central level, leaving regions have a reduced space to prioritise their own investments; 70% of investments in regions are determined on a sector-by-sector basis (MDS, 2015a) (see Annex) if regional and municipal investments are counted separately. Unlike in many other OECD countries, Chilean regional governments do not have an independent budget for regional investments, but rather depend on regionally defined grants from the central government, many of which are passed on to municipalities to finance local investments. SUBDERE breaks down regional investment into two categories: (1) "sectoral investment", defined centrally, and (2) "regionally defined investment" (*Inversión de Desición Regional*), decided upon at the regional level. However, for the regionally defined investment the classification might be misleading, as various of the instruments that fall into this category (FNDR, IRAL, CPs, Participative pavement, etc.) are mainly managed by the SEREMIs or Regional Services, which ultimately answer to their respective sectors more than to the region's priorities represented by the GORE (Acuña, 2009).

The Regional Fund for Regional Development (*Fondo Nacional de Desarrollo Regional* – FNDR) was conceived as a territorial fund, but its portfolio is largely based on individual projects. The primary source of non-sectoral funds for investment at the subnational level is the FNDR. Over the last 15 years the funding of the FNDR has been increasing, in 2015 reaching 75% of the total amount allocated to regions (MDS, 2015a) (see Figure 3.11 and Annex 2). One of the main advantages of the FNDR is its flexibility, which allows it to target issues and territories that other funds do not. However, there are two significant shortcomings associated with the FNDR: (1) while it was originally established as the primary funding source for long-term and comprehensive regional development initiatives, resources are in fact mainly allocated to individual municipal petitions; (2) it has become one of the main sources of municipal financing, as municipalities themselves are not able to raise enough revenues (OECD, 2009a). Although projects submitted for approval and funding through the FNDR are part of a comprehensive and integrated programme, they are evaluated on the project level for their cost/benefit, including social cost/benefit, rather than evaluated as an integrated whole. This could very well lead to one project being funded while another one that may be equally important (and potentially even linked), remains unfunded (OECD, 2013b). The FNDR portfolio thus becomes the sum of individual projects rather than the integration of different regional initiatives attached to the regional development strategy (OECD, 2014b).

The complexity of funding allocation for SNGs makes it difficult to achieve territorial synergies. From a municipal perspective, requests for FNDR funds must pass through a complex set of filters that can vary depending on the project's size. Larger projects, for example, may pass through regional governments, the Ministry of Social Development's SEREMI, and the Ministry of Finance, while smaller ones may only go through the regional government and a SEREMI (generally that of Social Development). The process lacks the flexibility and speed necessary to meet certain municipal demands for investment in basic services. Because requests for FNDR funds are subject to *ex ante* analysis on a project-by-project basis by national level actors (including SEREMI), it is very difficult to achieve synergies between investment projects (OECD, 2013a).

The FNDR has favoured investment in metropolitan regions, which might accentuate regional inequalities within the country. The FNDR assignment formula favours investments in regions with higher concentrations of population and poverty. This results in more FNDR resources for the relatively well-off metropolitan areas that concentrate the vast majority of employment opportunities but also the highest poverty levels. This in turn, may exacerbate spatial inequalities (Ahmad and Viscarra, 2016). Lagging regions are thus affected in two ways: (1) they are not favoured by FNDR funds, which go primarily to metropolitan areas with a high concentration of poor and female-headed households; and (2) they have lower capacities to present projects that meet the SNI criteria (see Chapter 4) (Ahmad and Zanola, 2015).

Other funding sources for subnational infrastructure investments also follow project-by-project allocation logic. The FNDR is not the only source for regional investments, although it is by far the largest. Regional governments can also enter into Programme Agreements (*Convenios de Programación*, CP) to fund regional and local investments (see below) or receive funds from the fund *Inversión Regional de Asignación Local* (IRAL). These funding sources represent a much lower proportion of regionally defined investments (CPs represent 21.6% of the total funds for regions, and IRAL only 3%). In some regions like Arica y Parinacota, O'Higgins and Aysen, the FNDR represents almost all regional funds[4] (Figure 3.11*)*. While highly valuable, these funds, like the FNDR, should incentivise and support comprehensive development needs rather than strictly sectoral ones.

Figure 3.11. Funds for Regions 2001-2015

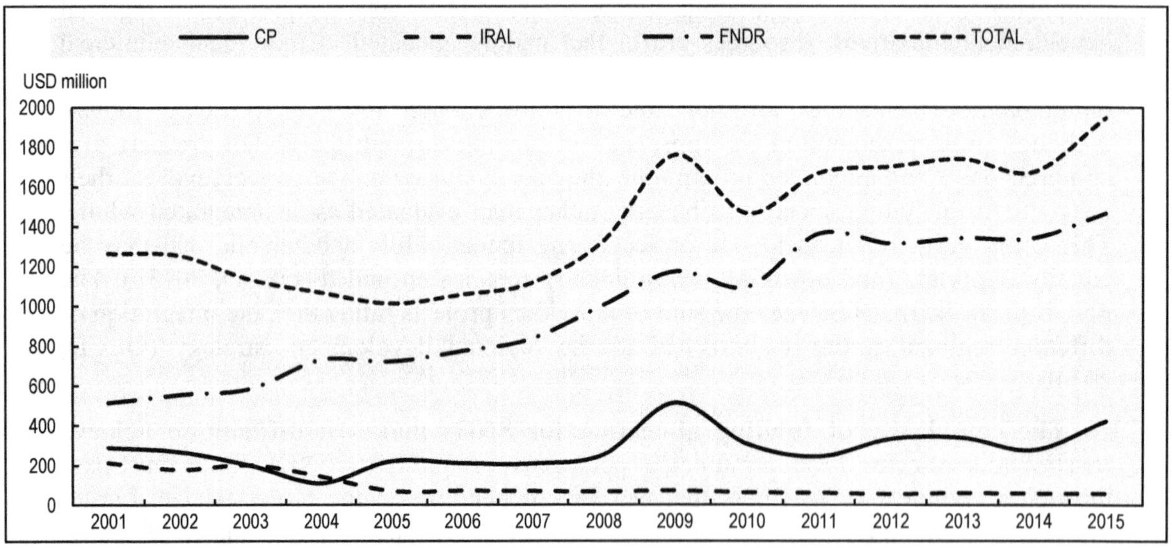

Source: MDS (2015b), "Serie de Inversión Pública Regionalizada 2001-2015".

Municipalities have limited financial autonomy and a reduced capacity to plan and implement infrastructure projects. Municipalities are responsible for a small percentage of public investment. OECD figures show that while approximately 12% of public investment occurred at the municipal level in Chile in 2013, the figure was a notably higher 56.4% weighted average in OECD unitary countries. An examination of data from the Ministry of Social Development leads to a similar conclusion: only 9% of total public investment is made by municipalities. Figures show a strong difference between municipal investments across the country; in Santiago this figure represents 14% of total public investment, whereas in Magallanes it is less than 2% (Figure 3.12*)*.

Figure 3.12. Sectorial, regional and municipal Investments in Chile (2015)

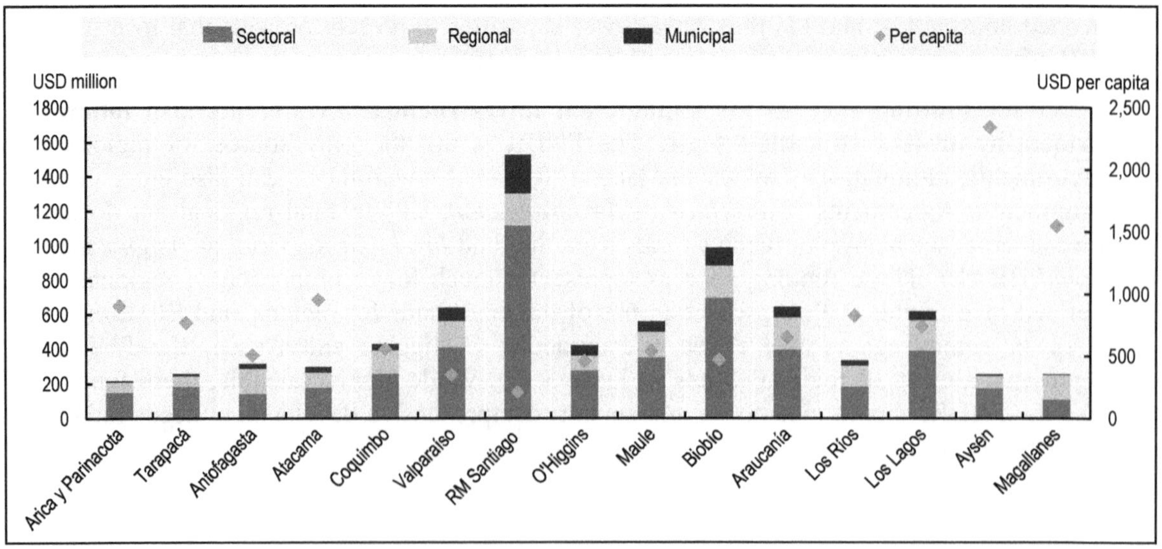

Source: MDS (2015b), "Serie de Inversión Pública Regionalizada 2001-2015".

Autonomy in deciding on and financing of infrastructure investments at municipal level is restricted by the inability to borrow. Under the Chilean the Constitution, municipalities may not borrow without Congressional approval, a prohibition that constrains their abilities to engage in larger infrastructure investments and gives rise to a disincentive, especially for bigger (and wealthier) municipalities, to design projects adapted to their needs. For some municipalities this is worsened by the lack of their own resources, even for recurrent expenditures, a situation that seriously undermines their capacity to undertake preventive maintenance of infrastructure and facilities. Postponed maintenance is compensated for with sporadic investments in the rehabilitation and "improvement" of facilities, as allowed under SNI rules, and with the use of sector funds available from the central government. This problem is noticeable in the widespread state of disrepair of public spaces, sidewalks and local roads under the purview of the municipalities (OECD, 2013a).

Investments at the municipal level are largely assigned on a competitive basis, which may handicap weak municipalities and prevent collaboration. A competitive process for disbursing funds is one way to manage a finite amount of financing, but it can also handicap the project development of weak municipalities. With limited resources, municipalities are particularly reliant on a long list of annual competitive intergovernmental transfers (Box 3.11, Figure 3.13). As noted before, the final allocation of funding does not necessarily follow the guidelines of multi-year planning documents, and there is uncertainty as to which funds will be received until the approval is given, leaving planners in limbo (OECD, 2013b). In this scenario, project prioritisation becomes critical but possibly risky for the municipality. It is critical because there are limited funds and it is important to concentrate its resources. At the same time, in an extreme scenario, if a municipality only presents its priorities and they are not approved or funded, it has few projects in its portfolio (*cartera*) to move infrastructure investment forward (OECD, 2013b). The competitive application process can also discourage inter-municipal co-operation and favour municipalities with greater technical capacity (OECD, 2013a).

Box 3.11. Main infrastructure investment funding sources for subnational governments in Chile

National Fund for Regional Development – *Fondo Nacional de Desarrollo Regional* (FNDR)

The FNDR constitutes the main funding source for investments at the regional and municipal level. Created in 1974, the objectives and functions of the National Fund for Regional Development have evolved gradually. The fund was originally established to standardise access to public investment funds across regions. However, SUBDERE has recently been working to shift the FNDR's orientation away from compensatory funds for infrastructure and towards regional development with a territorial approach. Under law, the main objectives of the FNDR are: (1) to finance investments that allow for regional development linked to social, cultural and socio-economic aspects; (2) to achieve equitable development in the region; and (3) to offer territorial compensation for regional development.

Municipal governments can apply to the GORE for a portion of these funds through a competitive process, presenting their projects to the GORE and the Regional Council. The main institutions/actors that intervene in the FNDR allocation process are:

- DIPRES: defines the special annotations (*glosas*) and provides instructions on how the funds are to be spent. For certain regions, DIPRES has to approve (*visar*) investments initiatives.
- SUBDERE: controls the execution of the FNDR and approves (*visar*) investment initiatives and its budget allocation through its Regional Units.
- GORE: is the manager and responsible for its implementation. The GORE, in accordance with the CORE, is responsible for the approval of investment projects, its prioritisation, control and monitoring.

Box 3.11. Main infrastructure investment funding sources for subnational governments in Chile (*cont.*)

- SEREMI: the involvement of SEREMIs in the FNDR varies across regions. In general, they are in charge of co-ordinating investment initiatives with services, as well as the articulation of the CPs and sectoral investments within the ARI.
- *Indentente*: in charge of doing a list of projects previously approved by the SNI to be presented to the CORE which will prioritise the projects to be executed during the year

Urban Improvement Programme (Programa de Mejoramiento Urbano, PMU)

This programme is administered by SUBDERE to finance municipal infrastructure and equipment in low income level municipalities. It finances rapid, small urban infrastructure projects to boost employment and quality of life in local population. It has a "traditional" and an "emergency" component. The former component represents 75% of the total amount. Funds infrastructure and equipment are distributed to regions based on the number of municipalities and unemployment rate. GOREs communicate the "budget framework" to the different municipalities, which then present projects to be financed by this "budget framework". The SUBDERE has to approve the projects.

Neighbourhood Improvement Programme (Programa de Mejoramiento de Barrios, PMB)

This programme is managed by the SUBDERE. Its main objective is to improve life quality of marginalised population, with a focus on improving basic service provision in poor neighbourhoods. The aim is to reduce the deficit in coverage of water supply and safe disposal of wastewater in rural areas. Since 2012, the programme has broadened its scope to target projects of "municipal interest". To be part of the programme, municipalities have to define certain projects and upload them onto PMB web platform to be revised. Regional representatives of SUBDERE are in charge of assessing the projects (legally and technically). The selected projects are sent to the Undersecretary of Regional Development for approval.

Regional Local Investment Fund (Fondo Regional de Inversión Local, FRIL)

This fund uses FNDR resources to finance minor infrastructure projects executed directly by municipalities, pending technical recommendations from the GORE and CORE. Among the projects to be financed by this Fund are squares, sidewalks and walkways. Every year, the GORE presents a proposal for the distribution of the FRIL to the CORE; after approval, the GORE communicates the amount to the municipalities, which then have 60 days to present their projects.

Investments for City Development Programme (Programa Inversión Desarrollo de Ciudades)

The main objective of the programme is to facilitate through reimbursable contributions the acquisition, construction, installation and repair of facilities and buildings linked to urban infrastructure. In order to be eligible for the programme, municipalities must meet a series of criteria. For example, they must be in the top 30% in terms of total population, be up to date on their municipal pension payments and contributions to the Municipal Common Fund, and have collected the enough surplus revenue over the three years prior to application to repay the debt by 31 December of the last year for which the loan is made. The programme provides loans for urban projects, including public spaces (e.g. roads, avenues, plazas, parks, bike lanes, pedestrian zones), lighting for streets and public spaces, traffic control systems, parking, equipment and facilities for the collection and sanitary disposal of solid waste, and for environmental protection, cultural centres (e.g. museums and theatres), civic centres, bus terminals, sports facilities, and open air and other markets.

Source: Acuña, E. (2009), Propuestas de Mejora al Diseño y Gestión del fondo Nacional de Desarrollo Regional; Centro de Políticas Públicas UC (2015), Asociatividad Municipal: herramienta para la inversión local", http://politicaspublicas.uc.cl/wp-content/uploads/2015/05/asociativad-municipal-2015-1.pdf ; Gobierno Regional Metropolitano de Santiago (2016), Instrumentos de Inversión Regional, www.gobiernosantiago.cl/instrumentos-de-inversion-regional; OECD (2013b), OECD Territorial Reviews: Antofagasta, Chile 2013, http://dx.doi.org/10.1787/9789264191808-en.

Figure 3.13. Funds for regional Investments by source (2015)

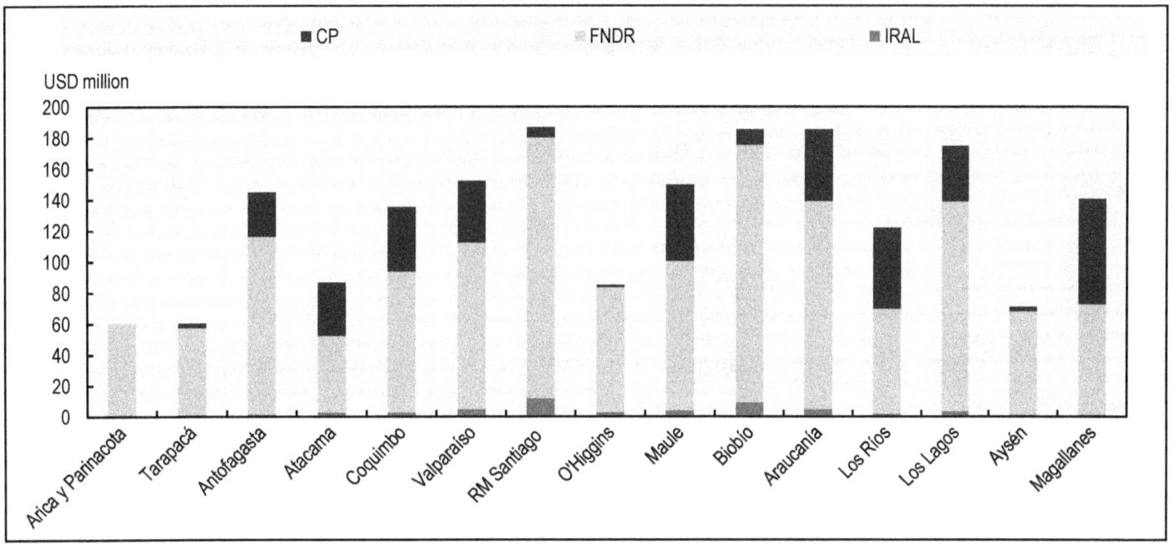

Source: MDS (2015b), "Serie de Inversión Pública Regionalizada 2001-2015".

Towards an articulated and strategic budgeting process

The funding mechanisms that are in place stand in the way of a comprehensive and strategic approach to infrastructure investments and its prioritisation. The investment process in Chile follows a sectoral logic, and the various projects that are in fact integrated initiatives risk being subjected to piecemeal evaluation independent of their master plans. The different approval stages a portfolio must go through, notably the filtering process of the CORE and the final evaluation by DIPRES, largely take place on a project-by-project basis. Different financing and budgeting practices could better support subnational development objectives and the investments designed to achieve them. With the country now facing infrastructure challenges that are much more linked to small projects than big infrastructures, the need to analyse a package of investments is even more acute. Challenges linked to funding and planning cannot be addressed separately, as funding is the key lever for co-ordination. If there are no monetary incentives, there is less likely to be co-ordination, and short-term, compartmentalised planning will prevail.

Annual budget allocation discourages medium- or long-term investment planning at the subnational level. This is partly why investment planning for Chilean municipalities is mostly restricted to the preparation of specific projects following the procedures of the National Investment System (*Sistema Nacional de Inversiones*, SNI) to be submitted for financing to whatever fund is available in a given year. Municipalities compete for these funds with projects which are not part of a strategic planning. Micromanagement of investment resources for by DIPRES is another obstacle to a portfolio based investment strategy (Waissbluth and Arredondo, 2011).

Chile needs to improve the connection between planning and budgeting to help prioritise infrastructure investment on a multi-year basis (see Box 3.12 to see how the EU deals with this matter). Neither the ERD, nor the PLADECO, nor the country's other infrastructure plans specify investments linked to budget lines. As territorial planning and strategies are the instruments that set the medium- and long term-horizon for development, the disconnection between planning and budgeting reinforces a system that functions on short-term plans and projects, unable to take decisions from a long-term, comprehensive perspective (see also Chapter 2). Medium-term budgeting frameworks (or multi-annual budget planning) provide a reasonable certainty that funds will allocated and carried over from year to year (see Chapter 2). This would be one mechanism to help address this issue, and it would strengthen the finance and planning capacity of sub-national authorities. Such a framework would allow for better management of investment projects. It would also help policy makers to see the medium-term consequences of their spending decisions more clearly and adapt investments to a territorial logic that makes it possible to finance integrated, multi-sectoral initiatives. To do so, it is necessary to articulate the diverse planning instruments, framed by a master plan which would act as the strategic umbrella guiding investment priorities (see Chapter 2).

Box 3.12. Articulating funding and planning: the case of the EU

With a budget of EUR 454 billion for 2014-20, the European structural and investment funds are the European Union's main investment policy tool. National co-financing is expected to amount to at least EUR 183 billion, with total investment reaching EUR 637 billion.

The post-crisis period has provided additional motivation for reforming the way the European structural and investment funds are planned and used. In a climate of declining overall investment, maximising the impact of these funds is a top priority, especially as they provide the majority of public investment in many countries.

Following the lessons learned from previous programming periods and taking into account the need for better use of European structural and investment funds, the 2014-20 regulations introduced several key reforms. There is a clear move towards a more focused policy approach, a stronger results orientation, solid framework conditions for investments, better co-ordinated use of funding through the common strategic framework, and improved links between EU priorities and regional needs.

Member states are required to draw up and implement strategic plans with investment priorities covering the five European structural and investment funds. These "partnership agreements" are negotiated between the European Commission and national authorities, following their consultation of various levels of government, representatives from interest groups, civil society, and local and regional representatives.

Partnership agreements outline each country's strategic goals and investment priorities, linking them to the overall aims of the Europe 2020 strategy for smart, sustainable and inclusive growth.

Once the partnership agreements have been adopted, the European Commission and the national authorities agree on programmes, setting out the priorities for each country, region or policy area concerned.

Combining different funds to finance local investment projects:

- Integrated territorial investments make it possible to combine funding from different European structural and investment fund programmes to support the implementation of territorial development strategies. Twenty member states will use integrated territorial investments in areas ranging from deprived urban neighbourhoods to metropolitan areas, from cultural heritage routes to sub-regions hit by economic restructuring.
- Community-led local development empowers local action groups to implement strategies creating jobs and growth and enhancing social inclusion by combining different EU funds. Over the programming period, multi-fund community-led local development is supported with more than EUR 12 billion. In rural development, more than 2 500 local strategies will reach out to half of the EU's rural population, while the European Maritime and Fisheries Fund will support some 280 such strategies in coastal and inland communities. Seventeen member states will support local development strategies in cohesion policy.

Source: OECD (2016), *Making the Most of Public Investment in Colombia: Working Effectively across Levels of Government*, OECD Publishing, Paris, http://dx.doi.org/10.1787/9789264265288-en.

Improving vertical co-ordination across levels of government

Strengthen institutions for vertical co-ordination

Strengthening the role of GOREs is crucial, as they can act as key interlocutors for vertical co-ordination. Acting as mere vehicles of central transfer for municipalities without their own resources, GOREs have restricted autonomy to invest at the regional scale, a limitation that will persist until funding mechanisms are enforced. However, within the current framework, the GORE planning unit should play a key role by sustaining co-ordination not only for the elaboration of the ERD, but also for all the planning instances in which the GORE is involved. GOREs are key players in vertical co-ordination, in the interaction between municipalities and the central government.

Regions could also take a more proactive role in supporting critical projects that require cross-jurisdictional cooperation, in particular those involving rural municipalities. GOREs could 129rotocol129ze municipal co-operation in investment projects by offering technical support and by acting as political facilitators. The GORE and CORE could encourage this co-operation by assigning resources to investment projects in which many municipalities are involved. This needs to go hand in hand with bolstering ERDs as master plans that effectively guide and frame infrastructure investments at the regional and local levels. In this role, regions may also be key partners for municipalities for technical and administrative support; limited regional own resources can hinder these responsibilities. The role of regions as integrators and brokers between municipalities and the national government should be fostered.

Deepening co-ordination through co-financing arrangements

In Chile, Programming Agreements (*Convenios de Programación,* CPs) have made great contributions to the development of regional infrastructure, and they are the unique tools that allow for multi-annual budgeting of infrastructure investments. To manage joint investments, Chile, like many other OECD countries, uses voluntary contracts to co-finance infrastructure investments between national and SNGs and co-ordinate projects involving different sectors. GOREs can enter into annual or multi-year CPs with each other, with one or more ministries, or with municipalities promoting collaboration across sectors and levels of government (Box 3.13). The two sectoral ministries that have historically most tended to use them are the Ministry of Public Works (MOP), which has mainly funded basic paving and rural drinking water; and the Ministry of Health (MINSAL), which has adopted a policy to plan and implement investment in primary, secondary and tertiary health infrastructure using CPs. In 2015, the MOP was the only ministry to contract CPs in as many as four regions, while the proportion of CPs contracted by MINSAL and MOP accounted for 50% each (Figure 3.14). To cite some interesting examples of these contracts, in 2009 the MOP and the Municipality of Antofagasta signed one for the improvement of the coastal shoreline and fishing infrastructure, and in 2004, the strategic Development Plan for the *silvoagropecuario* sector was signed with the Ministry of Agriculture (SUBDERE, n.d. a).

Box 3.13. Contracts in Chile

Programming agreements (*Convenios de Programación*, CPs) in Chile are formal binding agreements between one or more regional governments and one or more national ministries, detailing measures and procedures to be undertaken in projects of common interest over a specified period of time. These agreements can also include other public or private national, regional or local institutions. The subscription of an agreement does not imply new or complementary resources for the parties involved, but rather an allocation of their already approved budget to be spend through these agreements.

Box 3.13. Contracts in Chile (*cont.*)

Formally, the steps for signing a CP are: (i) identification of projects, (ii) signing of a protocol of purpose (*130rotocol de acuerdo*) that initiates negotiations between the parties and defines the objectives, areas of intervention and resources that each institution will contribute; (iii) deciding on investments that will be included in the agreement with the technical recommendation from the SNI); (iv) drafting the programming agreement and negotiation (technical); and (v) presentation of the agreement to the Regional Council for approval and signature. After the approval and execution of the agreement, there is formal a monitoring and evaluation stage in which a technical team with representatives of all parties involved is supposed to monitor its execution. Projects are carried out using the resources of both line ministries and regional governments (grants from the National Fund for Regional Development).

These agreements offer a useful legal framework for co-ordinating regional and national priorities and responsibilities. So far, they have mostly been used for shared planning and financing of large infrastructure projects.

Source: SUBDERE (n.d.), "Convenios de Programación", www.subdere.gov.cl/sites/default/files/documentos/articles-80573_archivo_fuente.pdf.

Figure 3.14. Public Investment in regions via Programming Agreements

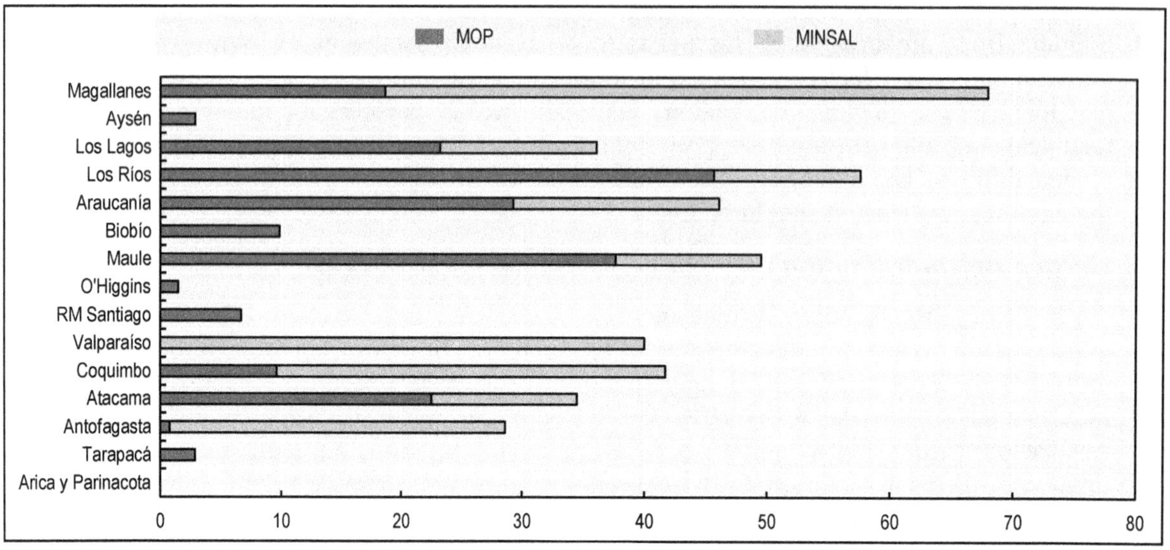

Source: MDS (2015b), "Serie de Inversión Pública Regionalizada 2001-2015".

Contracts can potentially ensure that national-level policy decisions and regional priorities cohere and "synergistically" contribute to national development targets. The benefits that they bring are multiple: (i) foster dialogue and share information; (ii) identify common targets, (iii) set clear and transparent objectives, (iv) make credible engagements; (v) promote municipal co-operation; (vi) improve monitoring and evaluation; and (vii)strengthen the capacities and practices to develop long term strategies (Charbit and Romano, forthcoming). However, these advantages have not been truly exploited in Chile. Although the *Convenios de Programación* represent a strong tool to co-finance investments, there are several shortcomings linked to their scope and implementation: (i) projects managed through these contracts tend to be highly fragmented and sector-driven; (ii) their use has been mainly restricted to large infrastructure initiatives (OECD, 2009a); (iii) some sectors have been reluctant to enter into this agreements; (iv) central government actors that do use CPs do so mostly to leverage regional resources for activities already in their sectoral plans (OECD, 2013a); (v) as a consequence, their connection with regional development strategies is limited; (vi) CPs at the subnational level compete for funding with FNDR projects.

In this scenario, some adjustments would be necessary in order to better use this instrument in a move from *sectoral-based* to *territorially-based* contracts, as in the examples of France and Colombia (Box 3.14). CPs need to be further developed and supported, which does not mean they need to be transformed in their essence, but rather that they can be adapted. Territorial contracts are a way for identifying relevant projects for competitiveness at the regional level that could enormously benefit productivity in lagging regions, thus enhancing the diversification of Chile's productive structure. To further develop contracts, some of the key elements to consider are:

- Specify territorial goals and regional development priorities that will be supported by the contract through a careful assessment of needs and opportunities in regions and municipalities (Charbit and Romano, forthcoming).
- Rebalance the top-down approach that has been dominant in the current framework, with a stronger bottom-up component through a consultation phase. The consultation should involve national and subnational actors, the private sector and civil society to establish priorities and actions by assessing regional development needs. In France for example, a two-year phase consultation allows the central and the regional government to agree on the Contract *État-Région* (Charbit and Romano, forthcoming).
- Encourage partnerships with Municipal Associations to support investments at a supra-municipal scale. This might help certain lagging regions that do not on their own have the capacity to enter into such contracts. Funding could be especially dedicated to contracts signed by Associations. Specific contractual arrangements might target metropolitan areas like city deals in the United Kingdom (Box 3.15).
- Include monitoring mechanisms and an evaluation phase in the initial contract to that allow for assessment of results and the potential impacts of contracts while learning from successes and failures and facilitating peer learning. Monitoring and evaluation are crucial to making enforcement possible with concrete incentives. For example, part of the funding could be allocated based on good performance (performance reserve, on the model of Italy or the EU).

Box 3.14. Contracts for investments: the case of France and Colombia

France

State-region planning contracts (*Contrat de plan État-région* – CPER) have been in operation since 1982 and are important tools in regional policy in terms of planning, governance and co-ordination. They are characterised by their broad thematic coverage and cross-sectoral nature, with a territorial approach being applied across diverse policy fields including industrial, environmental, and rural issues. The DATAR functions as the main national partner of the regions in developing and implementing these planning documents. The President of the Regional Council and Prefect as the representative of the central government different ministries make the contract. The co-financing of interventions is seen as an important co-ordination mechanism.

2007-2013 planning contracts: a new generation of state-region contracts was introduced in 2007 alongside the 2007-13 Structural Funds programmes, in order to increase links between French and EU regional policies. The new contracts have the same timeframe as the EU operational programmes, are based on a joint territorial analysis, and have integrated systems for monitoring. Similar to the Structural Funds, regions can decide that funding be de-committed 18 months after approval for projects if no commitment has been made. Contracts increased their focus on the Lisbon and Gothenburg agendas. They reflect three priority areas: the promotion of territorial competitiveness and attractiveness, the environmental dimension of sustainable development, and social and territorial cohesion. The emphasis on sustainable development has grown, with a consultation process launched in 2007 (*Grenelle de l'environnement*). Priority is given to soft functions (e.g. education, research and development) as well as infrastructures other than roads.

Box 3.14. Contracts for investments: the case of France and Colombia (*cont.*)

2014-2020 planning contracts: a new generation of State-region planning contracts 2014-2020 has been launched. Five topics have been selected: Higher education, research and innovation; National coverage by very high speed broadband and development of digital technologies usages; Innovation, promising niches and the factory of the future; Multimodal mobility; The environmental and energy transition. Being a priority for the Government, employment will be treated as cross-cutting issue in the contracts.

In order to ensure equality between territories within the regions, contracts will mobilise specific resources for priority areas: urban priority neighbourhoods, vulnerable areas undergoing major economic restructuring, areas facing a deficit of public services (rural areas), metropolitan areas and the Seine Valley. Inter-regional contracts for mountainous and fluvial basins will be re-conducted. The preparation of this new generation was conducted in two phases: a first phase of strategic thinking and co-preparation between the central government and the regions; a second phase of financial negotiation.

Colombia

Efforts to achieve better cross-sectoral co-ordination of investment among the three levels of government led to the introduction in the early 2010s of "*Contratos Plan*", investment programmes in specific areas. The programmes were defined jointly by the national government (which finances most of them), departments and municipalities. Seven *Contratos Plan* were developed as a first step in the 2010-2014 NDP (in 9 departments and 272 municipalities), and 17 are planned in the 2014-2018 NDP. They focus on lagging regions and on improving road connectivity and the delivery of services like education, healthcare and water sanitation. While Colombian contracts are inspired by the French "*contrats de projets État-région*", they differ from them in that the French system provides for simultaneous preparation of all the contracts, and each lasts for seven years. The *Contratos Plan* signed so far have different timings (from three to eight years) and different degrees of territorial coverage: some focus on a department (e.g. Santander); one focuses on a group of departments (Atrato-Gran Darien, covering 25 municipalities in the 3 departments of Chocó, Antioquia and Córdoba), and the majority focuses on groups of municipalities. For the seven pilot *Contratos Plan*, the parties had to come to a strategic agreement for the development of the territory.

The new generation of *Contratos Plan* have a specific focus on peace and post-conflict. They are now called "*Contratos Paz*" (*Contratos Plan para la Paz y el Posconflcito*), and they are being developed in the framework of Colombia's post-peace development agenda. They are currently being defined, matching the strategic importance of the areas for the country (areas affected by conflict and/or suffering from socio-economic and/or infrastructure gaps) and local demand. They focus on improving road connectivity and the delivery of services like education, healthcare and water sanitation. They will include long-term infrastructure projects, as well as other smaller development projects. They have a great potential for joint investments that contribute to building peace and, in this regard, other prioritisation variables, as the incidence of armed conflict will be taken into consideration.

Source: OECD (2016g), *Making the Most of Public Investment in Colombia: Working Effectively across Levels of Government*, http://dx.doi.org/10.1787/9789264265288-en.

Box 3.15. City Deals in United Kingdom

City Deals are agreements between government and a city that give the city control to: (1) take charge and responsibility of decisions that affect their area; (2) do what they think is best to help businesses grow; (3) create economic growth; (4) decide how public money should be spent.

The first wave of City Deals are with the 8 largest cities outside of London, known as the Core Cities. City Deals – Wave 2 involves 20 cities - the next 14 largest cities outside of London and their wider areas and the 6 cities with the highest population growth during 2001 to 2010. With the help of the Cities Policy Unit, these cities will negotiate deals with government – deals that give each city new powers in exchange for greater responsibility to stimulate and support economic growth in their area. Each city had to put forward a proposal by January 2013 that showed how they hope to do this.

Since late 2011, urban policy has been centred on a growing number of City Deals in England that are being implemented in waves. These deals allow a degree of "tailored" devolution of responsibility to English cities. City deals require better horizontal (across departments) and vertical (between the centre and the cities) co-ordination, and local capacity.

Source: OECD (2015b), *Recommendation on Effective Public Investment Across Levels of Government – Implementation Toolkit*, www.oecd.org/effective-public-investment-toolkit.

Improving dialogue with subnational actors

Chile has made important progress in fostering dialogue with regions. The MOP has started an interesting process of dialogue with regions for the design of the Plan Chile 30/30 to define infrastructure priorities to be included in the final package of the Plan. The efforts deployed throughout the country by the MOP have been very innovative in the OECD context and could effectively help Chile to build a place-based investment strategy. However, the role of municipalities in these dialogues remains weak. Municipalities, as the government level closest to citizens and local reality, should play a key role in the definition of investment priorities. Theses validation dialogues are a good first step toward multi-level co-ordination, one that needs to be institutionalised to maximise its potential to break with the prevailing silo and centralist culture.

Inter-ministerial committees have played a crucial role in facilitating cross-sectoral and multi-level dialogue in Chile. Chile has a strong tradition of inter-ministerial committees that bring together government institutions, civil society, experts and others to develop policies with widespread support. In many OECD countries, these consultative committees also promote dialogue between central and local actors, and this has also been the case in Chile. Both the PRIRH and the Regional Investment Plans were the result of consultative committees featuring local representatives. The regional COMICIVYT, if institutionalised, could foster dialogue over time; the COMICIVYT might evolve into a structure similar to the COAGG in Australia or the Executive GORE in Peru (Box 3.16), thus avoiding the creation of a new institution. It is important that Chile avoid the creation of a new institution for dialogue to diminish the risk of a *fatigue* of co-ordination bodies and to take advantage of the lessons learned when building the Regional Investment Strategies.

Box 3.16. Forums for dialogue: The examples of Peru and Australia

Peru

Following an OECD recommendation, Peru established a Council of Ministers, - the Executive GORE, including 19 line ministries and 25 Regional Governors, to try to offset information asymmetries between sectors and regions. The GORE holds quarterly meetings, where on the first day they conduct bilateral meetings to identify issues and opportunities for policy change and on the second identify and discussed shared strategic priorities.

Only two meetings have been conducted so far, in September and November. During the first meeting, the main topics discussed were the implementation of investment priorities that require viability, need financing in the private sector, seek public financing and / or require completion. The main objectives of the second meeting were the definition of priorities by territories, both to continue with the development of policies of intergovernmental coordination and to conduct a balance of the first Executive Gore that took place in September. The next meeting also includes follow-up/implementation etc.

Australia

The Council of Australian Governments (COAG) is the main forum for the development and implementation of inter-jurisdictional policy, comprising the Australian Prime Minister as its chair, State Premiers, Territory Chief Ministers and the President of the Australian Local Government Association. COAG meetings have been characterised by a high degree of collaborative efforts by state, territory and commonwealth political leadership as well as agency officials, who participate in COAG decision making through heads of government meetings, Ministerial Councils and working groups. In 2006, the States established a Council for the Australian Federation (CAF), comprising all the State Premiers and Territory Chief Ministers. The CAF aims to facilitate COAG based agreements with the Commonwealth by working towards a common position among the States, as well as common learning and sharing of experiences from state to state. In 2008, the COAG agreed to a new Intergovernmental Agreement on Federal Financial Relations (IGA). This agreement increased the financial autonomy of the states, moving from input control to the monitoring of outputs, and rationalising the payments made to the state into five broad areas (health, affordable housing, early childhood and schools, vocational educational and training and disability services). National Partnership Agreements outline mutually agreed policy objectives in areas of nationally significant reform or to achieve service delivery improvements, and define the outputs and performance benchmarks.

Box 3.16. Forums for dialogue: the examples of Peru and Australia (*cont.*)

Source: Carreño, I. (2016), "Ejecutivo y gobiernos regionales se unen para pedir facultades", *La República*, published online 3 September, http://larepublica.pe/impresa/politica/799543-ejecutivo-y-gobiernos-regionales-se-unen-para-pedir-facultades; El Peruano, (2016), "Confirman Segundo GORE Ejecutivo", *El Peruano*, published online 3 November, www.elperuano.pe/noticia-confirman-segundo-goreejecutivo-48051.aspx; OECD (2015b), *Recommendation on Effective Public Investment Across Levels of Government – Implementation Toolkit*, www.oecd.org/effective-public-investment-toolkit.

Co-operation across jurisdictions

Making the most of municipal associations

Like many other OECD countries, Chile has a weak culture of collaboration between municipalities, stemming in part from the fund allocations system in which municipalities are often called upon to compete. Municipal fragmentation in Chile does not represent a challenge in itself when compared to other OECD countries, as the size of Chilean municipalities is comparatively somewhat large on average; in Chile, almost 50% of municipalities have over 20 000 inhabitants, and only 5% have less than 2 000 (Figure 3.15). However, collaboration among municipalities is still relevant, especially due to strong inequalities in terms of resources and capacities (Box 3.17). The strong centralism has discouraged collaboration, as big projects that would need co-operation between local actors are mainly decided on at the central level. Funding allocation has also limited collaboration, as municipalities are often called on to compete instead of articulating investment priorities that could help municipalities to make the most of synergies obtained through co-operation and the building of a scale.

Box 3.17. Why is co-ordination across jurisdictions important?

Co-ordination across jurisdictions, both at the municipal and the regional level, is crucial to being in the right position to take advantage of spill-overs and to increasing efficiency through economies of scale. For infrastructure investments, this is even more the case, as for physical infrastructure the minimum efficient scale often transcends the boundaries of regions or municipalities. The small scale of public investment projects that regions or municipalities can often undertake can result in low returns and, as a result, prevent the local definition of infrastructure projects. To bridge this gap, formal mechanisms of collaboration allow municipalities and regions to identify the relevant functional scale of infrastructure investments, thereby reducing duplication of unsustainable investments due to inter-municipal competition. Overcoming jurisdictional barriers requires the capacity to see and execute opportunities while gathering the necessary political support.

Source: OECD (2015a), Recommendation on Effective Public Investment Across Levels of Government www.oecd.org/gov/regional-policy/recommendation-effective-public-investment-across-levels-of-government.htm

However, Chile has recognised that horizontal co-operation across jurisdictions is key to producing more strategic investments. To foster collaboration among municipalities, Law 20346 of 2009 gave a strengthened role to voluntarily constituted municipal associations (Box 3.18). This law grants municipalities the right to associate in order to establish not-for-profit organisations for different purposes. The experiences of municipal associations are diverse as the sets of objectives they have. As of 2015, 37 associations had been registered, and only two of them explicitly listed the development of infrastructure projects among their objectives: the *Asociación de Municipalidades de Punilla* and the *Asociación de Municipalidades Paisajes de Conservación para la*

Biodiversidad de la Región de los Ríos (SUBDERE, 2014). Meanwhile 16 have cited the execution of local development public works as an objective. Some of the experiences of these associations are in fact enhancing investments at the local level by designing joint investment projects.

Figure 3.15. Municipalities by population size in OECD

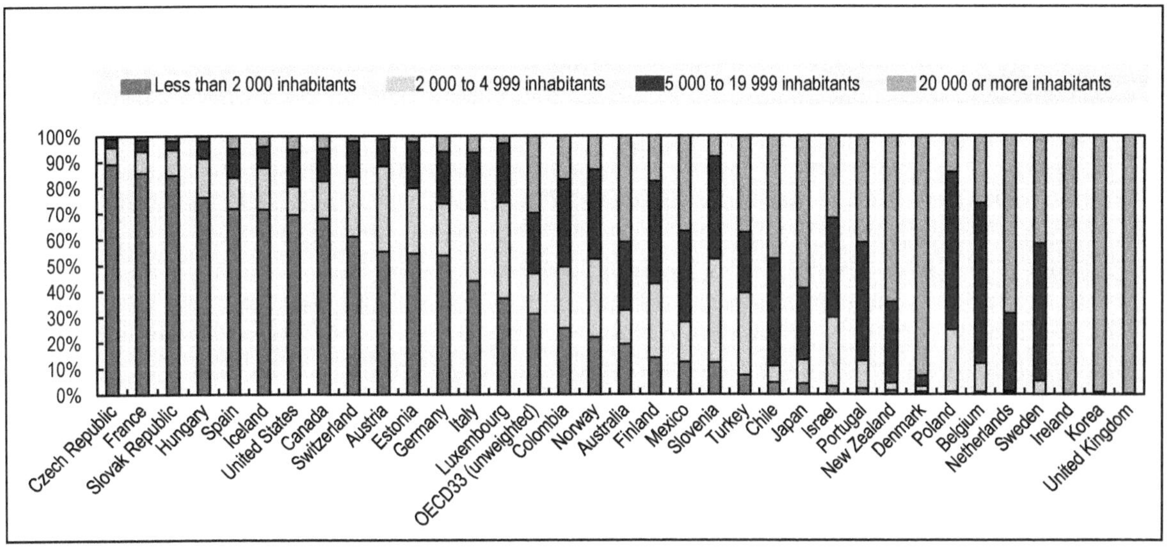

Note: The statistical data for Israel are supplied by and under the responsibility of the relevant Israeli authorities. The use of such data by the OECD is without prejudice to the status of the Golan Heights, East Jerusalem and Israeli settlements in the West Bank under the terms of international law.

Source: OECD (2016f), "Subnational government structure and finance", *OECD Regional Statistics* (database) http://dx.doi.org/10.1787/05fb4b56-en (accessed 2016); and OECD (2016b), "Subnational governments in OECD countries: Key data, 2016 edition", www.oecd.org/gov/regional-policy/Subnational-governments-in-OECD-Countries-Key-Data-2016.pdf (accessed November 2017).

Box 3.18. Municipal Associations in Chile

In Chile, Municipal Associations have existed since 1993 with the creation of the Chilean Municipal Association (Asociación Chilena de Municipalidades, AChM), which at that time grouped together 96% of Chilean municipalities. Its mission was the political and technical representation of municipalities at the national level. The AChM also has regional representations including all municipalities within each region. Thanks to the stimulus provided by the AChM and SUBDERE, other associations emerged for specific activities such as the co-management of services. The associations that have emerged group municipalities with similar issues and with clear and specific objectives. As of today, it is possible to identify four types of municipal associations:

- **National associations**: They represent municipalities politically at the national level. The main association is the AChM, grouping the vast majority of Chilean municipalities; it is the most important and widely recognised association in the country. The Association of Chilean Municipalities (*Asociación de Municipalidades de Chile*, AMUCH), existing since 2013, is also a national association, grouping around 40 municipalities with similar political affiliation.
- **Regional associations:** The AChM has regional representations which correspond to the associations of all municipalities within the region. The degree of development and autonomy of each of these regional associations varies among regions.
- **Territorial associations**: These associations group neighbouring municipalities with a common project. The vast majority of these associations form out of a common political will. In general, municipalities that form an association share a common identity in terms of culture or economic activities.

Box 3.18. Municipal Associations in Chile (*cont.*)

- **Thematic associations:** They group municipalities to address a specific, common issue (tourism, mining activities, productive development) or solve common problems such as waste management, or purchase of health material.

Source: PUC (2015), Asociatividad Municipal: herramienta para la inversión local; SUBDERE (2008), "Asociaciones Municipales: Lecciones y Aprendizajes Orientadores para una Política de Fortalecimiento", www.subdere.gov.cl/sites/default/noticiasold/articles-7601_recurso_1.pdf.

During their first years, Municipal Associations have proven they can effectively improve the investment process. Municipal associations can positively impact infrastructure projects in several ways: by strengthening municipalities' capacities to formulate projects, by allowing them to benefit from economies of scale, by leveraging resources for projects with greater local impact, and by increasing negotiation capacity with the regional and central government to get projects selected and approved, etc. The Centre of Public Policy at the Catholic University has shown that Municipal Associations have effectively attracted more skilled professionals than before to work in local government, sometimes using monetary incentives. With this, Associations manage to reduce rotation of specialists such as engineers or architects that play a key role in the formulation of infrastructure projects. At the same time, associated municipalities enhance the capacity to influence the regional government being better placed to leverage resources for investments and take advantage of peer learning, especially for smaller municipalities. As the study highlights, a key contribution of municipal associations is the possibility to jointly plan and formulate investment initiatives (PUC, 2015). This has resulted in better investment initiatives by municipal associations: smaller municipalities seem to benefit more from associations in light of an analysis of the number of projects with the approval (RS) of the National Investment System (*Sistema Nacional de Inversiones*, SNI), and associated municipalities also get more funding from the FNDR (PUC, 2015).

Box 3.19. Financial Incentives for cross-jurisdictional co-operation

At the sub-regional level in **Italy**, there is a long tradition of horizontal co-operation among municipalities, which takes the form of *Unione di Comuni*, intermediary institutions grouping bringing together municipalities to allow them to reach critical mass, reduce expenditures and improve the provision of public services. A recent law from April 2014 established new financial incentives for mergers and unions of municipalities. Functions to be exercised in co-operation include all the basic functions of municipalities. All municipalities with up to 5 000 inhabitants are obliged to the associated exercise of fundamental functions.

France has more than 36 000 communes, the basic unit of local governance. Although many are too small to be efficient, France has long resisted mergers. Instead, the central government has encouraged municipal co-operation. There are about 2 145 inter-municipal structures with own-source tax revenues aimed at facilitating horizontal co-operation. 99.8% of communes are involved in them. Each grouping of communes constitutes a "public establishment for inter-municipal co-operation" (EPCI). The EPCIs assume limited, specialised, and exclusive powers transferred to them by member communes. They are governed by delegates of municipal councils and must be approved by the State to exist legally. To encourage municipalities to form an EPCI, the central government provides a basic grant plus an "inter-municipality grant" to preclude competition on tax rates among participating municipalities. EPCIs draw on budgetary contributions from member communes and/or their own tax revenues.

Source: OECD (2015b), *Recommendation on Effective Public Investment Across Levels of Government – Implementation Toolkit*, www.oecd.org/effective-public-investment-toolkit.

While very important progress has been made, Chile needs to further encourage Municipal Associations and give them greater capacity to undertake infrastructure investments. Evidence shows that some municipalities are not aware of the possibility of engaging in one of these associations, while co-ordination between associations and the municipal planning divisions (*Secretaría de Planificación*, SECPLA) remains a challenge. A key element restricting the correct functioning of associations is directly linked to funding, as their budget coming from members' quotas only covers operational costs, a situation that prevents associations, for example, from directly hiring professionals (PUC, 2015). To encourage joint investments, it is crucial to create funding incentives through FNDR or other sources devoted exclusively to joint projects, or through special territorial contracts where associations are called upon to co-finance infrastructure projects. Many OECD countries like France (Box 3.19) have put in place such financial incentives for co-operation. In this process, peer learning within and among associations might be the key lever for more effective investments.

While collaboration between municipalities is gaining importance in Chile (Box 3.20), co-ordination among regions has partially been part of the discussion of joint investment initiatives. Given Chile's territorial characteristics and productive assets, an approach to the country through macro-regions could help in the definition of productive specialisations, which would lead to more territorially-oriented infrastructure development. "Zoning" the country is of course not without problems, as defining the boundaries of macro-regions might cause some complications, as no administrative frontiers have been established and similarities or differences between neighbouring territories are not always easy to assess.

Box 3.20. Co-operation across regions in Colombia

Colombia has developed two new types of institutions for regional planning: (1) Administrative and Planning Regions (*Regiones Administrativas de Planeación*, RAPs), which are associations between two or more adjacent departments whose purpose is the socio-economic development of a specific territory. They have a legally recognised status and manage their own resources, and the central government may co-finance strategic investment projects with the RAP. (2) Management and Planning regions (*Regiones de Planeación y Gestión*, RPG), which are a mechanism of co-operation between subnational governments (as well as the central government) to handle investment projects with regional impact. To this end, they are in charge of planning and executing the funds assigned from the royalties through the Regional Development Fund.

Source: OECD (2016g), *Making the Most of Public Investment in Colombia: Working Effectively across Levels of Government*, OECD Publishing, Paris, http://dx.doi.org/10.1787/9789264265288-en.

Planning at a macro-regional level could help Chile in the definition of place-based policies. Aware of the potential advantages of planning at a macro-regional level, the MOP has defined four macro-regions in the Plan Chile 30/30, which represents an important progress in the definition of place-based agendas. Each macro-region binds together four or five administrative regions to plan infrastructures for a territory with similar characteristics, acknowledging that the potential of infrastructure investment can be more fully exploited if territorial synergies exist. These macro regions might share a common identity, productive structures, and geographic and development challenges. To maximise the advantages of such macro-regions, existing regional planning instruments (Regional Development Strategies, Infrastructure Regional Plans, etc.) need to be fed into the final Plan. Planning in macro-regions also entails some important challenges. As has been pointed out earlier in this chapter, in Chile, co-ordination and collaboration among different administrations has been difficult; within a region, municipalities are called upon to compete with one another, and joint projects within an administrative boundary defined and headed by an Intendente are very difficult to undertake. The co-ordination role of regions is weak, although there are institutions – GORE and CORE – that are supposed to accomplish that role. In this sense, co-ordination across regions might be more challenging, as competition has also been part of the way regions operate and manage its funding. At the same time, with no macro-regional institutional head, collaboration between regions depends strongly on the political will of both, the GORE and the Intendente. The MOP will have to handle rigorously political imbalances that may arise in the process of defining macro-regional priorities.

Metropolitan governance gap

Urban investment at the national level is highly fragmented, putting at stake metropolitan administration. As pointed out previously in this chapter, metropolitan issues are siloed at the national level. Responsibility for urban development in Chile is distributed across several ministries and their public agencies, with the Ministries of Housing and Urban Planning (MINVU), Transport and Telecommunications (*Ministerio de Transporte y Telecomunicaciones*, MTT), and Public Works (*Ministerio de Obras Publicas*, MOP) all playing predominant roles. Central-level municipal management falls under the purview of the Ministry of Interior and Public Security's Sub-secretariat for Regional Development and Administration (*Subsecretaría de Desarrollo Regional y Administrativo*, SUBDERE). These institutions function effectively in a vertical dynamic. They do not, however, have a tradition of working horizontally in a co-ordinated or collaborative fashion, which leads to overlap and duplication in centrally generated sub-national policy and programming (OECD, 2013b).

An illustration of institutional fragmentation is transport policy in urban areas, where national and subnational authorities intervene in complementary areas. The MOP is responsible for managing urban highways (*vías expresas*), major road accesses to the city and the infrastructure concession programme, which includes several urban road projects. Its responsibilities also include bridges, tunnels and airports. The MINVU (through its regional implementing arm, SERVIU), normally builds and repairs most of the urban road network (*vías troncales* and *vías colectoras*), except minor connecting roads (*vías de servicio* and *vías locales*), which are generally managed and maintained by municipalities (with occasional intervention by the MINVU). The MTT is in charge of transportation operations, including granting bus route concessions, street sign standards and vehicle circulation bans. Prior to being allocated funds, a project must undergo a technical and economic analysis by the Ministry of Social Development. Municipal transit and urban directorates also intervene in the approval process, as do state-owned companies directly involved in transportation provision (e.g. Metro Santiago and Metro Valparaíso). Beyond transport policies, other institutions in closely related areas, such as land use and environment, play a role as well (see Chapter 5, Section on Road infrastructure) This fragmentation in road development, management and maintenance often makes it complicated to efficiently link urban highways with the urban road network (OECD, 2013a).

Co-operation across municipalities in urban areas is crucial for Chile, as the lack of a metropolitan body prevents a *whole-of-city* approach to investments. In metropolitan areas, each municipality has exclusive responsibility for enforcing all measures regarding transport, for implementing provisions regarding construction and city planning, and for the planning and urban regulation of the municipality. Fragmentation represents a particular challenge in infrastructure investments for the three main urban concentrations of the country – Santiago, Valparaíso and Concepción[5], where many municipalities, often with large inequalities among them, make up the metropolitan area. This challenge will be more acute in the years to come as some estimates foresee more growth of metropolitan areas in Chile by 2020, with the expansion of Iquique-Alto Hospicio, La Serena-Coquimbo, Rancagua-Machalí, Temuco-Padre Las Casas and Puerto Montt-Puerto Varas (*Política Nacional de Desarrollo Urbano* 2014). The challenge is twofold: on the one hand, municipalities do not have the right incentives to co-operate, and on the other, differences in administrative and financial capacity accentuate inequalities within the metropolitan areas, including socio-spatial segregation. It is thus of the utmost importance to manage such fragmentation through a territorially appropriate framework that helps to reconcile possible differences in development objectives, capacity and capability, and socio-economic disparities.

For several years, Chilean authorities and related stakeholders have been aware of the necessity to create some form of metropolitan institution to encourage more cohesive and harmonic development of metropolitan areas. The National Urban Policy launched in 2014, represented a very important step forward in this direction. The Policy recognises the need to create a metropolitan scale organisation responsible for metropolitan planning, specifically of transport systems and their administration, equipment and infrastructure, waste management, and governance, among others. The creation of a metropolitan scale implies a re-organisation of competences and responsibilities of both the regional and the municipal level. Still, this policy has not yet been translated into a law specifying the form and details of this eventual new metropolitan body.

The creation of a metropolitan body entails important challenges and faces political barriers that need to be carefully assessed. It is crucial that an institution managing metropolitan areas has very clearly ascribed, competences avoiding overlap with those of other levels of government, and that it has the sufficient managerial autonomy to execute its competences appropriately. In the Chilean context, the financial and fiscal autonomy of such an institution is highly challenging, as in order to be successful a metropolitan authority must enjoy a degree of decision-making authority over resources and have its own revenues. There is, in fact, evidence that metropolitan institutional structures that can generate own-source revenue (and have control over their finances) tend to flourish, while those that are held in check by their funders face greater difficulties (OECD, 2013a). Increased power for metropolitan areas in their relationship with the central government could create some tensions and power restructuring and imbalances. This is probably the main barrier that has impeded the National Urban Policy's being translated into specific Laws. However, a metropolitan body does not mean that the national government will fade into the background. Instead, the opportunity is created for the national level to focus on ensuring a more coherent approach to urbanism among central-level institutions – and in their relationship to sub-national institutions – through establishing the laws and regulations required for urban governance and acting as a mediator (OECD, 2013a).

A first step in strengthening metropolitan governance could be to better co-ordinate transport investment and management policies. A dedicated transport authority, overseen either by the Ministry of Transport or a devolved level of government, could be set up to address this gap. For example, Santiago, which has for decades struggled with its public transport system (see Chapter 4), could undertake the creation of a transport authority as means of building capacity for managing the region's transport system at the metropolitan scale, much like the Auckland Council that is in charge of developing the Auckland Plan which, amongst other things, sets out strategies for building infrastructure to reduce Auckland's congestion over the next thirty years (see Box B.6, Annex 3 Chapter 4). The authority could build on the experience of Plan Santiago and SECTRA. Such an intermediate step that involves the differentiated delegation of competences from the national and subnational levels avoids a "one size-fits-all" or homogeneous approach to the management of a heterogeneous set of functional urban areas. Urban governance needs an architecture that is sufficiently flexible to adapt to the various types and challenges of urban areas.

High disparities in subnational capacities

Strengthening capacities and skills for infrastructure investments at the SN level

Improving the capacities of regions and municipalities is crucial for the co-ordination mechanisms in place to work effectively. Defining, structuring, implementing and monitoring infrastructure investment requires a very diverse set of capacities and skills that enable the achievement of specific goals at the different stages of the investment cycle. As in many OECD countries, in Chile the capacity gap varies largely across subnational governments. Strengthening capacities at the subnational level is crucial, not only to improving the capabilities to design and implement infrastructure investments at the local level, but also to moving forward in the decentralisation agenda, as the capacity gap might be one of the main arguments standing in the way of the decentralisation process. The government's decentralisation reform needs to be accompanied by appropriate steps to ensure that the greater autonomy given to regions does not compound spatial inequalities (OECD, 2015e).

The low level of capacities in certain regions or municipalities is probably one of the most important obstacles to transformative and needed infrastructure investments at the subnational level. Several studies have analysed municipal performance in investment projects (Acuña, 2009; Avendaño, 2009; PUC, 2015) and concluded that municipalities do not have the sufficient capacity to create investment projects that can win the approval of the SNI. The study on Municipal Associations from the Catholic University of Chile shows that the percentage of municipal initiatives that obtain the "RS" was lower than the ratio for other institutions over the period 2002-2012 (PUC, 2015). Municipalities still have, on average, few resources and insufficient technical capacity to execute investment projects efficiently, a situation that is especially problematic for less developed localities. As of 2015, municipalities only executed 53.6% of their initial budget for investment (*Controlaría General de la República*, 2016) which can be partially explained by a lack of the sufficient skills to design investment projects able to be approved by the Ministry of Social Planning.

There are also important differences in local administrative capacity to undertake concession contracts, which may contribute to disparities within and among regions. The concession system has contributed to a significant improvement in Chile's infrastructure and access to basic public services, particularly for rural and remote areas. Despite these successes at the national level, this system may also contribute to inter- and intra-urban segregation on the municipal level. Local authorities have the possibility to enter into concession agreements with the private sector, for example to provide public parking garages. The actual capacity of municipalities to enter into such agreements, however, varies, and tends to be more common among wealthier municipalities. Thus, in a metropolitan area public services in adjacent municipalities may vary widely in type, variety and quality, in part due to concession agreements (OECD, 2013a).

In Chile, two of the main barriers to capacity building are associated with high staff turnover and low salaries at the local level. The capacity gap in Chile's subnational governments is linked to the relatively limited financial resources for hiring qualified staff, a challenge that is even more acute in poorer municipalities (Ahmad and Zanola, 2015; Contreras et al., 2011). Central government agencies offer higher wages and are thus able to attract the most highly trained personnel. Poor working conditions and high turnover of professionals leads to an insufficient level of professional specialisation. Officials in charge of designing infrastructure projects often leave their jobs after being trained (Contreras et al., 2011). Still, conditions vary greatly across the country; there are municipalities that only have one professional working in the planning division, while in other cases there is a multidisciplinary team with more than 30 professionals (Contreras et al., 2011).

Chile has made important progress in the professionalisation of the regional and municipal workforce. Training programmes are key to improving the design of appropriate investments projects, but also the overall skills of local level public servants (Box 3.21). For example, SUBDERE has a special department for municipal and regional training, the Academia de Capacitación Municipal y Regional, whose main objective is to promote continuous training for regional and municipal governments. It offers permanent and comprehensive training and technical assistance, building long-term capacities of SNG staff. The Academy manages a competitive fund devoted to helping municipal officials obtain technical or professional diplomas. The Academy also offers an annual programme of official training courses in different areas such as municipal management, decentralised co-operation and financial management, as well as short specialisation courses in areas like solid waste management (SUBDERE, 2016b). The National Investment System (SNI) offers specialised training courses on formulation and evaluation of public investment projects (*Capacitación en Formulación y Evaluación de Proyectos de Inversión Pública*) for national and subnational officials. It has a dedicated module on field training and regional workshops (*Capacitación en Terreno y Taller Regional*). In parallel, other central-level bodies have agreements with public or private institutions to hold workshops and provide diplomas, either through on-site or e-learning opportunities, and the Association of Chilean Municipalities also provides capacity-building opportunities through a variety of seminars, courses, workshops and fora (OECD, 2013b).

Box 3.21. Regional training for public investments in Chile

The National Investment System (Sistema Nacional de Inversiones, SNI) holds field training (*capacitaciones en terreno*) for entities in charge of formulating investment initiatives (*iniciativas de inversión*, IDI), mainly municipalities and other public services at the local level. The objective is to develop the appropriate competencies on the part of subnational civil servants in the formulation and preparation of investment projects, as well as in the methodologies of social evaluation (*evaluación social de proyectos*). The training sessions take place in the municipalities and are designed by investment analysts from the SEREMI of the Ministry of Social Development in each region. The timing is defined by the Regional Co-ordinator of Training (Coordinador Regional de Capacitación, CRC) with the Investment Co-ordinator from the SEREMI. Training sessions are designed for a group of two to eleven people.

Source: http://sni.ministeriodesarrollosocial.gob.cl/capacitacion/capacitaciones-en-terreno/ (accessed November 2016).

However, the multiplicity of tools and methodologies proposed by the central government, which are often not articulated, can act to constrain local governments instead of easing their tasks. The various technical assistance programmes need to be better articulated to avoid overlaps and a proliferation of different roadmaps. SUBDERE plays a key role in this process. With regard to infrastructure projects, a central level infrastructure advisory body (see Chapter 2) could be tasked with providing support to sub-national governments in direct collaboration with SUBDERE and the SNI. The role of regions and municipal associations in the articulation of municipal capacity building and technical support should also be better developed. Partnerships between regions and associations could be enhanced, including both the exchange of good practices among subnational governments and peer learning mechanisms

Box 3.22. Competences Assessment in Korea and Mexico

In 2006, the Korean government introduced a competency evaluation framework for the senior civil service. This framework has been used to appoint senior officials, regardless of seniority. Based on the successful operation among senior officials, the competency evaluation framework was expanded to division director-level officials in the second half of 2010. Competency evaluation has improved the reliability and fairness of human resource management. In addition, with the results of the competency assessment reflected in training, overall government competitiveness has been upgraded.

Competences subject to assessment include strategic decision making and commitment to change, as for high-ranking government officials, along with skills required for effective organisation management and efficient policy execution. Assessment focuses on work competency needed to run an organisation.

In Mexico, the National Council for Normalisation and Certification of Competences (Consejo Nacional de Normalización y Certificación de Competencias, CONOCER) is the authority in charge of establishing competence standards and managing the National Competences System, which aims to promote economic competitiveness and educational development. It issues the accreditation of several public and private institutions for the certification of competences. Also in Mexico, the Federal Electricity Commission (Comisión Federal de Electricidad, CFE) has been certifying procurement staff (*agentes compradores*) for more than 15 years. The result has been a rise in the standards of procurement, and it provides employees with ample room for a career in the profession.

Source: OECD (2013b*), OECD Territorial Reviews: Antofagasta, Chile 2013*, OECD Publishing, Paris, http://dx.doi.org/10.1787/9789264203914-en.

The recently approved Law 20922 on permanent municipal staff (planta municipal) opens a door for municipalities to strengthen subnational capacities. Municipalities are now allowed to designate their permanent municipal staff. This is a great opportunity for municipalities, which can now target professionals with the skills and capacities needed while offering improvement and the possibility to access more benefits through greater grades or financial incentives (bonos). For the implementation of this law, Chilean municipalities might follow the example of OECD countries like Korea (Box 3.22) which, in addition to performance management, increasingly take into account competency management to identify the capabilities that senior managers should bring to their jobs, set consistent standards and reinforce the desired values and culture of public service. Typically, the required profile includes leadership capabilities, management skills, the ability to achieve results and personal integrity. Competences are commonly used in recruitment and selection, succession planning, identification of potential future leaders among middle management ranks, performance management, training and leadership development. In fact, Chile should complement its training programmes with an adequate and rigorous competence assessment of the capacity gap of municipalities and/or regions, defining performance standards. These performance qualifications and standards should be assessed as the basis for granting an accreditation of having met the general expectations of the profession, and they should be monitored to maintain this accreditation and considered a continuous exercise. At the same time, subnational governments in Chile could turn to the Chilean central government's existing practices and consider adapting the principles for senior civil servants (*Sistema de Alta Dirección Pública*) to the local context (OECD, 2013b).

Devolving competences to strengthen subnational capacities

Devolving autonomy to regional and municipal governments is in fact necessary to start a process of progressive learning-by-doing. OECD experiences reveal that apart from mechanisms to strengthen performance and improve local officials' skills, building capacity clearly benefits from the progressive involvement of subnational governments in decision making (OECD, 2009a). The progressive devolution of competences to SNGs needs to be seen as part of a systemic strengthening of capacities and multi-level governance frameworks that will allow more efficient investments. In this process one of the most challenging factors in Chile is the existence of strong disparities among regions and municipalities. Some regions or localities may find it more difficult than others, in human and institutional terms, to cope with devolved responsibilities. In general terms, most developed localities will be better able to adapt and benefit from further devolution, while the least developed localities with weaker institutions and fewer financial and human resources for carrying out the enlarged mandate may find implementation more difficult (OECD, 2009a). This is why some countries have implemented this learning-by-doing framework gradually, by offering technical assistance and capacity building parallel to a progressive transfer of responsibilities. It is important to know that asymmetric governance approaches contain risks, as they might create institutional complexity or lead to preferential treatment for some, but at the same time they are ways to better take into account various territorial, political and cultural situations. If the process is clearly defined and transparent, such risks might be attenuated. Such an asymmetric approach is increasingly being adopted for various reasons in France, Italy, Sweden, the United Kingdom and recently Colombia (Box 3.23).

Box 3.23. Differentiated delegation of competencies in Sweden and Colombia

Since the late 1990s, Sweden has developed a rather unusual regionalisation process by proposing different options to different regions and pursuing asymmetrical decentralisation. In contrast with reforms driven by the central government in some other OECD countries, Sweden's regionalisation reforms have adopted a bottom-up approach based on a conscious choice to take the time to experiment, to achieve consensus through in-depth consultation and to learn from results. The result is a very heterogeneous map in which regional development responsibilities (notably the task of designing regional development programmes and regional growth programmes) have been variously assigned to: county councils (directly elected regional authorities) in two "pilot regions" since the late 1990s (Västra Götaland and Skåne, both urban regions in Southern Sweden); regional co-ordination bodies (indirectly elected associations of all municipalities in a county, called *kommunala samverkansorgan*) in two-thirds of counties through the 2000s; and to county administrative boards in one-fourth of counties (Norrbotten, Västernorrland, Jämtland, Västmanland and Stockholm).

One clear advantage of bottom-up regionalisation is that it allows a smooth decentralisation process on alearning-by-doing basis, with the right to experiment and to learn from the results. Various external assessments have been conducted since the late 1990s in the two pilot regions, and the outcome appears to be positive. However, their achievements are difficult to measure quantitatively, and lessons from Västra Götaland and Skåne, two metropolitan areas with almost a third of the total Swedish municipalities, cannot necessarily be extrapolated to all Swedish regions.

Between 2012 and 2015, nine local municipalities in Denmark were granted some exemptions from government rules and documentation requirements in order to test new ways of solving their tasks, in a policy experiment known as the "Free Municipality" initiative. The main focus was on simplification, innovation, quality and a more inclusive approach to the individual citizen, with many of the experiments focusing on the employment effort. The Free Municipality experiment is currently being evaluated, in order to form the basis for potential future legislation on de-bureaucratisation for all municipalities. The concept of Free Municipalities is to continue in an adjusted form until 2019, and is being extended to more municipalities.

Source: OECD (forthcoming), Monitoring Review of Sweden.

Chilean pilot experiences in the devolution of competences to Regional Governments (Box 3.24) are, in this sense, a very strong tool. Pilot experiences in Chile allow a *differentiated* devolution of responsibilities. As recognised by the OECD Better Policies Series, asymmetrical types of decentralisation allow for capacity building through different paths towards greater autonomy in decision making, and this could be in fact a solution for Chile (OECD, 2015e). In addition to dealing with disparities, pilot experiences allow for peer learning, as actors involved can take lessons from it. As Chile has a very strong centralist culture, pilot experiences can smooth the process and allow for an understanding of the main barriers, successes and failures of the process. It also allows regions, municipalities and the central government to adapt progressively to changes.

Box 3.24. Pilot decentralisation experiences in Chile

Among of the strategic pillars of decentralisation reforms in Chile are the pilot programmes for the devolution of competences in three areas: (1) productive development, (2) infrastructure and transport, (3) social and human development.

Pilot programmes for the transfer of productive development responsibilities started in the second semester of 2015 in three regions, Antofagasta, Bio Bio and Los Ríos. To this end, the government has started a co-ordination process between the Ministry of Economy, DIPRES, SUBDERE, CORFO and SERCOTEC, who together have defined a preliminary model for the transfer of productive development responsibilities. These pilot programmes are aimed at strengthening capacities of regional governments to allow them to take the lead in the diversification of productive activities, the strengthening of small and medium enterprises and the promotion of entrepreneurship and innovation.

To accomplish this, the new governance framework involves the creation of three kinds of institutions:

1. Regional executive tables (*Mesas Ejecutivas Regionales*): led by the *Intendente,* they bring together the authorities linked to productive development in a region. These are the main co-ordination bodies to articulate policies.
2. Productive development and industry divisions (*Divisiones de Fomento e Industria*): divisions within each GORE that are made up of three professionals. Their objective is to integrate policies productive development and those related with research, technology and innovation, thus encouraging investments in these areas and supporting regional decisions on resource allocation.
3. Productive development committees (*Comités de Desarrollo Productivo*, CDPR): entities in charge of managing and allocating resources of the 24 instruments transferred from CORFO and SERCOTEC to each GORE. The Directive Council of each CDPR includes 10 members; seven regional representatives and three national representatives (one each from CORFO, SERCOTEC and the Ministry of Economy). These Committees execute policies linked to productive development based on the objectives and strategies of regional governments articulated with national policies.

Source: SUBDERE (2016c), *Quinto pilar: Experiencias Pilotos en materia de descentralización*, www.descentralizacion.subdere.gov.cl/quintopilar.

Encourage stakeholder and citizen participation

Citizen engagement in Chile, especially for big infrastructure projects, has been more reactive than proactive. Reaction is particularly common for big controversial infrastructure projects that have prompted citizen mobilisation. Two examples are the successful anti-highway campaign that mobilised neighbourhood groups against the building of a major highway through communities in Santiago in 2000 (Sagaris, 2014), and the Barrancones environmental conflict wherein citizen action stopped the development of a hydroelectric plan in 2010 (Spoerer, 2014). Other examples include citizen action taken to stop the development of a shopping centre in one of Santiago's most affluent municipalities and community involvement to ensure that an existing park remained easily accessible to all residents (Fernández Prajoux, 2013). While citizen involvement in the participatory process may be growing, as seen in the proliferation of

CSOs, citizen engagement appears most successful in its ability to influence policy and programming when there is a real or perceived threat (OECD, forthcoming b). This is why it is of particular relevance for the government to integrate citizens into the early stages of the definition of infrastructure projects; the government needs to makeroom for citizens' voices by improving communication in the early planning stages of so that programmes do not reach the "threat" stage.

High levels of centralism and limited autonomy of subnational governments to decide on infrastructure investments make citizen and civil society engagement a difficult task. As the closest governmental level to citizens, which is where investment planning should start, municipalities must play a key role in promoting engagement. However, their limited ability to implement their own priorities and define their own investments may discourage participation of civil society and/or citizens; if decisions are made centrally, their input is likely to remain only on paper, with a limited real impact on the final decision. As the generation of participatory instances is costly for local governments, they might tend to involve citizens just to comply with the law and the required administrative processes. Subnational actors might see the requirement as an administrative burden imposed by the central government, resulting in a pro forma consultation that adds no real value to the policy process. One important concern at the local level is in fact the limited share of critical information about central or municipal government programming or plans that will affect specific neighbourhoods – for example the construction of a major road through a community, or of a shopping centre, etc. (Sagaris, 2014; Spoerer, 2014). Citizens do not always obtain the information from the proactive communication of local government officials, but because they heard the projects and sought it out (OECD, forthcoming b).

Within its top-down and centralist approach to designing investment strategies, Chile has made important progress in integrating stakeholders into the definition of priorities. The country has acknowledged that further understanding specific civil society preferences can help it to shape its infrastructure investments. A key step forward in engaging with citizens is the Law 20.500 of 2011 and the Presidential Instructive 007 of 2014, which institutionalise citizen participation and identify ways in which central government authorities can foster greater participation. A key initiative of this law is the creation of the Municipal Councils of Civil Society Organisations (*Consejos Comunales de la Sociedad Civil*, COSOC) at the local level, with whom national actors should maintain constant dialogue. The implementation of this law has been difficult. For example, it took until the end of 2013, two years after the law was introduced, for the 117 government ministries and dependent bodies to establish internal rules for participation. By 2015, 21% of the relevant organisations had yet to organise the required Civil Society Councils as part of their governance structure (Ministerio Secretaría General de Gobierno, 2015; OECD, forthcoming b).

Planning instruments have also a strong participatory component. At the subnational level, the ERD, the PLADECO and the Regulating Plan (*Plan Regulador*, PR) are supposed to define medium-term development strategies based on citizen and civil society input. SUBDERE strongly support both regions and municipalities with programmes or manuals to guide this processes. The 2010 *Manual for Citizen Participation in Regional Development Strategy Design of the* (*Manual Guía para la Participación Ciudadana en la Elaboración de la Estrategia Regional de Desarrollo*) is a very detailed and thorough methodological guide for regional governments on how and when citizens should be involved in the strategy design process. At the municipal level, participatory mechanisms are used to help shape municipal spatial and development plans. However, participation in the definition of the PR often comes late in the development process, limiting room for citizen input. Another limitation is that changes to the PRs are lengthy processes and occur on an irregular basis (OECD, 2013a).

The Ministry of Public Works is conducting a major initiative to involve citizens in the definition of infrastructure investment priorities through "regional validations" of Plan Chile 30/30. This is the first time the MOP has involved regional and local stakeholders in defining its agenda, and as such it represents an important breakthrough in terms of participation. The *validation* process consists of working groups (*mesas de trabajo*) in regions and regional and macro-regional workshops, in which private and public actors are involved. The MOP is also working on consultations with indigenous communities through the "Guide for Indigenous Communities: Consulting and Territories" (see Chapter 2) In OECD countries it is common practice to consult municipalities for the elaboration of a regional development strategy. However, involving citizens, academics and NGOs in the design of regional investment strategies is less common, and banks and private actors are the least involved in the design of these strategies (OECD, 2013c). In the OECD context, this regional validation stands out as an example of good practice for peer countries A further step could be a move from a consultation forum with the purpose of gathering public feedback to a collaborative platform where governments and citizens are partners and build consensus together (OECD, forthcoming b). In other words, Chile has still space to further move from top-down participation towards bottom-up initiatives.

The promotion of stakeholder engagement is highly fragmented, as it depends largely on isolated initiatives, and it follows a top-down logic. At the national level, two main ministries have responsibilities for encouraging participation. The first is the Social Organization Division (División de Organizaciones Sociales, DOS) of the Government General Secretariat (Ministerio Secretaría General de Gobierno), which co-ordinates government activity for citizen participation and is responsible for ensuring that normative frameworks are respected. The other is SUBDERE, which is responsible for promoting citizen participation at the municipal level through its Municipalities Division (especially for the formation of the COSOC), and through indications and normative frameworks to promote engagement at the subnational level. However, engagement of civil society is neither limited to nor integrally co-ordinated by these two entities. In parallel, line ministries, also promote engagement within their own sectors and have implemented a series of programmes encouraging participation, especially through specific programmes for the definition of investments or for the design process of development strategies (Box 3.25).

Box 3.25. Stakeholder engagement in investment-related initiatives in Chile

National Level

MINVU took another approach to stakeholder participation in its Participatory Paving Programme (Programa de Pavimentación Participativa). Here, the objective is to encourage citizen participation in the paving or repaving of streets, passageways and sidewalks. Residents of a community with public areas in need of paving or repaving can come together and form a paving committee to formally apply for the necessary support. If the application is successfully approved, 5%-30% of the project is financed by the requesting community, 5%-25% by the municipality in which the community is located, and the balance is financed by MINVU. The programme appears to be successful in that to date more than 3.5 million people have participated and more than 6 500 kilometres of pavement have been installed. However, it is an unorthodox approach to citizen participation where the participation includes community funding, and in a sense could be considered one way to reduce the cost of central and subnational government in the provision of arguably necessary infrastructure. This approach can also compound problems of inclusiveness, co-funding exceptions aside, as not all communities have the capacity to apply.

Box 3.25. Stakeholder engagement in investment-related initiatives in Chile (*cont.*)

The Ministry of Energy (Ministerio de Energía) has taken a participatory approach to developing its energy policy (Energía 2050), building a roadmap with the input not only of the ministry's civil society council, but also from a series of thematic and regional workshops and from an online virtual participation platform set up for direct and broad citizen input. The result was the Roadmap to 2050: Toward a Sustainable and Inclusive Energy (Hoja de Ruta al 2050: Hacia una Energía Sustentable e Inclusiva), a document setting out the basis for a long term energy policy that includes continuing to work with communities to ensure more robust, participative processes and strengthening local actors.

Local level

The *Intendencia* and Regional Government of Santiago lead the project *Nueva Alameda Providencia,* a project for the renewal of the main avenue of Santiago, with a length of almost 12km that passes through four very different municipalities (Lo Prado, Estación Central, Santiago and Providencia). Alameda-Providencia is considered the heart of the city. The renewal of this avenue is a major inter-sectoral project, as it is not only a transport project, but also one that considers planning and urban design, engineering, heritage, environment, etc., and it has an impact on the entire Metropolitan Region. The Management Council includes the Ministry of Transport, the Ministry of Housing, the Ministry of Public Works, the *Intendente* of the Metropolitan Region, and the four mayors of the relevant municipalities.

The project is based on citizen consultation and participation. The project's Participation Plan is an attempt to provide citizens with clear, comprehensive and meaningful information to generate space and opportunities for the participation of everyone interested, to ensure that the contributions are considered in the final design, and to clearly communicate how the contributions were incorporated. The Participation Plan considers three main spaces for participation: (1) consultation, (2) metropolitan meetings, and (3) territorial dialogues.

Source: Ministerio Secretaría General de Gobierno (2016), *Cuenta Pública de Participación Ciudadana*; MINVU (2014), *Programa de Pavimentación Participativa: Manual de Postulación,* www.minvu.cl/opensite_20070308155628.aspx; Gobierno Regional Metropolitano de Santiago (2016b), *Nueva Alameda Providencia*, www.nuevaalamedaprovidencia.cl.

Recent progresses have been important, but changing the way public policies are conceived takes time. While going in the right direction, stakeholder involvement still relies on formal requirements on paper. A critical element is that there are no explicit links between the plans participation on the one hand and performance or outcome objectives that could be used for accountability purposes on the other. As development strategies are not binding, and sectorial ministries are not required to follow their guidelines, a main risk is that participation might be perceived as a mere formal procedure, putting at stake future or long-term engagement. The existence of various dialogue and participation instances among the central and local levels with citizens and civil society is certainly valuable, but it also entails some risks. Chile has to be aware of the fact that multiplying consultations instance may cause what is known as "consultation fatigue". "Consultation fatigue" can occur if citizens are "over-solicited"– i.e. asked for their opinions in planning and processes repeatedly in short periods of time without knowing how their input is used. The tendency to over consult may be particularly accentuated in systems where the emphasis is placed on involving residents in short-term (e.g. one election cycle) programmes and projects rather than on developing long-term policy (OECD, forthcoming b). This is why stakeholder involvement needs to be strategic and co-ordinated, both among different levels of governments and horizontally at the national level to limit a fragmented approach.

Monitoring and evaluation of infrastructure investments

A well-developed *ex ante* assessment needs to be completed using effective monitoring and evaluations process, in particular in the current decentralisation reforms. Chile has a well-developed *ex ante* assessment system to evaluate infrastructure investments made at the national and subnational levels. While some adjustments to better integrate territorial dimensions and operational and maintenance costs in this *ex ante* evaluations need to be made (see Chapter 2), much attention to the monitoring and *ex post* evaluation of infrastructure investment is needed. Monitoring is a key piece of multi-level governance arrangements, as it allows actors to follow up on the implementation of investment portfolios and projects, to track the achievement of contractual obligations, to encourage performance, to make mid-course adjustments, and to identify medium-term outcomes (OECD, 2015a). This in turn encourages stakeholder engagement, as better information can be transformed in better accountability. Moving towards decentralisation of decision making brings along some risks of clientelism and corruption at the local level. While in Chile the Comptroller General of the Republic plays a key role by performing *ex ante* evaluations of infrastructure projects to ensure that they comply with the contract as well as applicable laws and regulations (see Chapter 2), monitoring and evaluation tools are also crucial pieces to prevent those behaviours. *Ex ante* control in Chile needs to be completed by *ex post* control for investments (see Chapter 1).

Ex post controls of infrastructure investments in Chile are mainly based on budget execution of national and subnational governments. In general, the performance of line ministries, but also of GOREs and municipalities, is judged by their capacity to execute the budget assigned by the annual budget law, as the assignation of annual budget depends mainly on the execution levels of the previous year. While this is not necessarily wrong, if subnational governments pay too much excessive attention to budget execution to ensure their annual budgets, there are two main elements that are being neglected: (i) execution in the field of investment; and (ii) the quality or impact of infrastructure investments.

Chile has developed a series of data repository and monitoring tools, apart from budget execution, for national and subnational investments, and they need to be further articulated (Box 3.26). These instruments, in general, take advantage of the central-level capacity to gather information from many sources and facilitate its sharing among central and subnational authorities (OECD, 2009a). While the existence of platforms to gather information on investments is valuable, the extent to which they are used, the information they provide, and the articulation between them remains limited. While some of these mechanisms complement each other, some provide partial pictures of investments, resulting in a fragmented and disperse set of information both for policy makers and citizens. Despite Chile's various indicator systems, and data collection by individual ministries, it is not clear whether and how the information is relayed to the subnational level and/or used by the central level to improve investment outcomes (OECD, 2009a). An exclusively top-down approach in the definition of indicators or information available may fail to reflect regional and local needs and challenges, and a strategy imposed by the centre in the absence of consultation may undermine the engagement and participation of subnational actors in the process (OECD, 2009a). To break the siloed approach, Chile should develop an integrated and unified monitoring system providing a comprehensive set of information available in a user-friendly way to encourage citizen use. The IDE provides a very good basis for such a development, and it could constitute the basis for an articulated platform, integrating information from the SNI, along the lines of the examples of Italy (Box 3.28). The final objective of such a platform should be the provision of usable and homogenised information.

Box 3.26. Investment data and monitoring tools in Chile

SINIM (SUBDERE)

While not only focused on infrastructure investments, the National System of Municipal Indicators (SINIM) - (managed by SUBDERE) – offers accessible information to the general public through its website (www.sinim.cl). It is the main tool used to monitor subnational performance. The SINIM provides over 150 standardised indicators for each of the municipalities in Chile, and some of them are linked to infrastructure investments such as the number of building permits and new housing investments. It is an interesting tool offering a comprehensive picture of each municipality through municipal profiles (*fichas comunales*) showing budget execution levels and transfer from the central government (FNDR, *Programa de Mejoramiento de Barrios*, etc.). Data available through this platform make it possible to compare the performance of all Chilean municipalities since 2001 and help the different stakeholders to make informed decisions.

The information available is not necessarily user-friendly. While it might be helpful as a repository of subnational data and useful to researchers for professional or academic purposes, it is not necessarily the type of information a majority of citizens seek.

ChileIndica (SUBDERE)

CHILEINDICA is an investment data repository that provides investment information about the central and regional government levels. It allows users to monitor the implementation of different projects at all levels, improving information flows between regional and sectoral public institutions and the management of investment. CHILEINDICA is an online platform providing the history of territorial interventions for regional governments and ministries in a transparent and timely manner. The information contained on this platform is not yet publicly available.

BPI – MAPI (MDS)

In parallel, the Ministry of Social Development provides investment information via the *Banco Integrado de Proyectos* (BIP), a platform that offers information on all National Investment System projects. It allows users to monitor the status of each project during the entire cycle of investment, from pre-investment through execution. The BIP breaks down public information on all investment projects (*iniciativas de inversión*, IDI) by region and municipality and by sector and thematic area.; For example, it allows users to see the percentage of projects that obtain approval (RS) from the SNI, that average number days that an initiative takes to be approved, etc. It gives a complete and comprehensive picture of all investments by territory. Based on the same data sources, the SNI has developed a new platform of investment projects maps (*mapas de proyectos de inversión*, MAPI) which allows for geo-referencing of national projects that have been approved by the SNI. These two platforms offer a cross-sectoral and territorial dimension of the investment projects being executed.

It is a good first step towards the regional localisation of investment projects, but there is no detailed information about the execution of projects. While it is thorough it needs to be simplified for easier usability if it is to act as an effective monitoring tool for investment projects.

National Geo-spatial Information Catalogue – *Infraestructura de Datos Geoespaciales* (IDE)

Led by the Ministry of National Assets (*Ministerio de Bienes Nacionales*, MBN), the IDE has been in operation since 2013 as a web platform providing territorial geospatial data. It includes all the institutions that generate and use geospatial information. The entity responsible for co-ordinating the IDE is the Council of Ministers of Territorial information (Consejo de Ministros de Información Territorial), featuring the Ministers of Finance, Economy, Social Development, Public Works, and Housing, among others. The IDE of the Ministry of Public Works is the Water Resource Infrastructure and Management Observatory (Observatorio de la Infraestructura y Gestión del Recurso Hídrico), which provides data on the existing infrastructure in the country. However, it does not offer information on projects under development or the agenda to monitor their execution. The IDE also has regional delegations, led by the *Intendente* and co-ordinated by the GORE, which main function is to facilitate the proper management of geospatial information in the region. Some municipalities have also developed their own IDE platforms (Maipu, Quillota, and San Antonio).

Source: SUBDERE (2016e), *Sistema Nacional de Información Municipal*, http://datos.sinim.gov.cl; SUBDERE (2016d), *Sistema de Información Territorial para las Regiones de Chile*, www.chileindica.cl; MDS (2016), *Mapa de Proyectos de Inversión*, http://sni.ministeriodesarrollosocial.gob.cl/mapa-de-proyectos-de-inversion; www.ide.cl/, OECD (forthcoming b), *Multi-level Governance Review of Chile: Modernisation of the Municipal System.*

Monitoring platforms can be more effective when they rely on solid performance indicators that can promote learning and point stakeholders towards results. In practice, well-defined indicators can help to address information asymmetries that arise between levels of government or between government and stakeholders, and they can reinforce accountability at all levels of government by improving transparency. In this sense, a unified platform in Chile needs to put emphasis on (i) ensuring coherence with the overall public investment strategy; (ii) ensuring technical and financial feasibility, sustainability and efficiency (including an appraisal of the impact of the investment on current expenditures). To accomplish this, it is crucial that development strategies and infrastructure plans incorporate monitoring indicators; Plan Chile 30/30 should specify the elements resulting from vertical collaboration that will allow for increased usefulness of indicator systems, and it should highlight the participatory arrangements that can make the system more effective. Specifying indicators in the Plan might clarify the outcomes to be achieved through infrastructure investments and encourage mechanisms to achieve them throughout the investment cycle. In order to take advantage of monitoring tools and for them to foster better and more efficient investments, they should be linked to rewards for good performance. Learning happens only if the information produced in one step is applied in a later one. In many OECD countries, such tools incentivise subnational governments to plan and implement projects efficiently. Chile could take a step forward in this direction by using performance monitoring to explicitly inform future investment decisions, as Europe does (Box 3.27).

Box 3.27. EU Performance Reserve 2014-2020

The EU Cohesion Policy 2014-2020 offers strong incentives to deliver Europe 2020 objectives through a result orientation based on three pillars. First, it requires a clear articulation of the objectives of programmes. It also defines that a number of framework conditions must be in place *ex ante* before the funds are disbursed (for instance, the proper functioning of public procurement systems) to ensure that investments can be made in the most effective manner. Third, progress towards the achievement of objectives will be closely monitored and measured against a set of milestones agreed as part of a performance framework.

The policy establishes that programmes and priorities which achieve milestones set for 2018 in the performance framework can benefit from the performance reserve after a review undertaken in 2019. The objective of the performance reserve is to ensure and reward good performance in the implementation of programmes. Where there is a serious failure to achieve milestones (i.e. serious under-performance compared to what was initially planned), the respective programmes and priorities cannot benefit from an allocation from the performance reserve. The European Commission agreed that the performance reserve will be 6% of the funding allocated in 2019 to programmes and priorities which have achieved 85% of their milestones.

Source: European Commission (2013), *Q&A on the legislative package for EU Cohesion Policy 2014-2020*, http://europa.eu/rapid/press-release_MEMO-13-678_fr.htm.

While Chile has made important progress in developing monitoring tools, *ex post* evaluations mechanisms are still limited. *Ex post* evaluations rely mainly on the Budget Office of the Ministry of Finance (DIPRES), which is mainly focused on programme evaluations. However, Chile has not developed investment evaluations tools to address the goals of investments, determine if intended outcomes were achieved and assess the role played by investment activities. For infrastructure investments, this is crucial, as the challenge is to identify real economic impacts that can benefit Chilean regions and come to an understanding of how and to what extent infrastructure investments can boost productivity in territories. Infrastructure and development strategies such as Plan Chile 30/30 and the ERD should include an evaluation phase from the very start. Ideally, monitoring and evaluation tools should be joined in a single device; a platform such as the IDE could bring together this information with a visualisation and georeferenced module for all public investment projects.

Box 3.28. Mapping investments: the case of Italy

The Open Coesione web portal provides analysis and monitoring on the use of regional policy resources, offering information, accessible to anyone, on what is funded, who is involved and where. The web portal contains information about every single project carried out to implement EU Cohesion Policy, and more specifically: funds used, places and categories, subjects involved and implementation timeframes. It concerns more than 700 000 investment projects (around EUR 17 billion, funded by national and local governments). Users can either download raw data or surf through interactive diagrams itemised by expenditure categories, places and type of intervention, as well as have access to files on single projects and subjects involved. Data on the local economy and social context are provided as well.

Source: OECD (2015f), *Effective public investment across levels of government: Principles for action*, https://www.oecd.org/effective-public-investment-toolkit/Effective-Public-Investment-Brochure.pdf.

Policy recommendations

Please see Table 3.2 for an overview of the main challenges and remedies for multi-level infrastructure governance.

1. A markedly geographic heterogeneity and strong territorial disparities

Chile should develop a place-based approach for infrastructure investments to tackle territorial inequalities and enhance productivity in all regions. A territorial approach will help Chile to make the most of its regional specificities, boosting competitiveness throughout the country.

2. Chile: a highly centralised country

Chile should pursue decentralisation reforms. The direct election of the *Intendente* needs to be complemented with the transfer of competencies and funding; otherwise limited autonomy could become a straitjacket for newly elected *Intendente*s.

The country should improve the financial autonomy of subnational government, and at the same time reinforce the decision-making capacity on infrastructure investments at the local level. Each municipality should be able to decide locally which infrastructure investments the commune needs, with more flexible funding in the use of grants and the possibility to combine different funding sources to finance infrastructure investment monitoring.

3. Improving the planning framework for infrastructure investments

The country needs to develop a long-term vision for regional development. What kind of regions do we want? Investment in infrastructure needs to be framed by a long-term strategy for regions. This should be articulated with a national strategy, identifying long-term development goals and a vision for the country.

Chile should strengthen the role of the ERD as an instrument to guide and articulate regional infrastructure investments. A unique strategy for infrastructure and spatial planning that is co-ordinated among sectors at the national and subnational levels would help Chile to streamline its infrastructure planning.

The role of the PLADECO as strategic planning tool needs to be strengthened and better articulated with the ERD.

To improve articulation between ministries and public agencies at the subnational level, the government should strengthen the role of the Sub-secretariat for Regional and Administrative Development (SUBDERE).

4. Linking budgeting and planning

Chile should develop a multi-year budgeting framework to improve the connection between planning and budgeting. In turn, this will facilitate an effective prioritisation of infrastructure projects.

The country needs to move from a project-based funding allocation framework to one that is programme based, in order to allow for the effective execution of place-based agendas.

5. Improving vertical co-ordination across the national and subnational governments

The role of regions could be expanded, allowing them to act as key brokers to foster vertical co-ordination and encourage co-ordinated investments. GOREs might be key levers to improve co-ordination in two dimensions:

- ✓ GOREs can act as key interlocutors for vertical co-ordination, as they have a privileged position in the interaction between municipalities and the central government.
- ✓ GOREs should support critical projects that require cross-jurisdictional cooperation, in particular with regard to rural municipalities

Programing agreements (*Convenios de Programación*) should be strengthened and transformed into territorial contracts. Some of the key steps to consider are:

- ✓ Specify territorial goals and regional development priorities for each contract.
- ✓ Consider a consultation phase involving national and subnational actors, the private sector and civil society to establish priorities and actions for the contract by assessing regional development needs.
- ✓ Clearly define the roles of the different institutions and authorities involved, ensuring collaboration on the ground.
- ✓ Chile should encourage partnerships with Municipal Associations to support investments at a supra-municipal scale. Funding could be especially set aside for contracts signed by Associations. Specific contractual arrangements might target metropolitan areas.
- ✓ Monitoring mechanisms and an evaluation phase should be put into place to allow for an assessment of contracts' results and potentially their impact.
- ✓ Incentives could be offered for contract enforcement, for example by allocating part of the funding based on good performance.

The role of regional COMICIVYTs could be further institutionalised by enhancing their competences. The COMICIVYTs could be placed in charge of analysing investment projects at the regional level to avoid redundancies in functions in executing projects and to monitor their execution. It is important that Chile avoid the creation of a new institution for dialogue to diminish the risk of fatigue of co-ordination instances. Regional COMICIVYTs could be regular committees with monitoring competences and accountable to citizens.

6. Co-operation across jurisdictions

Chile should further encourage Municipal Associations for infrastructure projects. To encourage joint investments, it is necessary to create funding incentives through FNDR, or other sources of funding devoted exclusively to joint projects, or to have special territorial contracts where associations are called on to co-finance infrastructure projects jointly.

To advance in the definition of place-based agendas, Chile might plan its infrastructure investments at a macro-regional level. To maximise the advantages of such macro-regions, existing regional planning instruments need to be fed into the final macro-regional strategy. It is crucial that the government rigorously confront the political imbalances that may arise in the process of defining macro-regional priorities.

To bridge the metropolitan gap, Chile could create an authority with specific and particular responsibilities as an intermediate step between the creation of a comprehensive metropolitan body and the current fragmented system. For example, Santiago, which has for decades struggled with its public transport system, could create a transport authority as means of building capacity for managing the region's transport system at the metropolitan scale.

7. Strengthen subnational capacities

Chile should streamline and articulate the various training programmes for investment capacities to avoid overlaps and a proliferation of different roadmaps. With regard to infrastructure projects, a central infrastructure advisory body (see Chapter 2) could take on this task. Regions and municipal associations also might be key levers to articulate capacity building and technical support.

Improving capacities needs to go along with adequate and rigorous competences and performance assessment to address the capacity gaps between municipalities and/or regions. It could also involve establishing acceptable qualifications and defining standards of performance for the different professions in the public service.

Subnational governments in Chile could turn to the Chilean central government's practices and consider adapting the principles for senior civil servants (*Sistema de Alta Dirección Pública*) to their local contexts.

For the *implementation* of Law 20.922, municipalities should develop a competence management framework to identify the capabilities that senior managers should bring to their jobs, set consistent standards and reinforce the desired values and culture of the public service.

The government should pursue capacity building on a learning-by-doing basis through pilot experiences. The devolution of infrastructure and transport competences should also be done gradually through pilot programmes.

The country should streamline participation spaces in order to avoid *consultation fatigue*. Boosting stakeholder engagement may rest on a re-evaluation of what is already in place (COSOS, committees, participation in ERD and PLADECO, workshops, etc.), better aligning government and citizen approaches and expectations, and consolidating consultation mechanisms to transform them into dialogue fora.

A well-developed ex-ante assessment needs to be completed by effective monitoring and evaluations process, in particular in the current decentralisation reforms. Chile should develop indicators that can help quantify change in areas where citizen input is sought.

Chile should develop an integrated and unique monitoring system that provides a comprehensive set of information available in a user-friendly way to encourage citizen use. The IDE provides a very good start for such a development and could constitute the basis for an articulated platform, bringing together information from the various existing platforms (BIP, SNI, SINIM, etc.). Infrastructure and development strategies such as Plan Chile 30/30 and the ERD should consider an *ex post* evaluation process to monitor their effectiveness and eventually their impact on territorial development.

Table 3.2. Main challenges and remedies for multi-level infrastructure governance

Pre-conditions	Main challenges for multi-level infrastructure governance	Recommendations
Decentralisation of infrastructure investments	• SNGs have limited own revenues and expenditure and play a very limited role in public investments compared to most OECD countries • Overlapping and unclear infrastructure competences across levels of government • Autonomy of regional governments is very limited by OECD standards • Weak co-ordination between subnational governments and private actors.	• Strengthen financial autonomy of subnational governments • Pursue decentralisation reforms and complement the direct election of the Intendente with transfer of competencies and funding • Clarify and if necessary readjust distribution of responsibilities across levels of government (policy making, planning and execution), • Pursue pilot projects on the devolution of competences to diminish transition costs • Involve subnational governments in the definition and tendering of infrastructure investments with the private sector
Place-based infrastructure investment planning framework	• Lack of institutionalised central guidance/strategy for infrastructure integrating territorial development goals/strategies • Weak cross-sectoral co-ordination at the national level concerning infrastructure investments with territorial impact • Weak co-ordination among sectoral ministries (SEREMIs) and services at the subnational level • Top-down approach in deciding infrastructure investments with poor involvement of subnational governments • The role of SUBDERE in promoting regional development and co-ordination for territorial policies is weak • Multiplicity of planning tools poorly, linked and not connected with budgeting • Insufficient integration between infrastructure and land use planning. • Weak role of regional and municipal development strategies (ERD and PLADECO), leading to poor prioritisation of projects	• Develop a long-term strategy/guidance for regional development to frame infrastructure planning across all levels of government • Strengthen the role of SUBDERE to improve collaboration between ministries and public agencies • Strengthen and further develop the role of COMICIVYTs in the definition and monitoring of regional investment strategies • Strengthen the role of the ERD and PLADECO to guide and articulate regional infrastructure investments • Streamline planning instruments at the national and subnational levels by articulating the ERD and PLADECO with a national and cross-sectoral regional development strategy

Table 3.2. Main challenges and remedies for multi-level infrastructure governance (*cont.*)

Pre-conditions	Main challenges for multi-level infrastructure governance	Recommendations
Linking budgeting and planning	• Allocation of budget for infrastructure investment is project-based • Subnational investment funding prevents comprehensive and strategic approach to infrastructure investments and their prioritisation • Annual budget allocation discourages medium- or long-term investment planning	• Move towards a programme-based funding allocation framework to allow the effective execution of place-based agendas • Develop a multi-year budgeting framework to improve the connection between planning and budgeting • Further prioritise investments framed by the ERD and PLADECO within a medium-term budgeting framework
Co-ordination across levels of government	• The role of GOREs in terms of competences and financing is weak; the authority and autonomy of GOREs are limited • The use of programming agreements (Convenios de Programación, CPs) is weak, highly concentrated in some sectors and focused on projects • The involvement of municipalities in CPs is limited • Dialogue across levels of governments depends largely on political will; platforms for dialogue are informal or ad hoc more than institutionalised • The role played by dialogue platforms as the COMICIVYTs has been crucial, but remains limited	• Strengthen GOREs (competences and resources) as key levers for improved co-ordination: • GOREs can act as key interlocutors for vertical co-ordination in the interaction between municipalities and the central government • GOREs should support critical projects that require cross-jurisdictional cooperation, in particular vis-à-vis rural municipalities • Strengthen programing agreements to transform them into territorial contracts. Some of the key steps to consider are: • Specify territorial goals and regional development priorities for each contract • Consider a consultation phase involving national and subnational actors, the private sector and civil society • Clearly define the role of the different institutions and authorities involved • Encourage partnerships with Municipal Associations to support investments at a supra-municipal scale through special funding for contracts signed by Associations. • Specific contractual arrangements for metropolitan areas • Incorporate monitoring mechanisms and an evaluation phase • Set incentives for contract enforcement, for example, allocate part of the funding based on good performance • Further institutionalise the role of regional COMICIVYTs by enhancing their competences. Regional COMICIVYT could be regular committees with monitoring competences and accountable to citizens.
Co-ordination across regions and municipalities	• Collaboration between regions and municipalities is limited; subnational governments are usually called on to compete for funding of infrastructure investments, hampering collaboration between them • Municipal Associations have encountered a series of challenges mainly linked to its funding • Involvement of Municipal Associations in infrastructure investments is limited. • Lack of financial incentives for co-ordination between municipalities and regions • Urban investments are highly fragmented • Lack of metropolitan governance framework	• Further encourage Municipal Associations for infrastructure projects through financial incentives: • Specific funding from FNDR (or other sources) dedicated exclusively to joint projects • Special territorial contracts where associations are called on to co-finance infrastructure projects. • Further encourage infrastructure investment planning at a macro-regional level articulated with existing regional planning instruments • Develop a metropolitan transport authority as a first step towards the creation of metropolitan governance bodies • Ensure a metropolitan governance architecture that is sufficiently flexible to adapt to the various types and challenges of Chilean urban areas.

Table 3.2. Main challenges and remedies for multi-level infrastructure governance (*cont.*)

Pre-conditions	Main challenges for multi-level infrastructure governance	Recommendations
Subnational capacities for infrastructure investments	• Low and unequal capacities of subnational governments to design and implement infrastructure projects - Main barriers for capacity building are high staff turnover and low salaries at the local level • Important differences in local administrative capacity to undertake concessions contracts • Multiple training programmes and methodologies weakly co-ordinated • Weak stakeholder involvement in the definition of infrastructure investments - Citizen engagement is more reactive than proactive • Multiple participatory spaces for different purposes with unclear outputs • Ex post evaluation is mainly based on budget execution assessment • Multiple data repositories with limited articulation	• Streamline and articulate the various training programmes for investment capacities. A central level Infrastructure Advisory Body (see Chapter 2) could assume this task. Regions and municipal associations also might be key levers to articulate capacity building and technical support. • Strengthen and adapt the permanent municipal staff (planta municipal) to local needs through Law 20.922 • Professionalise regional and municipal public servants: Subnational governments could consider adapting the principles for senior civil servants (Sistema de Alta Dirección Pública) to their local contexts • Assess subnational capacity gap with a competence and performance assessment framework that could involve defining standards of performance • Pursue capacity building through pilot projects (learning-by-doing) especially in the devolution of infrastructure and transport competences • Streamline participation spaces in order to avoid consultation fatigue by re-evaluating current participatory mechanisms and better aligning government and citizen approaches and expectations • Complete ex ante assessment needs with an integrated monitoring and evaluation system providing a comprehensive set of information available in a friendly way to encourage citizen use • Strengthen the IDE as an articulated platform, integrating information from the various existing platforms (BIP, SNI, SINIM, etc.). • Develop ex post evaluation process to monitor the effectiveness and eventually the impact on territorial development of infrastructure and development strategies such as Plan Chile 30/30

Source: Authors.

Notes

1. For Chile, subnational expenditures include only municipal expenditures.
2. According to the OECD (2013b), port governance in Chile is strongly influenced by private and central government actors with "little involvement at the regional or local level." Chile has 10 state-owned public use ports, 14 privately owned ports open to public use, and 32 private ports with private use (CPI, 2014). State-owned ports "are administered by public port authorities and owned by the state, which receives the port-related revenues… and has a central vision on which ports to expand, based on the national interest. As a result, Chile's ports tend to develop independently of the cities in which they are located" (OECD, 2013b: 138).
3. The election of regional councillors occurs at the time of presidential and parliamentary elections every four years.
4. This data comes from the MIDESOL and differs from the data provided by the Central Bank to the OECD.
5. The other functional urban areas (FUAs) of Chile each consist of only one municipality. While this sort of administrative fragmentation – i.e., the lack of correspondence between existing administrative borders and the spatial and functional organisation of social-economic relations –is not uncommon, even among Chile's urban areas, the variation in the number of individual municipalities comprising the metropolitan areas is significant: 47 in the case of Santiago, nine in Concepción and six in Valparaíso. Approximately half of all urban areas are comprised of one municipality, and thus do not face the same administrative fragmentation problems (or not to the same degree) as the metropolitan areas. In addition, each metropolitan region is composed of individual municipalities that themselves vary in territorial size and classification (core versus hinterland), and resource capacity, creating disparities within the metropolitan area that can often require "close to home", nuanced management (OECD Urban Review).

References

Acuña, E. (2009), *Propuestas de mejora al diseño y gestión del Fondo Nacional de Desarrollo Regional,* Memoria para Optar al título de Ingeniero Civil, Universidad de Chile, Santiago. www.sistemaspublicos.cl/wp-content/files_mf/1271449156PropuestasdeMejoraalFNDR.pdf.

Ahmad, E., Viscarra, H. (2016), *Public Investment for Sustainable Development in Chile. Building on the National Investment System,* IDB discussion paper nº IDB-DP-469, Inter-American Development Bank

Ahmad, E., Zanola, R. (2015), *Chile: Regional Investments, Convergence and Local Governance. Some Preconditions for Sustainable and Inclusive Growth*, London School of Economics, London.

Avendaño, C. (2009), *Estudio exploratorio de los elementos que afectan la formulación de proyectos a nivel municipal*, Memoria para optar al título de ingeniero civil industrial, Universidad de Chile, Santiago.

Banco Central de Chile (2015), *Cuentas Nacionales de Chile, PIB Regional 2015*, http://si3.bcentral.cl/estadisticas/Principal1/Informes/CCNN/regional/CCNNPIBregional2015.pdf.

Charbit, C. and O. Romano (forthcoming), *Contracts Across Levels of Government for Regional Development: An International Review*, OECD Regional Development Working Paper, OECD Publishing, Paris.

CCHC (2016), *Infraestructura Crítica para el Desarrollo 2016-2025*, Cámara Chilena de la Construcción, Santiago.

Centro de Políticas Públicas UC (2015), *Asociatividad Municipal: herramienta para la inversión local*", http://politicaspublicas.uc.cl/wp-content/uploads/2015/05/asociativad-municipal-2015-1.pdf

Comisión Asesora Presidencial en Descentralización y Desarrollo Regional (2014), *Propuesta de Política de Estado y Agenda para la Descentralización y el Desarrollo Territorial de Chile - Hacia un país desarrollado y justo.* Santiago.

Contraloría General de la República (2016), *Boletín Informativo de Ejecución Presupuestaria*, https://www.contraloria.cl/portalweb/documents/451102/2132612/boletin+biep+2015+%281%29.pdf/4d0b9a6d-8105-e95b-2ee1-64572ca7c47.

Contreras, E. et al. (2011), "Gestión del Conocimiento y Transparencia: Desafíos para la Inversión Pública a Nivel Local", *Revista Trend Managenent*, Vol. 13/4, Revista Trend Management, Santiago, pp. 44-52.

CPI (2014), *Análisis Crítico de los Planes de Infraestructura*, Consejo de Políticas de Infraestructura, Santiago.

EIU (2014), *Evaluating the environment for public-private partnerships in Latin America and the Caribbean: The 2014 Infrascope*, Economist Intelligence Unit, New York.

European Commission (2013), *Q&A on the legislative package for EU Cohesion Policy 2014-2020*, European Commission, Brussels, http://europa.eu/rapid/press-release_memo-13-678_fr.htm.

Fernández Prajoux, V. (2013), "Chapter 9: Whose Public Spaces? Citizen Participation in Urban Planning in Santiago, Chile," in *Participatory Learning and Action 66: Tools for Supporting Sustainable Natural Resource Management and Livelihoods,* International Institute for Environmental Development, London, http://pubs.iied.org/pdfs/G03664.pdf (accessed 1 June 2016).

Gobierno Regional Metropolitano de Santiago (2016*), Instrumentos de Inversión Regional*, Santiago, https://www.gobiernosantiago.cl/instrumentos-de-inversion-regional.

Gobierno Regional Metropolitano de Santiago (2016b), *Nueva Alameda Providencia,* Santiago, www.nuevaalamedaprovidencia.cl.

Government of Chile (2006), *DFL1, Ley Nro 18.695 Orgánica Constitucional de Municiaplidades*, Sub-secretariat of Regional Development and Administration, Ministry of Interior, Santiago, updated November 2016.

Government of Chile (2005), Law No. 19175, *Orgánica Constitucional sobre Gobierno y Administración Regional*, Sub-secretariat of Regional Development and Administration, Ministry of Interior, Santiago, updated October 2016.

Hooghe, L. et al. (2016), *Measuring global authority. Volume I: a postfuctionalist theory of governance,* Oxford University Press, Oxford, www.arjanschakel.nl/regauth_dat.html.

IMF (2015), "Chile: Selected Issues", *IMF Country Report No.15/228*, International Monetary Fund, Washington, D.C., www.imf.org/external/pubs/ft/scr/2015/cr15228.pdf.

IMF (2015), *The Macroeconomic Effects of Public Investment: Evidence from Advanced Economies*, IMF Working Paper, Research Department, International Monetary Fund, Washington, D.C. www.imf.org/external/pubs/ft/wp/2015/wp1595.pdf.

Marcel, M. (2008), *Modelos Alternativos de Decentralización y la Experiencia Chilena*, Corporación de Estudios para Latinoamerica (CIEPLAN), Santiago. www.cieplan.org/media/publicaciones/archivos/306/Paper.pdf.

McKinsey (2013), *Infrastructure productivity: How to save $1 trillion a year*, McKinsey & Company, www.mckinsey.com/industries/infrastructure/our-insights/infrastructure-productivity.

MDS (2016), *Mapa de Proyectos de Inversión,* Ministry of Social Development, Santiago, http://sni.ministeriodesarrollosocial.gob.cl/mapa-de-proyectos-de-inversion.

MDS (2015a), *Informe Anual de Inversión Pública 2014, Resúmen Ejecutivo [Annual Report on Public Investment, Executive Summary]*, División de Evaluación Social de Inversiones, Departamento de Metodologías y Estudios, Ministry of Social Development, Santiago.

MDS (2015b), "Serie de Inversión Pública Regionalizada 2001-2015" [Regionalized public investment series], Excel workbook, Ministry of Social Development, Santiago.

Ministerio Secretaría General de Gobierno (2015), *Cuenta Publica 2015: Ministerio Secretaría General de Gobierno, Ministerio Secretaría General de Gobierno*, Santiago de Chile, Chile, http://cuentapublica.msgg.gob.cl/#documentos

Ministerio Secretaría General de Gobierno (2016), *Cuenta Pública de Participación Ciudadana*, Dirección de Organizaciones Sociales, Ministerio Secretaría General del Gobierno, Santiago.

MINVU (2014), *Programa de Pavimentación Participativa: Manual de Postulación*, Ministerio de Vivienda y Urbanismo, Santiago, www.minvu.cl/opensite_20070308155628.aspx; www.minvu.cl/opensite_20070308155628.aspx.

MOP (2014), *Hacia un país con desarrollo equilibrado: Infraestructura y agua [Toward a country with balanced development: infrastructure and water]*, Planning Directorate, Ministry of Public Works, Santiago, www.dirplan.cl/centrodedocumentacion/documentosgenerales/Documents/libro/Hacia_un_pais_con_desarrollo_equilibrado.pdf.

MOP (2009), *Chile: Opportunities in infrastructure, 2009-2010*, Foreign Investment Committee, Ministry of Public Works, Santiago, www.mop.cl/Documents/chile%20opportunities%20in%20infrastructure.pdf.

OECD (n.d.), *OECD Regional Well-being* (database), www.oecd.org/gov/regional-policy/CHI.pdf

OECD (forthcoming a), *Multi-level Governance Review of Chile: Modernisation of the Municipal System*, OECD Publishing, Paris.

OECD (forthcoming b), *Monitoring Review of Sweden*, OECD Publishing, Paris.

OECD (2016a), *OECD Regional Outlook 2016: Productive Regions for Inclusive Societies*, OECD Publishing, Paris, http://dx.doi.org/10.1787/9789264260245-en.

OECD (2016b) *Subnational governments in OECD countries: key data*, OECD Publishing, Paris, www.oecd.org/gov/regional-policy/Subnational-governments-in-OECD-Countries-Key-Data-2016.pdf.

OECD (2016c), *Stronger Growth Remains Elusive: Urgent Policy Response is needed, Interim Economic Outlook*, OECD Publishing, Paris, http://pac-files.oecd.org/acrobatebook/1215071e.pdf.

OECD (2016e), *OECD Regions at a Glance 2016*, OECD Publishing, Paris, http://dx.doi.org/10.1787/reg_glance-2016-en.

OECD (2016f), "Subnational government structure and finance", OECD Regional Statistics (database), http://dx.doi.org/10.1787/05fb4b56-en.

OECD (2016g), *Making the Most of Public Investment in Colombia: Working Effectively across Levels of Government*, OECD Multi-level Governance Studies, OECD Publishing, Paris, http://dx.doi.org/10.1787/9789264265288-en.

OECD (2015a), Recommendation on Effective Public Investment Across Levels of Government www.oecd.org/gov/regional-policy/recommendation-effective-public-investment-across-levels-of-government.htm.

OECD (2015b), Recommendation on Effective Public Investment Across Levels of Government – Implementation Toolkit -- www.oecd.org/effective-public-investment-toolkit/.

OECD (2015e), *Chile Policy Priorities for Stronger and more equitable growth,* Better Policy Series, OECD Publishing, Paris, www.oecd.org/chile/chile-policy-priorities-for-stronger-and-more-equitable-growth.pdf.

OECD (2015f), *Effective public investment across levels of government: Principles for action*, OECD Publishing, Paris, www.oecd.org/effective-public-investment-toolkit/Effective-Public-Investment-Brochure.pdf.

OECD (2014a), *OECD Regional Outlook 2014: Regions and Cities: Where Policies and People Meet*, OECD Publishing, Paris, http://dx.doi.org/ 10.1787/9789264201415-en.

OECD (2014b), *OECD Rural Policy Reviews: Chile 2014*, OECD Publishing, Paris, http://dx.doi.org/10.1787/9789264222892-en.

OECD (2014c), *How's Life in Your Region?: Measuring Regional and Local Well-being for Policy Making*, OECD Publishing, Paris, http://dx.doi.org/10.1787/9789264217416-en

OECD (2014d), *OECD Territorial Reviews: Netherlands 2014*, OECD Publishing, Paris, http://dx.doi.org/10.1787/9789264209527-en.

OECD (2013a), *OECD Urban Policy Reviews, Chile 2013*, OECD Publishing, Paris, http://dx.doi.org/10.1787/9789264191808-en.

OECD (2013b), *OECD Territorial Reviews: Antofagasta, Chile 2013*, OECD Publishing, Paris, http://dx.doi.org/10.1787/9789264203914-en.

OECD (2013c), *Investing Together: Working Effectively across Levels of Government*, OECD Publishing, Paris, http://dx.doi.org/10.1787/9789264197022-en.

OECD (2009a), *OECD Territorial Reviews: Chile 2009*, OECD Publishing, Paris, http://dx.doi.org/10.1787/9789264060791-en.

OECD (2009b), *How Regions Grow: Trends and Analysis*, OECD Publishing, Paris, http://dx.doi.org/10.1787/9789264039469-en.

OECD (unpublished), *Regional Outlook Survey 2016*

OECD/UCLG (2016), *Subnational Governments around the world: Structure and finance.* United Cities and Local Governments, Barcelona.

PUC (2015), *Asociatividad Municipal: herramienta para la inversión local*, Centro de Políticas Públicas, Pontificia Universidad Católica de Chile, Santiago, http://politicaspublicas.uc.cl/wp-content/uploads/2015/05/asociativad-municipal-2015-1.pdf.

Raczynsky, D. and Serrano, C. (2001), *Descentralización: Nudos Críticos*, Corporación de Investigaciones Económicas para Latinoamérica (CIEPLAN), Santiago.

Rodríguez, J. and Granados, S. (2013), *Propuestas para avanzar en descentralización fiscal en Chile*, Documento de Trabajo N°7, Serie Estudios Territoriales, Programa Cohesión Territorial para el Desarrollo, Santiago.

Sagaris, L. (2014), "Citizen Participation for Sustainable Transport: the case of 'Living City' in Santiago, Chile (1997-2012)", *Journal of Transport Geography*, Elsevier, Amsterdam, http://dx.doi.org/10.1016/j.jtrangeo.2014.08.011.

Spoerer, M. (2014), "Paradoxes of Participatory Democracy: Citizen Participation, Collective Action and Political Influence in a Chilean Environmental Conflict", *Nuevo Mundo Mundos Nuevos,* online, http://Nuevomundo.revues.org/67153 (accessed 26 June 2016).

SUBDERE (n.d.), *Convenios de Programación*, Sub-secretariat of Regional and Administrative Development, Santiago, www.subdere.gov.cl/sites/default/files/documentos/articles-80573_archivo_fuente.pdf.

SUBDERE (2016a),*Descentralización*, Sub-secretariat of Regional and Administrative Development, Santiago, www.descentralizacion.subdere.gov.cl.

SUBDERE (2016b), *Programación Academia 2016*, Sub-secretariat of Regional and Administrative Development, Santiago, www.academia.subdere.gov.cl/wp-content/uploads/2016/06/Programacion2016_web.pdf.

SUBDERE (2016c), *Quinto pilar: Experiencias Pilotos en materia de descentralización,* Sub-secretariat of Regional and Administrative Development, Santiago, www.descentralizacion.subdere.gov.cl/quintopilar.

SUBDERE (2016d), *Sistema de Información Territorial para las Regiones de Chile*, Sub-secretariat of Regional and Administrative Development, Santiago, www.chileindica.cl.

SUBDERE (2016e), *Sistema Nacional de Información Municipal*, Sub-secretariat of Regional and Administrative Development, Santiago, http://datos.sinim.gov.cl.

SUBDERE (2014), *Registro Único de Asociaciones Municipales Con Personalidad Jurídica de Derecho Privado*, Sub-secretariat of Regional and Administrative Development, Santiago, www.subdere.cl/sites/default/files/documentos/registro_unico_de_asociaciones_municipales_con_personalidad_juridica_de_derecho_privado_11.08.2014.pdf.

SUBDERE (2008), *Asociaciones Municipales: Lecciones y Aprendizajes Orientadores para una Política de Fortalecimiento*, Sub-secretariat of Regional and Administrative Development, Santiago, www.subdere.gov.cl/sites/default/noticiasold/articles-7601_recurso_1.pdf.

Undurraga, A. (2015), *Agenda Chile 3030: Hacia un país con desarrollo equilibrado [Agenda Chile 3030: Toward a country with balanced development]*, presentation, Expo Regiones 2015, Santiago, www.exporegiones2015.cl/presentaciones-/21 (accessed 25 April 2016).

Valenzuela, J.P. and Rojas, E. (2012), "Urban Governance in Chile", background paper prepared for the OECD, Public Governance and Territorial Development Directorate, unpublished, as cited in OECD (2013), *OECD Urban Policy Reviews, Chile 2013*, OECD Publishing, Paris.

Villagran, V. (2013), *Regional Plans of Infrastructure and Water, Resource Management to 2021 (PRIGRH): Current Challenges to reach the Development of Integrated Regional Planning of Infrastructure*, presentation to the United Nations Centre for

Regional Development Expert Group Meeting on Integrated Regional Development Planning, 28 - 30 May 2013 Nagoya, Japan, www.uncrd.or.jp/content/documents/1058IRDP%20EGM%202013%20-%20P11_Chile.pdf (accessed 11 Feb 2016).

Villagran, V. et al. (2013), "Regional Infrastructure Planning in Chile: Challenges and Opportunities", *Regional Development Dialogue*, Vol. 34/2, United Nations Centre for Regional Development, Nagoya, Japan, pp. 130-143.

Waissbluth, M. and Arrendodo, C. (2011), *Descentralización en Chile: una trayectoria posible*, Nota Técnica Nro 4, Centro de Sistemas Públicos, Departamento de Ingeniería Industrial, Universidad de Chile, Santiago.

Annex 3A

Public investment at different levels of government in Chile, 2004-2015

Chile's Ministry of Social Development (MDS) provides an annual analysis of public investment at different levels of government. The definitions of public investment in these documents appear to differ from those used in the OECD Subnational Government Finance Dataset, producing public investment totals that are higher as a percent of GDP than those reported by the OECD. MDS classification of public investment derives from Chile's budget documentation, rather than national accounts. Moreover, it appears to include spending on maintenance and repair. As such, the findings from the latest MDS report are summarised here and the following page, separate from the main text. All USD figures are 2014 U.S. dollars.

According to the MDS, in 2014 public investment in Chile totalled USD 12.9 billion, equal to 5% of GDP – a percentage on par with 2013 and the highest level of the preceding decade. It accounted for 23.3% of total investment and translated to USD 724 per capita. Sectoral investments accounted for 47% of public investment, public enterprises 32%, regionalised investment 15%, and municipal investment 6%. Looking at the period from 2004 to 2014, public investment rose 63% in real terms. Sectoral investment rose steadily, regionally defined investment also rose, and municipal investment remained steady. Investment by public enterprises proved more volatile, but rose considerably between 2011 and 2013, before dropping off slightly in 2014.

Sectoral investment is heavily concentrated: the Ministry of Public Works (MOP) accounts for 40% of sectoral investment and the Ministry of Housing (MINVU) accounts for 38%. The remainder of investment is divided among the Ministry of Health (MINSAL; 8%), Ministry of Education (MINEDUC; 9%); and all others (5%). "Other" includes the Ministry of Transport and Telecommunications, which provided USD 102.2 mil in 2014 (most of which went to the Metro Santiago region). For state owned enterprises, spending is even more concentrated: in 2014, CODELCO Chile's state owned copper mining company, accounted for 74% of investment.

Regionally defined public investment is essentially central government spending directed to regions. This type of investment rose 57% in real terms between 2004 and 2014. By 2014, the overwhelming majority of regional public investment came via the National Regional Development Fund (FNDR) – 80% in 2014 compared to 68% in 2004. The amount of regional public investment occurring through Programme Agreements (Convenios de Programación, CP) peaked in 2009 but has since declined. In 2014, investment via CPs occurred in the Ministry of Public Works and Ministry of Health, and accounted for 17% of total regionally defined investment.

Municipal public investment is municipal spending of own funds. This type of investment tends to be volatile. It dropped considerably between 2004 and 2005, from USD 897 million to USD 676 million. Since 2005, spending rose to USD 768 mil in 2007 before dropping steadily through 2011 to USD 613 mil. It stood at USD 745 mil in 2014. Within regions, average municipal investment per capita is highest in Aisén (USD 133) and lowest in Arica y Parinacota (USD 20). The municipalities in the Santiago Metropolitan Region invest an average of USD 34 per capita.

Finally, aggregating 2014 sectoral, regional and municipal investment (and excluding public enterprises) by region **indicates that while the most populated region** (Metro Santiago) **has the highest level of overall investment** (e.g. USD 1 509 million), it also has **the lowest per capita** (e.g. USD 211). By contrast, the sparsely populated southern regions of Aisén and Magallanes have low levels of overall public investment (USD 240 mil and USD 245 mil, respectively), but the per capita values are highest (USD 2 260 and USD 1 502, respectively). Variability among the remaining regions in per capita public investment ranges from a low of USD 359 in Valparaiso to a high of USD 970 in Los Rios. Overall, national public investment per capita (sectoral, regional, and municipal) was USD 504 in 2014.

Chapter 4

Transport infrastructure

Productive investment in transport infrastructure is vital for prosperity. As a middle-income economy heavily geared towards exports, investment in a high-quality transport infrastructure base has contributed significantly to the Chile's development. A fully co-ordinated approach to infrastructure spending, with investment driven by transport policy goals that are integrated with land-use and sectoral development objectives, must accompany Chile's transition from a middle to a high-income economy and should address the potentially negative impacts on social and territorial equality and the environment associated with this transition. This Chapter analyses the current and projected gaps between Chile and its OECD peers based on the ITF/OECD methodology, and identifies policy priorities that should be set to achieve the goals of Plan Chile 30/30.

Infrastructure to support economic growth and territorial equality

The economic role of transport infrastructure

The impact on growth of investment in transport infrastructure varies in the different stages of a country's economic development (OECD, 2014). In low-income countries, investment in basic infrastructure provision can make a very large difference in access to education, jobs and services (UN, 2015). As incomes rise, better transport services are needed to support the growth of business activities, exports and value creation, and the focus for infrastructure investment shifts to supporting these sectors of the economy. In more mature economies, priorities tend to shift towards addressing issues of congestion and bottlenecks in reasonably complete networks, the upgrade and maintenance of existing assets, and providing for technological innovation. Typically, the economic impact of transport infrastructure is more transformative at lower levels of development, and the incremental impact of new investment decreases at more advanced stages of development (Eddington, 2006).

Transport infrastructure plays a critical role in the transition from a middle- to high-income economy. Theoretical and empirical studies have underscored the positive relationship between high-quality infrastructure and economy-wide productivity (IMF, 2015). This relationship is underpinned by a number of economic mechanisms triggered by improvements in transport infrastructure, including the following:

- High-quality infrastructure is a precondition for the provision of efficient transport services for both freight and passenger movements, which in turn supports core economic activities and removes geographic barriers to competition.
- Well-functioning logistics systems facilitate trade through lowering access costs to international markets and by improving the competitiveness of domestic firms (Arvis et al., 2014).
- Passenger transport connectivity enhances the productive capacity of the economy by widening and deepening labour markets and through agglomeration gains, facilitating industrial specialisation and enabling face-to-face interactions between businesses and specialised workers in high-value service sectors of the economy (Graham, 2014).
- Infrastructure can be an effective policy tool to address social and territorial imbalances by connecting rural and remote areas to larger centres of production and consumption, creating more economic opportunities for residents and reducing out-migration.

Investment in infrastructure to improve connectivity is most effective at delivering long-term growth when it relieves a constraint on productivity. The effectiveness of investment in generating growth and addressing inequality can be measured and compared to alternatives on the basis of good project selection methodologies, including high-quality appraisal and transparent selection procedures (ITF/OECD, 2007; Warner, 2014). Socio-economic cost-benefit assessment (CBA) is an important tool because it provides a quantitative measure of the extent to which, over its lifetime, a project or initiative will bring the community benefits that exceed the project's costs of construction and operation (Veryard, 2016). In this respect, CBA is a powerful framework for prioritisation, through which options can be compared and selected. However, CBA also suffers from limitations, and infrastructure investment will require additional analysis to ensure that the government's policies towards social and regional equity are accounted for in project selection and the allocation of resources. The prioritisation of effective investment in Chile is discussed in Box 4.1. Concerted efforts across the government, such as those led by the Road Division in the MOP to improve the link between CBA and territorial goals, are under way to reform assessment methodologies.

Box 4.1. Project appraisal and selection in Chile

As discussed in Chapter 2, Chile has an established national system of investment appraisal (SNI) that vets all public projects, and socio-economic cost-benefit analysis (CBA) lies at the heart of project evaluation. This system has several strengths, including a uniform approach to project selection throughout the country; a simple and clear target rate of return; well-documented methodologies for undertaking CBA; and a clear institutional separation of roles between project development, evaluation and approval. Regarding the latter point, sectoral ministries such as the Ministry of Public Works and the Ministry of Housing and Urbanisation prepare and deliver projects, while the Ministry of Social Development is responsible for reviewing and approving social cost-benefit evaluations. Chile's SNI exhibits a high degree of transparency. The various methodologies and processes for undertaking social evaluations are published on the Ministry of Social Development's website, as are the shadow prices used in those evaluations.

However, the SNI has been criticised for failing to take adequate account of externalities such as environmental impacts and for incorporating biases against poorer regions. Although the SNI makes some allowances for CO_2 emissions, it does not include other potential impacts of infrastructure investment. The main policy goal is economic growth, and the project appraisal method does not consider distributional effects and territorial inequalities. Thus, the SNI historically favours investment in areas with high vehicular flows and growing demand, such as congested metropolitan areas or mining areas. The National Fund for Regional Development (FNDR), which provides resources to regional governments, allocates funds for projects in regions with the highest poverty rates and the largest cost differentials in housing and infrastructure. Given the large concentration of poor households in larger cities, the FNDR nevertheless reinforces the concentration of investment in metropolitan areas. In addition, FNDR-funded projects are still subject to the same SNI assessment criteria.

Source: Ahmad and Zanola (2016).

Transport systems generate a range of external costs (Maibach et al., 2007; Bickel and Friedrich, 2013). These include congestion and its related costs (wasted time, impaired reliability and exacerbated air pollution); environmental impacts, both at the global level (greenhouse gas emissions) and the local level (noise and air pollution); health costs arising from air and noise emissions; and the costs associated with deaths and injuries from road crashes and accidents on other modes of transport. The importance placed upon these external costs when it comes to choosing between competing policy priorities rises along with a country's income. Some of these costs are already assessed as part of existing appraisal frameworks in Chile (e.g. congestion cost, greenhouse gas emissions), while others are not (e.g. noise and air pollution).

Each part of the national transport network contributes to economic development, but the benefit of transport systems as a whole is greater than the sum of their parts. Ports are gateways to international trade, but a well-equipped port system cannot adequately cater for trade unless maritime hubs have efficient transport connections to hinterland production and consumption centres. Likewise, intercity motorways can promote economic links between cities, but the positive effects of spatial concentration may be outweighed by rising congestion costs and increasing car trips in urban areas in the absence of efficient urban transport systems. Attention to intermodal interfaces (road-rail, road-port and rail-port) within a network-wide planning approach is critical to provide the physical connectivity needed to support economic growth.

To sum up, a gap in the provision and quality of transport infrastructure compared to optimal levels can undermine a country's competitiveness, equality and ultimately long-term economic growth. The notion of a gap, however, is not straightforward – it evolves as countries transition from middle to high income levels. Accordingly, any assessment of the presence and size of transport infrastructure gaps needs to be tailored to the national and regional context for economic development, as well as linked to national and regional policy goals, to guide decision makers in prioritising investments. This requires a shift in analytical focus – from focusing on infrastructure stock (most suited to earlier stages of development) to measures illustrating the role of the infrastructure in providing access to economic opportunities.

Chile's infrastructure challenge

Chile is a middle-income country with an open economy heavily reliant on trade and a complex geography coupled with uneven population and resource distribution. While Chile has a good transport infrastructure base thanks to investment carried out in recent decades, improvements in the capacity, quality and efficiency of public infrastructure will be necessary to support the country's transition to a high-income economy.

The Plan Chile 30/30 initiative, led by the Ministry of Public Works (MOP), links infrastructure investment to the long-term goals of higher incomes and greater equality, while simultaneously addressing different dimensions of transport and water infrastructure. Analysis undertaken by the International Transport Forum at the OECD (ITF) and presented in this chapter is designed to contribute to Plan Chile 30/30 by addressing the following key question: what are the policy priorities for infrastructure investment that should be set to achieve the Agenda's goals, given current and projected gaps between Chile and OECD comparator countries?

Previous examples of infrastructure gap assessments

Several approaches are available for assessing infrastructure needs, each dependent on data availability. The transport sector often lacks core data, and when data are available, their value for making international comparisons is often undermined by inconsistent definitions. This makes the assessment of potential infrastructure gaps particularly challenging.

Historically, most macro-level studies of the relation of infrastructure investment to productivity determined elasticities of GDP to infrastructure stock. Long-run elasticities represent the relationship between infrastructure stock measures and GDP/income measures over time. These can be derived either as ratios (based on historical and/or cross-country benchmarks) or as coefficients in econometric models.[1] In turn, elasticities are used to derive estimates of the level of infrastructure provision needed to satisfy consumer and producer demand, based on forecast levels of economic activity. Box 4.2 presents examples of the estimates derived.

Elasticity-based approaches raise a number of issues and questions. First, the measures of infrastructure stocks available and chosen to represent infrastructure indicators have some limitations. Taking road infrastructure gap assessments as an example, previous work has used the following:

- km of paved roads per km^2 of land (Fay and Yepes, 2003)
- km of roads (total) per worker (Calderón and Servén, 2004)

- km of roads (total) per km^2 of land (Liberini, 2006)
- km of roads (total) per 1 000 people (Andrés, 2014).

Box 4.2. Assessing infrastructure gaps through the estimation of long-run elasticities

Econometric analysis by the World Bank (Fay and Yepes, 2003) treats infrastructure in its dual role of input in the firm's production function and consumption services for individuals. Using GDP as a proxy for aggregate demand and controlling for underlying differences in economic and technological performance across countries, the authors define a model to predict how the evolution of GDP will affect infrastructure needs. Their model predicted the amount of "infrastructure demand" based on GDP forecasts for developing countries, which was equal to about USD 465 billion per annum – or 5.5% of developing countries' GDP over 2005-2010.

Liberini (2006) developed this framework further for Latin America by disaggregating the total demand function at the level of three core infrastructure sectors (telecommunications, power generation and transport). The relationship between GDP and each sector is captured through the estimation of sector elasticities. Further control variables are added, such as population density, the urbanisation rate and the size of the countries of interest. Rather than using GDP forecasts, the author uses estimates of potential GDP published by the OECD and the IMF, aiming to measure the gap between the optimal and the current infrastructure stock for the core sectors of interest. As far as road transport infrastructure is concerned, no statistically significant effect was detected in relation to transport sector output – suggesting the possibility that no gap exists for road infrastructure in Latin America.

Other studies rely on historical ratios of infrastructure stock and GDP to assess future needs. By way of example, recent research by McKinsey (2013) estimated that investment in economic infrastructure* has historically averaged 3.8% of GDP and that the ratio of infrastructure stock to GDP is around 70%. To maintain those flow-to-GDP and stock-to-GDP ratios, McKinsey forecast a global infrastructure investment requirement of USD 57 trillion between 2013 and 2030.

*Note:** Economic infrastructure includes roads, rail, airports, ports, energy, water and telecommunications infrastructure.

Source: Fay and Yepes, 2003; Liberini, 2006; Dobbs et al., 2013.

Measures of infrastructure density can penalise countries with a large land mass, while indicators of infrastructure stock per capita may show higher levels of infrastructure provision in areas hosting large-scale logistics operations (e.g. ports, international rail freight corridors), although such infrastructure may not enhance passenger connectivity. Hence, switching from one measure to another can lead to inconsistent estimates of infrastructure endowment. Moreover, stock indicators do not reflect characteristics such as capacity and quality that would better explain whether existing infrastructure is adequate to cater for specific connectivity and accessibility needs.

In addition**, elasticities based on historical relationships between infrastructure and GDP may not necessarily hold in the future**, particularly when there are changes in demographic and economic dynamics. Structural shifts such as the growth of international trade and increasing urbanisation cannot be easily incorporated in the estimation of gaps based on GDP or income forecasts only, although adjustments can be made going forward. These adjustments can include indicators of transport demand that more closely mirror pressures on transport networks, such as forecasts of international trade volumes.

Alternatively, gaps can be measured in investment terms, using either input or output measures. Input measures focus on what is considered an optimal budget dedicated to infrastructure, such as a given percentage of GDP.[2] A gap can also be expressed as the investment needed to reach identified standards or targets (output measure). In this case, the provision or quality of infrastructure is assessed against a given standard, such as the share of paved roads. Using average unit costs, a level of investment required to close the gap is then estimated.[3]

Financial estimations are subject to two types of bias. First, historical levels of infrastructure spending influence the assessment of needs, providing a reference point that may not have been optimal itself. Second, the share of GDP spent on infrastructure across different countries reflects differences in geography, transport intensity of the country's productive sector, budget constraints, private sector involvement in the financing of infrastructure and so on, all of which affect the consistency of those comparisons.

There is little point in focusing on measuring inputs such as investment without being able to measure and evaluate outputs and to relate outputs to inputs functionally (ITF/OECD, 2013). Therefore, it is preferable to develop long-term strategies with a focus on the key goals that infrastructure investment aims to meet, such as a given level of capacity to support export growth or a given level of road quality to reduce crashes. Feasibility and affordability considerations can be introduced at the next stages of assessment, moving from strategies to plans and from plans to projects.

The limitations of traditional methodologies point to the need to develop an approach that is better tailored to the specific conditions of Chilean infrastructure and that better suits long-term national objectives such as economic growth and greater equality. This requires an evidence-based, objectives-led framework that minimises the risk of developing inconsistent standards. Even in the presence of an infrastructure gap, governments need to appraise and prioritise investment options through a transparent framework to make the best use of the limited funds available. This includes selecting projects according to expected net welfare benefit and internal rate of return based on cost-benefit analysis (CBA) and developing portfolios of priority projects on this basis. New projects can still be welfare enhancing even if the stock of transport infrastructure assets is close to its optimum level. At the same time, as noted in Box 4.1, CBA will not fully reflect the potential benefits of projects in meeting the goals of national policy towards reducing social and regional inequality. Additional indicators for informing decision making will be required, or budgets will need to be structured to prioritise a number of projects designed to address inequality, regardless of the result of CBA.

ITF/OECD methodology to assess infrastructure gaps and set standards

An evidence-based framework for long-term planning

This study develops three streams of analysis to contribute to the development of realistic infrastructure standards that reflect long-term economic objectives: a top-down, modelling approach based on the ITF Global Freight Model; a bottom-up, benchmarking approach based on data collection and analysis across OECD countries; and a review of the literature, supported by interviews with stakeholders, across all sectors and information collected during the OECD mission to Chile.

The ITF Global Freight Model

The ITF Global Freight Model (GFM) is used to assess the presence of capacity constraints and future infrastructure needs based on forecast projected trade volumes up to 2030. In the flow of international trade, quality transport infrastructure plays a crucial role, together with efficient administration and cross-border procedures. Well-maintained and well-managed ports, highways, airports, rail links and related services connect trading partners and reduce transport costs. Given that exports account for around 30% of

Chile's GDP, it is important to identify whether infrastructure will be adequate to support trade, and in turn higher economic growth, by 2030.

A large body of literature, including studies by the World Bank and the OECD, relies on econometric analysis of historical trends to establish a positive relationship between infrastructure provision and GDP growth. Assuming historical relations hold, predictions of future needs can be made. The Global Freight Model allows us to move beyond historical relationships between transport infrastructure and growth. The model includes detailed data on existing port capacity, as well as estimated road and rail capacity, to examine future infrastructure capacity constraints and needs in light of projected GDP growth and trade activity.

The modelling framework is underpinned by the OECD's global trade scenarios (see Box 4.3), and it projects international freight transport activity up to 2050. The model includes the following six main components, also described in Figure 4.1:

- a general equilibrium model for international trade, developed by the OECD, covering 26 world regions and 25 commodities
- a global freight transport network model based on 2010-14 data and detailed capacity information by mode based on current national plans
- an international freight mode choice model calibrated using Eurostat and ECLAC data
- a weight/value model, using the same data, to convert trade value into weight, calibrated for each commodity and transport mode
- an equilibrium assignment model of freight cargo in the network model
- infrastructure capacity, based on existing and planned expansion of maritime and land-based transport infrastructure.

Combined, these components provide model outputs that forecast trade volumes by origin-destination (OD) pair, commodity type and ode. Comparing the projected flows against existing and planned capacity, gaps in infrastructure for trade-related flows are identified.

Box 4.3. Modelling framework for long-term global trade scenarios

The methodology used to design trade scenarios to 2060 combines two models. The long-run growth model in the OECD Economic Outlook (Johansson et al., 2013; OECD, 2013b) provides long-term projections for GDP, saving, investment and current accounts for OECD and non-OECD G20 countries, augmented with projections by Fouré et al. (2012) for other countries. The trade model is a version of MIRAGE, a multi-country, sectorial, dynamic micro-founded model developed by the Centre d'Etudes Prospectives et d'Informations Internationales (CEPII) (Fontagné and Fouré, 2013; for details see Château et al., 2014). This computable general equilibrium (CGE) model analyses the global evolution of bilateral trade and sectorial specialisation, and it covers the world economy for 147 countries and 57 industries, aggregated into 26 regions and 25 sectors in the ECO framework.

The OECD Economics Department (ECO) designed trade scenarios to 2060 using a framework integrating long-term macro projections for the world economy with a sectorial trade model reproducing the key evidence characterising the driving forces of past trends in trade and specialisation. The objective is to provide long-term trade scenarios on the assumption that past trends are to continue.

Box 4.3. Modelling framework for long-term global trade scenarios (*cont.*)

The combination of aggregate projections, which are based on a growth model, with the more detailed description of consumer and firm behaviour provided by the CGE model highlights how countries' specialisations are shaped by global trends (e.g. ageing, skill enhancement, capital investment, technology diffusion) and how structural and macro policies implemented in each country will affect future trade and specialisation patterns, taking into account inter-linkages across countries.

Combining aggregate projections and individual (consumers and firms) behaviours underlines the impact of both global trends and country-specific policies on future trade and specialisation patterns, acknowledging international spill-overs. Trade projections are presented in value terms, in constant 2004 USD.

Source: Chateau et al. (2014); Johansson and Olaberria (2014).

Figure 4.1. ITF Global Freight Model

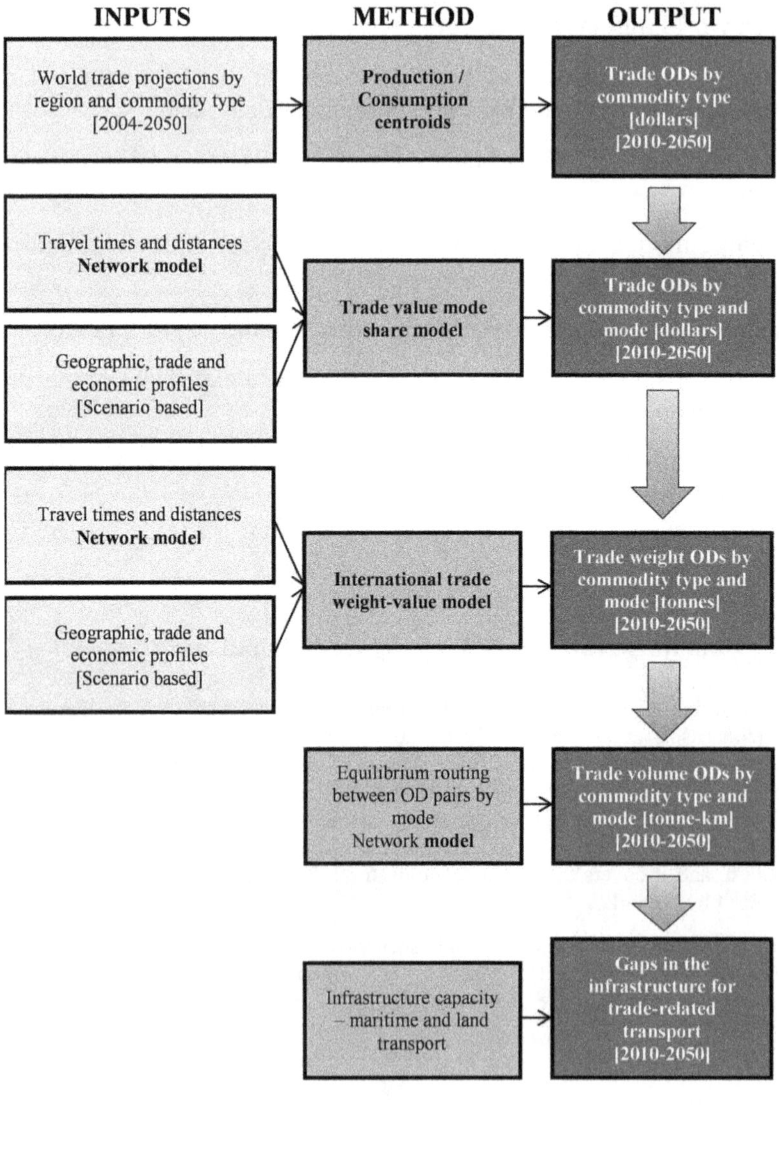

ITF/OECD International benchmarking indicators

The transport infrastructure characteristics in Chile can be assessed against several comparators:

- historical levels of infrastructure provision, coverage and quality
- countries with similar socio-economic characteristics
- policy targets and standards.

Comparisons of trends within the same country over time are potentially more appropriate for economies with high income levels and relatively low projected growth in population and income – for those countries, a key policy objective might be to maintain their current infrastructure stock, as exemplified by EU countries, where around 50% of public infrastructure budgets are spent on maintenance costs.

International benchmarking indicators are a more useful starting point for analysing Chile's infrastructure gap, provided that two conditions are met. First, meaningful indicators need to be selected to draw the appropriate links between comparative infrastructure performance and long-term national goals (considering data availability constraints). Second, comparator countries need to be selected to control, as far as possible, for factors exogenous to infrastructure provision and to improve the robustness of the analysis.

Selection of comparators

Comparator countries were selected on the basis of having similar demographic, geographic and industrial characteristics to Chile. Under the assumption that similar levels of economic activity, population density and trade patterns require similar levels of infrastructure provision and quality, the right comparison can minimise the influence of exogenous factors on transport infrastructure performance.

It may not always be optimal to benchmark national aggregate indicators for Chile, given the large differences between the country's regions in terms of demographic, geographic and economic structure. Thus, disaggregate comparisons are made between Chile's macrozones, selected OECD countries and regions of OECD countries. As far as possible, indicators for each Chilean macrozone are compared to the countries and/or regions as listed in Tables 4.1 and 4.2 below. The rationale for selecting each comparator is explained in greater detail in Annex B, which contains an overview of transport infrastructure in the selected OECD regions.

Table 4.1. Benchmark countries and regions

Chilean Macrozone	Comparator country (region if considered)
North	Australia (Western Australia)
Centre	Spain Italy (Southern Italy)
South	New Zealand
Austral	Sweden (North Sweden) Norway (North Norway)

Table 4.2. Definitions of Chilean macrozones and OECD regions

Macrozones / OECD regions	Regions	
Chile – North	Arica-Parinacota Tarapacá Antofagasta	Atacama Coquimbo
Chile – Centre	Valparaíso Region Metropolitana	O'Higgins Maule
Chile – South	Bío Bío La Araucanía	Los Ríos
Chile – Austral	Los Lagos Aysén	Magallanes
Sweden – North	European NUTS classification: SE31, SE32, SE33	
Australia – West	State of Western Australia	
Italy – South	European NUTS classification: ITG and ITF	
Norway – North	European NUTS classification: NOO7 and NOO6	

Figure 4.2. Population density and GDP per capita, 2004 and 2014

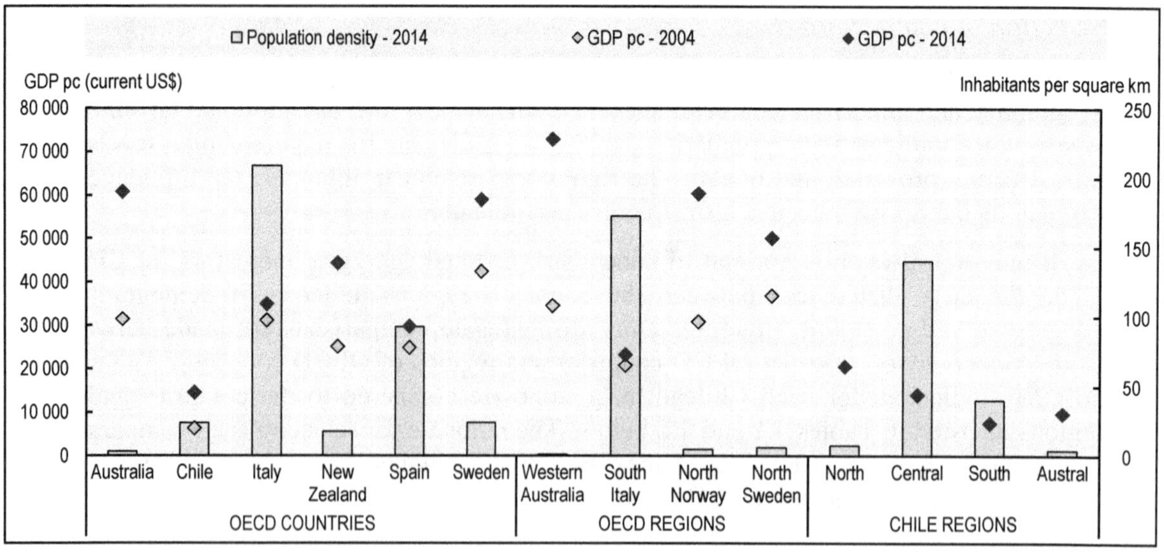

Source: Population: World Bank (2016a), Australia Bureau of Statistics (2016a), ISTAT (2016a), Statistics Norway (2016a), Statistics Sweden (2016a), Instituto Nacional de Estadísticas de Chile (2016a). Land area: World Bank (2016b), Australian Bureau of Statistics (2016b), OECD (2016b), Statistics Norway (2016a), Statistics Sweden (2016b), Instituto Nacional de Estadísticas de Chile (2016b). GDP: World Bank (2016c), Australian Bureau of Statistics (2016c), ISTAT (2016b), Statistics Norway (2016b), Statistics Sweden (2016c), Banco Central de Chile (2016).

The comparator countries and regions have already attained a level of economic development beyond Chile's national targets. Hence, the gaps identified by benchmarking today's levels of infrastructure are indicative and represent higher-end estimates rather than lower-end estimates. Since most comparators reached average incomes per capita of around USD 30 000 in the first half of the 2000s, we benchmark current infrastructure levels in Chile with levels in comparator countries both at the beginning of the century and for the most recently available year.

For each indicator and each transport sector, the benchmarking analysis points to the presence of gaps between Chile and OECD comparators, and in turn standards and goals. Gaps are not expressed in a common "currency" but rather in terms of the unit of measure used for each indicator. Most importantly, gaps translate into policy targets and standards that Chile's policy makers can use to support the development of the Plan Chile 30/30. In any case, gaps and standards should not be used in isolation but rather viewed as part of the wider narrative around the performance of transport infrastructure and its determinants.

Selection of indicators

For benchmarking indicators to provide the most useful and balanced information, a set of indicators, rather than a single indicator, is required. Performance indicators can play a key role in guiding policy, quantifying objectives and measuring progress, but they are open to misunderstanding and misuse (ITF/OECD, 2016b). A best-practice approach would involve a set of indicators that encompass measures of supply (physical network size, asset quality), demand (measures of traffic, user satisfaction) and externalities (environmental emissions and other external costs).

The number of indicators is naturally limited by the availability of comparable data across dimensions and countries, as this study does not include primary data collection. Although our work has previously highlighted the importance of macro-level transport infrastructure data to support policy-relevant research, major gaps in data availability persist. This, together with the lack of commonly agreed definitions and methods, undermines international comparators (ITF/OECD, 2013). We have also recently highlighted the presence of a significant data gap in Chile with respect to transport outputs (e.g. tonne-km, vehicle-km) and costs. The ITF and OECD (2016c) have previously suggested that a Logistics Observatory should be set up, which would fill the data gap in freight transport and related sectors (ITF/OECD, 2016c).

Acknowledging these limitations, our data collection efforts are focused on putting together a comprehensive set of benchmarking indicators across countries and regions, ensuring that the data chosen are comparable and derived from reliable sources. The following table summarises the benchmarking indicators selected for this study, by transport sector.

Table 4.3. Benchmark indicators

Sector	Indicator	Level of analysis
All transport infrastructure	GCI index	National
	LPI scores	National
Road infrastructure	Traffic intensity	National
	Road network density	National
	Share of paved roads	Macrozone
	Road quality (iRAP)	Macrozone
	Road safety	Macrozone

Table 4.3. Benchmark indicators (*cont.*)

Sector	Indicator	Level of analysis
Port infrastructure	Transport Intensity	National/Macrozone
	Turnaround times	Macrozone
	Inland transport modal share	Port level
Rail infrastructure	Traffic intensity	Macrozone
	Rail network density	Macrozone
	Utilisation rate	Macrozone
	Freight modal share	Macrozone
Airport infrastructure	Propensity to fly	National/Macrozone
	Surface access	Large airports
Urban accessibility and environmental indicators	Modal share	Urban level
	PM2.5 emissions	National/Macrozone
	NO emissions	Urban/rural areas
	CO_2 intensity	National

The following paragraphs provide a description of the indicators selected and some caveats on their interpretation to inform our analysis of gaps.

International infrastructure performance indicators – The World Economic Forum's Global Competitiveness Index (**GCI**) rests on unique data drawn from the Executive Opinion Survey, which surveys top business executives in all countries covered. Infrastructure is one of the 12 pillars of competitiveness covered by the index. The World Bank's Logistics Performance Index (**LPI**) is a multi-dimensional assessment of logistics performance and an international benchmarking tool focused on trade facilitation. The LPI is based on surveys of port operators, shippers and freight forwarders, producing a composite index reflecting responses to the questionnaire. Because of the nature of those surveyed, the LPI is oriented towards assessing the transport of manufactured goods rather than bulk commodities, and it is more applicable to higher-value goods. The LPI is most useful when used in conjunction with an in-depth assessment of trade and transport performance, and it has been used successfully in several countries to instigate discussions on the drivers of logistics performance and the areas in which barriers hinder performance (for example, see ITF/OECD, 2016b). Both the GCI and the LPI measure perceptions rather than physical availability or performance, and both suffer from year-on-year variations that depend on external factors (e.g. strikes, weather) as well as infrastructure quality. Nevertheless, if used in conjunction with an analysis of what determines efficiency on the ground, LPI scores can be a powerful stimulus for improvement.

Traffic intensity – Transport intensity (freight and passenger transport intensity) provides an indicator of how much freight and passenger activity "contributes" to the overall economy. However, the interpretation of these indicators is highly dependent on the type of economy and the geographical characteristics of the country. Unless these factors are controlled for, comparisons of transport intensity are better indicators of performance over time for the same entity than for comparing performance between countries. Transport intensity indicators can be calculated based on traffic data.

Network density – Indicators of network density for road and rail measure the stock of infrastructure with respect to land mass and/or population. As discussed above, these indicators can provide a distorted view of infrastructure provision. Estimates can be inconsistent across indicators depending on the choice of denominator, and they do not reflect characteristics such as capacity and quality. However, network density is often used in international comparisons, as it is often readily available from national statistics.

Share of paved roads – The share of roads that are paved is often used as an indicator of road infrastructure availability and quality, as paved roads can provide faster, safer and less vehicle-damaging links than unpaved roads, especially during extreme weather conditions such as high rainfall. However, the indicator quantifying paved roads fails to take account of road surface quality, including the status of maintenance, road support services, road connectivity to key centres and safety standards. Nevertheless, data on paved roads are readily available from national and regional authorities.

Road safety – While not an infrastructure indicator per se, road safety trends can shed light on the quality and reliability of the road network. In addition, road crashes represent a cost to the economy. Adopting safety standards that can be highlighted by benchmarking analysis can minimise this cost. The OECD hosts the IRTAD database, collecting detailed information on road safety worldwide.

Road quality – The international Road Assessment Programme (iRAP) is active in over 70 countries worldwide to measure the quality of road networks. iRAP Star Ratings involve an inspection of road infrastructure attributes that are known to have an impact on the likelihood of a crash and its severity. A ranking of between one star and five stars is awarded depending on the level of risk that is "built in" to the road. The lowest-risk roads (four- and five-star) have road safety attributes that are appropriate for the prevailing traffic speeds. The highest-risk roads (one- and two-star) do not have road safety attributes that are appropriate for the prevailing traffic speeds. Information about road attributes is collected by conducting video surveys of roads and subsequently recording data in categorical form at 100-metre intervals along the road. The road attributes include speed limit, curvature, intersections and sidewalks. Road attribute risk factors are combined with the road attribute data in multiplicative equations to produce Star Rating scores for vehicle occupants, motorcyclists, pedestrians and bicyclists for each 100-metre segment of road. These scores are then assigned range bands to produce Star Ratings, which therefore reflect a mix of road safety and road quality characteristics. The primary performance indicator being used worldwide is the percentage of travel on three-star or better roads for all road users. iRAP's indicators are linked to the UN Sustainable Development Goals.

Port turnaround times – The performance of port infrastructure is measured by a mix of commercially owned and publicly available indicators of efficiency. One of those measures is ship turnaround times, an indicator published by Lloyds Intelligence Unit, covering >95% of all vessels' movements. This captures the time spent by vessels at ports, including dwell time. Quicker turnaround and container loading times translate into more efficient port operations and lower costs for shipping lines. The average ship turn-around time of world container ports was 1.03 days in 2014. Although ship turnaround times give some indication of the efficiency of ports, some of the variation of the indicators could result from differences in ship size calling ports, which can only be addressed through detailed analysis.

Modal split – One of the indicators of the relative competitiveness of a transport mode compared to others is modal split. This is often used to characterise the road/rail/coastal shipping shares in domestic freight transport and the car/public transport shares for travel in cities. Modal split indicators need to be interpreted carefully. Among the most relevant issues is the "contestability" of traffic in a trade corridor. The availability or absence of competitive modes is fundamental to any comparison; in many cases, rail service may not be available or accessible because of an absence of track, sidings, terminals, etc. Second, mode split and choice need to be carefully assessed based on the commodities involved and the markets served. Some goods and commodities are much better suited to carriage by one mode than another. Supply chains and distribution patterns also determine which modes are relevant. Modal splits can be calculated based on overall traffic data, but splits are more meaningful when they are disaggregated into relevant markets.

Modal split and social inequality constitute a national policy priority. Providing high-quality public transport is frequently employed as a tool for promoting equality of opportunity to access jobs and services in urban areas. The availability and quality of public transport services, reflected in the modal split, are therefore relevant to social equality goals.

Environmental performance indicators – The performance of transport networks encompasses their ability to minimise negative externalities that are a common by-product of transport activity, including environmental externalities. The OECD Environment Directorate manages a database of transport-related emissions, allowing comparisons across countries and regions on relative environmental performance.

Other information sources

Further information collected through stakeholder interviews and a literature review supports the quantitative analysis undertaken as part of this study. Two OECD missions to Chile were organised to interview stakeholders in the public and private sectors. These sources were crucial to identifying examples of infrastructure gaps, framework conditions and long-term policies, as well as collecting missing information, particularly considering poor data availability for some sectors and/or macrozones.

In addition to identifying the sectors or areas in which Chile is lagging behind its comparators, we carry out **complementary analysis to shed light on the historical, financial and institutional arrangements that have determined investment levels and infrastructure performance in comparator countries**. Throughout the report and in Annex B, we provide some case-specific examples of those policy framework conditions that helped "best-in-class" comparators to achieve the levels of economic performance and infrastructure they currently enjoy. We also present examples of persisting challenges in OECD comparators.

Strategic assumptions

The analysis presented in this chapter and the policy recommendations that derive from it are based on the assumption that Chile's underlying economic and demographic trends will continue into the future. Given this assumption, the analysis and policy recommendations reflect a business-as-usual scenario, incorporating current elements such as a heavy reliance on exports for economic growth, high levels of urbanisation and uneven distribution of natural resources.

Planners and policy makers in Chile must prepare for a range of alternative scenarios considering the potentially disruptive impact that emerging trends may have on the country's economy, natural resources and population. These trends include climate change and its impact on water, arable land and temperatures; technological innovation in the form of digitalisation and automation; and demographic changes, including ageing and international migration. Considering the likelihood and magnitude of impacts from these trends is beyond the scope of this chapter, but such considerations should be part of the development and future-proofing of Plan Chile 30/30.

Analysis and results

Chile's transport infrastructure endowment, demand and capacity projections

Chile's transport infrastructure has improved considerably over past decades, and the country has a good transport infrastructure base. Concession-based PPPs have helped attract large private investment in the upgrades of motorways, ports and airports. Road infrastructure spending averaged 1.35% of GDP over 2008-2013 (more than double the share of GDP in comparator OECD countries, see Figures 4.3 and 4.4), container port capacity doubled between 2004 and 2013, and airports cater for record passenger numbers. In parallel, a number of initiatives have improved, upgraded or expanded the range of public transport in Chilean cities, with major improvements in Santiago.

However, gaps in the provision and quality of infrastructure and related services are still present, affecting all modes of transport. The following sections provide detail on the nature of the shortcomings and their extent in comparison to other OECD countries. By way of introduction, available international comparisons are helpful to set the scene, as they offer an indication of the extent to which Chile needs to improve its transport infrastructure and which sectors have the widest gaps with global comparators.

The World Economic Forum's Global Competitiveness Index (GCI) shows that Chile's overall infrastructure score is relatively high, with considerable variation across modes. Rail infrastructure is rated particularly low, and airport infrastructure is rated the highest. Looking at a more detailed breakdown of responses (Figure 4.5), the dissatisfaction with rail services is very clear. In comparison to selected OECD peers, Chile is second from the bottom, although road infrastructure is considered to be of better quality than that in Australia and New Zealand, and port infrastructure quality is higher than that in Italy. We highlight that the GCI reflects perceptions by business leaders rather than physical availability.

The World Bank's Logistics Performance Index (LPI) shows that Chile has been among the top 50 countries globally for logistics and customs in the past four editions of the index. The LPI is widely used to highlight the efficiency of the national logistics industry. The LPI score is based on a qualitative survey of the opinions of users of the transport and logistics systems. Therefore, the LPI is not an absolute indicator of efficiency, but it can be used for comparisons across 160 countries, particularly to identify challenges and opportunities related to transport infrastructure, logistics competence and the efficiency of supply chains. Multi-national companies use the LPI as an input for decisions on where to locate various types of operations (Ojala, 2015).

In conjunction, the GCI and the LPI results indicate that Chile's logistics competitiveness can be improved further. A gap emerges when Chile is compared to selected OECD countries. ITF/OECD (2016c) recently highlighted the determinants of logistics performance that are particularly weak. Analysis showed that these weaknesses include a host of variables related to trade facilitation and regulatory issues, rather than simply infrastructure provision, including ease of arranging shipments; quality and competence of services; timeliness of deliveries, especially for international transport; and high costs of cross-border shipments.

Figure 4.3. Rail and road investment and maintenance spending as a % of GDP, 2000-2014

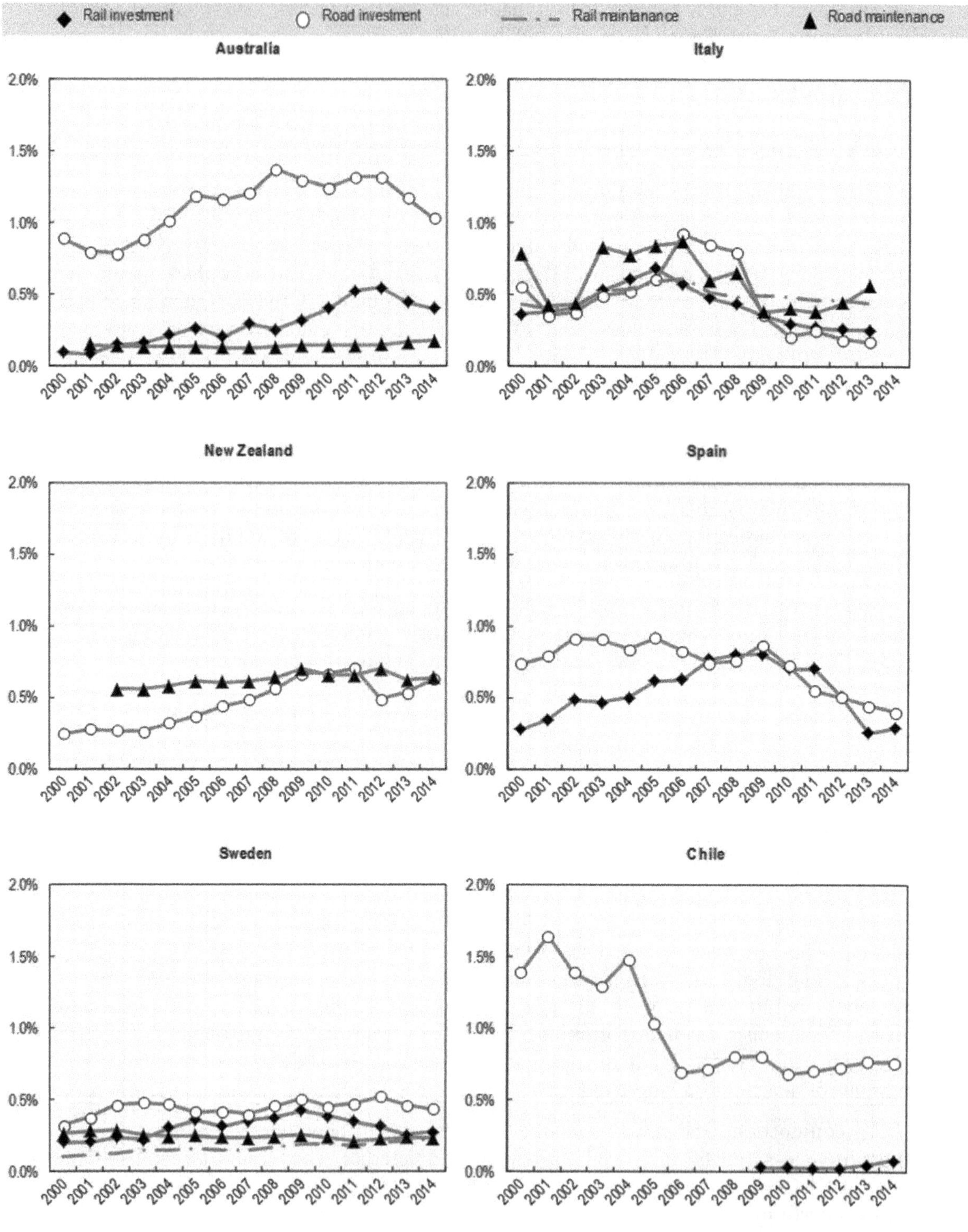

Notes: data include both private and government investment. Australia: road investment includes tarmac at airports. Chile: rail investment does not include metro. Italy: road investment and maintenance do not include urban roads. Sweden: road investment does not include private local roads; rail investment includes trams and metros. New Zealand: data refer to fiscal years ending on 30 June.

Source: OECD (2016c), Ministerio de Obras Públicas (2016b) and Grupo EFE (2016).

Figure 4.4. Rail and road average infrastructure investment as a % of GDP, 2000-2014

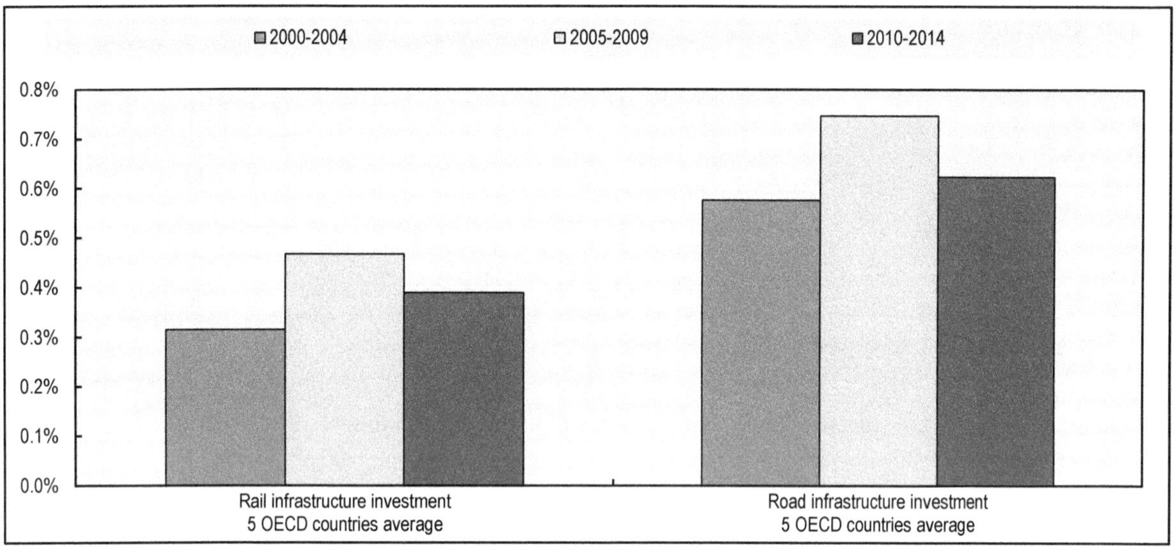

Notes: OECD average includes Australia, Italy, New Zealand, Spain and Sweden. Data include both private and government investment. Australia: road investment includes tarmac at airports. Italy: road investment and maintenance do not include urban roads. Sweden: road investment does not include private local roads; rail investment includes trams and metros. New Zealand: data refer to fiscal years endng on June 30.

Source: OECD (2016c).

Figure 4.5. Global Competitiveness Index (1 = worst, 7 = best), 2015-2016 edition

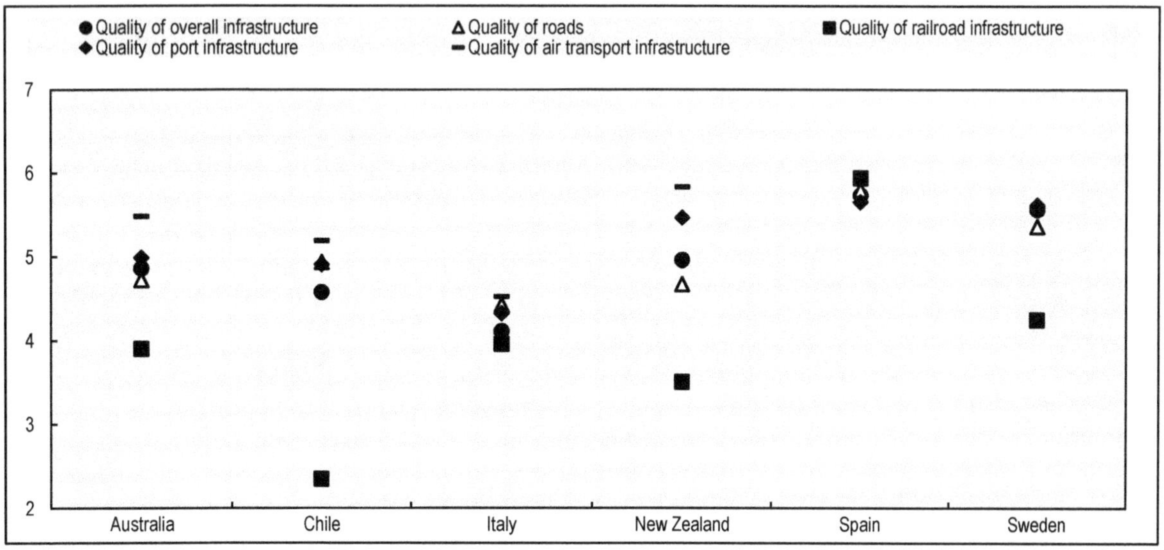

Source: World Economic Forum (2016).

Table 4.4. Quality of infrastructure, % of people responding low or very low, GCI 2015-16

	Chile	OECD average
Ports	0%	45%
Airports	17%	22%
Road	0%	25%
Rail	83%	48%
Warehousing	0%	10%
Telecommunications	29%	20%

Source: Chile's Productivity Commission (2016).

Figure 4.6. Logistic Performance Index (1= lowest, 5= highest), 2016 edition

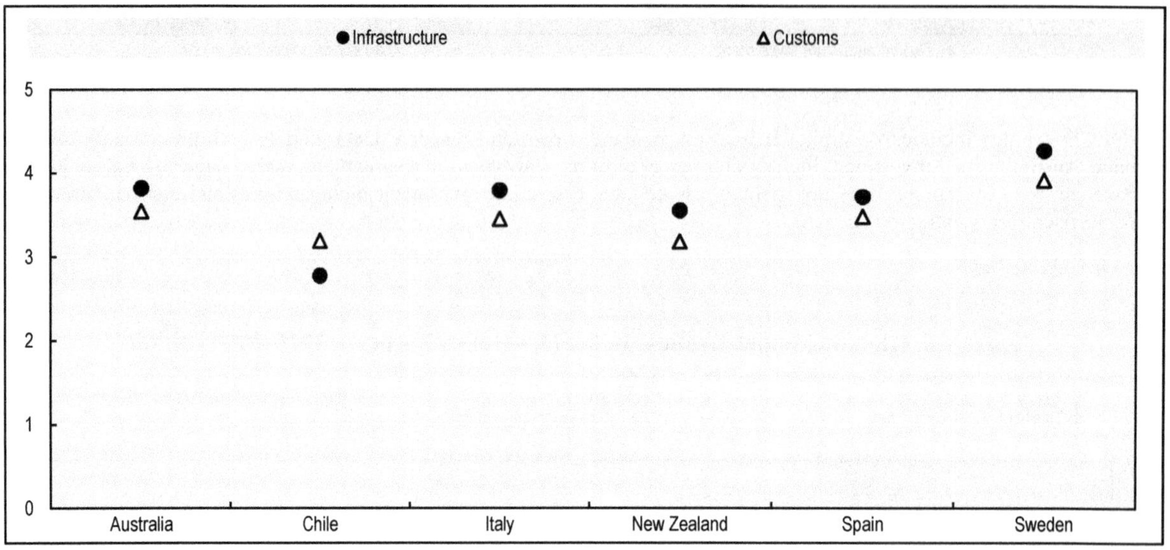

Source: World Bank (2016d).

Existing transport infrastructure in Chile needs to cope with continuous growth in transport demand. Figure 4.7 shows the growth in road traffic, port traffic and air traffic over the period 2005-2014. Freight-related movements by road and sea have grown at a similar pace (around 50% over the period), following a similar trend as average GDP. Passenger traffic by road (motorways only) and air has grown even faster over the same period.

Figure 4.7. Evolution of available transport volume indicators in Chile (2005 = 100)

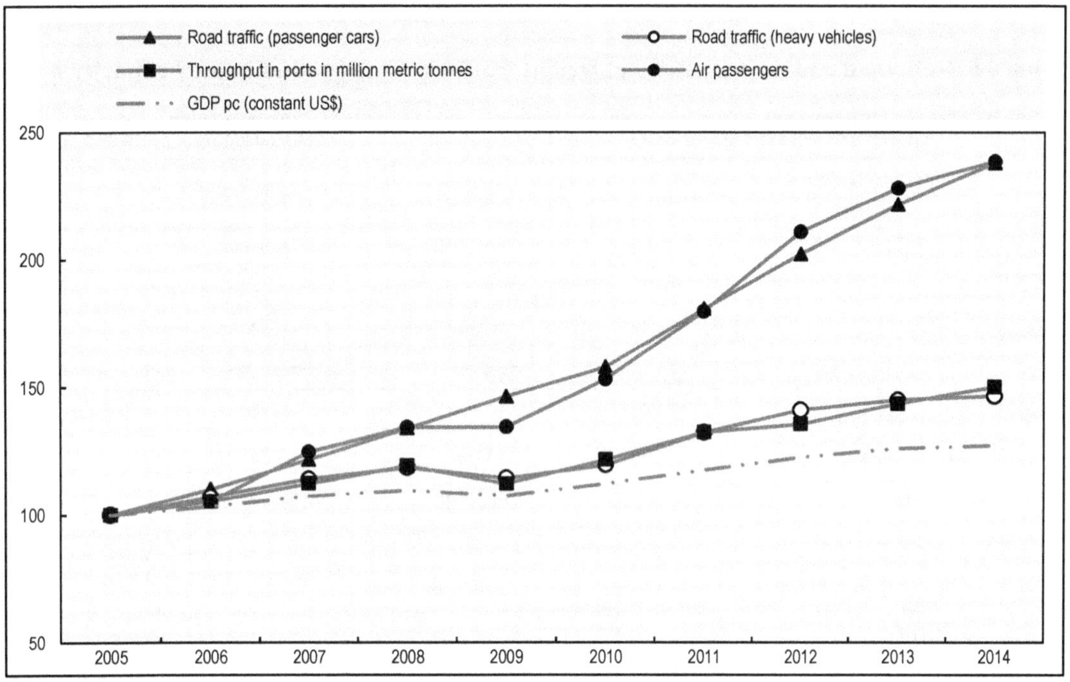

Note: road traffic is calculated as the number of vehicles counted at toll booths on inter-urban motorways.

Source: Road traffic: Instituto Nacional de Estadísticas de Chile (2016c). Throughput in ports: data elaborated by the ITF/OECD based on data from Lloyods Intelligence Unit. Air passenger: Junta de Aeronáutica Civil (2016). GDP: World Bank (2016e).

Looking ahead, the ITF Global Freight Model projections for Chile show a substantial increase in rail and road traffic linked to international trade between 2010 and 2030. Some of this growth has already materialised, although traffic growth has been weaker than expected since 2013, partly because of slower growth in trade volumes. The model indicates that:

- **rail infrastructure** will need considerable extra capacity to support projected growth – capacity will be needed for rail networks serving container ports and large cities
- **road infrastructure** serving international trade-related freight flows will be better able to cope with higher traffic levels – however, 27% extra capacity will be needed around key nodes
- capacity at **ports** will need to grow significantly – the projected capacity need (around 49% by 2030) is concentrated in the Central macrozone and will need to cater to larger container ships.

While these projections point to the need to increase capacity in selected infrastructure, they do not necessarily imply that nearly as much new infrastructure needs to be built. Chile's approach to capacity enhancements should reflect the current shift in transport policy from a "predict-and-provide" approach to a "demand-management" approach that combines investment, pricing and technological solutions to tackle capacity issues.4 The expansion of one type of transport infrastructure also affects the needs and hence the capacity required in other modes. Overall network capacity needs arise from the interaction of demand and modal split over time and across modes, thus requiring a co-ordinated approach to investment with a focus on key corridors and urban nodes.

Table 4.5. Rail, road and port (container) freight traffic in Chile, and estimated capacity needs

		Overall national estimate for Chile			Within 50 km from ports and large cities	
		Trade-related freight volumes	Capacity	% change	Capacity needs	% change
Rail		MO tonne-km	Track-km	Over 2010	Track-km	Over 2010
	2010	9 084	620	--	93	--
	2030	12 697	1 599	158%	291	211%
Road		MO tonne-km	Track-km	Over 2010	Track-km	Over 2010
	2010	59 653	17 240	--	1 760	--
	2030	84 652	19 066	11%	2 231	27%
Ports		MO TEUs	TEU capacity	Over 2010	TEU capacity	Over 2010
	2010	3.27	5.26	--	--	--
	2030	7.81	7.85	49%	--	--

Source: ITF/OECD (2016f).

These projections are also subject to several uncertainties, such as in relation to future economic growth and trade elasticities. The values provided should be viewed as the mid-point of a wide range. It is important to develop tools to adapt to these uncertainties. Tools include detailed national transport models to improve the precision of capacity projections. The possibility to adapt to uncertainties is served by flexible planning procedures within long-term strategic planning frameworks. In addition, it is critical for Chile to integrate the concepts of resilience and vulnerability, given the likelihood of natural disasters. Transport assets that integrate such considerations systemically can reduce potential uncertainties around supply shocks and temporary unavailability of infrastructure.

Road infrastructure

Key messages

Road infrastructure coverage and quality is uneven across Chile, and analysis suggests that targeted investment should be directed at addressing missing links and upgrading secondary roads. Some critical last-mile road links to ports and cities are missing, leading to bottlenecks, urban congestion and longer journey times for shippers.

Many regional and rural roads in all macrozones appear to be of low standards, although this is an issue linked not only to surface quality but also to safety features for all road users. Decisions on whether to pave more roads should be made in light of cost-benefit assessments; however, targeted investment is needed in rural and regional roads. Road authorities should adopt an incremental approach to road-paving solutions, taking into account connectivity needs, projected traffic growth and life-cycle costs, including future maintenance needs and safety implications (as Chile's performance is currently worse than OECD benchmarks). Over the next decade, maintenance needs will grow and could require a budget equivalent to that needed for investment. Multi-annual budgets that ring-fence routine maintenance of the road network should be introduced as in other OECD countries.

Sector overview

The Chilean road network is almost 80 500 km long and includes four main types of roads: private motorway concessions, publicly owned roads (categorised as national or regional, where the latter includes main, provincial, municipal and access roads). Notably, the MOP manages motorway concessions through its Concessions Division, and it designs, plans, builds and maintains public roads through its Roads Division.

Following a period of under-investment in road infrastructure, the government embarked on an ambitious franchising programme in the 1990s via build-operate-and-transfer (BOT) contracts. The main goal of the programme was to attract significant private investment to reduce the perceived deficit in road infrastructure (Engel et al., 2000). There is widespread agreement in Chile that the quality, capacity and resilience of Chile's motorway backbone is now of a high standard, thanks to the investment boost received in the 1990s and the provisions contained in long-term concession contracts to maintain the roads to high standards. Chile's road sector ranks 35th in the 2015 GCI (New Zealand: 43rd; Italy: 49th). This result may be disproportionately influenced by the good quality of motorways, as respondents to the GCI survey are more likely to use those roads.

Available data[5] show sustained growth in road transport over the past decade. Toll booth counts show a large increase in the number of vehicles travelling on motorways between 2005 and 2014 (+114% overall, with large increases in both cars and trucks). These figures match those on road motor vehicle fleets (Figures 4.8 and 4.9). The number of private cars has more than doubled over the past ten years, and there were 56% more registered trucks in 2014 than in 2005. Nonetheless, the number of passenger cars per 100 inhabitants in Chile is still 70% lower than in comparator countries in which average incomes have reached $30,000 per capita. Hence, growth in car ownership is expected to continue.

Figure 4.8. Stock of passenger cars per 100 inhabitants (2005 = 100)

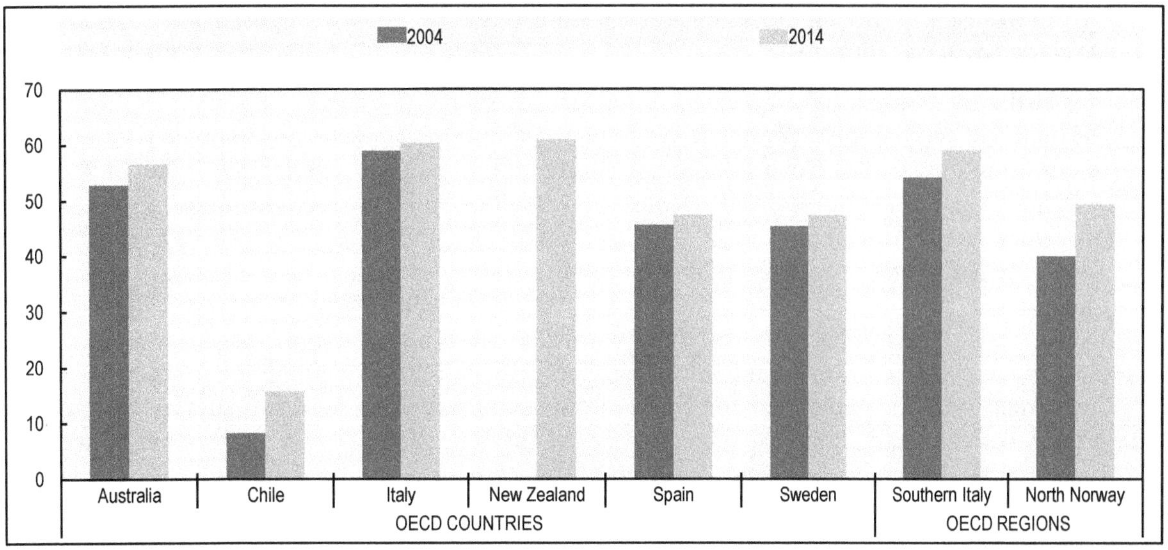

Source: Stock of passenger cars: ITF (2016a), ISTAT (2016c), Statistics Norway (2016c), Instituto Nacional de Estadísticas de Chile (2016d). Population: World Bank (2016a), ISTAT (2016a), Statistics Norway (2016a).

Figure 4.9. Stock of goods road motor vehicles per 100 inhabitants

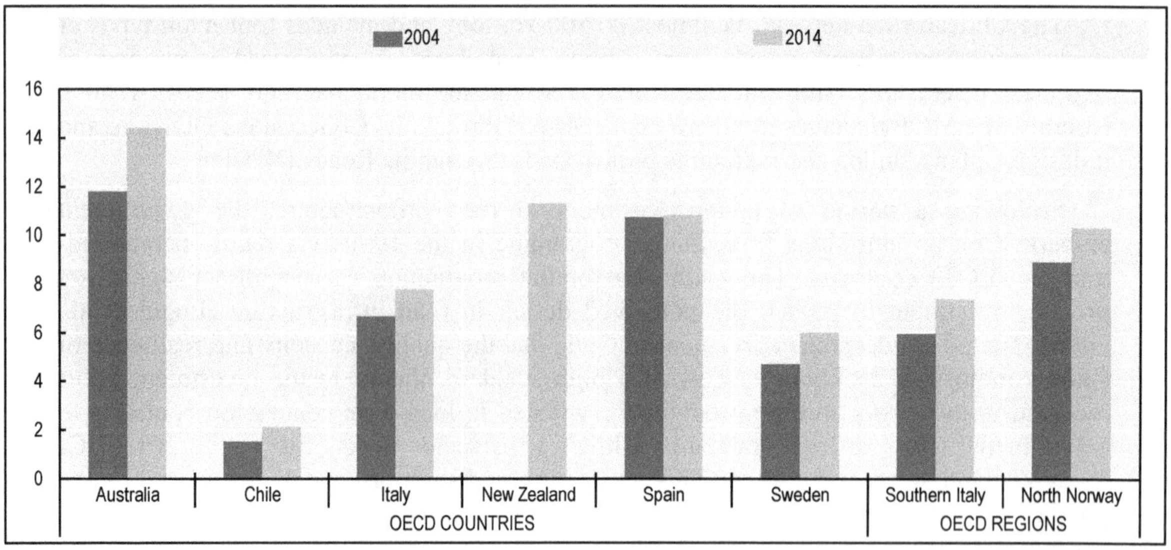

Note: goods road motor vehicles include vans, trucks, and road and agricultural tractors.

Source: Stock of passenger cars: ITF (2016a), ISTAT (2016c), Statistics Norway (2016c), Instituto Nacional de Estadísticas de Chile (2016d). Population: World Bank (2016a), ISTAT (2016a), Statistics Norway (2016a).

The maintenance and building of roads outside concession schemes receive around 80% of MOP's expenditures, with a strong focus on enhancing the standards of public roads. Targeted investment is being rolled out to improve the surface quality of rural roads in particular. Since the early 2000s, the MOP has deployed a large programme to provide lower-cost solutions ("*soluciones básicas*") to paving roads with traffic flows below 500 in average annual daily traffic (AADT).[6] This solution had been applied to over 10 000 km by 2014, and the programme aims to cover a further 15 000 km by 2018. Investment in *soluciones básicas* is not subject to the BCR thresholds normally imposed by the Ministry of Social Development and is considered of high importance to reduce isolation and inequality.

At the other end of the spectrum lie a number of mega-projects to enhance Chile's national and international connectivity. Some of the larger projects are planned in more remote areas of Chile. Road concessions have not previously been established in the extreme South and North of the country; therefore, the connectivity improvements necessary to reduce isolation and support trade in these regions rely on central government funding. There are plans to connect remote areas in Chile's Austral region, including a new bridge across the Chacao Channel and a new *Carretera Austral*. Developing international connectivity by road is also high on the agenda following agreements between Chile and its neighbours. Several passes along the border with Argentina will be upgraded or built from scratch with the aim of facilitating intra-American trade, some of those as part of the so-called *Corredor Bioceanico* (see Box 4.4). Connectivity between the northern macrozone and neighbouring states (Perú and Bolivia) will also be strengthened.

Box 4.4. The Bioceanic Corridor Mercosur Chile

The 1996 Economic Complementation Agreement between Chile and other Latin American countries stipulates that Mercosur states and Chile are committed to developing infrastructure links to strengthen so-called bioceanic corridors (Pacific Ocean to Atlantic Ocean). To do so, the countries are required to "improve and diversify" land connections and to stimulate the development of infrastructure such as greater port capacities.

This commitment implies greater international co-ordination in physical infrastructure and in trading rules. With respect to infrastructure, this translates into the need to upgrade the quality, capacity and resilience of road infrastructure across the Andes to facilitate trade-related freight flows, especially to the ports in central-southern Chile. Two key projects in the pipeline are:

Paso de Las Leñas, an 11-km base tunnel (altitude: 2 000 m) linking the southern part of Mendoza province in Argentina with the O'Higgins region in Chile.

Tunel de Agua Negra, a 14-km tunnel (altitude between 3 600 and 4 100 m) linking the province of San Juan in Argentina with the region of Coquimbo in Chile.

The new tunnels will enable freight movements even in extreme winter conditions and are intended primarily to serve trade flows to and from the port of San Antonio, providing an alternative to the Paso de Los Libertadores, situated closer to the Port of Valparaiso but often closed in the winter. As European experience shows, the success of international freight corridors depends on the ability of new infrastructure to address bottlenecks and offer an attractive alternative to existing routes.

As they strengthen bioceanic corridors, Chile and its neighbours should adopt an integrated, multi-modal approach to ensuring that the entire logistics chain benefits from targeted cross-border investment in terms of reduced congestion, faster journey times and more reliable travel conditions. Lessons from the EU show that, unless co-ordinated management and intermodal integration are achieved, the potential of international freight corridors will be unmet.

Source: Ministerio de Obras Públicas (2016), "*Hacia un país con desarrollo equilibrado*"; Ministerio de Transporte y Telecomunicaciones (2013), *"Conectando Chile"*.

Identified gaps

When looking at the overall density of roads per capita and by area (Figures 4.10 and 4.11), Chile ranks last among OECD comparators. However, the ITF Global Freight Model's projections show that road infrastructure serving international trade-related freight flows will need to increase by only around 10% by 2030 to cope with increased traffic. The implication of looking at these indicators in conjunction is that, although below OECD average, the overall road stock at the national level may be sufficient, but its varying degrees of quality and the presence of missing links require targeted investment.

The presence of gaps with respect to road infrastructure coverage, quality and capacity is better described in terms of geography and road type. In comparison to each benchmarking country or region, the Central and Southern macrozones in Chile show a lower road coverage by area and by population. Road density in the Northern macrozone is on par with Western Australia, but roads per capita are significantly lower. The Austral macrozone has similar levels of road provision to its comparators. From the point of view of road coverage, regional differences emerge, and the Central and Southern macrozones appear to have the largest gap.

Road coverage should be looked at in conjunction with road quality; the share of paved roads is one of the available quality indicators. Again, the national result for Chile shows that the share of paved roads is the lowest among comparators. However, it is the Southern and Austral macrozones that fare worst, with just 25% of paved roads, even when roads with thin surface layers are included in the paved category.

Figure 4.10. Density of road network (km of roads per km²), latest available year

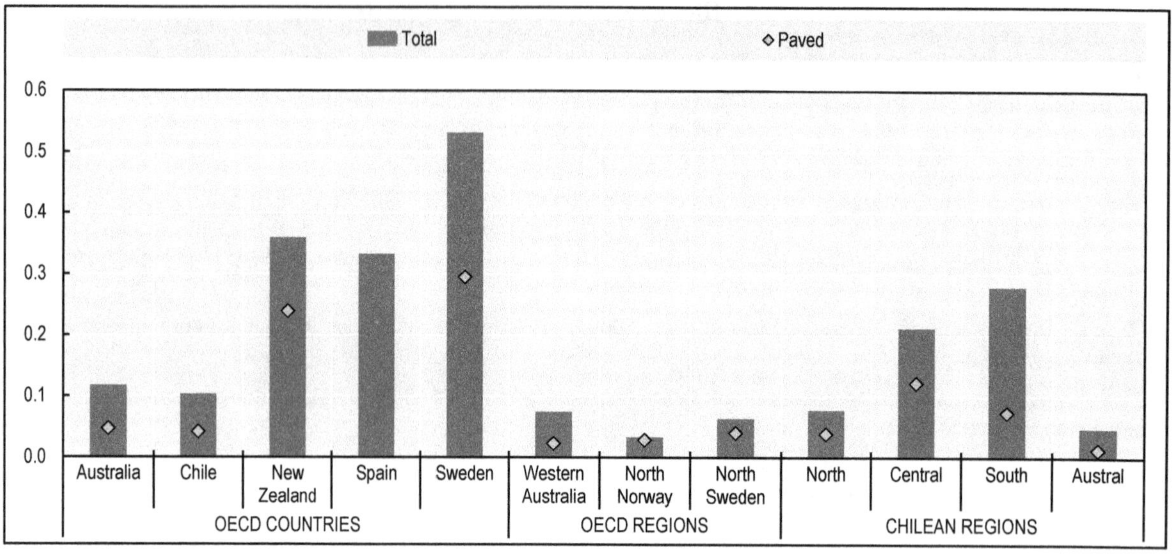

Source: Road network: BITRE (2013), Ministerio de Obras Públicas (2016c), ITF (2016b), Ministerio de Fomento (2016), Statistics Sweden (2016d), Mainroads Western Australia (2015), Roadex (2000), CIA (2016). Land area: World Bank (2016b), Australian Bureau of Statistics (2016b), Statistics Norway (2016a), Statistics Sweden (2016b), Instituto Nacional de Estadísticas de Chile (2016b).

Figure 4.11. Density of road network (km of roads per 1 000 inhabitants), latest available year

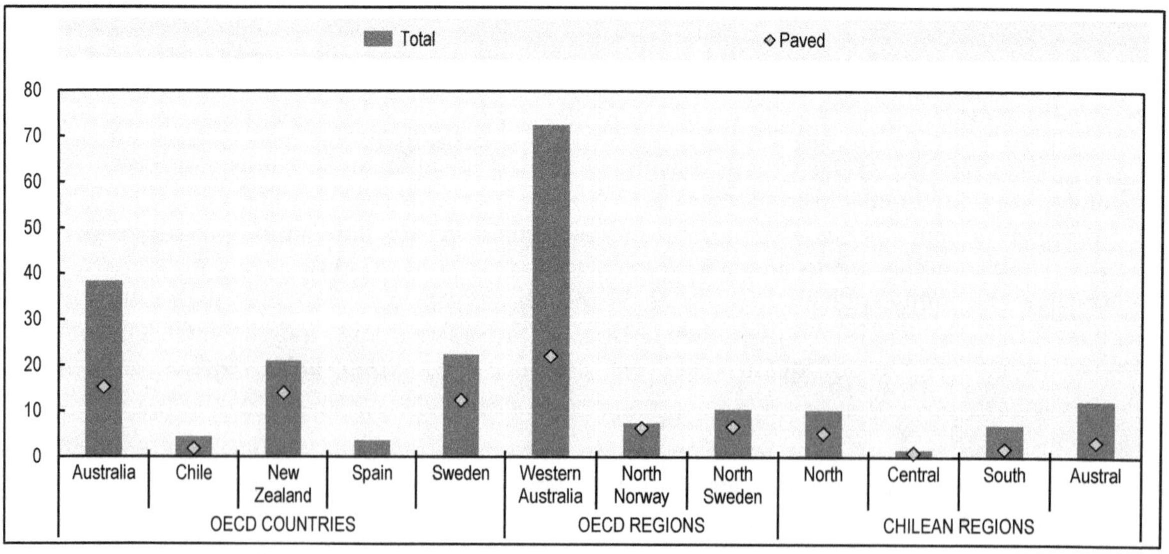

Source: Road network: BITRE (2013), Ministerio de Obras Públicas (2016c), ITF (2016b), Ministerio de Fomento (2016), Statistics Sweden (2016d), Mainroads Western Australia (2015), Roadex (2000), CIA (2016). Population: World Bank (2016a), Australia Bureau of Statistics (2016a), Statistics Norway (2016a), Statistics Sweden (2016a), Instituto Nacional de Estadísticas de Chile (2016a).

Private and public investment in those regions has been historically lower than in the North and Centre for different reasons. Concessions stopped at Puerto Montt given the low appetite for private investment in lower-density regions, and public actors have traditionally found it hard to justify government spending based on established socio-economic assessment criteria, due to low densities and fragmented territories.

Investment in infrastructure for regional development will often show relatively low internal rates of return. This does not mean that CBA should not be used to help establish priorities among projects, as higher rates of return reflect benefits to larger numbers of people, among other things. However, as discussed elsewhere, additional mechanisms will need to be employed to determine the distribution of public funds for infrastructure to address issues of equity.

When publicly funded investment in roads is determined to be needed for regional development, it does not follow that design standards should be lowered to reduce costs. In Italy, the southernmost stretch of the national highway network (A3 motorway) required direct investment, ownership and management by the State because expected returns were too low to support a private concession. However, the quality and safety design standards for the A3 motorway turned out to be sub-optimal following the car ownership boom of the 1970s and 1980s. Following piecemeal adjustments including widening, overhead bridges, improved safety and new emergency lanes, this has damaged the competitiveness of Southern Italy in two ways: first, by undermining connectivity on a key north-south axis for prolonged periods of time during makeover works; and second, by diverting financial resources away from other infrastructure projects in the area to fill this gap.

Figure 4.12. Share of paved roads, latest available year

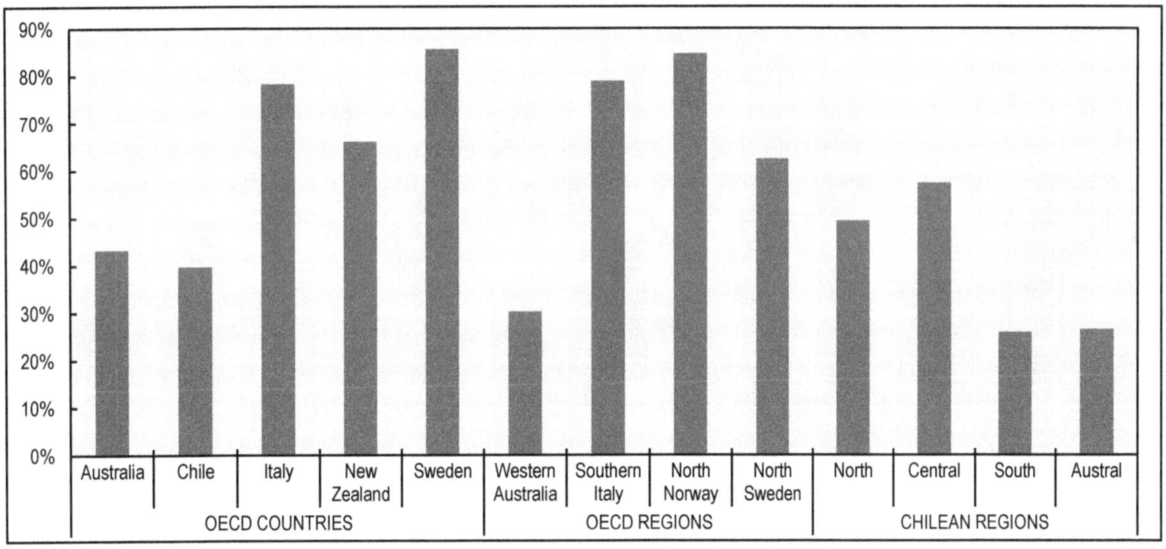

Notes: data exclude privately owned roads. In Chile, paved roads include "*soluciones básicas*".

Source: CIA (2016), Ministerio de Obras Públicas (2016c), SITEB (2012), Trafikverket (2016), Mainroads Western Australia (2015), Roadex (2000).

Within each macrozone, different types of roads show varying degrees of quality, as detailed by analysis carried out by iRAP. As Figure 4.13 shows, more than 60% of high-traffic-volume traffic roads are of good quality (three stars or above) in Central Chile. However, the share of undivided carriageway roads carrying low traffic volumes (encompassing most regional and rural roads) that is assessed to be of good quality is very low in the Southern and Austral regions compared to Central Chile (15%, 19% and 40%, respectively). In a different version of the iRAP assessment, which allows for international comparisons, even Central Chile is below best-in-class with respect to low-traffic, undivided roads. Only 24% of secondary roads are of good quality compared to 35% in Catalonia (for which data are available), although New Zealand has a worse score, with only 6% of these roads rated as good quality. Conversely, Northern Chile has higher ratings than both Central Chile and its comparators, including Western Australia.

Overall, iRAP ratings paint a national picture in which secondary roads are of much worse quality than primary roads in three macrozones, especially those with a lower share of paved roads. Within Chile, the analysis shows a 30% gap in road quality between the southern part of Chile and the centre. In an international perspective, however, Central Chile may in turn be lagging behind comparators such as Catalonia and hence might not be the standard setter. More in-depth analysis suggests the specific features that contribute to poor ratings for regional and rural roads. For instance, iRAP data show that more than 70% of curves on undivided rural roads where traffic flows at >80 km/h have hazardous roadsides across Chilean macrozones. The equivalent value for New Zealand and Catalonia ranges between 20% and 30% only. Roadsides need upgrading, and in the meantime, speeds should be restricted for compatibility with the design of the infrastructure.

Figure 4.13. Roads rated three stars or better for vehicle occupants (iRAP model V2)

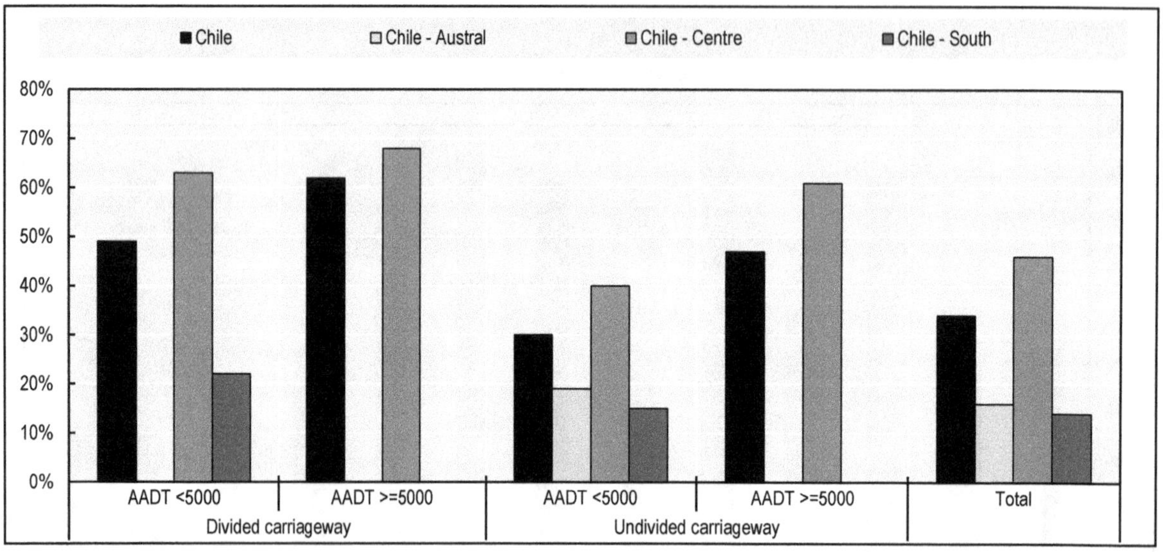

Notes: V2 and V3 stars are not directly comparable. AADT = average annual daily traffic.

Source: IRAP (2016).

Chile's road safety record also reflects the poor quality of these roads (see Box 4.5), whereby the highest number of fatalities arises on non-urban, non-motorway roads, despite lower levels of traffic. Chile has the worst rate of road fatalities (12 deaths per 100 000 inhabitants in 2014, 2.5 times higher than the average for our comparator countries) and the slowest rate of reduction of this indicator for the period 2004-2014 (-17% compared to -48% on average across OECD comparators).

Figure 4.14. Roads rated three stars or better for vehicle occupants (iRAP model V3)

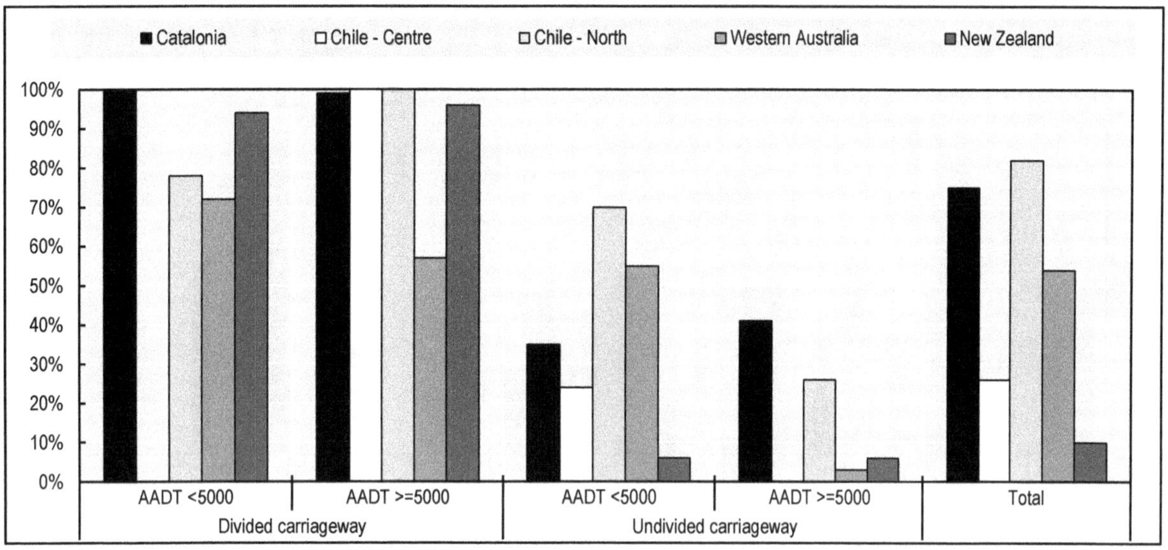

Notes: V2 and V3 stars are not directly comparable. AADT = average annual daily traffic.

Source: IRAP (2016).

Figure 4.15. Curves on rural roads on which traffic flows at >80 km/h that have hazardous roadsides

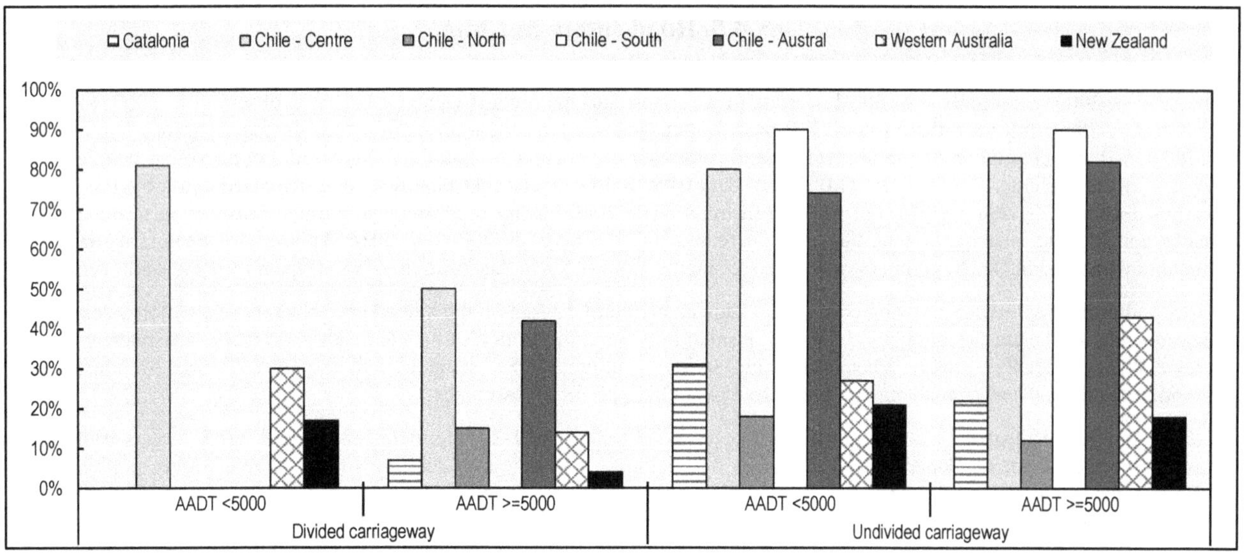

Note: AADT = average annual daily traffic.

Source: IRAP (2016).

Figure 4.16. Number of road fatalities per 100 000 inhabitants, 2004, 2010 and 2014

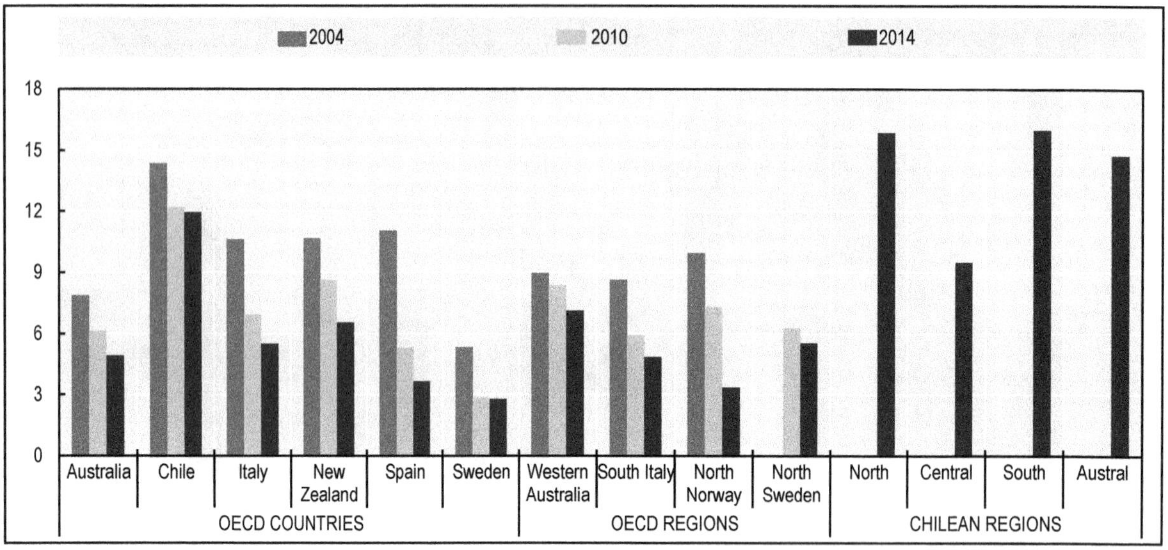

Note: Fatalities correspond to death within 30 days after the accident.

Source – Road fatalities: ITF (2016c), Instituto Nacional de Estadísticas de Chile (2016e), BITRE (2016a), ISTAT (2016d), Statistics Norway (2016d), Transportstyrelsen (2016). Population: World Bank (2016a), Australia Bureau of Statistics (2016a), ISTAT (2016a), Statistics Norway (2016a), Statistics Sweden (2016a), Instituto Nacional de Estadísticas de Chile (2016a).

Box 4.5. Road safety in Chile

Between 2000 and 2014, road fatalities in Chile fluctuated, with no clear trend emerging. The lowest value (1 960) was observed in 2009, potentially linked to lower traffic volumes, and the highest value (2 317) was observed in 2008. In 2014, the latest available full year, there were 2 119 road deaths. Year on year, the number of deaths decreased among cyclists and pedestrians but increased among motorcyclists and passenger car occupants. Fatalities increased among young people (0-14 years old) and the elderly (65+ years old). Initial data from 2015 indicate that fatalities have increased again by 1%. Injury crashes decreased by 2% in 2014, but the overall trend since 2000 has been an increasing one. Measured in terms of road deaths per 100 000 inhabitants, fatalities have decreased by 17% between 2004 and 2014. This rate of decline is far lower than that witnessed in OECD comparator countries, ranging from -37% in Australia to -67% in Spain over the same period.

Road deaths represent a growing cost for the Chilean economy. Based on the human capital approach, which assesses the consequences of the crashes based on the loss of productivity resulting from a statistical death, road crash costs were equal to around 0.2% of GDP in 2013. When killed and seriously injured (KSI) statistics and the related costs of injuries are considered, the total cost of road crashes grows to 3% of GDP, per iRAP estimates.

At the mid-point of the UN Decade of Action for Road Safety 2011-20, the inclusion of road safety targets in the UN Sustainable Development Goals (SDGs) enhances the visibility, urgency and ambition of global road safety policy. Most countries have national road safety strategies with ambitious targets in place, and many of these are aligned with the objectives of the Decade of Action. Notable examples are *Safe System* approaches in countries such as the UK and *Vision Zero* in countries such as Sweden. In April 2016, the UN General Assembly confirmed SDG 3.2 in Resolution 70/260, which aims to reduce global road traffic deaths and injuries by 50% by 2020 compared to their 2010 levels.

In 2012, the Chilean government introduced a new law on drinking and driving, setting the maximum permissible blood alcohol content (BAC) at 0.3 g/l. Two important measures were further implemented in 2014: the reform of the driving licence procedure, with new theoretical and practical exams, and the adoption of more severe punishment for drunk drivers who cause serious injuries or death (including one year or more in prison).

Building on these regulatory changes, Chile is currently developing a National Road Safety Strategy, led by the National Road Safety Commission (CONASET), aligned with the UN SDGs. The new strategy will need to ensure that legislation, education and construction efforts towards greater road safety are joined together. This could include developing a reference model based on criteria for safe road transport standards, setting the goal to close the gap between existing road quality standards and this reference model.

Source: ITF/OECD (2016d); iRAP (2016).

The second type of road infrastructure that shows some gaps with OECD comparators is connecting infrastructure, such as road links between ports and the motorway network, between urban motorway concessions and urban public roads, and between national and international roads. Numerous examples were provided by stakeholders during the interviews held in Chile, highlighting gaps between regions and cities of Chile. The examples of good practice provided in Annex B also show that investment in connecting infrastructure and "last-mile" has been made a top priority in the transport strategies of comparator OECD countries over the past decade.

For instance, the quality of port access roads can vary greatly, as is evident when comparing the roads linking the Port of San Antonio to Route 78 (where trucks need to drive through narrow city streets with road surfaces that are deteriorating fast due to the lack of maintenance) with the high-quality, dedicated tunnelled access to Route 68 from the Port of Valparaiso (*Camino de la Polvora*). Lower-quality access to the port of San Antonio increases congestion and pollution across the city, and it raises transport costs.

Figure 4.17. Road and rail links between Central ports and Santiago

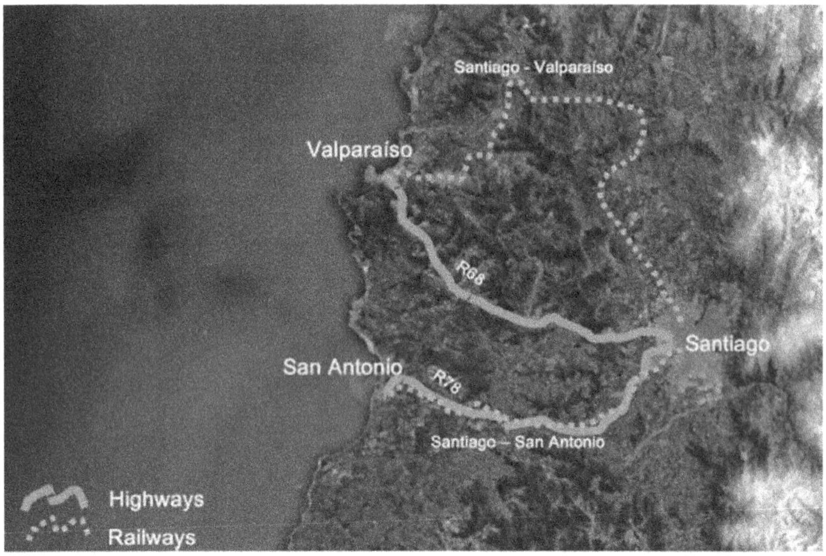

Source: MTT elaboration.

The interface between intercity motorways and urban roads is often problematic and creates bottlenecks at major access points in urban areas. Examples include links between motorway bypasses and urban arteries in Santiago, the incomplete ring-road in Valparaiso, and gaps in the trunk road network between the urban areas of Coquimbo and La Serena, including on roads carrying traffic to the port of Coquimbo along Route 5. The gaps in Coquimbo-La Serena create bottlenecks for urban residents when mixed car and truck traffic surges at peak times and results in longer journey times than would be the case with better links or specific policies aimed at targeting congestion.

Some of these gaps in Chile are the result of fragmented governance arrangements. For instance, port authorities only exercise their functions within port areas and are not responsible for access roads, whose funding relies on either MOP or municipal funding. The city authorities' ability to invest is hampered by financial constraints and unclear governance arrangements over the roles and responsibilities for those roads (see Chapter 2).

Examples of good practice encompass models of co-operation between ports and different tiers of government as well as restructuring of responsibilities. In Australia, the WestConnex project aims to provide progressive upgrades in the motorway network linked to the Port of Sydney between 2015 and 2023. The project is funded with a mix of distance-based tolls on all vehicles, including trucks; an availability charge from the New South Wales Government; and a grant from the Australian Government. In New Zealand, uncoordinated planning for transport and land use was the main rationale for merging the eight previous bodies governing the Auckland metropolitan area into a single body, the new Auckland Council. The council was required to develop the Auckland Plan, which, among other things, sets out co-ordinated strategies for building infrastructure to reduce Auckland's congestion, particularly in relation to port traffic, over the next 30 years.

Conclusions on road infrastructure

Results from the ITF Global Freight Model confirm the need to invest in additional road capacity around maritime and population hubs. Our projections suggest that one-quarter of the additional road capacity required by 2030 will be needed in the proximity of ports and large cities, translating into a 27% increase for these types of roads compared with 2010.

Importantly, the need for maintenance across all roads will grow over time. In the case of motorway concessions, existing contracts are already in place to ensure that the concession holders have asset management plans for the appropriate level of scheduled maintenance and that toll revenues provide sufficient funds for those activities.

A large-scale implementation of thin paving solutions could create a serious gap with respect to maintenance in the long run. For public roads, the ambitious roll-out plan for sealing surfaces at lower costs (*caminos básicos*) across the non-metropolitan areas of Chile is seen as a short-term option to address the current gap in road surface quality on secondary roads. However, these low-cost treatments are susceptible to accelerated wear and vulnerable to severe damage from excess loads, as the experience in Sweden in the 1980s has shown. Hence, the MOP would be required either to impose strict bans on heavy vehicles on these roads or to allocate an increasing share of its budget to road surface treatment (see Box 4.6), in addition to the increase in maintenance needs foreseen along the typical road wear cycle. A focus on incremental improvements to the network to standard levels of pavement quality and thickness, based on clearly defined criteria such as connectivity to transport hubs and current and projected traffic levels, would appear to be a more sustainable policy.

Box 4.6. To pave or not to pave, and to which standards? The case of Sweden

Decisions on whether to pave or not to pave roads, and to which standards, are often based on current and projected traffic flows. However, through neglecting future phases of the project lifecycle including operation and maintenance, countries run the risk of over-investing in new infrastructure, under-investing in maintenance, operating infrastructure inefficiently and under-estimating costs (see Chapter 2, Section 1.6). For road surfaces, a whole-of-life approach should be adopted to include the impact of different paving solutions on long-run maintenance needs and road users' safety.

The maintenance needs of a road network can be predicted fairly accurately from a set of structural characteristics, including age, climate, traffic, design standards, construction quality and subsequent maintenance. First, maintenance needs differ for paved and unpaved roads. For paved roads, there is a trade-off between higher investment costs at the time of paving and lower subsequent maintenance costs, and vice-versa. Unpaved roads, such as gravel roads, cost as much as three times less than paved surfaces to build but require more frequent maintenance, especially in areas with extreme weather conditions such as heavy rainfall.

Box 4.6. To pave or not to pave, and to which standards? The case of Sweden *(cont.)*

Experience from OECD countries shows that age is particularly important to the condition of paved roads because of the time path of their deterioration. Following a period of large-scale road construction, a grace period of several years – during which roads remain in good condition even without maintenance – is followed by a period in which the need for maintenance surges. In many European countries, the need for maintenance has coincided with budgetary pressures due to financial crises. The result has been a fast deterioration of road surface quality over the past decade. In countries with fast-expanding economies, traffic growth is instead one of the key determinants of road conditions.

In Sweden during the 1980s, most low-traffic-volume roads were paved with thinner and weaker structures, mainly using "Y1G" (surface dressing with one layer, 0-18 mm – a layer of stone is stuck with bitumen emulsion on the underlying gravel layer). The Y1G method was aimed at gravel roads to make the surface more even and reduce dust.

Although cheaper, the Y1G method revealed its limitations over time. Gravel roads on which the solution was applied were not built with the appropriate standards, and new surfaces were already subject to heavy damage after a few years, especially in frost-sensitive areas like Northern Sweden. It was then necessary to impose bearing capacity restrictions (12-ton maximum weight), particularly during the spring thaw. This negatively affected transport by heavy vehicles dependent on these roads.

Thin-layer paving solutions were almost entirely abandoned in Sweden as a result of this experience, which highlighted the risks of using thin layers directly on gravel roads. Thin layers today are used only for bituminous road surfaces and only when the road has good bearing capacity, a base course and good drainage. Importantly, thin layers are applied only on roads with very low AADT (below 250) and almost no heavy traffic. In Chile, some roads with AADT of up to 400 can be beneficiaries of *soluciones básicas*.

The experience of Sweden can provide valuable lessons to policy makers in Chile and points to the importance of a whole-cost approach when assessing options for road surfaces. While it is no substitute to applying sound CBA to sift and prioritise investment based on Net Present Values, this approach requires balancing considerations of the short-term benefits for road users and the future impacts, including on maintenance budgets. In the case of *soluciones básicas*, the appropriate standards should be set with a view on current and future traffic levels and the expected degree of deterioration given this forecast utilisation.

Source: World Bank (1988, 2005, 2009); Written submission to the ITF/OECD by Trafikverket officials.

Port infrastructure

Key message

Port infrastructure is fundamental to the success of Chilean exports, and improvements in port efficiency and investment in hinterland connectivity are needed to support projected growth. Given the expected growth in trade-related flows and changes in average vessel size, capacity for growth is needed, especially in the Central macrozone. Compared with ports in OECD countries, the efficiency of port operations in Chile shows room for improvement, particularly at southern ports. Across all macrozones, hinterland access upgrades are a priority to reduce costs for shippers, manage port-related traffic in cities and reduce congestion. As for other transport sectors, policies to complement infrastructure investment appear necessary, especially integrated transport and land-use development planning and the relaxation of cabotage restrictions.

Sector overview

Chile's economy is highly dependent on maritime transport, given that around 95% of external trade is handled through ports. Overall throughput was 144 million tonnes in 2015 (Directemar, Boletin Estadistico 2016), double the amount transported in 2000. Moreover, annual container traffic reached 4 million TEUs in 2015, which equates to four-fold growth over 15 years, pushed by the increased containerisation of trade flows.

As such, Chile has the highest ratio of maritime traffic per unit of GDP among comparator countries (Figure 4.18). Chilean ports mainly serve Asian Pacific Coast destinations. China is now Chile's largest trade partner – an entirely new phenomenon compared to the situation in the mid-1990s (OECD, 2015).

Figure 4.18. Maritime container transport intensity of the economy (TEUs per 100 000 units of GDP)

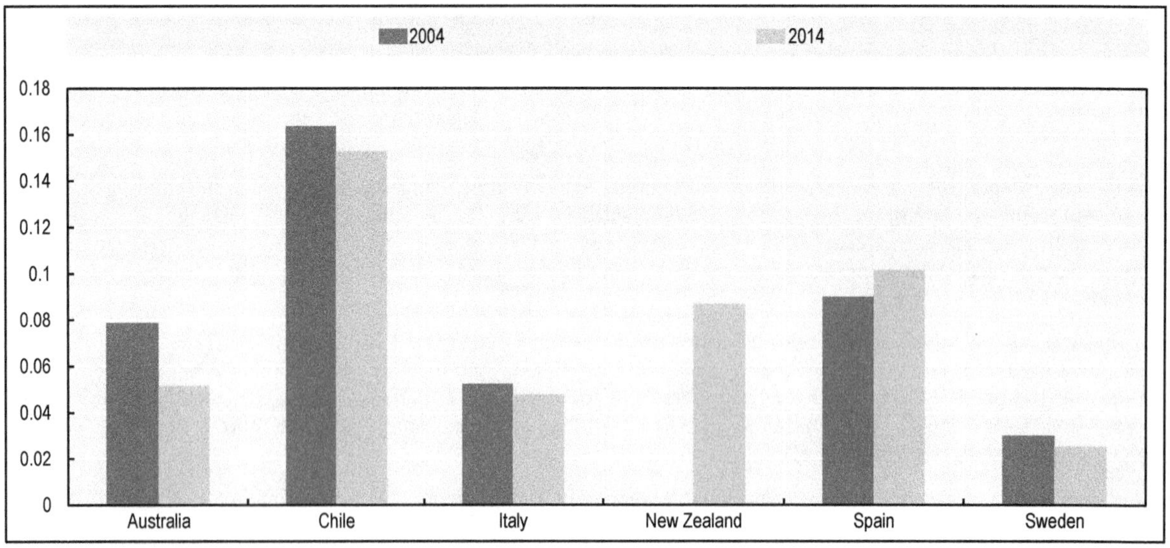

Source: Metric tonnes: data elaborated by the ITF/OECD based on data from Lloyds Intelligence Unit. GDP: World Bank (2016c).

More than 90 ports – some public and some private – are located along the 4 300-km coast of Chile. The largest ports are publicly owned, and the public sector's role is to manage and develop ports and terminals, either directly or through concessions to private terminal operators. There are also a number of private ports, some of which are vertically integrated with mining or industrial companies and specialise in the export of specific products – mostly bulk cargo of minerals, forestry and fuels. Many ports are located within or adjacent to urban areas. This is an advantage in terms of proximity to related services and workforce but a disadvantage due to the congestion and pollution impacts of port-related activities.

Chile has an implicit ports hierarchy. A strict maritime cabotage policy has meant that more than half of all container volumes are concentrated in the two largest ports: San Antonio and Valparaiso. Cabotage laws[7] hinder the development of coastal shipping, which accounted for less than 20% of tons moved in national ports in 2013. In the Northern macrozone, ports are specialised in the movement of mining products (mainly bulk cargo), but they are increasingly trading a larger share of containers. For instance, the ports of Iquique and Arica provide access to maritime trade for landlocked countries like Bolivia and Paraguay. In the Southern macrozone, maritime activities have a seasonal profile, as ports there specialise in forestry, fishery and agricultural products, many of which are perishable. In the Austral macrozone, maritime transport is often the only means of transport for both cargo and passengers.

In this context, the government views as necessary further port investment in the Central macrozone (MTT, 2013). The two largest ports are working on expansion and efficiency-enhancing projects to be implemented between 2015 and 2020. In addition, a consensus has been reached around the need for a mega-port to be developed (*Puerto de*

Gran Escala) in the Central macrozone. This will provide for longer and deeper terminals that are able to handle increasingly large container vessels (ITF/OECD, 2014). Many ports in the North are also adding capacity. ITF's Global Freight Model projections confirm the need to add 50% TEU capacity by 2030, with an emphasis on Central ports. The new port development will be located either in San Antonio or Valparaiso, with the final decision yet to be confirmed.

Identified gaps

The ITF/OECD has previously outlined (ITF/OECD, forthcoming) areas for improvement of Chile's port performance at the maritime, port and hinterland levels. Maritime connectivity depends on market decisions by shipping lines, but in turn, these decisions depend on the organisational and operational performance of ports and the quality of hinterland transport connections. Improvements to port operations can enhance performance even without investment in infrastructure. For example, changes to operational rules such as introducing port gate truck appointment systems are often the priority in the short term.

Investment in terminals can contribute to promoting operational efficiency. A measure of efficiency is ship turnaround time (Figure 4.19). Quick turnaround times reduce total trip costs; this is especially important for shipping lines' vessels. Chile's Central ports perform better than the rest of the country, but turnaround times are still about one-third longer than in comparator regions (Spain, Southern Italy). The performance of Northern ports is not far from Western Australia's port performance, while Southern ports lag further behind their comparators. Improvements in ship-to-shore operations, crane deployment and terminal layout can raise efficiency, including by reducing turnaround times (ITF/OECD, 2014).

For instance, in 2011, the New South Wales government introduced a range of measures at Port Botany to improve the operational efficiency of the supply chain through the port.[8] These measures included performance management standards to deal with truck congestion, whereby stevedores and truck carriers incur financial penalties if they do not meet those standards. In addition, a Cargo Movement Co-ordination Centre and teams of industry and government stakeholders in the road and rail sectors have been established, working to improve operations along the supply chain and at the port. The on-time performance of trucks arriving at Port Botany increased from 72% in February 2011 to 93% in March 2013.

Chile's maritime container port concessions regime has been effective in delivering optimal investment in container terminals. Concessions to develop container terminals inside the ports are awarded by competitive tender. Unlike other OECD countries, the concessions cover the development of wharves and piers as well as terminal buildings. Tenders are opened periodically and used to test demand: when there is insufficient interest to award a concession, this is taken as a signal that demand is not yet sufficient to warrant investment rather than signalling a failure of the tendering process. This mature approach has resulted in incremental expansion of capacity in step with demand, minimising investment risk and costs. Competition policy has ensured that no terminal operator holds significant market power in the overlapping hinterlands of competing ports. This regime is well suited to the expansion of capacity required to meet national goals in the context of Plan Chile 30/30.

The mega-port to be developed in the Central macrozone will require some additional attention, as a major breakwater will need to be built first and a series of terminals concessioned over time behind the breakwater. As discussed in ITF 2015, separating breakwater construction from concessions for terminal development would greatly simplify financing arrangements and allow competition for terminal concessions to proceed in the normal way. The life span and risk profile of such a breakwater is very different from terminal and pier infrastructure. Unbundling would allow the port authority to finance the breakwater and charge terminal concessions for its use on an equal basis. Construction might be financed by the MOP directly or through a separate concession. Opting for public finance would minimise the cost of finance; however, private finance might be preferred to transfer construction risk to a company with a recent track record in construction of similar projects (outside of Chile). A concession would also take the burden of paying for construction off the books of the port authority.

Figure 4.19. Average ship and container ship turnaround time (days), 2013

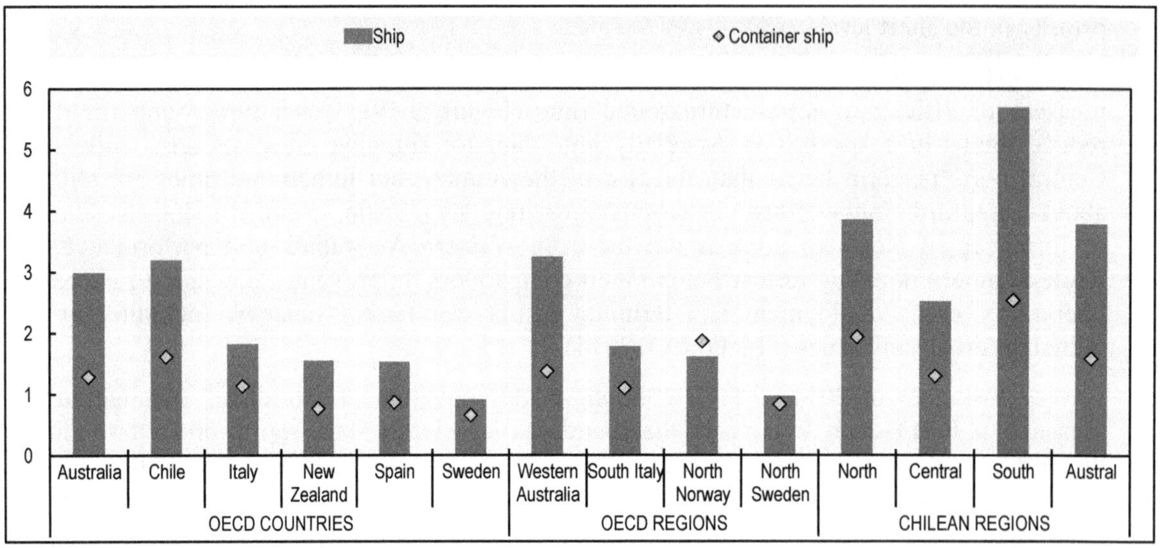

Note: global average is one day.

Source: data elaborated by the ITF/OECD based on data from Lloyds Intelligence Unit.

Infrastructure investment in areas that currently lie outside port authorities' jurisdiction is needed to promote the integration of port systems in multi-modal transportation networks and to improve market access and the fluidity of trade. Ports need efficient links between oceanic maritime port activities, inland terminals and the end-user markets they serve (Notteboom and Rodriguez, 2005). Poor hinterland access is often cited as an obstacle to efficient operations, raising the costs of international transport and thus trade competitiveness. Some Chilean ports have invested to create dry ports, freight corridors and port-information systems, such as the ZEAL logistics site 10 km from the Port of Valparaiso and the Portezuelo logistics platform in Antofagasta. However, there is no national policy on port hinterland connections, (OECD, forthcoming) and responsibilities for providing access to ports are fragmented.

In many OECD countries, investment in hinterland transport links has become the priority for the development of port systems. Ports such as Port Botany in Australia, Barcelona in Spain and Naples in Italy (see Box 4.9) have taken stakes in inland terminals and distribution centres, creating dry ports to facilitate hinterland transport and reduce congestion at port sites. While some of the investment comes directly from port operators, this is often accompanied by support from public authorities, either financially or through institutional facilitation of co-ordination, for the development of maritime-hinterland interfaces. With respect to hinterland transport, arrangements are similar across the three countries: typically, a private company develops and operates the inland terminal, and public funds complement it either by covering the capital costs of building new rail connections and adjusting existing lines, such as with new sidings, or by subsidising rail freight operations to improve their attractiveness.

Most of the transport of goods to and from ports is by road, with negative impacts on congestion and air pollution.[9] When Northern ports are excluded, the modal share of rail at Chilean ports is lower than at ports with similar characteristics in comparator countries (Figure 4.20). Some of the road traffic moving freight from Central Chilean ports to the North and South of the country could be shifted to other modes, notably short sea shipping. However, imports are concentrated in San Antonio and Valparaiso, as demand is centred in the Santiago region. From these ports, current rail links can only cater for a small proportion of containers going to Santiago. Congestion and pollution are likely to be exacerbated by growing trade volumes and the persistence of restrictive cabotage rules.

Figure 4.20. Modal share of rail at ports, latest available year

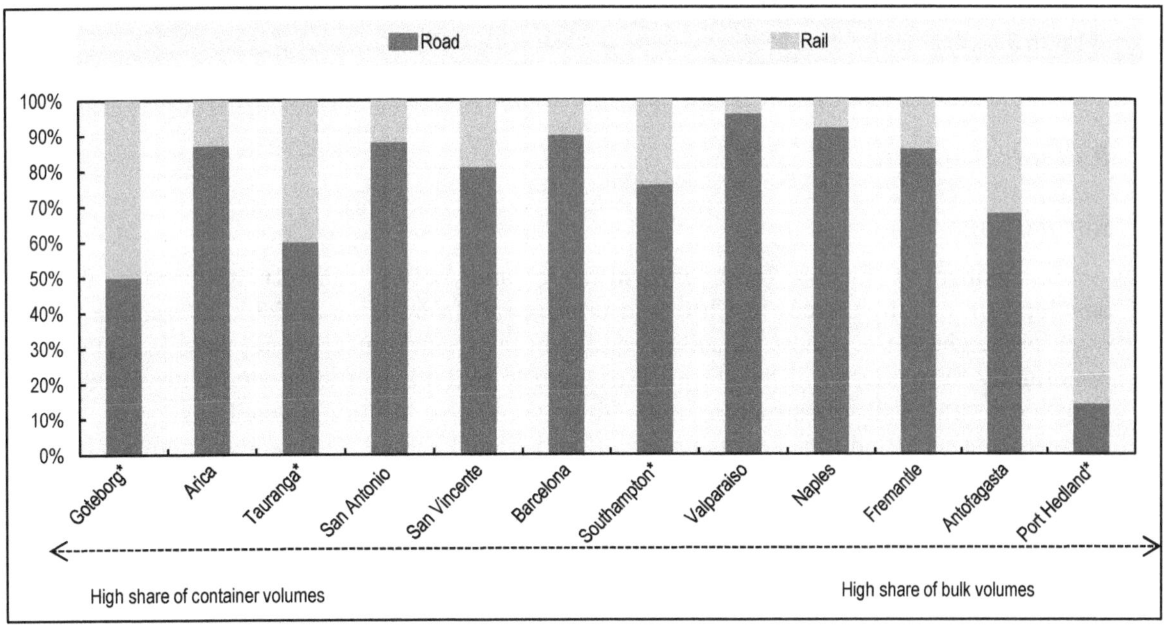

Note: * indicates the presence of dedicated port-hinterland rail shuttle services.

Source: European Parliament (2015), data elaborated by the ITF/OECD based on data from port authorities, BITRE (2014b), Ministerio de Transporte y Telecomunicaciones (2011).

Box 4.7. Trends and challenges in maritime transport in Latin America

Port development in Latin America and the Caribbean (LAC) has been driven by significant and continued growth of container movements, which in turn drives the development of liner shipping networks. Shipping lines may select the ports at which they operate according to the density of trade flows to and from the port/region, and port selection can be based on several criteria, from physical characteristics and geographical location to port efficiency, strategic carrier considerations and hinterland access. From the carrier's perspective, the economies of scale, scope and density in shipping, port operations, and inland operations would favour a very limited number of load centres in a region. However, there is some evidence that, in recent years, secondary ports in Latin America are starting to engage in more integrated development strategies that also include the consideration of logistics platform development.

The introduction of larger vessels on the world's mainline routes can be expected to initiate a process whereby vessels cascade down to the secondary LAC routes and create requirements for new infrastructure not only in the region's main ports but also in the secondary ones. A recent study forecasts that 13 000-TEU ships will start to call regularly on the coasts of South America between 2016 and 2020, which will have direct implications on the liner shipping networks and port infrastructure in the region.

If some of the secondary ports are unable to handle larger ships due to having insufficient handling capacity to accommodate them, this would support the growth of regional second-tier hubs, which can then serve the smaller ports either by smaller feeders or even land transport (thus raising issues relating to the quality and capacity of hinterland infrastructure links). Additionally, the introduction of ever larger vessels on mainline routes may be attractive for shipping lines but will strain ports severely. Ports invest large sums in upgrading their facilities and compete to receive vessel calls, but handling such demand spikes is difficult. Large container drops can result in inefficient crane utilisation, as the numerous large cranes required to service large ships are not all required between calls. Furthermore, moving this high number of containers in and out of the port will require new services, such as trunk rail shuttles, to be introduced.

Source: Adapted from Wilmsmeier et al., 2013.

Rail infrastructure

Key message

A number of factors (both infrastructure and policy related) hold back the development of rail services in Chile and prevent rail from being a viable alternative to road for freight. As new port capacity is added in the Central macrozone, there is a clear opportunity for modern rail freight infrastructure to be built and integrated with a wider logistics system. Rail infrastructure in the South could also be strengthened to support the competitiveness of industrial areas upon which the local economy depends. There is also an opportunity for the growth of passenger rail in specific suburban corridors, but this may require separate infrastructure for passenger and freight services to ensure that passenger train priority does not impair the development of freight services. Clearer policies and dedicated investment will be needed to turn around rail performance, currently below that of OECD comparator systems.

Sector overview

The share of goods and people carried by the rail network in Chile is relatively small. As a percentage of total inland transport, less than 10% of goods are carried by rail, and around 1% of passenger journeys are by train. In contrast, at the peak of their popularity in the 1950s, Chilean railways carried around one-third of the freight and passenger transport in the markets in which they operated (Soto, 2010). The success of railways then depended as much on the absence of suitable alternatives by road as the performance of rail transport. The average modal share of rail freight in comparator OECD countries was 25%[10] in 2013 (Table 4.6).

Table 4.6. Land transport – modal share of rail, 2013

	Freight rail modal share	Passenger rail modal share
Western Australia	63%	<1%
Chile North	17%	<1%
New Zealand	23%	<1%
Sweden	35%	9%
Chile Centre-South	6%	<1%

Source: data elaborated by the ITF/OECD based on data from Western Australia rail operators' reports and data from Grupo EFE, Ministerio de Transporte y Telecomunicaciones (2015), OECD (2016d), OECD (2016e).

The growth of some economic sectors such as forestry and especially mining is dependent on rail transport, and as a result, the private sector has invested in rail freight infrastructure. In Northern Chile, specialised private operators carry copper and other minerals from mines to ports over a network that is around 1 100 km long. These operators are often integrated with ports and/or mines, such as FERRONOR. In Central and Southern Chile, private operator FEPASA (owned by the Port of Ventanas) carries mainly cellulose and timber from inland forests to ports. Another private company (TRANSAP) is specialised in sulphuric acid transport to the port of San Antonio. FEPASA and TRANSAP use EFE's[11] network under a Railway Access Contract.

Passenger services by rail used to provide an alternative to roads. While many intercity passenger services have been cut back, new suburban services have been launched and are expanding. The national rail operator owns and manages the rail network in the Centre and South of Chile, which extends for over 2 100 km of tracks. It operates a limited number of long-distance intercity trains. Rail networks extend only as far as Puerto Montt in the South. Suburban services are provided by EFE's subsidiaries, mainly around the conurbations of Valparaiso and Concepción. In Valparaiso, this resulted in the rail line serving the port being converted to an urban metro, no longer suited to carrying containers[12]. In Santiago, sections of the rail network suitable for a rail freight alignment towards San Antonio are also used for passenger services. Suburban and long-distance operations are not integrated.

Clearer, better integrated policy objectives for railway development will be required if any of the nominal targets for expansion of rail services are to be met. Plans for rail infrastructure enhancement are fragmented. As emerged in discussions with stakeholders, EFE is currently unable to fund major investment and maintenance projects. Some of the government's plans to revitalise the network appear to be contradictory. For instance, the long-term plan (*PICAF*) presented by the MTT in 2013 lays out a vision for rail freight growth (reaching a 30% modal share), in contrast to the passenger-focused investment projects launched by EFE (with the goal of trebling passenger numbers by 2030) (MTT, 2013; EFE, 2015). Since freight and passenger share the same rail infrastructure in busy parts of the Central macrozone, achieving growth in both sectors will be impossible without major investment and some dedicated freight lines. In parallel, rail regulation needs reform. An update of rules on technical norms, safety and the environment is needed. Specific responsibilities for implementing today's general policy objectives need to be assigned.[13] The Ministry of Transport, or possibly a dedicated agency, should be charged with developing a detailed strategy. Underfunding and the lack of an integrated long-term strategy are some of the root causes of the gaps discussed in the following section.

Identified gaps

The role of rail passenger transport in Chile is clearly very marginal, but the gaps with OECD comparator countries differ by types of service. Two types of passenger services can be compared in more detail:

- Intercity services: compared to more densely populated European countries such as Italy and Spain that have built dedicated infrastructure to develop fast intercity links as an alternative to motorways, Chile has a large gap.
- Suburban services: conversely, countries with vast land areas and a complex geography, such as Australia and New Zealand, have prioritised investment in metropolitan rail services, and Chile's suburban rail infrastructure is comparable to that of those countries.

Given Chile's geography, an international comparison suggests that the development of higher-quality suburban railways may be a more suitable objective than reinstating intercity rail infrastructure. The majority of Chile's territory has similar geographic conditions and population densities to those seen in Australia and New Zealand. In both countries, fast intercity connections have been the object of detailed studies, but any decision to invest in this type of infrastructure has been put off following cost-benefit assessment. New investment in intercity rail passenger services should only be considered on the basis of robust cost-benefit analysis identifying large enough demand for such services, which compete with air and road alternatives. Decisions about investment in metropolitan rail services are more straightforward in the presence of large flows of commuters and other passengers from residential suburban areas to one or more centres of economic activity in the city.

Figure 4.21. Density of rail network by area and population, latest available year

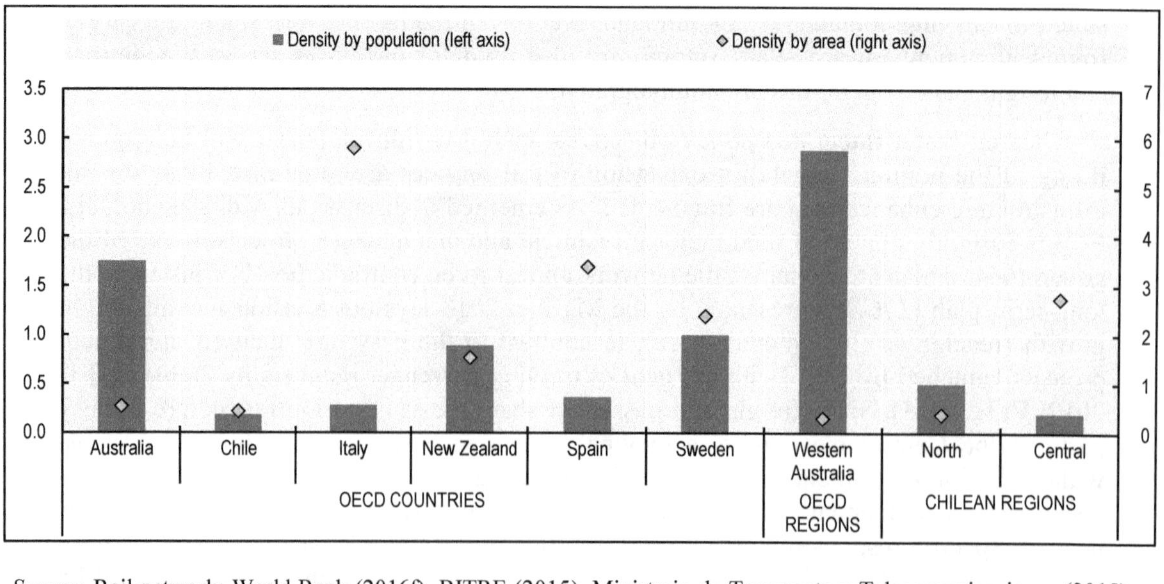

Source: Rail network: World Bank (2016f), BITRE (2015), Ministerio de Transporte y Telecomunicaciones (2015), data elaborated by the ITF/OECD based on data from Western Australia rail operators' reports. Population: World Bank (2016a), Australia Bureau of Statistics (2016a), Instituto Nacional de Estadísticas de Chile (2016a). Land area: World Bank (2016b), Australian Bureau of Statistics (2016b), Instituto Nacional de Estadísticas de Chile (2016b).

A more thorough analysis can be carried out in the case of rail freight transport, in which a gap in the provision and performance of infrastructure emerges. When the density of rail networks currently in use is analysed (Figure 4.21), Chile comes in at the bottom of the ranking. This is consistent with prior analysis showing that only around 15-20% of the original rail network in Chile is in use (Soto, 2010) and that operations are confined to self-contained networks over short distances.

Figure 4.22. Rail freight performance indicators, 2013

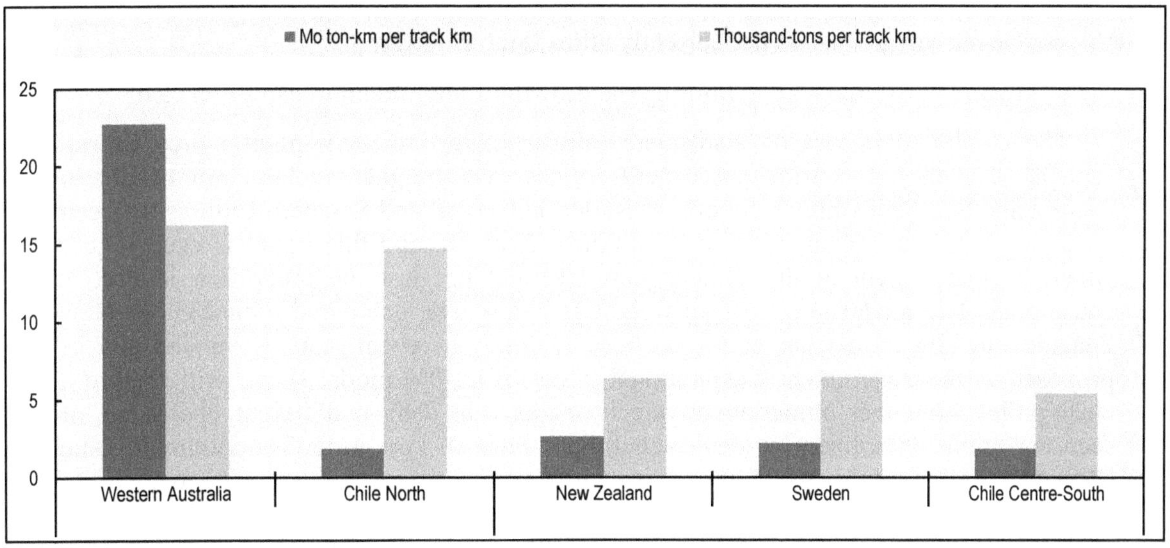

Source: Rail freight: data elaborated by the ITF/OECD based on data from Western Australia rail operators' reports and Grupo EFE, Ministerio de Transporte y Telecomunicaciones (2015), OECD (2016d). Rail network: World Bank (2016f), Ministerio de Transporte y Telecomunicaciones (2015), data elaborated by the ITF/OECD based on data from Western Australia rail operators' reports.

To ensure that the specificity of rail market segments (by product and geography) is taken into account and that only relevant comparisons are made, we benchmark the Central-Southern rail network carrying forestry and industrial products to that of Sweden and New Zealand, and we benchmark the Northern network serving mining ports to that of Western Australia (WA) (Figure 4.22).

Rail infrastructure in Northern Chile carries a similar number of tons per track-km as that in Western Australia, partly because the main product carried in Chile, copper, is denser than iron ore, the chief commodity carried in WA. However, given the much shorter distances of rail freight lines in Chile, tonne-km per track-km is 12 times as high in WA as in Northern Chile. The corresponding modal share of rail computed on this basis is thus lower in Northern Chile (17%) than in WA (63%). It should be emphasised that the performance of rail freight in the North falls outside of the public policy sphere of influence, given that networks are owned and operated by private companies.

EFE's network in Central-Southern Chile compared to Sweden and New Zealand. The network in use is far less dense in Chile than that in Sweden and New Zealand. The most apparent gap is in the provision of high-capacity, high-reliability rail infrastructure links to major public ports, resulting in a low proportion of freight transported by rail at the ports of San Antonio, Valparaiso and San Vicente. Existing rail infrastructure to these large container ports is often not ideal for the movement of containers themselves, given that the rail links share a number of unfavourable characteristics:

- Lines are predominantly single track.
- Low speeds are imposed (15-20 km/hour) given the lack of regular maintenance, compared to speeds of 50-60 km/hour in European rail corridors.
- Numerous bridges are not fit for carrying heavy trains, as exemplified by the collapse of the Pitrufquén viaduct in August 2016.
- Gauge restrictions do not currently allow double-stacking.
- Inland ports are lacking, limiting the growth of intermodal transport services.

The combined impact of inadequate infrastructure and an implicit policy of rail capacity allocation favouring passenger services over freight penalises rail freight in Central and Southern Chile. Network utilisation in Central and Southern Chile is between 15% and 25% lower than in Sweden and New Zealand, and this figure is even bigger when the total length of the Chilean network, and not just the proportion in use, is considered. The modal share of rail freight is below 6%, compared with 23% in New Zealand and 35% in Sweden, and it has been declining in recent years. Reversing this, as proposed in the government's aspirational target of a 30% modal share, will require a clear policy for either attracting private investment in dedicated freight operations or securing public investment in dedicated freight lines to key ports. The Bothnian Line (Box 4.8) is an example of such investment, as it aims to fill a clear gap in the availability of rail freight services for bulk exports from Northern Europe while introducing new passenger services. The approach adopted avoids mixing freight and passenger traffic while exploiting synergies in the construction and operation of this large rail corridor.

Box 4.8. The Bothnian Line in Northern Europe

The Bothnian Corridor extends along the Swedish and Finnish sides of the Gulf of Bothnia. The northern part of the corridor, which will extend between Umeå and Luleå, is recognised as a "missing link" in Sweden's strategic infrastructure. Original plans envisaged the construction of the North Bothnian Line as a key freight link, connecting to the existing Bothnian Line in the south for onward transport towards Europe, the Iron Ore Line in the west leading to Norway and the sea routes, and to the east via the Haparanda Line to the Finnish and Russian rail networks. Upon completion, the Bothnian Corridor would bring together several rail networks and facilitate potential east-west interchange of freight between the east coast of the United States and the Far East.

However, numerous studies during the 2000s showed that there would be considerable benefits for passengers travelling between Northern Swedish cities and towns as well. Currently, around 300 000 people live along the rail route, and all passenger movements take place by road. New rail services would significantly reduce journey times for different categories of users, including commuting trips for professionals, workers in key service sectors and students. For instance, travelling between Luleå and Umeå would be 20 minutes faster.

After years of delays linked to changes in political circumstances and budget availability, the presence of these large benefits for both freight and passenger services resulted in the project being reintroduced as a priority project by the Swedish government in 2014 and consequently marked as part of the part of the European Core Network, to be completed by 2030.

Construction of the 270-km North Bothnian Line is planned to commence in 2018 for a total estimated cost of around EUR 3 billion. The project will be co-funded by the European Union and some of the municipalities located along the line, which have pledged to contribute with direct funding as well as investment in related infrastructure such as railway stations. The Corridor is planned from the outset to accommodate both freight and passenger traffic on separate dedicated tracks, thus reducing potential conflicts.

Source: "The last link in the Bothnian Corridor" (2013), *European Railway Review*, Issue 5; written submission to the ITF/OECD by Trafikverket officials.

There may be an opportunity to develop a dedicated hinterland freight railway from the central ports to logistics centres in Santiago. The road congestion and air pollution issues identified in the sections on port and urban infrastructure could be relieved by investment in inland ports and logistics centres in the greater Santiago region served by rail links from the Central ports and the new mega-port. While rail service in Valparaiso has been compromised by the decision to cover over tracks, restrict loading gauge and run suburban passenger trains on the line through the port, in San Antonio, rail access to the terminal could be expanded substantially if land adjacent to the port is protected from encroachment by new urban development and rights of way are preserved. Given the potential for increased trade, private investors might be attracted to invest in a dedicated freight railway if national rail and port hinterland policy were developed to provide for such stand-alone investment. Alternatively, the government might invest in enhanced rail freight infrastructure. The scale of investment required might make private investment the preferred option. In either case, a clear separation of freight from passenger operations would be required. Positive examples of publicly and privately funded dedicated investment in port-rail connections are presented in Box 4.9, covering Australia, Spain and Italy.

Box 4.9. Hinterland ports

Investment in hinterland transport links has become the priority for the development of port systems in many OECD countries. Various ports have taken stakes in inland terminals and distribution centres, creating dry ports to facilitate hinterland transport. This is often accompanied by public authorities supporting, either financially or through institutional facilitation of co-ordination, the development of maritime-hinterland interfaces. Some of these developments are driven by policies to promote modal shift from road. Some examples are provided in this box.

Port Botany landside access, Australia

Port Botany is the largest container port in New South Wales (NSW), serving Sydney and the wider region. In 2014-15, the port handled approximately 2.28 million TEUs, including 0.14 million TEUs in trans-shipments. The port's private sector operator projects that this volume will grow to between 7.5 million and 8.4 million TEUs by 2045. Approximately 85% of containers originate from or are bound for a destination within 40 km of Port Botany. The rail mode share of container movements to and from Port Botany declined from 25% in 2002 to 14% in 2012. The NSW Government has set a target of doubling the rail mode share by 2020.

To improve landside access to the port, several actions have been pursued over the past five to seven years, including development of the Southern Sydney Freight Line (SSFL) at a cost of approximately AUD 1 billion to provide a dedicated rail line that improved access for interstate and intrastate freight trains passing through the southern part of the Sydney rail network. The project also extended an existing dedicated rail freight connection to a new intermodal terminal in southwestern Sydney (Moorebank), about 35 km from the port.

There has also been progressive upgrades of the motorway network, notably the development of the WestConnex project, which will be carried out over three stages between 2015 and 2023 (at a nominal cost of AUD 16.8 billion). The project will be funded with a mixture of: distance-based tolls on all vehicles, including trucks; an availability charge from the NSW Government; and a grant of AUD 1.5 billion from the Australian Government.

Development of intermodal terminals, both at an existing rail marshalling yard 15 km inland and at a new terminal at Moorebank, will be carried out on a 241 ha former military site. The terminal will operate as an open access facility. The site adjoins the dedicated freight rail network and the motorway network. The terminal is to be developed by Qube Holdings, a private operator, which is investing approximately AUD 1.5 billion in the project. The Australian Government is contributing a further AUD 370 million (principally for a rail connection to the SSFL) and leasing the land for the terminal. The terminal is expected to commence operations by the end of 2017.

Source: Written submission to the ITF/OECD by Infrastructure Australia officials.

Box 4.9. Hinterland ports (*cont.*)

Port of Barcelona's tmZ inland terminal

The Terminal Marítima de Zaragoza (tmZ) is an initiative that was led by the Port of Barcelona and Mercazaragoza, the largest food logistics platform in the Ebro Valley. This project is part of the wider Port of Barcelona strategy to extend its activities and services beyond the boundaries of the port to facilitate hinterland connectivity and ensure high service quality as part of its strategic development plan. The tmZ is strategically located within the Mercazaragoza Logistics Area and at the crossroads of some of the country's main road corridors. Between Barcelona and Madrid, it lays within a 300-km range of some of Spain's most important industrial areas. This project enables the port to bring together port services with other maritime logistics services to the largest importers and exporters of the region. Combining tmZ's ability to transfer containers to all these destinations with Barcelona's deep-sea shipping connections offers logistics solutions that are efficient, economical and environmentally sustainable.

The first part of the facility was opened in 2001 as an inland logistics centre. A direct rail connection between the terminal and the Port of Barcelona was later completed in 2007. The Port of Barcelona is still contributing a large chunk of the infrastructure, such as the facilities for refrigerated goods. It will also continue to fund the 10 to 12 railway sidings of at least 750 meters in the railway corridor Barcelona-Zaragoza-Madrid, through the Fondo Financiero de Accesibilidad Terrestre Portuaria, an initiative led by the Ministry of Development that plans to dedicate over EUR 450 million to the development of port hinterland projects throughout the country between 2016 and 2019. The operation of the rail connection was granted to Depot tmZ Services S.L., owned by Spanish companies Terminal de Contenedores de Barcelona (TCB, 45%), tmZ (35%) and Hutchinson since 2015 through its subsidiary BEST, the company's new Barcelona semi-automated terminal and a competitor of TCB (20%).

The terminal has been a success, with considerable traffic increases since its creation. Between 2013 and 2015, traffic more than doubled, from 135 000 TEUs to over 305 000 TEUs, in part due to container traffic increases at the Port of Barcelona, which is now connected to tmZ by six trains per day. In total, 125 000 containers where moved by rail between the port and the terminal in 2014. Along with other factors such as the inclusion of the Opel Mokka assembly lines within the Zaragoza General Motors plant, this led tmZ's board to approve expansion projects in 2015 to double the terminal's capacity to be able to accommodate growing demand for the services it offers. Since the beginning of this project, the Port of Barcelona has decided to invest in other logistics platforms along strategic supply chains for the port, including across the border in France.

Source: ITF/OECD, 2016e.

Naples' hinterland port, Italy

The Port of Naples is one of the largest in Southern Italy, with a capacity of just over 500 000 TEUs. More than 430 000 TEUs, mainly container traffic for import goods, have been handled annually at the port (traffic has remained fairly constant since the early 2000s), which operates close to capacity. Only 8% of all goods are typically moved to and from the port by rail. In this context, plans for an "extended Port of Naples" were developed over the past few years, focusing on two twinned objectives: increasing the modal share of rail and decongesting the port by moving some key functions inland.

The plan has taken shape with the creation of a large hinterland logistics centre around the existing rail freight depot of Nola, about 30 km inland from Naples. Owned by a private company (Interporto Campano), Naples' hinterland port occupies an area of 3 million m^2, hosting a large intermodal terminal (7.5 ha) and parking areas that can accommodate up to 3 000 trucks. It sits at the intersection of the A30 and A16 motorways. However, road transport only makes up 20% of traffic at the site. The port is linked to the national rail freight network by a short stretch of 13 railway lines, of which six are electrified; in turn, this is linked to a major European Freight Corridor. Daily rail shuttles have been introduced to move containers arriving on different ships from the Port of Naples to the hinterland port as a single load, achieving the densities needed to make rail the preferred mode of transport. Inland ports further away, linked to Naples by rail, have similarly been developed, for example in Bologna. Such initiatives are particularly successful when customs and other inspection activities can be moved to the inland port, relieving overstretched or inefficient services in the ports.

The hinterland port can reduce capacity constraints at the Port of Naples and decrease road congestion in and around the city. The site will be strengthened through new rail services planned by national freight operators and the expansion of border control facilities. The hinterland facility, however, would not have been possible without the close co-operation between public actors and the private sector, with respect to co-ordinated planning across modes and to financing. For instance, state contributions amounted to around 30% of the start-up costs of new rail services.

Source: Interporto Campano website, ACAM (2015), European Commission C (2009) 4508.

Urban accessibility and environmental quality

Key message

Chile's ability to address its economic, social and environmental challenges largely depends on developing the right investment and planning policies at the urban level. A prerequisite is improved co-ordination, which involves planning and governance reforms as discussed in other chapters of this report. However, a shift in infrastructure investment priorities is also necessary to address inequality of access between and within urban areas. Public transport risks a decline in ridership with rapid growth in car ownership towards levels seen in other OECD countries. In parallel, congestion and pollution from transport activities are affecting the health of urban residents and the quality of life in cities. Investment in higher-quality public transport and urban spaces, together with more integrated land-use and transport planning to manage car use, will need to become a more prominent part of urban strategies.

Issues overview

Around 90% of Chile's population lives in urban areas. The metropolitan region of Santiago hosts more than 40% of the total population and jobs, and it accounts for over 45% of national GDP. From the 1990s onwards, urban expansion also took place in other regional centres, typically port cities such as Valparaiso, Concepcion and Antofagasta. The concentration of economic activities in urban areas has attracted internal migration from rural areas to regional centres, accelerating the pace of urban population growth (Ahman and Zanola, 2016).

The challenge of providing access to jobs and services for a growing urban population has predominantly been met by the growth of private motorised transport. Chilean cities increasingly face the challenge of providing access to jobs and services, including health and education, for a growing number of urban residents and daily commuters. The number of passenger cars per inhabitant in Chile doubled between 2004 and 2014, and urban congestion has increased. The response to growing car traffic has often been the construction or widening of road infrastructure, such as Santiago's East-West road links and the ring road in Valparaiso.

Considerable investment has also been directed at public transport systems, although mainly concentrated in the capital. In Santiago, the reorganisation of the Transantiago bus network is considered one of the largest public policy experiments ever conducted in Chile, and it has set a precedent for improving public transport provision.[14] In parallel, the capital's metro has continuously expanded since the 1970s. In other cities, while buses remain the most popular public transport mode, local stakeholders believe that the quality standards of these services are far lower than in Santiago as a result of insufficient funding. Plans are nonetheless in place to expand suburban rail systems in Valparaiso (new stations along the corridor that goes from Valparaiso to the East joining several small centres to the regional capital) and Concepcion (*Biotrén* extension to Coronel), providing better-quality access for residents of the cities' conurbations.

Chile's weak land use planning framework and fragmented urban governance (see Chapter 3) negatively affect the ability to improve urban accessibility. Given the lack of co-ordination between land-use and transport policies, housing and transport investment have often not been carefully managed. This has resulted in urban sprawl, fuelled by the growing cost of living in central areas, the unbalanced provision of transport and urban amenities between neighbourhoods in the same city (Salazar-Burrows and Cox, 2014), and failures to set aside land that could facilitate the future expansion of transport assets such as airports, ports and logistics centres. Improved accessibility therefore relies not only on more investment in urban infrastructure and public transport but also on better governance at the metropolitan level to tackle the root causes of inequality.

The presence of large ports and clusters of maritime activity is a further challenge for policy makers. According to a recent study (Zrari and Alvarez, 2015), 66% of actors in the port system (including port authorities, municipalities and regional *Intendentes*) believe that ports in Chile have not developed in a harmonious way with cities, and only 4% of respondents consider that the relationship between ports and cities has been "very harmonious". Conflicts arise when port-related traffic exacerbates congestion in cities at peak times, as exemplified in areas of San Antonio in relation to truck traffic and Antofagasta in relation to rail traffic on a system without grade separation. In a similar fashion, the growth of national and regional airports can raise co-ordination challenges with respect to surface access, land use and negative externalities such as noise.

Identified gaps

The growth in urban population and city-based economic activities will continue to exert considerable pressure on urban transport infrastructure in Chile. If the country follows a similar path to other OECD members, the number of private motor vehicles in the country could double or even treble by 2030. In addition, in cities hosting large ports, infrastructure will come under increased pressure given the projected growth in truck movements under a business-as-usual scenario. Likewise, the expected growth of the aviation sector will exacerbate urban traffic conditions in the proximity of airports and may raise conflicts over land use.

Figure 4.23. Modal share in cities, latest available year (2012-2014)

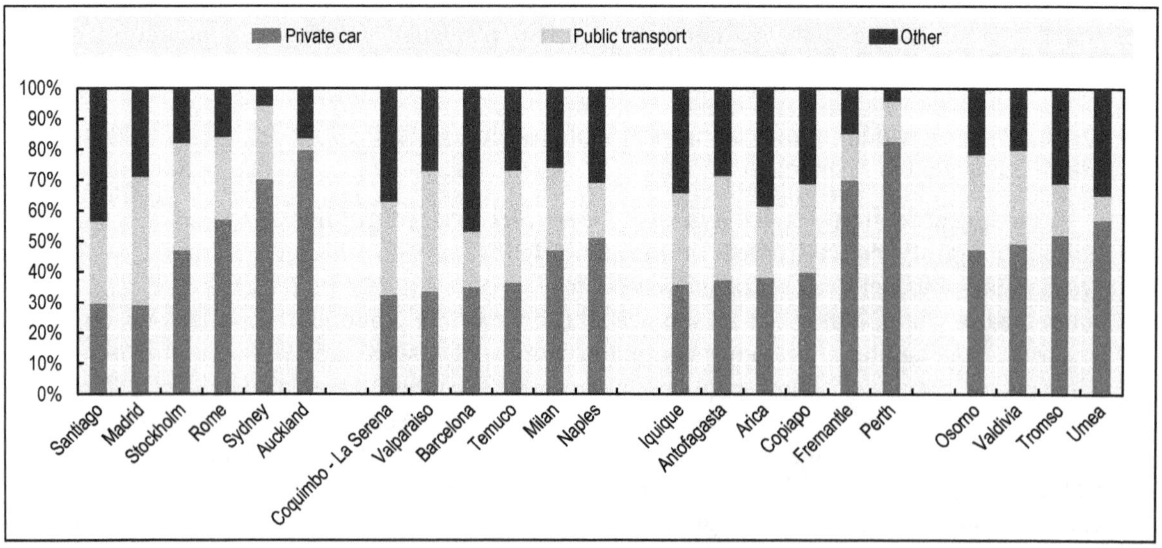

Note: Modal share calculations may differ on survey methodology adopted.

Source: SECTRA (2016), Ministero dell'Economia e delle Finanze (2016), data elaborated by the ITF/OECD based on data from national travel surveys.

The costs associated with growing road congestion are wide ranging, and they can hold back economic growth and increase inequality. Evidence from the United States, United Kingdom and France shows that the rise of negative externalities such as urban congestion translates into lower potential and actual economic growth, for instance by discouraging investment in cities, lowering productivity and inflating the costs of goods and services (INRIX, 2014). In addition, greater congestion can lead to poorer accessibility to jobs and services for the "captive users" of public transport, particularly the poorer section of urban populations, as exemplified by the case of Santiago described in the following section. In the capital, the car ownership gap is stark: there are 0.38 cars per person in households earning less than USD 1 000 per month and 1.27 cars per person in households with incomes above USD 2 000 (Hurtubia et al, 2016) (rates elaborated based on SECTRA, 2015).

Box 4.10. Urban congestion in New Zealand

Road carries the majority of traffic in New Zealand, especially in and around cities. There is heavy reliance on private motorised vehicles for urban transport. Public transport accounts for only 2.8% of all trips. Private vehicles account for almost 80%.

There are several factors that appear to encourage private vehicle use in New Zealand cities. These include:

- Spread-out, low-density urban areas (hindering cost effectiveness of public transport)
- historical low levels of public investment in infrastructure, including public transport
- administrative boundaries not matching the real boundaries of built-up areas (hindering planning co-ordination).

Together with economic and population growth, along with New Zealand's geography, the factors encouraging private vehicle use have resulted in substantial congestion in New Zealand's main cities. In fact, congestion in New Zealand's main cities is higher than comparable, though larger, cities in Australia (Tom Tom Index 2016).

Auckland especially suffers from high levels of congestion. Just over 90% of Aucklanders commute to work by car, and the number of kilometres travelled by car has increased by 30% since 2000. In addition, the policy drive for greater asset utilisation has created larger traffic volumes at the port of Auckland. However, the port is adjacent to the city's central business district. Thus, land near the port is limited, and an increased number of truck movements has been exacerbating congestion in the area in recent years.

Therefore, the New Zealand government has sought to address congestion and other issues in Auckland through a range of interventions including:

- increased investment in transport infrastructure, including public transport infrastructure – motorways, busways and electrified urban rail have been introduced or expanded in recent years
- reforming governance and planning systems, such as merging the eight previous bodies governing the Auckland metropolitan area into a single body, the new Auckland Council, since 2010, and creating a new agency for urban mobility – Auckland Transport
- requiring the Auckland Council to develop the Auckland Plan, which, among other things, sets out strategies for building infrastructure to improve Auckland's congestion over the next 30 years.

While there are signs of improvement, the Auckland Plan acknowledges that forecast population growth means that congestion will worsen over the next 30 years, even with very substantial investments in transport infrastructure.

Source: Tom Tom Index 2016, Auckland Plan 2012.

Recent work in the area of accessibility and inequality sheds light on the extent to which Santiago's public transport system meets the need for access to opportunities and basic services (Ibid). In the capital, the north-eastern area hosts the richest section of the population, and this area has grown much faster than the rest of the city in recent decades, attracting productive activities, commerce and services that were historically concentrated in the central business district (CBD). In parallel, poorer households have been offered social housing in the periphery of Santiago and have moved away from informal settlements closer to the centre.

These trends have resulted in longer journeys by public transport for poorer residents to access jobs and services, not just those located in the north-east of the city but also in the historical CBD. Higher infrastructure spending per capita in richer districts increases the accessibility gap across the city, negatively affecting lower-income areas and thus increasing the inequality of travel conditions.[15] For example, whereas pavements and metro entrances are constructed to high quality in the wealthier neighbourhoods, pavements are frequently absent in poorer districts, making access to bus stops difficult and sometimes dangerous.

A related issue affecting the attractiveness of public transport is over-crowding. Using the example of Santiago again, comparisons of overall utilisation between the capital's metro and similar metro systems in other OECD cities show that utilisation is far higher on average in Santiago. Further analysis has confirmed that the most negative attribute of the city's metro system is that it is too crowded at peak times, with over-crowding acting as a deterrent for people to choose public transport over cars. An increase in public transport convenience often reduces the generalised cost of travel and thus provides benefits to passengers that is equivalent to an increase in speed (ITF/OECD, 2014).

Figure 4.24. Passenger utilisation of selected metro networks, 2014

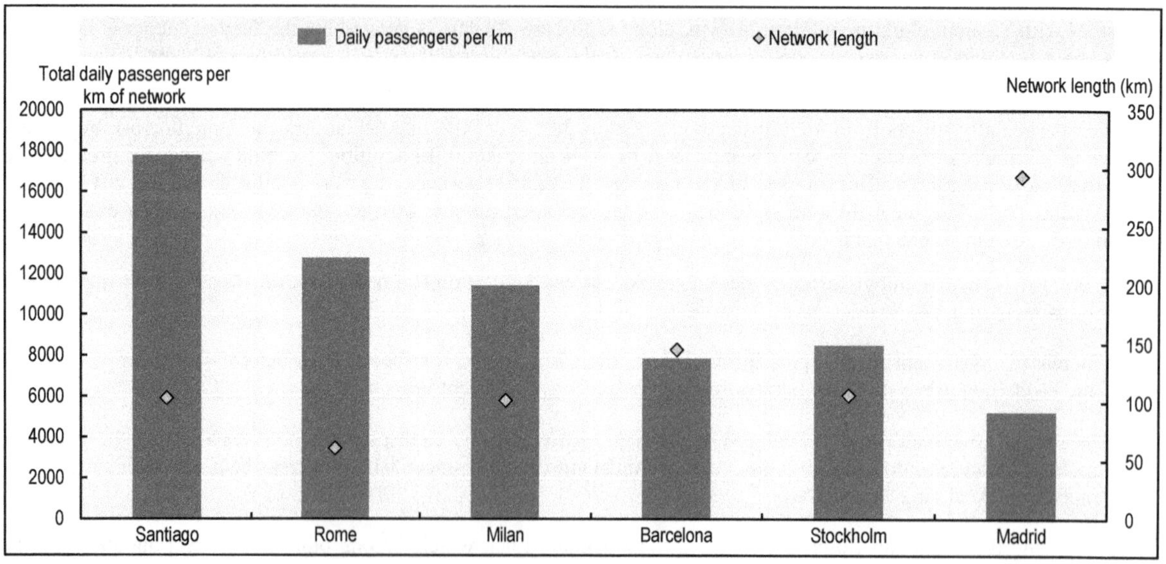

Source: data elaborated by the ITF/OECD based on data from cities' annual reports.

Another dimension of accessibility relates to the ability of people who are mobility impaired[16] to travel using public transport. While legal instruments to guarantee universal accessibility are in place (*Ley no. 20.422*), Chilean cities have been slow in the implementation of measures such as lifts, bus ramps, pedestrian walkways, visual and audio information, and other elements that enhance the accessibility of urban public transport systems. Investment in accessible transport, when co-ordinated with better access to public spaces, homes and offices, has a direct impact on equality of opportunities for mobility-impaired passengers and yields benefits to all passengers in terms of comfort, reliability, quality and information provision.

Mainly as a result of road traffic, urban residents in Chile are exposed to air pollution levels well above OECD comparator countries. In line with the UN Sustainable Development Goals, we compare air pollution levels as measured by the population-weighted annual mean levels of small particulate matters (PM2.5) in cities (Figure 4.25) and by prolonged exposure to photochemical smog (NO_x and NO_2). The World Health Organisation (WHO) estimates the health impact, in terms of mortality and morbidity, attributable to these emissions. The latest estimates for Chile show that 2 822 deaths were attributable to ambient air pollution in 2012. This translates into 13 deaths per 100 000 inhabitants (age adjusted), on par with Italy but above Spain (7), New Zealand, Sweden and Australia (all three countries have rates between 0.2 and 0.3) (WHO, 2016). Our analysis shows that the Central macrozone has the highest levels of air pollution from PM2.5 given the high concentration of population and activities in large metropolitan areas and that Chilean cities are second only to Italian cities with respect to photochemical smog.

Transport-related greenhouse gas emissions per capita are on an upward trend, as shown in Figure 4.27. Transport is the second largest contributor to CO_2 emissions in Chile, accounting for 30% of emissions from fuel use. Over 90% of those transport emissions are from road transport. Although the average fuel efficiency of Chile's vehicle fleet is improving, this is not enough to offset the increasing demand for road-based travel. Under a business-as-usual scenario, the climate change mitigation action plans (MAPS) for Chile project an increase in transport-related greenhouse gas emissions by 61% to 95% by 2030, depending on GDP growth (OECD/ECLAC, 2016).

Modal shift targets in cities need to be set, and strategies should be implemented to reduce reliance on car movements. Policies to restrict the use of cars, including through pricing mechanisms and the introduction of stringent environmental standards, as well as investment to improve infrastructure for cycling and walking and to attract people to public transport through higher-quality services and reserved road space for buses and BRT systems, are essential elements of the policy mix needed to reduce car movements and contain emissions.

Figure 4.25. Mean population exposure to PM2.5 (micrograms per cubic metre), 2005 and 2013

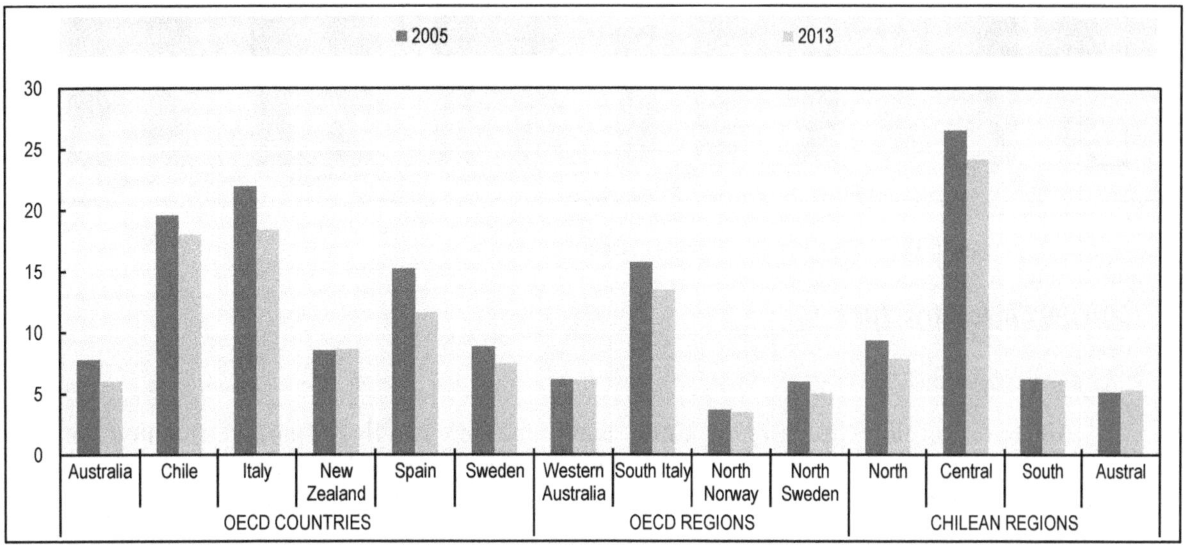

Source: OECD (2016f).

Figure 4.26. NO_2 Emissions (10^n molecules/cm^2) in urban, intermediate and rural areas, 2012

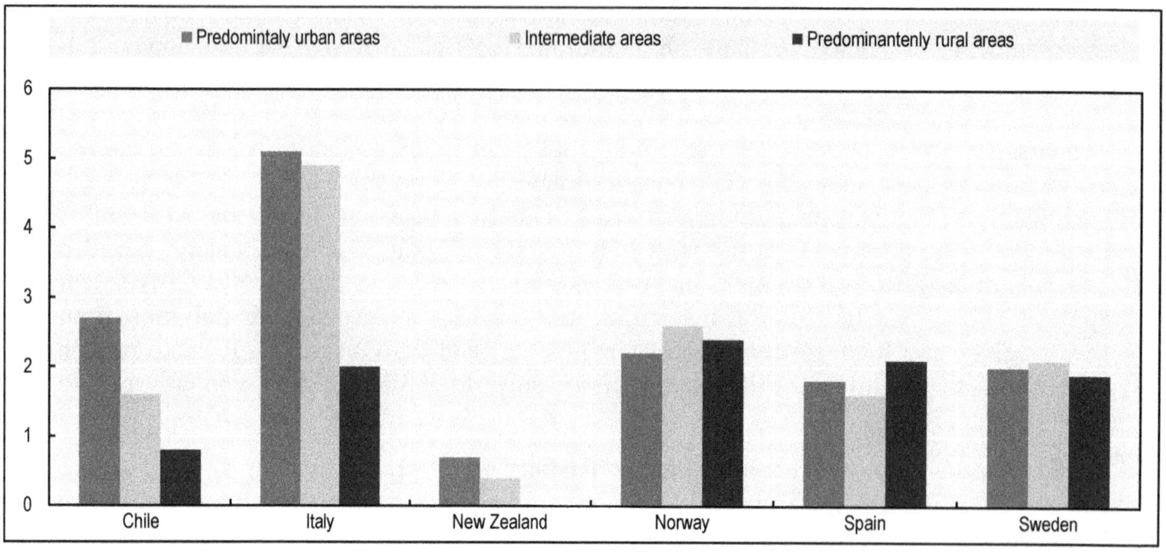

Source: OECD (2016g).

Figure 4.27. Transport-related greenhouse gas emissions (CO_2 equivalent tonnes) per inhabitant, 1994, 2004 and 2013

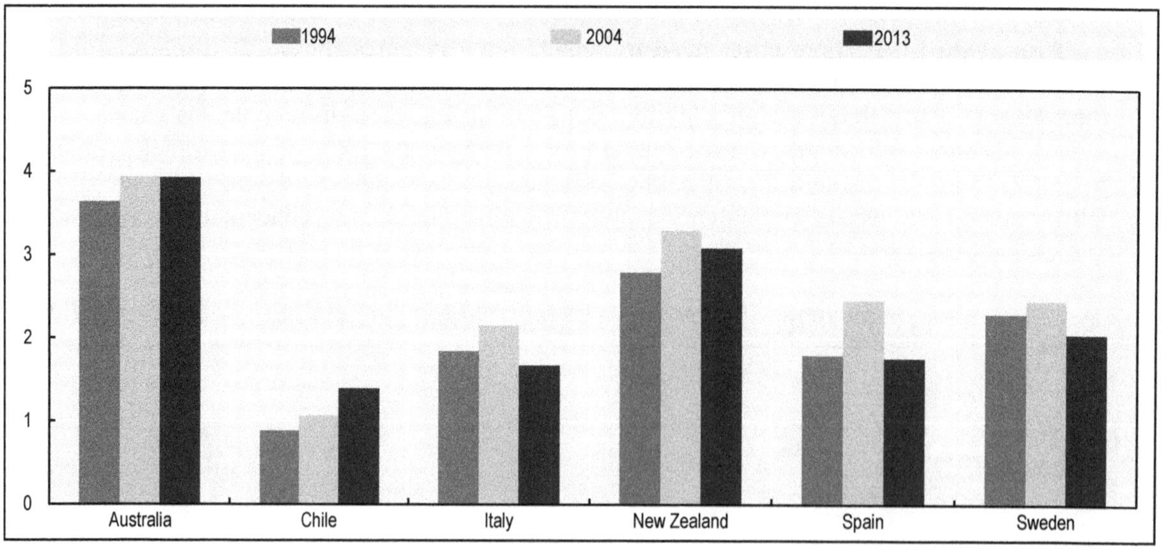

Source: CO2 emissions: IEA (2016). Population: World Bank (2016a).

Airport infrastructure

Key message

Air transport infrastructure in Chile plays an increasingly important function in connecting the country to the rest of the world, different parts of the country to each other and remote areas without land-based connections to regional capitals. The continued development of air connectivity relies on a stable regulatory framework that is conducive to attracting bidders at airports under concessions to further develop airport infrastructure and to attracting air carriers to strengthen connectivity and promote competition and new routes.

The priorities for this sector should encompass a range of strategic elements in Chile's airport system. These include greater integration of urban planning and airport development in large cities to accommodate growth and reduce negative externalities, ensuring that public funds currently cross-subsiding non-commercially viable airports are spent efficiently, and providing adequate surface access alternatives by public transport to reduce congestion. In light of continued growth, detailed analysis at the airport system level should continue to be carried out to ensure that investment and regulation are tailored to the changing strategic needs and to the role that aviation will play in ensuring national and international connectivity.

Sector overview

Most cities and towns in Chile are served by airports and airfields, with Santiago's airport acting as a national hub. The airports sector comprises 15 primary airports, operating under concessions, seven of which serve international destinations; a secondary network of airports and airfields linking regional capitals to international hubs and local airfields; and other local, very small airports linking remote areas and operating under "public service obligations" established by the State.

Airport services are provided by a public body, the General Civil Aviation Authority (DGAC), while the Ministry of Public Works is responsible for tendering and monitoring airport terminal concessions awarded to private bidders. Other ministries are also included in this process, and the Ministry of Finance ultimately approves all concession contracts. Airport BOT contracts were promoted from the mid-1990s onwards, with the goal of attracting private investment (ICAO, 2013). An innovative aspect of private concessions in Chile is the bundling of profitable and unprofitable airports into a single concession, as is the case for the airports of Punta Arenas and Balmaceda.

Companies operating across the country rely on air connectivity for short journeys between cities, particularly for business trips between Santiago and regional centres. Flying between these cities and Santiago is always a faster alternative than driving, except when travelling within Central Chile.

Air connectivity is also particularly important for those remote regions without any land-based transport links to the rest of the country. Smaller airports, even if not financially viable, can provide an essential service to their community and support the existence of local economic activities.

As Chileans are flying increasingly for work and leisure, expansion plans are in place at airports to cater for continuous growth in the number of passengers. More than 15 million passengers travelled to and from the country's airports in 2014, an increase of 170% over 2000. Around 70% of passenger movements are handled at Santiago's Arturo Merino Benitez airport. When the airport's concession was re-let in 2013, covering the period 2015-2030, the agreement included a plan to expand terminal capacity given the projected doubling of passengers by 2030. Similarly, terminal expansion is planned for other airports, from Iquique to Los Lagos.

Several factors have contributed to passenger growth and the development of national and international connectivity. Some of these factors include rising incomes and a growing number of destinations offered by airlines at more competitive prices as a result of open-skies agreements, with new entries to the market, including from low-cost carriers and the building of global alliances by national airlines. Improvements in airport infrastructure can also attract air carriers to develop new routes, as shown by the introduction of two direct flights from Santiago to Puerto Natales following the expansion of terminal capacity in the small airport of the Austral macrozone.

Identified gaps

National forecasts predict continued growth in air passenger numbers (CChC, 2016), and our benchmarking analysis confirms that this is a likely trend (Figure 4.28). The propensity to fly in Chile was just under one flight per person per year in 2014/15, vis-à-vis an average of 3.3 for OECD comparators. When incomes in OECD comparators were around the USD 30 000 mark in 2004, propensity to fly was already 2.5 on average, and this continued to grow over the following decade. Regional differences are wide, however: while Northern and Central Chile have a score in line with the national average, the propensity to fly is much higher in the Austral macrozone (similar to levels seen in Southern Italy). Levels are well below average in the Southern macrozone. These differences reflect underlying differences in average incomes, as well as the high dependency on air transport and the growing tourism market in the more remote Austral regions.

Figure 4.28. Propensity to fly, 2004 and 2014/15

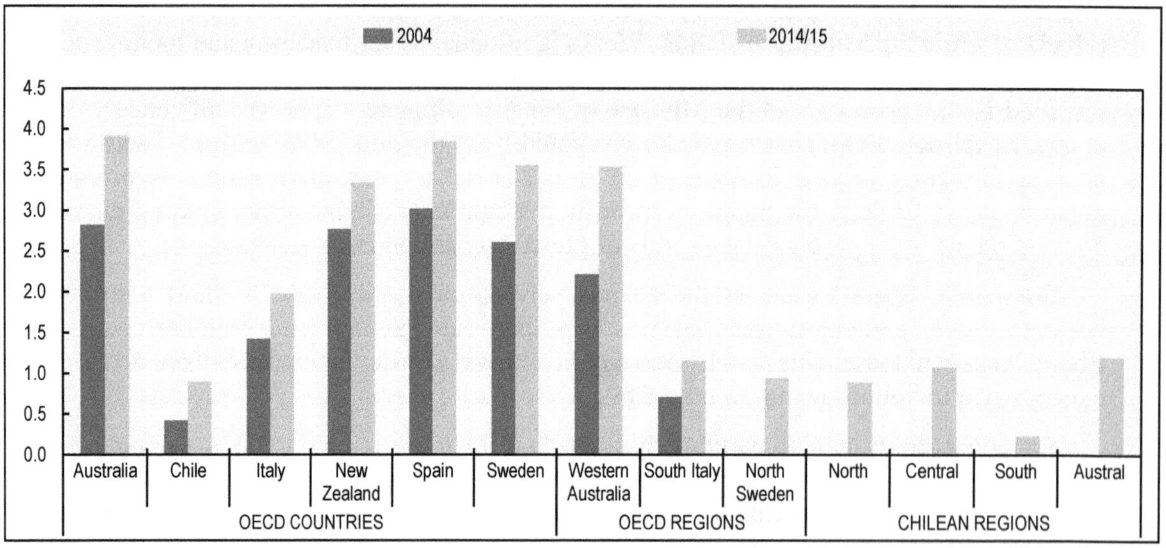

Note: propensity to fly is the ratio of the number of national and international passengers in the country/region to the population.

Source: Number of passenger: BITRE (2016b), Junta de Aeronáutica Civil (2016), ISTAT (2016e), World Bank (2016g), AENA (2016), Statistics Sweden (2016e) Population: World Bank (2016a), Australia Bureau of Statistics (2016a), ISTAT (2016a), Statistics Sweden (2016a), Instituto Nacional de Estadísticas de Chile (2016a).

The development of air connectivity relies on a stable regulatory framework that is conducive to attracting bidders at airports under concessions to further develop airport infrastructure and to attracting air carriers to strengthen connectivity and promote competition and new routes. The following strategic elements need to be examined in more detail as the national airport system grows:

- **Integrating land-use development and transport planning with airport site planning in large cities.** Land-use conflicts are common when airport sites are located in close proximity to large urban areas. Integrated development plans can ensure that potential conflicts are contained and that land uses are clearly assigned to accommodate both airport and urban growth. Integrated planning should also address issues such as noise and air pollution that are typically associated with air traffic growth. Major airports are large generators of road traffic. Transport to and from Santiago International Airport is entirely by private cars. Public transport options, beginning with bus services, will be required to cope with demand in the future.
- **Providing public funds to support non-commercially viable airports**. At present, cross-subsidies are allocated from profitable to unprofitable airports, a policy that differs from most OECD countries (see Box 4.11). Using revenues from profitable activities to expand networks with investments that show a positive socio-economic return but are not viable on purely commercial terms is a system successfully applied to France's passenger railway, but it always bears the risk of overextending the system and building unsustainable infrastructure.

Box 4.11. Cross-subsidies for smaller airports in Chile

Airports are characterised by having high fixed capital costs, relatively low marginal operating costs and capacity that is expanded in steps rather than incrementally. Airports also face numerous costs derived from maintaining a safe and compliant facility, even when there is no direct return on investment from meeting regulatory requirements. For airports to achieve economies of scale and declining cost curves, they need a critical mass of traffic. This poses significant financial challenges for small regional airports.

ACI (2014) shows that profit margins for airports with less than 1 million passengers per year (MPA) fell by 11.9% in 2013, compared to industry average growth of 15.9%. The most profitable airports were those in the 15-25 MPA range and those with over 40MPA. Adler et al. (2013), in a sample 85 regional airports worldwide, modelled a financial break-even point for airports at 463 569 passengers per year. This was more than double the 200 832-passenger threshold in 2002.

Regional airports, even if not financially viable, can provide an essential service to their community and support the existence of local economic activities. In Chile, they provide these communities with connectivity to Santiago and from there the rest of the world. However, regional airports require long-term financial support to absorb financial losses and remain operational. Support in Chile is at present provided in the form of cross-subsidies from more profitable airports such as Santiago's Arturo Merino Benitez.

Abeyrante (2009) presents a number of arguments for and against cross-subsidies. While there may be advantages for small airports to operate as part of a network to share some common costs, there is an inherent issue of fairness in having users of one airport pay for infrastructure in another airport that they do not use. The International Civil Aviation Organization discourages making passengers pay for infrastructure they do not use in its guidance on airport charges (ICAO, 2012). Cross-subsidisation also results in passengers on one carrier subsidising passengers on another. It can also foster inefficiencies, as the airport being subsidised has less incentive to achieve profitability by reducing its own costs. At the same time, cross-subsidies can result in lower air fares for travel from the smaller airports, stimulating demand and supporting a larger number of routes. Miller et al. (2016) found that this could create a feedback effect whereby the welfare gains from subsidies might outweigh the value of the subsidy.

In Norway, the state-owned company Avinor operates 46 airports under a cross-subsidisation model. A study by GAP (2012) found that the break-even point for its airports grew four-fold between 2002 and 2010 to reach 800 000. During that period, real operating costs doubled, and the value of cross-subsidies tripled. The study proposed a management or franchised contract model with competition to replace the system and drive efficiency. Studies in other countries with large networks and cross-subsidies (e.g. Spain and Portugal) found that operating efficiencies were much lower at airports that were being subsidised.

Box 4.11. Cross-subsidies for smaller airports in Chile (*cont.*)

Preserving regional connectivity for smaller, less financially viable airports may be achieved by way of direct subsidies by the state instead. For instance, the Australian Government announced a four-year fund for remote aerodrome updates in the 2015-16 budget. Complementary measures include the Remote Air Services Subsidy (RASS) scheme, which subsidises a regular weekly air transport service for the carriage of passengers and goods such as educational materials, medicines, fresh foods and other urgent supplies to communities in remote and isolated areas of Australia.

Compared to cross-subsidies from larger airports, direct subsidies are more transparent in accounting terms and enable the fiscal burden of providing what is essentially a public service to be spread across the entire taxpayer base. Direct subsidies can be combined with regulatory regimes that incentivise cost and revenue optimisation. For instance, governments can tender out the management of smaller airports and provide a subsidy cap.

Source: Abeyrante, 2009; Miller et al, 2016.

Figure 4.29. Surface access to airports, passenger modal share and travel time (minutes)

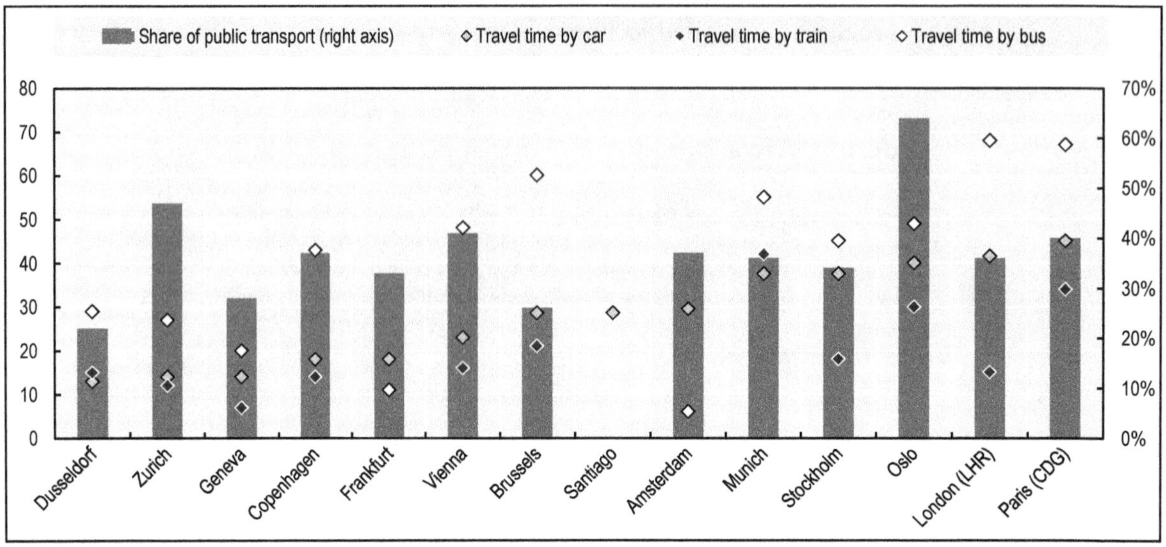

Note: travel times are calculated for a trip on Tuesday leaving from the city centre at 9AM.

Source: Share of public transport: ACRP (2008), data elaborated by ITF/OECD based on data from Google Maps.

One of the issues that could become more pressing as the economy grows is the lack of infrastructure for surface access to airports by public transport. Travel to and from airports in Chile takes place almost exclusively by car and taxi. Public investment in surface access plays a complementary role to airport development in many OECD countries (see Box 4.12), in which the share of passengers reaching airports in capitals by public transport ranges from 22% to 64% (Figure 4.29).

Alternatives to private vehicles can encompass dedicated bus routes to start with, maximising timetabling and fare integration opportunities with existing public transport systems. An additional benefit of comprehensive public transport access is that it maximises the catchment area of an airport, reducing time and cost for passengers in neighbouring areas to reach the airport site. Improving surface access by public transport should be a priority for Santiago and could be considered at some of the regional airports. At higher levels of demand, rail links may be considered if the flow of passengers to and from the airport is high enough to justify investment.

A number of countries that, like Chile, have not yet developed strategic plans to incorporate airports and surface access in their wider transport strategies are also aiming to rectify this. In New Zealand, surface access to Auckland International Airport has been a growing concern, given the increasing difficulty that passengers, staff and businesses experience in accessing the airport. Airport managers commissioned a surface access study in 2005, and the study confirmed the presence of severe travel-time delays to and from the airport as a result of bottlenecks on the regional road network. It also highlighted the weaknesses in public transport services. A number of planning and feasibility studies are under way to prepare for the construction of a dedicated public transport link, possibly by rail, to better serve the airport and reduce congestion.

Box 4.12. Airport surface access – the role of public transport

Large transport flows to and from main airports are generated by the movement of passengers, airport workers and freight traffic to and from airport sites. These flows can have negative impacts on road traffic congestion and air pollution. When airport operations expand in the absence of complementary surface access investment, these impacts can worsen and affect the reliability of travel times and hence depress demand at the airport itself.

Most OECD capital cities have developed strategic transport plans and land-use planning controls applicable to large property and infrastructure developments (including airports). These typically make the approval of construction projects conditional upon the provision of adequate surface access, including by public transport and rail. Additionally, limits may be set regarding acceptable levels of air quality. In some systems, infrastructure managers also directly contribute to the funding of access links.

As a result, airports in OECD capital cities are generally linked to urban areas by bus, metro and/or rail links. In Australia, Sydney's Kingsford Smith Airport was connected to the existing rail network by a tunnelled rail link in 2000, ahead of the Olympic Games. At London Heathrow Airport, the prominent role of public transport surface access can be seen in the planning, design and layout of Terminal 5, which opened in 2008. Before construction, the terminal's design directly incorporated a station and rail tunnels for extensions to existing rail services (Heathrow Express/Connect and the Piccadilly Line). The station also embeds two additional platforms to allow for the potential future (westward or southern) expansion of the rail network. Incheon Airport in Korea opened in 2010 and is served by 117 bus lines as well as a railway station that is integrated into the existing national and regional railroad network.

Even in smaller cities such as Bari, Southern Italy, airport rail links are being built. Bari Airport handles 4 million passengers per year, travelling to both national and international destinations. Over the summer months, it is one of the main points of entry for tourists arriving to the region. The rail link was built over 2009-2012 as a spur of the existing regional rail network. The airport rail link is 8 km long and fully electrified, and it adopts an automatic train control system. Trains can reach maximum speeds of 110 km/hour, but on average, they travel at 60 km/hour. The overall cost of the link was just over EUR 80 million, co-financed by the Region of Apulia and the European Commission. The new infrastructure connects the airport to the city of Bari in 15 minutes, as well as to other regional cities and towns.

Ultimately, fast and reliable access is one of the conditions for an airport's long-term success. A reduction in the share of journeys by car and taxi also contributes to reducing air pollution and congestion, with positive effects across the city as well as at the airport site.

Source: UK Airport Commission (2015), https://www.gov.uk/government/publications/airports-commission-final-report-surface-access; New South Wales Parliament (2014); Ferrovie.it (2013).

Summary of the analysis

The analysis of infrastructure gaps by transport sector reveals that gaps in the provision, quality and efficiency of transport infrastructure are present across the macrozones of Chile. Notable deficiencies and emerging themes from the analysis are described in this section and summarised in Table 4.7.

Last-mile connectivity gaps exist at the interface of different modes and limit the efficiency of transport networks as a whole:

- Suburban motorways are not always linked to urban roads, and bottlenecks are present along key access routes to large cities.
- There is a lack of high-quality links between ports and the national highway network in San Antonio and Concepcion, resulting in heavy vehicles using inadequate and inappropriate urban streets to access port terminals.
- The quality of rail freight connections to ports is poor, and the logistics network lacks inland ports and distribution centres connected to the ports by trunk rail or road links, especially in the Central and Southern macrozones.
- Access to all major airports is exclusively car based, and public transport options are not integrated with urban mobility systems.

Large differences exist in the quality of infrastructure and accessibility across the country and in cities:

- The capacity of port infrastructure is under pressure from increasing trade flows and the emergence of larger container ships, particularly in the Central macrozone, where the development of a new port will be necessary.
- Gaps in surface quality and safety standards of roads exist not just between Chile and OECD comparators but also between Chilean macrozones and within these zones, as seen by large differences in road paving rates and road crash rates.
- Even starker differences are evident across areas of large cities, such as in Santiago, where poorer neighbourhoods are not only located further away than richer ones from jobs and services but also suffer from lower-quality infrastructure, such as the lack of pavements and other infrastructure for pedestrians.

The potential for rail services to contribute to passenger mobility and logistics is not fulfilled:

- On the one hand, the rail network's ability to accommodate both passenger and freight services has been undermined by low investment and the lack of a national strategy for rail transport, in turn undermined by ineffective institutional governance of the sector.
- This leads to low utilisation of existing tracks, particularly in Central and Southern Chile, where the potential for rail to move freight to and from ports is high and there is extra pressure on road infrastructure.
- On the other hand, rail services are not considered an integral part of the transport network, apart from mining railways in the North. Unclear choices for investment and capacity allocation raise conflicts between passenger and freight services that are detrimental to the development of both services.

Across all sectors, data for policy making are not collected systematically:

- The lack of comprehensive data (e.g. on freight and passenger flows, origin-destination movements, quality of services and users' satisfaction) hinders the compilation of transport statistics and the development of performance indicators and related analysis.

The external costs of transport (safety, congestion and environmental impacts) are a growing challenge in urban areas:

- Chile's transport networks are generating high external costs, reflected in the number of deaths caused by road crashes, the exposure of urban residents to pollutants at levels higher than in OECD comparators and growing transport-related greenhouse gas emissions.
- Externalities derive from an over-reliance on road transport for both freight and passenger movements. Public transport and infrastructure for walking and cycling are often inadequate in major cities, and traffic demand management systems are not in place.
- The rise of negative externalities such as urban congestion translates into lower potential and actual economic growth, and it has a negative effect on quality of life.

The need for maintenance across all transport modes is growing:

- Experience from OECD countries shows that, following a period of large-scale road construction, a grace period of several years – during which roads remain in good condition even without maintenance – is followed by a period in which the need for maintenance surges.
- In many European countries, the need for maintenance has coincided with budgetary pressures due to financial crises. The result has been a fast deterioration of road surface quality over the past decade. Maintenance needs are already evident in Chile's rail infrastructure and will grow as road, port and airport assets age.
- In addition, extreme weather events linked to climate change and natural disasters will continue to be a challenge for the resilience of transport networks across the country.
- Greater priority should be assigned to maintenance in multi-annual infrastructure budgets.

Table 4.7. Chilean transport infrastructure scorecard – strengths and challenges

Sector	Strengths	Current challenges	Future challenges
All transport infrastructure	Some good-quality assets following high investment	Inequality in the provision of infrastructure	Accommodating economic growth while fostering competitiveness across economic sectors
		Gaps at the interface of different modes	Resilience to extreme weather and natural disasters
		Missing data for assessment and strategy	Changing socio-economic appraisal methodologies to reflect policy goals
Primary road network	Good asset condition	Unreliable cross-border connections	
	Good intercity connectivity (C, S)	Missing links to ports and cities	Missing links to growing ports and cities
		Lower quality standards (N, A)	Congestion and bottlenecks
	Good safety record		Worsening of safety
Secondary road network	Good asset condition (N)	Low share of paved roads (N, C, S)	Poor asset condition
		Poor asset condition (S, A)	Maintenance bulge
		Poor safety record	Worsening of safety

Table 4.7. Chilean transport infrastructure scorecard – strengths and challenges (*cont.*)

Sector	Strengths	Current challenges	Future challenges
Port infrastructure	Good asset condition (N, C)	Efficiency gap (S, A)	Capacity for larger vessels Maintenance bulge
	Good global connectivity	Low rail modal share (C, S)	Poor hinterland connections
Rail infrastructure		Poor asset condition	Network assets decline (C, S)
		Lack of interconnections	Lack of intermodal options for freight transport (C, S)
		Low utilisation rate	No passenger services
Urban accessibility and environmental quality	High modal share of public transport	Lack of integrated planning leading to inequality of access	Growing motorisation levels displacing public transport Road maintenance bulge
		High levels of transport-related emissions and air pollution	Growing emissions from higher traffic volumes Impacts of emissions and congestion
Airport infrastructure	Good asset condition at most airports	Lack of surface access by public transport	Sustainability of concession models and cross-subsidies

Note: Letters in brackets indicate macrozones where the strength/challenge is particularly relevant. N = North; C = Centre; S = South; A = Austral.

Policy recommendations

The challenges ahead

Productive investment in transport infrastructure is vital to keep Chile on the road to greater prosperity. As the country transitions to a high-income economy and the population continues to grow, it is likely that today's gaps and negative externalities will worsen. The potential impacts of not addressing Chile's infrastructure gaps through an integrated infrastructure strategy are three-fold:

- First, national economic growth would be constrained, as deteriorating infrastructure can negatively affect the competitiveness of export industries and inflate the prices of imported goods. Poor connectivity can also act as a drag on labour and capital productivity.
- Second, disparities in economic performance between regions and within metropolitan areas could widen. Investment in public transport and infrastructure for cyclists and pedestrians is a key policy for improving equity in cities. Targeted investment in standard-quality road infrastructure will be more sustainable in rural and remote areas than large-scale programmes to surface roads with low standards.
- Third, future resources that could be allocated to strategic infrastructure investment may need to be diverted towards actions to reduce the deterioration of inadequate infrastructure.

In the context of the new Plan Chile 30/30, the government needs to devise targeted and co-ordinated actions to address the identified gaps and raise the standards of transport infrastructure. ITF/OECD policy recommendations are presented through six strategic themes based on the quantitative and qualitative analysis presented in this chapter.

There are limits to what infrastructure investment alone can do without co-ordinated government policies across ministries, a consistent framework for pricing and regulation (including subsidy reforms), and integrated transport policy and land-use planning and development strategies. There are numerous examples from OECD countries as to how an effective planning system can be established.

For instance, Western Australia has a detailed hierarchy for developing long-term planning strategies across all sectors of its economy, including for the development of transport infrastructure. The Western Australian Planning Commission works in consultation with a range of government and non-government stakeholders to produce long-term planning strategies. The strategy is the highest-order planning instrument. While the document does not bind government agencies to specific actions, it is used to guide, shape and inform a hierarchy of State, regional and local planning tools, instruments and decisions within the Western Australian planning system. All other planning documents seek to be consistent with the planning strategy.

The recent *Red Logística de Gran Escala* joint initiative between the Ministry of Public Works and the Ministry of Transport and Telecommunications with the State Railway Company, which will focus on developing logistics centres and a rail link to the San Antonio port, is an excellent initiative in this respect. A new institutional approach to rail infrastructure can build on the experience accumulated in other transport sectors to attract private investment and develop sustainable long-term financial plans for the construction, maintenance and operations of new connections.

Strategic recommendations

1. The development of an integrated logistics strategy is a priority to support trade and growth

- To ensure well-functioning logistics, Chile should develop a national multi-modal strategy. The main goal of the strategy should be to identify, upgrade and interconnect the assets that contribute to trade competitiveness. The priorities already highlighted in this chapter include addressing last-mile connectivity issues and providing better intermodal links to ports.
- The national logistics strategy should aim to co-ordinate new infrastructure investment and land-use planning. Specifically, the *Puerto de Gran Escala (PGE)* provides a nationally significant opportunity to develop a logistics system to improve trade competitiveness in central Chile that includes ports, inland ports and dedicated freight corridors. Rail and highway rights of way should generally be preserved in the land-use development plans of the major port cities.
- The national logistics strategy should have medium-term and long-term goals that link to the Plan Chile 30/30 objectives. This will be an opportunity to assess different options for funding and financing of new infrastructure and long-term maintenance needs, as well as to develop new governance models to streamline decision making at the central level while devolving responsibility for implementation at the regional level – as detailed in Chapters 2 and 3.

OECD comparator countries have developed multi-modal and long-term strategies to strengthen logistics competitiveness, either as part of a national transport strategy or by joining up road, rail and port planning. Strategies range from a 12-year plan in Sweden to a 30-year strategy in New Zealand to a vision towards 2050 in Western Australia.

2. Infrastructure planning and investment should be better co-ordinated at the metropolitan level

- Chile's prosperity inevitably depends on the success of its cities, where most of the population and economic activities are concentrated. Metropolitan authorities need to be better equipped with transport infrastructure planning instruments and co-ordinate transport and land-use policies to ensure the effectiveness of comprehensive strategies to relieve congestion bottlenecks and improve the attractiveness of public transport and active modes.
- This requires reforms that strengthen planning powers at the right metropolitan level of authority, such as by overcoming district-based decision making on strategic issues. In parallel, further better co-ordination of investment across ports, airports and urban transport assets is needed to align investment in metropolitan areas.
- Two priorities at the urban level are the provision of more equitable access to jobs and services for all citizens and the reduction of negative externalities from transport systems. Both priorities can be addressed through targeted investment in higher-quality public transport and urban spaces, coupled with policies to manage car and truck traffic flows.

Issues such as congestion, pollution and inequality of access are a common feature across OECD metropolitan areas. Most urban authorities have been given a mix of planning and financial instruments to tackle these challenges through co-ordinated policies at the appropriate level of governance. Particularly in Europe, priorities have progressively shifted from simply providing more road capacity to investing in public transit.

3. A territorial approach is needed to promote targeted investment and reduce inequality

- More productive investment in transport infrastructure for logistics and metropolitan areas will not exempt policy makers from addressing the needs of rural and isolated populations in remote regions where the availability and quality of transport infrastructure shows significant gaps with the rest of the country.
- A territorial approach requires targeted investment to make the most of the public funds spent to address these gaps. This requires specific allowances to be made in national and regional budgets, or appraisal methodologies could be reformed to better address territorial inequalities.
- Specifically, road-paving solutions can be rolled out incrementally in more peripheral regions, taking into account connectivity needs, projected traffic growth (by vehicle type), life-cycle costs including future maintenance needs and safety implications. With this in mind, the share of paved roads can be increased over time where appropriate.
- In addition, many remote regions in Chile are not accessible by land transport and rely on connections by sea and air. The provision of public funds to support non-commercially viable airports should be carefully monitored to ensure that the system does not lead to building unsustainable infrastructure and that investment is funded in a transparent way.

OECD countries with remote and isolated areas have been developing targeted strategies to promote investment. Examples include direct subsidies for the local airports providing essential connectivity to the residents of North Sweden, changes to the national system of transport project appraisal that recognise the importance of "life line" infrastructure in Australia and co-funding of infrastructure projects by local Maori communities in New Zealand.

4. A life-cycle approach needs to promote the long-term resilience of the transport network

- Long-term investment strategies require the introduction of asset-management techniques by all authorities responsible for transport assets in Chile, learning from sectors that already do so. Investment in public roads is an example of how a systemic approach to asset management would help decision makers assess what level of paving is best for secondary roads.
- Better data can support the mapping of asset conditions and key service-level outcomes, which in turn will feed into an asset-management strategy for rural roads, rail infrastructure, etc. The strategy needs to be linked to long-term financial planning. The risk of not doing so is that, as assets age, maintenance funding will not be available when needed.
- Besides making allowances for what can be foreseen, Chile needs to develop studies to map and quantify the potentially disruptive impacts of natural disasters and climate change. Based on the findings of these studies, mitigation and adaptation strategies should be developed. In addition, the cumulative impact of deferred maintenance increases the transport network's vulnerability to local or systemic disruptions.

A challenge for virtually all OECD countries is applying a whole-of-life perspective to infrastructure investment, especially when asset conditions are subject to uncertainties such as earthquakes and extreme weather events. Some of the initiatives undertaken include measures to identify alternative lifeline infrastructure such as parallel roads or complementary ports in the case of a natural disaster in New Zealand, as well as linking maintenance needs to long-term budgets in Australia.

5. The external impacts of transport activity need to be minimised

- Reducing transport-related emissions, which are already above OECD average despite relatively lower levels of motorisation, should be a made a policy priority across sectors. Measures to reduce emissions include modal shift and technological efficiency. Actions targeted at shifting transport activity from road to other modes include the following:
- promote rail transport to meet freight and passenger demand by providing reliable infrastructure and dedicated links that support commercial speeds and accommodate higher loads and by reducing conflicts in the allocation of capacity between freight and passenger traffic.
- develop costal shipping, including by liberalising cabotage, as an alternative to land-based transport, especially for imports that arrive at deep-sea ports in Central Chile but carry goods going to other regions.

- contain the growth of private motorised vehicles in urban areas in favour of public transport options and active modes, including by adding surface access alternatives at airports.
- These measures can be effective at reducing emissions while tackling congestion and bottlenecks, mainly on the road network and around key economic hubs such as ports.
- In parallel, the development of Chile's National Road Safety Strategy will need to ensure that legislation, education and infrastructure investment efforts towards greater road safety are joined up and adhere to international best practices.

Efforts to tackle externalities from transport activity have been wide ranging in OECD comparator countries. These include initiatives to raise the attractiveness of rail transport for shippers sending cargo to and from major ports in Spain, Italy and Australia, as well as policies to promote integrated public transport solutions for commuters and for travellers to and from airports. Long-term road safety strategies that include specific targets are also very common in OECD countries.

6. Policy makers will need better data to make better decisions

- Data availability, particularly in relation to transport demand and performance measures, has been a limitation of this review and affects policy making in Chile more generally. Standardised data-collection methodologies should be deployed across transport sectors, and a key goal should be bridging the knowledge gap between private and public actors, as well as between different government agencies.
- To this end, ITF/OECD (2016c) have suggested that a Logistics Observatory for Chile should be set up, and this would contribute to fill the knowledge gap in freight transport and related sectors. This recommendation can be strengthened and broadened to support the creation of a transport infrastructure observatory in the near future.
- Data-collection efforts should focus on several Key Performance Indicators (KPIs), in line with most OECD countries. Table 4.8 provides some examples of KPIs by sector, beyond those presented in the rest of the chapter. These KPIs could be developed further in each macrozone.

Table 4.8. Key Performance Indicators by mode

Sector	Sample indicator	Market	Indicators units
All transport modes	Traffic	Freight/Passenger	Traffic volumes (by user and vehicle types where appropriate); distances travelled
	Modal share	Freight/Passenger	Evolution over time of traffic share of each passenger and freight mode
	Life-cycle costs	Freight/Passenger	Life-cycle costs of maintenance regime
	Customer satisfaction	Freight/Passenger	Regular surveys of users for each mode (passenger) and logistics sector (freight)
	Time to market	Freight	Average export and import lead times in days
	Accessibility indices	Passenger	Contour indices or location-based indices that express access to jobs and services in terms of time/cost

Table 4.8. Key Performance Indicators by mode

Sector	Sample indicator	Market	Indicators units
Road	Congestion	Passenger	Lane occupancy rate, travel speed, idle time spent in traffic for an average journey, variability over expected travel time
	Reliability	Freight	Travel speed; average delays of shipments, such as average lost time per truck-km
	Asset condition	Freight/Passenger	Surface roughness, rutting and cracking; skid resistance; bridge load capacity; height and width clearance
Port	Productivity	Containers	Truck and vessel turnaround time, TEUs per berth area and/or port area
	Productivity	Bulk	Vessel turnaround time, tonnes per hour and/or berth occupancy rate
Rail	Crowding	Passenger	Number of passengers in excess of capacity at peak time
	Punctuality	Passenger	Share of late services compared to schedule, such as >10-minute delay for journeys >1 hour
	Reliability	Freight	Average speed, average delays of shipments

Box 4.13. Reforming regional road project appraisal and funding in Australia

In 2013-14, Australia spent approximately AUD 19 billion maintaining, expanding and operating its extensive road network. Despite constant growth in expenditure in recent years, parts of the road network are poorly maintained, particularly in remote and regional areas. In the same areas, accessibility is a concern, as some roads experience closures on a routine basis mainly due to flooding. Future road expenditure liabilities are large, and inaction will lead to further deterioration of road performance.

The current economic evaluation system is based on conventional traditional cost-benefit analysis (CBA) techniques. Prioritisation of investment is based on two main types of benefits, namely time savings and operating cost reductions. However, the system used to prioritise road project funding in Australia is not well suited to ensure that future funding streams are allocated to roads in remote and regional areas.

The rationale for investment in these roads is not based on reducing travel times and vehicle operating costs. Based on these criteria, remote road projects have very low net present values. Given lower traffic volumes, road projects in remote areas generate lower benefits than in densely populated urban areas. In addition, construction costs are higher for roads of equivalent standards due to the higher cost of inputs, access to contractors and the impact of extreme weather events.

Instead, road projects in remote and regional areas yield other types of benefits, such as direct cost savings thanks to road improvements (such as reduced storage costs for food and fuel, avoided costs of delivering goods by barge/air) and access to jobs and services in the nearest towns and cities. If those benefits are not taken into account, standard economic evaluation techniques will fail to prioritise projects that improve accessibility and are of high value to the communities and regions that they support.

In this context, the Australian Transport and Infrastructure Council has committed to reviewing the National Guidelines for Transport System Management and investigating new approaches to the appraisal of remote and regional transport infrastructure projects. The new approaches are part of a wider nationally co-ordinated effort to address key transport infrastructure that is specific to remote and regional Australia, known as the National Remote and Regional Transport Strategy (August 2016). The strategy aims to raise the profile of these areas and highlight the challenges to growth and development, so as to maximise investment opportunities in transport infrastructure and services.

One of the proposed approaches consists of a Risk Indicator to support the evaluation of "Life Line" freight routes. These are roads that do not deliver high positive outcomes under CBA but whose resilience and reliability is critical for more remote populations. The Risk Indicator has been developed to help road managers identify whether routes qualify as a "Life Line" and hence determine which roads have greater justification for receiving upgrade funding, rather than relying on assessments based on CBA. The Risk Indicator uses a scoring methodology (1 to 5) examining:

- the sizes and needs of the communities and the establishments they service
- the availability of alternative routes that could be used if the route in question is unavailable
- the likelihood that the alternative routes are also closed

Box 4.13. Reforming regional road project appraisal and funding in Australia (*cont.*)

- historical incidence and duration of events that close or restrict operations on the route
- assessment of responses to previous events, including costs and impacts in the regions serviced.

Going forward, the proposed methodology could be introduced, together with alternatives such as greater weight given to resilience against natural hazards. More effectively linking assessment to overall policy objectives can result in better prioritisation in more peripheral areas, counterbalancing the risk of being excluded from future funding allocations.

Table 4.9. Transport infrastructure gaps and remedies

Theme	Gaps	Recommendations
Last-mile connectivity	• Last-mile connectivity gaps exist at the interface of different modes and limit the efficiency of transport networks as a whole. • Suburban motorways are not always linked to urban roads, and bottlenecks are present along key access routes to large cities. • The lack of high-quality links between ports and the national highway network results in heavy vehicles using inadequate and inappropriate urban streets to access port terminals. • Access to all major airports is exclusively car based, and public transport options are not integrated with urban mobility systems.	• Develop a national multi-modal strategy. The main goal of the strategy is to identify, upgrade and interconnect the assets that contribute to trade competitiveness. • Priorities should cover addressing last-mile connectivity issues and providing better intermodal links to ports, including the nationally significant opportunity to develop a logistics system in central Chile. • Give metropolitan authorities transport infrastructure planning instruments to develop comprehensive strategies and better co-ordinate investment across ports, airports and urban transport assets.
Inequalities in infrastructure provision and quality	• Gaps in surface quality and safety standards of roads exist not just between Chile and OECD comparators but also between Chilean macrozones and within these zones, as seen by large differences in secondary road quality and road crash rates. • Even starker differences are evident across areas of large cities, where poorer neighbourhoods are not only located further away than richer ones from jobs and services but also suffer from lower-quality infrastructure such as the lack of pavements and other infrastructure for pedestrians.	• Provide more equitable access to jobs and services for all citizens by investing in higher-quality public transport and urban spaces, coupled with policies to manage car and truck traffic flows. • Target investment to make the most of the public funds spent to address gaps in remote regions, either with specific allowances in national and regional budgets or by reforming appraisal methodologies. • Roll out road-paving solutions incrementally in more peripheral regions, taking into account connectivity needs, projected traffic growth (by vehicle type), life-cycle costs and safety implications.
Rail transport potential	• Low investment, unclear capacity allocation choices and the lack of a national strategy for rail transport undermine the rail network's ability to accommodate both passenger and freight services. • The quality of rail freight connections to ports is poor, and the logistics network lacks inland ports and distribution centres connected to the ports by trunk rail or road links, leading to low utilisation of existing tracks, particularly in Central and Southern Chile.	• Promote rail transport to meet freight demand by providing reliable infrastructure and dedicated links that support commercial speeds and accommodate higher loads. • Develop a coherent strategy that reduces conflicts in the allocation of capacity between freight and passenger traffic. • Identify opportunities for new rail passenger services, especially at the suburban level.
Collection, dissemination and analysis of data	• The lack of comprehensive datasets for most transport sectors hinders the compilation of transport statistics and the development of performance indicators and related analysis.	• Deploy standardised data-collection methodologies across transport sectors by bridging the knowledge gap between private and public actors, and between different government agencies. • Set-up a Logistics Observatory in charge of compiling and disseminating statistics and Key Performance Indicators to guide policy.

Table 4.9. Transport infrastructure gaps and remedies (*cont.*)

Theme	Gaps	Recommendations
External impacts of transport	• Transport networks are generating high external costs, reflected in the number of deaths caused by road crashes, the exposure of urban residents to pollutants and growing greenhouse gas emissions. • Externalities derive from an over-reliance on road transport for freight and passenger movements, as well as low-quality public transport alternatives.	• Contain the growth of private motorised vehicles in urban areas by promoting modal shift to public transport and active modes. • Develop costal shipping, including by liberalising cabotage, as an alternative to road transport for imports that arrive at deep-sea ports in Central Chile but carry goods going to other regions. • Develop the National Road Safety Strategy to ensure that legislation, education and infrastructure investment efforts towards greater road safety are joined up and adhere to international best practices.
Focus on performance over lifetime of asset	• Maintenance needs are already evident in Chile's rail infrastructure, and given large-scale construction in recent years, needs will grow as road, port and airport assets age. • Extreme weather events linked to climate change and natural disasters will continue to be a challenge for the resilience of transport networks across the country.	• Assign greater priority to maintenance in future infrastructure budgets based on foreseen needs; develop studies to map and quantify the potentially disruptive impacts of natural disasters and climate change. • Introduce asset-management techniques across all modes to better assess what level of investment is best for each category of infrastructure.

Notes

1. Econometric techniques with panel data (over time and across observations) are designed to estimate elasticities while controlling for external factors such as population growth, urbanisation and economic changes.

2. UNECLAC has adopted this approach in the estimation of the investment gap in Latin America and the Caribbean, based on a comparison with the share of GDP invested in a selection of East Asian countries.

3. The Camara Chilena de Construcción (CChC) employs a similar methodology in its studies of infrastructure needs for Chile (2012 and 2016).

4. For instance, rail freight capacity can be increased by improving both track and train utilisation. In turn, track utilisation can be improved through demand management (e.g. access charges and timetabling) and technology (e.g. modern signalling systems and automation).

5. Data on road traffic flows are not regularly collected, and there is no standard processing of the limited available data to develop regular and comprehensive traffic indices in Chile

6. These include different technical solutions such as a thin layer of asphalt (~5 cm) or a compacted granular base. These solutions are cheaper than more advanced paving techniques and are applied to roads with lower utilisation, as measured by average annual daily traffic (AADT).

7. Laws stipulate that cabotage should be carried out by Chilean-flagged ships: Chilean companies with Chilean crew. Foreign companies can apply for a waiver, but transaction costs are high enough to discourage entry.

8. Port Botany Landside Improvement System (PBLIS)

9. For example, truck waiting times are high; trip length for a truck transporting fruit from the Curico zone to ports in the Central macrozone is estimated to be 28 hours (round trip), of which 7 hours is driving and 21 hours is waiting (CAMPORT, 2015, citing a study by KOM).

10. The average is affected by the high share of rail freight traffic in Australia, supported by large mining and related rail operations.

11. Empresa de los Ferrocarriles del Estado, the state-owned national rail company supervised by the MTT

12 The urban metro operates at night with cargoes to the port (11pm until dawn) (Information provided by Direplan, September 2017)

13. Railway laws in force today are the Ley General de Ferrocariles (1931) for private operators and the Ley Organica de la Empresa de los Ferrocariles del Estado (1993) for EFE's network and concessions.

14. New buses were introduced in February 2007, with routes restructured around hubs with trunk-and-feeder ines. The aim was to formalise, rationalise and improve public transport quality. Transantiago's fleet is less polluting, less accident prone and more accessible than the previous system. However, the system has also been criticised for its rigidity, leading to higher journey times for some passengers, and for the faulty implementation of some key elements, such as the lack of reserved bus lanes across the city. Plans are now at an advanced stage for addressing these weaknesses, improving safety and adapting routes to the changing pattern of demand in the fast-growing city.

15. Tiznado et al. use a corrected accessibility measure (CAM), taking into account comfort and number of transfers, to compare accessibility to the CBD from the San Miguel district in the south and from the Las Condes district in the north-east. Based on CAM, travel time is 22 minutes faster from Las Condes than San Miguel.

16. Factors such as age, mental and physical disability, and to a different extent travelling with young children or heavy luggage are all barriers to people's mobility and, in turn, their ability to access jobs, services and other activities (ITF/OECD, forthcoming).

References

Abeyratne, R. (2009, "Airport business law", Authorhouse.

ACAM (2015), "Rapporto sulle infrastrutture in Campania", Napoli.

ACRP (2008), "Public transportation mode shares to European and Asian airports", in Ground Access to Major Airports by Public Transportation, http://aci-na.org/static/entransit/acrp_access_to_airports.pdf.

Adler, N., Ülkü, T., & Yazhemsky, E. (2013) "Small regional airport sustainability: Lessons from benchmarking". Journal of Air Transport Management, 33, pp. 22-31.

AENA (2016), "Tráfico por año" [Yearly traffic], Estadísticas de tráfico aéreo [Statistics on air traffic], www.aena.es/csee/Satellite?c=Page&cid=1113582476715&pagename=Estadisticas%2FEstadisticas (accessed 13 May 2016).

Ahmad, E., Zanola, R. (2015), Chile: Regional Investments, Convergence and Local Governance. Some Preconditions for Sustainable and Inclusive Growth, London School of Economics, London.

Andrés, L., D. Biller and J. Schwartz (2014), "The infrastructure gap and decentralization", Working Paper 14-06, International Center for Public Policy.

Arvis, J-F., L. Ojala, B. Shepherd, D. Saslavsky, C. Busch and A. Raj (2014), Connecting to Compete 2014: Trade Logistics in the Global Economy: The Logistics Performance Index and Its Indicators, The World Bank.

Auckland Council (2012), The Auckland Plan.

Australian Bureau of Statistics (2016a), "Table 4. Estimated Resident Population, States and Territories (Number)", Australian Demographic Statistics, Dec 2015, www.abs.gov.au/ausstats/abs@.nsf/detailspage/3101.0dec%202015?opendocument (accessed 23 February 2016).

Australian Bureau of Statistics (2016b), "Land area (ha)", Western Australia (S/T), http://stat.abs.gov.au/itt/r.jsp?regionsummary&region=5&dataset=abs_regional_asgs&geoconcept=region&measure=measure&datasetasgs=abs_regional_asgs&datasetlga=abs_regional_lga&regionlga=region&regionasgs=region (accessed 23 February 2016).

Australian Bureau of Statistics (2016c), "Table 6. Expenditure, Income and Industry Components of Gross State Product, Western Australia, Chain volume measures and current prices", Australian National Accounts: State Accounts, 2014-15, www.abs.gov.au/ausstats/abs@.nsf/detailspage/5220.02014-15?opendocument (accessed 23 February 2016).

Banco Central de Chile (2016), "PIB regional" [Regional GDP], Cuentas Nacionales [National Accounts], http://si3.bcentral.cl/Siete/secure/cuadros/arboles.aspx (accessed 23 February 2016).

Bickel, P., and R. Friedrich (eds.) (2013), Environmental External Costs of Transport, Springer Science & Business Media, Stuttgart.

BITRE (2016a), "Fatalities", Australian Road Deaths Database, https://bitre.gov.au/statistics/safety/fatal_road_crash_database.aspx (accessed 13 May 2016).

BITRE (2016b), "Airport Traffic Data 1985-86 to 2015-16", Airport traffic data, https://bitre.gov.au/publications/ongoing/airport_traffic_data.aspx (accessed 13 May 2016).

BITRE (2015), "Route-kilometres of open railway", in Yearbook 2015 – Australian infrastructure statistics, https://bitre.gov.au/publications/2015/files/BITRE_yearbook_2015_full_report.pdf.

BITRE (2014a), "Road and rail freight: competitors or complements?", Information Sheet 34.

BITRE (2014b), Freightline 2 – Australian iron ore freight transport, https://bitre.gov.au/publications/2014/files/Freightline_02.pdf.

BITRE (2013), "Total road length by state/territory, by road type", in Yearbook 2013 – Australian infrastructure statistics, https://bitre.gov.au/publications/2013/files/infra1886_r_bitre_infrastructure_yearbook_0813_web.pdf.

Calderon, C. and L. Serven (2004), "The effects of infrastructure development on growth and income distribution", Policy Research Working Paper, Series no. 3400, The World Bank.

Cámara Chilena de la Construcción (CChC) (2016), Infraestructura Critica para el Desarrollo.

Cámara Marítima y Portuaria de Chile (2016), Una Nueva Vuelta de Tuerca, Cámara Marítima y Portuaria de Chile (CAMPORT)

Cámara Marítima y Portuaria de Chile (2015), Desafíos De La Conectividad Para El Comercio Exterior, Cámara Marítima y Portuaria de Chile (CAMPORT), www.camport.cl/sitio/wp-content/uploads/2016/09/Camport-Desafiosparalaconectividad-baja.pdf

Château, J., Dellink, R., & Lanzi, E. (2014). An overview of the OECD ENV-Linkages model. OECD Environment Working Paper; Paris

CEPAL/UNECLAC (2011), "The economic infrastructure gap in Latin America and the Caribbean", Comisión Económica para América Latina y el Caribe/United Nations Economic Commission for Latin America and the Caribbean. FAL Bulletin n. 293.

CIA (2016), "Roadways", The World Factbook, www.cia.gov/library/publications/the-world-factbook/fields/2085.html (accessed 13 May 2016).

Consejo Político de Infraestructura (2016), Políticas Públicas de Infraestructura.

Chile's Productivity Commission (2016), Indice de Competitividad Global 2015-16, www.productividadchile.cl/indice-de-competitividad-global-2015-2016/.

Dobbs, R., Pohl, H., Lin, D. Y., Mischke, J., Garemo, N., Hexter, J. and Nanavatty, R. (2013). Infrastructure productivity: how to save $1 trillion a year. McKinsey Global Institute.

Directemar, Boletín Estadístico, 2016, http://web.directemar.cl/estadisticas/maritimo/2016/BEAM2016.pdf

Eddington, R. (2006), The Eddington Transport Study: Transport's Role in Sustaining the UK's Productivity and Competitiveness, H. M. Treasury, London.

Engel, E., R. Fischer and A. Galetovic (2000), "Franchising of infrastructure concessions in Chile: A policy report", Serie Economía n 88.

European Parliament (2015), "Modal share in selected ports (overall throughput)", in Modal share of freight transport to and from EU ports, www.europarl.europa.eu/RegData/etudes/STUD/2015/540350/IPOL_STU(2015)540350_EN.pdf.

European Parliament (2014), EU Road Surfaces: Economic and Safety Impact of the Lack of Regular Road Maintenance.

Fay, M. and T. Yepes (2003), "Investing in infrastructure: What is needed from 2000–2010", Policy Research Working Paper 3102, The World Bank.

Gómez-Lobo, A. (2012), "The ups and downs of a public transport reform: the case of Transantiago", Serie Documentos de Trabajo SDT354, Universidad de Chile, Departamento de Economía, Santiago, Chile.

Graham, D. (2014), Causal Influence for Ex-Post Evaluation of Transport Interventions, International Transport Forum, Paris.

Grupo EFE (2016), "Inversión real de la Empresa de los Ferrocarriles del Estado" [Current investment of the State Enterprise of Railways].

Grupo EFE (2015), Memoria Anual.

Hurtubia, R., Muñoz, J.C. and Tiznado-Aitken, R. (2016), "How Equitable is Access to Opportunities and Basic Services Considering the Impact of the Level of Service?" ITF/OECD Discussion Paper 2016-15, OECD Publishing, Paris.

IEA (2016), "CO2 emissions by product and flow", IEA CO2 emissions from fuel combustion statistics, http://stats.oecd.org/BrandedView.aspx?oecd_bv_id=co2-data-en&doi=data-00430-en (accessed 13 May 2016).

ICAO (2012), ICAO's Policies on Charges for Airports and Air Navigation Services, International Civil Aviation Organization, www.icao.int/publications/Documents/9082_9ed_en.pdf

IMF (2015), Making Public Investment More Efficient.

INRIX (2014), Urban Mobility Scorecard Annual Report: Europe.

Instituto Nacional de Estadísticas de Chile (2016a), "País y regiones por áreas urbana-rural: actualización población 2002-2012 y proyecciones 2013-2020" [Country and regions by urban/rural areas: actual population 2002-2012 and projections 2013-2020], www.ine.cl/estadisticas/demograficas-y-vitales (accessed 23 February 2016).

Instituto Nacional de Estadísticas de Chile (2016b), "Superficie de la tierra por tipo de uso, según region. 2015" [Land area by use and region. 2015], in Medio Ambiente – Informe Annual 2016 [Environment – Annual Report 2016], http://historico.ine.cl/medioambiente/descargas/2016/medio_ambiente_2016.pdf.

Instituto Nacional de Estadísticas de Chile (2016c), "Plazas de Peaje Nacional y Pórticos de Autopistas Urbanas" [National Tolls and Urban Highway Gates], Transporte y Comunicaciones [Transport and Communication], www.ine.cl/estadisticas/economicas/transporte-y-comunicaciones?categoria=Encuesta%20estructural%20de%20transporte%20por%20carretera%20anual (accessed 13 May 2016).

Instituto Nacional de Estadísticas de Chile (2016d), "Anuario/Parque de Vehículos" [Yearbook/Vehicle fleet], Transporte y Comunicaciones [Transport and Communication], www.ine.cl/estadisticas/economicas/transporte-y-comunicaciones?categoria=Parque%20de%20veh%C3%ADculos (accessed 13 May 2016).

Instituto Nacional de Estadísticas de Chile (2016e), "Accidentados en el transíto, por tipo de consecuencia, según región y prefecturas" [Road casualties by consequence, region and province], Cuadros estadísticos Infrome Anual de Carabineros [Statistical tables in the annual report of police], www.ine.cl/estadisticas/sociales/informe-anual-de-carabineros (accessed 13 May 2016).

IRAP (2016), ad-hoc request.

IRAP (2009), Chile Country Report, (updated information as of 2015).

ISTAT (2016a), "Population - Resident population on 1st January", I.Stat –Population and households, http://dati.istat.it/?lang=en (accessed 23 February 2016).

ISTAT (2016b), "Regional accounts – Gross domestic product supply (millions of euro)", I.Stat – National Accounts, http://dati.istat.it/?lang=en (accessed 23 February 2016).

ISTAT (2016c), "Road accidents – Vehicles – Public Register of Motor-vehicles", I.Stat – Health Statistics, http://dati.istat.it/?lang=en (accessed on13 May 2016).

ISTAT (2016d), "Road accidents", I.Stat – Health Statistics, http://dati.istat.it/?lang=en (accessed on13 May 2016).

ISTAT (2016e), "Air transport, rail transport, maritime transport, road transport – Air transport", I.Stat – Services, http://dati.istat.it/?lang=en (accessed on13 May 2016).

ITF (2016a), "Vehicles (thousands)", IRTAD Road Safety Database, www.itf-oecd.org/irtad-road-safety-database (accessed 13 May 2016).

ITF (2016b), "Road length (km) by road type", IRTAD Road Safety Database, www.itf-oecd.org/irtad-road-safety-database (accessed 13 May 2016).

ITF (2016c), "Casualties by age and road use", IRTAD Road Safety Database, www.itf-oecd.org/irtad-road-safety-database (accessed 13 May 2016).

ITF/OECD (2016a), "Capacity to grow, transport infrastructure needs for future trade growth", CPB Report. OECD Publishing, Paris.

ITF/OECD (2016b) "Logistics development strategies and performance measurement", Roundtable Report 158. OECD Publishing, Paris.

ITF/OECD (2016c) "A logistics observatory for Chile", Country-Specific Policy Analysis. OECD Publishing, Paris.

ITF/OECD (2016d) "Road safety annual report 2016", IRTAD, http://dx.doi.org/10.1787/irtad-2016-en.

ITF/OECD (2016e), "Chile ports policy review", Country-Specific Policy Analysis.

ITF/OECD (2016f), "Global Freight Model".

ITF/OECD (2015), ITF Transport Outlook 2015, OECD Publishing, Paris.

ITF/OECD (2014), "Valuing convenience in public transport", ITF Round Tables, No. 156, OECD Publishing, Paris, http://dx.doi.org/10.1787/9789282107683-en.

ITF/OECD (2013) "Understanding the value of transport infrastructure", Task Force Report, OECD Publishing, Paris.

ITF/OECD (2007), "Transport infrastructure investment and economic productivity", Roundtable Report 132, OECD Publishing, Paris.

Johansson, A. and E. Olaberria (2014), Long-Term Patterns of Trade and Specialisation, OECD Economics Department Working Papers, No. 1136, OECD Publishing. http://dx.doi.org/10.1787/5jz158tbddbr-en.

Junta de Aeronáutica Civil (2016), "Pasajeros totals por año" [Total passenger by year], in Anuario 2014 de transporte aéreo [Annual report 2014 of air transport].

Kohon, J. (2013), "Información estadística sobre los ferrocarriles de carga de Latinoamérica y el Caribe", Banco Interamericano de Desarrollo, Observatorio Regional de Carga y Logistica.

Liberini, F. (2006), Economic Growth and Infrastructure Gap in Latin America",Rivista di Politica Economica, 96(11/12), 145-186.

Maibach, M., Schreyer, C., Sutter, D., Van Essen, H. P., Boon, B. H., Smokers, R. and Bak, M. (2008). Handbook on estimation of external costs in the transport sector. CE Delft.

Mainroads Western Australia (2015), "Road Classification (as at 30 June 2015)", in Annual Report 2015, www.mainroads.wa.gov.au/Documents/2015%20Annual%20Report%20PDF.RCN-D15%5E23624789.PDF.

Michea, A. (2013), "Puerto de Gran Escala: The case for a New Container Terminal in Central Chile", International Transport Forum Discussion Papers, No. 2013/20, OECD Publishing, Paris. DOI: http://dx.doi.org/10.1787/5jz40rzftr0x-en

Miller, E.B., Dewey, F. and Denslow, D. "A welfare analysis of subsidies for airports." Journal of Air Transport Management 50 (2016): 83-90.

Ministerio de Energía (2015), Energía 2050 – Politicas Energética de Chile. Available at www.energia.gob.cl/sites/default/files/energia_2050_-_politica_energetica_de_chile.pdf.

Ministerio de Fomento (2016), "Evolucíon desde 1970" [Trends since 1970], Catálogo y evolución de la red de carretteras [Overview and trends of road network], www.fomento.es/mfom/lang_castellano/direcciones_generales/carreteras/catyevo_red_carreteras/evolucion/ (accessed 13 May 2016).

Ministerio de Obras Públicas (2016a), "Hacia un país con desarrollo equilibrado", www.dirplan.cl/centrodedocumentacion/documentosgenerales/Documents/libro/Hacia_un_pais_con_desarrollo_equilibrado.pdf.

Ministerio de Obras Públicas (2016b), "Inversión MOP y Sistema de Concesiones en Proyectos Viales v/s PIB (2000-2014)" [MOP investment and concessions in road transport infrastructure related to GDP (2000-2014)].

Ministerio de Obras Públicas (2016c), "Longitud de la Red Vial según región y tipo de carpeta" [Length of road network by region and type of roads].

Ministerio de Transporte y Telecomunicaciones (2015), "Oferta de vías férreas y participación de mercado" [Supply of railway lines and market participation], in Plan de impulso a la carga ferroviaria [Plan to boost rail transport], www.mtt.gob.cl/wp-content/uploads/2014/02/picaf_29_01_14.pdf.

Ministerio de Transporte y Telecomunicaciones (2013), Conectando Chile, www.mtt.gob.cl/vision-estrategica.

Ministerio de Transporte y Telecomunicaciones (2011), "Partición modal" [Modal share], in Análisis de la Competitividad entre el Transporte Caminero y Ferroviario respecto del Accesso a Puertos [Analysis of Competitiveness of Rail and Road Transport in the Access to the Ports], www.subtrans.cl/subtrans/doc/Informe%20Final%20Acceso%20a%20Puertos%20VF.pdf.

Ministero dell'Economia e delle Finanze (2016), "Ripartizione modale della mobilità urbana: confronti internazionali" [Urban modal share: international comparison], in Documento di economia e finanza 2016 [Document of economy and finance 2016], www.dt.tesoro.it/modules/documenti_it/analisi_progammazione/documenti_programmatici/W-_Del-_Allegato_-_INFRASTRUTTURE.pdf.

Monios, J. (2011), "The role of inland terminal development in the hinterland access strategies of Spanish ports", Research in Transportation Economics, 33 (1): 59-66.

Muñoz, J. C., Batarce, M., & Hidalgo, D. (2014), "Transantiago, five years after its launch", Research in Transportation Economics, 48, 184-193.

Niehaus, M., P. Galilea and R. Hurtubia (2016), "Accounting access equity impacts for transport projects: Towards a wider assessment in the Latin American context", WCTR 2016 Shanghai.

Notteboom, T. E., and J. P. Rodrigue (2005), "Port regionalization: towards a new phase in port development", Maritime Policy & Management, 32(3), 297-313.

NSW Ports (2015a), Navigating the Future: NSW Ports' 30 Year Master Plan.

OECD (2005), Economic Evaluation of Long-Life Pavements – Phase 1, OECD Publishing, Paris.

OECD (2016a), The Productivity-Inclusiveness Nexus, OECD Publishing, Paris.

OECD (2016b), "Regional statistics - Regional demography", OECD.Stat – Regions and Cities, http://stats.oecd.org/Index.aspx?DataSetCode=REGION_DEMOGR (accessed 23 February 2016).

OECD (2016c), "Transport infrastructure - Transport infrastructure investment and maintenance spending", OECD.Stat – Transport, http://stats.oecd.org/Index.aspx?Datasetcode=itf_inv-mtn_data (accessed 23 February 2016).

OECD (2016d), "Transport Measurement - Goods transport", OECD.Stat – Transport, http://stats.oecd.org/index.aspx?datasetcode=itf_goods_transport (accessed 13 May 2016).

OECD (2016e), "Transport Measurement – Passenger transport", OECD.Stat – Transport, http://stats.oecd.org/index.aspx?datasetcode=itf_passenger_transport (accessed 13 May 2016).

OECD (2016f), "Air quality and health – Exposure to air pollution", OECD.Stat – Environment, http://stats.oecd.org/index.aspx?datasetcode=exp_pm2_5 (accessed 13 May 2016).

OECD (2016g), "Regional statistics – Regional social and environmental indicators", OECD.Stat – Regions and cities, http://stats.oecd.org/index.aspx?datasetcode=region_social (accessed 13 May 2016).

OECD (2015), Chile – Policy Priorities for Stronger and More Equitable Growth, OECD Publishing, Paris.

OECD/ECLAC (2016), OECD Environmental Performance Reviews, Chile 2016, OECD Publishing, Paris.

Roadex (2000), "The share of gravel vs. paved roads in each road district", in Road Condition Management of Low Traffic Volume Roads in the Northern Periphery, www.roadex.org/wp-content/uploads/2014/01/roadexspa0007.pdf.

Sabonge, R. and E. Lugo (2014), Diagnóstico y Pronóstico – Sobre la Oferta y Demanda de Servicios de Transporte Marítimo de Naves de Línea Regular, Entre Chile y el Mundo.

Salazar Burrows, A. and T. Cox Oettinger (2014), "Accesibilidad y valor de suelo como criterios para una localización racional de vivienda social rural en las comunas de San Bernardo y Calera de Tango, Chile", Revista INVI, 29(80), 53-81.

SECTRA (2016), "Encuestas de movilidad" [Travel surveys], www.sectra.gob.cl/encuestas_movilidad/encuestas_movilidad.htm.

SITEB (2012), "Estensione della rete stradale italiana – Anno 2007" [Length of Italian road network – Year 2007], in Il valore delle nostre strade [The value of our road network], www.siteb.it/new%20siteb/documenti/rassegna/7112_1.pdf.

Sinclair, E. (2013), "The last link in the Bothnian Corridor", European Railway Review, Issue 5, 2013, www.globalrailwayreview.com/article/21521/the-last-link-in-the-bothnian-corridor/.

Soto, R. (2010), "End of the line: railroads in Chile", Documento de Trabajo N 391, Instituto de Economia. Pontificia Universidad Católica de Chile, Santiago.

Statistics Norway (2016a), "Population and area", Population and population changes, www.ssb.no/statistikkbanken/selecttable/hovedtabellHjem.asp?KortNavnWeb=folkemengde&CMSSubjectArea=befolkning&PLanguage=1&checked=true (accessed 23 February 2016).

Statistics Norway (2016b), "Main result regional accounts", Regional accounts, www.ssb.no/statistikkbanken/selecttable/hovedtabellHjem.asp?KortNavnWeb=fnr&CMSSubjectArea=nasjonalregnskap-og-konjunkturer&PLanguage=1&checked=true (accessed 23 February 2016).

Statistics Norway (2016c), "Registered vehicles, by type of vehicle and trade mark (M)", Registered vehicles, www.ssb.no/statistikkbanken/selecttable/hovedtabellHjem.asp?KortNavnWeb=bilreg&CMSSubjectArea=transport-og-reiseliv&PLanguage=1&checked=true (accessed 13 May 2016).

Statistics Norway (2016d), "Persons killed or injured in road traffic accidents by police district (M)", i, www.ssb.no/statistikkbanken/selecttable/hovedtabellhjem.asp?kortnavnweb=vtu&cmssubjectarea=transport-og-reiseliv&planguage=1&checked=true (accessed 13 May 2016).

Statistics Sweden (2016a), "Population 1 November by region, age and sex. Year 2002-2016", Population statistics - Number of inhabitants, www.statistikdatabasen.scb.se/pxweb/en/ssd/start__be__be0101__be0101a/folkmangdnov/table/tableViewLayout1/?rxid=04da7b70-7b24-4563-890f-ef1a88bb26a3 (accessed 23 February 2016).

Statistics Sweden (2016b), "Land and water area 1 January by region and type of area. Year 2012-2016", Environment – Land and water area, www.statistikdatabasen.scb.se/pxweb/en/ssd/start__mi__mi0802/areal2012/?rxid=04da7b70-7b24-4563-890f-ef1a88bb26a3 (accessed 23 February 2016).

Statistics Sweden (2016c), "Gross Regional Domestic Product (GRDP), number of employed and wages and salaries (ESA2010) by region (NUTS1-3). Year 2000-2015", Regional accounts, annual estimates, www.statistikdatabasen.scb.se/pxweb/en/ssd/start__nr__nr0105__nr0105a/nr0105ens2010t01a/?rxid=04da7b70-7b24-4563-890f-ef1a88bb26a3 (accessed 23 February 2016).

Statistics Sweden (2016d), "Road length in km after region and road category. Year 2010", Land used for transport infrastructure, www.statistikdatabasen.scb.se/pxweb/en/ssd/start__mi__mi0816/vaglangdkategori/table/tableviewlayout1/?rxid=19b9b838-0a08-4cf1-abc3-b4243d6062a9 (accessed 13 May 2016).

Statistics Sweden (2016e), "Number of arriving and departing passengers at Swedish airports where scheduled and non-scheduled traffic is conducted", in Civil Aviation 2015, www.trafa.se/globalassets/statistik/flygtrafik/luftfart-2015.pdf?.

Straub, S. (2008), "Infrastructure and development: A critical appraisal of the macro level literature", Policy Research Working Paper 4590.

TomTom Traffic Index, 2016, Available at: www.tomtom.com/en_gb/trafficindex/list?citysize=large&continent=all&country=all (accessed 14 March 2017).

Trafikverket (2016), ad-hoc request.

Transport for NSW (2013), Port Botany Landside Improvement Strategy.

Transportstyrelsen (2016), ad-hoc request.

United Nations (2015), Transforming our World: The 2030 Agenda for Sustainable Development, New York.

UK Airports Commission (2015) "Surface Access, Final Report", London available at www.gov.uk/government/publications/airports-commission-final-report-surface-access

Veryard, D. (2016) "Quantifying the socio-economic benefits of transport", Discussion Paper n. 2016-06, ITF/OECD Publishing, Paris.

Warner, A. (2014), Public Investment as an Engine of Growth, IMF Working Paper No 14/148.

WEF (2016), The Global Competitiveness Report 2015–2016, World Economic Forum.

Wilmsmeier, G. (2013). Liner shipping markets, networks and strategies: "The implications for port development on the West Coast of South America", Discussion Paper n. 2013-22, ITF/OECD Publishing, Paris

WHO (2016), Ambient Air Pollution: A Global Assessment of Exposure and Burden of Disease", World Health Organization.

World Bank (2016a), "Population, total", World Development Indicators, http://databank.worldbank.org/data/reports.aspx?source=world-development-indicators (accessed 23 February 2016).

World Bank (2016b), "Land area (sq. km)", World Development Indicators, http://databank.worldbank.org/data/reports.aspx?source=world-development-indicators (accessed 23 February 2016).

World Bank (2016c), "GDP (current US$)", World Development Indicators, http://databank.worldbank.org/data/reports.aspx?source=world-development-indicators (accessed 23 February 2016).

World Bank (2016d), "Logistic Performance Index Dataset", http://lpi.worldbank.org/ (accessed 23 February 2016).

World Bank (2016e), "GDP (constant US$)", World Development Indicators, http://databank.worldbank.org/data/reports.aspx?source=world-development-indicators (accessed 23 February 2016).

World Bank (2016f), "Rail lines (total route-km)", World Development Indicators, http://databank.worldbank.org/data/reports.aspx?source=world-development-indicators (accessed 13 May 2016).

World Bank (2016g), "Air transport, passengers carried", World Development Indicators, http://databank.worldbank.org/data/reports.aspx?source=world-development-indicators (accessed 13 May 2016).

World Bank (2015), Doing Business 2015: Going Beyond Efficiency, The World Bank.

World Economic Forum (2016), "Global Competitiveness Index Dataset", http://reports.weforum.org/global-competitiveness-report-2015-2016/downloads/ (accessed 23 February 2016).

Zrari S. and M. Álvarez (2014), Asesoría Subsecretaria de Transportes. Consejos de Coordinación Ciudades Puerto.

Annex 4A

Quantitative benchmarking indicators

Table 4A.1. Population density and GDP per capita, 2004 and 2014

		Population density 2014	GDP per capita (current USD)	
		(inhabitants per km²)	2014	2004
OECD countries	Australia	3	61 925	31 472
	Sweden	24	58 887	42 442
	New Zealand	17	44 342	25 104
	Italy	209	34 960	31 190
	Spain	93	29 767	24 920
	Chile	23	14 528	6 324
OECD regions	Western Australia	1	86 262	34 578
	North Norway	4	67 045	30 888
	North Sweden	6	50 068	36 896
	Southern Italy	172	23 296	20 775
Chilean regions	Chile - North	7	20 559	--
	Chile - Central	140	13 979	--
	Chile - Austral	4	9 693	--
	Chile - South	40	7 435	--

Source: Population: World Bank (2016a), Australia Bureau of Statistics (2016a), ISTAT (2016a), Statistics Norway (2016a), Statistics Sweden (2016a), Instituto Nacional de Estadísticas de Chile (2016a). Land area: World Bank (2016b), Australian Bureau of Statistics (2016b), OECD (2016b), Statistics Norway (2016a), Statistics Sweden (2016b), Instituto Nacional de Estadísticas de Chile (2016b). GDP: World Bank (2016c), Australian Bureau of Statistics (2016c), ISTAT (2016b), Statistics Norway (2016b), Statistics Sweden (2016c), Banco Central de Chile (2016).

Table 4A.2. Rail and road infrastructure investment and maintenance spending as a percentage of GDP, 2000-2014

		2000	2005	2010	2014
Australia	Rail investment	0.10%	0.26%	0.40%	0.40%
	Road investment	0.89%	1.19%	1.25%	1.03%
	Total investment	**0.99%**	**1.45%**	**1.65%**	**1.43%**
	Rail maintenance	na	na	na	na
	Road maintenance	na	0.13%	0.15%	0.18%
	Total maintenance	**na**	**0.13%**	**0.15%**	**0.18%**

Table 4A.2. Rail and road infrastructure investment and maintenance spending as a percentage of GDP, 2000-2014 (*cont.*)

		2000	2005	2010	2014
Italy	Rail investment	0.37%	0.68%	0.30%	0.26%
	Road investment	0.56%	0.62%	0.21%	0.18%
	Total investment	**0.93%**	**1.30%**	**0.51%**	**0.43%**
	Rail maintenance	0.43%	0.60%	0.49%	0.45%
	Road maintenance	0.78%	0.84%	0.40%	0.57%
	Total maintenance	**1.22%**	**1.44%**	**0.89%**	**1.02%**
New Zealand	Rail investment	na	na	na	na
	Road investment	0.25%	0.38%	0.67%	0.63%
	Total investment	**0.25%**	**0.38%**	**0.67%**	**0.63%**
	Rail maintenance	na	na	na	na
	Road maintenance	na	0.62%	0.66%	0.64%
	Total maintenance	na	**0.62%**	**0.66%**	**0.64%**
Spain	Rail investment	0.28%	0.62%	0.71%	0.29%
	Road investment	**0.74%**	**0.92%**	**0.73%**	**0.41%**
	Total investment	1.03%	1.54%	1.44%	0.70%
	Rail maintenance	na	na	na	na
	Road maintenance	na	na	na	na
	Total maintenance	na	na	na	na
Sweden	Rail investment	0.21%	0.36%	0.39%	0.28%
	Road investment	0.32%	0.41%	0.45%	0.43%
	Total investment	**0.53%**	**0.77%**	**0.84%**	**0.71%**
	Rail maintenance	0.11%	0.16%	0.20%	0.23%
	Road maintenance	0.27%	0.25%	0.24%	0.24%
	Total maintenance	**0.37%**	**0.41%**	**0.43%**	**0.46%**

Notes: Data include both private and government investment. Australia: road investment includes tarmac at airports. Chile: rail investment does not include metro. Italy: road investment and maintenance do not include urban roads. Sweden: road investment does not include private local roads; rail investment includes trams and metros. New Zealand: data refer to fiscal years ending on June 30.

Source: OECD (2016c), Ministerio de Obras Públicas (2016b) and Grupo EFE (2016).

Table 4A.3. Global Competitiveness Index (1 = worst, 7 = best), 2015-2016 edition

	Quality of overall infrastructure	Quality of roads	Quality of railroad infrastructure	Quality of port infrastructure	Quality of airport infrastructure
Australia	4.86	4.72	3.90	4.99	5.48
Chile	4.57	4.93	2.35	4.91	5.19
Italy	4.11	4.42	3.96	4.32	4.52
New Zealand	4.96	4.68	3.50	5.47	5.84
Spain	5.73	5.80	5.95	5.65	5.89
Sweden	5.56	5.36	4.25	5.62	5.60

Source: World Economic Forum (2016).

Table 4A.4. Quality of infrastructure, percentage of people responding low or very low, GCI 2015-2016

	Chile	OECD
Ports	0%	45%
Airports	17%	22%
Road	0%	25%
Rail	83%	48%
Warehousing	0%	10%
Telecommunications	29%	20%

Source: Chile's Productivity Commission (2016).

Table 4A.5 Logistics Performance Index (1= worst, 5=best), 2016 edition

	Infrastructure	Customs
Australia	3.82	3.54
Chile	2.77	3.19
Italy	3.79	3.45
New Zealand	3.55	3.18
Spain	3.72	3.48
Sweden	4.27	3.92

Source: World Bank (2016d).

Table 4A.6 Rail, road and port (container) freight traffic in Chile, and estimated capacity needs

		Overall national estimate for Chile			Within 50km from ports, large cities	
		Trade-related freight volumes	Capacity	% change	Capacity needs	% change
Rail		MO tonne-km	Track-km	Over 2010	Track-km	Over 2010
	2010	9 084	620	--	93	--
	2030	12 697	1 599	158%	291	211%
Road		MO tonne-km	Track-km	Over 2010	Track-km	Over 2010
	2010	59 653	17 240	--	1 760	--
	2030	84 652	19 066	11%	2 231	27%
Ports		MO TEUs	TEU capacity	Over 2010	TEU capacity	Over 2010
	2010	3.27	5.26	--	--	--
	2030	7.81	7.85	49%	--	--

Source: ITF/OECD (2016f).

Table 4A.7 Road, rail and port freight transport intensity of the economy, 2004 and 2013

	Road tonne-km per current US$ GDP			Rail tonne-km per current US$ GDP			TEUs at ports per current 1000US$ GDP		
	2004	2013	Growth rate	2004	2013	Growth rate	2004	2013	Growth rate
Australia	0.25	0.14	-44%	0.27	0.24	-11%	1.00	0.85	-14%
Chile	--	0.21	--	--	0.02	--	0.89	0.56	-37%
Italy	0.09	0.06	-36%	0.01	0.01	-31%	0.23	0.21	-10%
New Zealand	0.19	0.11	-39%	0.06	0.03	-43%	0.39	0.30	-24%
Spain	0.21	0.14	-32%	0.01	0.01	-52%	0.32	0.31	-2%
Sweden	0.09	0.07	-22%	0.05	0.04	-34%	0.36	0.29	-20%

Source: Road and rail ton-km: OECD (2016d), data elaborated by the ITF/OECD based on data from Western Australia rail operators' reports and Grupo EFE, Ministerio de Transporte y Telecomunicaciones (2015). Metric tonnes at ports: data elaborated by the ITF/OECD based on data from Lloyds Intelligence Unit. GDP: World Bank (2016c).

Table 4A.8 Road and rail passenger transport volumes per inhabitant

	Road passenger transport (thousand passenger-km per inhabitant)		Rail passenger transport (thousand passenger-km per inhabitant)	
	2004	2013	2004	2013
Australia	13.87	12.53	0.59	0.66
Chile	--	--	0.05	0.05
Italy	14.14	12.00	0.85	0.81
Spain	8.94	7.90	0.47	0.51
Sweden	12.95	12.17	0.96	1.24

Source: Passenger transport: OECD (2016e), Ministerio de Transporte y Telecomunicaciones (2015). Population: World Bank (2016a).

Table 4A.9 Stock of road motor vehicles per 100 inhabitants, 2004 and 2014

		Passenger cars		Goods road motor vehicles	
		2004	2014	2004	2014
OECD countries	Australia	52.81	56.61	11.80	14.40
	Chile	8.19	15.71	1.52	2.13
	Italy	58.89	60.32	6.67	7.77
	New Zealand	--	60.94	--	11.32
	Spain	45.53	47.47	10.73	10.83
	Sweden	45.31	47.33	4.69	6.01
OECD regions	Southern Italy	54.13	59.05	5.97	7.38
	North Norway	39.94	49.34	24%	8.89

Note: goods road motor vehicles include vans, trucks, road and agricultural tractors.

Source: Stock of passenger cars: ITF (2016a), ISTAT (2016c), Statistics Norway (2016c), Instituto Nacional de Estadísticas de Chile (2016d). Population: World Bank (2016a), ISTAT (2016a), Statistics Norway (2016a).

Table 4A.10 Density of road network by area and population, latest available year

		Km of road network per km²		Km of road network per 1000 inhabitants	
		Total	Paved	Total	Paved
OECD countries	Australia	0.12	0.05	38.32	15.17
	Chile	0.10	0.04	4.38	1.74
	New Zealand	0.36	0.24	20.95	13.92
	Spain	0.33	--	3.58	--
	Sweden	0.53	0.29	22.33	12.37
OECD regions	Western Australia	0.07	0.02	72.61	21.94
	North Norway	0.03	0.03	7.41	6.27
	North Sweden	0.06	0.04	10.50	6.55
Chilean regions	North	0.08	0.04	10.32	5.10
	Central	0.21	0.12	1.51	0.87
	South	0.28	0.07	6.99	1.81
	Austral	0.05	0.01	12.37	3.28

Source: Road network: BITRE (2013), MOP (2016b), ITF (2016b), Ministerio de Fomento (2016), Statistics Sweden (2016d), Mainroads Western Australia (2015), Roadex (2000), CIA (2016). Land area: World Bank (2016b), Australian Bureau of Statistics (2016b), Statistics Norway (2016a), Statistics Sweden (2016b), Instituto Nacional de Estadísticas de Chile (2016b). Population: World Bank (2016a), Australia Bureau of Statistics (2016a), Statistics Norway (2016a), Statistics Sweden (2016a), Instituto Nacional de Estadísticas de Chile (2016a).

Table 4A.11 Share of paved roads, latest available year

OECD countries	Australia	43%
	Chile	40%
	Italy	78%
	New Zealand	66%
	Spain	86%
	Sweden	30%
OECD regions	Western Australia	79%
	Southern Italy	85%
	North Norway	62%
	North Sweden	49%
Chilean regions	North	57%
	Central	26%
	South	26%
	Austral	43%

Notes: Data exclude privately owned roads. In Chile, paved roads include "*soluciones básicas*".

Source: CIA (2016), Ministerio de Obras Públicas (2016c), SITEB (2012), Trafikverket (2016), Mainroads Western Australia (2015), Roadex (2000).

Table 4A.12. Roads rated three stars or better for vehicle occupants (iRAP model V2)

Carriageway	Divided		Undivided		Total
AADT	<5 000	>=5 000	<5 000	>=5 000	
Chile	49%	62%	30%	47%	34%
Chile - Austral	0%	0%	19%	0%	16%
Chile - Centre	63%	68%	40%	61%	46%
Chile - South	22%	0%	15%	0%	14%

Notes: V2 and V3 stars are not directly comparable. AADT = average annual daily traffic.

Source: IRAP (2016).

Table 4A.13. Roads rated three stars or better for vehicle occupants (iRAP model V3)

Carriageway	Divided		Undivided		Total
AADT	<5 000	>=5 000	<5 000	>=5 000	
Catalonia	100%	99%	35%	41%	75%
Chile - Centre	N/A	100%	24%	N/A	26%
Chile - North	78%	100%	70%	26%	82%
Western Australia	72%	57%	55%	3%	54%
New Zealand	94%	96%	6%	6%	10%

Notes: V2 and V3 stars are not directly comparable. AADT = average annual daily traffic.

Source: IRAP (2016).

Table 4A.14. Curves on rural roads where traffic flows at >80 km/h that have hazardous roadsides

Carriageway	Divided		Undivided	
AADT	<5 000	>=5 000	<5 000	>=5 000
Catalonia	N/A	7%	31%	22%
Chile - Centre	81%	50%	80%	83%
Chile - North	N/A	15%	18%	12%
Chile - South	N/A	N/A	90%	90%
Chile - Austral	N/A	42%	74%	82%
Western Australia	30%	14%	27%	43%
New Zealand	17%	4%	21%	18%

Note: AADT = average annual daily traffic.

Source: IRAP (2016).

Table 4A.15 Number of road fatalities per 100 000 inhabitants, 2004, 2010 and 2014

		2004	2010	2014	% change
OECD countries	Australia	7.86	6.14	4.92	-37%
	Chile	14.35	12.19	11.93	-17%
	Italy	10.61	6.94	5.51	-48%
	New Zealand	10.67	8.62	6.54	-39%
	Spain	11.05	5.32	3.64	-67%
	Sweden	5.34	2.84	2.79	-48%
OECD regions	Western Australia	8.96	8.37	7.13	-20%
	Southern Italy	8.63	5.94	4.86	-44%
	North Norway	9.94	7.30	3.35	-66%
	North Sweden	--	6.28	5.54	--
Chilean regions	North	--	--	15.86	--
	Central	--	--	9.48	--
	South	--	--	15.98	--
	Austral	--	--	14.74	--

Note: fatalities correspond to death within 30 days after the accident.

Source: Road fatalities - ITF (2016c), Instituto Nacional de Estadísticas de Chile (2016e), BITRE (2016a), ISTAT (2016d), Statistics Norway (2016d), Transportstyrelsen (2016). Population: World Bank (2016a), Australia Bureau of Statistics (2016a), ISTAT (2016a), Statistics Norway (2016a), Statistics Sweden (2016a), Instituto Nacional de Estadísticas de Chile (2016a).

Table 4A.16 Average ship and container ship turnaround time (days), 2013

		Ship	Container ship
OECD countries	Australia	2.99	1.28
	Chile	3.20	1.61
	Italy	1.82	1.13
	New Zealand	1.55	0.76
	Spain	1.53	0.86
	Sweden	0.91	0.65
OECD regions	Western Australia	3.25	1.37
	Southern Italy	1.78	1.09
	North Norway	1.61	1.86
	North Sweden	0.97	0.83
Chilean regions	North	3.85	1.93
	Central	2.52	1.29
	South	5.69	2.53
	Austral	3.78	1.58

Note: global average is one day.

Source: data elaborated by the ITF/OECD based on data from Lloyds Intelligence Unit.

Table 4A.17 Modal share of rail at ports, latest available year

Port	Country/macrozone	Road	Rail
Naples	Italy	92%	8%
Barcelona	Spain	90%	10%
Fremantle	Australia	86%	14%
Livorno	Italy	76%	24%
Tauranga*	New Zealand	60%	40%
Goteborg*	Sweden	50%	50%
Port Hedland*	Australia	14%	86%
Antofagasta	North	68%	32%
Arica	North	87%	13%
Ventanas	Centre	75%	25%
San Antonio	Centre	88%	12%
Valparaiso	Centre	96%	4%
Coronel	South	48%	52%
San Vicente	South	81%	19%

Note: * indicates the presence of dedicated port-hinterland rail shuttle services.

Source: European Parliament (2015), data elaborated by the ITF/OECD based on data from port authorities, BITRE (2014b), Ministerio de Transporte y Telecomunicaciones (2011).

Table 4A.18 Land transport – modal share of rail, 2013

	Freight rail modal share	Passenger rail modal share
Western Australia	63%	<1%
Chile North	17%	<1%
New Zealand	23%	<1%
Sweden	35%	9%
Chile – Central/South	6%	<1%

Source: data elaborated by the ITF/OECD based on data from Western Australia rail operators' reports and data from Grupo EFE, Ministerio de Transporte y Telecomunicaciones (2015), OECD (2016d), OECD (2016e).

Table 4A.19 Density of rail network by area and population, latest available year

	Km of rail network per 10 km2	Km of rail network per 1 000 inhabitants
Australia	0.53	1.75
Chile	0.43	0.18
Italy	5.79	0.28
New Zealand	1.52	0.89
Spain	3.37	0.36
Sweden	2.38	1.00
Western Australia	0.29	2.88
Chile – North	0.37	0.50
Chile – Central/South	2.73	0.19

Source: Rail network: World Bank (2016f), BITRE (2015), Ministerio de Transporte y Telecomunicaciones (2015), data elaborated by the ITF/OECD based on data from Western Australia rail operators' reports. Population: World Bank (2016a), Australia Bureau of Statistics (2016a), Instituto Nacional de Estadísticas de Chile (2016a). Land area: World Bank (2016b), Australian Bureau of Statistics (2016b), Instituto Nacional de Estadísticas de Chile (2016b).

Table 4A.20 Rail freight performance indicators, 2013

	Mo tonne-km per track km	1 000 tonnes per track km
Western Australia	22.7	16.2
Chile North	1.8	14.7
New Zealand	2.6	6.4
Sweden	2.2	6.4
Chile – Central/South	1.8	5.4

Source: Rail freight: data elaborated by the ITF/OECD based on data from Western Australia rail operators' reports and Grupo EFE, Ministerio de Transporte y Telecomunicaciones (2015), OECD (2016d). Rail network: World Bank (2016f), Ministerio de Transporte y Telecomunicaciones (2015), data elaborated by the ITF/OECD based on data from Western Australia rail operators' reports.

Table 4A.21 Modal share in cities, latest available year

	Private car	Public transport	Other
Santiago	26%	24%	39%
Madrid	29%	42%	29%
Stockholm	47%	35%	18%
Rome	57%	27%	16%
Sydney	68%	23%	6%
Auckland	79%	4%	16%
Coquimbo - La Serena	32%	30%	37%
Valparaiso	33%	39%	27%
Barcelona	35%	18%	47%
Temuco	35%	36%	26%
Milan	47%	27%	26%
Naples	51%	18%	31%
Iquique	36%	30%	34%
Antofagasta	37%	34%	29%
Arica	38%	23%	38%
Copiapo	39%	29%	31%
Fremantle	70%	15%	15%
Perth	79%	13%	4%
Osorno	46%	31%	21%
Valdivia	49%	30%	20%
Tromso	52%	17%	31%
Umeå	57%	8%	35%

Note: Modal share calculations may differ on survey methodology adopted.

Source: SECTRA (2016), Ministero dell'Economia e delle Finanze (2016), data elaborated by the ITF/OECD based on data from national travel surveys.

Table 4A.22 Modal share in cities, latest available year

	Daily passengers per km	Network length
Santiago	17 759	103
Rome	12 740	60
Milan	11 386	101
Barcelona	7 833	144.3
Stockholm	8 502	105.7
Madrid	5 236	293

Source: data elaborated by the ITF/OECD based on data from cities' annual reports.

Table 4.A.23 Mean population exposure to PM2.5 (micrograms per cubic metre), 2005 and 2013

		2005	2013	% change
OECD countries	Australia	7.8	6.0	-22%
	Chile	19.6	18.0	-8%
	Italy	22.0	18.4	-16%
	New Zealand	8.5	8.6	1%
	Spain	15.2	11.7	-24%
	Sweden	8.8	7.5	-16%
OECD regions	Western Australia	6.2	6.1	0%
	South Italy	15.8	13.5	-15%
	North Norway	3.7	3.5	-5%
	North Sweden	6.0	5.1	-16%
Chile regions	North	9.3	7.9	-16%
	Central	26.5	24.2	-9%
	South	6.2	6.1	-1%
	Austral	5.1	5.3	4%

Source: OECD (2016f).

Table 4.A.24 NO_2 Emissions (10^n molecules/cm^2) in urban, intermediate and rural areas, 2012

	Predominantly urban areas	Intermediate areas	Predominantly rural areas
Chile	2.7	1.6	0.8
Italy	5.1	4.9	2
New Zealand	0.7	0.4	--
Norway	2.2	2.6	2.4
Spain	1.8	1.6	2.1
Sweden	2	2.1	1.9

Source: OECD (2016g).

Table 4.A.25 Transport-related greenhouse gas emissions (CO2 equivalent tonnes) per inhabitant, 1994, 2004 and 2013

	1994	2004	2013	% change 2013-2004
Australia	3.63	3.93	3.93	0%
Chile	0.88	1.06	1.39	31%
Italy	1.84	2.15	1.67	-22%
New Zealand	2.79	3.29	3.08	-6%
Spain	1.80	2.46	1.76	-28%
Sweden	2.29	2.45	2.05	-16%

Source: CO2 emissions: IEA (2016). Population: World Bank (2016a).

Table 4.A.26 Propensity to fly, 2004 and 2014

		2004	2014	% change
OECD countries	Australia	2.82	3.91	39%
	Chile	0.42	0.90	116%
	Italy	1.42	1.98	39%
	New Zealand	2.77	3.34	21%
	Spain	3.02	3.85	27%
	Sweden	2.61	3.55	36%
OECD regions	Western Australia	2.21	3.53	59%
	Southern Italy	0.70	1.16	64%
	North Norway	--	7.81	--
	North Sweden	--	0.95	--
Chilean regions	North	--	0.89	--
	Central	--	1.07	--
	South	--	0.23	--
	Austral	--	1.20	--

Note: propensity to fly is the ratio of the number of national and international passengers in the country/region divided by the population.

Source: Number of passenger: BITRE (2016b), Junta de Aeronáutica Civil (2016), ISTAT (2016e), World Bank (2016g), AENA (2016), Statistics Sweden (2016e) Population: World Bank (2016a), Australia Bureau of Statistics (2016a), ISTAT (2016a), Statistics Sweden (2016a), Instituto Nacional de Estadísticas de Chile (2016a).

Table 4A.27 Surface access to airports, passenger modal share and travel time

	Share of public transport (rail and bus)	Average travel time by car (mins)	Average travel time by rail (mins)	Average travel time by bus (mins)
Düsseldorf	22%	13	15	29
Zurich	47%	14	12	27
Geneva	28%	14	7	20
Copenhagen	37%	18	14	43
Frankfurt	33%	18	11	11
Vienna	41%	23	16	48
Brussels	26%	29	21	60
Santiago	--	29	--	45
Amsterdam	37%	30	6	6
Munich	36%	38	42	55
Stockholm	34%	38	18	45
Oslo	64%	40	30	49
London (LHR)	36%	42	15	68
Paris (CDG)	40%	45	34	67

Source: Share of public transport: ACRP (2008), data elaborated by ITF/OECD based on data from Google Maps.

Annex 4B

Overview of transport infrastructure investment and policies in selected comparator OECD regions

4B.1 Western Australia

4B.1.1 Economic and demographic profile

Western Australia is the largest of Australia's States and Territories, covering 2.5 million km^2 or 33% of Australia's land mass (Australian Bureau of Statistics, 2014: 3). At that size, Wetern Australian has over three times more territory than Chile. However, like Chile, Western Australia's north-south coverage leads to substantial diversity in its climate, landscape and vegetation. Western Australia has a monsoonal tropical climate in the north, arid northern coastal and inland areas, and a temperate and Mediterranean climate in the south west. Unlike Chile, most of Western Australia is a flat, low plateau (Australian Bureau of Statistics, 1998: 16).

Almost 80% of WA's 2.5 million residents live in the capital city Perth (Australian Bureau of Statistics, 2014: 3). Therefore, the majority of the state is sparsely populated. Greater Perth has a population density of 315 people per km^2, while the rest of Western Australia has 0.2 people per km^2. On average, across the state, Western Australia has an average population density of 1 person per km^2 (Australian Bureau of Statistics, 2013-14).

Western Australia is a high-income state. In 2012-13, its Gross State Product (GSP) per capita was USD 93 825, which was 1.5 times greater than Australia's GDP per capita (Australian Bureau of Statistics, 2014-15). Arguably, Western Australia's high income is mainly related to the boom in recent years in the state's key exports – minerals and petroleum products. In 2012-13, Western Australia's exports totalled USD 104 166 million, which represented 47% of Australia's total exports. Of these exports, 46% were iron ore, 13% were gold products and 10% were natural gas (ibid).

Western Australia's key iron ore and natural gas production is located in the Pilbara region in the north and its surrounding waters. The Pilbara region constitutes 20% of WA's land mass, roughly equivalent in size to Spain. The main town in the Pilbara is Port Hedland, which is located on the coast 1 312 km north of Perth (1 638 km by road) (Main Roads Western Australia, 2013: 12). Iron ore mines are located inland, up to 425 km from Port Hedland (Bureau of Transport, Infrastructure and Economics, 2013: 23).

These characteristics make Western Australia a good comparator for the North of Chile. (Australian Bureau of Statistics, 2013-14)

Table 4B.1 Characteristics of Western Australia

	Year	Western Australia	Australia	Northern Chile
GDP per capita (current USD)	2004	34 578	31 472	
	2014	93 825	60 806	20 559
Population density (inhabitants per km²)	2004	0.79	2.62	
	2014	1.02	3.06	7.46
Main exports (by value, latest available)	1.	Iron	Wholesale and retail trade hotels and restaurants	Copper and iron
	2.	Gold	Transport and storage, post and telecommunication	
	3.	Natural gas	Food products, beverages and tobacco	

Source: Population: World Bank (2016a), Australian Bureau of Statistics (2016a), Instituto Nacional de Estadísticas de Chile (2016a). Land area: World Bank (2016b), Australian Bureau of Statistics (2016b), Instituto Nacional de Estadísticas de Chile (2016b). GDP: World Bank (2016c), Australian Bureau of Statistics (2016c), Banco Central de Chile (2016). Exports: OECD (2016), Direccion Nacional de Adunas (2016).

4B.1.2 Overview of transport infrastructure and key issues

Western Australia has extensive transport infrastructure, both near the main population centre in Perth and throughout the state. The following is an overview of the transport infrastructure in Western Australia.

Road

Western Australia's size and sparse population density affects the make-up of its road infrastructure. Of its 186 308 km of roads, only 10% are urban roads (Bureau of Infrastructure, Transport and Regional Economics, 2015: 44). Many of the roads link regional centres with Perth and each other. Unsurprisingly, most of the road network is in the state's south west (Department of Transport Western Australia, 2014: 23), which also has most of the state's population.

Only 30% Western Australia's main roads are paved (Main Roads Western Australia, 2015: 147). These include only some of the substantial freight routes carrying heavy vehicles. For example, the Goldfields Highway that links Kalgoorlie to a port at Esperance is unpaved. There are only medium-term plans to pave this road. However, those plans include paving the road to the full standard. There are also similar medium-term plans for the Marble Bar Road in the Pilbara region to assist with the development of new iron ore mines (Department of Transport Western Australia, 2014: 51-52).

Figure 4B.1 Map of Western Australia's road network

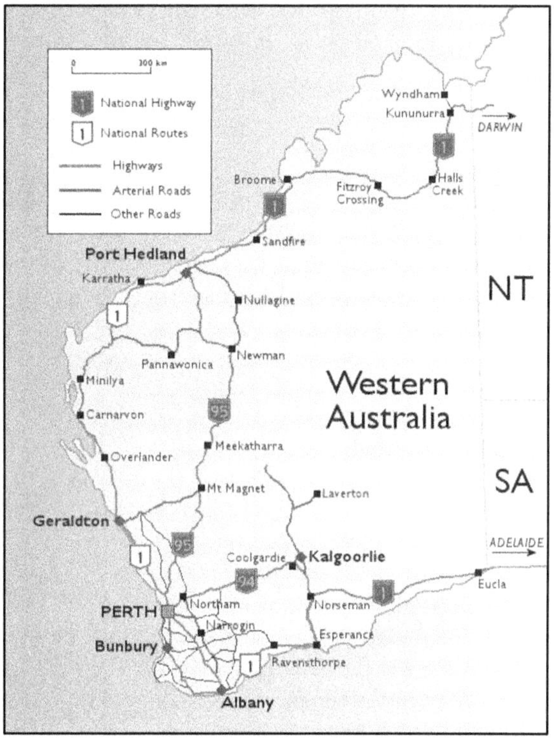

Source: Australian1.com.

Rail

Western Australia has 7 391 route-km of railway (Bureau of Infrastructure, Transport and Regional Economics, 2015: 96). The railways can be considered in two sections.

The first section covers the southern half of the state. It includes:

- the urban public transport rail network in Perth
- a freight network linking regional centres to Perth, each other and various ports
- a link to the rest of the Australian mainland (Economic Regulatory Authority of Western Australia, 2017).

This network undertakes a range of tasks, including transporting general freight and limited passenger services (Brookfield Rail). However, its main transport tasks involve transporting export commodities such as minerals and grain to ports (Department of Transport Western Australia, 2014).

Most of this network is government owned and privately operated by Brookfield Rail under a lease that is in force until 2049. Brookfield provides open access to its part of the network for above rail operators and is responsible for providing track infrastructure and train control services (*ibid*). The link to the rest of the Australian mainland is also an open-access multi-user network. The Perth public transport rail network is government owned and operated (Economic Regulatory Authority of Western Australia, 2017).

The second section is the Pilbara railways. These are heavy-haulage rail lines that transport iron ore from mines up to 425 km inland to export ports on Western Australia's coast (Bureau of Infrastructure, Transport and Regional Economics, 2013:23).

The Pilbara railways are privately owned and operated by iron ore mining companies and their joint venture partners as an integrated part of the iron ore supply chain. There is a more detailed discussion on the Pilbara railways and their integration with port infrastructure below.

Ports

With a mainland coastline of 12 889 km (Geoscience Australia), WA has the largest network of ports of any Australian state or territory. There are 17 government-owned ports. However, nine of these are privately operated, and many of the government-operated ports have substantial privately owned and operated infrastructure within them (Department of Transport Western Australia, 2014a: 23).

Western Australia is also home to the world's biggest iron ore port at Port Hedland (Department of Transport Western Australia, 2015: 28). Most of Western Australia's port activities are commodity export oriented.

The state's biggest general cargo port is at Fremantle near Perth, which handles almost all of Western Australia's container trade. As with many ports in urban areas, the Port of Freemantle has suffered from congestion and issues arising from trucks using local roads. The Western Australian government has sought to alleviate these issues by providing a rail subsidy for freight moved by rail between the Port of Freemantle and an intermodal hub in Forrestfield, an industrial suburb of Perth. From 2002 to 2013, the share of containers entering/exiting the Port of Freemantle by rail increased from 2% to 14%, equating to an estimated 100 000 fewer truck movements annually on roads linking with the port (Buswell, 2013). The Western Australian government has extended the subsidy to 2021-22 (Freemantle Ports, 2016) and has a target of 30% of containers reaching the port by rail in the long term (Buswell, 2013).

Airports

WA's size and low population density can result in aviation being the only practical way to transport people around the state (Department of Transport Western Australia, 2015: 4). Thus, Western Australia has one major international airport at Perth and 12 regional airports. Perth International Airport is also the main airport for domestic connections to other Australian states and territories (Department of Transport Western Australia, 2014: 51).

To ensure the viability of some regional air services, the Western Australian government holds tender processes and grants exclusive rights to operate certain air routes from Perth to particular regional towns. The Western Australian government does not provide subsidies for this policy (Department of Transport Western Australia, 2015: 5).

Box 4B.1 Port Hedland and Newcastle – two approaches to an integrated supply chain

Port Hedland – separately owned and operated supply chains

The Port of Port Hedland is the world's largest bulk port. While the port dates back to 1896, large-scale development only began in 1965 with the commencement of iron ore exports (Bureau of Transport, Infrastructure and Economics, 2013:20). There is strong integration across the iron ore export supply chain. The railways that service the port are the world's highest-capacity bulk railways. The newest railway involves trains of up to 33 000 tonnes, with 234 wagons operating under a 40-tonne axle load limit (ibid: 27). Railways come all the way to the port, unloading iron ore at large stockpiling facilities located close to berths. The railways at the port have balloon loops to maximise efficiency in turnaround times. The iron ore is blended at the port and moved to loading facilities by relatively short conveyer belts. While there are shared facilities available, BHP Biliton and Fortescue Metal Group each own and operate separate supply chain infrastructure from mine to ship. Vertical integration facilitates planning and day-to-day logistics maximise efficiency (ibid: 23). Port Hedland is a relatively remote location, which had little major development prior to iron ore exports commencing. Arguably, this provided substantial land away from a large population centre in which to build infrastructure to optimise the integration of supply chains.

Newcastle – shared infrastructure and central supply chain co-ordination

The Port of Newcastle (on Australia's east coast in the State of New South Wales) is the world's largest coal export port (ibid: 39). Supply integration at the Port of Newcastle takes a different approach from that of Port Hedland. While railways come all the way to the port, the rail network linking coal mines to the port is operated by a single infrastructure company with access arrangements to provide for above rail competition. The presence of the city of Newcastle limits the port's ability to expand. In the past, there was no central planning or co-ordination for moving coal through the supply chain. This resulted in substantial delays and inefficiency. Over the course of several years, all stakeholders, including coal producers, above and below rail operators, coal terminals, and the port developed a co-ordination system. The Hunter Valley Coal Chain Coordinator (HVCCC) was established to plan and co-ordinate the daily operation of the coal logistics chain. It co-ordinates vessel berthing, stockpile layouts and train sequencing to fulfil customers' orders efficiently. It also models future developments to predict future constraints in the supply chain and work with other stakeholders to keep them from occurring (Hunter Valley Coal Chain Coordinator, 2013: 1, 3).

4B.1.3 A co-ordinated approach to port hinterland transport – Port Botany, Sydney, Australia

The Australian and New South Wales (NSW) Governments have collaborated over several years to improve land transport connections to Port Botany in Sydney. The collaboration involves:

- expansion of the port itself (funded on a commercial basis) and subsequent privatisation of the port (in 2013)
- introduction of a third stevedore (commenced operations in July 2014)
- funding of extensions and upgrades to an existing dedicated rail freight line between the port and parts of western Sydney (primarily by the Australian Government)
- facilitating development of intermodal freight terminals
- joint funding of upgrades of the motorway network between the port and key freight hubs in western Sydney.

Port Botany is the largest container port in NSW, and it serves Sydney (-population 5.0 million in mid-2016) and regional NSW. In 2014-15, the port handled approximately 2.28 million TEUs, including 0.14 million TEUs in transhipments (NSW Ports, 2015). The port's private-sector operator forecasts that this volume will grow to between 7.5 million and 8.4 million TEUs by 2045 (NSW Ports, 2015a).

Approximately 85% of containers originate from or are bound for a destination within 40 kilometres of Port Botany. The rail mode share of container movements to and from Port Botany declined from 25.0% in 2001-02 to 14.1% in 2012 (NSW Government, 2013). The NSW Government has set a target of doubling the rail mode share by 2020.

To improve landside access to the port, several actions have been pursued over the past five to seven years, and they continue to be developed. These are shown on Figure B.2. The most significant developments are:

1. Development of the Southern Sydney Freight Line (at a cost of approximately AUD 1 billion) to provide a dedicated freight rail line, which achieved the following:
   - improved access for interstate and intrastate freight trains passing through the southern part of the Sydney rail network (the network carries large passenger loads on weekdays; there were curfews on freight trains entering the network before the SSFL; there are still are curfews on parts of the network that do not have a dedicated freight line)
   - extended an existing dedicated rail freight connection (between Port Botany and Enfield) to a new intermodal terminal to be developed on a 241-ha. site at Moorebank in south-western Sydney (about 35 km from the port).
2. Progressive upgrades of the motorway network, notably the development of the WestConnex project, which will be developed over three stages between 2015 and 2023 (at a nominal cost of AUD 16.8 billion).[1] The project will be funded with a mixture of:

   a. distance-based tolls on all vehicles, including trucks

   b. an availability charge from the NSW Government

   c. AUD 1.5 billion grant from the Australian Government.

Figure 4B.2. Map of existing and potential future infrastructure supporting Port Botany

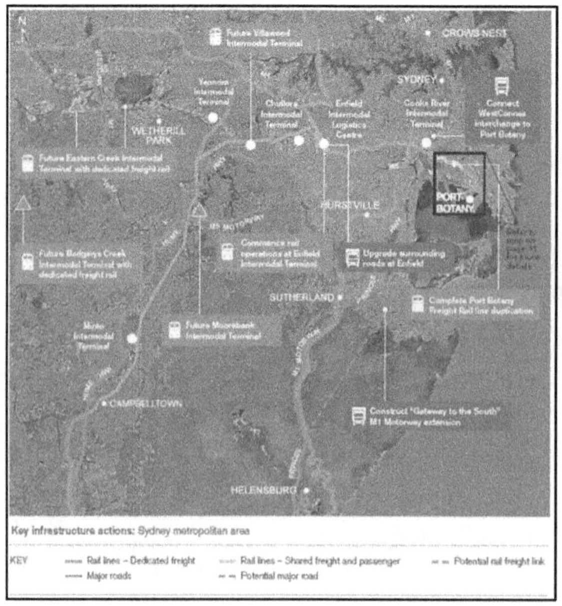

Source: NSW Ports (2015a), p. 37.

Figure 4B.3. Map of WestConnex

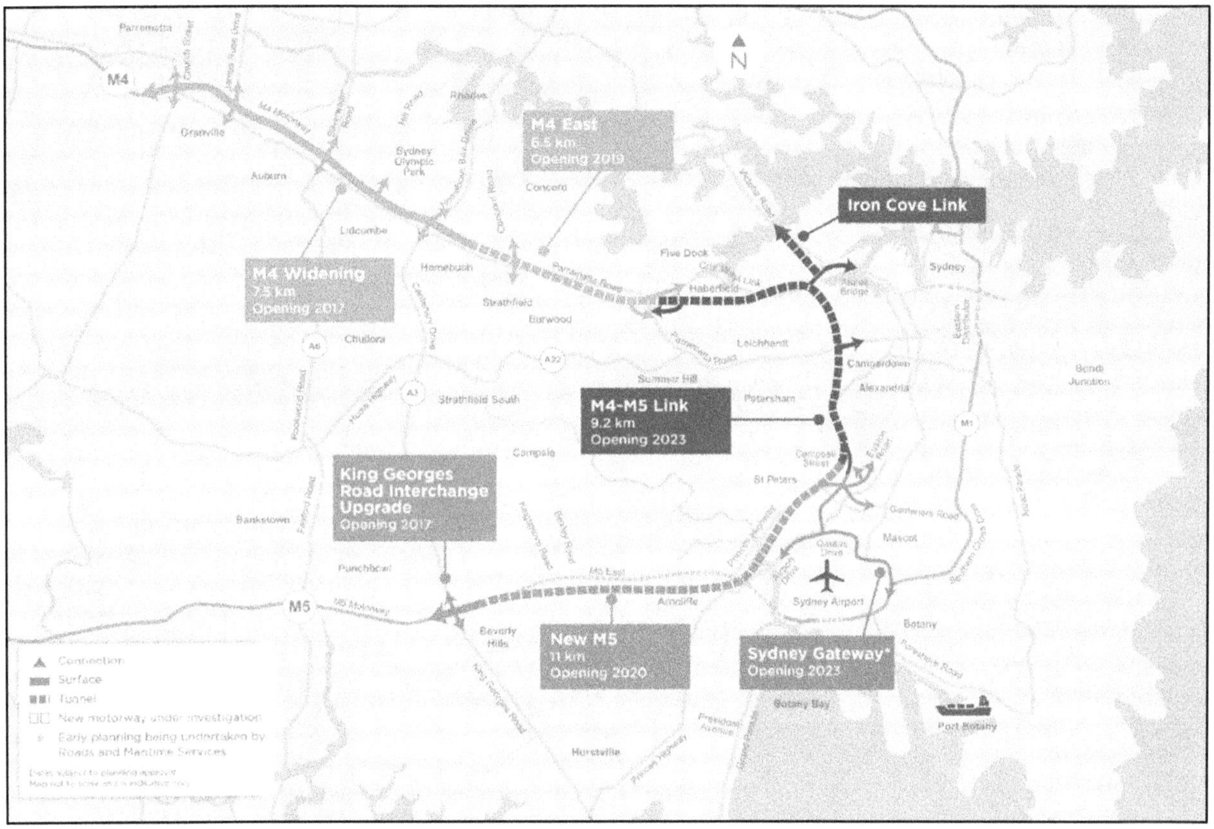

Source: Sydney Motorway Corporation (2016)

3. Development of intermodal terminals:

   a. on an existing rail marshalling site at Enfield (approximately 15 km inland from the port). The terminal is being operated by the rail operator, Aurizon, in partnership with the port corporation; the port corporation presently has environmental planning approval to handle 300 000 TEUs per year through the terminal

   b. a new terminal for port-related containers and interstate rail traffic at Moorebank, on the site of a former military training facility; the terminal will operate as an open-access facility with capacity for up to 1.05 million import-export and 500 000 interstate freight containers per year by 2030; the site adjoins the dedicated freight rail network and the motorway network; the terminal is to be developed by Qube Holdings, a private operator, which is investing approximately AUD 1.5 billion in the project (Australian Department of Infrastructure and Regional Development, 2015); the Australian Government is contributing a further AUD 370 million (principally for a rail connection to the SSFL) and leasing the land for the terminal; the terminal is expected to commence operations by the end of 2017.

In addition to the infrastructure upgrades, the NSW Government has established a range of measures to improve the operational efficiency of the supply chain through the port (the Port Botany Landside Improvement System – PBLIS). These include the following:

4. Most notably, since February 2011, a range of Operational Performance Measurement standards have been applied to truck movements at the port. The standards are applied by NSW Government regulation. Stevedores and truck carriers incur reciprocal financial penalties for poor performance against the standards. The system provides:

- an independent data source
- truck tracking
- information to assist with traffic and congestion management
- transparency and visibility for carriers and stevedores
- user capable reporting (Penalty Trend, Truck Trip Arrival Performance, Truck Spread)
- online training.

5. Consideration has been given to applying a similar regime to rail operations at the port:

- establishment of a Cargo Movement Co-ordination Centre and establishment of teams of industry and government stakeholders in the road and rail sectors, working to improve operations along the supply chain and at the port (Transport for NSW, 2015)
- use of "TruckCams" at selected locations around the port to provide timely information on traffic movements to assist port users in better managing their business.

Figure 4B.4 below shows the improvement in truck turnaround times at the two stevedores – DP World and Patrick – following the introduction of the PBLIS system. The on-time performance of trucks arriving at Port Botany increased from 72% before PBLIS to 93% in March 2013 (Transport for NSW, (2013).

Figure 4B.4 Turnaround times comparison by stevedore

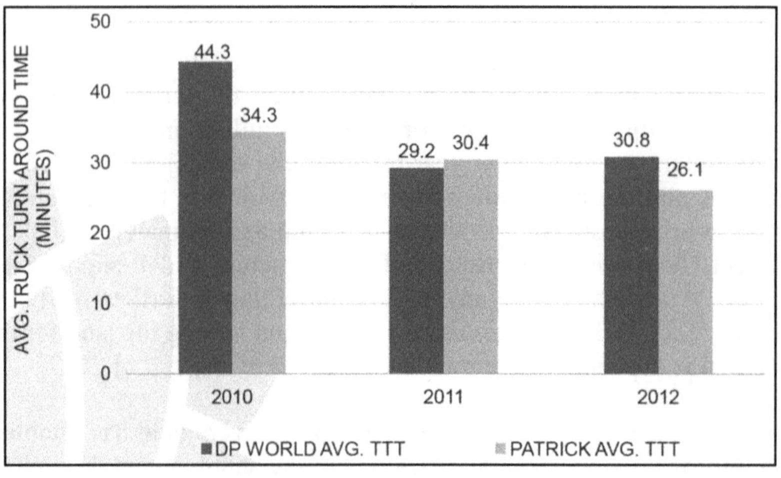

Source: Transport for NSW, 2013.

4B.1.4 Overview of framework conditions (policy, planning, co-ordination)

Western Australia has a detailed hierarchy for developing long-term planning strategies across all sectors of its economy, including for the development of transport infrastructure. The Western Australian Planning Commission works in consultation with a range of government and non-government stakeholders to produce long-term planning strategies. Western Australia has been issuing these since 1997 (Western Australian Planning Commission, 2014: 7).

The most recent strategy was issued in 2014 and seeks to develop strategies until 2050. The State Planning Strategy is the highest-order planning instrument in the Western Australian planning system (ibid: 8). While the document does not bind government agencies to specific actions, it is used to guide, shape and inform a hierarchy of state, regional and local planning tools, instruments and decisions within the Western Australian planning system (ibid: 7). All other planning documents seek to be consistent with the planning strategy.

In the transport space, Western Australia has also developed other long-term planning documents. These include:

- the Western Australian Regional Freight Transport Network Plan 2031
- the Perth Transport Plan for 3.5 million people and beyond
- the Western Australian State Aviation Strategy 2015.

In addition, the Western Australian Government has quarantined revenue from the iron ore mining boom to plan and fund regional development, including transport infrastructure, as part of the *Royalties for Regions* programme (see Box 4B.2).

Box 4B.2. Royalties for regions

Since December 2008, the Western Australian Government has allocated a set proportion of revenue from mining royalties to regional development, as an addition to funding provided out of the ordinary state budget. The Royalties for Regions programme is a fund, enshrined in legislation, which ensures that 25% of forecast royalty income for each year (up to a cap of AUD 1 billion per annum) is allocated to development of Western Australia's regional areas (Royalties for Regions Act, 2009, (WA) ss. 3, 6(2) and 8). The fund consists of three subaccounts relating to local government, regional community services and regional infrastructure (ibid s. 5(11)). Funds from the Royalties for Regions programme may be used for the following purposes:

- to provide infrastructure and services in regional Western Australia
- to develop and broaden the economic base of regional Western Australia
- to maximise job creation and improve career opportunities in regional Western Australia (ibid s. 9(11).

The Royalties for Regions programme has a regional grants scheme, which allows the nine regional development commissions to administer and allocate some funds directly within their regions (Department of Regional Development, n.d.). Much of the funding under the scheme is allocated by the Minister for Regional Development. An independent advisory board, The Regional Development Trust, provides recommendations and advice to the minister on how to allocate funding and operate the programme (Royalties for Regions Act, 2009 (WA) s. 12).

Since its commencement in December 2008, the Western Australian Government has allocated AUD 6.1 billion to the Royalties for Regions programme and used on more than 3 600 projects (Department of Regional Development, 2015: 6).

One project being funded through Royalties for Regions is the Infrastructure Audit and Investment Fund. The Department of Regional Development has commissioned an infrastructure audit to improve supply chains and the opportunity for Western Australian producers to export premium quality food and fibre products from regional Western Australia. Once the audit it complete, it will be used to identify and fund necessary transport, freight, storage, packaging and processing infrastructure and to alleviate other supply chain constraints (Department of Regional Development, n.d.).

Note

1. The overall project is very large. By the time it is finished, there will around 25 km of motorway standard tunnel, as well as approximately 8 km of surface motorway. The expected cost of the project has increased since it was first announced, and there is speculation that, by the time the project is finished, the costs will increase further.

References

Australian Bureau of Statistics (2016a), "Table 4. Estimated Resident Population, States and Territories (Number)", Australian Demographic Statistics, Dec 2015, www.abs.gov.au/AUSSTATS/abs@.nsf/DetailsPage/3101.0Dec%202015?OpenDocument (accessed 23 February 2016).

Australian Bureau of Statistics (2016b), "Land area (ha)", Western Australia (S/T), http://stat.abs.gov.au/itt/r.jsp?regionsummary&region=5&dataset=abs_regional_asgs&geoconcept=region&measure=measure&datasetasgs=abs_regional_asgs&datasetlga=abs_regional_lga&regionlga=region&regionasgs=region (accessed 23 February 2016).

Australian Bureau of Statistics (2016c), "Table 6. Expenditure, Income and Industry Components of Gross State Product, Western Australia, Chain volume measures and current prices", Australian National Accounts: State Accounts, 2014-15, www.abs.gov.au/ausstats/abs@.nsf/detailspage/5220.02014-15?OpenDocument (accessed 23 February 2016).

Australian Bureau of Statistics (2014-15), 5220.0: Australian National Accounts: State Accounts. www.abs.gov.au/ausstats/abs@.nsf/mf/5220.0 (accessed 14 March 2017).

Australian Bureau of Statistics (2014), 1306.5: Western Australian at a Glance, www.abs.gov.au/ausstats/abs@.nsf/mf/1306.5 (accessed 14 March 2017).

Australian Bureau of Statistics (2013-14), 3218.0: Regional Population Growth, Australia, www.abs.gov.au/ausstats/abs@.nsf/mf/3218.0 (accessed 14 March 2017).

Australian Bureau of Statistics (1998), 1300.5: Western Australian Yearbook, www.abs.gov.au/AUSSTATS/abs@.nsf/mf/1300.5 (accessed 14 March 2017)

Australian Department of Infrastructure and Regional Development (2015), Moorebank Intermodal Freight Terminal, http://investment.infrastructure.gov.au/funding/projects/rail.aspx (accessed 14 March 2017).

Banco Central de Chile (2016), "PIB regional" [Regional GDP], Cuentas Nacionales [National Accounts], http://si3.bcentral.cl/Siete/secure/cuadros/arboles.aspx (accessed 23 February 2016).

Brookfield Rail, "About us: our network", www.brookfieldrail.com/about-us/our-network/.

Bureau of Infrastructure, Transport and Regional Economics (2015), Yearbook 2015: Australian Infrastructure Statistics.

Bureau of Infrastructure, Transport and Regional Economics (2013), Research Report 135: Maritime - Australia's Bulk Ports.

Buswell (2013), "State Govt adds support for rail to move freight", 5 February 2013.

Department of Infrastructure and Regional Development Australia (n.d.), "Designated international airports in Australia", https://infrastructure.gov.au/aviation/international/icao/desig_airports.aspx (accessed 14 March 2017).

Department of Regional Development (n.d.), "How to access royalties for regions investment, www.drd.wa.gov.au/rfr/howtoapplyrfr/Pages/default.aspx (accessed 14 March 2017).

Department of Regional Development (n.d.), "Infrastructure Audit and Investment Fund", www.drd.wa.gov.au/projects/Agriculture/Pages/Infrastructure-Audit-and-Investment-Fund.aspx (accessed 14 March 2017).

Department of Regional Development (2015), Royalties for Regions Progress Report: July 2014-June 2015, p. 6.

Department of Transport Western Australia (2015), Review of Regulated Regular Public Transport Air Routes in Western Australia Final Public Report 2015.

Department of Transport Western Australia (2015), Ports Handbook Western Australia 2015.

Department of Transport Western Australia (2014), Western Australian State Aviation Strategy.

Department of Transport Western Australia (2014a), Western Australian Regional Freight Transport Network Plan.

Direccion Nacionales de Adunas (2016), "Principales rubros de exportación por région de embarque, 2014-2015" [Main exports by loading region, 2014-2015], in Anuario Estasístico 2015 [Annual statistics report 2015], www.aduana.cl/aduana/site/artic/20150624/asocfile/20150624160021/anuario_estadistico_servicionacionaladuanas_2015.pdf.

Economic Regulatory Authority of Western Australia (n.d.), "Rail access", www.erawa.com.au/rail/rail-access (accessed 14 March 2017).

Freemantle Ports (2016), "WA port operations task force meeting papers June 2016", p. 2.

Geoscience Australia (n.d.), "Border lengths – states and territories", www.ga.gov.au/scientific-topics/national-location-information/dimensions/border-lengths (accessed 14 March 2017).

Hunter Valley Coal Chain Co-ordinator (2013), The History of the Hunter Valley Coal Chain Co-ordinator.

Instituto Nacional de Estadísticas de Chile (2016a), "País y regiones por áreas urbana-rural: actualización población 2002-2012 y proyecciones 2013-2020" [Country and regions by urban/rural areas: actual population 2002-2012 and projections 2013-2020], www.ine.cl/estadisticas/demograficas-y-vitales (accessed 23 February 2016).

Instituto Nacional de Estadísticas de Chile (2016b), "Superficie de la tierra por tipo de uso, según region. 2015" [Land area by use and region. 2015], in Medio Ambiente – Informe Annual 2016 [Environment – Annual Report 2016], http://historico.ine.cl/medioambiente/descargas/2016/medio_ambiente_2016.pdf.

Main Roads Western Australia (2013), Distance Book: Distances to Towns and Localities in Western Australia Edition 13.

NSW Ports (2015), Public Reporting 2014-15, www.nswportsbotany.com.au/news/publications/ (accessed 14 March 2017).

NSW Ports (2015a), Navigating the Future: NSW Ports' 30 Year Master Plan, www.nswports.com.au/publications/ (accessed 14 March 2017).

NSW Government (2013), NSW Freight and Ports Strategy, http://freight.transport.nsw.gov.au/strategy/index.html (accessed 14 March 2017).

OECD (2016), "Trade in Value Added TiVA)", OECD.Stat – International Trade and Balance of Payments, http://stats.oecd.org/Index.aspx?DataSetCode=TIVA_2016_C1 (accessed 13 May 2016).

Royalties for Regions Act (2009) (WA).

Sydney Motorway Corporation (2016), www.westconnex.com.au/library/key_documents_and_maps.html (accessed 14 March 2017).

Transport for NSW (2015), "CMCC news, events and contacts", http://freight.transport.nsw.gov.au/network/cmcc/pblis-news-contacts.html (accessed 14 March 2017).

Transport for NSW (2013), "PBLIS program keeps on rolling for the NSW freight network", www.transport.nsw.gov.au/media-releases/pblis-program-keeps-rolling-nsw-freight-network (accessed 14 March 2017).

Western Australian Planning Commission (2014), State Planning Strategy 2050.

World Bank (2016a), "Population, total", World Development Indicators, http://databank.worldbank.org/data/reports.aspx?source=world-development-indicators (accessed 23 February 2016).

World Bank (2016b), "Land area (sq. km)", World Development Indicators, http://databank.worldbank.org/data/reports.aspx?source=world-development-indicators (accessed 23 February 2016).

World Bank (2016c), "GDP (current US$)", World Development Indicators, http://databank.worldbank.org/data/reports.aspx?source=world-development-indicators (accessed 23 February 2016).

4B.2 Southern Italy – Il Mezzogiorno

4B.2.1 Economic and demographic profile

The Italian Mezzogiorno is a macrozone comprising an area of 121 364 km^2 in the South of Italy. Around 20.5 million people live in the area, and the population density is 172 inhabitants per km^2. Incomes in Sothern Italy are lower than the national average, with GDP per capita of USD 23 304 in 2014. GDP growth has been stagnant after a sharp decline in the 2008-09 recession. Unemployment is high at 18% (2015), compared to 12% nationally.

The economy relies heavily on public services, agriculture and specialised industries such as food processing and the extraction of raw materials. Only 12% of Italy's exports are produced in the South, and export composition reflects the industry mix. However, the Mezzogiorno plays a key role in Italy's logistics chains, including by handling a large share of imports through its ports. The population is concentrated in and around main cities. More than 3 million people live in Napoli's metropolitan area.

These characteristics make the Italian Mezzogiorno a good comparator for Central Chile. However, it is worth noting that the income trajectory of Central Chile is on an upward trend, compared to a stagnant economy in Southern Italy. Therefore, the key challenge for infrastructure in Southern Italy is not to cope with growth but rather to cater for changing economic needs and to boost competitiveness against the threat of continued decline.

Table 4B.2 Characteristics of Southern Italy

	Year	Southern Italy	Italy	Central Chile
GDP per capita (current USD)	2004	20 775	31 190	
	2014	23 004	34 909	13 979
Population density (inhabitants per km²)	2004	169	196	
	2014	172	208	139
Main exports (by value, latest available)	1.	Extractive minerals	Chemicals and non-metallic mineral products	Copper and iron
	2.	Food and beverage	Wholesale and retail trade, hotels and restaurants	Fruits
	3.	Transport machinery	Machinery and equipment	Food

Source: Population: World Bank (2016a), ISTAT (2016a), Instituto Nacional de Estadísticas de Chile (2016a). Land area: World Bank (2016b), OECD (2016a), Instituto Nacional de Estadísticas de Chile (2016b). GDP: World Bank (2016c), ISTAT (2016b), Banco Central de Chile (2016b). Exports: OECD (2016), Direccion Nacional de Adunas (2016).

4B.2.2 Overview of transport infrastructure and key issues

Historically, transport connectivity has been a challenge for the Mezzogiorno given its complex geography – a peninsula with mountainous areas and two large islands. Following a period of high public investment over the 1970s and 1980s, the backbone of transport infrastructure has been provided across all transport modes. However, the decoupling of investment between the Centre and North and the South of Italy (Figure 4B.5) that has existed since the early 1990s is often blamed for the lack of progress in the coverage and quality of infrastructure in Southern Italy compared to the Centre and North.

Figure 4B.5. Investment in public infrastructure, constant million EUR 2005

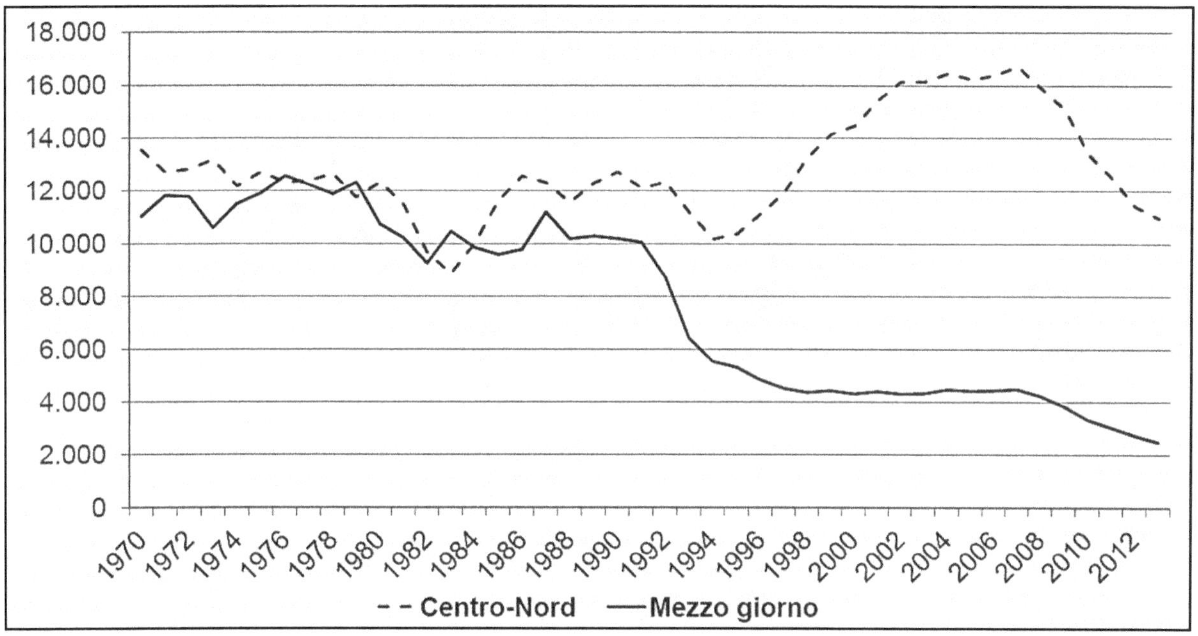

Note: it includes transport, water and energy networks and reconstruction following natural disasters.

Source: SVIMEZ (2015b).

As a result, passenger transport infrastructure in the South of Italy is perceived as being worse than the rest of the country, and it is often blamed for holding back the economic potential of the area (SVIMEZ, 2015). However, large variations exist within the Mezzogiorno; for instance, the A1 motorway and the High-Speed Rail lines have been extended to the city-region of Naples (which is therefore well connected to the rest of Italy) but not further South. Figure 4B.6 shows that passenger connectivity to population centres and jobs is worse for most areas in the South than the rest of the country when considering all modes of transport.

Similarly, freight transport infrastructure coverage and quality is uneven across the Mezzogiorno. Some large port systems have been developed, sometimes integrated with intermodal services via hinterland ports. Overall, Southern ports handle around half of Italy's maritime traffic. Nonetheless, the development of freight transport in the South is hampered by the under-provision of some critical infrastructure links, such as the A3 motorway between Salerno and Reggio Calabria, and rail/road connections for the ports of Sicily and Apulia.

Despite a general trend of decline in investment, some improvements in passenger infrastructure have been made in recent decades, especially by strengthening rail services in and around cities and to and from transport hubs. Some of the sector-specific issues for transport infrastructure in Southern Italy are discussed next. We also present case studies on the A3 motorway, Naples' hinterland port and Bari's airport rail link.

Figure 4B.6 Accessibility to population and jobs – indicators for Italy, based on 2014 data

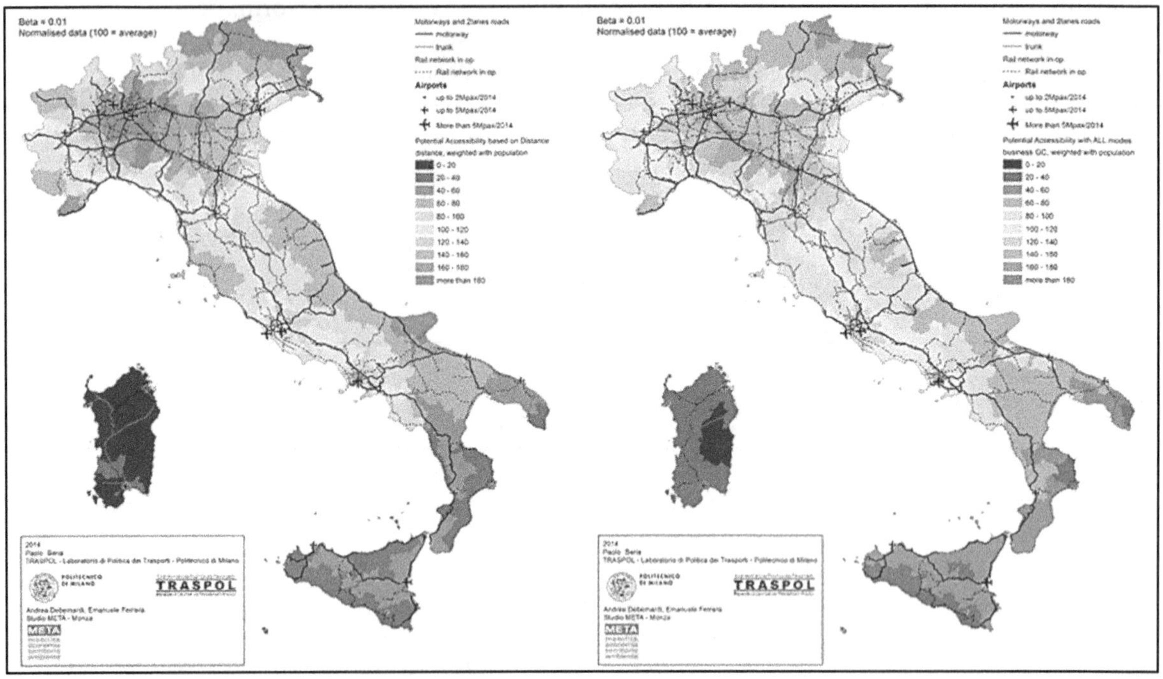

Notes: Medium light-grey areas in northern Italy and areas around Rome and Naples indicate good connectivity; dark grey to black indicates poor connectivity. Left: distance-based indicator weighted by population. Right: generalised cost-based indicator (business travel) weighted by population. All modes are included.

Source: Beria et al. (2016).

Road

The road network of Southern Italy comprises 357 686 km of roads, of which around 1% are motorways and 79% are paved. The stock of roads per 10 000 inhabitants is 37 km, above the Italy average of 30 km (Uniontrasporti, 2011).* While road network length has been stable over the past 15 years, two key challenges have emerged with respect to road infrastructure: completing the A3 motorway and maintaining the existing network.

Some view the A3 motorway as a missed opportunity for the economic development of Southern Italy. The motorway may finally be completed in 2016-17 after 20 years of works that were necessary to upgrade it. When the motorway is completed, the north-south backbone infrastructure of Southern Italy will still need to be strengthened to improve the connectivity of Sicily with the rest of the country. Infrastructure needs include the Palermo-Messina connections and potentially a suspension bridge between Messina and Reggio Calabria, for which only preparatory work has been carried out.

The need for road maintenance emerges over time and tends to be directly proportionate to the size of infrastructure stocks, and inversely proportionate to the quality of those stocks. Against a large stock of roads, maintenance budgets have been repeatedly cut under budgetary pressures in Italy; between 2008 and 2012, annual maintenance spending by ANAS decreased from EUR 1.65 billion to EUR 1.15 billion (European Parliament, 2014). Adequate funding for road surfaces is a key pledge of the 2016 Ministry of Transport Plan (Ministero dei Trasporti, 2016), responding to pressures by users and stakeholders on the declining quality of roads.

* Figures exclude urban and other municipal roads

Box 4B.3. The importance of getting investment right
The A3 motorway's EUR 10 billion makeover

The A3 motorway connects Naples to the southernmost city of the Italian peninsula, Reggio Calabria. The A3 was initially planned in the 1950s as the continuation of the A1 motorway (Milan-Naples), which was built and operated (with toll payments) by private investors in partnership with the Italian State. Unlike the A1, however, the A3 was viewed as a public interest project to connect the poorer regions of the South to the Centre-North of Italy. As such, it was wholly financed and built by the State, through its wholly controlled company ANAS, free of charge for users.

The A3 motorway was designed to be single carriageway, with no emergency lanes, and have a length of 440 km, 30% of which was tunnelled given the local morphology. Following the car ownership boom of the 1970s and 1980s, the infrastructure standards of the A3 were revealed to be insufficient, with constant congestion and safety problems. New projects were thus devised to widen the road by adding extra lanes and to improve safety by building new emergency lanes, overhead bridges and tunnels. Works began again in 1997, and after years of delays, they are expected to be finished by 2016-2017.

The case of the A3 motorway illustrates the risks in under-funding infrastructure built to promote regional development. The estimated investment for 1997-2015 is around EUR 10 billion. The makeover of the A3 motorway has damaged the competitiveness of Southern Italy in two ways: first, by reducing connectivity for a prolonged period, with associated high journey times and low safety standards on a key north-south axis; and second, by diverting financial resources away from other infrastructure projects in the area to fill this gap.

Source: "La storia siamo noi" RAI, 2015; Floris, 2010.

Rail

The coverage and quality of rail infrastructure in the Mezzogiorno is below national standards. In addition to the lack of High-Speed Rail connections south of Naples, regional and suburban lines have a low share of electrification (40% in the South compared with 70% nationally) and a high share of single-track lines (RFI, n.d.).

Therefore, passenger services are slower in the South (Uniontrasporti, 2011) than in the rest of the country, and efficiency is held back by the over-reliance on diesel trains. The average age of rolling stock in the South was 20.4 years as opposed to 16.6 years in the North, and more than 50% of trains running in the Mezzogiorno are more than 20 years old (Legambiente, 2015).

Rail freight has historically been marginal in the movement of goods in Southern Italy; however, new investment has been directed to freight in recent years (see Box 4B.3*)*.

Airports in the Mezzogiorno lacked dedicated rail links until recently, when services were opened in the Palermo (2001), Reggio Calabria (2013) and Bari airports (see Box 4B.4). As with roads, Naples is well connected to the Centre and North. As well as the high-speed passenger line, there is an important freight link to the logistics hubs of the north between Bologna and Verona, connecting on to the rail networks of Austria and northern Europe. Customs facilities have been established in Bologna's Hinterport to operate dry port services for Naples for bonded containers, bypassing delays at the Naples port, although labour interests in the customs and inspection services have hampered the use of these facilities.

Figure 4B.7 Density of double-track, electrified lines (left) and single-track, non-electrified lines right)

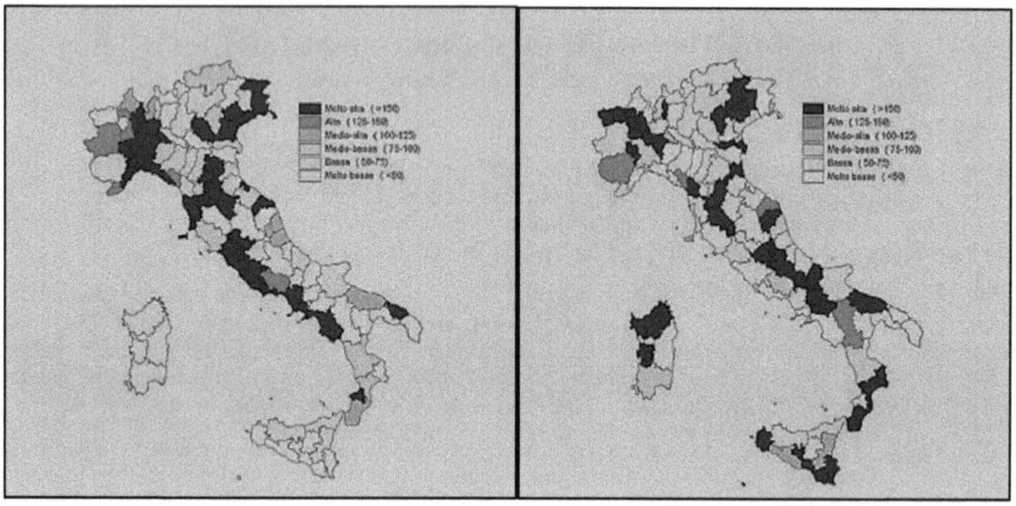

Notes: dark grey = high density, white = low density.

Source: ISTAT (2006).

Box 4B.4. Integrating Bari Airport with the regional rail network

Airports in the Mezzogiorno carry around 24 million passengers annually. While most airports are served by public transport to and from the nearest city, Bari Airport was the first Southern airport to open a rail link in 2013. Located in Apulia, Bari Airport handles 4 million passengers per year, travelling to both national and international destinations. Over the summer months, it is one of the main points of entry for tourists arriving to the region.

The rail ink was built over 2009-2012 as a spur of the existing regional rail network. The rail link is 8 km long and fully electrified, and it adopts an automatic train control system. Trains can reach maximum speeds of 110 km/hr but on average travel at 60 km/hr. The overall cost of the link was just over EUR 80 million, co-financed by the Region Apulia and the European Commission.

The new infrastructure connects Bari Airport to the city of Bari in 15 minutes, as well as to other regional cities and towns with direct services. A notable feature of the new line at the planning stage was the creation of a stop between Bari and the airport in correspondence with the newly created headquarters for tax authorities (*Cittadella della Finanza*), encouraging land-use and transport integration.

Source: "All'aeroporto di Bari in treno", Ferrovie.it, 2013; FerrovieNordBarese website; Bari Airport website

Ports

Around half of all national maritime traffic is handled at ports in the South of Italy, equivalent to 5 million TEUs per year. The majority of container traffic goes through the port of Gioia Tauro in Calabria, which is the largest transhipment port in Italy. The second and third largest ports by volumes are Taranto and Naples. Naples is the largest import port, specialising in containers and liquid bulk.

Inward connectivity by road and rail to the main ports is one of the national priorities for the ports (Ministero dei Trasporti 2016). Implementing this plan will require close cooperation between public companies (such as port authorities and the rail network manager – RFI), private actors (including intermodal terminal owners) and transport users. The Italian Ministry also stresses the importance of linking all core ports by rail, ultimately to the European freight corridors, to maximise the potential for long-distance Ro-Ro traffic from Southern Italian ports (Ministero dei Trasporti 2014).

Box 4B.5. Intermodal infrastructure – Naples' extended port

The Port of Naples is one of the largest ports in Southern Italy, with a capacity of just over 500 000 TEUs. More than 430 000 TEUs, mainly container traffic for import goods, have been handled annually at the port (traffic has remained fairly constant since the early 2000s), which therefore operates close to capacity. Only 8% of all goods were moved by rail to and from the port. In this context, plans for an "extended Port of Naples" were developed over the past decade, focusing on two key objectives: increasing the modal share of rail and decongesting the port by moving some key functions inland.

The plan has taken shape with the creation of a large hinterland site for port logistics around the existing rail freight depot of Nola, about 30 km inland from Naples. Owned by a private company and known as "*Interporto Campano*", the logistics site occupies an area of 3 million m^2, hosting a large intermodal terminal and parking areas that can cater for up to 3 000 trucks. However, road transport makes up only 18% of traffic at the site. The site is linked to the national rail freight network by a short stretch of electrified railway lines; this in turn is linked to the European TEN-T Corridor 1. Between 10 and 12 weekly rail shuttles have been introduced to move containers arriving on different ships from the Port of Naples to the *Interporto Campano* under a single load, achieving the densities needed to make rail the preferred mode of transport.

Evidence from other OECD countries suggests that Naples' extended port could become a success story for the Mezzogiorno. The hinterland port can reduce capacity constraints at the Port of Naples and road congestion in and around the city. The site will be strengthened through new rail services planned by national freight operators and the expansion of border control facilities. The *Interporto Campano*, however, would not have been possible without the close co-operation between public actors and the private sector, both with respect to co-ordinated planning across modes and to financing. For instance, state contributions amounted to around 30% of the start-up costs of new rail services.

Source: Interporto Campano website, Port of Naples website, European Commission C(2009) 4508

Bibliography

ACAM (2015), "Rapporto sulle infrastrutture in Campania", Napoli

"All'aeroporto di Bari in treno", Ferrovie.it, 2013, Available at: www.ferrovie.it/portale/articoli/1194 (last accessed 14 March 2017)

Beria, P., Debernardi, A., Ferrara, E. (2016), "Measuring the long-distance accessibility of Italian cities", World Conference on Transport Research - WCTR 2016, Shanghai. 10-15 July 2016.

European Parliament (2014), "EU Road surfaces: economic and safety impact of the lack of regular road maintenance", DG for internal policies, Policy department B: structural and cohesion policies

Floris, G. (2015) "Zona retrocessione: perché l'Italia rischia di finire in Serie B", Rizzoli editore

ISFORT (2015), "Sviluppo dell'intermodalitá – Autostrade del mare 2.0 e combinato marittimo"

ISTAT, National Institute for Statistics of Italy, www.istat.it/en/

"La storia siamo noi", (2015) RAI Documentary, can be viewed at: www.lastoriasiamonoi.rai.it/ puntate/salerno-reggio-calabria/816/default.aspx (last accessed 3 July 2016)

Legambiente (2015), "Rapporto Pendolaria – La situazione e gli scenari del trasporto ferroviario pendolare in Italia" Available at: https://www.legambiente.it/sites/default/files/docs/pendolaria_2016.pdf (last accessed 14 March 2017)

Ministero dei Trasporti (2016), Connettere l'Italia – Strategie per le infrastrutture di trasporto. Available at: www.mit.gov.it/sites/default/files/media/notizia/2016-07/Strategie%20per%20le%20infrastrutture_2016.pdf (last accessed 14 March 2017)

Ministero dei Trasporti (2014), Programma Operativo Nazionale – Infrastrutture e reti

SVIMEZ (2015), "Rapporto 2014 sull'economia del Mezzogiorno". Available at: https://www.cliclavoro.gov.it/Barometro-Del-Lavoro/Documents/Rapporto%20Svimez%202014.pdf (last accessed 14 March 2017)

Uniontrasporti (2011), "Rapporto sullo stato delle infrastrutture in Italia; criticitá di oggi, prioritá di domani", Available at: www.uniontrasporti.it/writable/news/pdf/Uniontrasporti_I%20Rapporto%20sulle%20infrastrutture_Presentazione.pdf (last accessed 14 March 2017).

4B.3 New Zealand

4B.3.1 Economic and demographic profile

New Zealand is an island nation in the south-western Pacific Ocean, covering 263 310 km^2. It is similar in size to the United Kingdom (UK), with no part of New Zealand being greater than 130 km from the sea. New Zealand's main populated territories are its North and South Island, which sit on the Pacific rim. This location gives those islands volcanoes and makes them prone to earthquakes. It has a largely temperate climate (Statistics New Zealand, 2015: 2).

In 2014, New Zealand's population was 4 509 700, with most of the population living on the North Island. Its only large city by international standards is Auckland. The city is home to one-third of the New Zealand population (1.4 million), hosts the country's major commercial and manufacturing centres, and serves as the logistical trade node. Auckland hosts New Zealand's largest two largest export platforms by value (Port of Auckland and Auckland International Airport).

New Zealand has two other regional cities. The capital, Wellington, has less than one-third of Auckland's population at 398 200, and the only other city with a population of about 300 000 is Christchurch at 381 800 (Statistics NZ, 2015a). New Zealand's average population density is 17.13 people per km^2.

New Zealand is a high-income country. In 2014, its Gross Domestic Product (GDP) per capita was USD44 342. Of New Zealand's GDP, 28% is derived from exports. New Zealand's main exports by value include agricultural goods and services.[1] It also has a substantial forestry export industry.

These characteristics make New Zealand a good comparator for the Southern Chile.

Table 4B.3 Characteristics of New Zealand

	Year	New Zealand	Central Chile
GDP per capita	2004	25 104	
(current USD)	2014	44 342	7 435
Population density	2004	15.52	
(inhabitants per km^2)	2014	17.13	39.91
Main exports	1.	Food products, beverages and tobacco	Paper, paper products
(by value, latest available)	2.	Wholesale and retail trade, hotels and restaurants	Forestry
	3.	Transport and storage, post and telecommunication	Food

Source: Population: World Bank (2016a), Instituto Nacional de Estadísticas de Chile (2016a). Land area: World Bank (2016b), Instituto Nacional de Estadísticas de Chile (2016b). GDP: World Bank (2016c), Banco Central de Chile (2016). Exports: OECD (2016), Direccion Nacional de Adunas (2016).

4B.3.2 Overview of transport infrastructure and key issues

New Zealand has extensive transport infrastructure and substantial plans to improve its transport infrastructure for the next 30 years. At present, the New Zealand Government subsidises the road and rail networks. It requires ports and airports to have a commercial focus, and a similar focus increasingly applies to rail (National Infrastructure Unit, 2015: 20).

Figure 4B.8 Map of transport networks in New Zealand

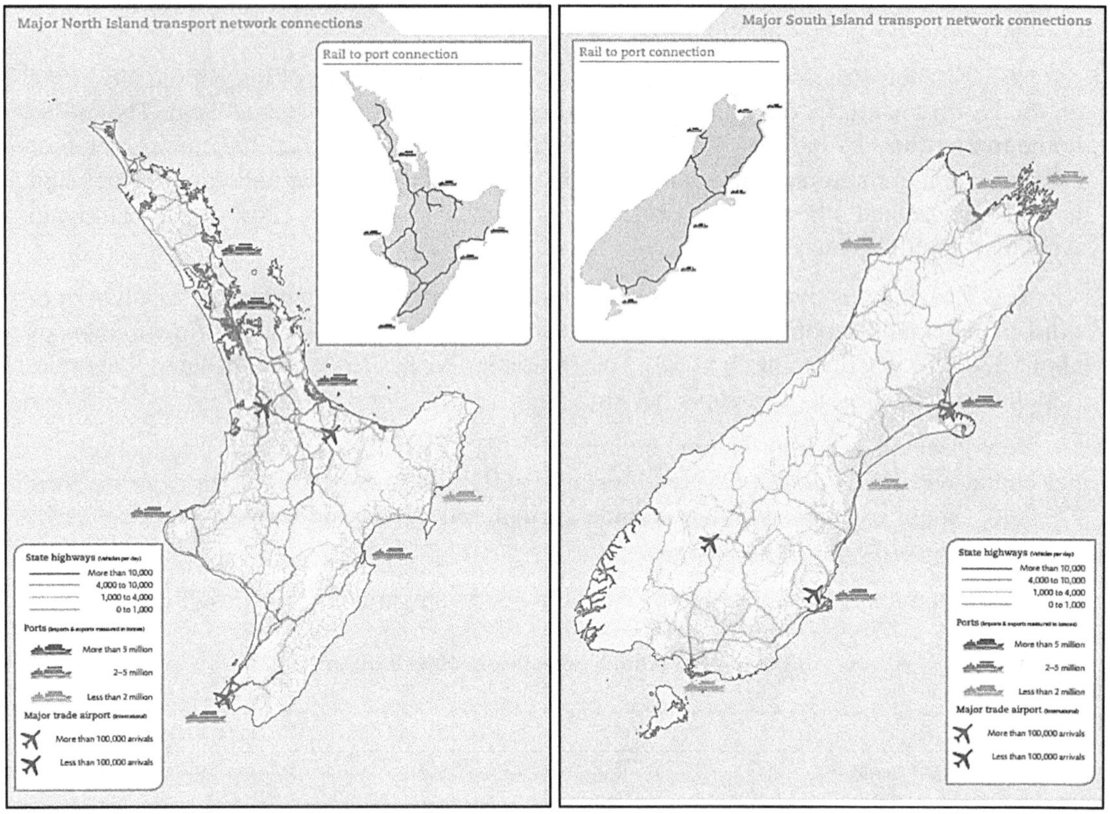

Source: NZ Ministry of Transport.

The following provides an overview of the transport infrastructure in New Zealand.

Road

New Zealand has approximately 95 000 km roads, two-thirds of which are paved (ibid: 3). New Zealand's roads can be considered in two categories. The State Highway network is made up of 11 000 km of highways that link cities and towns and provide access to transport hubs, such as ports. Despite being only 11.6% of roads, the State Highway network carries almost half of all road travel kilometres in New Zealand. The State Highway network is funded and operated by the national government through the New Zealand Transport Authority. Approximately 27.5 km of the network is tolled (New Zealand Transport Agency, n.d.).

All other roads are the responsibility of local and regional governments. However, much of this is subsidised by the national government.

Box 4B.6 Small but congested cities

The drive for greater asset utilisation has created larger volumes at some ports, such as Auckland. However, the Port of Auckland is adjacent to the city's central business district. Therefore, land near the port is limited, and an increased number of trucks travelling to the port is exacerbating congestion in the area.

Road carries the majority of traffic in New Zealand, especially in and around cities. There is heavy reliance on private motorised vehicles for urban transport. Public transport accounts for only 2.8% of all trips. Private vehicles account for almost 80%. There are several factors that appear to encourage private vehicle use in New Zealand cities. These include:

- spread-out, low-density cities (hindering cost effectiveness of public transport)
- historically low levels of public investment in infrastructure for public transport
- administrative boundaries not matching the real boundaries of built-up areas (hindering planning co-ordination).

Together with economic and population growth, as well as New Zealand's geography, the factors encouraging private vehicle use have resulted in substantial congestion in New Zealand's main cities. In fact, congestion in New Zealand's main cities is higher than that in most Australian cities that have higher populations.

Starting to address congestion in Auckland

Just over 90% of Aucklanders commute to work by car, and the number of kilometres travelled by car has increased by 30% since 2000.

The New Zealand government has sought to address congestion and other issues in Auckland through a range of mechanisms including:

- increased investment in transport infrastructure, including public transport infrastructure; motorways, busways and electrified urban rail have been introduced or expanded in recent years
- reforming governance and planning systems, such as merging the eight previous bodies governing the Auckland metropolitan area into a single body, the new Auckland Council
- requiring the Auckland Council to develop the Auckland Plan, which, among other things, sets out strategies for building infrastructure to improve Auckland's congestion over the next 30 years.

While there are signs of improvement, the Auckland Plan acknowledges that forecast population growth means that congestion will deteriorate over the next 30 years, even with very substantial investments in transport infrastructure.

Rail

New Zealand has approximately 3 500 route-km of railway (KiwiRail, Annual Integrated Report, 2016: 6), down from a peak of 5 695km in 1952 (Asia-Pacific Economic Co-operation, 2011:231). At present, the railways focus on linking New Zealand's main industrial and agricultural centres and ports. There has been an increased focus on freight activities, and several segments of the passenger network have been closed in recent years (National Infrastructure Unit, 2015: 4, 8).

Following the privatisation of railways for a relatively short period (1993-2008), the New Zealand government bought back the national railway operator, currently branded KiwiRail (Kiwi Rail, n.d.). The operator is vertically integrated, operating and maintaining rolling stock and rail infrastructure services. Local governments own the rolling stock that provides urban public transport and contract with KiwiRail for those services (ibid: 4). KiwiRail's above rail operations are cash positive. However, the New Zealand government provides a subsidy (NZD 210 million in 2016) to fund the rail infrastructure (KiwiRail, 2016: 21).

While the government is addressing road congestion through improved rail public transport, land-use limitations at the Port of Auckland incentivise moving more freight by rail to inland ports. Passenger and freight services share rail infrastructure in Auckland. Thus, congestion on Auckland's railways is increasing, undermining reliability for both passenger and freight services. In turn, this undermines government attempts to move passenger and freight transport from road to rail. In November 2016, KiwiRail proposed that the New Zealand government fund construction of separate freight rail lines in central Auckland to ease congestion for both passenger and freight trains (KiwiRail, 2016: 41). So far, the New Zealand government has not made any decisions on the proposal.

Box 4B.7 Governance structures and policy objectives changed; underlying economics did not

Over the past 40 years, New Zealand's rail industry has experienced several reforms. Originally, the New Zealand Railways Department built infrastructure and operated services. Rail was viewed as a public service to link sparsely populated communities and industries to population centres and ports. It was protected from competition by restrictions on road haulage. However, protection did not prevent competition from trucking and domestic shipping. In turn, from the 1920s onwards, rail in New Zealand required increasing government funding as operating profits declined and turned negative.

In 1982, New Zealand corporatised rail into a vertically integrated government business enterprise – the New Zealand Rail Corporation (NZRC). This improved efficiency, reducing staffing by 54%, closing some uneconomic lines and steadying rail's decline. However, this was not enough to stop the downward trend, especially after protections were removed in 1986. In 1990, the NZRC transferred operations to NZ Rail to prepare for privatisation.

In 1993, a new government privatised rail, and NZ Rail became Tranz Rail. The government sought to maximise access of the new company to private funding and avoid further government investment by selling an integrated monopoly with no access regime. This provided incentives for investment, which improved productivity.

Tranz Rail was unable to sell any land under the rail network, and in 2002, another new government prevented it from closing any of the 41% of rail lines that Tranz Rail considered to be uneconomic. In 2002, this resulted in Tranz Rail on-selling the railway at a discount to Toll Rail.

In 2004, Toll Rail returned the unprofitable rail infrastructure to the government (NZRC) and began paying an access charge for rail operations. Tension over the access charge followed. The government sought increases to fund infrastructure enhancements. Toll Rail sought decreases to keep rail freight competitive with road. Toll Rail's ability to withdraw operations gave it greater bargaining power, reducing access charges and, in turn, increasing subsidies.

In 2005, New Zealand enacted a limited access regime for freight lines that Toll was underutilising.

The government was prepared to subsidise rail to provide the extensive national rail network that it considered necessary to meet its goals relating to regional development, primary industry exports and the environment. However, it considered it preferable to provide subsidies to a government entity rather than a foreign, private company. Thus, in 2008, the government bought back the operations for NZD 690 million.

A month later, the government changed again. This government expected a commercial rate of return and that any subsidies would be transparent. Further efficiencies followed, including substantial line closures. Network length has been reduced from 4 000 km in 2008 to 3 500 km in 2016. Above rail operations are cash positive, while below rail operations continue to require substantial subsidies (NZD 210 million in financial year 2016).

The various reforms to the New Zealand rail sector demonstrate how structural changes cannot remedy fundamental economic issues. New Zealand's low population density, together with its legacy network's layout and narrow gauge, make government subsidies a necessity if there is to be an extensive national passenger and freight rail network. It is advisable to identify the underlying circumstances driving challenges in a country's rail network and addressing those directly and transparently, rather than assume that corporatisation, privatisation or open access will cure all issues.

Furthermore, New Zealand's experience indicates the importance of setting and holding true-to-policy objectives over the long term. New Zealand's rail reforms may have been more successful if the original efficiency objectives were maintained throughout the period. This would have allowed the railways to focus on areas such as bulk freight on a limited number of profitable lines where they provide greatest benefit to the community, rather than needing to provide a broader range of services. Coincidentally, these are often also the areas providing commercial returns and operating on an environmentally sustainable basis.

Source: APEC, 2011 (pp. 230-253); KiwiRail, 2016 (pp. 6, 21).

Ports

As an island nation, New Zealand's international trade relies heavily on port infrastructure. Of New Zealand's international trade, 99% is shipped through sea ports (National Infrastructure Unit, 2015: 10). It has 16 ports that service domestic and international ship movements. More than two-thirds of throughput volume at New Zealand ports is bulk, rather than containerised freight. However, containerised freight is 80% of the value of exports (ibid: 4-5).

New Zealand's biggest container freight and passenger port is adjacent to the Auckland central business district (Ports of Auckland, 2015: 3). Approximately 200 km away, the Port of Tuaranga has expanded from its previous focus on forestry exports to compete with the Port of Auckland for container transport.

Most ports are owned by local governments (there is also some private ownership), with each port serving a local hinterland. However, over time, international ships have called at fewer ports to obtain greater asset utilisation.

Box 4B.8 Inland port competition

The drive for greater asset utilisation has created larger volumes at some ports, such as Auckland. However, the Port of Auckland is adjacent to the city's central business district. Therefore, land near the port is limited, and an increased number of trucks travelling to the port was exacerbating congestion in the area.

The Port of Auckland responded to these challenges by creating an inland port, located in the south of Auckland close to its manufacturing and industrial activities. Containers are moved by rail from the Port of Auckland to the Wiri Inland Port, reducing truck traffic in central Auckland, while helping to address congestion and difficulties with limited space at the port.

The Port of Tuaranga, 200 km by road from Auckland on the east coast, has sought to compete with the Port of Auckland. It has also built an inland port, MetroPort, in southern Auckland, which has a rail link to the Port of Tuaranga (Port of Tuaranga, 2015: 2).

A third inland port, valued at NZD 3.3 billion, will shortly be built at Ruakura, east of Hamilton, 125 km south of Auckland. Ruakura will have rail links to both the ports of Auckland and Tuaranga. Unlike the ports of Auckland and Tuaranga, which have substantial local government ownership, the Ruakura inland port is being funded by Tainui Group Holdings (TNH), which is the investment arm of a local Maori organisation, Waikato-Tainui. Since 1995, TNH has grown an initial settlement payment of NZD 170 million under the Treaty of Waitangi into over NZD 1.1 billion of assets (National Infrastructure Unit, 2015:17). Profits from the Ruakura inland port will form part of TNH's dividends, which are used to support the community through a range of activities including funding for employment and scholarships (Waikato-Tainui, 2016: 4).

Airports

New Zealand has five airports receiving international flights and 26 receiving domestic flights (National Infrastructure Unit, 2015: 4). Auckland International Airport has the largest passenger and cargo operations. It is the second largest cargo port by value in New Zealand (ibid: 25). New Zealand's other key international passenger airports are in Wellington and Christchurch. Most airports in New Zealand are owned by local governments. There is also some central government or private ownership of airports. The three key international airports are subject to light-handed economic regulation.

Surface access to Auckland International Airport has been a growing concern, given the increasing difficulty that passengers, staff and businesses have experienced in accessing the airport. Airport managers commissioned a surface access study in 2005, and the study confirmed the presence of severe travel-time delays to and from the airport as a result of bottlenecks on the regional road network. It also highlighted the weaknesses in public transport services. A number of planning and feasibility studies are under way, paving the way for the construction of a dedicated public transport link, possibly by rail, to better serve the airport and reduce congestion.

4B.3.3 Overview of framework conditions (policy, planning, co-ordination)

New Zealand has detailed mechanisms to undertake transport infrastructure planning. The National Infrastructure Unit within the New Zealand Treasury works with a range of stakeholders to develop, monitor and update the National Infrastructure Plan (NIP) and the supporting evidence base, which cover infrastructure across all sectors of the economy. The most recent 30-year plan and supporting evidence were released in 2015. They include a vision for infrastructure over the life of the plan and more detailed objectives that explain the vision. In addition, the plan sets out the strategic context, current state of infrastructure and the responses that the plan proposes.

In addition to the NIP, the **2003 Land Transport Management Act** (LTMA) sets out the requirements for the operation, development and funding of the land transport system. Through the Government Policy Statement on Land Transport (GPS), the central government sets the overall objectives and long-term results sought over a ten-year period, as well as expenditure ranges for each class of transport activity. The New Zealand Transport Agency (NZTA) then develops a three-year National Land Transport Programme, which outlines the activities that will receive funding from the National Land Transport Fund. These activities are selected from proposals prepared by regional land transport committees. Activities proposed for funding must form part of a ten-year Regional Land Transport Plan (RLTP). All RLTPs must be consistent with the GPS. There are also requirements to consult Maori affected by these plans.[2]

Notes

1. New Zealand includes travel, commercial and transportation services under the service category. Commercial services include financial and insurance services, telecommunication and computer services, and other business services. Government services are also included; see Statistics New Zealand, New Zealand in profile, 2015, p. 2.
2. Land Transport Management Act 2003 ss. 18F and 18G.

References

APEC (2011), "Rail Transport in New Zealand," in The Impacts and Benefits of Structural Reforms in Transport, Energy and Telecommunications Sectors. Asia-Pacific Economic Co-operation, http://publications.apec.org/publication-detail.php?pub_id=1113 (accessed 14 March 2017).

Auckland Council (2012), The Auckland Plan, http://theplan.theaucklandplan.govt.nz/ (accessed 14 March 2017).

Banco Central de Chile (2016), "PIB regional" [Regional GDP], Cuentas Nacionales [National Accounts], http://si3.bcentral.cl/Siete/secure/cuadros/arboles.aspx (accessed 23 February 2016).

Direccion Nacionales de Adunas (2016), "Principales rubros de exportación por région de embarque, 2014-2015" [Main exports by loading region, 2014-2015], in Anuario Estasístico 2015 [Annual statistics report 2015], www.aduana.cl/aduana/site/artic/20150624/asocfile/20150624160021/anuario_estadistico_servicionacionaladuanas_2015.pdf.

Instituto Nacional de Estadísticas de Chile (2016a), "País y regiones por áreas urbana-rural: actualización población 2002-2012 y proyecciones 2013-2020" [Country and regions by urban/rural areas: actual population 2002-2012 and projections 2013-2020], www.ine.cl/estadisticas/demograficas-y-vitales (accessed 23 February 2016).

Instituto Nacional de Estadísticas de Chile (2016b), "Superficie de la tierra por tipo de uso, según region. 2015" [Land area by use and region. 2015], in Medio Ambiente – Informe Annual 2016 [Environment – Annual Report 2016], http://historico.ine.cl/medioambiente/descargas/2016/medio_ambiente_2016.pdf.

KiwiRail (2016), Annual Integrated Report, www.kiwirail.co.nz/uploads/Publications/Annual%20Integrated%20Report%202016.pdf (accessed 14 March 2017).

KiwiRail (n.d.), Rail Privatisation, www.kiwirail.co.nz/about-us/history-of-kiwirail/150yearsofrail/stories/rail-privatisation.html (accessed 14 March 2017).

National Infrastructure Unit (2015), Infrastructure Evidence Base 2015 Refresh. www.infrastructure.govt.nz/plan/evidencebase (accessed 14 March 2017).

National Infrastructure Unit (2015a), Thirty Year New Zealand Infrastructure Plan. www.infrastructure.govt.nz/plan/2015/nip-aug15.pdf (accessed 14 March 2017).

New Zealand Transport Agency (n.d.), "Where the toll roads are", www.nzta.govt.nz/roads-and-rail/toll-roads/toll-road-information/where-the-toll-roads-are/ (accessed 14 March 2017).

OECD (2016), "Trade in Value Added TiVA)", OECD.Stat – International Trade and Balance of Payments, http://stats.oecd.org/Index.aspx?DataSetCode=TIVA_2016_C1 (accessed 13 May 2016).

Ports of Auckland (2005), Annual Review.

Port of Tuaranga (2015), Annual Report.

Statistics New Zealand (2015), New Zealand in Profile.

Statistics NZ (2015a), Estimated Resident Population for Urban Areas at 30 June 2015.

TomTom Traffic Index, 2016, www.tomtom.com/en_gb/trafficindex/list?citySize=LARGE&continent=ALL&country=ALL (accessed 14 March 2017).

Waikato-Tainui (2016), Puurongo-Aa-Tau (Annual Report) o Waikato Tainui 2016.

World Bank (2016a), "Population, total", World Development Indicators, http://databank.worldbank.org/data/reports.aspx?source=world-development-indicators (accessed 23 February 2016).

World Bank (2016b), "Land area (sq. km)", World Development Indicators, http://databank.worldbank.org/data/reports.aspx?source=world-development-indicators (accessed 23 February 2016).

World Bank (2016c), "GDP (current US$)", World Development Indicators, http://databank.worldbank.org/data/reports.aspx?source=world-development-indicators (accessed 23 February 2016).

4B.4 Northern Sweden – The Sub-Arctic

4B.4.1 Economic and demographic profile

This area of Sweden stretches from the north-eastern border with Finland to the inland mountainous areas marking the border with Norway on the West. To the east, the coastal region along the Baltic Sea is relatively flat, with several island archipelagos. The area has a sub-arctic climate, with cold winters and mild summers. The inland territories receive abundant precipitation.

Northern Sweden had a population of 1 714 342 inhabitants in 2014 and a population density of just under 6 inhabitants per km^2. The largest county is Norrbotten, representing one-quarter of Sweden's total land area. Three-quarters of the population is concentrated along the coast, and Umeå, the biggest city, has 100 000 inhabitants. The inland regions are very sparsely populated.

The area is rich in mineral resources, notably iron ore, and forests, with a large production of timber. Almost 90% of the entire European supply of iron ore is extracted in Norrbotten. Forests cover almost 60% of the area of Västerbotten County area and 35% of Norrbotten County. The forests provide raw materials for the sawmill, carpentry, cellulose and energy industries, and they are also significant for biodiversity, ecosystem-related services and experiencing nature. Other business activities include industries such as gold and hydropower. Tourism is on the rise. Between 2004 and 2014, GDP per capita grew by more than one-third in Northern Sweden; average incomes are slightly below the national average.

These characteristics make Northern Sweden an appropriate comparator for Chile's Austral marcozone. Although the southernmost regions of Chile have an even more irregular territory and lower population density, the geographic and climatic conditions of Northern Sweden are not too dissimilar. These, coupled with economic activities such as forestry, result in similar demands for local transport networks. A notable difference is that Northern Sweden has a highly developed mineral extraction industry.

Table 4B.4 Characteristics of Northern Sweden

	Year	Northern Sweden	Sweden	Chile Austral
GDP per capita (current USD)	2004	36 896	42 442	
	2014	50 068	58 939	9 693
Population density (inhabitants per km²)	2004	5.97	22.08	
	2014	5.99	23.79	3.82
Main exports (by value, latest available)	1.	Forestry	Chemicals and mineral products	Food products
	2.	Chemicals and mineral products	Wholesale and retail trade, hotels and restaurants	Forestry
	3.		Real estate	

Source: Population: World Bank (2016a), Statistics Sweden (2016a), Instituto Nacional de Estadísticas de Chile (2016a). Land area: World Bank (2016b), Statistics Sweden (2016b), Instituto Nacional de Estadísticas de Chile (2016b). GDP: World Bank (2016c), Statistics Sweden (2016c), Banco Central de Chile (2016). Exports: OECD (2016), Direccion Nacional de Adunas (2016).

4B.4.2 Overview of transport infrastructure and key issues

Transport infrastructure in Northern Sweden is designed to meet the needs of extractive industries such as iron ore extraction and forestry, as well as for passenger connectivity within the region and with the rest of Sweden. Road and rail networks need to be resilient enough to accommodate both freight and passenger flows throughout the year considering very low temperatures and heavy snowfalls.

Road

The road network is Northern Sweden covers 18 000 km of publicly owned roads, characterised by a large share of roads with low traffic volumes (<1 000 AADT) and high seasonal fluctuations (ROADEX, n.d.). Fluctuations correspond to production peaks for extractive industries and to periods of high tourist activity. In mountainous areas, for instance, spring time is when passenger car traffic is the highest, corresponding to the peak season for frost-related road damage. Road deformations and restrictions can have high economic impacts on local industries. Northern Sweden has reduced the number of road fatalities in recent years to low levels, but the rate is still double that for Sweden as a whole.

Around two-thirds of all roads in Northern Sweden are paved, and around one-third are gravel roads. Meeting the requirements of heavy haulage on secondary roads (that are often not paved) is a specific challenge of this area. Design standards are based on traffic flow, as well as stress and strain calculations; layer thickness is dependent on the chosen construction type, the number of equivalent standard axles,* and the type of material in the subgrade and the climatic zone. The highest road standards are set for roads with >2,000 AADT and prescribe a rock-bitumen pavement. For roads to be considered as suitable for paving, traffic must be higher than 250 AADT.

In Sweden during the 1980s, most low-traffic-volume roads were paved with thinner and weaker structures, mainly using "Y1G" (surface dressing with one layer, 0-18 mm – a layer of stone is stuck with bitumen emulsion on the underlying gravel layer). The Y1G method was aimed at gravel roads to make the surface more even and reduce dust.

Although cheaper, the Y1G method revealed its limitations over time. The gravel road beds on which the solution was applied were not built to appropriate standards, and new surfaces were already subject to heavy damage after only a few years, especially in frost-sensitive areas. It was then necessary to impose bearing capacity restrictions (12-ton maximum weight), particularly during the spring thaw. This negatively affected heavy vehicles relying on these roads.

Thin-layer paving solutions were almost entirely abandoned in Sweden as a result of this experience, which highlighted the risks of using thin layers directly on gravel roads. Thin layers are only used today when the road has good bearing capacity, a base course and good drainage. Importantly, thin layers are only applied on roads with very low AADT and almost no heavy traffic.

* This number is calculated from AADT, the percentage of heavy vehicles, the number of standard axles per vehicle and the assumed changes in traffic during the intended lifetime of the road.

Rail

The rail network is approximately 1 670 km long in Northern Sweden. One of the main railway lines is the Ore Railway, between Luleå (Sweden) and Narvik (Norway), which carries iron ore products from the extraction sites to areas of industrial refinement in Sweden to export ports in Norway. Norwegian fish products are also carried into Sweden on the line. Half of Sweden's tonnage of railway freight is transported from Kiruna to Riksgränsen and on to Narvik.

Other important freight links run east-west, for instance carrying ore from the interior to the coast where steel factories are located, and north-south, carrying those metal products to Southern Sweden for value-added manufacturing. Thus, the share of rail freight transport is high in Northern Sweden (38% of all tonne-km are moved by rail.).

Passenger services are provided along the north-south axis running inland because of strategic, historical decisions not to build rail lines along the coast. Services subsidised by the State include two overnight trains per day linking the North to Stockholm and Goteborg. One of the largest infrastructure projects in Northern Sweden is linked to the construction of the North Bothnian Line, which will complete the coastal railway line, connecting the major population centres in the region and reducing journey times between them and to the rest of the country (see Box 4B.9).

Box 4B.9 The North Bothnian Line

The Bothnian Corridor extends along the Swedish and Finnish sides of the Gulf of Bothnia. The northern part of the corridor, which will extend between Umeå and Luleå, is recognised as a "missing link" in Sweden's strategic infrastructure.

Original plans envisaged the construction of the North Bothnian Line as a key freight link, connecting to the existing Bothnian Line in the south for onwards transport towards Europe, the Iron Ore Line in the west leading to Norway and the sea routes, and to the east via the Haparanda Line to the Finnish and Russian rail networks. Upon completion, the Bothnian Corridor would bring together several rail networks and enable transport to the east-west interchange between the east coast of the US and the Far East.

However, a number of studies during the 2000s showed that there would be considerable benefits for passengers travelling between Northern Swedish cities and towns as well. Currently, around 300 000 people live along the rail route, and all passenger movements take place by road. New rail services would significantly reduce journey times for different categories of users, including commuting trips for professionals, workers in key service sectors and students. For instance, travelling between Luleå and Umeå would be 20 minutes faster.

After years of delays linked to changes in political circumstances and budget availability, the presence of these large benefits for both freight and passenger services resulted in the project being reintroduced as a priority project by the Swedish government in 2014 and consequently marked as part of the part of the European Core Network, to be completed by 2030.

Construction of the 270-km North Bothnian Line is planned to commence in 2018 for a total estimated cost of around EUR 3 billion. The project will be co-funded by the European Union and some of the municipalities located along the Line, which have pledged to contribute with direct funding as well as investment in related infrastructure such as railway stations.

Source: European Railway Review (2013); Trafikverket (2016).

Ports

The largest commercial port is located in Luleå. Luleå is Sweden's leading bulk goods terminal. Iron ore constitutes more than half of the volumes traded. An effective icebreaker service enables the ports of Piteå and Luleå to remain open all year round for the intensive shipping. The harbour in Kalix also has year-round shipping, although on a smaller scale than Luleå and Piteå. Shipping is crucial for export competitiveness: for example, 95% of all the overseas exports from Västerbotten County (measured in tonnes of goods) are moved by ships.

Passenger ferry services are also important to connect isolated communities. Where it is not possible to build bridges, the Swedish government provides ferry services free of charge for the local population. With respect to international connectivity, the Kvarken route, a ferry line between Umeå and Vaasa, provides an important year-round link with Finland.

Airports

There are 11 airports in Northern Sweden, three of which are part of the primary network operated by Swedavia and eight of which are owned by local municipalities. Sweden's Transport Agency is responsible for procuring non-commercially viable services at these airports. These services are directly subsidised by the government. Luleå Airport is the sixth largest airport in Sweden, and the air route to Stockholm/Arlanda is the busiest domestic route in Sweden. The next largest airports are in Umeå and Kiruna.

4B.4.3 Overview of framework conditions (policy, planning, co-ordination)

The Ministry of Enterprise, Energy and Communications has responsibility over transport matters in Sweden. The ministry, together with the Swedish Parliament (Riksdag), sets the overall direction for transport policies through the Direction Plan, within the framework of Policy Goals and Policy Principles (see Box. 4B.10).

The Swedish Transport Administration (Trafikverket) operates under the authority of the ministry and has overseen all modes of transport since 2010. Based on the Direction Plan, it is tasked with preparing an Infrastructure Proposal to cover how Swedish roads, railways and infrastructure for shipping and aviation should develop and be managed over a period of 12 years. The Proposal, with its associated budget, is sent to Parliament by the government. This offers Parliament the opportunity to modify the proposal, balancing the interests of stakeholders with different political and regional goals.

Once the Proposal is approved, the government tasks Trafikverket with preparing a National Transport Plan to implement the projects and measures developed. Over a period of approximately one year, the Administration develops concrete investment and maintenance plans, and it ensures that regional inputs from Sweden's 21 counties are included. These inputs are the result of analysis on specific local issues and often give rise to the definition of smaller schemes, always within the framework of national priorities.

The latest National Transport Plan 2014-2025 was released in April 2014. It is associated with a budget envelope of around SEK 58 billion (EUR 5.8 billion). Approximately SEK 9.5 billion is for operation and maintenance of the railways, with SEK 17 billion for operation and maintenance of the roads and SEK 31 billion for infrastructure development in line with regional plans.

The allocation of funds is not based on any territorial criteria, nor on per capita spending rules. Nonetheless, the process gives rise to a fairly balanced distribution of investment across Swedish regions, as shown in Figure 4B.9 This is the result of the ability of local project sponsors to identify investment proposals that meet the national strategic objectives and that are supported by a wide range of stakeholders, including local municipalities and private businesses. One such project is investment in increasing the load-bearing capacity of roads ahead of the introduction of 74-tonne trucks in Northern Sweden.

Figure 4B.9 Transport investment per capita (thousands of SEK) in Northern Sweden and Sweden

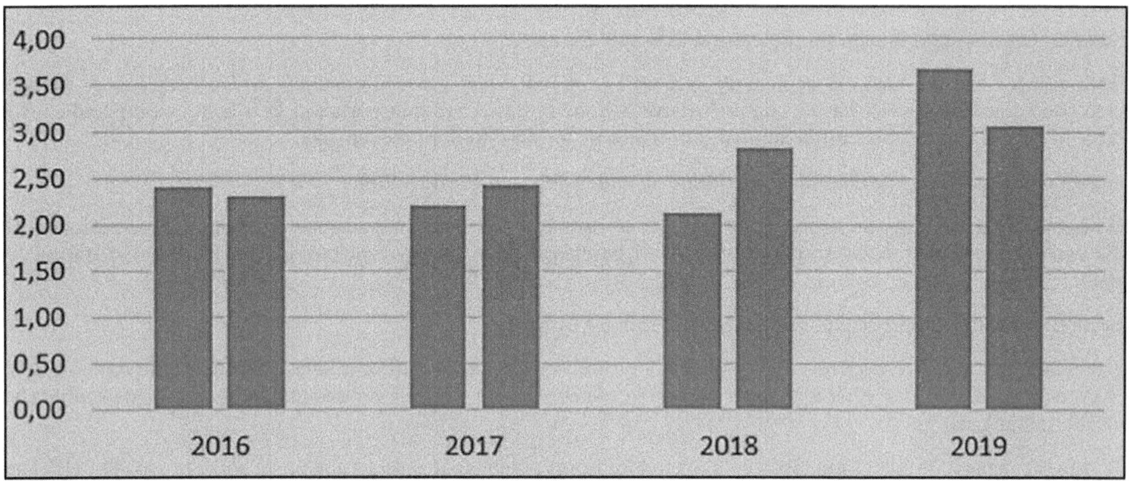

Note: Left bars = Northern Sweden; Right bars = all Sweden.

Source: Trafikverket (2016).

Figure 4B.10 From transport policy goals to implementation

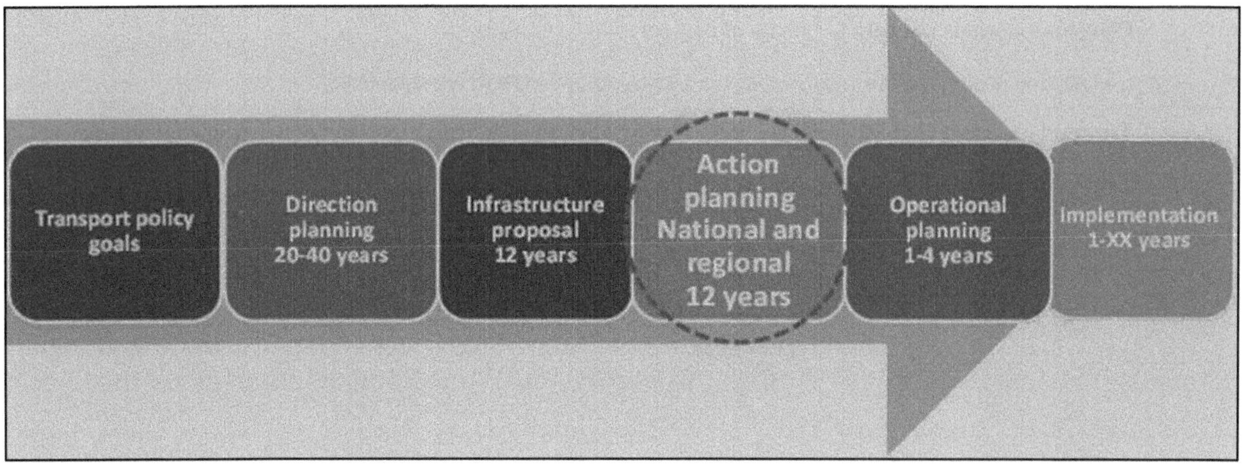

Source: Trafikverket (2016).

Box 4B.10 Sweden's transport policy vision, goals and principles

The national vision for transport infrastructure in Sweden establishes that "everyone shall arrive in a smooth, green and secure way". The vision is further explained as follows:

Smooth: Our transport system is efficient and available for all

Both citizens and the business community, regardless of individual preconditions and where they live or work, have access to good connectivity. We have a comprehensive attitude to travel and transportation. It is both smooth and convenient to be able to choose and combine different modes of transport for door-to-door movements.

Green: Our transport system takes the environment and health into consideration

When we are developing the transport system, we always consider health aspects and give due consideration to people and the countryside/nature. The transport system shall be clean, quiet, energy-efficient and have a limited impact on the climate.

Secure: Our traffic environments feel secure and safe for everyone

The whole journey, irrespective of how we travel or are transported in traffic, is safe, and our traffic environments are perceived as being secure. Together with other players in society, we are working for unambiguous safety goals with a Vision Zero as our guiding star.

Within the context of this vision, Sweden's overall transport policy goal is set to guarantee an economically efficient and effective transport supply system for citizens and the business community, which is sustainable in the long term throughout the whole country. The current functional goal of transport policy is **availability**. This goal needs to be balanced by transport policy considerations around **safety, the environment and health**.The following guiding principles complement the vision and goals:

- Customers should be given freedom to decide how they want to travel.
- Decisions on transport production should take place in a decentralised manner.
- Co-operation within and between modes of transport will be promoted.
- Competition between railway undertakings and transport options will be promoted.
- Transport costs to society should be the main consideration when designing transport policy regulatory instruments.

Source: Trafikverket, 2016.

References

Banco Central de Chile (2016), "PIB regional" [Regional GDP], Cuentas Nacionales [National Accounts], http://si3.bcentral.cl/Siete/secure/cuadros/arboles.aspx (accessed 23 February 2016).

Direccion Nacionales de Adunas (2016), "Principales rubros de exportación por région de embarque, 2014-2015" [Main exports by loading region, 2014-2015], in Anuario Estasístico 2015 [Annual statistics report 2015], www.aduana.cl/aduana/site/artic/20150624/asocfile/20150624160021/anuario_estadistico_servicionacionaladuanas_2015.pdf.

Instituto Nacional de Estadísticas de Chile (2016a), "País y regiones por áreas urbana-rural: actualización población 2002-2012 y proyecciones 2013-2020" [Country and regions by urban/rural areas: actual population 2002-2012 and projections 2013-2020], www.ine.cl/estadisticas/demograficas-y-vitales (accessed 23 February 2016).

Instituto Nacional de Estadísticas de Chile (2016b), "Superficie de la tierra por tipo de uso, según region. 2015" [Land area by use and region. 2015], in Medio Ambiente – Informe Annual 2016 [Environment – Annual Report 2016], http://historico.ine.cl/medioambiente/descargas/2016/medio_ambiente_2016.pdf.

Ministry of Transport (2014), "Review of international transport planning and funding frameworks", New Zealand Government Paper submitted to ITF/OECD.

OECD (2016), "Trade in Value Added TiVA)", OECD.Stat – International Trade and Balance of Payments, http://stats.oecd.org/index.aspx?datasetcode=tiva_2016_c1 (accessed 13 May 2016).

ROADEX (n.d.), Sub-Project A Phase 1, "Road Condition Management of Low Traffic Volume Roads in the Northern Periphery", Project supported by European Regional Development Funds, www.roadex.org.

Statistics Sweden (2016a), "Population 1 November by region, age and sex. Year 2002-2016", Population statistics - Number of inhabitants, www.statistikdatabasen.scb.se/pxweb/en/ssd/start__be__be0101__be0101a/folkmangdnov/table/tableviewlayout1/?rxid=04da7b70-7b24-4563-890f-ef1a88bb26a3 (accessed 23 February 2016).

Statistics Sweden (2016b), "Land and water area 1 January by region and type of area. Year 2012-2016", Environment – Land and water area, www.statistikdatabasen.scb.se/pxweb/en/ssd/start__mi__mi0802/areal2012/?rxid=04da7b70-7b24-4563-890f-ef1a88bb26a3 (accessed 23 February 2016).

Statistics Sweden (2016c), "Gross Regional Domestic Product (GRDP), number of employed and wages and salaries (ESA2010) by region (NUTS1-3). Year 2000-2015",

Regional accounts, annual estimates, www.statistikdatabasen.scb.se/pxweb/en/ssd/start__nr__nr0105__nr0105a/nr0105ens2010t01a/?rxid=04da7b70-7b24-4563-890f-ef1a88bb26a3 (accessed 23 February 2016).

"The last link in the Bothnian Corridor" (2013), European Railway Review, Issue 5, 2013.

Trafikverket (2016), presentation to the ITF/OECD on "The planning process - from transport policy goals to implementation", October 2016, Lulea, Sweden.

World Bank (2016a), "Population, total", World Development Indicators, http://databank.worldbank.org/data/reports.aspx?source=world-development-indicators (accessed 23 February 2016).

World Bank (2016b), "Land area (sq. km)", World Development Indicators, http://databank.worldbank.org/data/reports.aspx?source=world-development-indicators (accessed 23 February 2016).

World Bank (2016c), "GDP (current US$)", World Development Indicators, http://databank.worldbank.org/data/reports.aspx?source=world-development-indicators (accessed 23 February 2016).

Chapter 5

The governance of water infrastructure in Chile

This chapter identifies Chile's main water-related infrastructure and governance challenges in urban and rural areas, including rainwater infrastructure and desalination, as well as irrigation systems and dams. The chapter highlights the prominent water risks faced by Chile, as well as drivers that influence water demand and supply, including climate change, economic development, energy, urbanisation, demographic trends and territorial development. The chapter points to some infrastructure deficits both in quantity and type, and it makes some suggestions on how to move forward, including low-cost options such as green and natural infrastructure, demand management techniques and rainwater harvesting. The chapter includes a rudimentary assessment of Chile's institutional water framework against the OECD Principles for Water Governance and makes some recommendations on how water can drive sustainable growth.

* The statistical data for Israel are supplied by and under the responsibility of the relevant Israeli authorities. The use of such data by the OECD is without prejudice to the status of the Golan Heights, East Jerusalem and Israeli settlements in the West Bank under the terms of international law.

Water infrastructure and Plan Chile 30/30

The Plan Chile 30/30 was conceived with the objective of developing the level of infrastructure (transport, water, ports, etc.) that Chile needs to overcome the middle income trap and reach USD 30 000 GDP per capita in 2030. The objective of the Ministry of Public Works (MOP) is to quantify the infrastructure gap by benchmarking Chile against countries that face similar challenges to Chile's macro-zones,[1] and plan investments accordingly for the coming 15 years. It is worth noting though that while the Agenda 30/30 focused primarily on *economic growth* as an outcome, the Plan Chile 30/30 has started to change its paradigm towards a broader understanding of wellbeing and development, coming closer to the OECD's regional well-being framework, which encompasses both material conditions (income, jobs, and housing) and non-material conditions (health, education, environment, community, life satisfaction, civic engagement, safety, and access to services). In that context, the efforts to boost infrastructure should continue to be conceived as a systemic effort to contribute to the three pillars of sustainable development now and in the future, namely economic prosperity, social inclusion and environmental protection.

The Plan Chile 30/30 is a responsibility of the MOP, thus placing infrastructure under its area of competence. The MOP is the ministry with the broadest portfolio in Chile, which ranges from road and port infrastructure to certain areas of urban transportation and to water infrastructure. Other strategic areas fall under the competence of other ministries like the Energy Ministry, which plans and executes energy infrastructure, or the private sector, which offers water services in urban areas. The Plan Chile 30/30 does not consider all types of water-related infrastructure (e.g. hydropower infrastructure and urban water services are excluded), but primarily focuses on water services in rural areas (essentially drinking water supply, with plans to include wastewater treatment), irrigation, rainwater and flood protection infrastructure. These areas fall under the responsibility of the Directorate of Hydraulic Infrastructure (DOH), a department within MOP (Box 5.1).

Urban water services are a key area of infrastructure that falls outside the purview of the MOP, and is regulated by the Superintendence of Sanitation Services (SISS). Chile's urban water services, i.e. drinking water supply and wastewater treatment, operate using in a concessional regime to the private sector, which means different private utilities are responsible for providing water services and thus responsible for maintaining, renovating and building the distribution network.

The Agenda 3030, which was conceived as a support document for the discussions and development of the Plan Chile 30/30, calls for some investments that might help bridge some infrastructure gaps. For instance, the Agenda 3030 includes an investment programme in a series of big reservoirs that will increase water supply capacity and hence the country's irrigated surface area by 220 000 hectares at a cost of USD 3.2 billion over 15 years. There is also a plan to improve and increase small reservoirs, which the initial period of 2015–18 alone will invest USD 174 million (Ministry of Public Works, 2014). Moreover, it is projected to invest USD 58.6 million annually to improve rainwater infrastructure in 54 cities. All these investments represent efforts to provide solutions that will last for 20, 30, or 40 years, and they must therefore be carefully planned, since they come at an important cost and may have impacts on territorial development and land use.

Box 5.1. Who does what in Chile's water policies

Chile counts over 40 water-related institutions delivering 100+ functions, thus making it one of the most fragmented countries for water management in the OECD region (OECD, 2012). Chile is among the OECD countries that give the most dominant role to central government and limited prerogatives to the subnational level when it comes to water resources management. Key players in Chile's water institutional mapping include:

- **General Directorate of Water (Ministry of Public Works):** responsible for water resources planning; monitoring and information dissemination; issuing and regulating water rights under the Water Code; monitoring the execution of those rights; granting permission for major works; implementing policies and conducting surveillance of water in natural channels; supervising the operation of water user organizations; and developing the Public Water Registry.
- **Directorate of Hydraulic Works (Ministry of Public Works):** delivers water infrastructure to efficiently exploit water resources and protects populations against floods and other extreme events. In particular, the Directorate of Hydraulic Works is responsible for delivering irrigation dams and channels, rainwater and fluvial protection, and rural drinking supply systems. The Rural Potable Water Programme aims at supplying drinking water to rural areas.
- **Directorate for Planning (Ministry of Public Works):** responsible for short-, medium- and long-term planning of infrastructure, including water infrastructure.
- **Superintendence of Sanitation Services, established in 1990 as the main regulatory and enforcement body of water supply and sanitation services:** decides on tariffs for drinking water and sanitation services. For concessions, the Superintendent's Office works with private sector operators to ensure service quality and monitor industrial sites producing liquid waste.
- **Ministry of Health:** responsible for overseeing water quality standards and environmental regulations in the industrial sector.
- **National Hydraulic Institute (Ministry of Public Works):** research institute that investigates hydraulics matters and whose mission is to provide guidance to the national government by enriching knowledge on water resources. It is located within the Ministry of Public Works.
- **Ministry of Environment:** responsible for the design and implementation of environmental policies and programmes to protect and conserve ecosystems, as well as natural and water resources.
- **Superintendence of Environment:** oversees the compliance with all environmental and fiscal instruments included in the Law 19.300 (Law on Environmental Requirements). It also promotes and encourages stakeholders to comply with these instruments.
- **Service of Environmental Evaluation:** responsible for overseeing the System of Environmental Impact Assessment and ensuring that the environmental evaluations conducted in public and private projects are transparent, of good technical quality and efficient. It also promotes citizen participation in environmental evaluations.
- **National Irrigation Commission:** responsible for all irrigation issues, from policy design to infrastructure provision.
- **Chilean Commission of Copper:** develops, implements and supervises natural resource exploitation policies, including for water management in the mining sector.

Source: OECD (2012), *Water Governance in Latin America and the Caribbean: A Multi-level Approach*, OECD Publishing, Paris, http://dx.doi.org/10.1787/9789264174542-en.

Water infrastructure investments need to be closely coordinated with other policy areas and sectoral plans to account for externalities in other sectors, as well as for the impact that other sectors in turn have on the water system. The development of rainwater infrastructure, water services or flood protection infrastructure has a direct impact, for example, on land use policies, and vice versa. The way in which the city and its hinterland will evolve is directly linked to the existence and the development of basic infrastructure that provides water safety and universal coverage. For instance, frequent floods in Chile, such as in March 2015, reveal that urban planning and rainwater harvesting have not been optimally co-ordinated in the past, and that cities have developed without taking water risks into account (UCHILE, 2016). In the particular case of urban water services, the coordination with private water utilities is also key to ensuring that urban development strategies and plans feature water-related constraints, especially in the peri-urban areas. Moreover, many decisions taken outside the area of water policy (land use, energy, agriculture, industry) have significant impacts on water, and vice-versa. For instance, it is not clear how water aspects feature in the energy agenda that has been outlined through 2050. The expansion of the agriculture frontier has been planned, but without evaluating related impacts and needs in terms of water resources. A thorough assessment of the distributional impacts of decisions taken on water-related policy areas is essential to identifying contradictory incentives and fostering policy complementarities, especially when it comes to exploring synergies in terms of future infrastructure. Also, in light of the multipurpose potential of the infrastructure that may be built in the future, it is essential to make the most of investments and foster policy complementarities across water-related domains, which requires effective inter-ministerial coordination. For instance, large dams can primarily serve to supply water for irrigation, but also as tourist attractions and to generate electricity or regulate floods.

Infrastructure should be considered a means to an end. The Plan Chile 30/30 cannot deliver its ultimate objective of developing the level of infrastructure that Chile needs to overcome the middle income trap, if it does not build concomitantly on the "3Is", namely infrastructure, institutions and information. While infrastructure can certainly play a role in Chile in securing sustainable access to water resources and services in the future, it alone cannot meet a challenge of the magnitude posed by all the country's water-related risks. Investments in physical infrastructure will need to be accompanied by robust governance frameworks, supported by strong institutions, and improved information systems in order to effectively guide decision making at all levels.

Key factors that affect water management in Chile

Water demand in Chile is projected to rise in the coming decades, unlike in other OECD countries where it is expected to decrease by 2050 (OECD, 2012a). Over the last few decades, water demand has increased in Chile, linked to the period of dynamic economic growth and the high specialisation of the economy in water-intensive sectors including mining, agriculture and forestry, and fish farming. COCHILCO (2009) reported that the mining sector alone is expected to increase its demand for water by 45% in 2020,[2] while forecasts indicate that agriculture will require an additional 4 km^3 over the next 40 years. These trends raise the issues of how to match supply with demand geographically, how to maintain water sustainability in the future, and how to minimise competition for water by transitioning further from water supply to water demand management approaches (OECD, 2016b), especially in the northern regions between mining and agriculture.

Chile faces water challenges that will require action to maintain current levels of supply and meet increasing demands. A new report *OECD Water Risk Hotspots for Agriculture* ranks Chile as the 10th country out of 142 (4th among OECD countries just after US, Mexico and Australia) subject to more severe water risks (OECD, forthcoming). The following long-term drivers in particular, affect the capacity of the system to manage too much, too little water or too polluted water, and to secure universal coverage in terms of water supply and sanitation services in the future:

- **Climate change** will continue to have noticeable effects over the next 50 years and will deplete the available resources, particularly in those areas of the country that suffer from the greatest shortages. The Directorate of Meteorology of Chile (DMC, 2015) estimates that in 2050 the minimum temperature in northern Chile will rise 2 °C on average, with an even greater increase in the stretch between Copiapó and Concepción, where the minimum temperature in the mountainous areas is expected to increase by 3°C. Meanwhile, total annual rainfall will decrease by between 200 mm and 500 mm in Central Chile. Geographic and climatologic variability will act as a compounding factor to these trends. While in the north, average rainfall is 87 mm/year and water availability barely reaches 510 m^3/person/year, the south of Chile has an average rainfall of 2 963 mm/year and water availability of 2 340 227 m^3/person/year (DGA, 2016).
- **Urbanisation and demographic growth** keep increasing at a fair rate. Currently, nearly 90% of the total population lives in cities, and this share will approach 95% by 2050 (OECD, 2013). Between 2002 and 2012, the mean annual national population growth was above the OECD average (1.04% vs. 0.67%) (OECD, 2016a).
- **Economic development** continues to be tightly linked to the performance of water-intensive sectors. In 2014, 92% of water resources were used for mining (11% of GDP), agriculture (3%) and manufacturing (11%). Governmental plans to expand the agricultural frontier and increase the importance of mining in central regions will further exacerbate the current tensions due to competing water demand.
- **Energy.** The *Energy 2050 Policy* (2015) calls for an increase in the use of renewable energies, where hydropower is meant to play an important role in the coming years. One of the goals of the energy policy is to boost the amount of electricity production from renewable energy sources to 60% of the electricity matrix by 2035, and to at least 70% by 2050 (currently, it is 30%) (Ministry of Energy, 2015).

Territorial specificities

Geographic and climate variability in Chile raise a number of challenges in terms of water resources management. The country extends longitudinally over 4 300 km, and its widest part is 445 km. The climate of the country varies from the driest region in the world, including the Atacama Desert extending over 180 000 km2 in the north, to numerous glaciers and humid weather in the south. The country has about 1 251 rivers that flow from the mountains to the sea, forming 101 small-scale hydrographic basins. The Andes, the Coastal Mountainous Chain and the intermediate depression create a special morphology that influences the rivers' paths, creating a complex water system to manage. These small-scale river basins are often at the same time the water source for users, which creates an interconnected system that is difficult to manage. The large number of rivers and the mountainous terrain provide a considerable potential for hydropower.

Chile is overall a water-rich country, where per capita availability of water resources largely exceeds the OECD average, but the water is unevenly distributed. Renewable resources in Chile, accounting for long-term averages, are approximately 55 640 m3/capita, which is close to double the OECD average (31 360 m^3/capita)

(Figure 5.1). Disparities between the north and centre (where most of the people live and work) and the south (where most of the water resources are located) are noteworthy. The four macro-zones used by the MOP to differentiate the infrastructure and development challenges that the country faces also apply when considering water and hydrological conditions (DGA, 2016):

1. **North Macro-Zone**: characterised by an arid to semi-arid climate (more arid to the north) with an average rainfall of 87 mm/year, the lowest per capita availability among the four macro-zones (510 m^3/person/year), and includes the Atacama desert, one of the driest spots in the world.

2. **Centre Macro-Zone**: characterised by Mediterranean climate conditions, with an average rainfall of 943 mm/year, which is mainly concentrated in the winter season (3 to 4 months). Average water availability per capita is 3 169 m^3/person/year, with important disparities between Valparaíso area (around 1 000 m^3/person/year) and farther south in the region of Maule (7 000 m^3/person/year).

3. **South Macro-Zone**: characterised by a mild rainy and maritime rainy climate, with abundant rainfall (average 2 420 mm/year), which is higher to the south. Water availability is 56 799 m^3/capita/year.

4. **Austral Macro-Zone**: rich in water resources, rather sparsely populated and with low economic activity. The macro-zone has the highest average rainfall (2 963 mm/year) and water availability (2 340 227 m^3/capita/year).

Figure 5.1. Total renewable freshwater resources per capita, long-term annual average values

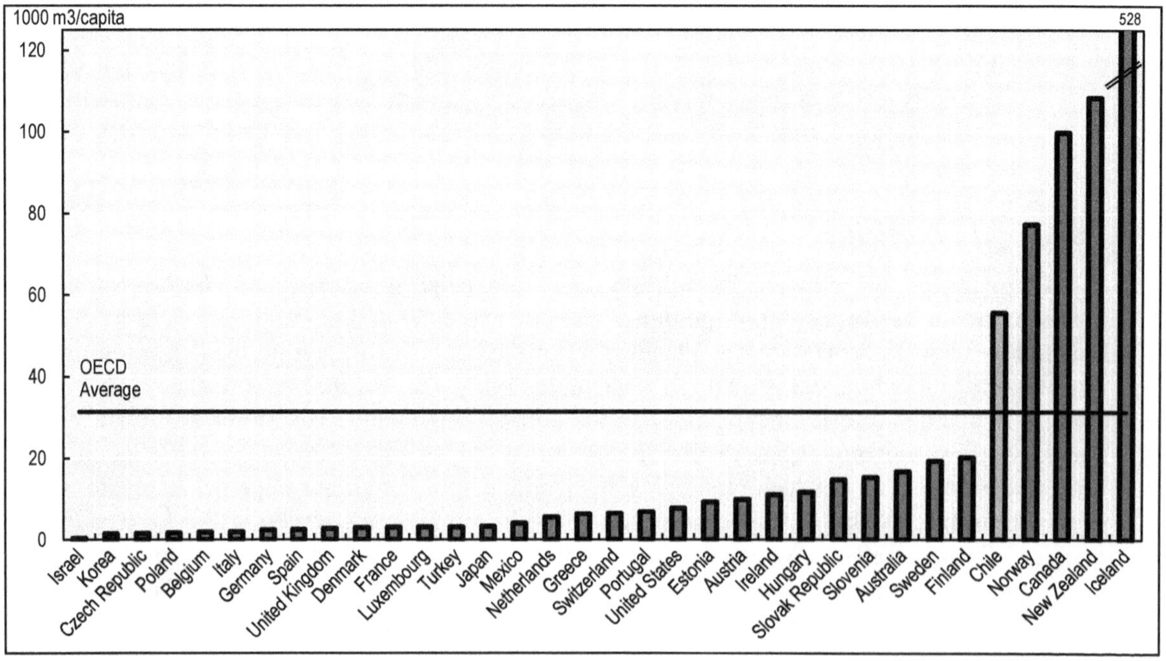

Source: OECD (2015), "Total renewable freshwater resources per capita, long-term annual average values", in *Environment at a Glance 2015*, OECD Publishing, Paris, http://dx.doi.org/10.1787/9789264235199-graph23-en.

The diversity of geographic and climatological conditions in Chile requires place-based policy responses. The infrastructure needed in the north of Chile is different from that required in central Chile, or in the southern parts of the territory. Whereas the North Macro-zone suffers from severe water shortages, this is less true for the centre, and not an issue at all in the south. Thus, northern and central Chile need policies that target scarcity, through both increasing supply and reducing demand. The former can be costly, e.g. dams or desalination plants that require large investments, and have an impact on the environment. Water demand policies, such as more efficient irrigation techniques, awareness campaigns or reuse of wastewater, are usually more cost-efficient and less disruptive. Lastly, the south of Chile is less developed and has different needs, such as securing access to water supply and sanitation to rural population and improving rainwater infrastructure in less developed cities.

Demographic trends

Over the past 25 years, Chile has experienced a 50% increase in population and become highly urbanised. In 1950, 58% of the total Chilean population (3.5 million people) was living in urban areas. In 2010, approximately 15.2 million people lived in urban areas, representing around 89% of its population. Using the OECD definition of functional urban areas[3] (FUAs), approximately 77% of Chileans live in cities at present (OECD, 2013). Of the 26 functional urban areas, 15 can be classified as small urban areas[4], eight as medium-sized urban areas, two metropolitan areas (Valparaíso and Concepción), with only one large metropolitan area (Santiago de Chile). Small urban areas host 11% of the total national population, medium urban areas 15%, Valparaíso and Concepción are home to 11% of the national population, and Santiago is the biggest metropolitan area, accounting for 39% of the Chilean population (OECD, 2013).

Chile is above the OECD average in terms of population growth. National population grew at an average annual rate of 1.04% between 2002 and 2012, which is higher than the 0.67% registered on average for the OECD area (Figure 5.2). Demographic trends show an average growth rate (2002-12) of 1.2% in cities (OECD, 2013). The urban population continues to grow more rapidly than the total national population, and it is projected that 90% of Chileans will live in urban areas by 2025 (OECD, 2013).

Figure 5.2. Mean annual population growth rate 2002-12

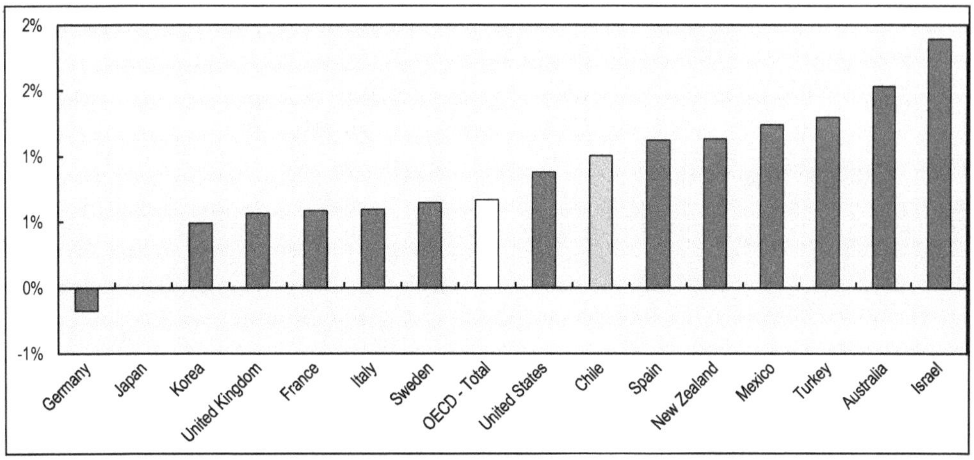

Source: OECD (2016a), OECD Regional Statistics (database) Demography and Population, https://stats.oecd.org/ (accessed September 2016).

Drinking water supply and sanitation services represented 8% of consumptive water use in Chile in 2014. Approximately 44% of the water rights for drinking water are located in the Metropolitan Region of Santiago, and 12% in Valparaíso (Government of Chile, 2014). Domestic water consumption in 2014 accounted for 8% of water use (Figure 5.4), and water demand is expected to rise if population trends continue.

A water-intensive socioeconomic profile, geographically concentrated

The socioeconomic structure of the country puts pressure on available water resources. Mining, agriculture and manufacturing are the backbones of Chile's economic development and well-being, but they are water-intensive (Figure 5.3)[5]. Agriculture represents 82% of freshwater abstractions, human consumption accounts for 8%, industrial uses for 7% and mining for 3%. Agriculture and mining continue to develop in the north and centre of the country where the resource is scarce. Mining activities are geographically located close to the main copper reserves. The central region (IV, V, RM, VI), is home to 60% of the country's population, 16% of the world's copper reserves and 50% of the country's mining potential (CNID, 2014), and it represented almost 66% of national output in 2013 (Figure 5.5).

Water use varies significantly from north to south in Chile, according to the economic specialisation of the different regions. Economic activities in the North Macro-Zone are mainly dedicated to mining, though mining is less dominant in the north than agriculture is elsewhere (Figure 5.6). Agriculture has a predominant role in the Centre Macro-Zone and in the South Macro-Zone, while industrial and mining activities both play an important role in the Austral Macro-Zone (Figure 5.6). The North Macro-Zone accounts for 6.45% of total water use in Chile and 48.52% of the total water allocated to mining. The Central Macro-Zone concentrates 74.64% of Chile's total water use, 79.06% of the total water allocated to agriculture and 73.05% of drinking water, (mainly in the metropolitan areas of Santiago and Valparaíso) (Table 5.1). The South Macro-Zone represents 16.16% of total allocated water, and the most significant demand corresponds to the industrial sector (26.07% of total water allocated to industry). The Austral Macro-Zone has the lowest water demand (2.74% of total water), of which 19.27% and 21.66 are allocated to industry and mining, respectively.

Table 5.1. Water use as % of total allocated water to each use by Macro-Zone, 2011

	North Macro-Zone	Centre Macro-Zone	South Macro-Zone	Austral Macro-Zone	
			%		
Agriculture	4.61%	79.06%	15.79%	0.54%	100
Drinking water	7.66%	73.05%	15.54%	3.76%	100
Industry	7.96%	46.70%	26.07%	19.27%	100
Mining	48.52%	23.76%	6.05%	21.66%	100
Total	6.45%	74.64%	16.16%	2.74%	100

Source: DGA (2016), *Atlas del Agua: Chile 2016*, Dirección General de Aguas, www.dga.cl/atlasdelagua/Paginas/default.aspx.

Figure 5.3. Contribution to GDP by sector, 2014

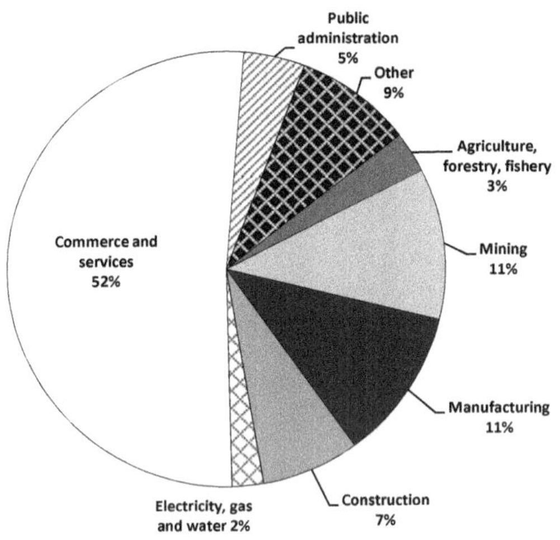

Source: OECD/ECLAC (2016), *OECD Environmental Performance Reviews: Chile 2016*, OECD Publishing, Paris, DOI: http://dx.doi.org/10.1787/9789264252615-en.

Figure 5.4. Freshwater abstractions in Chile, 2013

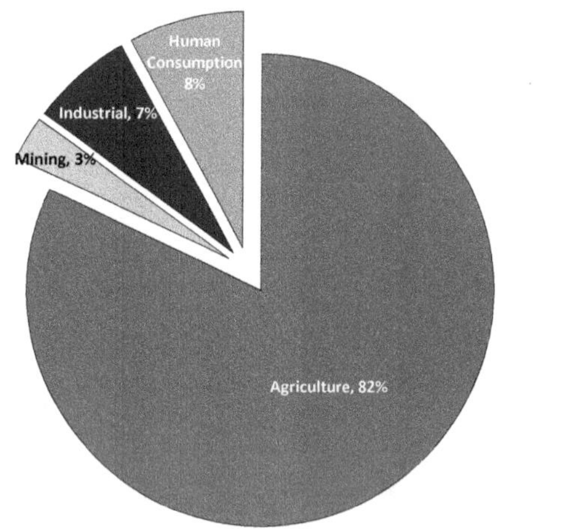

Source: OECD (2015b), "Water: Freshwater abstractions", *OECD Environment Statistics* (database). https://stats.oecd.org/Index.aspx?DataSetCode=WATER_RESOURCES ; OECD (2014a) *Historical population data and projections statistics* (database). http://stats.oecd.org/.

Figure 5.5. Regional contribution to national GDP (%) and population

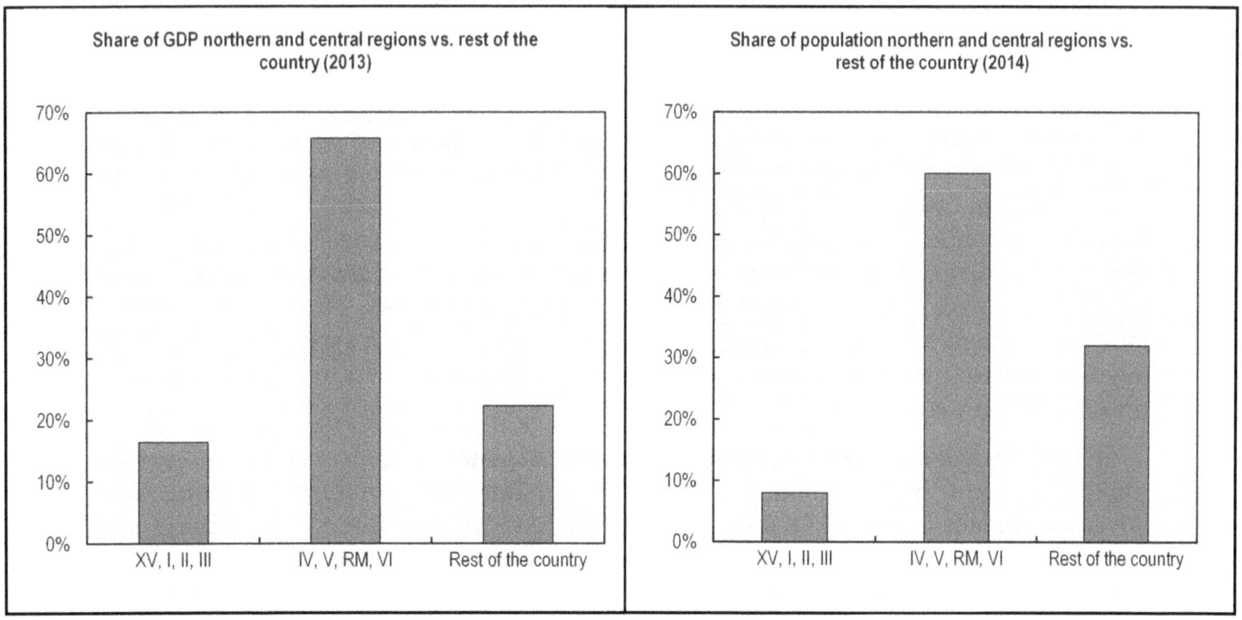

Source: OECD (2016a), OECD Regional Statistics (database) Demography and Population, Regional Accounts, https://stats.oecd.org/ (accessed September 2016).

Figure 5.6. Water use per region, 2011

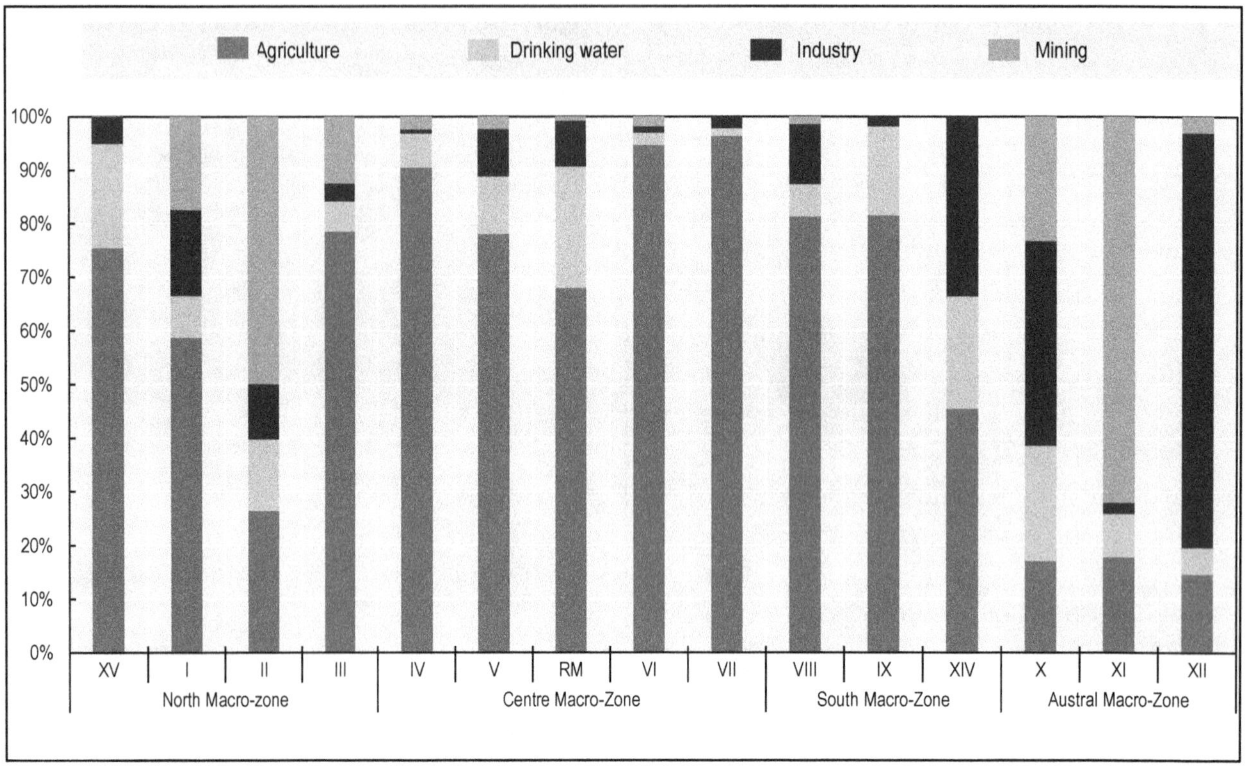

Source: DGA (2016), *Atlas del Agua: Chile 2016*, Dirección General de Aguas, www.dga.cl/atlasdelagua/Paginas/default.aspx.

The geographic concentration of activities in the north and centre has an impact on competition over water demand. Water demand exceeds water supply in northern and central regions such as Arica, Parinacota, Antofagasta, Tarapacá, Atacama, and Coquimbo. Particularly in Antofagasta (Region II), where the mining sector accounted for 66% of GDP in 2010 (OECD, 2011), the water deficit was the largest in Chile in 2016 (-5.3 m^3/s). The cities of Valparaíso and Santiago also suffer from water stress with values near from incurring deficit[6] (Figure 5.7). From region VI to X, south of the metropolitan region of Santiago, agriculture represents on average around 14% of GDP and 27% of total employment, while mining is below 1.32% of GDP. Although agriculture is a water-intensive activity, the higher availability of water resources in these regions reduces the pressure on the water system.

Chile's economic and social development depends heavily on the country's ability to meet water demands for its water-intensive economic sectors. The government plans to expand 10 000 ha of agriculture to increase Chile's national exports, and domestic water consumption together with urbanisation are expected to keep rising in the coming decade. Moreover, over time mining has gained traction in the north and is further developing in the central areas. Given the depletion of the northern reserves where mining activities were traditionally located, within the next 50 years mining is expected to shift further towards the central regions. There will be large investments taking place in the northern mining areas (USD 100 000 million) over the next 10-15 years to increase water supply (OECD, 2014) including investments in desalination plants.

Figure 5.7. Water deficit per region in Chile (2016)

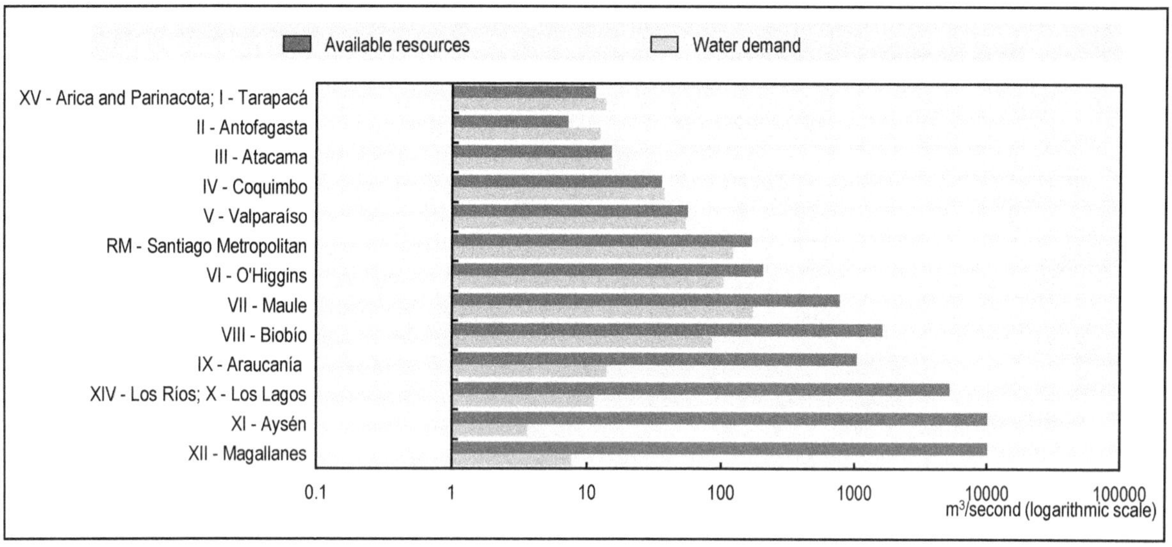

Source: Based on data from DIRPLAN & INH (2016), "Análisis de Requerimiento de Largo Plazo en Infraestructura Hídrica", Dirección de Planeamiento del Ministerio de Obras Públicas (DIRPLAN) e Instituto Nacional de Hidráulica (INH).

In the face of these future trends, Chile needs robust and adaptive water policies to transition from supply to demand management, and from crisis to risk management. Whereas increasing supply through dedicated infrastructure might work in the short term, climate change and related uncertainties threaten the status quo in the medium and long term. A change of model towards a rebalancing of water supply and demand by using demand management approaches will be a more effective and efficient development strategy for the country, as explored later in this chapter.

Energy supply

In the face of rising energy prices and scarcity of energy resources, energy security is a crucial concern for Chile's current administration. Recent debates around environmental sustainability and climate change, as well as commitments to the reduction of CO2 emissions following the Paris Agreement, have raised further the profile of energy on the national political agenda. Chile imports 60% of its primary energy, which makes the country vulnerable to price instability, volatility of markets and supply constraints. Energy availability is considered by the Chilean government as a necessary condition for economic growth and development, as well as for a move toward better social inclusion.

The development of the Chilean energy sector is intrinsically linked to water resources management. Chile has historically generated a large share of its electricity from renewable sources. In the 1980s, no less than 80% of energy generation was hydroelectric. However, droughts caused frequent cuts in supply, which is why in the 1990s the national government decided to diversify the energy matrix by incorporating natural gas from Argentina as a new source of electricity. After Argentina restricted natural gas exports in 2004, Chile started relying on coal and thermal plants for its electricity production, thus resulting in a reduction in the share of hydroelectric generation in its electricity matrix. While over the past five years, the average share of hydroelectric generation was 32%, Energy Policy 2050 (Box 5.2) aims to raise the share of renewable energy to 60% of the electricity generation matrix by 2035, and at least 70% by 2050.

Box 5.2. Energy Policy 2050

The Ministry of Energy launched the "Energy 2050" initiative in July 2014, as a result of a participatory process, and the plan proposes a vision for Chile's energy sector in which the country will achieve a reliable, inclusive, competitive and sustainable energy system by 2050. The Energy Policy is built on four pillars: i) Quality and Security of Supply, ii) Energy as a Driver of Development, iii) Environmentally-friendly Energy, and iv) Energy Efficiency and Energy Education. Within Pillar 3, Environmentally-friendly Energy, one of the policy goals by 2050 is to achieve an energy matrix where renewable energy sources represent 70% of total electricity generation. The fundamental guidelines identified in the Energy Policy to reach this goal by 2050 are:

- promote a greater contribution from renewable energy sources (conventional and non-conventional) to the electricity matrix
- promote sustainable hydroelectricity development, to increase renewable energy's share of the electricity matrix
- promote the share in energy matrix of fuels with low GHG emissions and atmospheric pollutants.

Increasing hydroelectric power generation is therefore one of the central pillars in the Ministry's plan for the coming 35 years.

Source: Ministry of Energy (2016), "Energy 2050: Chile's Energy Policy", www.energia2050.cl/wp-content/uploads/2016/08/Energy-2050-Chile-s-Energy-Policy.pdf

Mining and industry account for the largest share of energy use (38%) (Figure 5.8). Energy demand in these sectors increased by 50% over the period from 2000-13, driven by the energy-intensive mining industry and paper and pulp production (OECD, 2016). Projections show that the mining industry's electricity consumption may increase by 81% by 2025 (COCHILCO, 2015). Other pressing energy demands are related to the development of alternative water sources (such as desalination and reuse) which consume large quantities of energy.

Figure 5.8. Energy consumption by sector in Chile

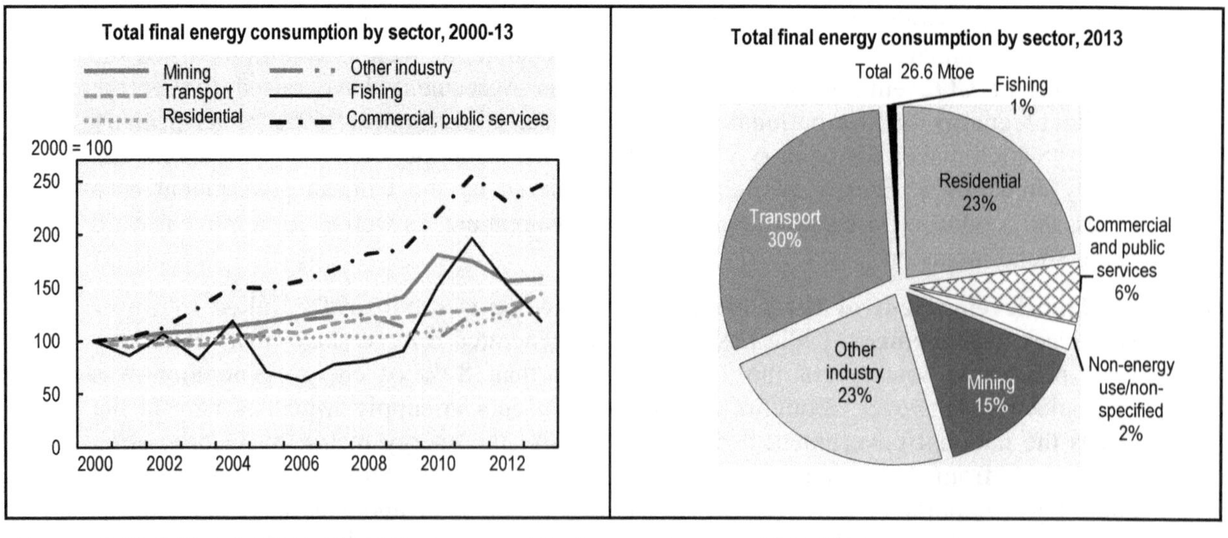

Source: OECD/ECLAC (2016), *OECD Environmental Performance Reviews: Chile 2016*, http://dx.doi.org/10.1787/9789264252615-en.

Better co-ordination and planning across water and energy policies are needed. As the Ministry of Energy targets 70% of electricity production through hydropower in the coming three decades, releasing water resources from dams in central and northern parts of the country where much of the hydropower potential is located will be unavoidable. The Agenda 3030, which was conceived as a support document for the discussions and development of the Plan Chile 30/30, aims at increasing water supply through dams to expand 300 000 ha of irrigated land by 2030, but Central and North Macro-Zone are already under water stress. Although hydroelectricity will use water from reservoirs when irrigators downstream do not need them, there is no explicit co-ordination between the Agenda 3030 (nor the development of the Plan Chile 30/30) and Energy Policy 2050. Both strategies were conceived in parallel, with rather limited inter-ministerial consultations, which could cause some implementation bottlenecks. Moreover, the mining industry keeps developing in the north and central parts of the country, and future plans include the development of desalination plants to deal with water scarcity. The latter initiatives will increase energy demands in already water-scarce and energy-scarce areas. This is why better co-ordinated policies in the water and energy domains would be desirable to make the most of policy complementarities. For instance, multi-purpose reservoirs that serve different policy areas (agriculture, energy, domestic supply, mining) when operated through consensus-based agreements, can increase efficiency in the use of the resource. Moreover, they help create economies of scale by pulling financial resources from different sources (private and public sectors) and sectors.

Climate change

Climate change forecast models project higher variability in water resource availability between the north and the south. The Directorate of Meteorology of Chile (DMC) estimates that in 2050, the minimum temperature in northern Chile will increase 2°C, with a 3°C rise in the stretch between Copiapó and Concepción. With respect to precipitation, it is expected that total annual rainfall will decrease between 200 mm and 500 mm in Central Chile and increase around 400mm in Southern Chile. The National Climate Change Adaptation Plan (2014) identifies a range of potential impacts on water and energy (Box 5.3). The plan states that the frequency of hot days will increase, and temperatures experienced once every 20 years will occur every two years in most regions of Chile by the end of the century. The majority of climate model simulations predict that floods and droughts (defined as two consecutive years of low precipitation) will become much more frequent (OECD, 2016). Floods will be particularly intense in the central region where most of the population lives, while droughts should increase in central and northern regions, thus generating more intense competition among domestic, agriculture and industrial water uses. Moreover, reduction of hydropower potential will put more pressure on Chile's energy system.

Box 5.3. Potential impacts from climate change in Chile

The National Climate Change Adaptation Plan (2014) identifies a range of potential impacts arising from reductions in water availability, rising temperatures and extreme weather events:

- Lack of water could constrain hydropower, with CEPAL (2012) estimating potential reductions in electricity generation in the range of 10% to 22%. Less available water for cooling could also affect thermal generation. Patterns of consumption will shift, as demand for cooling increases and that of heating decreases
- Increased soil erosion would negatively affect agricultural production. Pests are likely to be more prevalent, while some diseases could diminish. The zones of suitability for forestry, fruit and wine production will shift. Irrigated land could become more productive as temperatures rise, provided enough water is available.

Box 5.3. Potential impacts from climate change in Chile (*cont.*)

- Negative impacts on biodiversity could arise as the pace of climate change exceeds species' ability to adapt. It could take several centuries for ecosystems to find a new equilibrium following the disruption caused by climate change.
- Risk of flooding could increase. For example, CEPAL (2015) estimates that coastal floods that now occur in Valparaíso once every 50 years will occur every 11 years by 2070.

Monetary estimates show that overall, economic losses would amount to 1.1% of GDP under a higher-warming scenario (equivalent to a global temperature increase of 3.4 C) from now until 2100. These estimates pointed to economic benefits for agriculture and forestry, but net costs for fruit growing, livestock, hydropower and drinking water provision. A range of important impacts, however, were not considered. These include increased deaths in hot weather (either directly or as a result of interactions between temperatures and air quality), extreme weather, impacts on businesses and biodiversity. As such, these monetary estimates only capture a fraction of the potential costs of climate change in Chile.

Source: OECD/ECLAC (2016), *OECD Environmental Performance Reviews: Chile 2016*, http://dx.doi.org/10.1787/9789264252615-en.

Managing water risks

The previous sections revealed key trends that will altogether increase pressure in the existing water resources, and which will threaten water security in Chile. In the case of Chile as for many OECD countries, four types of water challenges need particular attention now and in the future to ensure sustainable and inclusive growth in the country.

- **Too much water:** Floods are becoming more frequent and also affect households supply and water quality. Floods affecting urban areas will have a bigger impact in Santiago and Valparaíso, which account for most of national output and 60% of total population. For instance, the heavy rains in central Chile in April 2016 have left an estimated 4 million people without drinking water. In Santiago, the national emergency response agency declared a red alert for the city of more than seven million people due to dirty water caused by the flooding. In May 2015 floods in northern Chile (Atacama region) caused 31 casualties and left 16 588 people homeless (ONEMI, 2015). The Chilean government estimated recovery costs of at least USD 1.5 billion (O'Brien and Esposito, 2015). According to the Chamber of Construction, in the last 30 years, eight of the ten biggest natural disasters measured by number of deaths were related to floods in urban areas or rivers beds.
- **Too little water:** The current drought, which began in 2007, is hampering the Chile's copper production, although it remains the world's top exporter. The drought is exacerbating forest fires, driving energy prices higher and having an impact on agriculture. This has economic implications, as Chile is among the countries with the largest difference in economic growth between drought years and non-drought years, with GDP varying by 1-2% (OECD/GWP, 2015).
- **Too polluted water**: Water quality levels vary across the country, and differences are noticeable from the south to the north. In the far south of Chile, where 80% of the 16 000 lakes and lagoons in the country are located, water quality is in general terms very good, mainly due to low population density and limited economic activities. In central Chile, large urban settlements like Santiago and Valparaíso have limited access to tertiary wastewater treatment, which together with large

agricultural runoff has caused eutrophication of coastal lakes, wetlands and estuaries. Also in central Chile, mining activity has elevated copper and salinity levels in some rivers, including in the Maipo River, which is the major source of irrigation and drinking water for the Santiago Metropolitan Region and Valparaíso. In the northern regions, surface waters often exceed permissible or recommended limit values of heavy metals and sulphates, mainly due to mining effluent (OECD/ECLAC, 2016).

- **Universal coverage of water services:** a key challenge in Chile is providing access to water supply and sanitation in rural settlements. According to the Joint Monitoring Programme, 7% of Chile's rural population currently lacks access to improved drinking sources and 9% to improved sanitation. Future trends in terms of urbanisation and population growth, together with infrastructure ageing in cities, will also increase the pressure on urban drinking water systems.

While infrastructure can help manage the above water risks, it cannot be the only response. Constructing more dams, upgrading channels to have less leakage, and installing efficient irrigation systems will certainly all contribute to increased water availability and reduce risks of too little water. Rainwater systems with larger capacity and higher coverage will help manage higher peak flows and therefore diminish the risk of floods in cities as well as reduce the impact on the environment, urban infrastructure such as water services infrastructure, and the society at large. Higher quality treatments in wastewater treatment plants will also diminish the risks of disrupting freshwater systems. However, investments in physical infrastructure will need to be integrated into wider governance frameworks, accompanied by sound water institutions and improved information systems. For instance, if rainwater systems are enlarged in Santiago but are not operated and maintained properly due to the fragmentation of competences across the state and municipalities, the system will not deliver on its intended goals. Dams that are not operated for multiple uses might supply water for one specific use, but they could miss out on generating benefits for other categories of users as well.

Due to Chile's particular water rights regime and water market, the space for public action in water management is somewhat limited. The National Water Code of 1981 created a unique system of water rights, known as one of the world's most pro-market systems. The National Water Code allowed for the development of a water market with the objective of achieving greater economic efficiency and water conservation. Whereas the former was achieved by allocating rights to productive activities, the latter is claimed to have failed due to monopolies and speculation. Water rights have been allocated by the national government to private users upon their request, free of cost. They were allocated for indefinite time periods, with the possibility of being passed down in inheritance from one individual to another. When there is more than one claim made on the same water source and not enough resources to satisfy them all, the right is allocated following a bidding/auction process. The right is tradable, with the goal of assigning the right of water access to those initiatives with the greatest market value. Once private parties are in possession of their water rights, they are responsible for the management and distribution of their water. In most Chilean rivers, these private parties are organised in Water Users Organisations (WUOs) (see Box 5.5) which are century-old institutions that have acquired the experience and social acceptance to manage water resources. However, WUOs focus on managing surface water resources for irrigation purposes in a specific river, and often do not have control over all rivers, tributaries, and groundwater resources that together form a basin. Thus, the government loses its power to establish integrated planning and a long-term vision, as it has no faculty over water allocation regimes and the prioritisation of uses. For instance, such an institutional framework limits the role of the state to manage trade-offs between upstream/downstream, current/future generations, water producers/water users, energy/agriculture /households /mining users. Given the current and future trends' impact on water demand and supply, these trade-offs need to be addressed as a shared responsibility across the public, private and non-profit sectors. The state's role in this context is to facilitate the effective and efficient functioning of the market through providing clear rules and standards to ensure that sufficient water is allocated for human consumption and the preservation of natural ecosystems, and facilitating access to sound information to guarantee that actors in the market can take the right decisions.

In 2005 and 2011, important efforts to reform the water code have been undertaken by Chilean administration. Since the 2005 reform, which established ecological flows, the state has been able to deny requests for water rights to preserve environmental minimum values. In addition, the reform included the possibility of creating water reserves under exceptional circumstances, the need for a justification in a water rights application, a fee in the case of non-use of water rights, and the obligation to report transactions on water rights. However, the 2005 reform did not change the basics of the allocation model and water trading as defined in the 1981 Code. This is why a new reform, which started in 2011, seeks to reinforce the role of water as a national public good and has the objective to facilitate public action in managing water risks in Chile. It was given legislative priority in 2014 and is now under discussion in the Senate's Special Commission for Water Resources, Desertification and Droughts, after having passed Congress on 22 November 2016The draft bill foresees a number of provisions, which are difficult to assess at the time of the drafting, but any attempt at strengthening the current institutional framework towards more sound public governance in Chile's water management is a significant step forward to set sound framework conditions to manage water risks.

The ongoing process to reform the Water Code also provides a good opportunity to engage stakeholders in the development of a country-wide strategy for water. The process should be used as a catalyst for developing a country-wide, national strategic vision on how water can contribute to sustainable and inclusive growth over the short, medium and long term. Raising the profile of water management on the national and local political agenda is essential to sustain Chile's productive matrix and to ensure the well-being of citizens.

An overview of water governance gaps in Chile

The following sections detail the most prominent gaps in Chile's water governance, measured against the *OECD Principles on Water Governance* (Box 5.4).

Box 5.4. OECD Principles on Water Governance

The 12 OECD Water Governance Principles aim to enhance water governance systems that help manage "too much", "too little" and "too polluted" water in a sustainable, integrated and inclusive way, at an acceptable cost, and in a reasonable time-frame. The Principles consider that governance is good if it can help to solve key water challenges, using a combination of bottom-up and top-down processes while fostering constructive state-society relations. It is bad if it generates undue transaction costs and does not respond to place-based needs.

Box 5.4. OECD Principles on Water Governance (*cont.*)

Coping with current and future challenges requires robust public policies, targeting measurable objectives in pre-determined time-schedules at the appropriate scale, relying on a clear assignment of duties across responsible authorities and subject to regular monitoring and evaluation. Water governance can greatly contribute to the design and implementation of such policies, in a shared responsibility across levels of government, civil society, business and the broader range of stakeholders who have an important role to play alongside policy-makers to reap the economic, social and environmental benefits of good water governance.

The OECD Principles on Water Governance intend to contribute to tangible and outcome-oriented public policies, based on three mutually reinforcing and complementary dimensions of water governance:

- **Effectiveness** relates to the contribution of governance to define clear sustainable water policy goals and targets at all levels of government, to implement those policy goals, and to meet expected targets.
- **Efficiency** relates to the contribution of governance to maximise the benefits of sustainable water management and welfare at the least cost to society.
- **Trust and Engagement** relate to the contribution of governance to building public confidence and ensuring inclusiveness of stakeholders through democratic legitimacy and fairness for society at large.

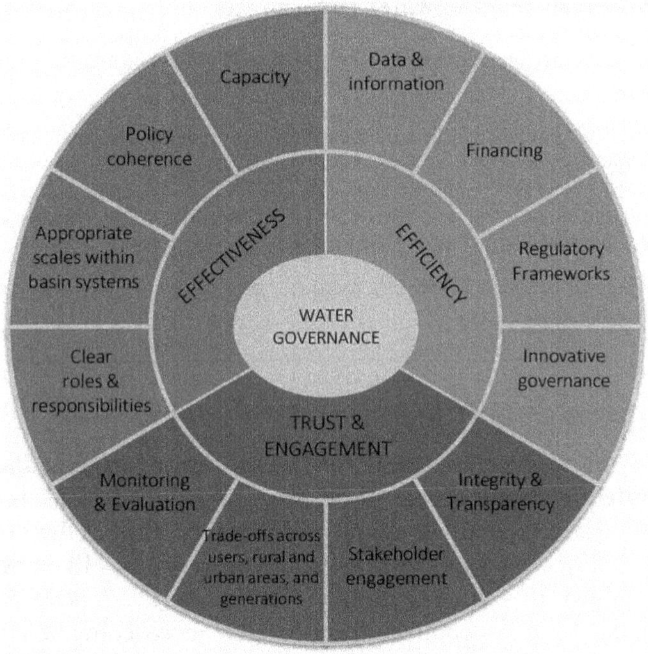

Enhancing the effectiveness of water governance

- Principle 1. Clearly allocate and distinguish roles and responsibilities for water policymaking, policy implementation, operational management and regulation, and foster co-ordination across these responsible authorities.
- Principle 2. Manage water at the appropriate scale(s) within integrated basin governance systems to reflect local conditions, and foster co-ordination between the different scales.
- Principle 3. Encourage policy coherence through effective cross-sectoral co-ordination, especially between policies for water and the environment, health, energy, agriculture, industry, spatial planning and land use.
- Principle 4. Adapt the level of capacity of responsible authorities to the complexity of water challenges to be met, and to the set of competencies required to carry out their duties.

Box 5.4. OECD Principles on Water Governance ***(cont.)***

Enhancing the efficiency of water governance

- Principle 5. Produce, update and share timely, consistent, comparable and policy-relevant water and water-related data and information, and use it to guide, assess and improve water policy.
- Principle 6. Ensure that governance arrangements help mobilise water finance and allocate financial resources in an efficient, transparent and timely manner.
- Principle 7. Ensure that sound water management regulatory frameworks are effectively implemented and enforced in pursuit of the public interest. Principle 8. Promote the adoption and implementation of innovative water governance practices across responsible authorities, levels of government and relevant stakeholders.
- Principle 8. Promote the adoption and implementation of innovative water governance practices across responsible authorities, levels of government and relevant stakeholders.
- Principle 9. Mainstream integrity and transparency practices across water policies, water institutions and water governance frameworks for greater accountability and trust in decision making.

Pillar 3: Enhancing trust and engagement in water governance

- Principle 10. Promote stakeholder engagement for informed and outcome-oriented contributions to water policy design and implementation.
- Principle 11. Encourage water governance frameworks that help manage trade-offs across water users, rural and urban areas, and generations.
- Principle 12. Promote regular monitoring and evaluation of water policy and governance where appropriate, share the results with the public and make adjustments when needed.

Source: OECD (2015c), OECD Water Governance Principles, available at: https://www.oecd.org/gov/regional-policy/OECD-Principles-on-Water-Governance-brochure.pdf.

Fragmentation of responsibilities in water-related competences

Chile has one of the highest levels of fragmentation of responsibilities when it comes to water-related competences. More than forty institutions are involved in delivering over 100 water-related functions. Both the 2012 OECD study *Water Governance in Latin America and the Caribbean* and other studies like one by the World Bank in 2013 highlighted this fragmentation and raised awareness among Chilean stakeholders. Within the MOP, several authorities have core competencies over water management, including DGA, DOH, and the Planning Directorate. In the past, the DGA and the DOH have seldom been involved in the planning of water infrastructure, but the Plan Chile 30/30 offers an opportunity to combine perspectives and identify needs for water-related infrastructure. It is critical for DGA to be able to control and monitor water rights, and DOH to execute infrastructure within the framework of an integrated vision. One way forward that Chile is currently considering to strengthen the institutional and coordination framework for water management is the establishment of an Under-Secretariat for Water Resources within the MOP. While such a figure might help solve the compartmentalisation within the MOP, there would still need to be effective coordination mechanisms with agencies and ministries outside the MOP. For the time being, such coordination is done informally through the Committee of Water Ministers established in 2014 as an operational body to bring together the ministries of agriculture, mining, energy, environment and public works. A step forward could be the formalisation of that Committee following a similar approach as the Under-Secretariat of Tourism, which relies on a formal inter-ministerial committee that ensures co-ordination with relevant sectors to tourism such as public works, environment, and transport.

Fragmentation, or the high number of responsible authorities, is not bad per se, if the right co-ordination mechanisms are in place and work properly (OECD, 2016). The traditional co-ordination mechanism for irrigation policies in Chile has been an inter-ministerial committee called the National Irrigation Commission (CNR) (Box 5.19), which operates under the umbrella of the Ministry of Agriculture. The Commission is in charge of designing irrigation policies and is led by a Council of Ministers. The Council is chaired by the representative of the Ministry of Agriculture, and gathers several ministries including the representatives of the Ministries of Economy, Finance, Public Works and Social Development. However, this mechanism has been claimed to be insufficient to effectively coordinate water policies across responsible authorities in Chile (OECD 2012, World Bank, 2013). In 2014, a Presidential Delegate for Water Resources was appointed to advise the President and Ministers on how to improve water resources management in Chile. At the time, it reflected a certain commitment to raising the profile of water in Chile, but the mandate of the Presidential Delegate ended in May 2016 before any National Water Resource Policy could be agreed upon by the different competent ministries and stakeholders. The views of the Presidential Delegate have however been captured in a document entitled "National Water Resources Policy", some guidelines of which are summarised below in Boxes 5.6 and 5.8. However, it is worth noting that, to date, this document has not been vetted by all competent authorities as a National Water Policy per se.

A lack of functional and hydrological scale in water management

A striking feature of the Chilean water management model is the absence of integrated basin governance systems that can provide for a functional and territorial approach to water risks. This can be very much explained by the specific geographical context (north/south asymmetry and very small-scale basins due to the mountain/sea specificity), but also by the high degree of centralisation in most of Chile's public policies, including water. In the absence of proper river basin governance, Water Users Organisations (WUOs) (Box 5.5) manage water in a rather fragmented way, and limited consideration is given to the need for conjunctive management of surface and groundwater. These century-old institutions have acquired the experience and social acceptance to manage effectively water resources. Though most of them have control over an entire river, they do not generally have control over all rivers and tributaries that together form a basin. These organisations focus on managing surface water resources for irrigation purposes, and they often do not coordinate with users withdrawing groundwater. As a result, the hydrological interconnection between the river and the aquifers is neglected. One of the reasons for the lack of coordination is the limited number of groundwater user organisations. OECD countries experience shows that effective groundwater management can provide a natural storage of water if properly managed, particularly in areas with unconfined sedimentary aquifers. There is therefore a need to seek alternatives to enhance basin governance in Chile, and the conjunctive management of groundwater and surface water within the current water rights context.

Box 5.5. Water Users' Organisations in Chile

Water Users Organisations (WUOs) have played a key role in water infrastructure development since the 19th century and operate and maintain a large share of it today. They manage a network of roughly 100 000 km channels without translating their operation and maintenance costs to the State. However, the development of this network was largely supported through different State subsidies (see Box 5.19).

The main types of Water Users' Organisations in Chile are:

- **Water Channels Associations** (*Asociaciones de Canalistas*): formed by water rights owners sharing the operation of a water infrastructure that takes water from a natural source and distributes water among the users
- **Surface Water Communities** (*Comunidad de Aguas superficiales*): formed by water rights owners that withdraw, channel and distribute water from the same water source
- **Groundwater Communities** (*Comunidad de Aguas Subterráneas*): formed by water rights owners that abstract water from the same groundwater source. These organisations control abstractions and manage information on wells and availability of water
- **Control Boards** (*Juntas de Vigilancia*): organisations with jurisdiction over a basin or part of a basin, which are formed by surface water communities, water channels associations and individuals that execute their water rights

Source: DGA (2016), *Atlas del Agua: Chile 2016*, Dirección General de Aguas, available at: www.dga.cl/atlasdelagua/Paginas/default.aspx.

Several policies, including the reflections captured by the Presidential Delegate for Water in the document entitled "National Water Resources Policy" (Box 5.6), have been aimed at promoting river basin management, but they have had little success. For instance, a series of Territorial Roundtables (*Mesas Territoriales*) were set up throughout 2014-15 to coordinate with the subnational authorities the implementation of national goals at local level and strengthen the role of WUOs. The roundtables included public and private actors, as well as universities and representatives of civil society, and were formed through an incremental approach. First, a broad-based meeting with public water authorities in the region was held to explain the role of the appointed subnational Delegate, the underlying goal of the roundtable and its methods of work. Second, relevant private sector actors, academics and civil society groups were invited to be part of the tables. Representatives were appointed in each region to set up the Territorial Roundtable, with the support of the Ministry of Interior, which appointed "subnational Presidential Delegates", and of the *intendentes* of the regions, who provided them with logistical support to carry out their functions (i.e. offices, vehicles, etc.). However, due to budget cuts in the Ministry of Interior in 2015, only a limited number of Territorial Roundtables remained, namely in Coquimbo, Valparaíso, Bio-Bio, La Auracania, Los Rios, and Los Lagos, because authorities in these regions decided to cover related operation costs.

There have also been attempts to develop integrated water resources management (IWRM) plans for individual basins. The Government of Chile and the World Bank worked towards an IWRM plan in Choapa, in the Region of Coquimbo, which was ultimately not implemented due to budgetary constraints. The project, which was revived by the DGA, foresees the participation of WUOs, civil society organisations and regional and local authorities together with the national government. The plan involves using hydrological models that include climate change scenarios, developing a platform that visually displays water resource information about the basin and proposing a coordination mechanism to help improve water governance in the basin in the long-term (Agua, 2016). Similar efforts are also being considered in the Copiapo River Basin.

Box 5.6. Provisions on river basin management in the Presidential Delegate's "National Policy for Water Resources" document

The latest policy statement of the Government of Chile on water management, issued by the Presidential Delegate, recognises river basins as a unit of territorial management and calls for:

- promoting integrated water resources management through place-based approaches in each basin, in order to account for the singularities of each basin in terms of future challenges, with the Territorial Roundtables to be implemented in each region as the first step forward
- studying the possibility of developing a normative framework for the implementation of integrated water resources management in Chile
- instruments for territorial management that consider basins as the unit for planning and management of water resources
- territorial development plans that consider the basin as the planning unit.

Source: Government of Chile (2015), "National Water Resources Policy 2015", www.interior.gob.cl/media/2015/04/recursos_hidricos.pdf

Policy incoherence across sectors

Chile's central government is characterised by a high degree of compartmentalisation. Sectoral ministries work in insulated silos, with limited mechanisms for ensuring alignment and integration across policy areas and investments. The lack of horizontal co-ordination is particularly challenging in water management, as many decisions taken in other policy domains (e.g. land use, energy, agriculture, industry) generate water risks and vice-versa. For instance, it is not clear how water management has been taken into account in the development of the energy infrastructure agenda spanning through 2050. It is also unclear how the National Commission for Irrigation has planned the expansion of the agriculture frontier and how relevant water stakeholders have been consulted and engaged (e.g. Ministry of Environment, Ministry of Energy, WUOs, etc.). A thorough assessment of the distributional impacts of decisions taken in water-related policy areas is essential to fostering policy complementarities, especially when it comes to exploring synergies in future infrastructure.

A Committee of Water Ministers was established to coordinate actions in policy areas with an impact on water. The Committee was promoted by the Ministry of Public Works, which is responsible for its Secretariat, and it was designed as an operational body to discuss trade-offs across the five water-related ministries: agriculture, mining, energy, environment, and public works. The National Presidential Delegate to Water Resources also sat on the Committee until the end of his mandate. To some extent, the Water Committee has supported policy coherence on a case-by-case basis rather than systematically. A notable case is the conflict among users regarding the Reservoir of Laja Lake, in the Bio-Bio Region. This 5 000 Mm^3 natural lake of environmental value (there is a waterfall that is a popular touristic attraction) is an important water source for the agricultural activity in the region, but the reservoir is managed by the National Energy Company ENDESA (*Empresa Nacional de Electricidad Sociedad Anónima*), as it holds the water rights. The conflict started when ENDESA was privatised in 1989 and used water rights to maximise its profits from the installed hydropower plant. This put additional pressure on the available water resources, and two main conflicts arose: first, agricultural users could not access the water resources the needed to keep up production, and second, the environmental sustainability of the waterfalls was threatened. In this context, the Council met and agreed upon an operational rule for the management of the lake's resources, which was first discussed by the ministries with a higher stake, i.e. Energy, Environment, and Agriculture, together with the users and stakeholders. Each ministry negotiated and liaised with their constituencies prior to holding discussions with their peers on the need to reconsider some of the water allocation entitlements.

The Water Committee is an informal mechanism rather than an institutionalised body. While this has allowed some flexibility and confidentiality when discussing sensitive issues, the absence of formalisation could call into question its accountability and sustainability over time. Relevant ministries argue that any formalisation would reduce its operability and delay implementation of measures. However, a more formal coordination body would also be better able to outlast political cycles and serve as a robust coordination mechanism, where trade-offs and conflicting interests could be managed effectively. In addition, a variety of complementary co-ordination mechanisms used by OECD countries can be considered in the case of Chile (Box 5.7).

Box.5.7. Menu of options for co-ordinating policies across ministries, public agencies and levels of government

In **France**, the Inter-ministerial Committee for Sustainable Development was created by decree in 2003. Presided over by the Prime Minister, it meets annually and is made up of the ministers responsible for interior affairs, social affairs, employment, foreign affairs, European affairs, defense, youth, education, research, economy, finances, industry, transport, housing, tourism, health, agriculture, culture, state reform, territorial development, cities and local communities, sports, and overseas territories. A representative of the President also takes part in the activities of the inter-ministerial committee. Its role is to define and monitor the implementation of governmental orientations to foster sustainable development, including regarding greenhouse gases and the prevention of major natural risks. It also ensures alignment the national strategy and action plans for sustainable development with the country's commitment in that field at European and international levels. The committee prepares an annual evaluation report on the implementation of the strategy and actions plans.

In **Australia**, the Council of Australian Governments (COAG) is the peak intergovernmental forum. The members of COAG are the Prime Minister, state and territory premiers and chief ministers and the President of the Australian Local Government Association (ALGA). The Prime Minister chairs the COAG. The role of the COAG is to promote policy reforms that are of national significance, or which need coordinated action by all Australian governments. The COAG is supported by inter-jurisdictional, inter-ministerial councils that facilitate consultation and co-operation between the Commonwealth and the states and territories in specific policy areas such as health, education, indigenous rights and the economy. Together, these councils constitute the COAG Council System. COAG councils pursue and monitor priority issues of national significance and take joint action to resolve issues that arise between governments. Councils also develop policy reforms for consideration by the COAG, and oversee the implementation of policy reforms agreed by the COAG. The COAG has been the co-ordinating and driving force behind the water reforms undertaken across Australian jurisdictions for more than 20 years.

In **Mexico**, there has been notable progress in addressing institutional fragmentation of water policy at the federal level. Some of these efforts were undertaken through the National Water Commission (CONAGUA)'s Technical Council. The council is an inter-ministerial body in charge of approving and evaluating the commission's programmes, projects, budget and operations, as well as co-ordinating water policies and defining common strategies across multiple ministries and agencies (SEMARNAT; SEDESOL; Secretary of Agriculture, Livestock, Rural Development, Fisheries and Food [SAGARPA.]; Treasury; Energy; CONAFOR; and IMTA).

Israel, the Water Authority Council created in 2007 is responsible for all decision making and policy setting by the Israeli Water Authority. It seeks to co-ordinate the actions of the ministries of Environmental Protection, Health, Finance, Foreign Affairs, and Infrastructure, which used to be collectively responsible for the decision-making process over matters concerning water and sewage. Under the previous arrangement, important decisions were often impossible to reach because of the diverging interests of each agency/ministry and a lack of incentives for compromise, which posed a risk of a lack a collective sense of responsibility for national decision making on water and wastewater management. The Water Authority Council was

Box.5.7. Menu of options for co-ordinating policies across ministries, public agencies and levels of government (*cont.*)

established to alleviate these frequent deadlocks.All policies and plans that the Israeli Water Authority or any other ministry proposes must be presented to the Water Authority Council Forum for approval before they can be passed. The efficiency of the Water Authority Council is founded upon two criteria – creating equal representation of all interested groups, and ensuring that effective and timely decision-making is their priority. This unifies the responsibility for decision making on national water and wastewater management and has substantially improved the efficiency and timing of decision making.

The National Water Council in **Spain** is a high-level consultative agency created in 2009 which includes autonomous communities, local entities, river-basin authorities, and professional and economic unions related to water. Horizontal co-ordination of water policies is ensured by the participation of the main directors-general of the Ministry of Environment, Rural and Maritime affairs (water, quality and environmental protection, sustainable development and rural affairs).

Source: OECD (2015d), *Water Resources Governance in Brazil*. OECD Publishing, Paris, http://dx.doi.org/10.1787/9789264238121-en ; OECD (2011), *Water Governance in OECD Countries: A Multi-level Approach*, http://dx.doi.org/10.1787/9789264119284-en.

Data and information gaps

Chile has made important efforts to produce its Water Atlas, which provides an overall picture of the stock of water resources but, in general terms there are still data and information gaps on water resources management and planning that hinder decision making. Raw data is dispersed among a wide range of sources, which include the public sector, water operators, agricultural users and industry (i.e. mining and others). Often, the government has to provide estimates and, at the same time, misses basic indicators such as abstraction rate by use or the household drinking water consumption rate in rural areas. In particular, the Ministry of Agriculture reports that there is a need to improve measurement of water demands in the agricultural sector as currently volumetric abstraction is measured through water rights. Water rights in Chile are often not used entirely and there are also situations where users go over their assigned amount of water. The lack of enforcement and monitoring of water abstractions, both from surface and groundwater sources, hinders the exact measurement of water volumes for agriculture. In addition, there is little data online in workable format, and time series tend to be limited. A final concern is the inconsistencies, or the lack of convergence, between official sources of data and those produced by the private sector, in addition to the fact that the information produced with existing data does not always serve to guide decision making.

Chile is already taking action to address its information gap, but further progress is needed. These steps include the action guidelines produced by the Presidential Delegate in the document entitled "National Water Resources Policy", particularly those aimed at improving the country's water information system (Box 5.8). However, there has been no specific follow-up on the implementation of these action guidelines. More can be done to improve data production and the use of data to inform water resources planning and management processes. International standards and data quality measures implemented in OECD countries could serve as a compass to guide Chile.

Box 5.8. Provision on information systems in the Presidential Delegate's "National Policy for Water Resources" document

The National Policy acknowledges that access to clear and precise water-related information is critical for evidence-based decision making by both institutions and private water users. In particular, it calls for the following actions:

- establish an integrated National Public Water Resources Information System
- strengthen the role of the DGA in information systems, so that they are capable of implementing a complete public stock of water, with temporal reliable time series and updated data, and complete the water rights record, which is currently incomplete
- modernise and expand the programme of river gauges, rainwater meters, groundwater monitoring systems, reservoir level meters and quality measurements
- ensure private actors share water-related information by placing incentives through collaboration agreements
- develop a national research agreement between public and private actors, including universities, technological centres, WUOs and others, with the objective of enhancing water-related information and developing new information and technologies.

Source: Government of Chile (2015), "National Water Resources Policy 2015", www.interior.gob.cl/media/2015/04/recursos_hidricos.pdf.

An overview of water infrastructure gaps in Chile

The following sections capture the most prominent gaps in Chile's water infrastructure as measured against international standards. The types of water infrastructure analysed in this Chapter include: i) water supply and sanitation services, both in urban and rural areas; ii) infrastructure for non-conventional water sources; and, iii) irrigation and water resources infrastructure.

Water and sanitation services

Table 5.2. Access to water and sanitation services, 1990 and 2015

	Drinking water coverage					
	Urban (%)		Rural (%)		Total (%)	
	1990	2015	1990	2015	1990	2015
Piped onto premises	98	100	38	93	88	99
Other improved source	1	0	10	0	2	0
Other unimproved	1	0	25	7	5	1
Surface water	0	0	27		5	
	Sanitation coverage estimates					
	Urban (%)		Rural (%)		Total (%)	
	1990	2015	1990	2015	1990	2015
Improved+Shared facilities	91	100	53	91	85	99
Other unimproved	5	0	41	8	10	1
Open defecation	4	0	6	1	5	0

Source: WHO/UNICEF (2015), Join Monitoring Programme for Water Supply and Sanitation (database). https://www.wssinfo.org/documents/?tx_displaycontroller[type]=country_files.

As an OECD country, Chile is close to universal coverage of drinking water supply and sanitation, but has some important territorial disparities, in particular between rural and urban areas. The Joint Monitoring Programme (led by the World Health Organization and UNICEF) estimated that Chile reached 99% access to improved water sources and sanitation facilities in 2015 (Table 5.2). However, while in urban areas access to improved drinking water and sanitation services is 100%, in rural areas drinking water coverage in 2015 was 93%, with 91% for sanitation (Table 5.2).

Urban water supply and sanitation

Water services in urban areas are delivered by private concessions and regulated by the Superintendence of Sanitation Services (SISS) (Box 5.9). Chile's urban water services, i.e. drinking water supply and wastewater treatment, are in a concessional regime to the private sector, which means that different private utilities are responsible for providing water services under the regulation of the SISS. There are two types of concession regimes in Chile:

- **Concessions assigned for an indefinite time period.** Between 1998 and 2000, the State sold strategic participation of public companies to private water service providers. These private companies bought an important part of the public companies' stake and participated in capital increases. The main public companies where privatised using this scheme, including the service providers in Santiago de Chile and the regions of O´Higgins, Los Lagos and Biobío.

- **Concessions assigned for 30 years**. In 2001, the government decided to change the privatisation scheme by only transferring the private sector the right to exploit and manage water services concessions, and not the property. Rights for exploitation were assigned for 30 years under the agreement of undertaking the necessary investments, particularly in sanitation infrastructure. Under this scheme, between 2001 and 2004 the remaining eight public companies were concessioned to the private sector.

The delegation of urban water services to private providers worked for the expansion of urban sanitation services, which was the government's main goal. Chile restructured its water supply and sanitation services in the 1990s to make up for the backlog of public investment in sanitation infrastructure. Access to sewerage treatment increased from 20.85% to 73.30% between 2000 and 2005 and from 73.30% to 90.59% between 2005 and 2011 (Figure 5.9). In 2014, it is reported that 96.58% of households had access to sewage systems, with primary, secondary or tertiary treatment.

Box 5.9. Superintendence of Sanitation Services

The Superintendence of Sanitation Services (SISS) was established in 1990 as a public, decentralised, regulatory entity with command and control functions for water supply and sanitation services. Its responsibilities include oversight and auditing of service providers, enforcement of norms, control of industrial wastewater discharges and tariff setting. The regulator carries out the following activities:

- revise, propose and monitor the implementation of technical norms related to design, construction and operation of WSS
- implement and enforce norms related to tariffs of services delivered by the concessioners, according to the legal tariff framework

Box 5.9. Superintendence of Sanitation Services (*cont.*)

- implement the concessions regime and ensure concessioners' compliance with SISS legal norms and resolutions, and take part in the initialisation, exploitation, transference and extinction phases of the concession regime
- Monitor industrial wastewater discharges, in particular enforcing quality standards
- enforce penalties and sanctions.

Source: SISS (2016), Historia del Sector Sanitario en Chile, www.siss.gob.cl/577/w3-article-3681.html.

Figure 5.9. Evolution of Chile's access to sewerage by percentage of population

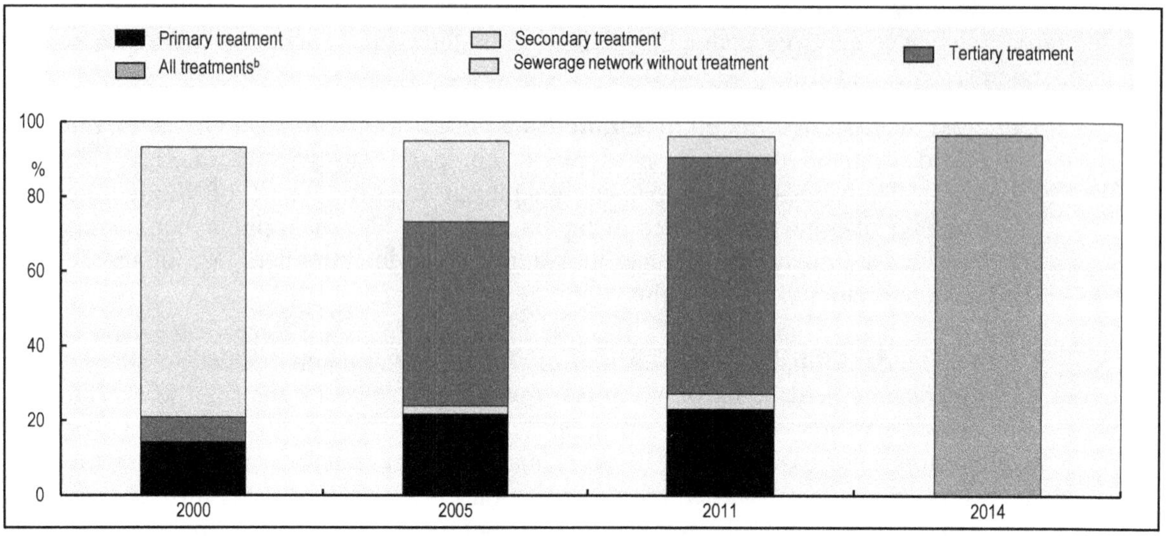

Notes: Primary treatment: Physical and/or chemical process involving settlement of suspended solids, or other in which the BOD5 of the incoming wastewater is process reduced by at least 20% before discharge and the total suspended solids are reduced by at least 50%. Secondary treatment: process generally involving biological treatment with a secondary settlement or other process, with a BOD removal of at least 70% and a COD removal of at least 75%. Tertiary treatment: treatment of nitrogen and/or phosphorous and/or any other pollutant affecting the quality or a specific use of water (microbiological pollution, colour, etc.).

Source: OECD/ECLAC (2016), *OECD Environmental Performance Reviews: Chile 2016*, http://dx.doi.org/10.1787/9789264252615-en.

Chile's urban water supply and sanitation challenges are similar to those faced by other OECD countries and mainly relate to the infrastructure upgrade and the renewal needed to sustain current levels of service delivery and water safety. In OECD countries with relatively low GDP per capita, infrastructure development is ongoing and requires investment on the order of 1% of GDP (OECD, 2015a). An OECD survey of 48 metropolitan areas in 2015 showed that over 90% of cities reported ageing or lacking infrastructure as a prominent challenge. The latter can threaten universal coverage of drinking water and sanitation and diminish the capacity to protect citizens against water-related disasters. Similarly to other OECD countries and cities, Chile needs to modernise its facilities to deliver high-quality wastewater treatment. Currently, in Chile the norm that sets the quality of the service (SEGPRES N°90/2000) does not require treatment plants to have tertiary level treatment. Countries which have already raised levels of tertiary treatment include Austria, Germany, Luxembourg, the Netherlands,

Spain, Switzerland and the United Kingdom (OECD, 2016). In European cities, this performance is high due to the EU Directive 91/271/EEC on urban wastewater treatment, which sets higher standards than the Chilean norm.

Selected benchmarks

Water infrastructure gaps are not easy to assess in general, as water systems are complex structures that depend not only on the "quantity" of infrastructure, but also on the type of infrastructure, its quality, its location, and how is it managed. Moreover, there is an overall lack of indicators for many types of infrastructure. For instance, there are no indicators for rainwater systems, green infrastructure, or natural infrastructure (i.e. ecosystem services). To assess the performance of this type of infrastructure there is a need to conduct individual cost-benefit analyses. For instance, a rainwater system is adequately designed and managed if it prevents flooding in a city and therefore saves losses to citizens and businesses. Ecosystem services can help improve water quality, protect from flooding and increase water availability by recharging aquifers.

Ageing water networks have negative impacts in terms of efficiency and generate failures to deliver the service. The indicator used to measure efficiency levels in urban water supply systems across OECD cities is water loss. Another indicator that has been used by the SISS to evaluate the quality of a network is the number of pipelines breaks every 100 km. Leaking pipes generate additional costs, both in environmental (more freshwater is used and lost, and some wastewater returns to the environment untreated) and financial terms (through the opportunity cost of leakage and the cost of treating water that leaks before it reaches the consumer, thereby increasing the unit treatment cost). In Chile, the future availability of water resources is predicted to decrease due to the effects of climate change, presumably driving up the future value of water, which could make further improvement of infrastructure efficiency more cost-effective (OECD, 2016).

In the following section, Chile's largest metropolitan areas are compared to equivalent cities in terms of water loss[7] and domestic consumption (Table 5.3). Chilean metropolitan areas are defined using the OECD definition of Functional Urban Areas (FUAs)[8], which are not bound by administrative boundaries of cities, but rather defined according to where people work and live (using commuting flows). According to this definition, Chile has 26 FUAs that altogether encompass 100 municipalities. In the case of Chile, FUAs included the large metropolitan area of Santiago de Chile (above 1.5 million), the metropolitan areas of Concepción and Valparaíso are (between 500 000 and 1.5 million), and the medium-sized urban areas of Coquimbo and Antofagasta (between 200 000 and 500 000)[9].

Table 5.3. Clustering of benchmarked cities by size

No. of inhabitants	Cities
More than 5 million	Mexico City, New York City, Paris, Hong Kong, Rio de Janeiro, Singapore, Santiago de Chile
Between 1.5 and 5 million	Amsterdam, Athens, Barcelona, Belo Horizonte, Budapest, Daegu, Lisbon, Marseille, Milan Montreal, Naples, Phoenix, Rome, Suzhou, Zibo.
Less than 1.5 million	Acapulco, Bologna, Calgary, Chihuahua, Cologne, Copenhagen, Culiacan, Edinburgh, Glasgow, Grenoble, Hermosillo, Kitakyushu, Krakow, Liverpool, Malaga, Nantes, Okayama, Oslo, Prague, Queretaro, San Luis Potosi, Stockholm, Turin, Toluca, Tuxla, Veracruz, Zaragoza, Valparaíso, Concepción, Antofagasta, Coquimbo-La Serena

Source: Based on Total Population of the urban core of the functional urban area (OECD, 2012b) and data provided by surveyed cities from non-OECD countries.

Water losses in Chile's major cities are higher than in most peer cities. Valparaíso (42.9%) performs slightly better than Mexican cities such as Tuxtla (65%) San Luis Potosi (50.9%), Chihuahua (45%) and Mexico City (44%), which feature at the bottom of the ranking. The city of Concepción also registers relatively high levels of water losses (34.4%), similar to Belo Horizonte (35.8%), Oslo (35.3%), Toluca (35%) and Montreal (33%). Santiago, with a share of 29.5%, has a higher rate than equivalent metropolitan areas such as Rome (25.8%), Hong Kong (18%), Milan (9.6%) and Paris (7.7%). It is worth noting that Antofagasta (25.5%) and Coquimbo-La Serena (22.5%) have the lowest rates out of the five Chilean metropolitan areas studied (Figure 5.10).

The evolution of water leakage differs across Chile's metropolitan areas. In Valparaíso, water losses increased from 36.2% to 42.9% between 2000 and 2012, and in Santiago from 28.1% to 29.5% in the same period. Valparaíso registered the largest increase in water losses among cities that provided data for years 2012 and 2000 (Figure 5.11). However, Coquimbo-La Serena, Concepción and Antofagasta have managed to reduce these losses in absolute terms: 2.3%, 6.3% and 7.4%, respectively.

Figure 5.10. Water losses in selected OECD and non-OECD cities

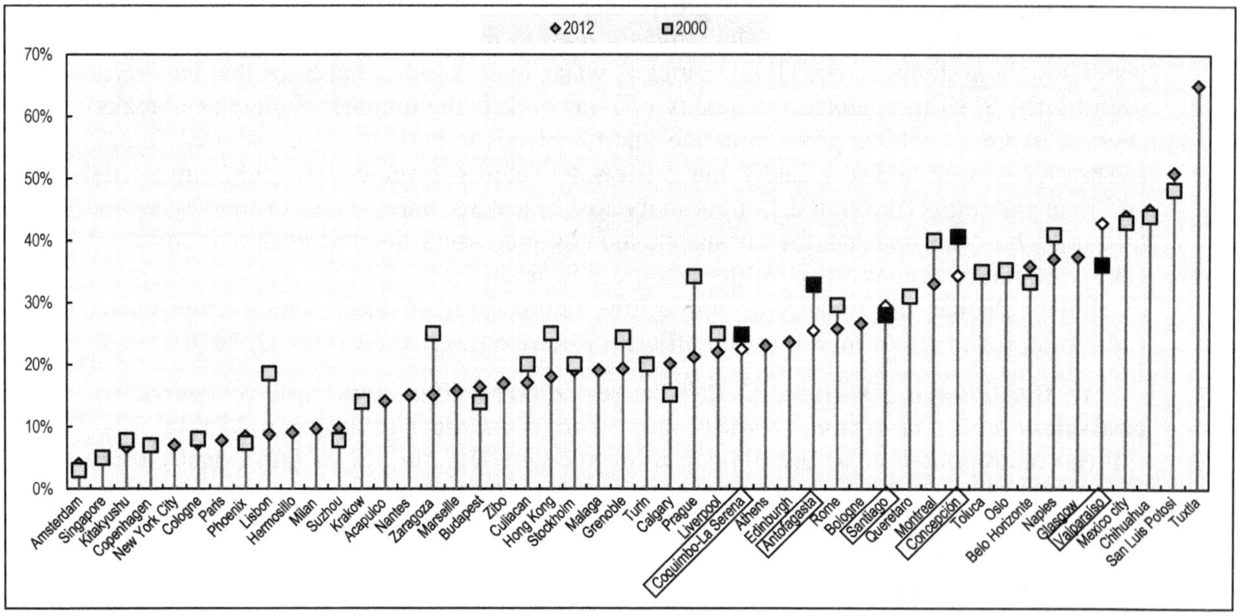

Notes:

1) from the surveyed cities: Budapest (data 2013); Liverpool (2012 figure is actual loss for Liverpool. 2000 and 1990 values are based on UU's regional data); Singapore (unaccounted-for-water: PUB monitors the UFW which comprises two components i.e. real losses [leakage] and apparent losses [metering]).

2) for Chile's metropolitan areas data is aggregated for municipalities within the Functional Urban Areas and with available data for water losses. Santiago de Chile (Maipú, Gran Santiago, Las Condes, Estación Central , Colina, Lo Barnechea, Huechuraba, Vitacura, Peñaflor, Talagante, Buin, Cerrillos,Paine, Lampa, Padre Hurtado, Isla de Maipo, El Monte, Curacaví, Calera de Tango, San José de Maipo), Valparaíso (Viña del Mar, Valparaíso, Quilpué, Villa Alemana, Concón, Limachean), Concepción (Concepción, Talcahuano, Chiguayante, Coronel, San Pedro de la Paz, Tomé, Penco, Hualqui).

3) Data corresponds to percentage of population served by urban water operators with respect to total population living within the area covered.

Source: Ministry of Public Works (2016c). Official statistics provided in the OECD Questionnaire for this report: Data Request on Water in Chile (2016); and OECD (2016), Water Governance in Cities. DOI: http://dx.doi.org/10.1787/9789264251090-en.

The economically optimal level of water losses in municipal networks is estimated to be on average between 10% and 20%, depending on the nature of individual systems (OECD, 2016a). The optimal level of leakage is reached at the point at which the cost of reducing it further is equal to the benefit gained (OECD, 2016). The value of water per unit is expected to rise in Chile due to the decrease of water availability in water-stressed areas. A more efficient network could thus contribute to saving water and increasing availability.

Figure 5.11. Evolution of water losses from 2000 to 2012

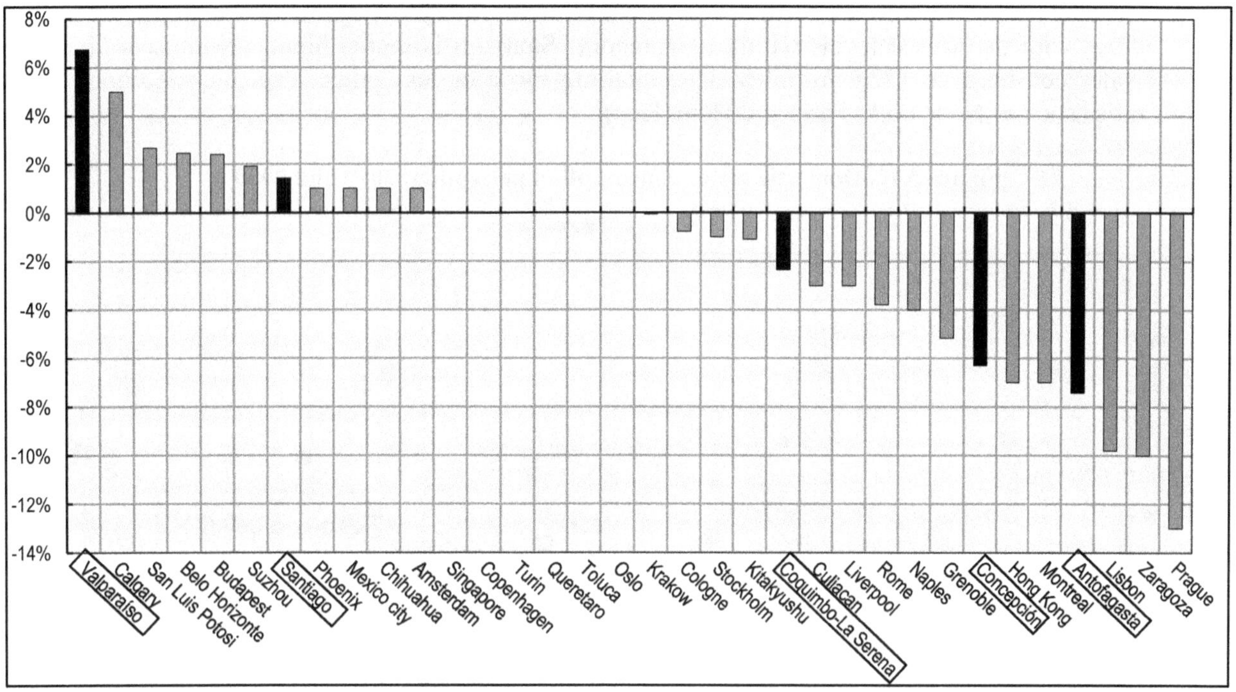

Notes:

1) from the surveyed cities: Budapest (data 2013); Liverpool (2012 figure is actual loss for Liverpool. 2000 and 1990 values are based on UU's regional data); Singapore (unaccounted-for-water: PUB monitors the UFW which comprises two components i.e. real losses [leakage] and apparent losses [metering]).

2) for Chile's metropolitan areas data is aggregated for municipalities within the Functional Urban Areas and with available data for water losses. Santiago de Chile (Maipú, Gran Santiago, Las Condes, Estación Central , Colina, Lo Barnechea, Huechuraba, Vitacura, Peñaflor, Talagante, Buin, Cerrillos,Paine, Lampa, Padre Hurtado, Isla de Maipo, El Monte, Curacaví, Calera de Tango,San José de Maipo), Valparaíso (Viña del Mar, Valparaíso, Quilpué, Villa Alemana, Concón, Limachean), Concepción (Concepción, Talcahuano, Chiguayante, Coronel, San Pedro de la Paz, Tomé, Penco, Hualqui).

3) Data corresponds to percentage of population served by urban water operators with respect to total population living within the area covered.

Source: Ministry of Public Works (2016c). Official statistics provided in the OECD Questionnaire for this report: Data Request on Water in Chile (2016); OECD (2016), Water Governance in Cities. DOI: http://dx.doi.org/10.1787/9789264251090-en

The average number of breaks of the Chilean urban water supply system was 20.9 (breaks) every 100 km in 2015 (SISS, 2015). The number of breaks differs greatly across water services providers in Chile recording a highest value of 34.6 breaks every 100 km and a lowest value of 0 breaks every 100 km (SISS, 2015). Based on international studies, SISS's Water Services Management Report (2014) argues that 40 breaks or more every 100 km indicates that the network is in a poor state, networks with 20 to 39 breaks have acceptable level of breaks, and networks below 20 breaks every 100 km have high standards.

Chilean cities are among the lowest domestic water consumers when compared with cities of similar size (Figure 5.12). Considering 2012 data, Concepción (43.21 m^3/inh/year), Coquimbo-La Serena (45.44 m^3/inh/year), and Antofagasta (46.25 m^3/inh/year) are among cities with the lowest domestic water consumption of the sample surveyed. Consumption levels in these three cities are similar to those in Malaga, Grenoble, Nantes and Krakow. Valparaíso (51.36 m^3/inh/year) also ranks among the cities with the lowest levels within its category. Santiago is a step higher in household water consumption (72.6 m^3/inh/year), equalling more or less other large metropolitan cities such as New York, Paris and Hong Kong.

Figure 5.12. Domestic water consumption per capita, 2012 and 2000

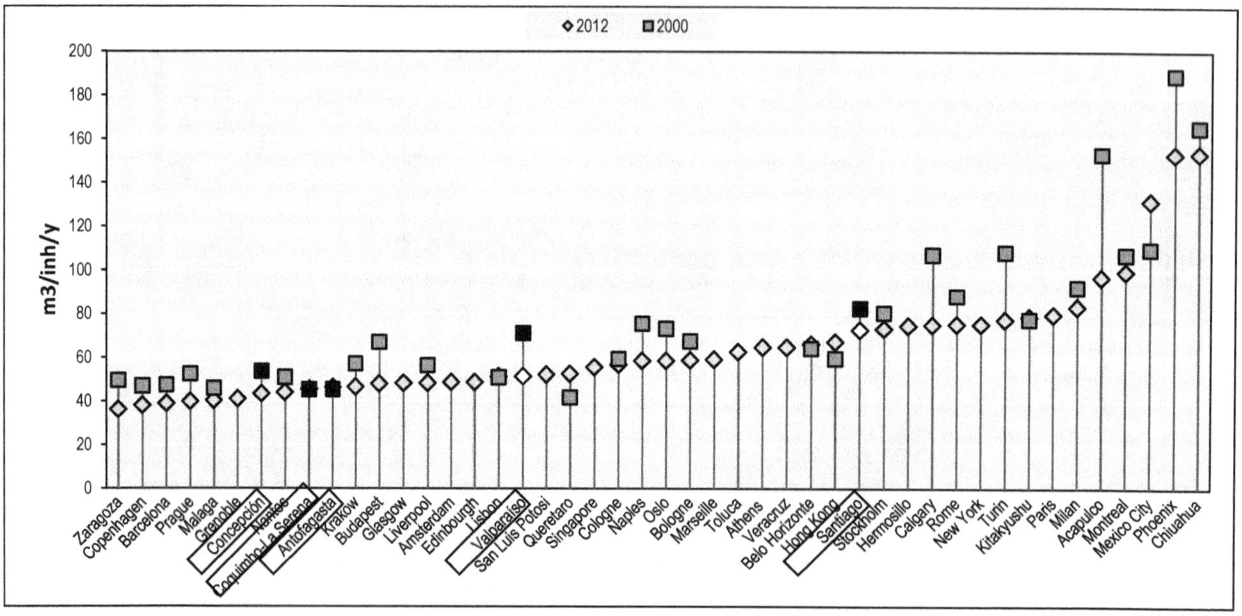

Notes:

1) for Chile's metropolitan areas data is aggregated for municipalities within the Functional Urban Areas and with available data for domestic water consumption. Santiago de Chile (Maipú, Gran Santiago, Las Condes, Estación Central, Colina, Lo Barnechea, Huechuraba, Vitacura, Peñaflor, Talagante, Buin, Cerrillos,Paine, Lampa, Padre Hurtado, Isla de Maipo, El Monte, Curacaví, Calera de Tango,San José de Maipo), Valparaíso (Viña del Mar, Valparaíso, Quilpué, Villa Alemana, Concón, Limachean), Concepción (Concepción, Talcahuano, Chiguayante, Coronel, San Pedro de la Paz, Tomé, Penco, Hualqui)

2) Data corresponds to percentage of population served by urban water operators with respect to total population living within the area covered.

Source: Ministry of Public Works (2016c). Official statistics provided in the OECD Questionnaire for this report: Data Request on Water in Chile (2016); OECD (2016), Water Governance in Cities,. DOI: http://dx.doi.org/10.1787/9789264251090-en.

Figure 5.13. Domestic water consumption in large metropolitan areas, 2012

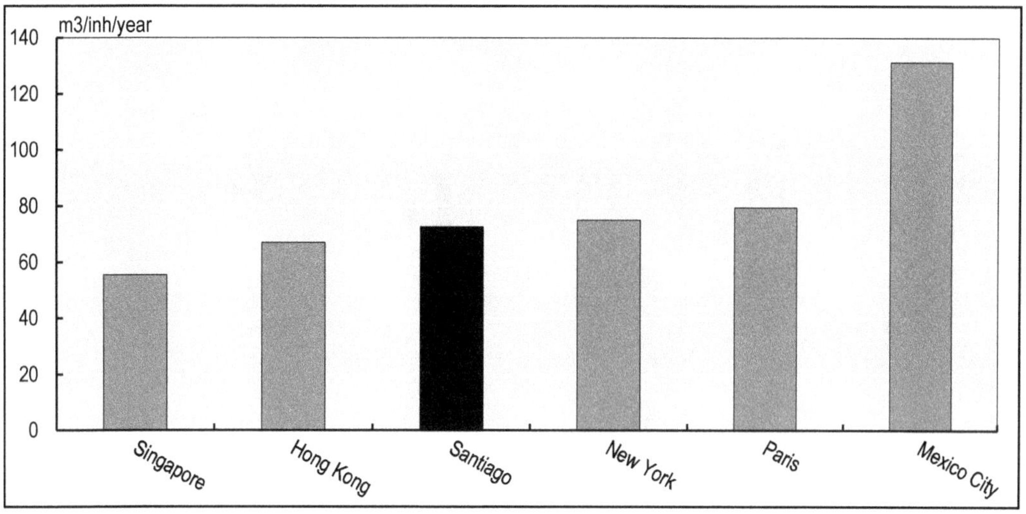

Notes:

1) for Chile's metropolitan areas data is aggregated for municipalities within the Functional Urban Areas and with available data for domestic water consumption. Santiago de Chile (Maipú, Gran Santiago, Las Condes, Estación Central, Colina, Lo Barnechea, Huechuraba, Vitacura, Peñaflor, Talagante, Buin, Cerrillos,Paine, Lampa, Padre Hurtado, Isla de Maipo, El Monte, Curacaví, Calera de Tango, San José de Maipo)

2) Data corresponds to percentage of population served by urban water operators with respect to total population living within the area covered.

Source: Ministry of Public Works (2016c). Official statistics provided in the OECD Questionnaire for this report: Data Request on Water in Chile (2016); and OECD (2016), Water Governance in Cities. DOI: http://dx.doi.org/10.1787/9789264251090-en.

Trends in domestic water consumption differ across Chile's largest cities. Between 2000 and 2012, Santiago reduced domestic water consumption from 82.55 to 72.60 m^3/inh/year. During the same period, Concepción and Valparaíso also lowered consumption from 53.58 m^3/inh/year to 43.21 m^3/inh/year and from 71.04 to 51.36 m^3/inh/year, respectively. In terms of percentage change, Valparaíso registered the largest fall in consumption (-27.70%), followed by Concepción (-19.36%) and Santiago (-12.05%). In Coquimbo-La Serena and Antofagasta changes in domestic water consumption since 2000 have been minimum – with an increase of 0.64% and 2.10%, respectively.

Figure 5.14. Domestic water consumption per capita, percentage change 2000-12

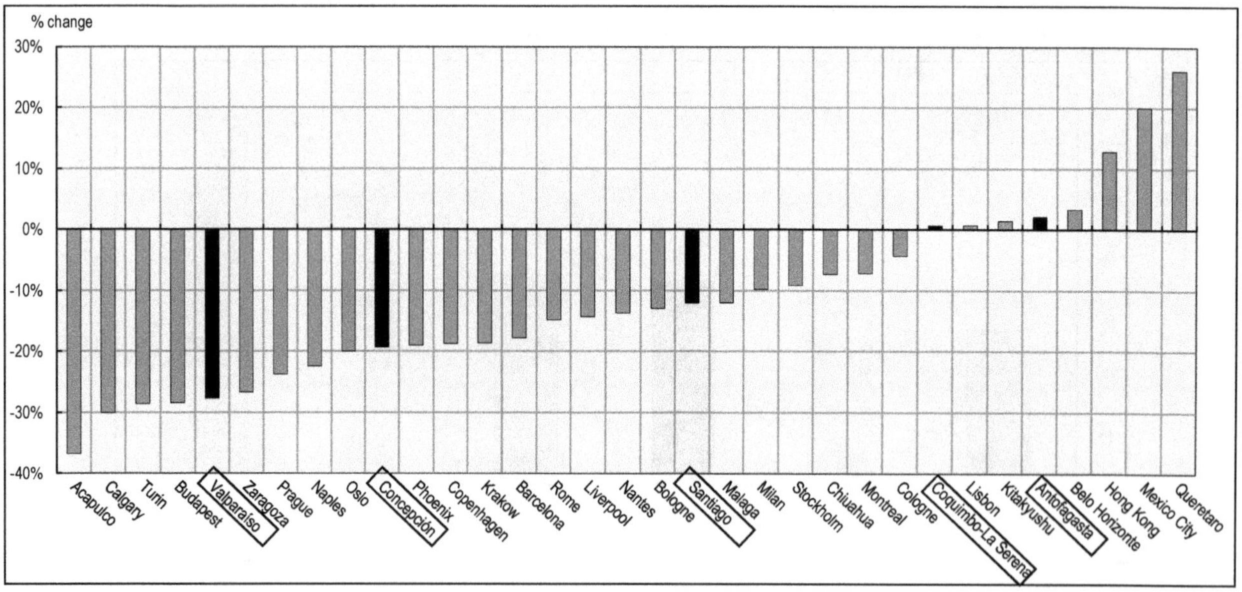

Notes: For Chile's metropolitan areas data is aggregated for municipalities within the Functional Urban Areas and with available data for domestic water consumption. Santiago de Chile (Maipú, Gran Santiago, Las Condes, Estación Central, Colina, Lo Barnechea, Huechuraba, Vitacura, Peñaflor, Talagante, Buin, Cerrillos,Paine, Lampa, Padre Hurtado, Isla de Maipo, El Monte, Curacaví, Calera de Tango,San José de Maipo), Valparaíso (Viña del Mar, Valparaíso, Quilpué, Villa Alemana, Concón, Limachean), Concepción (Concepción, Talcahuano, Chiguayante, Coronel, San Pedro de la Paz, Tomé, Penco, Hualqui); Data corresponds to percentage of population served by urban water operators with respect to total population living within the area covered.

Source: Ministry of Public Works (2016c). Official statistics provided in the OECD Questionnaire for this report: Data Request on Water in Chile (2016); and OECD (2016), *Water Governance in Cities*, http://dx.doi.org/10.1787/9789264251090-en.

Urban sanitation services are assessed in terms of the quality of wastewater treatment. The challenge OECD countries face, including Chile, is no longer related to access to sanitation services in urban areas, but rather the quality of the water resulting from the treatment process. The greater the quality of the treatment, the more opportunities arise to reuse the treated water. This reuse contributes to better efficiency of the water supply and can drive the tariff cost down. This recycling can be for alternative uses with less stringent water quality demands (e.g. watering gardens, cleaning streets, irrigation etc.). Chile ranks among the countries in the OECD with the highest access to sewerage systems with some level of treatment (96%) (Figure 5.15). However, the SISS 2015 Water Services Management Report indicates that a total of 37% of the country's wastewater treatment plants (109) are considered "vulnerable". This implies that these plants are at risk, as they are operating close to their design limit, if not beyond. These limitations encompass both hydraulic capacity and organic treatment capacity, with excess therefore putting companies at risk of non-compliance with quality standards, which can eventually result in negative externalities such as bad smells (SISS, 2015). Wastewater treatment in Chile is not as high in quality as in other high-level income OECD countries. While in the Netherlands, Germany, Denmark and Sweden the share of tertiary treatment was above 80% in 2011, in Chile it is lower (63% for the same year) (Figure 5.16).

Figure 5.15. Access to sewerage and type of treatment in selected countries, 2013 or latest available data

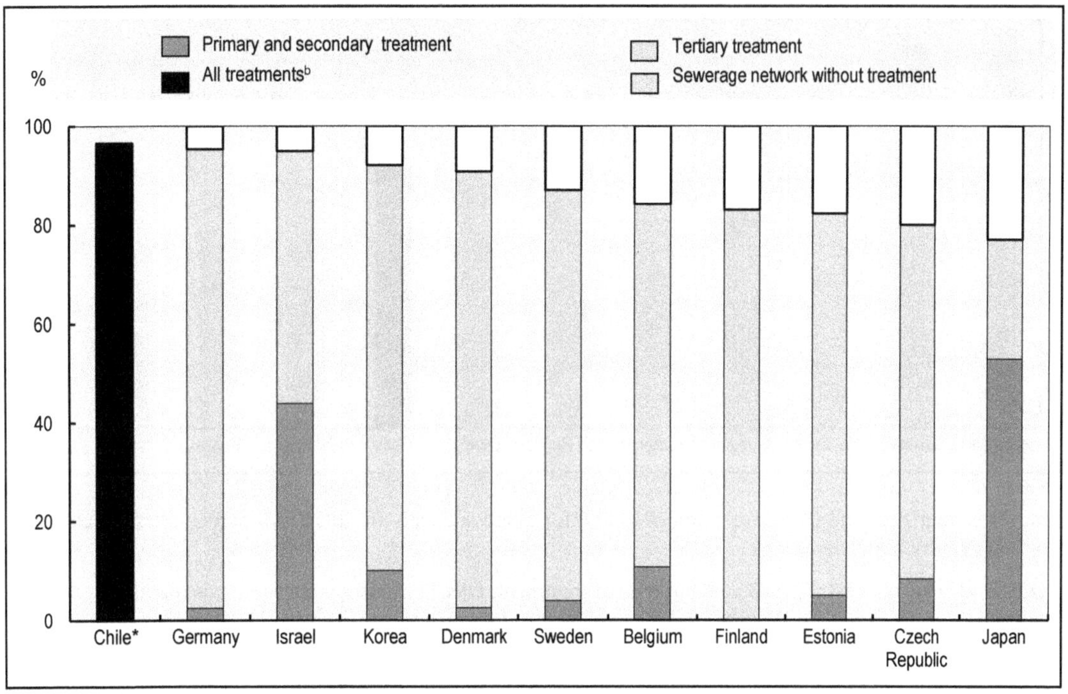

Note: Chile's data is for year 2014 and there is no disaggregation by treatment type. All percentages are calculated with respect to total country population.

Source: OECD (2015e), Access to sewerage and type of treatment, OECD Environment Statistics (database). http://stats.oecd.org/ OECD (2014a), Historical population data and projections statistics (database), http://stats.oecd.org/

Access to sewerage varies across Chile's largest cities, from 99.90% in Antofagasta, 98.74% in Coquimbo-La Serena and 98.59% in Santiago de Chile, to 93.91% in Concepción, where significant progress was achieved between 2000 and 2012 (Figure 5.17). The metropolitan area of Santiago de Chile registers the largest variability among its municipalities in terms of access to sewerage, especially in low income municipalities such as San José de Maipo (43.80%), Lampa (70.40%) and Calera de Tango (52.70%) (Figure 5.18).

Figure 5.16. Tertiary Treatment in selected countries, 2011

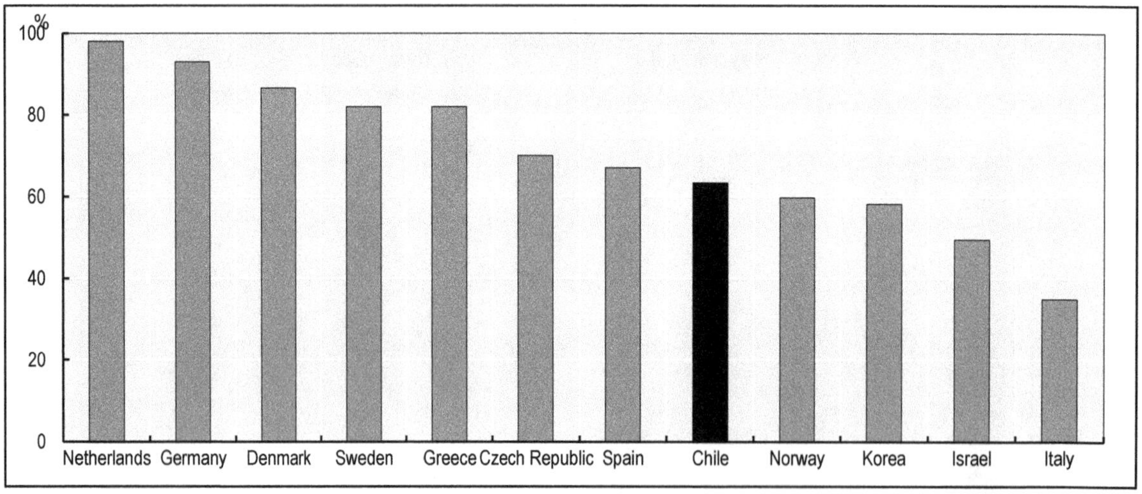

Note: Data for Netherlands and Germany is for 2010 and for Spain and Italy for 2012. All percentages are calculated with respect to total country population.

Source: OECD (2015e), Access to sewerage and type of treatment, OECD Environment Statistics (database), http://stats.oecd.org/

Figure 5.17. Selected FUAs' access to sewage systems in Chile

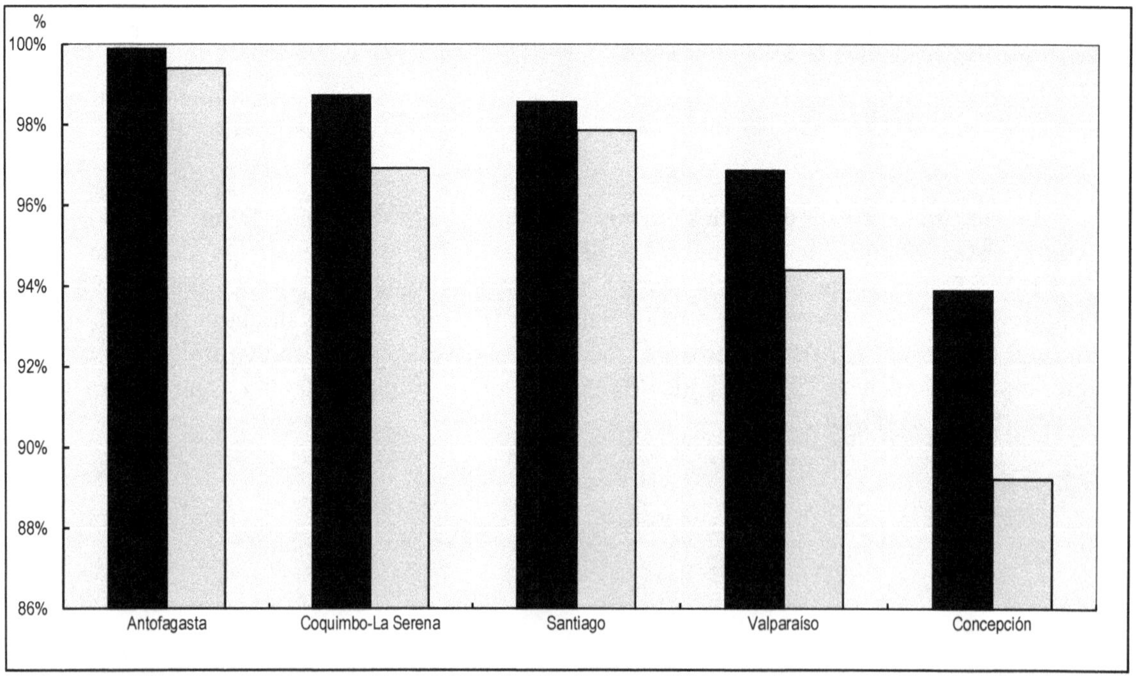

Note: for Chile's metropolitan areas data is aggregated for municipalities within the Functional Urban Areas and with available data for domestic water consumption. Santiago de Chile (Maipú, Gran Santiago, Las Condes, Estación Central, Colina, Lo Barnechea, Huechuraba, Vitacura, Peñaflor, Talagante, Buin, Cerrillos,Paine, Lampa, Padre Hurtado, Isla de Maipo, El Monte, Curacaví, Calera de Tango,San José de Maipo); Data corresponds to percentage of population served by urban water operators with respect to total population living within the area covered.

Source: Ministry of Public Works (2016c). Official statistics provided in the OECD Questionnaire for this report: Data Request on Water in Chile (2016)

Figure 5.18. Income and access to sewerage, selected municipalities in Santiago FUA, (2012)

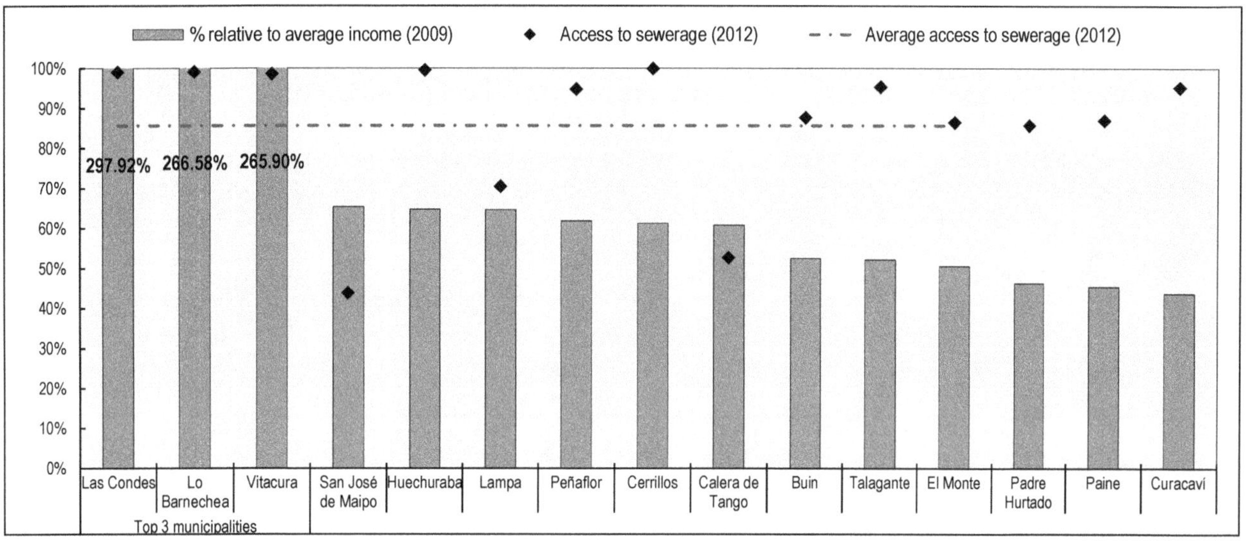

Note: Data corresponds to percentage of population served by urban water operators with respect to total population living within the area covered.

Source: Ministry of Public Works (2016c). Official statistics provided in the OECD Questionnaire for this report: Data Request on Water in Chile (2016)

Addressing Chile's urban water and sanitation infrastructure gaps

In its 2015 Water Services Management Report, the SISS also highlights the need for infrastructure renewal in certain areas of the water supply and sanitation networks. It is currently estimated that 40.4% of the water supply network in Chile was constructed of asbestos cement between 1950 and 2000 and has an estimated life span of 40 years, if maintenance activities are done regularly and effectively (SISS, 2015). This implies that a great part of the network must be closely looked at, and the same holds true for sewage systems constructed of pre-stressed concrete or cement. Moreover, some drinking water supply pipes that are over 60 years old and will require a specific diagnosis and, when needed, replacement (SISS, 2015). In 2015, the replacement rate was reported to be 0.32%, which implies that it would take 312 years to renew the entire network if such a rate remains constant (SISS, 2015). The current level of breakage rate (20.8 breaks per 100 km) could increase if the replacement rate remains constant. Thus, it is necessary to increase the monitoring ageing pipelines and pay closer attention to drinking water supply networks with higher breakage rate, which according to SISS 2015 data varies across concessions from 34.6 to 0.0 per 100 km of pipes.

It is not clear now how Chile will face renewing and modernising urban water services to ensure an efficient and effective system that is up to the standards of developed countries. The execution of investment plans to renew water supply infrastructure by private concessions in Chile has decreased during the last 3 years. Investment plans are agreed upon and negotiated between SISS and private concessions, and failure to comply with them can entail penalties. Between 2007 and 2010, private concessions carried out an average of over 90% of planned investments. This is reported to be due to the strong monitoring and enforcement of penalties and fines carried out by

SISS during that period (SISS, 2015). However, starting in 2012, the percentage of executed investments during the fiscal year (i.e. natural years)has been decreasing, and on average private concessions executed less than 70% of planned works each year (Figure 5.19). It is

worth noting however that there is currently no mechanism whereby delayed investments executed at a later stage of the plan period are reported in the following fiscal years

Figure 5.19. Execution of investment plans (%) by private concessioners in Chile, 2007-15

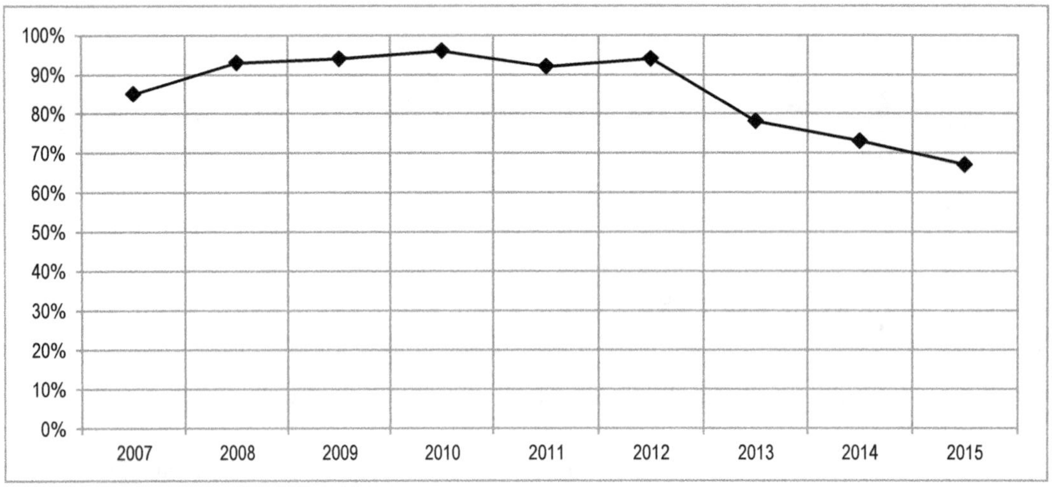

Source: SISS (2015), Informe de Gestión del Sector Sanitario 2015, www.siss.cl/577/articles-15784_inf_gest.pdf.

Perception surveys, which have been conducted by the SISS on a yearly basis since 2008, show that users are becoming less satisfied with water services. Since 2009, there has been a decline in the score given by users to drinking water services, which reached its lowest level in 2015 (10.2%) (Figure 5.20). According to the SISS survey, other basic services, such as gas, phone and electricity registered higher scores in 2015 (60.8%, 37.0% and 42.0%). This low level of users' satisfaction for drinking water supply in Chile is likely due to deficits in quality and quantity. Other studies, such as ProCalidad, show some differences with respect to the surveys conducted by SISS. For example, in the ProCalidad survey, which uses a different interviewing methodology (but the same scoring system: "net satisfaction"), electricity (38%) and internet (20%) services are not better ranked than water services (42%) (ProCalidad, 2017). Furthermore, the net satisfaction for phone services (43%) has only one point percentage difference with water services, versus 20 percentage points in the SISS Survey.

Figure 5.20. User Perception Surveys for Gas, Drinking Water, Phone and Electricity, 2008 - 2015

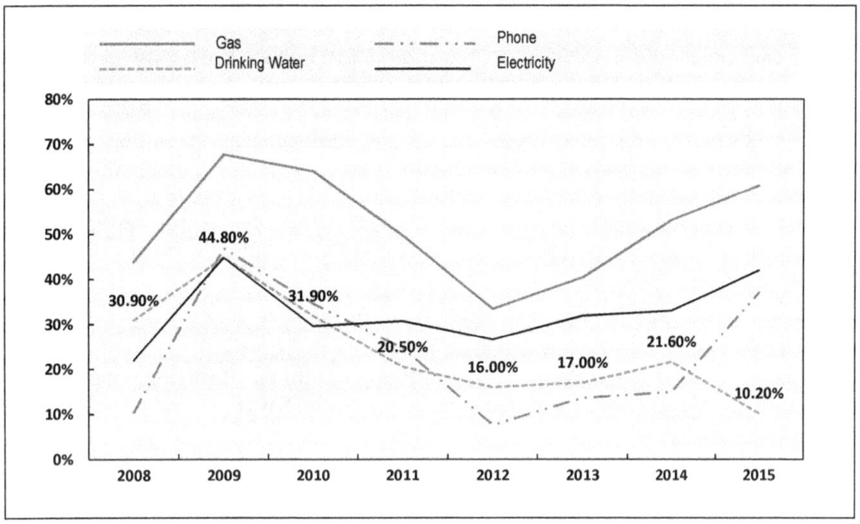

Note: The survey's sample consisted of 10 036 households in the 15 regions which are served by the 27 biggest concessioners in Chile. For each concessioner the sample used had a statistical confidence level of 95% and a sample error of 1%. User perception is measured as "Net satisfaction", which corresponds to the difference between the % of satisfied clients (clients that give grades of 6 or 7) and the % of unsatisfied clients (clients that give grades equal or below 4).

Source: SISS (2017), *User Perception Surveys*, www.siss.cl/577/w3-propertyvalue-3452.html (accessed 7 February 2017).

Investments in water infrastructure are capital intensive, and they can be recovered only over a period of time only. When investing in water infrastructure, seeking the highest value for money is therefore critical. Water loss can be distributed throughout the water supply system, which in big cities means hundreds of kilometres of pipelines, and real-time data is critical to identifying, locating and quantifying the leakage. OECD cities that have managed to improve their water information systems have been more effective at tackling leakages. Two good practices in the OECD area are New York City's plan to replace a portion of a critical aqueduct in the city's water supply system as well as Zaragoza's (Spain) policy to control and monitor leakages, which led to a 40% of reduction of water losses (Box 5.10).

Box 5.10. Fixing the institutions that can fix the pipes in OECD cities

Infrastructure renewal helps to slow the increase of environmental and operative treatment costs of treatment caused by leakages. Improving the information system, flow monitoring and the use of performance indicators related to water losses can also reduce inefficiencies and related environmental and financial costs. In **Zaragoza**, for example, consistent investments were made to reduce and control water loss, including rehabilitation of the pipeline network and pressure management controls. By 2008, losses from the system were reduced by over 40% compared to 1997, leading to yearly water savings of 20 million m^3 (Philip, 2011). Other cities have also significantly reduced water losses since the 1990s (Cologne, Grenoble, Kitakyushu, Lisbon, Liverpool, Montreal, Naples, Oslo, Prague, Rome and Stockholm).

Box 5.10. Fixing the institutions that can fix the pipes in OECD cities (*cont.*)

Since the 1990s, The Department of Environmental Protection (DEP) in **New York City** has been monitoring leaks in a portion of the aqueduct that connects the Rondout Reservoir in Ulster County to the West Branch Reservoir in Putnam County. There are two areas of significant leakage in the Rondout-West Branch Tunnel (RWBT) portion of the Delaware Aqueduct, the Wawarsing and Roseton crossings. Together, they leak approximately 35 million gallons of water per day. In response, the DEP plans to construct a bypass tunnel around the leaking areas in Roseton, which would consist of a new tunnel segment to bypass the leaking section and two shafts at each end. This work was started in 2013 and should be completed in 2023. Once the shafts and bypass tunnel are constructed, the aqueduct would be shut down and unwatered. At s: Chile 2016, OECD Publishing, Paris. DOI: ⊥‼ HYPERLINK "http://dx.doi.org/10.1787/9789264252615-en" ¶ http://dx.doi.org/10.1787/9789264252615-en.

OECD/GWP (2015), Securing Water, Sustai

*Source: OECD (2016), Water Governance in Cities,*http://dx.doi.org/10.1787/9789264251090-en; UKRN (2015*), "Innovation in regulated infrastructure sectors"*, available at: www.ukrn.org.uk/wp-content/uploads/2016/07/20150112InnovationInRegInfrSec.pdf; Philip R. (2011), "Reducing water demand and establishing a water saving culture in the City of Zaragoza", *Case study:* Zaragoza, Spain, SWITCH Training Kit, www.switchtraining.eu/fileadmin/template/projects/switch_training/files/Case_studies/Zaragoza_Case_study_preview.pdf.

Upgrading Chile's urban water and sanitation infrastructure is a shared responsibility across public and private sectors. Chile has the peculiar challenge that all its urban water supply system is concessioned to private utilities, which has helped improve the efficiency of water and sanitation systems. Although Chile has been successful in mobilising investment for the development of infrastructure thus far, the current challenges that the country faces renewing and modernising infrastructure require new responses. The Chilean government must consider low-cost options, such as investing in information systems to identify and target with better knowledge leakages and problems in the network, and further resort to green and multipurpose infrastructure to make the most of policy complementarities between drinking water and other domains and minimise liabilities for future generations. For instance, the Development Plan for 2015-2029 of Aguas Andinas in Santiago (*Plan de Desarrollo 2015 – 2029 Sistema Gran Santiago*) includes a Plan of Hydraulic Efficiency that has the objective to tackle those segments of the Greater Santiago water supply network that register high unaccounted water losses, i.e. an average of 30%. The plan includes investments in information systems to better identify water losses and, once located in the system, installing equipment to reduce those losses. However, the latter does not imply that no large investments are needed, some systems are ageing and require more capital intensive solutions, but rather that these must be coupled with low-cost infrastructure solutions.

Low-cost alternatives: Natural infrastructure and demand management techniques

Investing in natural infrastructure can contribute to managing risks of too polluted water. There is a general misconception that ecosystem services are only relevant to water users such as the agricultural sector or rural communities. However, ecosystem services are also a valuable part of the stock of facilities, services and equipment needed to ensure water security in cities. For instance, in central Chile, where mining activity has raised copper and salinity levels in some rivers like the Maipo, ecosystem services could help increase water quality and reduce operation costs of water treatment plants. If water abstracted for the drinking water supply is of higher quality, then treatment requirements are lower and there is a lesser need to use chemical processes in treatment plants. This can also drive electricity savings, as treatment processes are shorter. Demand management techniques such as education, raising awareness or reuse of water are also lower cost alternatives than developing large infrastructure. However, they require improvements in resource monitoring and water use databases.

Showcasing the benefits of ecosystem services is important to raise awareness of stakeholders. The use of ecosystems economic valuations is increasing as tested tools for analysis. With ecosystem values in hand, decision makers can then weigh up the costs and benefits of alternate choices for water infrastructure (Emerton, L. and Bos, E., 2014). Moreover, if ecosystem valuations encourage relevant stakeholders to participate, i.e. water service providers, rural communities, agricultural users, better informed and consensus-based decisions can be made. A combination of natural and hard infrastructure can drive more sustainable and climate resilient projects (Emerton and Bos, 2014). Innovative experiments with payment for environmental services were carried out in the city of Quito, Ecuador for example (Box 5.11).

Box 5.11. Mobilise innovative financing for water resource management in Quito, Ecuador

The city of Quito, Ecuador, provides an example of how to make sustainable funding for water resource management. By 2025 the city's population is expected to reach nearly 4 million, increasing the demand for water by almost 50%. The municipal government and NGOs recognised the value of watershed services for the city and provided seed money to form the Water Protection Fund for Quito (FONAG). Water users (agricultural, energy, utilities, etc.) pay a fee to the fund that depends on their water consumption, where the largest share comes from the Quito Water Utility. By 2009 the fund held more than US$ 7 million. Using interest accrued, FONAG pays to protect and maintain ecosystem services. Short term benefits can already be counted, including the conservation of 730 000 hectares, improved water quality and supply for more than 13 million people, 52% of whom are poor, and economic benefits for 1 800 people associated with watershed management and conservation. Long-term (80 year) funding focuses on environmental education, research and watershed conservation.

Source: Smith, M. et al. (2006). *Pay – Establishing payments for watershed services*, http://mtnforum.org/sites/default/files/publication/files/5381.pdf.

Recycling rainwater and greywater are good options for water savings, but quality standards need to be set to avoid health-related issues (OECD, 2016) (Box 5.12). For the reuse of wastewater, a precondition is that urban and rural sewage and the treatment of effluent is of high enough standards to preserve the quality of water sources. The technical choices of treatment are defined according to the intended uses of such water, which could be direct outfall to rivers to maintain water levels, irrigating green spaces, cereal crops, tree planting, coolants for industry or aquifer replenishment (GWP, 2012). The development of wastewater reuse depends greatly on the pressure on resources and the costs (especially energy costs), and on how they compare with those of primary sources of water resources.

Box 5.12. Water reuse in Singapore

In 2003, the Public Utilities Board (PUB), Singapore's national water agency, introduced NEWater as one of Singapore's Four National Taps.[1] It is high-grade reclaimed water produced from treated used water that has undergone stringent purification and treatment process using advanced dual-membrane (microfiltration and reverse osmosis) and ultraviolet technologies. It has passed over 130 000 scientific tests and exceeds the drinking water standards set by the World Health Organisation and the US Environmental Protection Agency. NEWater is used primarily for non-potable industrial purposes at wafer fabrication parks, industrial estates and commercial buildings. During dry months, NEWater is used to top up the reservoirs and blended with raw water before undergoing treatment at the waterworks and then being used for the drinking water supply.

Box 5.12. Water reuse in Singapore (*cont.*)

Prior to the development of NEWater, Singapore had to rely heavily on local catchments and imported water from Johor in Malaysia as its key water sources. However, these two traditional sources are weather-dependent. While reclaiming used water is not a new concept, what is significant for Singapore is the wide-scale implementation and widespread public acceptance of NEWater for indirect potable use. This is part of an overall strategy to raise awareness among the population, stressing a new approach to water management by communicating to the public the need to look at water as a renewable resource that can be used over and over again. The price of NEWater is cheaper than that of potable water, and this has encouraged many industries to switch to NEWater. Strict enforcement of used water discharge also plays an important role in ensuring that water reclamation plants are able to function as designed and to supply part of the treated effluent to the NEWater plants. Water reclamation technology is relevant to other water-scarce regions. From an energy perspective, it uses about one quarter of what desalination would require. It is from this perspective that NEWater holds tremendous promise for developing cities.

1. The other three are local catchment water, imported water and desalinated water.

Source: OECD (2016), *Water Governance in Cities*, http://dx.doi.org/10.1787/9789264251090-en.

Rural water supply and sanitation services

Chile has engaged in significant efforts over the last few decades to foster access to water supply and sanitation in rural areas. Although sewage and wastewater treatment infrastructure partly exist in rural Chile[10], evaluating the percentage of the population covered in dispersed settlements is a daunting task. Official sources report that this is the most pressing challenge in Chile's rural water programme. The Rural Drinking Water Programme (APR Programme) has been active since 1964, and it has been operated by the Under-Directorate of Rural Drinking Water within the DOH since 2011. The DOH delivers rural water services infrastructure, but citizens benefitting from the APR Programme are responsible for managing, operating and maintaining the systems through an APR Committee or co-operative. However, co-operatives and committees do not always have the necessary resources to cover the operation and maintenance costs of infrastructure, which is why DOH dedicates parts of its APR Programme budget to improving, renewing, expanding and maintaining the networks.

The results of the APR Programme in terms of access to drinking water supply have been noticeable. When the programme started back in 1964, coverage of drinking water supply in rural areas was marginal, around 6%, whereas currently over 93% of the rural population has access to improved water sources (Government of Chile, 2016). Since 1980, the total served population by this programme has increased from 400 000 people to over 1 600 000 (Figure 5.21). The two macro-zones with the most beneficiaries of the APR programme are the Central Macro-zone, with over one million people, and the South Macro-Zone, accounting for close to 400 000 people (Figure 5.21).

In 2015, the Chilean government reported that while concentrated rural communities have overall access to drinking water, sparsely populated areas still struggle to access basic water services. The APR Programme has been successful in securing access for the largest rural settlements, 100% of which are reported to have access to drinking water (Government of Chile, 2016), but there are still significant challenges in small or more disperse rural settlements (Figure 5.22).

Figure 5.21. Total rural population served in Chile, by macro-zone

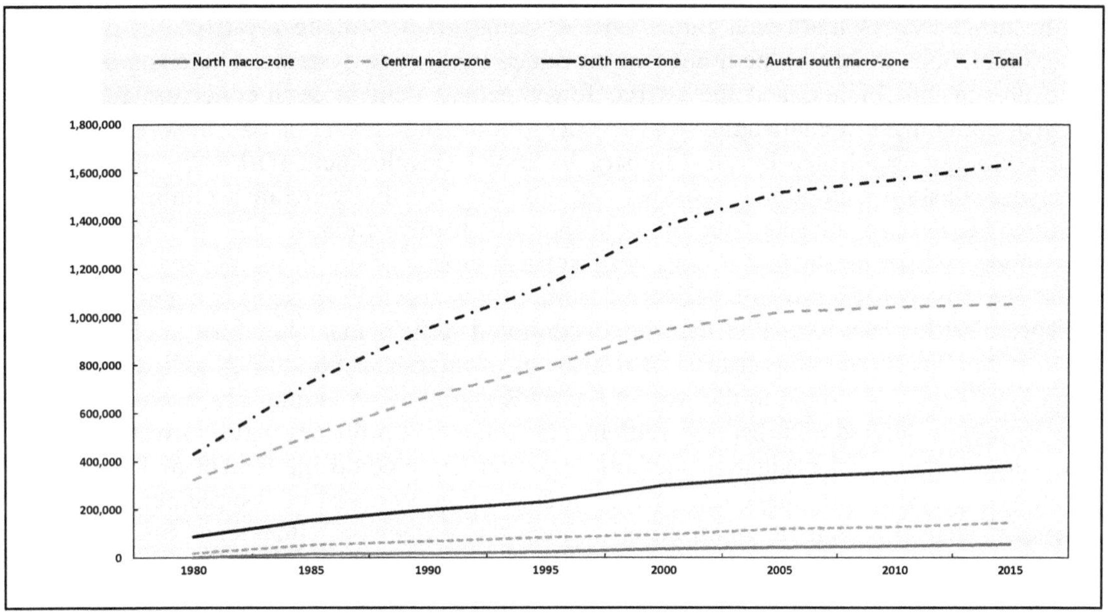

Source: Ministry of Public Works (2016c), Official statistics provided in the OECD Questionnaire Data Request on Water in Chile for this report: "Review of the Gaps, Standards and Governance of Public Infrastructure in Chile".

Figure 5.22. People in sparsely populated areas served by APR

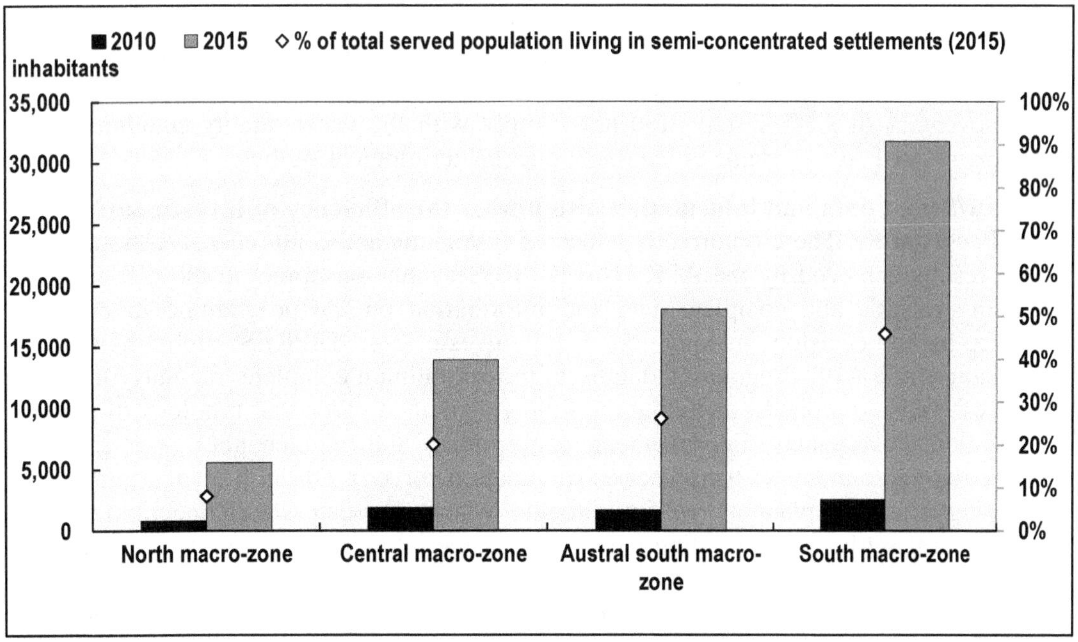

Source: Ministry of Public Works (2016c), Official statistics provided in the OECD Questionnaire Data Request on Water in Chile for this report: "Review of the Gaps, Standards and Governance of Public Infrastructure in Chile".

The renewed challenge to the APR programme is to secure access for the population living in semi-concentrated and disperse areas. Whereas in semi-concentrated areas traditional rural water systems might still be effective, in disperse agglomerations there will be a need to introduce innovative systems. The costs of these are presumably higher, and they serve fewer people than in semi-concentrated areas, which could make it challenging for projects to meet the criteria of the social evaluation methodology established by the Ministry of Social Development (DIPRES, 2015). The social evaluation methodology ensures that only projects that generate a minimum social return, i.e. in terms of economic or social outputs, receive funding from the Ministry of Economy, which means that it does not prioritise infrastructure in remote regions, given that the cost-benefit ratio of delivering rural water services in semi-concentrated and disperse settlements is smaller than in concentrated settlements. Therefore, such projects would not easily meet the criteria of the social evaluation methodology and qualify for funding. This could stand in the way of the APR's goal of providing rural water services to semi-concentrated and disperse settlements. Chapter 2 proposes ways forward for the revision of the social evaluation methodology that Chile could implement as it faces its renewed infrastructure challenges. These methods might consist of complementing cost-benefit analysis with a multi-criteria analysis framework that can be used to accommodate more long-term goals, strategic issues, and to improve alignment with broader policy priorities.

The Budget Directorate (Dirección de Presupuesto, DIPRES) evaluation report (2015) highlights noticeable damage and ageing of APR systems, creating obstacles to the reliability of the quality and quantity of water supply. Between 2011 and 2014, 22.1% of unexpected maintenance and operation costs arose due to the deterioration of APR systems. This is mainly due to the uneven distribution of technical, financial and managerial skills across different APR committees and co-operatives. Although all committees have the obligation to use planning instruments such as annual financial statements and activity plans, many do not have them in practice (DIPRES, 2015). As a result, over 5% of APR systems did not comply with the water quality standards, and more than 9% of APR systems failed to conduct bacteriological studies.

Insufficient data and information also hinder the efficiency of investments in the APR Programme. There is currently a lack of systematic and comprehensive monitoring of the results achieved by the APR. The DIPRES evaluation points to the difficulty of accessing reliable and complete data and information on the programme to enhance evidence-based decision making on rural investments. DIPRES recommends an expansion of the APR Programme database, incorporating a complete, regularly updated record of executed projects, including the following data in particular: typology of project (installation, enlargement, improvement, conservation and maintenance), start and end dates, costs and number of beneficiaries (population served). DIPRES also recommends promoting strategic planning of investments when targeting semi-concentrated and disperse rural settlements; building capacity, managerial skills and technical knowledge of cooperatives and committees responsible for operating, maintenance and financing of the APR system; and implementing monitoring and evaluation techniques by improving data and information production.

A future objective of the APR Program is to extend access to drinking water and improved rural sanitation services to 560 semi-concentrated settlements that represent 220 000 inhabitants. This should be enabled by the New Law on Rural Sanitation Services adopted in January 2017 with the following objectives:

- strengthen the management capacity of committees and co-operatives, while preserving their participatory component
- establish the rights and obligations of committees and co-operatives, based on the principles of solidarity and non-discrimination as to the rights to access rural water services
- establish and clarify the regulatory functions of the State in rural water services, including the methodology for calculating and revising tariffs for the services
- create an Underdirectorate for Rural Water Services (within the DOH) with the responsibility to develop a policy to support and promote committees and co-operatives' activities
- encourage the participation of the management staff of committees and co-operatives in the to-be-established National and Regional Councils
- incorporate the less densely populated rural areas in the scope of the Rural Water Programme, focusing first on areas with water stress
- incorporate improved rural sanitation services in the scope of the Rural Water Programme, and appoint a technical body to study the best solutions on a case-by-case basis, i.e. to decide between sanitation networks or localised systems.
- involve communities in the decision as to find the best solution.
- reduce fragmentation by having only one water operator per rural settlement for both drinking water and sanitation services.
- Bridging the rural water services gap.

The DOH should conduct regular monitoring of the APR Programme to anticipate supply cuts and the need for costly investments due to infrastructure replacements, and it should co-ordinate with Regional Councils to establish investment priorities. Financing of rural water services in Chile is done through the National Budgetary Law. The MOP provides regional governments with a list of projects and a certain amount of funds, and the Regional Councils (CORE) are in charge of prioritising them. The Rural Infrastructure Funds of the SUBDERE are channelled through the regional governments under DOH's responsibility to supervise the technical execution of the projects. Closer cooperation between the CORE and MOP would help identify dysfunctional or not properly operated or maintained rural water systems, as well as the most urgent investment needs in semi-concentrated and disperse settlements. The National Budgetary Law has provided flexibility for the APR Programme to make investments in small works and enabled CLP 2.5 billion Chilean pesos of investment per year between 2007 and 2011, with a peak of CLP 82 680 million in 2016 (over 400 rural drinking water supply systems registered maintenance works financed with this mechanism) (SAFI, 2017). This mechanism will therefore be key to preventing the collapse of rural water systems. In addition, the MOP could conduct a re-evaluation of the technical standards required for rural water systems to last longer, and it could identify network enlargement requirements in rural settlements with noticeable population growth.

The lessons gleaned from OECD countries' experiences can help in the choice of the right infrastructure to face the challenge of delivering water services to semi-concentrated and disperse settlements. While reflecting on future infrastructure needs, most countries now recognise that large-scale centralised systems may no longer be the optimal solution due to high maintenance costs and resource needs; this holds particular true for rural settlements where small distributed systems make more sense. The expansion of sanitation services within the framework of the Rural Drinking Water Programme is instead built around localised wastewater management systems serving individual or small groups of properties (Box 5.13). They require less upfront investment than larger-scale, centrally piped infrastructures and are more effective at coping with the need to expand services, as it is the current case of Chile.

Box 5.13. Localised sanitation services in OECD countries

Localised water supply and sanitation can be used to serve populations not connected to public systems. Rich countries with large metropolitan areas but low population density, e.g. Australia and the United States, still have significant populations served by private individual or community systems. The situation in Europe is more diverse: the proportion of households not connected to sewers is higher in low-density or low-revenue countries or regions – e.g. Portugal and Spain, southern Italy and Greece, eastern European and Nordic countries, Ireland and even some German *Länders*. In these areas, populations are not yet fully connected to public water systems. Ireland has officially kept a large number of grouped water schemes, providing water to 8% of the population at small community scales (OECD, 2013c).

Localised sanitation systems are not merely a remedy to the limited number of centrally piped systems. They are increasingly used in countries such as the United States, where on-site sanitation now comprises some 40% of all new developments (USEPA, 2002). Sustainable neighbourhoods in cities are partly – or fully – replacing traditional public systems with decentralised technologies. Paradoxically, these innovations are taking place in the richer and higher-density European States (OECD, 2013c). The performance of localised systems can compare with that of centrally piped infrastructures. For instance, an evaluation of localised systems in Ireland shows that despite difficulties in meeting the standards now imposed at the European level, such schemes sometimes operate better than public water systems, and the population they serve is largely committed to keeping them (Brady and Gray, 2013).

Innovation can contribute to improved performance of localised systems. Research is ongoing to provide communities reliant on individual and community systems with robust and simplified treatment systems, equipped with real-time ICTs, to help set up community services operated from distant centres (e.g. work by Yoram Cohen, UCLA Institute of the Environment and Sustainability). These developments explain the renewed interest for localised, on-site sanitation. The Australian Academy of Technological Sciences and Engineering (ATSE), for example, recommends that Australian governments encourage investment and uptake of such systems (ATSE, 2012).

Source: (OECD, 2013c), Brady and Gray (2013), and ATSE (2012) adapted from OECD (2015a), *Water and Cities: Ensuring Sustainable Futures*. DOI: http://dx.doi.org/10.1787/9789264230149-en.

Rainwater infrastructure

Under the current legal framework, rainwater infrastructure involves multiple players at the national level. According to Law 19.525, adopted in 1997, DOH (under MOP) is in charge of the primary network, while the Ministry of Housing is responsible for the secondary network. Moreover, each urban centre with more than 50 000 inhabitants must design its own master plan, defining the primary and secondary rainwater network of the city. A key fact is that rainwater infrastructure is not included in the concession regime to private utilities in urban areas.

While rainwater infrastructure exists in Chile's main cities, like Valparaíso, Concepción and Santiago, it is not does not function effectively against heavy rain episodes. Given trends in climate change and population growth in urban areas, efficient and effective rainwater collection systems are much needed in Chile. Flooding episodes cause material, human and economic losses. Flood risk from storm water is particularly high in areas where storm-water infrastructure has not been adapted to elevated runoff in creeks coming from mountains, as in Santiago. Urban expansion in the eastern part of

Santiago towards the Andean piedmont has also increased the amount of impermeable surfaces, contributing to increased risks from flood hazards (Romero and Mendoça, 2014). Medium-sized growing cities, such as Valparaíso or Antofagasta, must also consider further developing and maintaining this type of infrastructure in order to prepare for the future.

Urban flooding is a very local issue in water management, which could be under local responsibility considering the current process of decentralisation in Chile. Such a transfer of prerogatives to cities in Chile should go along with new availability of financial resources, either via national transfers from the central government or through the administrative capacity to raise revenues at the sub-national level. Chapter 3 depicts the necessary framework conditions and capacities of subnational administrations to ensure infrastructure investment at subnational level is effective and achieves pre-established objectives. OECD countries such as France have considered a range of options to raise revenue to account for rainwater infrastructure, including fiscal instruments (Box 5.14).

Low-cost alternatives also exist to reduce the impact of an insufficiently developed urban rainwater system, especially urban green infrastructure. As for the case of rural water services, decentralised systems also apply to rainwater drainage. In the OECD area, there is a growing use of "source control" technologies that handle rainwater near the point of generation (OECD, 2015a). For instance, green roofs or pervious surfaces capture rainwater before it runs onto polluted pavements and streets. These solutions have several benefits. First, they help alleviate peak flows: water is captured at the source so it does not run off into the streets and sewer networks, which mitigates the effects of urban floods, as it reduces the probability of experiencing an overflow in the sewer. Second, they help reduce pollution by stopping rainwater from getting polluted while flowing on the streets. Third, these methods can also help improve the quality of water returned to the environment: for instance, pervious surfaces allow rainwater to trickle through the ground and recharge aquifers. Lastly, they help adapt rainwater infrastructure to climate change, since decentralised drainage reduces urban flooding peak flows conveyed through the sewers, which helps alleviate the need for investing on the extension of sewage collection and wastewater treatment infrastructure (OECD, 2015a). Several OECD cities have developed full-fledged strategies to develop urban green infrastructure systems. One of them is San Francisco, which was among the pioneer cities ten years ago where a multilateral agreement was signed among the utilities' association, the city's building agency and the public health department to coalesce efforts in promoting decentralised systems (Box 5.15).

Box 5.14. Financing urban rainwater management in France

The failure to properly manage rainwater affects the capacity of French local authorities to achieve the "good ecological status" mandated by the European Water Framework Directive. Thanks to a dedicated fiscal instrument introduced in 2011, French local authorities have the capacity to set up a new public service dedicated to urban rainwater management, which can be financed in full or in part by earmarked revenues from a dedicated tax.

The tax is based on impervious surfaces, in urban areas or future development areas, whether or not the surfaces are connected to a drainage system. It is paid by the owner of the land or property when the property is larger than a minimum area set by the local authority. The tax rate is set by the local government and cannot exceed EUR 1 square metre per year (EUR/ m^2/year). It can be reduced, in full or in part, where facilities are in place to reduce run-off. The reduction is meant to reflect the decreased run-off. Several adjacent property owners can join the mechanism if they build and operate a common facility.

Box 5.14. Financing urban rainwater management in France (*cont.*)

This new tax principally aims to create incentives for managing rainwater close to the source and limiting run-off by implementing measures that mitigate the consequences of impervious surfaces. It also aims to raise revenues earmarked for long-term urban rainwater management. In the long term, the revenues generated by the tax are bound to decrease as the objectives are met – a trend that local authorities need to anticipate and factor in. Local authorities have the opportunity when engaging in feasibility studies to reflect on the level of ambition of their urban rainwater management policy and the policy packages (zoning, standards, information, tax, etc.) they wish to implement. Stakeholder consultation should feature prominently in the process.

Source: OECD (2015a), *Water and Cities: Ensuring Sustainable Futures*, http://dx.doi.org/10.1787/9789264230149-en.

Given that floods are becoming more frequent in Chile, and affect households' supply and water quality with important economic impacts due to high recovery costs, a full-fledge strategy to deal with floods is much needed, beyond rainwater systems. Several OECD countries have an excellent track record at dealing with floods or the risk of submersion, such as the Netherlands. The Netherlands' flood protection policy is rooted in the 1950s when the first Delta Committee developed starting points and standards for flood safety, which were laid down in the Flood Defence Structures Act. Currently, the Delta Programme is the main policy instrument aimed at preventing floods (Box 5.16).

Box 5.15 San Francisco's rainwater harvesting

In 2008, San Francisco's Public Utilities Commission (SFPUC), Department of Building Inspection (DBI), and Department of Public Health (DPH) signed a Memorandum of Understanding (MOU) for the permitting requirements for rainwater harvesting systems located within the City and County of San Francisco. The MOU encouraged rainwater harvesting and its reuse for non-potable applications without requiring treatment to potable water standards. It also defined the roles of the participating agencies. Line of actions have included:

- The SFPUC has created and distributed guidance and material on rainwater harvesting. The material covers system design, system components, allowable uses, owner responsibilities, and permitting requirements. The SFPUC has encouraged all rainwater harvesters to notify the SFPUC with the design specifications of their systems for research purposes.
- DBI has issued permits for construction of properly designed rainwater harvesting systems for non-potable uses that meet the minimum criteria described in the MOU and in guidance materials prepared by the SFPUC. DBI has been responsible for the review of permit applications and inspection of rainwater harvesting systems that required permits.
- DPH has reviewed rainwater harvesting projects that propose any residential indoor uses of rainwater other than toilet flushing to assure the protection of public health.

System design, maintenance and use are the responsibility of the system owner. The MOU classified rain barrels and cisterns and defined the allowable uses of harvested rainwater. Water from rain barrels may be used for irrigation and vehicle washing; it is prohibited to connect rain barrels to indoor or outdoor plumbing. Water from cisterns connected to indoor plumbing may be used for irrigation, vehicle washing, heating and cooling, and toilet flushing. If a cistern is not connected to indoor plumbing, it cannot be used for toilet flushing. The MOU also included safety and maintenance requirements, required system components, labelling requirements, and DBI permit requirements.

Source: EPA (2008), Managing Wet Weather with Green Infrastructure, Municipal Handbook: Rainwater Harvesting Policies, available at: https://www.epa.gov/sites/production/files/2015-10/documents/gi_munichandbook_harvesting.pdf.

Box 5.16. The Delta Programme

The Delta Programme is a national planning instrument that aims to achieve two priority goals for a country "safe now and in the future": protect the Netherlands against flooding and ensure freshwater supply. It is a joint endeavour between the central government, the provinces, municipal councils and regional water authorities, in close co-operation with social organisations and business. The Delta Programme is implemented through a Delta Act (legislation), a Delta Fund (financial resources) and a Delta Commissioner with ministerial ranking (leadership) The implementation of the Delta Programme consists in a series of short- and long-term flexible projects. The first Delta Programme was presented to the House of Representatives in 2010 and introduced a new flexible approach to water management, based on measurements and scenarios carried out by the Royal Netherlands Meteorological Institute in 2006. The second edition of the Delta Programme was presented in September 2011 with a new important element: the definition of five Delta Decisions, or priority areas for action in flood risk management and freshwater supplies. Building on multi-stakeholder dialogues, and technical calculations and assumptions, these decisions structure the Delta Programme and provide direction for the measures to be taken in the following areas:

- Water safety: updating safety standards and developing regionally oriented safety strategies
- Freshwater strategy: elaborating a strategy for the sustainable supply of freshwater
- Water level management in the IJsselmeer region: a decision regarding the long-term water level management of the IJsselmeer, focused on water safety and freshwater supply
- Rhine-Meuse delta: a strategy for the protection of the Rhine-Meuse delta and solutions for the freshwater supply
- Spatial adaptation: a national policy framework for the (re)development of built-up areas and recommendations regarding flooding and heat stress.

The Delta Act on Flood Risk Management and Freshwater Supplies that came into effect in January 2012 as an amendment to the Water Act is the backbone of the Delta Programme. It mandates a Delta Commissioner, appointed by the government, to lead the Delta Programme and submit a yearly proposal for action to the Cabinet, in consultation with the relevant authorities, social organisations and the business community. This annual report provides an overview of all measures, facilities, studies and ambitions related to flood risk management and freshwater supplies. The Delta Act also enshrines a Delta Fund, separated from the Infrastructure Fund, to finance the implementation of the Delta Programme and related projects and reduce the risk that too much or too little is invested in water safety and freshwater supply. The Delta Fund is split across five budget articles (Arts. 1-5) related to:

- investing in flood risk management
- investing in freshwater supplies
- management, maintenance and replacement
- experimenting
- network-related costs and other expenses.

The Minister of Infrastructure and the Environment bears final responsibility for the expenditures under the Delta Fund. The first official Delta Fund budget was sent to the Dutch House of Representatives together with the third Delta Programme report in 2013. In Budget Day 2016, the House of Representatives received the seventh edition of the Delta Programme, which presents the progress in implementation of the five Delta Decisions as well as other concrete measures for improving flood defence and securing freshwater supply.

Source: OECD (2014b), Water Governance in the Netherlands: Fit for the Future?, OECD Publishing, Paris, http://dx.doi.org/10.1787/9789264102637-en.

Infrastructure for non-conventional water sources

In Chile, desalination has expanded in the past two decades, mainly in the North macro-zone. Desalination for drinking water supply has developed in the five regions of the North Macro-Zone, where it increased by 2 500% in the last 15 years (Figure 5.23).

Newly available resources have been mainly used to satisfy urban water needs in the region of Antofagasta (Figure 5.24), where there has been a rapid development of volume supplied by this alternative source (from 2 Mm^3/year in 2005 to over 20 Mm^3 in 2015). Increases in rural drinking water supply by desalination have also been noticeable, particularly in Coquimbo, where it has increased from 0.1 Mm^3/year to over 0.4 Mm^3 (Figure 5.25).

While desalination plants provide reliable, large supplies of quality drinking water, they are expensive and energy intensive. This type of water supply technique is independent of the hydrological cycle and does not reduce the amount of water available for other uses, as it uses brackish water or seawater. Its development has mainly been seen in countries with arid and semi-arid climates, such as Chile's North and Central Macro-zones. For instance, in the Mediterranean region, countries with severe water stress such as Spain, Algeria or Israel have explored the utilisation of this water source to increase the availability of water resources without depleting already over-exploited aquifers or surface waters (Box 5.16). However, investing in desalination to increase water supply is costly, and not all countries can afford it. GWP (2012) reports that the cost of water produced by large-scale desalination plants is between EUR 0.40 and 0.60/m^3 (and from EUR 0.20 to 0.30/m^3 if it is brackish water), without considering the high initial capital investment requirements. The cost is roughly twice that of conventional water sources, i.e. withdrawals from freshwater sources, and one and a half times that of reused water (wastewater that is used for other purposes after appropriate treatment).

Figure 5.23. Evolution of total drinking water supply from desalination

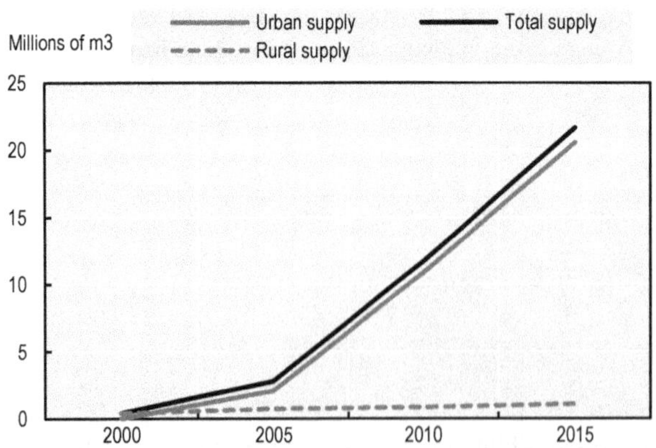

Source: Ministry of Public Works (2016c), Official statistics provided in the OECD Questionnaire Data Request on Water in Chile for this report: "Review of the Gaps, Standards and Governance of Public Infrastructure in Chile".

Figure 5.24. Evolution of drinking water supply from desalination in region II - Antofagasta

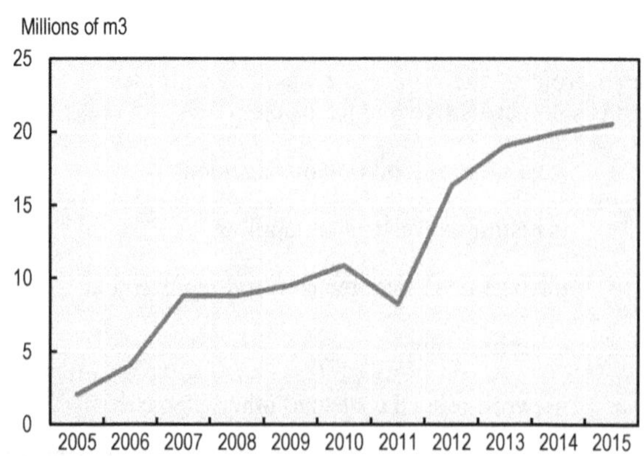

Source: Ministry of Public Works (2016c), Official statistics provided in the OECD Questionnaire Data Request on Water in Chile for this report: "Review of the Gaps, Standards and Governance of Public Infrastructure in Chile".

Figure 5.25. Rural drinking water supply from desalination per region in Chile

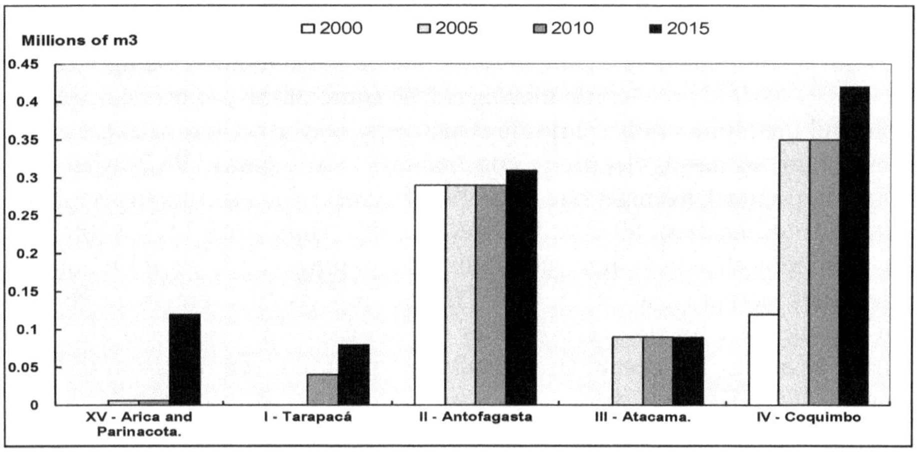

Source: Ministry of Public Works (2016c), Official statistics provided in the OECD Questionnaire Data Request on Water in Chile for this report: "Review of the Gaps, Standards and Governance of Public Infrastructure in Chile".

There are plans to expand desalination in the north of Chile for mining activities. Increasing water demand in mining is being met in the North Macro-Zone with the construction of desalination plants. The Chilean Commission of Copper (COCHILCO, Comisión Chilena del Cobre) suggests that the water consumption of the mining industry will increase by 66% by 2020 over 2014 totals (Figure 5.26). In absolute terms, this will mean an increase of 10 Mm^3/year in the requirements of freshwater for mining activities. COCHILCO also expects that the majority of the increase will be covered by desalination plants constructed by major mining companies. In 2014, it is reported that 1.7 Mm^3 out of the 14.8 Mm^3 used by the mining industry was seawater (roughly 11%). However, in 2025 the percentage is expected to increase to 33%. In absolute terms, this will mean that of the 10 Mm^3 increase expected by 2025, 7.7 Mm^3 will be desalinated water. This will have an impact on the energy needed to operate these plants.

Box 5.17. Desalination in semi-arid countries in the Mediterranean region

Spain has a diverse climatological profile where the northern parts of the country are humid and have plenty of water and the east and south suffer from severe water stress. For example, e.g. the Jucar River Basin, located on the eastern Mediterranean coast, records 87% water stress. Spain ranks 4th worldwide in terms of desalination installed capacity (more than 1500 desalination plants and 2.5 Mm^3/day installed capacity). The country allocates a great proportion of these water resources from desalination to supply greenhouse agriculture production, which is mainly located in the region of Almeria (southeast coast).

Israel is the country that has made the biggest commitment to desalination for its supply of water to meet current and future demands. Until 2004, Israel's water supply system was completely dependent on groundwater sources and rainwater, which was not enough to satisfy existing demands. It therefore started an ambitious desalination expansion programme with the construction of four plants that now represent 40% of the country's total water availability. In early 2015, Israel started operating the biggest desalination plant in the world, called Sorek. It cost USD 500 million and at full strength is capable of producing 627 000 m^3/day. The country plans to keep increasing production of desalinated water to 2 Mm^3/day in 2020 and 4.25 Mm^3/day in 2050, which should meet 70% and 100% of drinking water supply, respectively.

Algeria's desalination capacity is focused on urban water supply to the big urban centres of the country: Algiers, Oran and Skikda. Existing cheap energy in the country enables the economic viability of these projects, and the current total capacity installed in only these 3 cities is over 0.4 Mm^3/day.

Source: Adapted from GWP (2012), "Water Demand Management: The Mediterranean Experience", *Technical Focus Paper*, www.gwp.org/en/ToolBox/PUBLICATIONS/Technical-Focus-Papers/.

The coming developments of desalination infrastructure in Chile have had an impact on the forecasts as to the mining sector's energy consumption. COCHILCO's forecast for energy consumption considered three different scenarios: the maximum scenario, with all mining investment projects under consideration being executed; the expected scenario, based on uncertainties regarding some of the projects considered in the simulation; and the minimum scenario, in which only confirmed projects are carried out. For the maximum scenario, electricity consumption will increase 98.7% between 2014 and 2025, at an annual average rate of 6.4% (Figure 5.27). In the expected scenario, consumption would increase 80.6% at a rate of 5.5%. Thus, 16.5 TWh is the additional energy consumption that with high probability the mining sector would require to carry out its activities normally in 2025. COCHILCO reports that the increase is mainly explained by the new treatment processes of minerals in Chile and the increasing requirements of energy for desalination plants and pumping stations from the seaside to the mining pits (COCHILCO, 2015).

Figure 5.26. Projected water consumption by the mining industry in Chile, 2014-20

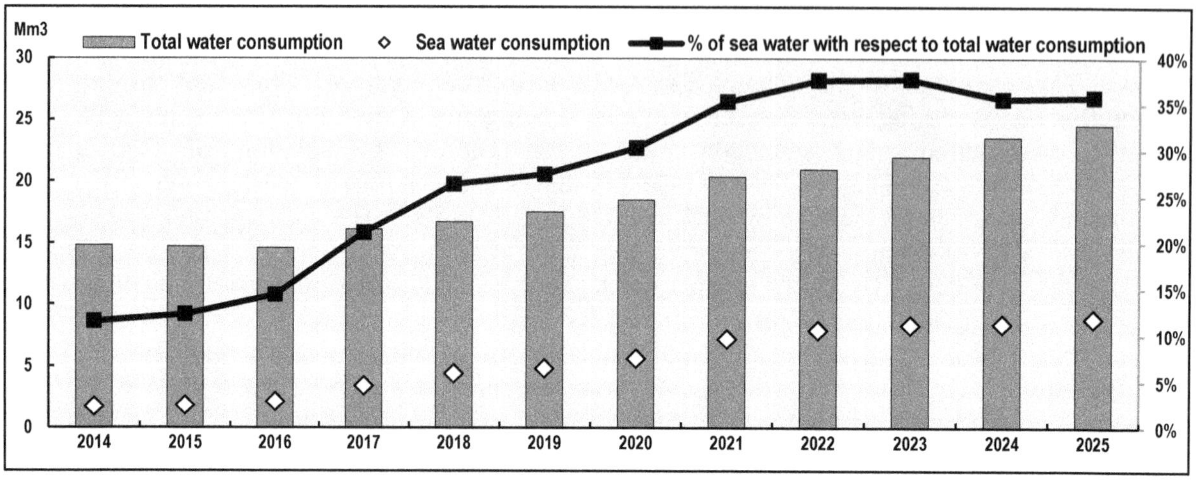

Source: COCHILCO (2015), *Factores clave para el desarrollo de la minería en Chile*, https://www.cochilco.cl/Recopilacin%20de%20Estudios/2015.pdf

Energy constraints have already had an impact on Chile's mining sector. In the region of Atacama, some important energy projects such as the Castilla project (estimated generation capacity of 2 100 MW) or the Punta Alcalde (740 MW) have been stalled due to uncertainty and lack of confidence among mining investors. In the absence of a sound water-energy coordination and strategic combination, if energy prices keep increasing due to rising demand, the competitiveness of Chile's mining sector might decline compared to others in Latin American such as Peru.

Figure 5.27. Forecasted energy consumption in Chile's mining sector, 2014 - 2025

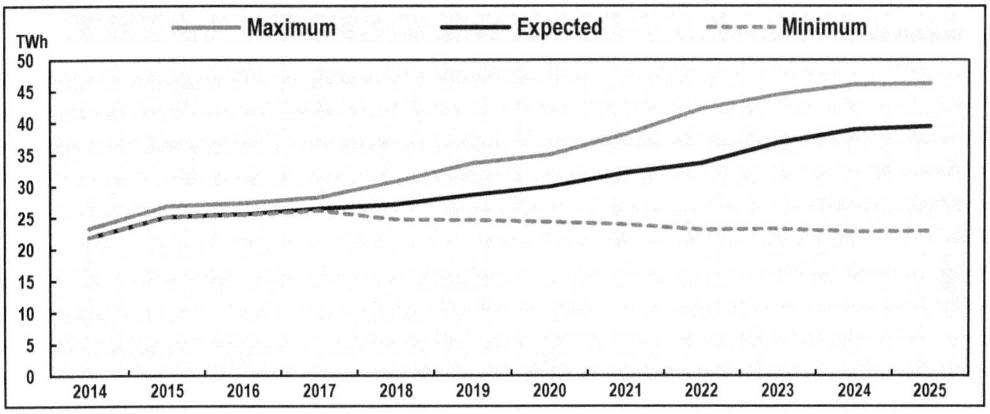

Source: COCHILCO (2015), "Factores clave para el desarrollo de la minería en Chile", https://www.cochilco.cl/Recopilacin%20de%20Estudios/2015.pdf.

Energy shortfalls and climate change require thinking of how energy will be delivered to desalination plants and how much this will cost. It is therefore crucial to minimise energy consumption and GHG emissions. An option for Chile could be exploring low CO2 emission options, i.e. reverse osmosis plants, and combining this infrastructure with energy recovery systems and higher performing membranes (which only need 3 to 4 kWh of electricity per m^3 of water produced). The use of renewables for desalination (wind, photovoltaic, solar and concentrated solar thermal) could be a way forward, particularly in the North Macro-Zone, where the potential for solar renewable energy is huge (Ministry of Energy, 2015). However, renewables are only an attractive option if used to supply small desalination plants at isolated sites. Worldwide, about 100 desalination plants, coupled to renewable energy sources, have been built in the past 20 years, several in the Mediterranean (Algeria, Egypt, Spain, Tunisia) (GWP, 2012). These low-capacity solar and wind-powered desalination plants are well designed and operated and supply sites cut off from quality water. The costs are immediately attractive. Desalination therefore appears to be an option to adapt to climate change, but it must not replace other sustainable possibilities, such as rational use of water. It should also primarily produce drinking water for human consumption.

When investing in costly infrastructure like desalination plants, future projections of costs and benefits become even more crucial. Desalination plants, besides requiring a high initial capital investment, are costly to maintain throughout their entire life-cycle. Desalination requires large amounts of energy and generates greenhouse gas emission when electricity does not come from renewable sources. As a result, it can be a costly option depending on energy prices, particularly in countries like Chile with energy supply shortfalls. Moreover, the variability of costs is high when the energy markets are volatile due to the dependence on external energy sources, as in Chile, and where the effects of climate change could potentially reduce the country's energy potential. Countries with uncertainties associated with variable costs might not be the ideal to places to develop large amounts of desalination water supply. These uncertainties hinder solid investment assessments in desalination, as future costs cannot be forecasted with a high enough level of confidence. Thus, long-term quality feasibility studies could entail great savings if they shed light on the opportunity for investment. Some OECD countries, such as Australia, have developed desalination projects that have not turned out to be profitable in either economic or social terms (Box 5.17).

Box 5.18. Investing in desalination in Sydney, Australia

In 2007, a contract for a desalination plant was signed in Sydney due to concerns over water shortages. However, the construction of the plant took several years, during which the end of the drought alleviated some of the water security concerns. Following the construction of the plant, water prices increased by 50% from 2007 to 2010 to cover the costs of investment. By contrast, if scarcity prices had been introduced in Sydney prior to building the desalination plant, the market would have sent signals about the optimal time to invest in desalination. By estimating the optimal time to invest in desalination based on efficient volumetric prices, Grafton and Ward (2010) found that the investment in desalination in Sydney was made prematurely, and led to welfare losses valued at hundreds of millions of US dollars per year. These losses arose from the costs associated with using mandatory water restrictions rather than dynamically efficient pricing and, ultimately high volumetric water prices needed to cover the high capital costs associated with the premature construction of the desalination plant.

Source: Grafton and Ward (2010) adapted from OECD (2013b), *Water Security for Better Lives*, OECD Publishing, Paris, http://dx.doi.org/10.1787/9789264202405-en.

Innovation in cities' water cycles can also help mitigate energy shortages and make energy available for other purposes. Electricity is a heavy feature of the annual budget of water utilities, due to operations such as pumping from withdrawal and to treatment plants, which often occur outside of populated areas (OECD, 2016). To make up for these requirements, increasing efficiency of the water-energy cycle is becoming an important goal for water managers, and innovative practices have emerged to foster greater coherence among water and energy policies at the local level. For instance, in Budapest, legal requirements are used for coordination between water utility supply and the energy sectors. In Singapore England, and Chile (Box 5.19), important investments have been dedicated to innovative water-energy-waste projects. Further innovations can be encouraged through experimentation and pilot testing.

Box 5.19. Innovation in water-energy-waste projects

In Singapore, energy consumption is and will continue to be a challenge to water supply and used water operations. The PUB, Singapore's national water agency, seeks to mitigate the impact of energy on the processes through a long-term water supply strategy known as the "Four National Taps" – (i) Local catchment water from the reservoirs; (ii) Imported water from Malaysia; (iii) NEWater: ultra-clean, high-grade reclaimed water; (iv) Desalinated water.

Among the Four National Taps, desalination is the one with the highest energy consumption. With the aim of cutting current energy use at least by half, PUB has partnered with Evoqua Technologies (previously Siemens Water Technologies Corporation) to pilot electrically-driven processes to desalt seawater and move forward with other innovations. PUB is looking into building rooftop solar panels at waterworks and installing floating solar systems on the reservoir to explore alternative and sustainable energy sources. By 2025, the country plans to construct Tuas Water Reclamation Plant (TWRP), which will incorporate technologies to improve energy efficiency and manpower requirements. It will be located within the National Environment Agency's (NEA)'s Integrated Waste Management Facility to reap the potential synergies of the Water-Energy-Waste nexus. This co-location marks Singapore's first initiative to integrate used water and solid waste treatment processes to maximise both energy and resource recovery while minimising land footprint.

Box 5.19. Innovation in water-energy-waste projects (*cont.*)

England has also engaged in cross-sector technical innovation by generating energy from waste. In 2011, Thames Water opened a GBP 1.5 million sewage sludge dryer at its water treatment plant in Slough, Berkshire. Previous attempts to generate power from sludge at the company's Crossness sewage works in southeast London had been limited by the high water content of the sludge collected (75%). The main role of this process was therefore to reduce waste more efficiently. With the new dryer, the water content is reduced to 5% and the sludge is produced as flakes or granules. This enables it to be burnt like wood chip, and requires less gas to burn it and generate electricity. The electricity is used to power Thames Water's operations, generating GBP 300 000 a year of operational cost reductions and reducing carbon emissions by 500 tonnes a year.

Chile's second biggest wastewater treatment plant, Mapocho-Trebal, which treats an average flow of 6.6 m^3/s generates energy from waste. The treatment plant generates biogas that is then used as fuel for engines of electric energy co-generation, and the resulting electricity is mainly used for self-consumption. In the Mapocho-Trebal plant biogas generates thermal energy that is used in the wastewater treatment process. In 2013, the plant started a modernisation process to improve energy efficiency and resulted in the certification of the ISO 50.001 norm that specifies the requirements for establishing, implementing, maintaining and improving an energy management system. Chile has also included innovation in pipelines where the existing hydraulic energy within the system is used to generate hydropower. This is the case for instance of the regulator valve in San Antonio which is installed in the drinking water supply system linked to the drinking-water plant of San Enrique.

Source: OECD (2016), *Water Governance in Cities*. DOI: http://dx.doi.org/10.1787/9789264251090-en ; UKRN (2015), "Innovation in Regulated infrastructure sectors", available at: www.ukrn.org.uk/wp-content/uploads/2016/07/20150112InnovationInRegInfrSec.pdf ; Aguas Andinas (2015), "*Reporte de Sustentabilidad 2015*", available at: https://www.aguasandinas.cl/la-empresa/desarrollo-sustentable/reportes-de-sustentabilidad

It is crucial to monitor and evaluate closely the impact of desalination projects on the local environment to ensure sustainability in the medium and long-term. Desalination produces an effluent of salty water with around double the salt content of the average of oceans in the world, which when released into the ocean raises salinity and can affect the marine environment. Desalination projects located along the coastline discharge their effluent to the marine ecosystems, raising the salinity of the water. To ensure that this highly concentrated brine does not disrupt natural ecosystems there have been some recent developments to install diffuser systems that will control dilution of brine with sea water and reduce the impact area. Continuous monitoring of the membrane of desalination infrastructure and of fauna and flora in marine ecosystems are called for to avoid environmental catastrophes (GWP, 2012). A way forward would consist of strengthening the institutional, legal and regulatory framework that governs desalination infrastructure, in particular in three areas:

- **Environmental impact assessments and permits**: this area seems ideally suited to meeting the challenges of developing desalination in Chile. Desalination projects must undergo environmental impact assessments conducted by the Environmental Evaluation Service (Servicio de Evaluación Ambiental, SEA). Only after this body grants its approval can the desalination plants be executed. Given the plans to develop more desalination projects in Chile, there might be a need to expand the scope of the environmental impact assessments to also take into account the expected aggregated effects if several projects are undergoing the impact assessment at the same time. The Ministry of National Defense is in charge of monitoring, regulating and supervising the coastline and territorial sea of Chile. It is therefore the competence of this ministry to grant the necessary permits (duration of 50 years) to use any land within its jurisdiction.

- **National policy and private investment**: the development of desalination projects has responded to the necessities of private users rather than to a co-ordinated strategy by the Chilean government. Thus, there is currently no coherent land use planning strategy for Chile's northern coastline to develop these projects. There is also no co-ordinated approach to managing trade-offs among water users in the north of Chile, with desalination as part of a response. A coherent national policy could set the guidelines in this area.
- **Legal status of desalinated water**: the Water Code only regulates land water resources, and not water resources resulting from seawater treatment. Although, seawater is considered a public good in Chile, there is neither a regulation nor a regulatory authority that oversees the management and use of the water resulting from desalination processes (iAgua, 2015). Thus, there is no clear framework that sets rules and holds investors and public authorities accountable. Key questions then arise on the nature and scope of the entitlements that mining companies or water service providers use to desalinate sea water, on whether desalinated water used to recharge aquifers or lakes can be considered as land water resources, and as to whether the desalinating plant or the public authorities will be held accountable if there is a breach (Rojas and Delpiano, 2015).

Irrigation and water storage infrastructure

Agriculture is the main water user in Chile, as most countries worldwide. In 2013, Chile withdrew 1159 m^3/capita of freshwater overall, which is second highest in the OECD, below only Estonia (Figure 5.29). Chile aims to be one of the leading countries in exports of agricultural products and is the OECD country with the highest share of water dedicated to agriculture (82%). Only Turkey (81%) and Mexico (73%) come close to this level (Figure 5.28). This fact is explained by Chile's economic structure and the importance of its water-intensive sectors, particularly agriculture, is reflected in the shares of water allocation by use. There are plans to expand the agricultural frontier by an additional 300 000 ha, which will raise a range of issues, posing significant challenges for water resources management prompting calls for irrigation efficiency.

Chile's agricultural sector has been an integral part of the country's development in the last 25 years, and it is based on a subsidised irrigation infrastructure policy. Figure 5.31 shows that between 1990 and 2012, Chile's irrigated area increased by over 65%, with over a 20% increase just since the year 2000. Chile's irrigation infrastructure development has been based on subsidies for the private sector with a view to increasing the irrigated surface. In 1985, Law 18 450 on the Promotion of Private Investment in Drainage and Irrigation Works laid the groundwork for a new irrigation policy through subsidising the cost of new equipment to increase expand irrigation. In 1990, the law was modified to also include irrigation infrastructure in the subsidy scheme (up to 75% of the infrastructure cost was eligible to be subsidised). The three main guidelines of the modified law were the Large Irrigation Works Programme, the Medium-sized Irrigation Works Programme and the Small-scale Irrigation Works Programme. The first two focused on the promotion of dams and major channels, while the latter targeted the promotion of distribution systems. Almost all efforts between 1990 and 1999 were focused on increasing water security. They included improvements in water availability for an area of 12 000 ha thanks to the Santa Juana dam, and an increase in irrigated surface by 11 200 ha with the construction of the Pencahue channel (FAO, 2015).

Figure 5.28. Freshwater abstractions by major primary uses in selected OECD countries, 2013 or latest available data

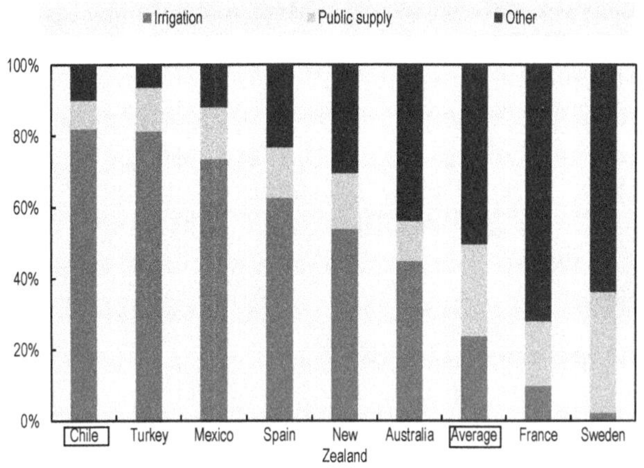

Source: Ministry of Public Works (2016c), Official statistics provided in the OECD Questionnaire Data Request on Water in Chile for this report: "Review of the Gaps, Standards and Governance of Public Infrastructure in Chile"; OECD (2016), OECD Environment Statistics (database) Freshwater abstractions, https://stats.oecd.org/ (accessed September 2016).

Figure 5.29. Freshwater abstraction per capita in selected OECD countries, 2013 or latest available data

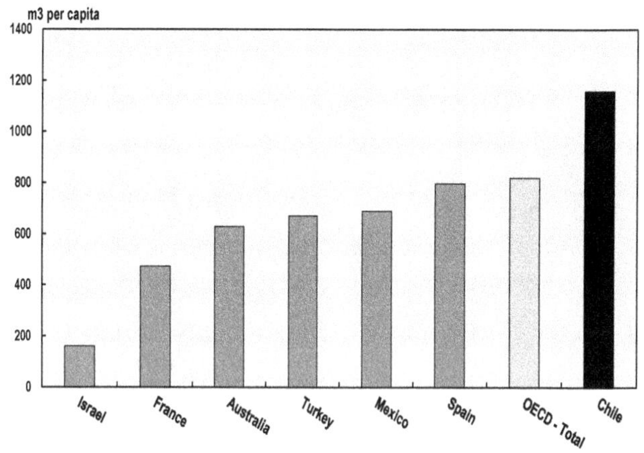

Source: Ministry of Public Works (2016c), Official statistics provided in the OECD Questionnaire Data Request on Water in Chile for this report: "Review of the Gaps, Standards and Governance of Public Infrastructure in Chile"; OECD (2016), OECD Environment Statistics (database) Freshwater abstractions, https://stats.oecd.org/ (accessed September 2016).

Figure 5.30. Percentage of irrigated area as arable land in selected OECD countries, 2012

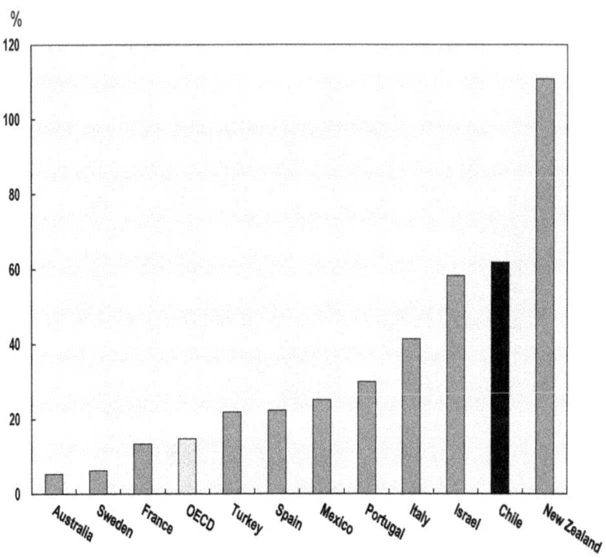

Source: Ministry of Public Works (2016c), Official statistics provided in the OECD Questionnaire Data Request on Water in Chile for this report: "Review of the Gaps, Standards and Governance of Public Infrastructure in Chile"; OECD (2017), Environmental Performance of Agriculture (Edition 2013), OECD Agriculture Statistics (database). http://dx.doi.org/10.1787/data-00660-en (accessed April 2017).

Figure 5.31. Change in irrigated area as a percentage of arable land in selected OECD countries

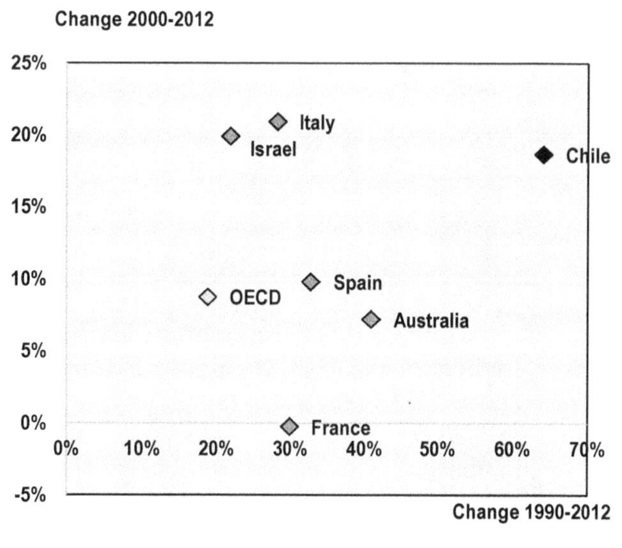

Source: Ministry of Public Works (2016c), Official statistics provided in the OECD Questionnaire Data Request on Water in Chile for this report: "Review of the Gaps, Standards and Governance of Public Infrastructure in Chile"; OECD (2017), Environmental Performance of Agriculture (Edition 2013), OECD Agriculture Statistics (database). http://dx.doi.org/10.1787/data-00660-en (accessed April 2017).

The Law on the Promotion of Private Investment in Drainage and Irrigation Works (passed in 1985) remains the instrument supporting private endeavours in Chile. The main objectives of the law are to: i) increase irrigated surface; ii) improve water supply in irrigated areas suffering water stress; iii) improve quality and efficiency in the use of water; iv) recover irrigated areas in bad conditions. The consensus around this strategy is clear, and it has been renewed until 2022, with an allocation of USD 85 million. One of the main impacts since 1997 has been the increase in the coverage of new irrigation techniques from 90 000 ha in that year to 300 000 ha in 2007 (FAO, 2015). The National Irrigation Commission (CNR) organises a public tender every year to assign subsidies to irrigation infrastructure projects (Box 5.19). The DOH, under MOP, is responsible for monitoring the execution of the works and ensuring that quality and technical requirements are met.

Box 5.20. National Irrigation Commission (CNR)

The National Commission of Irrigation was created in 1975 to increase and improve the country's irrigated area. The CNR is run by a council of ministers councils headed by the Minister of Agriculture, and rounded out by representatives of the ministries of Economy, Finance, Public Works and Social Development. The CNR's main functions include:

- contributing to the design of the national irrigation policy
- oversee and control the investment of funding included in the national budget items which are planned to be invested in irrigation works
- improving the efficiency of irrigation processes through development and productive transformation projects
- focusing on the development of remote areas of the country and producers in a disadvantaged position
- promoting private investment in irrigation infrastructure by optimising investments and allocating subsidies for irrigation and drainage
- evaluating the technical and economic feasibility of investments in irrigation infrastructure in the country's river basins
- administering the application of Law 18450 on the Promotion of Private Investment in Drainage and Irrigation Works, ever since the passage of the law in 1985.

Source: CNR (2016), "Historia: Comisión Nacional de Riego", www.cnr.gob.cl/Conozcanos/Paginas/Historia.aspx (accessed November 2016).

Chile's rate of freshwater abstraction per hectare of irrigated land is among the highest in the OECD (Figure 5.32). Chile abstracts 12 761 m^3/ha/year, which is well above OECD average (6 821 m^3/ha/year), and second only to Japan, with 21 450 m^3/ha/year. Other countries such as Mexico (9 450 m^3/ha/year), Turkey (7 790 m3/ha/year), Spain (6 150 m^3/ha/year), New Zealand (4 120 m^3/ha/year) or Australia (2 480 m^3/ha/year) withdraw less freshwater per hectare while also allocating large shares of their water resources to agriculture (Figure 5.32). These figures depend on the meteorological effect (i.e. irrigation water abstractions can be complementary to net precipitation in the country), the water resource effect (i.e. farmers can change their irrigation patterns depending on the seasonal availability of water resources), and the composition effect (i.e. relative shares of agricultural activities or crops grown), and the efficiency of water resources use (i.e. upgrade of irrigation systems or better weather information systems) (OECD, forthcoming 2017a). With regards to efficiency, Law 18450 contributed to the improvement of irrigation efficiency in Chile, but the country is still lagging behind other countries such as Italy, Brazil and France, which have managed to develop more modern irrigation systems in their agricultural sectors (Figure 5.33). Specifically, in contrast to modern techniques such as pressurised irrigation, traditional surface irrigation technique still dominates most of Chile's hectares (72.29%).

Improving the irrigation system's efficiency should be a priority, particularly in the Central Macro-Zone where most agricultural activities are concentrated. The share of irrigated land in the Central Macro-Zone plus region VIII (Biobio) adds up to over 89% of the total irrigated land in the country. A distinction should be made when analysing irrigation techniques in Chile, as the climatological conditions of the areas where the irrigated land is located vary significantly from north to south. For example, in region IV (Coquimbo) water availability is around 35.9 m^3/s, and in region VII (Biobio) this number is around 767 m^3/s (see Figure 5.7). Traditional irrigation techniques still dominate irrigation in this area. Figure 5.33 shows that only in region V (Valparaiso) is the share of hectares irrigated with new irrigation techniques larger than the share of traditional irrigation (58% vs. 42%), while in region IV (Coquimbo) the totals are about the same (51% versus 49%). It is likely that intense competition for water resources in regions IV (Coquimbo) and V (Valparaiso) has driven the agricultural sector to be more efficient. Nevertheless, there is still room to promote more efficient practices in regions with large shares of irrigated land, particularly in Santiago Metropolitan Region (RM) (34% hectares with new irrigation techniques and 12.5% of total irrigated land) and in the region of O'Higgins (VI) (28% of hectares with new irrigation techniques and 19.2% of total irrigated land). If subsidies are set to promote efficiency, these must be combined with soft measures (irrigation and watershed conservation plans) in order to prevent farmers to switch to water-intensive crops or expand irrigated areas that could lead to an increase in the overall consumption of water.

Figure 5.32. Abstractions per area of irrigated land in selected OECD countries, 2013 or latest data

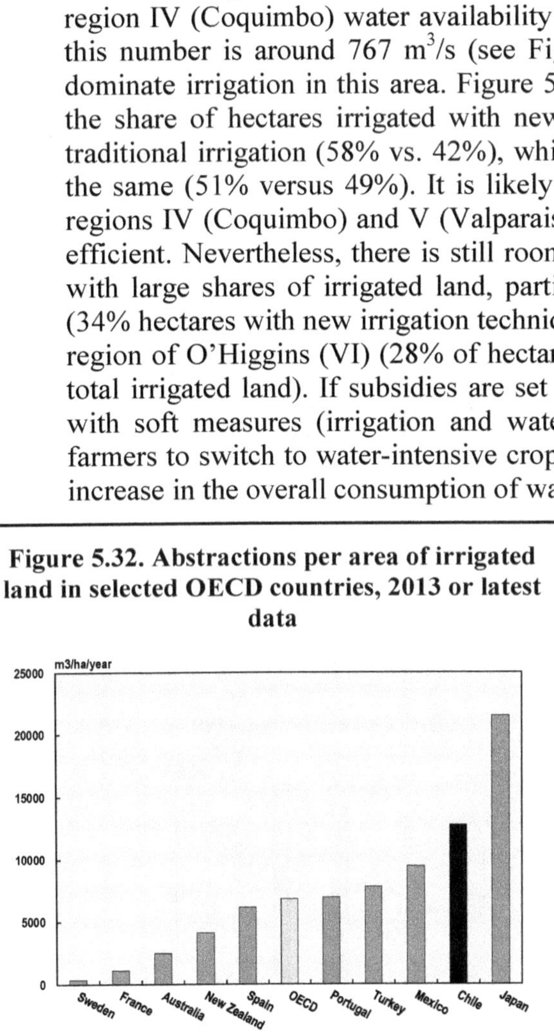

Source: Ministry of Public Works (2016c), Official statistics provided in the OECD Questionnaire Data Request on Water in Chile for this report: "Review of the Gaps, Standards and Governance of Public Infrastructure in Chile"; OECD (2017), Environmental Performance of Agriculture (Edition 2013), OECD Agriculture Statistics (database). http://dx.doi.org/10.1787/data-00660-en (accessed April 2017).

Figure 5.33. Irrigation systems in selected OECD and non-OECD countries, 2007 or latest data

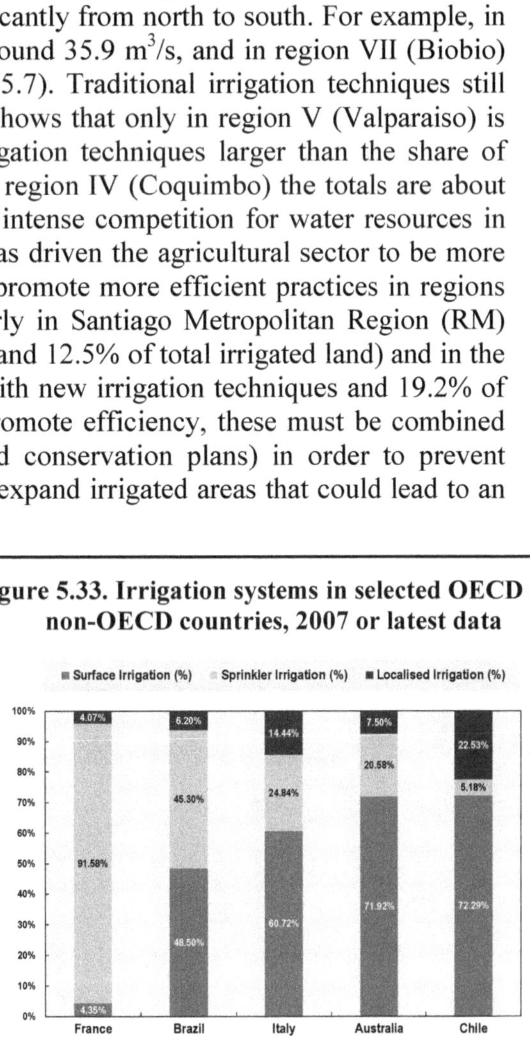

Note: Italy, Chile and France data dates back to 2007, Brazil and Australia to 2010

Source: FAO (2016), Aquastat: Irrigation and drainage database, www.fao.org/nr/water/aquastat/irrigationdrainage/index.stm.

Water resources infrastructure is complex to quantify and assess. While dams or groundwater pumping stations can be inventoried, such a stock-taking does not provide evidence that such infrastructure can meet water demands in the agricultural or mining sectors. Another way of quantifying irrigation infrastructure can be to count the current kilometres of channels. However, a country can have a large number of dams for water storage, which may not work if not designed adequately to fit the water availability and demand (e.g. oversized dams) or not managed and operated effectively. For instance, large empty dams suffer from cracks and fissures, as the structural design considers certain levels of water height calculated under specific hydrological scenarios. This can result in costly investments in maintenance and operation. On the contrary, if irrigation systems have canals with craks these can in fact be an important vector of groundwater recharge, so moving to better infrastructure can reduce recharge and contribute to further depletion of groundwater. Thus, each infrastructure assets needs to be carefully assessed against the territorial specificities of its location.

In the face of climate, economic and urban trends, some infrastructure could contribute to better water supply management for irrigation. Selected dams and aqueducts could contribute to keeping up the level of current water consumption and to an extent to meeting increasing demand. Investments under consideration include pumping infrastructure for groundwater sources, building and upgrading channels and improving irrigation systems, and developing in the medium-term small-scale desalination plants and dams to supply drinking water (*Plan de Embalses Pequeños*). The Plan Chile 30/30 should combine these investments with softer and less capital intensive measures, i.e. wastewater reuse from cities or better groundwater management. For instance, in the Southwest United States, under a similar agro-ecological and climatic conditions as in North and Central Chile, an OECD study that look in-depth on water risks for agriculture called for a combined set of measures: i) increasing efficiency in agriculture and urban water management; ii) more refined groundwater management; iii) investment in water banks and recycled wastewater systems; and, iv) well-defined water transfers (Cooley H. et al., 2016).

Figure 5.34. Irrigation systems in Chilean regions

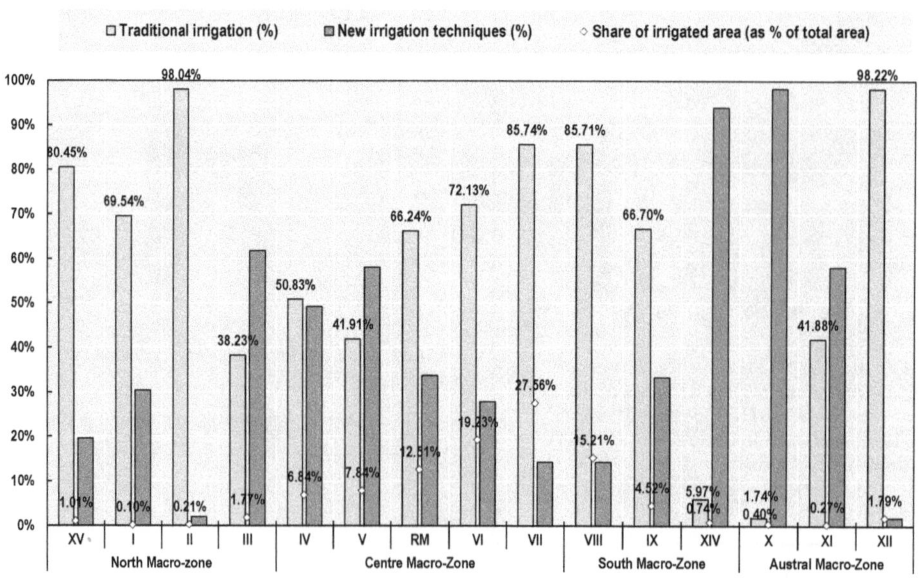

Source: INE (2007), "Censo Agropecuario 2007", Instituto Nacional de Estadísticas de Chile, www.ine.cl/canales/chile_estadistico/censos_agropecuarios/censo_agropecuario_07.php.

Strategic thinking about the type of infrastructure that would be the best fit for Chile's future is essential to making the most of policy complementarities. Multipurpose reservoirs are designed and/or operated to serve complementary purposes such as hydropower generation, flood control, water supply, ecosystem services, and irrigation. They are increasingly being used in OECD and non-OECD countries (Box 5.20). This type of infrastructure interconnects related sectors in a long-term and integrated way and strives to share costs and benefits across users efficiently. Successful stories of multipurpose dams bringing together energy and irrigation already exist in Chile (e.g. the Ancoa Reservoir). As Chile is looking to develop hydropower, multi-purpose reservoirs can have other uses besides irrigation.

Stakeholder engagement in infrastructure-related choices and decisions is critical to preventing social conflicts and building the needed social acceptance. In recent years, many large infrastructure projects, in Chile particularly hydroelectric ones, have faced severe conflicts and attracted a considerable amount of public resistance (e.g. HidroAysen, Barrancones). These deadlocks have contributed to a strategic shift towards increased investment in coal power plants, which are easier to realise given the lower rate of hydroelectricity as compared to the 1980s. Large infrastructure projects involve a wide range of private and non-profit actors. The corporate sector plays an important role in building, operating and maintaining these infrastructures, with several companies involved, such as ENDESA, AES Gener, Colbún S.A., Suez Energy Andino, E.E. Guacolda and Pacific Hydro. National and local NGOs act as watchdogs and have gained socio-political capital. However, some categories of stakeholders often get omitted and remain under-represented, such as urban and rural communities whose lives and activities are often the most affected by energy projects. Indigenous peoples are also seldom recognised in energy-related policy decisions at local and national levels, and they often lack the institutional structures and capacities to promote their interests outside their communities.

Box 5.21. Examples of multipurpose reservoirs in OECD and non-OECD countries

Multipurpose reservoirs and risks of too much and too little water

Wivenhoe Dam in Brisbane, Australia. Over the last 40 years, the city of Brisbane has experienced significant problems with both drought and flooding. After severe floods in 1974, the Wivenhoe dam was built to reduce the impacts of future floods and to store water during times of scarcity. The dam was designed to meet the region's drinking water supply with an additional 125% excess capacity to also cope with flood prevention. The design of the dam creates risk-risk trade-offs, i.e. the more water is stored the lesser chance of water scarcity, however, there is less capacity to capture flood water.

In 2008, during a drought period, the water level fell to around 17% and the dam operating rules focused on managing water scarcity. After several months of intense rains in 2010 the water level rose, which led to significant flooding throughout the city and surrounding area. While the dam reduced the impact of the floods, the operational rules resulted in water being stored when it could have been released earlier. Earlier release would have reduced the impact of the flooding and helped mitigate property damages worth about AUD 0.5 billion. The experience of Brisbane highlights the complex trade-offs that are present in flood management schemes.

Multipurpose reservoir: hydropower, irrigation, fisheries and recreation.

Arthurs Lake is a very good example of multipurpose water uses of reservoirs in **Tasmania, Australia**. The multiple purposes that Arthurs Lake can deliver are hydropower, recreation, a fishery and irrigation. Irrigation is a new purpose, after approval of the Midlands Water Scheme in August 2014. Farm Water Access Plans are in place and ensure the environmental sustainability of the scheme. Water price and supply in the irrigation district are underpinned by a water supply agreement between Tasmanian Irrigation and Hydro Tasmania. The agreement recognises that water taken from Arthurs Lake would have otherwise been used to generate electricity at Hydro Tasmania's Poatina and Trevallyn Power Stations, and considering

Box 5.21. Examples of multipurpose reservoirs in OECD and non-OECD countries (*cont.*)

the economic and financial benefits (and costs) was a key step to change the storage operating rules. With respect to accommodating irrigation needs, Hydro Tasmania evaluated the implications on electricity generation and associated revenues and developed a water pricing instrument to consider water sharing among users.

Lake Arenal Rica, Costa Rica. The wetland provides benefits related to several uses: hydropower generation, irrigation, tourism and fishing. Arenal Lake was declared a Ramsar site on 16 March 2000. The concerns about the lake, including the stability of its watershed, problems of deforestation and possible premature sedimentation, led the Government to create the Lake Arenal Watershed Management and Development Plan in 1996, and a was created Commission to implement the plan in 1997. The Commission offers a platform for dialogue involving all the interested parties and institutions. The environmental outcomes have been mixed, i.e. negative from disruptions caused by construction of the dam and irrigation project, and positive efforts to protect the forests and introduce a sustainable development approach to the management of the lake.

Source: OECD (2013b), *Water Security for Better Lives*, OECD Publishing, Paris, http://dx.doi.org/10.1787/9789264202405-en; EDF/WWC (2014), Multipurpose Water Uses of Hydropower Reservoirs, "Sharing the water uses of multipurpose hydropower reservoirs: the SHARE concept", https://www.hydropower.org/sites/default/files/publications-docs/Multi-purpose%20water%20uses%20of%20hydropower%20reservoirs.pdf.

Early engagement of all those who have a stake in the outcome, may be directly or indirectly affected, and/or have the ability to influence the outcome positively or negatively is critical to these projects. The parties involved raise awareness, share information, identify hotspots and take collective action, including through compensation measures to mitigate unintended consequences. This is particularly relevant as a recent survey the Ministry of Energy, for instance, conducted as part of the development of its Energy Policy 2050 revealed that communities would not reject the construction of renewable energy technology, provided it complies with international environmental standards (Ministry of Energy, 2015). 97% of survey respondents indicated a willingness to support the construction of wind or solar power plants in their communities or in nearby communities, if they complied with the strict environmental and social requirements applied in developed countries and the offered concrete benefits. 90% of respondents concurred when asked about tidal power plants, 71% for geothermal power plants, and 57% and 56% for hydroelectric power plants using reservoirs and for run-of-river hydroelectric power plants, respectively (Ministry of Energy, 2015).

Conclusions and policy recommendations

Current and future climate, urban, population and economic trends are putting pressure on Chile's water resources, especially for the water-intensive sectors that are also sources of productivity, mining and agriculture. The energy policy aimed at increasing the share of renewable sources in Chile's energy matrix, particularly through the promotion of hydropower, is a compounding factor, especially as droughts become more frequent, with lower levels of reservoirs having a negative effect in hydroelectricity production.

Additional investments in hard, physical infrastructure will undoubtedly be needed to solve some of the country's water challenges. Urban water pipes are ageing and leaking and need to be upgraded, properly operated and maintained. Sparsely populated areas and settlements need to be equipped with rural water and sanitation infrastructure. Rainwater infrastructure is currently insufficient and results in costly damages when floods occur. The efficiency of irrigation systems needs to be improved. In some cases, multipurpose infrastructure can combine several of the above needs. A critical way forward is to consider policy complementarities to make the most of these large sunk costs, which can be recovered only over the long run and generate liabilities for future generations.

Coupling the development of grey infrastructure in cities (e.g. tertiary treatment in wastewater plants) with natural infrastructure (ecosystem services) can make investments more cost-efficient by reducing treatment requirements. In turn, this will offer benefits including contributing to a reduction in electricity consumption and the use of chemicals. Promoting green infrastructure in cities through rainwater harvesting systems will also contribute to limiting the need for grey infrastructure. Localised rainwater systems reduce peak flows in times of urban flooding and contribute to better water quality because rainwater is quickly disposed of from street pavements. As such, this makes rainwater systems more resilient and cities have to resort less to wastewater treatment.

In addition to investment in hard infrastructure, Chile will need to strengthen its institutional framework for water management to overcome fragmentation, scale and policy coherence challenges. While important steps have been taken with the ongoing reform of the Water Code (pending discussion and approval in the Senate), the recent attempts to foster coordination across water-related policies and raise the profile of water on the national agenda through the Presidential Delegate for Water Resources and the Committee of Water Ministers have proven insufficient to meet their intended goals. In addition, the lack of a sound basin governance system allowing for a functional approach to water management, and the inconsistencies across agriculture, land use, energy, mining and water policies, are both important challenges Chile must address for to ready itself for the future. The country must put in place a territorial approach to water planning and management. Further action needs to be taken to better coordinate actions across public, private and non-profit sectors, to engage all levels of government in water-related decisions, to manage trade-offs across users, to regulate grey areas such as desalination expansion, and to engage stakeholders for greater acceptance of infrastructure and policy choices.

What follows is a set of recommendations for water to drive Chile's future economic development and well-being. This will require a focus on a combination of policy responses, addressing water infrastructure gaps, not only in quantity, but also, and most importantly, in type. It will also mean improving water governance practices for infrastructure to deliver the intended outcomes.

A) Raise the profile of water management on Chile's national political agenda for water to contribute to sustainable growth and development.

1. **Design and implement a consensus-based national water resources policy that involves sound consultation across water-related ministries and public agencies, between levels of government, and with the private sector and society at large.** Chile's specific institutional framework based on water markets and the resulting atomisation of water rights should not stand in the way of the design and implementation of a solid national framework for water resources management, with clear guidelines, priorities and strategies for water to drive economic, social and environmental outcomes. Previous attempts at doing so, including the document "National Water Resources Policy" developed by the Presidential Delegate under the Ministry of Interior, can provide food for thought and a baseline. Such a national policy would help foster co-ordination of

otherwise fragmented actors and provide a framework for aligning objectives across sectors.

2. **Use the ongoing process to reform the Water Code as a good opportunity to engage stakeholders in the development of a country-wide strategy for water.** Building on the 2005 water code reform, which established requirements for ecological flows, the reform that started in 2011 has the potential to open a wider debate on how to place water as a key factor for national development and facilitate public action in managing water risks in Chile.

3. **Consider incentives to foster effective basin governance to reconcile administrative and hydrological boundaries.** Chile has a number of specificities in terms of climate variability (combining deserts and numerous glaciers), small-scale hydrographic basins formed by the 1 251 rivers flowing from the mountains to coast, and the special morphology that influences the river paths, creating a water system that is complex to manage. In this context, water users' organisations are critical players in the management of water resources, as long as these associations operate at the appropriate scale and are endowed with the needed prerogatives and resources to play fully their role. Chile could push forward a basin governance framework tailored to the territorial specificities of each basin. Raising awareness on the benefits of managing water resources at the basin level could be done through promoting the value of ecosystem services, for instance.

4. **Strengthen water information systems and use them to guide planning and decision making.** Improved information access, quality and disclosure across levels of government is a prerequisite for better water policy decision making, monitoring and evaluation. A common frame of reference should be set across institutions to foster data gathering on social, economic and environmental trends, in line with international standards and OECD best practice. Chile should also strengthen data collection on basic indicators such as abstraction rate by use and household consumption rate for rural drinking water. There is also little data online in a workable format, and time series tend to be limited. Another way forward is to address inconsistencies between official sources of data and those produced by the private sector and ensure that water-related data and information effectively guide decision making.

B) Invest in the right infrastructure mix, both in quantity and type, while favouring a tailored approach according to water management functions, and place-based needs and opportunities.

Urban Water Supply and Sanitation Services

1. **Develop a strategy and catalyse needed finance to upgrade, renew and maintain drinking water supply and sanitation infrastructure.** Engagement with utilities and end users will be needed to clarify who pays for what over the short, medium and long-term.

2. **Enhance efforts to transition from water supply to water demand management, especially in cities, to better manage risks.** This can rely on a combination of hard and soft measures, such as exploring possibilities to reuse rainwater and greywater, with the precondition that quality standards are put in

place to avoid health-related issues; enhancing public education on water conservation through awareness campaigns; and promoting the use of water saving devices (e.g. use of seawater for toilet flushing).

Rural Water Supply and Sanitation Services

1. **Consider further alternatives to large-scale centralised systems in semi-concentrated and disperse agglomerations**. OECD countries' experience in rural access to water and sanitation services indicate that localised systems can perform as well as centrally piped infrastructures. This applies both to drinking water supply systems and sanitation services.
2. **Strengthen the implementation of the APR programme to meet the challenges of delivering services to semi-concentrated and disperse populations,** building on three sets of actions:

- Improve strategic planning and tailor investments in the APR Programme to take into account specific type of infrastructure needs of the new target population living in semi-concentrated and disperse agglomerations.
- Revise the social evaluation methodology for Chile to face the renewed challenges of the APR Programme. For instance, complementing the cost-benefit analysis with a multi-criteria analysis framework that can be used to accommodate more long-term goals, strategic issues, and improve alignment with broader policy priorities.
- Enhance technical, managerial and financial skills and capacities in APR committees and cooperatives, both to ensure that existing systems do not age at a faster pace than initially planned and to improve the efficiency of new systems.

3. **The DOH should conduct regular monitoring of the APR Programme to anticipate supply cuts and costly future investments due to infrastructure replacements, and it should coordinate with Regional Councils (CORE) to establish investment priorities.** Closer cooperation between MOP (DOH) and CORE will then be instrumental in identifying dysfunctional rural water systems and prioritising investments according to the most pressing needs.

Rainwater infrastructure

1. **Promote lower cost alternatives such as urban green infrastructure,** for example by employing "source control" technologies that handle rainwater near the point of generation, green roofs or pervious surfaces that capture rainwater before it runs onto polluted pavements and streets.
2. **Develop local or metropolitan strategies in Chile's large urban centres (Santiago, Valparaíso, Concepción) to foster resilience and adaptive capacity of water systems in the face of climate, economic and urban trends.**

- This can be achieved through engagement with relevant stakeholders and working to boost rainwater harvesting, set incentives to better co-ordinate water and land use policies and raise awareness of the current levels of water risks and the shared responsibility to manage them.

Desalination

While desalination can generate a large amount of available resources, its impacts on the environment can be high, and its operation costs are driven by high energy consumption. In that sense, desalination should not preclude the country from making the most of water demand management instruments and the low-cost options explored in the chapter. Should Chile pursue the desalination avenue, several actions should be considered:

1. **Strengthen the institutional, legal and regulatory framework for desalination to contribute to a coherent strategy that respects the environment.**

   - Develop a national policy on desalination that sets planning guidelines to ensure private investment is done right. Due to the cross-sectoral nature of desalination projects, such a strategy should not only be developed in conjunction with mining companies and water utilities, but also include the energy and agricultural sector, as well as environmental NGOs.
   - As the environmental threats of desalination are well-documented, it is important to put in place clear, transparent and proportionate enforcement rules, procedures, incentives and tools (including rewards and penalties) to promote compliance.

2. **Future investments in desalination need to be carefully evaluated through sound feasibility studies that take into account initial capital investments as well as uncertainties in operating costs (related to energy prices) throughout the life cycle of the project.** Chile's energy shortfall and the effects of climate change require a process of reflection as to how energy will be delivered to desalination plants and what it will cost. Two concrete actions will help deal with energy constraints:

   - Encourage the use of renewable energy sources (wind, photovoltaic, solar and concentrated solar thermal energy) for small desalination plants at isolated sites, particularly in the North Macro-Zone, where the potential for solar renewable energy is high.
   - Drive innovation in cities that can help mitigate energy shortages, and make this energy available for other purposes. Electricity is a heavy feature of the annual budget of water utilities, due to operations such as pumping from withdrawal and to treatment plants, which are often outside populated areas.

3. **Closely monitor and evaluate the impacts of desalination projects on the local environment to ensure sustainability in the medium and long term.** Ensure that the highly concentrated brine does not disrupt natural ecosystems by installing cutting-edge technologies and reducing impact area. Continuous monitoring of fauna and flora in marine ecosystems is also needed to avoid environmental catastrophes.

Irrigation and water storage infrastructure

Selected dams and aqueducts could contribute to maintaining the level of current water consumption and to an extent to dealing with increasing demand.

1. Irrigation systems could be upgraded in Central Chile, where most of the water allocated to agriculture is used, but demand management should also be boosted in parallel to make the most of available resources and foster water use efficiency. International benchmarks show that Chile is below OECD countries in terms of irrigation efficiency (it is the country with the 2nd highest water abstraction per irrigated area, and above 70% of irrigation infrastructure still relies on traditional techniques). However, this upgrade should be done on a case-by-case basis, as efficiency in irrigation is also associated with lower recharge of aquifers.

2. Engage stakeholders in infrastructure-related choice and decisions, and strive to share costs and benefits across users in an efficient way. In a context, as Chile is looking to further develop hydroelectricity generation and expand its irrigation frontier, multi-purpose reservoirs offer opportunities to combine other benefits with irrigation. The Chilean government has an important role to play in establishing an institutional environment that encourages exchange and more bottom-up decision making to build social and political acceptance, mitigate conflicts, and empower communities and subnational governments in order for all parts of Chilean society to benefit from infrastructure projects.

Table 5.4. Water Governance and Infrastructure gaps and responses

Place water governance high in Chile's agenda for long-term sustainable development		
Theme	Gaps	Recommendations
Water governance	• Chile's central government is characterised by high degree of compartmentalisation. Sectoral ministries work in insulated silos, with limited mechanisms for ensuring alignment and integration across policy areas and investments. The lack of horizontal co-ordination is particularly challenging in water management as where many decisions taken in other policy domains (e.g. land use, energy, agriculture, industry) generate water risks and vice-versa. • A striking feature of the Chilean water management model is the absence of integrated basin governance systems that can provide the baseline for a functional and territorial approach to water risks. • Chile has made important efforts to produce the Water Atlas, which provides an overall picture of the stock of water resources but, overall, data and information gaps on water resources management and planning hinder decision-making.	• Establish a consensus-based National Water Resources Policy that involves sound consultation across water-related ministries and public agencies, between levels of government, and with the private sector and society at large. • Use the ongoing process to reform the Water Code as an opportunity to engage stakeholders in the development of a country-wide strategy for water resources management. • Consider incentives to foster effective basin governance that can help reconcile administrative and hydrological boundaries. There is room for building on the experience of the Territorial Roundtables and strong water users organisations already in place as well as lessons learned from past attempts. • Strengthen water information systems and use them to guide planning and decision-making. Improved access, quality and disclosure of information across levels of government is a prerequisite for better decision making, monitoring and evaluation in water policy.

Table 5.4. Water Governance and Infrastructure gaps and responses (*cont.*)

Choosing the right water infrastructure, both in quantity and type. Water infrastructure is heterogeneous and requires different approaches		
Theme	Gaps	Recommendations
Urban Water Supply and Sanitation Services	• Chile's challenges in urban water supply and sanitation relate to infrastructure upgrade and renewal needed to sustain current levels of service delivery and water safety. Water losses in Chilean major cities are higher than in most peer cities, and wastewater treatment is not as high-quality as in other high-level income OECD countries.	• Develop a strategy and catalyse needed finance to upgrade, renew and maintain drinking water supply and sanitation infrastructure. Engagement with utilities and end-users will be needed to clarify who pays for what over the short, medium and long-term. • Enhance efforts to transition from water supply to water demand management, especially in cities, to better manage risks now and in the future.
Rural Water Supply and Sanitation Services	• The renewed challenge in the APR programme is to secure access for population living in semi-concentrated and disperse area. In 2015, the Chilean government reported that while concentrated rural communities have overall access to drinking water, sparsely populated areas still struggle to access basic water services. • Insufficient data and information hinders the efficiency of investments in the APR Programme. There is currently a lack of systematic and comprehensive monitoring of the results achieved by the APR	• Consider further alternatives to large-scale centralised systems in semi-concentrated and disperse agglomerations. OECD countries' experience in rural access to water and sanitation services indicate that localised systems can perform as centrally piped infrastructures • Strengthen the implementation of the APR programme by: i) improving strategic planning; ii) revising the social evaluation methodology; iii) enhance technical, managerial and financial skills and capacities in committees and cooperatives. • Conduct regular monitoring of the APR Programme to anticipate supply cuts, and costly investments due to infrastructure replacements, and coordinate with Regional Councils (CORE) to establish investment priorities
Rainwater infrastructure operation and maintenance and expanding the network	• Rainwater infrastructure exists in Chile's main cities, such as Valparaíso, Concepción or Santiago, but it is not effectively functioning against heavy rain episodes • Medium-size growing cities must consider further developing and maintaining rainwater infrastructure to be fit for the future	• Promote lower cost alternatives such as urban green infrastructure resorting for instance to "source control" technologies green roofs or pervious surfaces. • Develop local or metropolitan strategies in Chile's large urban centres (Santiago, Valparaíso, Concepción) to foster resilience and adaptive capacity of water systems in the face of climate, economic, and urban trends.
Desalination projects	• There is no current land use planning strategy of the Chile's northern coastline to coherently develop desalination projects. • There is no co-ordinated approach to manage trade-offs across water users in the north of Chile, with desalination as part of a response • There is no clear legal framework that sets rules and holds investors and public authorities accountable. The Water Code only regulates land water resources and not water resources resulting from sea water treatment. There is neither a regulation nor a regulatory authority that oversees the management and use of the resulting water from desalination processes. • Energy shortfalls in Chile and climate change require thinking of how and at which cost energy will be delivered for desalination plants. Desalination requires large amounts of energy and as a result, it can be a costly option depending on energy prices.	• Strengthen the institutional, legal and regulatory framework for desalination to contribute to a coherent strategy that respects the environment. Actions include: i) developing a national policy on desalination that sets planning guidelines to ensure private investment is done right; and, ii) setting clear, transparent and proportionate enforcement rules, procedures, incentives and tools (including rewards and penalties) to promote compliance • Future investments in desalination need to be carefully evaluated through long-term sound feasibility studies, which take into account initial capital investments as well as uncertainties related to energy prices in operating costs during the life-cycle of the project • Closely monitor and evaluate the impact of desalination projects on the local environment to ensure sustainability in the medium and long term. Ensure that the highly concentrated brine does not disrupt natural ecosystems by installing cutting-edge technologies and reducing impact area. Continuously monitor fauna and flora in marine ecosystems to avoid environmental catastrophes.

Table 5.4. Water Governance and Infrastructure gaps and responses (*cont.*)

Choosing the right water infrastructure, both in quantity and type. Water infrastructure is heterogeneous and requires different approaches		
Theme	Gaps	Recommendations
Irrigation and water resources infrastructure	• Chile's rate of freshwater abstraction per hectare of irrigated land is among the highest in the OECD region. Although the Law 18450 contributed to the improvement of irrigation efficiency in Chile, it is still lagging behind other countries such as Italy, Brazil, or France. • In the face of climate, economic and urban trends, some infrastructure could contribute to better water supply management for irrigation. Selected dams and aqueducts could contribute to keep up the level of current water consumption and deal, to some extent, with increasing demand.	• Irrigation systems could be upgraded in Central Chile, where most of the water allocated to agriculture is used, but demand management should also be boosted in parallel to make the most of available resources and foster water use efficiency. This upgrade should be done on a case-by-case basis, as efficiency in irrigation is also associated to lower recharge of aquifers • Engage stakeholders in multipurpose infrastructure choice and decisions to and strive to share costs and benefits across users in an efficient way. The Chilean government has an important role to play in establishing an institutional environment that encourages exchange and more bottom-up decision-making.

Notes

1. The MOP has grouped Chile's 15 regions into four macro-zones according to their similarities in terms of territorial specificities, such as productive structure, climate conditions and demographic development. They are: i) North (XV, I, II, III); ii) Central (IV, V, RM, VI, VII), iii) South (VIII, IX, XIV); and, iv) Austral (X, XI, XII).

2 The study COCHILCO (2009) "Proyección consumo de agua en la minería del cobre 2009-2020" is the most updated source for future mining water demand. The MOP reports that the data could be outdated due to changes in copper prices, but the Ministry has no other available information or data source.

3. For details, see OECD (2012) "Redefining "urban": A new way to measure metropolitan areas," OECD Publishing, Paris.

4. Small urban areas are those with a population of less than 200 000 people; medium-sized urban areas are those with a population of between 200 000 and 500 000; metropolitan areas are those with a population of between 500 000 and 1.5 million; and large metropolitan areas are those with a population of over 1.5 million.

4. Small urban areas are those with a population of less than 200 000 people; medium-sized urban areas are those with a population of between 200 000 and 500 000; metropolitan areas are those with a population of between 500 000 and 1.5 million; and large metropolitan areas are those with a population of over 1.5 million.

5. It is worth mentioning that during the interviews with stakeholders as part of this policy dialogue, the Ministry of Agriculture emphasised the need to improve the quality of the measurements for volumes used in agricultural activities in Chile to foster water use efficiency.

6 In OECD/ECLAC (2016), the same graph with 2011 data registered water deficits for both Valparaíso (-15 m3/s) and Santiago Metropolitan Region (-13 m3/s)

7. Proportion of water loss as a percentage of net water production (delivered to the distribution system) reported by the surveyed cities.

8. The definition of Functional Urban Area (FUA) can be found at: www.oecd.org/gov/regional-policy/Definition-of-Functional-Urban-Areas-for-the-OECD-metropolitan-database.pdf, and the complete list of FUAs by country at www.oecd.org/gov/regional-policy/all.pdf.

9 Antofagasta (Antofagasta), Coquimbo-La Serena (Coquimbo, La Serena, Andacollo), Valparaíso (Viña del Mar, Valparaíso, Quilpué, Villa Alemana, Concón, Limache), Santiago (Maipú, Puente Alto, La Florida, San Bernardo, Las Condes, Pudahuel, Peñalolén, La Pintana, Quilicura, Santiago, El Bosque, Ñuñoa, Cerro Navia, Recoleta, Renca, La Granja, Providencia, Estación Central, Conchalí, Lo Espejo, Macul, Pedro Aguirre Cerda, Colina, Lo Prado, La Reina, Lo Barnechea, Quinta Normal, San Ramón, San Joaquín, Huechuraba, Vitacura, Peñaflor, La Cisterna, San Miguel, Talagante, Buin, Cerrillos, Paine, Independencia, Lampa, Padre Hurtado, Isla de Maipo, El Monte,

Curacaví, Calera de Tango, Pirque, San José de Maipo), Concepción (Concepción, Talcahuano, Chiguayante, Coronel, San Pedro de la Paz, Tomé, Hualpén, Penco, Hualqui).

10. The definition is constructed by the National Statistical Institute (INE) and classifies localities as either urban or rural. Urban localities are considered to be places with over 2 000 persons, or between 1 001 and 2 000 persons when 50% or more of the economically active population is engaged in secondary or tertiary activities. As a special case, tourism and recreation centres which have at least 250 clustered dwellings, but fail to meet the required population standard may also be classified as urban. The APR program has established its own definition for rural areas: i) Concentrated areas: population between 100/150 and 3 000 inhabitants with a minimum concentration of 15 households per km of drinking water supply pipe: ii) Semi-concentrated areas: disperse areas: minimum of 80 inhabitants and a minimum concentration of 8 households per future km of drinking water supply pipe.

References

Agua (2016), "*DGA licita estudio para desarrollar Plan de Gestión Integrada de Recursos Hídricos en cuenca del río Choapa*", available at: www.revistagua.cl/2016/09/08/dga-licita-estudio-para-desarrollar-plan-de-gestion-integrada-de-recursos-hidricos-en-cuenca-del-rio-choapa/ (published online on 8 September 2016).

Aguas Andinas (2015), "*Reporte de Sustentabilidad 2015*", available at: https://www.aguasandinas.cl/la-empresa/desarrollo-sustentable/reportes-de-sustentabilidad

Aguas Andinas (2015), *"Actualización Plan de Desarrollo Gran Santiago 2015 – 2029"*,

ATSE (2012), *Sustainable Water Management. Securing Australia's Future in a Green Economy*, Australian Research Council, Academy of Technological Sciences and Engineering, Melbourne.

Brady, J. and N.F. Gray (2013), "Analysis of water pricing in Ireland and recommendations towards a more efficient water sector", Water Policy, IWA Publishing, Vol. 15, pp. 435-437.

CCHC (2016), "*Cámara Chilena de la Construcción: Infraestructura Crítica para el Desarrollo 2016-25*", Santiago. www.cchc.cl/uploads/archivos/archivos/CChC-ICD_2016_(FINAL).pdf.

CEPAL (2015), *The Effects of Climate Change in the Coastal Areas of Latin America and the Caribbean Chile*, UN Economic Commission for Latin America and the Caribbean, Santiago. http://repositorio.cepal.org/handle/11362/39866

CNID (2014), "Minería: Una Plataforma de Futuro para Chile", Consejo Nacional de Innovación y Competitividad, Santiago. http://programaaltaley.cl/wp-content/uploads/2015/10/Mineria-_Una_Plataforma_de_Futuro_para_Chile_web.pdf.

CNR (2016), "Historia: Comisión Nacional de Riego", www.cnr.gob.cl/Conozcanos/Paginas/Historia.aspx (accessed in November 2016).

COCHILCO (2015), *Factores clave para el desarrollo de la minería en Chile*, Comisión Chilena del Cobre. https://www.cochilco.cl/Recopilacin%20de%20Estudios/2015.pdf.

COCHILCO (2009), *Gestión del Recurso Hídrico y la minería en Chile: Proyección Consumo de Agua en la Minería del Cobre 2009 – 2020*, Comisión Chilena del Cobre, www.aih-cl.org/articulos/Proyeccion-consumo-agua-en-mineria-del-Cobre-2009-2020-COCHILCO-(2009).pdf.

Cooley, H., et al. (2016), "Water risk hotspots for agriculture: The case of the southwest United States", OECD Food, Agriculture and Fisheries Papers, No. 96, OECD Publishing, Paris. DOI: http://dx.doi.org/10.1787/5jlr3bx95v48-en

DGA (2016), *Atlas del Agua: Chile 2016*, Dirección General de Aguas, Santiago. www.dga.cl/atlasdelagua/Paginas/default.aspx.

DMC (2015), “Análisis de los Resultados Convenio Alta Dirección Pública, Director, Dirección Meteorológica de Chile, Objetivo N°3”. http://archivos.meteochile.gob.cl/portaldmc/meteochile/documentos/SintesisInformeClima.pdf.

DIPRES (2015), “Evaluación de Programas Gubernamentales: Programa Infrastructura Hidráulica Potable Rural”, Dirección de Presupuestos, Ministerio de Hacienda. www.dipres.gob.cl/574/articles-141243_r_ejecutivo_institucional.pdf.

DIRPLAN & INH (2016), “Análisis de Requerimiento de Largo Plazo en Infraestructura Hídrica”, Dirección de Planeamiento del Ministerio de Obras Públicas (DIRPLAN) e Instituto Nacional de Hidráulica (INH).

EDF/WWC (2014), Multipurpose Water Uses of Hydropower Reservoirs, “Sharing the water uses of multipurpose hydropower reservoirs: the SHARE concept”. https://www.hydropower.org/sites/default/files/publications-docs/Multi-purpose%20water%20uses%20of%20hydropower%20reservoirs.pdf.

Emerton, L. and Bos, E. (2014) *Value. Counting Ecosystems as an Economic Part of Water Infrastructure*. IUCN, Gland, Switzerland and Cambridge, UK. https://cmsdata.iucn.org/downloads/value_en.pdf.

EPA (2008), *Managing Wet Weather with Green Infrastructure, Municipal Handbook: Rainwater Harvesting Policies*. https://www.epa.gov/sites/production/files/2015-10/documents/gi_munichandbook_harvesting.pdf.

FAO (2016), Aquastat: Irrigation and drainage database, Food and Agriculture Organisation. www.fao.org/nr/water/aquastat/irrigationdrainage/index.stm.

FAO (2015), Chile Country Profile, Food and Agriculture Organisation. www.fao.org/nr/water/aquastat/countries_regions/CHL/index.stm.

Ferro, G. and Mercadier, A.C. (2016), “Technical efficiency in Chile's water and sanitation providers”, *Utilities Policy, 43, 97-106.* http://dx.doi.org/10.1016/j.jup.2016.04.016

Government of Chile (2016), “Programa de Agua Potable Rural: 1964 – 2015”. www.clocsas.org/assets/historia-del-programa-de-agua-potable-rural-en-chile.pdf.

Government of Chile (2015), National Water Resources Policy 2015, www.interior.gob.cl/media/2015/04/recursos_hidricos.pdf.

Grafton, R.Q. and M.B.Ward (2010), “Dynamically Efficient UrbanWater Policy”, CWEEP Research Paper, No. 10-13, Australia National University.

GWP (2012), “Water Demand Management: The Mediterranean Experience”, Technical Focus Paper. www.gwp.org/en/ToolBox/PUBLICATIONS/Technical-Focus-Papers/

iAgua (2015), “Desalación de Agua para la minería en Chile”. www.iagua.es/blogs/guillermo-donoso/desalacion-agua-mineria-chile (published online in September 2015).

INE (2007), “Censo Agropecuario 2007”, Instituto Nacional de Estadísticas de Chile. www.ine.cl/canales/chile_estadistico/censos_agropecuarios/censo_agropecuario_07.php.

Jiménez Shaw, C. (2003), *Régimen Jurídico de la desalación de agua marina*, Tirant lo Blanch, Valencia. www.tirant.com/editorial/libro/regimen-juridico-de-la-desalacion-del-agua-marina-concepcion-jimenez-shaw-9788484427599

Ministry of Agricutlure (2015), "Política Sectorial", Santiago. www.gob.cl/cuenta-publica/2015/sectorial/2015_sectorial_ministerio-agricultura.pdf.

Ministry of Energy (2015), Energy 2050: Chile's Energy Policy, Santiago. www.energia2050.cl/wp-content/uploads/2016/08/Energy-2050-Chile-s-Energy-Policy.pdf

Ministry of Public Works (2016a), Dirección de Obras Hidráulicas, www.doh.gov.cl/AcercadelaDireccion/Paginas/default.aspx (accessed 17 November 2016)

Ministry of Public Works (2016b), "Análisis de Requerimientos de largo plazo en infraestructura hídrica",

Ministry of Public Works (2016c), Official statistics provided in the *OECD Questionnaire Data Request on Water in Chile* for this report: "*Review of the Gaps, Standards and Governance of Public Infrastructure in Chile*".

Ministry of Public Works (n.d.a), "Objetivos del Programa de Agua Potable Rural". www.doh.gov.cl/APR/AcercadeAPR/Documents/ObjetivosDelProgramaDeAguaPotableRural.pdf.

Ministry of Public Works (n.d.b), "Desafíos para la próxima década". www.doh.gov.cl/APR/AcercadeAPR/Documents/Desafíosparalapróximadécada.pdf.

Ministry of Public Works (2014), "Hacia un país con desarrollo equilibrado: Infraestructura y Agua". www.dirplan.cl/centrodedocumentacion/documentosgenerales/Documents/libro/Hacia_un_pais_con_desarrollo_equilibrado.pdf.

Ministry of Public Works (2003), "El Riego en Chile", Santiago. www.doh.gov.cl/publicacionesyestudios/Documents/historia_del_riego_en_chile.pdf

O'Brien, R. and A. Esposito (2015), "Chile's Bachclct says to cost $1.5 bln to repair flood damages", Reuters. www.reuters.com/article/2015/04/08/chile-weather-bachelet-idUSC0N0UE00A20150408 (accessed 30 August 2015).

OECD (2017), *Environmental Performance of Agriculture* (Edition 2013), OECD Agriculture Statistics (database). http://dx.doi.org/10.1787/data-00660-en (accessed April 2017)

OECD (2016), *Water Governance in Cities*, OECD Publishing, Paris. DOI: http://dx.doi.org/10.1787/9789264251090-en.

OECD (2016a), *OECD Regional Statistics* (database) Demography and Population, OECD Publishing, Paris. https://stats.oecd.org/ (accessed September 2016).

OECD (2016b), OECD Council Recommendation on Water, https://www.oecd.org/environment/resources/Council-Recommendation-on-water.pdf

OECD (2015), *Total renewable freshwater resources per capita, long-term annual average values*, in Environment at a Glance 2015, OECD Publishing, Paris. DOI: http://dx.doi.org/10.1787/9789264235199-graph23-en

OECD (2015a), *Water and Cities: Ensuring Sustainable Futures*, OECD Publishing, Paris. DOI: http://dx.doi.org/10.1787/9789264230149-en.

OECD (2015b), *Water: Freshwater abstractions,* OECD Environment Statistics (database). https://stats.oecd.org/Index.aspx?DataSetCode=WATER_RESOURCES

OECD (2015c), *OECD Water Governance Principles*, available at: https://www.oecd.org/gov/regional-policy/OECD-Principles-on-Water-Governance-brochure.pdf.

OECD (2015d), *Water Resources Governance in Brazil*. OECD Publishing, Paris. DOI: http://dx.doi.org/10.1787/9789264238121-en.

OECD (2015e), *Access to sewerage and type of treatment*, OECD Environment Statistics (database). http://stats.oecd.org/

OECD (2014), *OECD Rural Policy Reviews: Chile 2014*, OECD Publishing, Paris. DOI: http://dx.doi.org/10.1787/9789264222892-en

OECD (2014a), *Historical population data and projections statistics* (database). http://stats.oecd.org/

OECD (2014b), Water Governance in the Netherlands: Fit for the Future?, OECD Publishing, Paris. DOI: http://dx.doi.org/10.1787/9789264102637-en

OECD (2013), *OECD Urban Policy Reviews, Chile 2013*, OECD Publishing, Paris. DOI: http://dx.doi.org/10.1787/9789264191808-en.

OECD (2013a), *OECD Territorial Reviews: Antofagasta, Chile 2013*, OECD Publishing, Paris. DOI: http://dx.doi.org/10.1787/9789264203914-en.

OECD (2013b), *Water Security for Better Lives*, OECD Publishing, Paris. DOI: http://dx.doi.org/10.1787/9789264202405-en.

OECD (2013c), *New Modes of Water Supply and Sanitation Management and Emerging Business Models*, OECD, Paris. www.oecd.org/officialdocuments/publicdisplaydocumentpdf/?cote=ENV/EPOC/WPBWE/RD%282013%297&docLanguage=En

OECD (2012), *Water Governance in Latin America and the Caribbean: A Multi-level Approach*, OECD Publishing, Paris. DOI: http://dx.doi.org/10.1787/9789264174542-en.

OECD (2012a), *OECD Environmental Outlook to 2050: The Consequences of Inaction*, OECD Publishing, Paris. DOI: http://dx.doi.org/10.1787/9789264122246-en

OECD (2012b), *Population in cities*, Regions and Cities, Metropolitan Areas (Database). http://stats.oecd.org/

OECD (2011), *Water Governance in OECD Countries: A Multi-level Approach*. OECD Publishing, Paris. DOI: http://dx.doi.org/10.1787/9789264119284-en.

OECD (2009), *OECD Territorial Reviews: Chile 2009,* OECD Publishing, Paris. DOI: http://dx.doi.org/10.1787/9789264060791-en.

OECD (forthcoming), *Water Risk Hotspots for Agriculture,* OECD Publishing, Paris.

OECD (forthcoming a), Agri-Environmental Indicators: Agricultural Water Use and Irrigation, OECD Publishing, Paris.

ORGANISATION FOR ECONOMIC CO-OPERATION AND DEVELOPMENT

The OECD is a unique forum where governments work together to address the economic, social and environmental challenges of globalisation. The OECD is also at the forefront of efforts to understand and to help governments respond to new developments and concerns, such as corporate governance, the information economy and the challenges of an ageing population. The Organisation provides a setting where governments can compare policy experiences, seek answers to common problems, identify good practice and work to co-ordinate domestic and international policies.

The OECD member countries are: Australia, Austria, Belgium, Canada, Chile, the Czech Republic, Denmark, Estonia, Finland, France, Germany, Greece, Hungary, Iceland, Ireland, Israel, Italy, Japan, Korea, Latvia, Luxembourg, Mexico, the Netherlands, New Zealand, Norway, Poland, Portugal, the Slovak Republic, Slovenia, Spain, Sweden, Switzerland, Turkey, the United Kingdom and the United States. The European Union takes part in the work of the OECD.

OECD Publishing disseminates widely the results of the Organisation's statistics gathering and research on economic, social and environmental issues, as well as the conventions, guidelines and standards agreed by its members.

OECD PUBLISHING, 2, rue André-Pascal, 75775 PARIS CEDEX 16
(04 2017 07 1 P) ISBN 978-92-64-27886-8 – 2017

www.ingramcontent.com/pod-product-compliance
Lightning Source LLC
Chambersburg PA
CBHW061157240926
51846CB00006B/1039